Upgrading & Troubleshooting Networks: The Complete Reference

About the Author

Craig Zacker is a writer, editor, and networker whose computing experience began in the halcyon days of teletypes and paper tape. After making the move from minicomputers to PCs, he worked as an administrator of Novell NetWare networks and as a PC support technician, while operating a freelance desktop publishing business. After earning a Masters degree in English and American literature from NYU, Craig worked extensively on the integration of Windows NT into existing NetWare internetworks, and was employed as a technical writer, content provider, and Webmaster for the online services group of a large software company. Since devoting himself to writing and editing full time, Craig has authored or contributed to many books on operating systems and networking topics, and has published articles with top industry publications including *Windows NT Magazine*, for which he is a contributing editor.

Upgrading & Troubleshooting Networks: The Complete Reference

Craig Zacker

Osborne/**McGraw-Hill**

Berkeley New York St. Louis San Francisco
Auckland Bogotá Hamburg London Madrid
Mexico City Milan Montreal New Delhi Panama City
Paris São Paulo Singapore Sydney
Tokyo Toronto

Osborne/**McGraw-Hill**
2600 Tenth Street
Berkeley, California 94710
U.S.A.

For information on translations or book distributors outside the U.S.A., or to arrange
bulk purchase discounts for sales promotions, premiums, or fund-raisers, please
contact Osborne/**McGraw-Hill** at the above address.

Upgrading & Troubleshooting Networks: The Complete Reference

1234567890 DOC DOC 019876543210

ISBN 0-07-212256-0

Publisher
    Brandon A. Nordin

**Associate Publisher and
Editor-in-Chief**
    Scott Rogers

Acquisitions Editor
    Jane Brownlow

Project Editor
    Emily Rader

Acquisitions Coordinator
    Tara Davis

Technical Editors
    Chris Prosise and Ariel Silverstone

Copy Editors
    William F. McManus
    Marcia Baker

Proofreader
    Linda Medoff

Indexer
    Rebecca Plunkett

Computer Designers
    Jani Beckwith
    Roberta Steele

Illustrators
    Beth Young
    Bob Hansen
    Michael Mueller

This book was composed with Corel VENTURA ™ Publisher.

For LJ, with love

Contents at a Glance

Contents

Part I

Network Basics

Part II

Network Hardware

Part III

Network Protocols

Part IV

Network Operating Systems

Part VII

Network Services

Part VIII

Network Administration

Introduction

Computer networking is an enormous subject—one in which the more you learn, the more you realize there is to learn. To cover everything there is to know would require a library, or at least a good-sized bookcase. No single volume can cover everything, but this book tries to provide an overview of networking technologies and sufficient background to help you begin to understand what's going on "under the hood" of your network. It is only by understanding a process that you can effectively improve or repair it.

- Part I outlines networking basics. Chapter 1 explains essential networking terminology and introduces some of the fundamental concepts that you will build on in later chapters. You'll learn about some of the primary components that make up a network and how the technology came about. Chapter 2 introduces the OSI reference model, a theoretical tool that compartmentalizes the networking functionality of a computer into seven discrete layers. These layers work together to enable the computer to communicate effectively with the other computers on the network. In this chapter, you'll also get your first glimpses of the technologies that will be examined in much greater detail later in the book.

■ Part II explains the hardware used to construct a network. Chapter 3 examines network interface cards, which enable you to connect a computer to a network. These include the various types of cards you can buy to suit your computer's hardware configuration, your network type, and the role of your system on the network. In Chapter 4, you'll learn about the cables used to connect computers together to form a network. The type of cable you choose determines how easy or difficult network installation and maintenance will be, how long the cable can run, and how well your network will perform. Chapter 4 also examines the standards that should guide your cable installation, and some of the tools you'll need to do the job.

Chapter 5 describes other hardware components that might be needed on your network, such as repeaters, hubs, and bridges. These are devices you can use to expand your network to support a greater number of workstations and users. Chapter 6 examines routers and switches, high-end devices that are used to connect different types of networks together and improve network efficiency. In Chapter 7, you learn about the various technologies used to create wide area network connections, such as leased lines, ISDN, and frame relay.

■ Part III is about the protocols used at various layers of the OSI reference model. Chapter 8 examines Ethernet, the most popular data link–layer protocol used in the world today. Chapter 9 addresses other contenders, such as Token Ring and 100VG-AnyLAN. Chapter 10 discusses high-speed technologies used to form network backbones, such as Fiber Distributed Data Interface (FDDI), Gigabit Ethernet, and Asynchronous Transfer Mode (ATM).

Chapter 11 begins coverage of the network and transport layers by outlining the TCP/IP protocols used on the Internet and on the majority of private networks today. Chapter 12 examines the proprietary IPX protocols created by Novell for use with its NetWare operating system. In Chapter 13, you'll learn about the NetBIOS, NetBEUI, and Server Message Blocks (SMB) protocols, which are integral components of Windows networks.

■ Part IV examines networking aspects of operating systems most commonly used on today's networks, such as Windows NT and Windows 2000 (Chapter 14), Novell NetWare (Chapter 15), and UNIX (Chapter 16). Chapter 17 explains client capabilities that workstations need in order to access resources hosted by various other operating systems. For example, it describes how to connect Macintosh and UNIX systems to Windows and NetWare networks.

■ Part V discusses some of the most important administrative services used on today's networks. Chapter 18 covers the Dynamic Host Configuration Protocol (DHCP), which you can use to automatically configure TCP/IP clients on your network, and Chapter 19 covers the Windows Internet Naming Service (WINS). Windows NT networks use WINS to resolve the NetBIOS names Windows systems are known by into IP addresses necessary to communicate on a TCP/IP network. Chapter 20 examines the Domain Name System (DNS), which is used on the Internet and on private TCP/IP networks to resolve host names into IP addresses.

■ Part VI discusses the various types of directory services used to store information about networks, their users, and their applications. These services include Novell Directory Services (NDS), the first commercially successful enterprise directory service (Chapter 21), the domains used to organize Windows NT networks (Chapter 22), and Active Directory, the long-awaited enterprise directory service from Microsoft, which is included with Windows 2000 (Chapter 23).

■ Part VII shows you how to improve your network by adding some of the most useful services available, such as World Wide Web and FTP servers (Chapter 24), network printing (Chapter 25), and access to the Internet (Chapter 26).

■ Part VIII covers the tools and techniques you can use to administer your network. Chapter 27 outlines Windows-specific network administration techniques, and Chapter 28 discusses network troubleshooting and management tools.

This book provides complete coverage of networking basics and technology, including hardware, protocols, administrative and directory services, and administration techniques. For that reason, this book is useful on several levels. As a reference work, it presents information about a wide variety of networking technologies. Its structured form makes it easy to locate the material you need. As a learning tool, the book provides a high-level overview of the networking process and then drills down into the specifics of the most useful elements of a network. As an administrator's companion, the book provides the information you need to learn how to improve network efficiency and usefulness, and how to solve problems yourself rather than paying a high-priced expert to do it for you.

The book is intended for beginners, as well as experienced network professionals. I hope that, in addition to the uses mentioned above, it will lead you to learn more about the computer systems you use everyday.

The
Complete
Reference

Upgrading
&
Troubleshooting
Networks

Part I

Network Basics

The Complete Reference

Upgrading & Troubleshooting Networks

Chapter 1

What Is a Network?

Simply put, a *network* is a group of computers connected together by cables or some other medium; but, the networking process is anything but simple. When computers are able to communicate, they can work together in a variety of ways: by sharing their resources with each other, by distributing the workload of a particular task, or by exchanging messages. This book examines in detail how computers on a network communicate; what functions they perform; and how to go about building, upgrading, and troubleshooting them.

The original paradigm for collaborative computing was to have a single large computer connected to a series of terminals, each of which services a different user. This is the basis for mainframe computing. In this arrangement, the terminals are simply communications devices; they accept input from users through a keyboard or other device and send it to the computer. When the computer returns a result, the terminal displays it on a screen or prints it out on paper. This type of terminal is sometimes called a *dumb terminal,* because it doesn't perform any calculations of its own. The communications between the terminals and the computer are relatively simple on this type of network, because each terminal can only communicate with one device, the computer; terminals never communicate with each other.

Local Area Networks

As time passed and technology progressed, engineers began to connect computers together so that they could communicate; at the same time, computers were becoming smaller and less expensive, giving rise to mini- and microcomputers. The first computer networks used individual links, such as telephone connections, to connect two systems together. Soon after the first IBM PCs hit the market in the 1980s and rapidly became accepted as a business tool, the advantages of connecting these small computers together became obvious. Rather than supplying every computer with its own printer, a network of computers might be able to share a single one. When one user needed to give a file to another user, a network could eliminate the need to swap floppy disks. The problem, however, was that connecting a dozen computers in an office with individual point-to-point links was not practical. The eventual solution to this problem was the *local area network (LAN).*

A LAN is a group of computers connected together by a shared medium, usually a cable. By sharing a single cable, each computer requires only one connection, and can conceivably communicate with any other computer on the network. A LAN is limited to a local area by the electrical properties of the cables used to construct them and by the relatively small number of computers that can share a single network medium. LANs are generally restricted to operation within a single building or, at most, a campus of adjacent buildings. Some technologies, such as fiber optics, have extended the range of LANs to one or two kilometers, but it isn't possible to use a LAN to connect computers in distant cities, for example. This is the province of the *wide area network (WAN),* as discussed later in this chapter.

In most cases, a LAN is a baseband, packet-switching network. Understanding the terms *baseband* and *packet switching,* which are examined in the following sections, is necessary to understand how data networks operate, because these terms define how data is transmitted over the network medium.

Baseband Versus Broadband

A *baseband* network is one in which the cable or other network medium can carry only a single signal at any one time. A *broadband* network, on the other hand, can carry multiple signals simultaneously, using a discrete frequency for each signal. As an example of a broadband network, consider the cable television service that you probably have in your home. Although only one cable runs to your TV, it supplies you with dozens of channels at the same time. If you have more than one television connected to the cable service, the installer probably used a splitter to run the single cable entering your house to two different rooms. The fact that the TVs can be tuned to different programs at the same time over the same cable proves that the cable is providing a separate signal for each channel at all times.

A baseband network uses pulses applied directly to the network medium to create a single signal that carries binary data in encoded form. Compared to broadband technologies, baseband networks span relatively short distances, because they are subject to degradation caused by electrical interference and other factors. The maximum length of a baseband network cable segment diminishes as its transmission rate increases. This is why local area networking protocols such as Ethernet have strict guidelines for cable installations.

Packet Switching Versus Circuit Switching

LANs are called *packet-switching networks* because their computers divide their data into small, discrete units called *packets* before transmitting it. There is also a similar technique called *cell switching,* which differs from packet switching only in that cells are always a consistent, uniform size, whereas the size of packets is variable. Most LAN technologies, such as Ethernet, Token Ring, and Fiber Distributed Data Interface (FDDI), use packet switching. Asynchronous Transmission Mode (ATM) is the only cell-switching LAN protocol in common use.

Segmenting the data in this way is necessary because the computers on a LAN share a single cable, and a computer transmitting a single unbroken stream of data would monopolize the network for too long. When you examine the data being transmitted over a packet-switching network, you can see that the data stream consists of packets generated by many different systems, intermixed on the cable. It is normal on this type of network for packets that are part of the same message to take different routes to their destination and even to arrive at the destination in a different order than they were transmitted. The receiving system, therefore, must have a mechanism for reassembling the packets into the correct order and recognizing the absence of packets that may have been lost or damaged in transit.

The opposite of packet switching is *circuit switching,* in which one system establishes a dedicated communication channel to another system before any data is transmitted. In the data networking industry, circuit switching is used for certain types of wide area networking technologies, such as Integrated Service Digital Network (ISDN) and frame relay. The classic example of a circuit-switching network is the telephone system. When you place a call to another person, a physical circuit is established between your telephone and theirs. This circuit remains active for the entire duration of the call, and no one else can use it, even when it is not carrying any signal (that is, when no one is talking). In the early days of the telephone system, every phone was connected to a central office with a dedicated cable, and operators using switchboards manually connected a circuit between the two phones for every call. Today, the process is automated, but the principle is the same.

Networks and Internetworks

LANs were originally designed to connect a small number of computers together into what later came to be called a *workgroup.* Rather than investing a huge amount of money into a mainframe computer and the support system needed to run it, business owners came to realize that they could purchase a few computers, cable them together, and perform most of the computing tasks they needed. As the capabilities of personal computers and applications grew, so did the networks, and the technology used to build them progressed as well.

Cables and Topologies

Most LANs are built around copper cables that use standard electrical currents to relay their signals. Originally, most LANs consisted of computers connected with coaxial cables; but eventually, the twisted-pair cabling used for telephone systems became more popular. Another alternative is fiber-optic cable, which doesn't use electrical signals at all, but instead uses pulses of light to encode binary data. Other types of network infrastructures eliminate cables entirely and transmit signals using what is known as *unbounded media,* such as radio waves, infrared, and microwaves.

Note   *For more information about the various types of cables used in data networking, see Chapter 4.*

LANs connect computers using various types of cabling patterns, called *topologies* (see Figure 1-1), which depend on the type of cable used and the protocols running on the computers. The most common topologies are as follows:

- **Bus** A bus topology takes the form of a cable that runs from one computer to the next one in a daisy-chain fashion, much like a string of Christmas tree lights. All of the signals transmitted by the computers on the network travel along the bus in both directions to all of the other computers. The two ends of the bus must be terminated with electrical resistors that nullify the voltages reaching them, so that the signals do not reflect back in the other direction. The primary drawback of the bus topology is that, like the string of Christmas lights it resembles, a fault in the cable anywhere along its length splits the network in two and prevents systems on opposite sides of the break from communicating. Most coaxial cable networks, such as the original Ethernet LANs, use a bus topology.

- **Star** A star topology uses a separate cable for each computer that runs to a central cabling nexus called a *hub* or *concentrator.* The hub propagates the signals entering through any one of its ports out through all of the other ports, so that the signals transmitted by each computer reach all of the other computers. A star network is more fault-tolerant than a bus, because a break in a cable affects only the computer to which that cable is connected, not the entire network. Most twisted-pair cable networks use the star topology, such as 10BaseT Ethernet.

- **Ring** A ring topology is functionally equivalent to a bus topology with the two ends connected together so that signals travel from one computer to the next in a circular fashion. However, the communications ring is only a logical construct, not a physical one. The physical network is actually cabled using a star topology, and a special hub implements the logical ring by taking each incoming signal and transmitting it out through the next downstream port only (instead of through all of the other ports, like a star hub). Each computer, upon receiving an incoming signal, processes it (if necessary) and sends it right back to the hub for transmission to the next station on the ring. Because of this arrangement, systems that transmit signals onto the network must also remove the signals after they have traversed the entire ring. Networks configured in a ring topology can use several different types of cable. Token Ring networks, for example, can use twisted-pair cables, while FDDI networks use the ring topology with fiber-optic cable.

- **Star Bus** A star bus topology is one method for expanding the size of a LAN beyond a single star. In this topology, a number of star networks are joined together using a separate bus cable segment to connect their hubs. Each computer can still communicate with any other computer on the network, because each of the hubs transmits its incoming traffic out through the bus port as well as the other star ports. Designed to expand 10BaseT Ethernet networks, the star bus is less common today because of the speed limitations of coaxial bus networks, which can function as a bottleneck that degrades the performance of faster star network technologies such as Fast Ethernet.

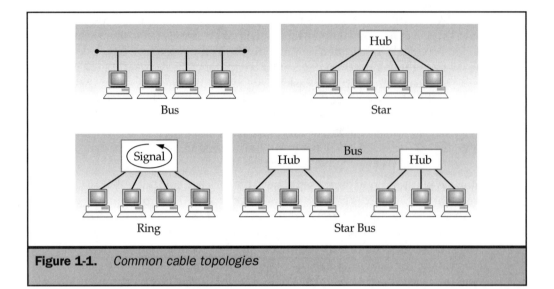

Figure 1-1. *Common cable topologies*

Media Access Control

When multiple computers are connected to the same baseband network medium, there must be a *media access control (MAC)* mechanism to arbitrate access to the network, to prevent systems from transmitting data at the same time. A MAC mechanism is a fundamental part of all local area networking protocols. The two most common MAC mechanisms are Carrier Sense Multiple Access with Collision Detection (CSMA/CD), which is used by Ethernet networks, and token passing, which is used by Token Ring, FDDI, and other network types. These two mechanisms are fundamentally different, but they accomplish the same task by providing each system on the network with an equal opportunity to transmit its data. For more information about these MAC mechanisms, see Chapter 8 for CSMA/CD and Chapter 9 for token passing.

Addressing

In order for systems on a shared network medium to communicate effectively, they must have some means of identifying each other, usually some form of numerical address. In most cases, the network interface card (NIC) installed into each computer has an address hardcoded into it at the factory, called its *MAC address* or *hardware address,* which uniquely identifies that card among all others. Every packet that each computer transmits over the network contains its address and the address of the system to which the packet is intended.

In addition to the MAC address, systems may also have other addresses operating at other layers. For example, the TCP/IP protocol requires that each system be assigned a unique IP address in addition to the MAC address it already possesses. Systems use the various addresses for different types of communications. For more information on MAC addressing, see Chapter 3; for more information on IP addressing, see Chapter 11.

Repeaters, Bridges, Switches, and Routers

LANs were originally designed to support only a relatively small number of computers—30 for thin Ethernet networks, and 100 for thick Ethernet—but the needs of businesses quickly outgrew these limitations. To support larger installations, engineers developed products that enabled administrators to connect two or more LANs together into what is known as an *internetwork,* which is essentially a network of networks that enables the computers on one network to communicate with those on another.

Note   *Don't confuse the generic term* internetwork *with the Internet. The Internet is an example of an extremely large internetwork, but any installation that consists of two or more LANs connected together is also called an internetwork.*

This terminology is confusing, because it is so often misused. Sometimes, what users mean when they refer to a network is actually an internetwork, and at other times, what may seem to be an internetwork is actually a single LAN. Strictly speaking, a LAN or a network segment is a group of computers that share a network cable so that a broadcast message transmitted by one system reaches all of the other systems, even if that segment is actually composed of many pieces of cable. For example, on a typical 10BaseT Ethernet LAN, all of the computers are connected to a hub using individual lengths of cable. Regardless of that fact, this arrangement is still an example of a network segment or LAN.

Individual LANs can be connected together using several different types of devices, some of which simply extend the LAN while another creates an internetwork. These devices are as follows:

■ **Repeaters**   A repeater is a purely electrical device that extends the maximum distance a LAN cable can span by amplifying the signals passing through it. The hubs used on star networks are sometimes called *multiport repeaters* because they have signal amplification capabilities integrated into the unit. Standalone repeaters are also available for use on coaxial networks, to extend them over longer distances. Using a repeater to expand a network segment does not divide it into two LANs or create an internetwork.

■ **Bridges**   A bridge provides the amplification function of a repeater, along with the ability to selectively filter packets based on their addresses. Packets that originate on one side of the bridge are propagated to the other side only if they are addressed to a system that exists there. Because bridges do not prevent broadcast messages from being propagated across the connected cable segments, they, too, do not create multiple LANs or transform a network into an internetwork.

■ **Switches**   Switches are revolutionary devices that in many cases eliminate the need for a shared network medium entirely. A switch is essentially a multiport repeater, like a hub, except that instead of operating at a purely electrical level, the switch reads the destination address in each incoming packet and transmits it out only through the port to which the destination system is connected. Switches can operate at different layers, connecting networks into either a single LAN or an internetwork.

■ **Routers**   A router is a device that connects two LANs together to form an internetwork. Like a bridge, a router only forwards traffic that is destined for the connected segment; but unlike repeaters and bridges, routers do not forward broadcast messages. Routers can also connect different types of networks together (such as Ethernet and Token Ring), whereas bridges and repeaters can only connect segments of the same type.

> **Note**   *For more information on repeaters, hubs, and bridges, see Chapter 5. For more information on routers and switches, see Chapter 6.*

Wide Area Networks

Internetworking enables an organization to build a network infrastructure of almost unlimited size; but in addition to connecting multiple LANs together in the same building or campus, an internetwork can also connect LANs at distant locations, through the use of wide area network (WAN) links. A WAN is a collection of LANs, some or all of which are connected using point-to-point links that span relatively long distances. A typical WAN connection consists of two routers, one at each LAN site, connected using a long-distance link such as a leased telephone line. Any computer on one of the LANs can communicate with the other LAN by directing its traffic to the local router, which relays it over the WAN link to the other site.

WAN links differ from LANs in that they do not use a shared network medium and they can span much longer distances. Because the link connects only two systems, there is no need for media access control or a shared network topology. An organization with offices located throughout the world can build an internetwork that provides users with instantaneous access to network resources at any location. The WAN links themselves can use technologies ranging from telephone lines to public data networks to satellite systems. Generally speaking, WAN connections are slower than LANs, sometimes much slower, and are more expensive, sometimes much more expensive. As a result, one of the goals of the network administrator is to maximize the efficiency of WAN traffic by eliminating unnecessary traffic and choosing the best type of link for the application.

Note *For more information on WAN technologies, see Chapter 7.*

Protocols and Standards

The communications between the computers on a network are defined by *protocols,* standardized languages that the software programs on the computers have in common. These protocols define every part of the communications process, from the signals transmitted over network cables, to the query languages that enable applications on different machines to exchange messages. Networked computers run a series of protocols, called a *stack,* that spans from the application user interface at the top to the physical network interface at the bottom. The stack is traditionally split into seven layers, the functions of which are defined by the Open Systems Interconnection (OSI) reference model, a document that defines the functions of each layer and how the layers work together to provide network communications.

Note *For more information on the OSI reference model, see Chapter 2.*

Early networking products tended to be proprietary solutions created by a single manufacturer, but as years passed, interoperability became a greater priority and organizations were used to develop and ratify networking protocol standards. Most of these bodies are responsible for large numbers of technical and manufacturing standards in many different disciplines. Today, most of the protocols in common use are standardized by these bodies, some of which are as follows:

- **Institute of Electrical and Electronic Engineers (IEEE)** U.S.-based society responsible for the publication of the IEEE 802 working group, which includes the standards that define the protocols commonly known as Ethernet and Token Ring, as well as many others.

- **International Organization for Standardization (ISO)** Worldwide federation of standards bodies from over 100 countries, responsible for the publication of the OSI reference model document.

- **Internet Engineering Task Force (IETF)** Ad hoc group of contributors and consultants that collaborate to develop and publish standards for Internet technologies, including the TCP/IP protocols.

- **Telecommunications Industry Association/Electronic Industry Association (TIA/EIA)** Two organizations that have joined together to develop and publish the Commercial Building Telecommunications Wiring Standards, which define how the cables for data networks should be installed.

Clients and Servers

PC networking is based on the client/server principle, in which the processes needed to accomplish a particular task are divided between computers functioning as clients and servers. This is in direct contrast to the mainframe model, in which the central computer did all of the processing and simply transmitted the results to a user at a remote terminal. A *server* is a computer running a process that provides a service to other computers when they request it. A *client* is the computer running a program that requests the service from a server.

For example, a LAN-based database application stores its data on a server, which stands by waiting for clients to request information from it. Users at workstation computers run a database client program in which they generate queries that request specific information in the database and transmit those queries to the server. The server responds to the queries with the requested information and transmits it to the workstations, which format it for display to the users. In this case, the workstations are responsible for providing a user interface and translating the user input into a query language understood by the server, as well as for taking the raw data from the server and displaying it in a comprehensible form to the user. The server may have to service dozens or hundreds of clients, so it is still a powerful computer; but by offloading some of the application's functions to the workstations, its processing burden is nowhere near what it would be on a mainframe system.

Operating Systems and Applications

Clients and servers are actually software components, although some people associate them with specific hardware elements. This confusion is due to the fact that some network operating systems (such as Novell NetWare) require that a computer be dedicated to the role of server and that other computers function solely as clients. This is a client/server operating system, as opposed to a peer-to-peer operating system, in which every computer can function as both a client and a server. The most basic client/server functionality provided by network operating systems (NOSs) is the ability to share file system drives and printers, and this is what usually defines the client and server roles. For example, Windows NT comes in both Server and Workstation versions, but it's still a peer-to-peer operating system, because any Windows NT computer can access resources on another NT computer and share its own resources, regardless of whether it is running Server or Workstation. A Novell NetWare server, however, can share its drives and printers, but it can't access shared resources on other drives, nor can NetWare clients share their own resources. NetWare clients can communicate with servers only, not with other clients (see Figure 1-2).

Note   *For more information on Windows NT, see Chapter 14. For more information on Novell NetWare, see Chapter 15.*

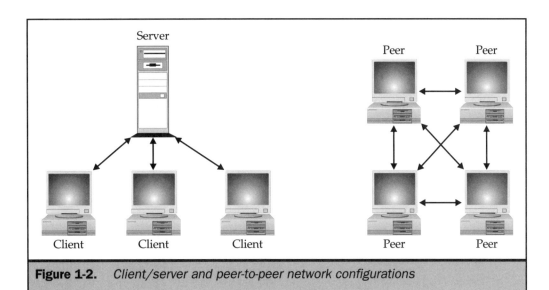

Figure 1-2. *Client/server and peer-to-peer network configurations*

Apart from the internal functions of NOSs, many LAN applications and network services also operate using the client/server paradigm. Internet applications, such as the World Wide Web, consist of servers and clients, as do administrative services such as the Domain Name System (DNS).

From Here

This chapter introduced some of the basic concepts and terminology that you need to know to learn more about computer networking. In the next chapter, you begin your examination of networking in detail with the OSI reference model, the blueprint for the communications capabilities built into LAN computers.

The
Complete
Reference

Upgrading
&
Troubleshooting
Networks

Chapter 2

The OSI Reference Model

Network communications take place on many levels, and can be complicated to understand, even for the knowledgeable administrator. The Open Systems Interconnection (OSI) reference model is a theoretical construction that separates network communications into seven distinct layers, as shown in Figure 2-1. Each computer on the network uses a series of protocols to perform the functions assigned to each layer. The layers collectively form what is known as the *protocol stack* or *networking stack*. At the top of the stack is the application that makes a request for a resource located elsewhere on the network, while at the bottom is the medium that actually connects the computers and forms the network, such as a cable.

The OSI reference model was developed in two separate projects by the International Organization for Standardization (ISO) and the Consultative Committee for International Telephone and Telegraphy (CCITT), which is now known as the Telecommunications Standardization Sector of the International Telecommunications Union (ITU-T). These two bodies each developed its own seven-layer model, but the two projects were combined in 1983, resulting in a document called "The Basic Reference Model for Open Systems Interconnection" that was published by the ISO as ISO 7498 and by the ITU-T as X.200.

The OSI stack was originally conceived to be the model for the creation of a protocol suite that would conform exactly to the seven layers, but this suite never materialized and the model has since been used as a teaching, reference, and communications tool. Networking professionals, educators, and authors frequently refer to protocols, devices, or applications as operating at a particular layer of the OSI model, because using this model breaks down a complex process into manageable units that provide a common frame of reference. Many of the chapters in this book use the layers of the model to help define networking concepts. However, it is important to understand that none of the protocol stacks in common use today conform exactly to the layers of the OSI model. In many cases, protocols have functions that overlap

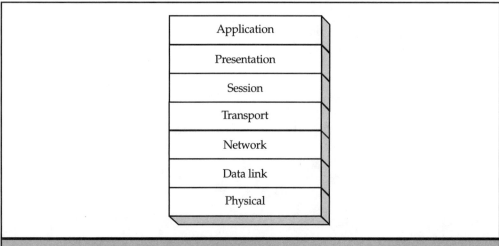

Figure 2-1.   *The OSI reference model*

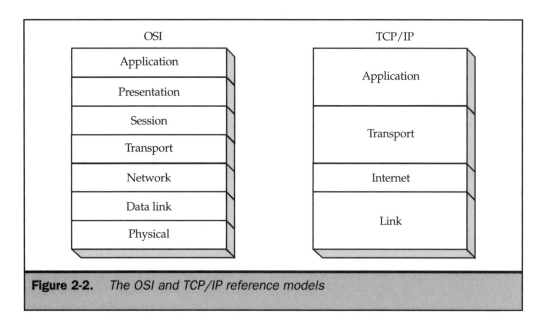

Figure 2-2. *The OSI and TCP/IP reference models*

two or more layers, such as Ethernet, which is considered a data link–layer protocol but also defines elements of the physical layer.

The primary reason why real protocol stacks differ from the OSI model is that many of the protocols used today (including Ethernet) were conceived before the OSI model documents were published. In fact, the TCP/IP protocols have their own layered model, which is similar to the OSI model in several ways, but uses only four layers (see Figure 2-2). In addition, developers are usually more concerned with practical functionality than with conforming to a preexisting model. The seven-layer model was designed to separate the functions of the protocol stack in such a way as to make it possible for separate development teams to work on the individual layers, thus streamlining the development process. However, if a single protocol can easily provide the functions that are defined as belonging in separate layers of the model, why divide it into two separate protocols just for the sake of conformity?

Interlayer Communications

Networking is the process of sending messages from one place to another, and the protocol stack illustrated in the OSI model defines the basic components needed to transmit messages to their destinations. The communication process is complex, because the applications that generate the messages have varying requirements. Some message exchanges consist of brief requests and replies that have to be exchanged as quickly as possible and with the minimum amount of overhead. Other network transactions, such as program file transfers, involve the transmission of larger amounts of data that must reach the destination in perfect condition, without a single bit value altered. Still other transmissions, such as streaming audio or video, consist of huge amounts of data that can survive the loss of an occasional packet, but that must reach the destination in a timely manner.

The networking process also includes a number of conversions that ultimately take the API calls generated by applications and transform them into electrical charges, pulses of light, or other types of signals that can be transmitted across the network medium. Finally, the networking protocols must see to it that the transmissions reach the appropriate destinations in a timely manner. Just as you package a letter by placing it in an envelope and writing an address on it, the networking protocols package the data generated by an application and address it to another computer on the network.

Data Encapsulation

To satisfy all the requirements just described, the protocols operating at the various layers work together to supply a unified quality of service. Each layer provides a service to the layers directly above and below it. Outgoing traffic travels down through the stack to the network medium, acquiring the control information needed to make the trip to the destination system as it goes. This control information takes the form of headers and sometimes footers that surround the data received from the layer above, in a process called *data encapsulation*. The headers and footers are composed of individual *fields* that contain control information used to get the packet to its destination. In a sense, the headers and footers form the envelope that carries the message received from the layer above.

In a typical transaction, an application-layer protocol (which includes presentation- and session-layer functions) generates a message that is passed down to a transport-layer protocol. The protocol at the transport layer has its own packet structure, called a *protocol data unit (PDU)*, which includes specialized header fields and a Data field that carries the payload. In this case, the payload is the data received from the application-layer protocol. By packaging the data in its own PDU, the transport layer *encapsulates* the application-layer data, and then passes it down to the next layer.

The network-layer protocol then receives the PDU from the transport layer and encapsulates it within its own PDU by adding a header and using the entire transport-layer PDU as its payload. The same process occurs again when the network layer passes its PDU to the data link–layer protocol, which adds a header and a footer. To a data link–layer protocol, the data within the frame is treated as payload only, just as postal employees have no idea what is inside the envelopes they process. The only system that reads the information in the payload is the system possessing the destination address. That system then either passes the network-layer protocol data contained in the payload up through its protocol stack or uses that data to determine what the next destination of the packet should be. In the same way, the protocols operating at the other layers are conscious of their own header information, but are unaware of what data is being carried in the payload.

Once it is encapsulated by the data link–layer protocol, the completed packet is then ready to be converted to the appropriate type of signal used by the network medium. Thus, the final packet, as transmitted over the network, consists of the original application-layer data plus several headers applied by the protocols at the succeeding layers, as shown in Figure 2-3.

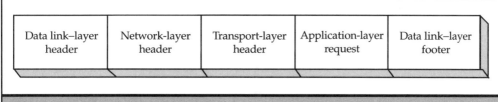

Figure 2-3. *Application requests are encapsulated for transmission by multiple protocol headers*

Horizontal Communications

In order for two computers to communicate over a network, the protocols used at each layer of the OSI model in the transmitting system must be duplicated at the receiving system. When the packet arrives at its destination, the process by which the headers are applied at the source is repeated in reverse. The packet travels up through the protocol stack, and each successive header is stripped off by the appropriate protocol and processed. In essence, the protocols operating at the various layers communicate horizontally with their counterparts in the other system, as shown in Figure 2-4. The horizontal connections between the various layers are logical; there is no direct communication between them, but the information included in each protocol header by the transmitting system is a message that will be carried to the same protocol in the destination system.

Vertical Communications

The headers applied by the various protocols implement the specific functions carried out by those protocols. In addition to communicating horizontally with the

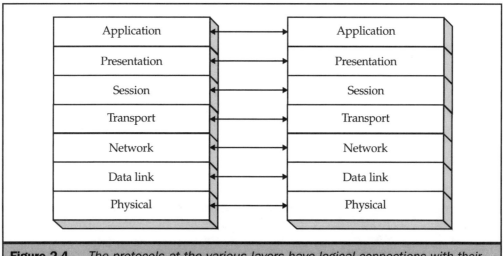

Figure 2-4. *The protocols at the various layers have logical connections with their equivalents on other systems*

same protocol in the other system, the header information also enables each layer to communicate with the layers above and below it (see Figure 2-5). For example, when a system receives a packet and passes it up through the protocol stack, the data link–layer protocol header includes a field that identifies which network-layer protocol the system should use to process the packet. The network-layer protocol header in turn

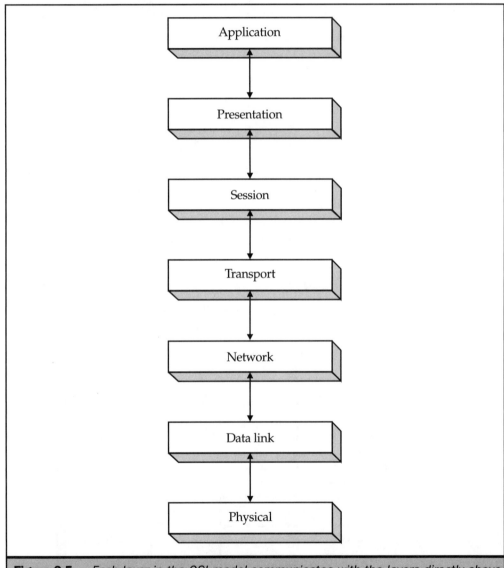

Figure 2-5.   *Each layer in the OSI model communicates with the layers directly above and below it*

specifies one of the transport-layer protocols, and the transport-layer protocol identifies the application for which the data is ultimately destined. This vertical communication makes it possible for a computer to support multiple protocols at each of the layers simultaneously. As long as a packet has the correct information in its headers, it can be routed on the appropriate path through the stack to the intended destination.

Encapsulation Terminology

One of the most confusing aspects of the data encapsulation process is the terminology used to describe the PDUs generated by each layer. The term *packet* specifically refers to the complete unit transmitted over the network medium, although it also has become a generic term for the data unit at any stage in the process. Most data link–layer protocols are said to work with *frames,* because they include both a header and a footer that surround the data from the network-layer protocol. The term *frame* refers to a PDU of variable size, depending on the amount of data enclosed. A data link–layer protocol that uses PDUs of a uniform size, such as Asynchronous Transfer Mode (ATM), is said to deal in *cells.*

When transport-layer data is encapsulated by a network-layer protocol, the resulting PDU is called a *datagram.* During the course of its transmission, a datagram might be split into *fragments,* each of which is sometimes incorrectly called a datagram. The terminology at the transport layer is more protocol specific than at the lower layers. TCP/IP, for example, has two transport-layer protocols. The first, called the *User Datagram Protocol (UDP),* also refers to the PDUs it creates as *datagrams,* although these are not synonymous with the datagrams produced at the network layer. When the UDP protocol at the transport layer is encapsulated by the IP protocol at the network layer, the result is a datagram packaged within another datagram.

The difference between UDP and the Transmission Control Protocol (TCP), which also operates at the transport layer, is that UDP datagrams are self-contained units that contain the entirety of the data generated by the transport-layer protocol. UDP is therefore used to transmit small amounts of data. TCP, on the other hand, is used to transmit larger amounts of data that usually do not fit into a single packet. As a result, each of the PDUs produced by the TCP protocol is called a *segment,* and the collection of segments that carry the entirety of the application-layer protocol data is called a *sequence.* The PDU produced by an application-layer protocol is typically called a *message.* The session and presentation layers are usually not associated with individual protocols. Their functions are incorporated into other elements of the protocol stack, and they do not have their own headers or PDUs.

All of these terms are frequently confused, and it is not surprising to see even authoritative documents use them incorrectly. The following sections examine each of the seven layers of the OSI reference model in turn, the functions that are associated with each, and the protocols that are most commonly used at those layers. As you proceed through this book, you will learn more about each of the individual protocols and their relationships to the other elements of the protocol stack.

The Physical Layer

The physical layer of the OSI model defines the actual medium that is used to carry data from one computer to another. The most common physical-layer type used in data networking is a copper-based electrical cable, although fiber-optic cable is becoming increasingly popular. There are also a number of wireless physical-layer implementations that use radio waves, infrared, lasers, microwaves, and other technologies. The physical layer includes the type of technology used to carry the data, the type of equipment used to implement that technology, the specifications by which the equipment should be installed, and the nature of the signals that should be used to encode the data for transmission.

For example, one of the most popular physical-layer standards used for local area networking today is 10BaseT Ethernet. Ethernet is primarily thought of as a data link–layer protocol; but as with most protocols functioning at the data link layer, it is intimately related to specific physical-layer implementations, and the standards for the protocol define the elements of the physical layer as well. 10BaseT refers to the type of cable used to form a particular type of Ethernet network. The Ethernet standard defines 10BaseT as an unshielded twisted-pair cable containing four pairs of wires enclosed in a single sheath.

However, the construction of the cable itself is not the only physical-layer element involved. The standards used to build an Ethernet network also define how the cable is to be installed, including maximum segment lengths and distances from power sources. The standards specify what kind of connectors are used to join the cable, the type of network interface card (NIC) to install in the computer, and the type of hub used to join the computers in the star topology. Finally, the standard specifies how the NIC should encode the data generated by the computer into electrical impulses that can be transmitted across the cable.

Thus, you can see that the physical layer encompasses much more than a type of cable. However, you generally don't have to know the details about every element of the physical-layer standard. When you buy Ethernet NICs, cables, and hubs, they are already constructed to the Ethernet specifications and designed to use the proper signaling scheme. Installing the equipment, however, is more complicated.

Physical-Layer Specifications

The installation of a network's physical layer is a job that is increasingly being outsourced to specialized contractors. While it is relatively easy to learn enough about a LAN technology to purchase the appropriate equipment, installing the cable (or other medium) is much more difficult, because you must be aware of all the specifications that affect the process. For example, the Ethernet standards published by the IEEE 802.3 working group specify the basic wiring configuration guidelines that pertain to the protocol's media access control (MAC) and collision detection mechanisms. These rules specify elements such as the maximum length of a cable segment, the distance between workstations, and the number of repeaters permitted on a network.

These guidelines are common knowledge to Ethernet network administrators, but these rules alone are not sufficient to perform a large cable installation. The American National Standards Institute/Electronic Industry Association/Telecommunication Industry Association (ANSI/EIA/TIA) 568, "Commercial Building Telecommunication Cabling Standard," defines in much greater detail how the cabling for data networks of various types should be installed. In addition, there are local building codes to consider, which might have a great effect on a cable installation. For these reasons, large physical-layer installations should in most cases be performed by professionals who are familiar with all of the standards that apply to the particular technology involved.

Note *For more information on network cabling and its installation, see Chapter 4.*

Physical-Layer Signaling

The primary operative component of a physical-layer installation is the transceiver found in NICs, repeating hubs, and other devices. The transceiver, as the name implies, is responsible for transmitting and receiving signals over the network medium. On networks using copper cable, the transceiver is an electrical device that takes the binary data it receives from the data link–layer protocol and converts it into signals of various voltages. Unlike all of the other layers in the stack, the physical layer is not concerned in any way with the meaning of the data being transmitted. The transceiver simply converts zeros and ones into voltages, pulses of light, radio waves, or some other type of signal, but it is completely oblivious to packets, frames, addresses, and even the system receiving the signal.

The signals generated by a transceiver can be either *analog* or *digital.* Most data networks use digital signals, but some of the wireless technologies use analog radio transmissions to carry data. Analog signals transition between two values gradually, forming the sine wave pattern shown in Figure 2-6, while digital value transmissions are immediate. The values of an analog signal can be determined by variations in amplitude, frequency, phase, or a combination of these elements.

The use of digital signals is much more common in data networking, however. All of the standard copper and fiber-optic media use various forms of digital signaling. The signaling scheme is determined by the data link–layer protocol being used. All Ethernet networks, for example, use the Manchester encoding scheme, whether they are running over twisted-pair, coaxial, or fiber-optic cable. Digital signals transition between values almost instantaneously, producing the square wave shown in Figure 2-7. Depending on the network medium, the values can represent electrical voltages, the presence or absence of a beam of light, or any other appropriate attribute of the medium. In most cases, the signal is produced with transitions between a positive and a negative voltage, although some use a zero value as well. The actual voltage is not relevant; it is the transitions that create the signal.

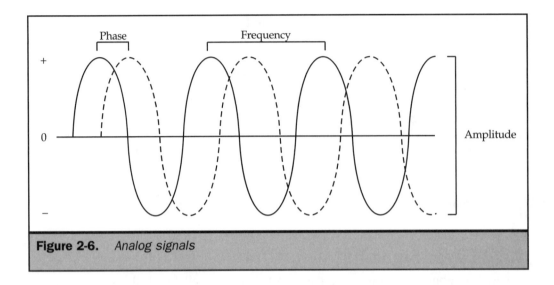

Figure 2-6. *Analog signals*

Figure 2-7 illustrates a signaling scheme called *polar signaling*. In this scheme, the signal is broken up into units of time called *cells*, and the voltage of each cell denotes its binary value. A positive voltage is a zero, and a negative voltage is a one. This

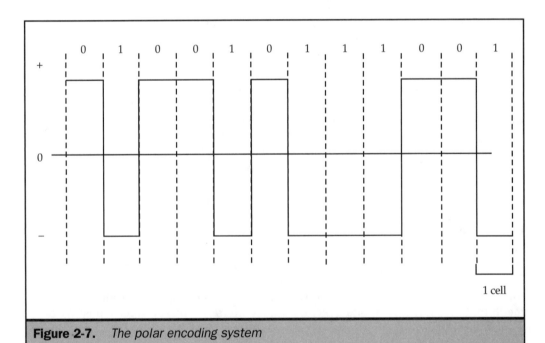

Figure 2-7. *The polar encoding system*

signaling code would seem to be a simple and logical method for transmitting binary information, but it has one crucial flaw, and that is timing. When the binary code consists of two or more consecutive zeros or ones, there is no voltage transition for the duration of two or more cells. Unless the two systems communicating have clocks that are precisely synchronized, it is impossible to tell for certain whether a voltage that remains continuous for a period of time represents two, three, or more cells with the same value. Remember that these communications occur at incredibly high rates of speed, so the timing intervals involved are extremely small.

Some systems can use this type of signal because they have an external timing signal that keeps the communicating systems synchronized. However, most data networks run over a baseband medium that permits the transmission of only one signal. As a result, these networks use a different type of signaling scheme that is *self-timing*. In other words, the data signal itself contains a timing signal that enables the receiving system to correctly interpret the values and convert them into binary data.

The *Manchester encoding scheme* used on Ethernet networks is a self-timing signal, by virtue of the fact that every cell has a value transition at its midpoint. This delineates the boundaries of the cells to the receiving system. The binary values are specified by the direction of the value transition; a positive-to-negative transition indicates a value of zero, and a negative-to-positive transition indicates a value of one (see Figure 2-8). The value transitions at the beginnings of the cells have no function other than to set voltage to the appropriate value for the midcell transition.

Token Ring networks use a different encoding scheme called *Differential Manchester*, which also has a value transition at the midpoint of each cell. However, in this scheme,

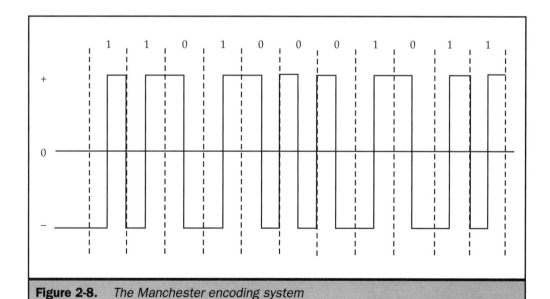

Figure 2-8. *The Manchester encoding system*

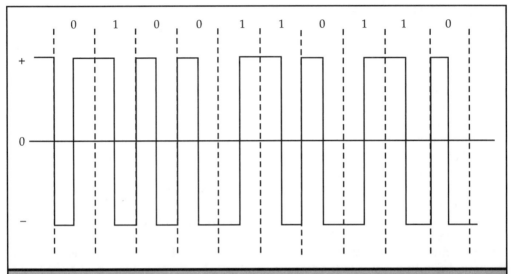

Figure 2-9. *The Differential Manchester encoding system*

the direction of the transition is irrelevant; it exists only to provide a timing signal. The value of each cell is determined by the presence or absence of a transition at the beginning of the cell. If the transition exists, the value of the cell is zero; if there is no transition, the value of the cell is one (see Figure 2-9). As with the midpoint transition, the direction of the transition is irrelevant.

The Data Link Layer

The data link–layer protocol provides the interface between the physical network and the protocol stack on the computer. A data link–layer protocol typically consists of three elements:

- The format for the frame that will encapsulate the network-layer protocol data.
- The mechanism that regulates access to the shared network medium.
- The guidelines that should be used to construct the network's physical layer.

The header and footer applied to the network-layer protocol data by this protocol are the outermost on the packet as it is transmitted across the network. This frame is, in essence, the envelope that carries the packet to its next destination and, therefore, provides the basic addressing information needed to get it there. In addition, data link–layer protocols usually include an error-detection facility and an indicator that specifies the network-layer protocol that the receiving system should use to process the data included in the packet.

On most LANs, multiple systems access a single shared baseband network medium. This means that only one computer can transmit data at any one time. If two or more systems transmit simultaneously, a collision occurs and the data is lost. The data link–layer protocol is responsible for controlling access to the shared medium and preventing an excess of collisions.

Because protocols are operating at multiple layers of the stack simultaneously, there can be confusion between them, and data link–layer protocols are sometimes referred to by incorrect names in order to distinguish them from the protocols operating at the other layers. For example, Ethernet is sometimes called a *topology*, when the topology actually refers to the way in which the computers on the network are cabled together. Some forms of Ethernet use a *bus topology*, in which each of the computers is cabled to the next one in a daisy-chain fashion; while the *star topology*, in which each computer is cabled to a central hub, is more prevalent today. A *ring topology* is a bus with the ends joined together, and a *mesh topology* is one in which each computer has a cable connection to every other computer on the network. These last two types are mainly theoretical; networks today do not use them. Token Ring networks use a logical ring, but the computers are actually cabled using a star topology.

This confusion is understandable, since most data link–layer protocols include elements of the physical layer in their specifications. It is necessary for the data link–layer protocol to be intimately related to the physical layer, because media access control mechanisms are highly dependent on the size of the frames being transmitted and the length of the cable segments.

Addressing

The data link–layer protocol header contains an address of the computer sending the packet and the computer that is to receive it. The addresses used at this layer are the hardware (or MAC) addresses that in most cases are hardcoded into the network interface of each computer and router by the manufacturer. On Ethernet and Token Ring networks, the addresses are 6 bytes long, the first 3 bytes of which are assigned to the manufacturer by the Institute of Electrical and Electronic Engineers (IEEE), and the second 3 bytes of which are assigned by the manufacturer itself. A few older protocols, such as ARCNET, use addresses that are assigned by the network administrator, but the factory-assigned addresses are more efficient, insofar as they ensure no duplication can occur.

Data link–layer protocols are not concerned with the delivery of the packet to its ultimate destination, unless that destination is on the same LAN as the source. When a packet passes through several networks on the way to its destination, the data link–layer protocol is only responsible for getting the packet to the router on the local network that provides access to the next network on its journey. Thus, the destination address in a data link–layer protocol header always references a device on the local network, even if the ultimate destination of the message is a computer on a network miles away.

The data link–layer protocols used on LANs rely on a shared network medium. Every packet is transmitted to all of the computers on the network segment, and only the system with the address specified as the destination reads the packet into its memory buffers and processes it. The other systems simply discard the packet without taking any further action.

Media Access Control

Media access control is the process by which the data link–layer protocol arbitrates access to the network medium. In order for the network to function efficiently, each of the workstations sharing the cable or other medium must have an opportunity to transmit its data on a regular basis. This is why the data to be transmitted is split into packets in the first place. If computers transmitted all of their data in a continuous stream, they could conceivably monopolize the network for extended periods of time.

Two basic forms of media access control are used on most of today's LANs. The *token passing* method, used by Token Ring and FDDI systems, uses a special frame called a *token* that is passed from one workstation to another. Only the system in possession of the token is permitted to transmit its data. A workstation, on receiving the token, transmits its data and then releases the token to the next workstation. Since there is only one token on the network (assuming it's functioning properly), it isn't possible for two systems to transmit at the same time.

Note   *For more information on token passing, see Chapter 9.*

The other method, used on Ethernet networks, is called *Carrier Sense Multiple Access with Collision Detection (CSMA/CD)*. In this method, when a workstation has data to send, it listens to the network cable and transmits if the network is not in use. On CSMA/CD networks, it is possible (and even expected) for workstations to transmit at the same time, resulting in packet collisions. To compensate for this, each system has a mechanism that enables it to detect collisions when they occur and retransmit the data that was lost.

Note   *For more information on CSMA/CD, see Chapter 8.*

Both of these MAC mechanisms rely on physical-layer specifications for the network to function properly. For example, an Ethernet system can only detect collisions if they occur while the workstation is still transmitting a packet. If the network segment is too long, a collision may occur after the last bit of data has left the transmitting system, and thus may go undetected. The data in that packet is then lost and its absence can only be detected by the upper-layer protocols in the system that is the ultimate destination of the message. This process takes much longer and significantly reduces the efficiency of the network. Thus, while the OSI reference model might create a neat division between the physical and data link layers, in the real world, the functionality of the two is more closely intertwined.

Protocol Indicator

Most data link–layer protocol implementations are designed to support the use of multiple network-layer protocols at the same time. This means that there are several possible paths through the protocol stack on each computer. To use multiple protocols at the network layer, the data link–layer protocol header must include a code that specifies the network-layer protocol that was used to generate the payload in the packet. This requirement is so that the receiving system can pass the data enclosed in the frame up to the appropriate network-layer process.

For example, on a network that uses both Windows NT and Novell NetWare servers, there might be some packets carrying IP datagrams and others using the IPX protocol at the network layer. To distinguish between the two, the DIX Ethernet II specification called for a header field called the Ethertype, which contains a code identifying the network-layer protocol. The IEEE 802 specifications use a Sub-Network Access Protocol (SNAP) field to perform the same function, using the same codes as the Ethertype field.

Error Detection

Most data link–layer protocols are unlike all of the upper-layer protocols in that they include a footer that follows the payload field in addition to the header that precedes it. This footer contains a *frame check sequence (FCS)* field that is used to detect any errors that have occurred during the transmission. To do this, the system transmitting the packet computes a cyclical redundancy check (CRC) value on the entire frame and includes it in the FCS field. When the packet reaches its next destination, the receiving system performs the same computation and compares its results with the value in the FCS field. If the values do not match, the packet is assumed to have been damaged in transit and is silently discarded.

The receiving system takes no action to have discarded packets retransmitted; this is left up to the protocols operating at the upper layers of the OSI model. This error-detection process occurs at each hop in the packet's journey to its destination. Some upper-layer protocols have their own mechanisms for end-to-end error detection.

The Network Layer

The network-layer protocol is the primary end-to-end carrier for messages generated by the application layer. This means that, unlike the data link–layer protocol, which is concerned only with getting the packet to its next destination on the local network, the network-layer protocol is responsible for the packet's entire journey from the source system to its ultimate destination. A network-layer protocol accepts data from the transport layer and packages it in a datagram by adding its own header. Like a data link–layer protocol header, the header at the network layer contains the address of the destination system, but this address identifies the packet's final destination. Thus, the two destination addresses in the data link–layer and network-layer protocol headers may actually refer to two different computers. The network-layer protocol datagram is essentially an envelope within the data link–layer envelope, and while the data link–layer envelope is opened by every system that processes the packet, the network-layer envelope remains sealed until the packet reaches its final destination.

In addition to addressing, the network-layer protocol also performs some or all of the following functions:

- Routing
- Fragmenting
- Error checking
- Transport-layer protocol identification

Routing

Network-layer protocols use different types of addressing systems to identify the ultimate destination of a packet. The most popular network-layer protocol, the Internet Protocol (IP), provides its own 32-bit address space that identifies both the network on which the destination system resides and the system itself. NetWare's Internetwork Packet Exchange (IPX) protocol uses a separate network address and relies on the hardware address coded into each network interface to identify particular systems.

An address by which individual networks can be uniquely identified is vital to the performance of the network-layer protocol's primary function, which is *routing*. When a packet travels through a large corporate internetwork or the Internet, it is passed from router to router until it reaches the network on which the destination system is located. A properly designed network will have more than one possible route to a particular destination, for fault-tolerance reasons, and the Internet has literally thousands of possible routes. Each router is responsible for determining the next router that the packet should use to take the most efficient path to its destination. Because data link–layer protocols are completely ignorant of conditions outside of the local network, it is left up to the network-layer protocol to choose an appropriate route with an eye on the end-to-end journey of the packet, and not just the next interim hop.

The network layer defines two types of computers that can be involved in a packet transmission: end systems and intermediate systems. An *end system* is either the computer generating and transmitting the packet or the computer that is the ultimate recipient of the packet. An *intermediate system* is a router or switch that connects two or more networks and forwards packets on the way to their destinations. On end systems, all seven layers of the protocol stack are involved in either the creation or the reception of the packet. On intermediate systems, packets arrive and travel up through the stack only as high as the network layer (see Figure 2-10). The network-layer protocol chooses a route for the packet and sends it back down to a data link–layer protocol for packaging and transmission at the physical layer.

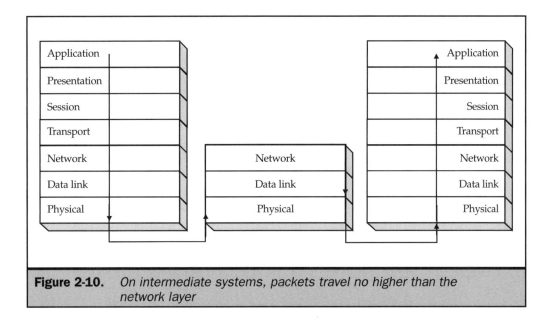

Figure 2-10. *On intermediate systems, packets travel no higher than the network layer*

When an intermediate system receives a packet, the data link–layer protocol checks it for errors and for the correct hardware address, and then strips off the data link header and footer and passes it up to the network-layer protocol identified by the Ethertype field or its equivalent. At this point, the packet consists of a datagram; that is, a network-layer protocol header and a payload that was generated by the transport layer of the source system. The network-layer protocol then reads the destination address in the header and determines what the packet's next destination should be. If the destination is a workstation on a local network, the intermediate system transmits the packet directly to that workstation. If the destination is on a distant network, the intermediate system consults its routing table to select the router that provides the most efficient path to that destination.

The compilation and storage of routing information in a reference table is a separate network-layer process that is performed either manually by an administrator or automatically by specialized network-layer protocols that routers use to exchange information about the networks to which they are connected. Once it has determined the next destination for the packet, the network-layer protocol passes the information down to the data link–layer protocol with the datagram, so that it can be packaged in a new frame and transmitted. When the IP protocol is running at the network layer, an additional process is required in which the IP address of the next destination is converted into a hardware address that the data link–layer protocol can use.

Fragmenting

Because routers can connect networks that use different data link–layer protocols, it is sometimes necessary for intermediate systems to split datagrams into fragments to transmit them. If, for example, a workstation on a Token Ring network generates a packet containing 4,500 bytes of data, then an intermediate system that joins the Token Ring network to an Ethernet network must split the data into fragments no larger than 1,500 bytes, because that is the largest amount of data that an Ethernet frame can carry.

Datagrams that are fragmented by intermediate systems are not reassembled until they reach their final destinations. Depending on the data link–layer protocols used by the various intermediate networks, the fragments of a datagram may be fragmented themselves.

Connection-Oriented and Connectionless Protocols

There are two types of end-to-end protocols that operate at the network and transport layers: connection-oriented and connectionless. The type of protocol used helps to determine what other functions are performed at each layer. A *connection-oriented* protocol is one in which a logical connection between the source and the destination systems is established before any upper-layer data is transmitted. Once the connection is established, the source system transmits the data, and the destination system acknowledges its receipt. A failure to receive the appropriate acknowledgments serves as a signal to the sender that packets have to be retransmitted. When the data transmission is completed successfully, the systems break down the connection. By using this type of protocol, the sending system is certain that the data has arrived at the destination successfully. The cost of this guaranteed service is the additional network traffic generated by the connection establishment, acknowledgment, and termination messages.

A *connectionless protocol* simply packages data and transmits it to the destination address without checking to see whether the destination system is available and without expecting packet acknowledgments. In most cases, connectionless protocols are used when the guaranteed delivery and other services provided by a connection-oriented protocol are supplied by another layer of the stack. These additional services can include flow control, error detection, and correction.

Most of the LAN protocols operating at the network layer, such as IP and IPX, are connectionless, because in both cases, various protocols are available at the transport layer to provide both connectionless and connection-oriented services. There have been a few connection-oriented network-layer protocols, such as X.25; but the widespread adoption of TCP/IP, which supports only connectionless IP communications, has all but eliminated this type of protocol from the network layer. Despite its being connectionless, however, the IP protocol has an error-detection mechanism, but it checks only the IP header fields for errors, leaving the data to be checked by the protocols at the other layers.

The Transport Layer

Once you reach the transport layer, the process of getting packets from their source to their destination is no longer a concern. The transport-layer protocols and all the layers above them rely completely on the network and data link layers for addressing and transmission services. As discussed earlier, packets being processed by intermediate systems travel only as high as the network layer, so the transport-layer protocols only operate on the two end systems. The transport-layer PDU consists of a header and the data it has received from the application layer above, which is encapsulated into a datagram by the network layer below.

One of the main functions of the transport-layer protocol is to identify the upper-layer process that generated the message at the source system and that will receive the message at the destination system. The transport-layer protocols in the TCP/IP suite, for example, use port numbers in their headers to identify upper-layer services. Other functions that can be performed at the transport layer include error detection and correction, flow control, packet acknowledgment, and other connection-oriented services.

Protocol Service Combinations

Data link– and network-layer protocols operate together interchangeably; you can use almost any data link–layer protocol with any network-layer protocol. However, transport-layer protocols are closely related to a particular network-layer protocol, and cannot be interchanged. The combination of a network-layer protocol and a transport-layer protocol provides a complementary set of services that is suitable for a specific application. As at the network layer, transport-layer protocols can be connection oriented (CO) or connectionless (CL). The OSI model document defines four possible combinations of CO and CL protocols at these two layers, depending on the services required, as shown in Figure 2-11. The process of selecting a combination of protocols for a particular task is called *mapping* a transport-layer service onto a network-layer service.

The selection of a protocol at the transport layer is based on the needs of the application generating the message and the services already provided by the protocols at the lower layers. The OSI document defines five theoretical classes of transport-layer protocol, which are as follows:

- **TP0** No additional functionality. Assumes that the protocols at the lower layers already provide all of the services needed by the application.

- **TP1** Signaled error recovery. Provides the capability to correct errors that have been detected by the protocols operating at the lower layers.

- **TP2** Multiplexing. Includes codes that identify the process that generated the packet and that will process it at the destination, thus enabling the traffic from multiple applications to be carried over a single network medium.

- **TP3** Signaled error recovery and multiplexing. Combines the services provided by TP1 and TP2.

- **TP4** Complete connection-oriented service. Includes error detection and correction, flow control, and other services. Assumes the use of a connectionless protocol at the lower layers that provides none of these services.

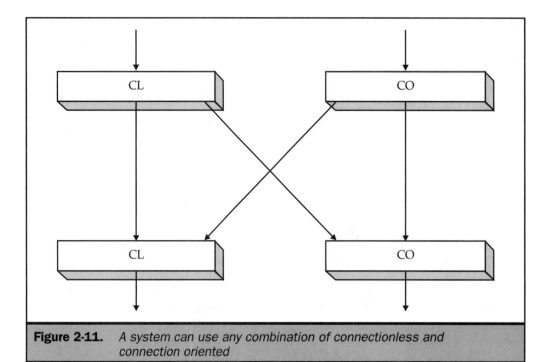

Figure 2-11.   *A system can use any combination of connectionless and connection oriented*

This classification of transport-layer services is another place where the theoretical constructs of the OSI model differ substantially from reality. None of the protocol suites in common use have five different transport-layer protocols conforming to these classes. Most of the suites, like TCP/IP, have two protocols that basically conform to the TP0 and TP4 classes, providing connectionless and connection-oriented services, respectively.

Transport-Layer Protocol Functions

The UDP protocol is a connectionless service that, together with IP at the network layer, provides minimal services for brief transactions that do not need the services of a connection-oriented protocol. Domain Name System (DNS) transactions, for example, generally consist of short messages that can fit into a single packet, so no flow control is needed. A typical transaction consists of a request and a reply, which functions as an acknowledgment, so no other guaranteed delivery mechanism is needed. UDP does have an error-detection mechanism in the form of a checksum computation performed on both the source and destination systems, however. Because the UDP protocol provides a minimum of additional services, its header is only 8 bytes long, adding very little additional control overhead to the packet.

The TCP protocol, on the other hand, is a connection-oriented protocol that provides a full range of services, but at the cost of much higher overhead. The TCP header is 20 bytes long, and the protocol also generates a large number of additional packets solely for control procedures, such as connection establishment, termination, and packet acknowledgment.

Segmentation and Reassembly

Connection-oriented transport-layer protocols are designed to carry large amounts of data, but the data must be split into segments to fit into individual packets. The segmentation of the data and the numbering of the segments is a critical element in the transmission process and also makes functions like error recovery possible. The routing process performed at the network layer is dynamic; and in the course of a transmission, it is possible for the segments to take different routes to the destination and arrive in a different order from that in which they were sent. It is the numbering of the segments that makes it possible for the receiving system to reassemble them back into their original order. This numbering also makes it possible for the receiving system to notify the sender that specific packets have been lost or corrupted. As a result, the sender can retransmit only the missing segments and not have to repeat the entire transmission.

Flow Control

One of the functions commonly provided by connection-oriented transport-layer protocols is *flow control,* which is a mechanism by which the system receiving the data can notify the sender that it must decrease its transmission rate or risk overwhelming the receiver and losing data. The TCP header, for example, includes a Window field with which the receiver specifies the number of bytes that it can receive from the sender. If this value decreases in succeeding packets, the sender knows that it has to slow down its transmission rate. When the value begins to rise again, the sender can increase its speed.

Error Detection and Recovery

The OSI model document defines two forms of error recovery that can be performed by connection-oriented transport-layer protocols. One is a response to *signaled errors* detected by other protocols in the stack. In this mechanism, the transport-layer protocol does not have to detect the transmission errors itself. Instead, it receives notification from a protocol at the network or data link layer that an error has occurred and that specific packets have been lost or corrupted. The transport-layer protocol only has to send a message back to the source system listing the packets and requesting their retransmission.

The more commonly implemented form of error recovery at the transport layer is a complete process of error detection and correction that is used to cope with *unsignaled errors,* which are errors that have not yet been detected by other means. Even though most data link–layer protocols have their own error-detection and correction mechanisms, they only function over the individual hops between two systems. A transport-layer error-detection mechanism provides error checking between the two end systems and includes the capability to recover from the errors by informing the sender which packets have to be resent. To do this, the checksum included in the transport-layer protocol header is computed only on the fields that are not modified during the journey to the destination. Fields that routinely change, such as a Time-to-Live indicator that is incremented by every router processing the packet, are omitted from the calculation.

The Session Layer

When you reach the session layer, the boundaries between the layers and their functions start to become more obscure. There are no discrete protocols that operate exclusively at the session layer. Rather, the session-layer functionality is incorporated into other protocols, with functions that fall into the provinces of the presentation and application layers, as well. NetBIOS (Network Basic Input/Output System) and NetBEUI (NetBIOS Extended User Interface) are two of the best examples of these protocols.

The boundary to the session layer is also the point at which all concern for the transmission of data between two systems is transcended. Questions of packet acknowledgment, error detection, and flow control are all left behind at this point, because everything that can be done has been done by the protocols at the transport layer and below.

The session layer is also not inherently concerned with security and the network logon process, as the name seems to imply. Rather, the primary functions of this layer concern the exchange of messages between the two connected end systems, called a *dialog.* There are also numerous other functions provided at this layer, which really serves as a multipurpose "toolkit" for application developers.

The services provided by the session layer are widely misunderstood, and even at the time of the OSI model's development, there was some question concerning whether they should be allotted a layer of their own. In fact, 22 different services are provided by the session layer, grouped into subsets such as the Kernel Function Unit, the Basic Activity Subset, and the Basic Synchronization Subset. Most of these services are of interest only to application developers, and some are even duplicated as a result of a compromise that occurred when the two committees creating OSI model standards were combined.

Communications between the layers of the OSI reference model are facilitated through the use of *service request primitives,* which are the tools in the toolkit. Each layer provides services to the layer immediately above it. A process at a given layer takes advantage of a service provided by the layer below by issuing a command using the appropriate service request primitive, plus any additional parameters that may be required. Thus, an application-layer process issues a request for a network resource using a primitive provided by the presentation layer. The request is then passed down through the layers, with each layer using the proper primitive provided by the layer below, until the message is ready for transmission over the network. Once the packet arrives at its destination, it is decoded into *indication primitives* that are passed upward through the layers of the stack to the receiving application process.

The two most important services attributed to the session layer are dialog control and dialog separation. *Dialog control* is the means by which two systems initiate a dialog, exchange messages, and finally end the dialog while ensuring that each system has received the messages intended for it. While this may seem to be a simple task, consider the fact that one system might transmit a message to the other and then receive a message back without knowing for certain when the response was generated. Is the other system responding to the message just sent or was its response transmitted before that message was received? This sort of *collision case* can cause serious problems, especially when one of the systems is attempting to terminate the dialog or create a checkpoint. *Dialog separation* is the process of inserting a reference marker called a *checkpoint* into the data stream passing between the two systems so that the status of the two machines can be assessed at the same point in time.

Dialog Control

When two end systems initiate a session-layer dialog, they choose one of two modes that controls the way they will exchange messages for the duration of the session: either two-way alternate (TWA) mode or two-way simultaneous (TWS) mode. Each session connection is uniquely identified by a 196-byte value consisting of the following four elements:

- Initiator SS-USER reference
- Responder SS-USER reference
- Common reference
- Additional reference

Once made, the choice of mode is irrevocable; the connection must be severed and reestablished in order to switch to the other mode.

In TWA mode, only one of the systems can transmit messages at any one time. Permission to transmit is arbitrated by the possession of a *data token.* Each system, at the conclusion of a transmission, sends the token to the other system using the S-TOKEN-GIVE primitive. On receipt of the token, the other system can transmit its message. There is also an S-TOKEN-PLEASE primitive that a system can use to request the token from the other system. The use of TWS mode complicates the communication process enormously. As the name implies, in a TWS mode connection, there is no token and both systems can transmit messages at the same time.

Note	*It is important to understand that the references to tokens and connections at the session layer have nothing to do with the similarly named elements in lower-layer protocols. A session-layer token is not the equivalent of the token frame used by the Token Ring protocol, nor is a session-layer connection the equivalent of a transport-layer connection such as that used by TCP. It is possible for end systems to terminate the session-layer connection while leaving the transport-layer connection open for further communications.*

The use of the token prevents problems resulting from crossed messages and provides a mechanism for the *orderly termination* of the connection between the systems. An orderly termination begins with one system signaling its desire to terminate the connection and transmitting the token. The other system, on receiving the token, transmits any data remaining in its buffers and uses the S-RELEASE primitive to acknowledge the termination request. On receiving the S-RELEASE primitive, the original system knows that it has received all of the data pending from the other system, and can then use the S-DISCONNECT primitive to terminate the connection.

There is also a *negotiated release* feature that enables one system to refuse the release request of another, which can be used in cases in which a collision occurs because both systems have issued a release request at the same time, and a *release token* that prevents the occurrence of these collisions in the first place by enabling only one system at a time to request a release.

All of these mechanisms are "tools" in the kit that the session layer provides to application developers; they are not automatic processes working behind the scenes. When designing an application, the developer must make an explicit decision to use the S-TOKEN-GIVE primitive instead of S-TOKEN-PLEASE, for example, or to use a negotiated release instead of an orderly termination.

Dialog Separation

Applications create checkpoints in order to save their current status to disk, in case of a system failure. This was a much more common occurrence at the time that the OSI model was developed than it is now. As with the dialog control processes discussed earlier, checkpointing is a procedure that must be explicitly implemented by an application developer as needed.

When the application involves communication between two systems connected by a network, the checkpoint must save the status of both systems at the same point in the data stream. Performing any activity at precisely the same moment on two different computers is nearly impossible. The systems might be performing thousands of activities per second, and their timing is nowhere near as precise as would be needed to execute a specific task simultaneously. In addition, the problem again arises of messages that may be in transit at the time the checkpoint is created. As a result, dialog separation is performed by saving a checkpoint at a particular point in the data stream passing between the two systems rather than at a particular moment in time.

When the connection is used in TWA mode, the checkpointing process is relatively simple. One system creates a checkpoint and issues a primitive called S-SYNC-MINOR. The other system, on receiving this primitive, creates its own checkpoint, secure in the knowledge that no data is left in transit at the time of synchronization. This is called a *minor synchronization* because it works with data flowing in only one direction at a time and requires only a single exchange of control messages.

It is still possible to perform a minor synchronization in TWS mode, using a special *minor synchronization token* that prevents both systems from issuing the S-SYNC-MINOR primitive at the same time. If it was possible to switch from TWS to TWA mode in midconnection, the use of an additional token would not be necessary, but mode switching is not possible. This is something that many people feel to be a major shortcoming in the session-layer specification.

In most cases, systems using TWS mode communications must perform a *major synchronization*, which accounts not only for traffic that can be running in both directions, but also for expedited traffic. A primitive called S-EXPEDITED enables one system to transmit to the other using what amounts to a high-speed pipeline that is separate from the normal communications channel. To perform a major synchronization, the system in possession of yet another token called the *major/activity token* issues a primitive called S-SYNC-MAJOR and then stops transmitting until it receives a response. However, the system issuing this primitive cannot create its checkpoint yet, as in a minor synchronization, because there may be traffic from the other system currently in transit.

On receiving the primitive, the other system is able to create its own checkpoint, because all of the data in transit has been received, including expedited data, which has to have arrived before the primitive. The receiving system then transmits a confirmation response over the normal channel and transmits a special PREPARE message over the expedited channel. The system that initiated the synchronization procedure receives the PREPARE message first and then the confirmation, at which time it can create its own checkpoint.

The Presentation Layer

Unlike the session layer, which provides many different functions, the presentation layer has only one. In fact, most of the time, the presentation layer functions primarily as a *pass-through service*, meaning that it receives primitives from the application layer and issues duplicate primitives to the session layer below, using the Presentation Service Access Point (PSAP) and the Session Service Access Point (SSAP). All the discussion in the previous sections of applications utilizing session-layer services actually involves the use of the pass-through service at the presentation layer, because it is impossible for a process at any layer of the OSI model to communicate directly with any layer other than the one immediately above or beneath it.

While the basic functions of the primitives are not changed as they are passed down through the presentation layer, they can undergo a crucial translation process that is the primary function of the layer. Applications generate requests for network resources using their own native syntax, but the syntax of the application at the destination system receiving the request may be different in several ways. For example, a connection between a PC and a mainframe may require a translation between the ASCII and EBCDIC bit-coding formats. The systems might also implement encryption and/or compression for the data to be transmitted over the network.

This translation process occurs in two phases, one of which runs at the presentation layer on each system. Each computer maintains an *abstract syntax*, which is the native syntax for the application running on that system, and a *transfer syntax*, which is a common syntax used to transmit the data over the network. The presentation layer on the system sending a message converts the data from the abstract syntax to the transfer syntax and then passes it down to the session layer. When the message arrives at the destination system, the presentation layer converts the data from the transfer syntax to the abstract syntax of the application receiving the message. The transfer syntax chosen for each abstract syntax is based on a negotiation that occurs when a presentation-layer connection is established between two systems. Depending on the application's requirements and the nature of the connection between the systems, the transfer context may provide data encryption, data compression, or a simple translation.

Note	*As with the session layer, the presentation-layer connection is not synonymous with the connections that occur at the lower layers, nor is there direct communication between the presentation layers of the two systems. Messages travel down through the protocol stack to the physical medium and up through the stack on the receiver to the presentation layer there.*

The syntax negotiation process begins when one system uses the P-CONNECT primitive to transmit a set of *presentation contexts*, which are pairs of associated abstract contexts and transfer contexts supported by that system. Each presentation context is numbered using a unique odd-numbered integer called a *presentation context identifier*. With this message, one system is essentially informing the other of its presentation-layer capabilities. The message may contain multiple transfer contexts for each abstract context, to give the receiving system a choice.

Once the other system receives the P-CONNECT message, it passes the presentation contexts up to the application-layer processes, which decide which of the transfer contexts supported by each abstract context they want to use. The receiver then returns a list of contexts to the sender with either a single transfer context or an error message specified for each abstract context. On receipt by the original sender, this list becomes the *defined context set*. Error messages indicate that the receiving system does not support any of the transfer contexts specified for a specific abstract context. Once the negotiation process is completed, the systems can propose new presentation contexts for addition to the defined context set or remove contexts from the set using a primitive called P-ALTER-CONTEXT.

The Application Layer

As the top layer in the protocol stack, the application layer is the ultimate source and destination for all messages transmitted over the network. All of the processes discussed in the previous sections are triggered by an application that requests access to a resource located on a network system. Application-layer processes are not necessarily synonymous with the applications themselves, however. For example, if you use a word processor to open a document stored on a network server, then you are redirecting a local function to the network. The word processor itself does not provide the application-layer process needed to access the file. In most cases, it is an element of the operating system that distinguishes between requests for files on the local drive and those on the network. Other applications, however, are designed specifically for accessing network resources. When you run a dedicated FTP client, for example, the application itself is inseparable from the application-layer protocol it uses to communicate with the network. Some of the other protocols that are closely tied to the applications that use them are as follows:

- **DHCP** Dynamic Host Configuration Protocol
- **TFTP** Trivial File Transfer Protocol
- **DNS** Domain Name System
- **NFS** Network File System
- **RIP** Routing Information Protocol
- **OSPF** Open Shortest Path First
- **BGP** Border Gateway Protocol

In between these two extremes are numerous application types that access network resources in different ways and for different reasons, and the tools that make that access possible are located in the application layer. Some applications use protocols that are dedicated to specific types of network requests, such as the Simple Mail Transport Protocol (SMTP) and Post Office Protocol (POP3) used for e-mail, the Simple Network Management Protocol (SNMP) used for remote network administration, the Hypertext Transfer Protocol (HTTP) used for World Wide Web communications, and the Network News Transfer Protocol (NNTP) used for USENET news transfers. As you have seen in this chapter, the bottom four layers of the OSI reference model perform functions that are easily differentiated, while the functions of the session, presentation, and application layers tend to bleed together. Many of the application-layer protocols listed here contain functions that rightly belong at the presentation or session layers, but it is important not to let the OSI model assert itself too forcibly into your perception of data networking. The model is at this point a tool for understanding how networks function, and not a guide for the creation of networking technologies. Manufacturers are not interested in designing their products to conform to the arbitrary divisions of a theoretical model, and you should not expect them to.

The
Complete
Reference

Upgrading
&
Troubleshooting
Networks

Part II

Network Hardware

The
Complete
Reference

Upgrading & Troubleshooting Networks

Chapter 3

Network Interface Adapters

E very computer that participates on a network must have an interface to that network, using either a cable or some form of wireless signal that enables it to transmit data to the other systems. The most common form of network interface is an adapter card that connects to the computer's expansion bus and to a network cable, typically referred to as a *network interface card* or *NIC* (see Figure 3-1). The NIC is usually a separate product that you can insert and remove from the computer, but quite a few systems today integrate the network adapter into the motherboard design. Modems are also a form of network interface, even when the network is nothing more than two computers joined together. The Windows operating systems, for example, treat modems as a part of their networking architecture, just like a NIC, but with a different set of hardware features.

NIC Functions

The *network interface adapter,* in combination with the network adapter driver, implements the data link–layer protocol used on the computer, such as Ethernet or Token Ring, as well as part of the physical layer. The NIC also provides the link

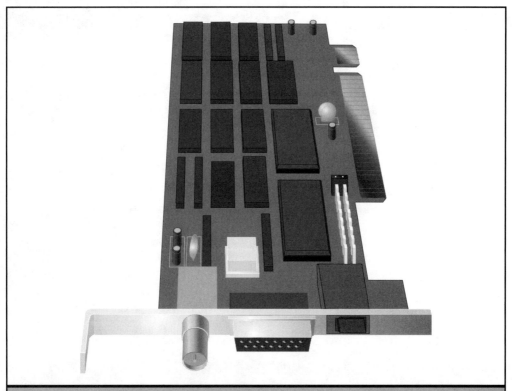

Figure 3-1.   *A typical network interface adapter card*

between the network layer protocol, which is implemented completely in the operating system, and the network medium, which is usually a cable connected to the NIC.

The NIC and its driver perform the basic functions needed for the computer to access the network. The process of transmitting data consists of the following steps (which, naturally, are reversed during packet reception):

1. **Data transfer**   The data stored in the computer's memory is transferred to the NIC across the system bus using one of the following technologies: *direct memory access (DMA)*, shared memory, or programmed I/O.

2. **Data buffering**   The rate at which the PC processes data is different from the transmission rate of the network. The NIC includes memory buffers that it uses to store data so it can process an entire frame at once. A typical Ethernet NIC has 4KB of buffer space, divided into separate transmit and receive buffers of 2KB each, while Token Ring and higher-end Ethernet cards can have 64KB of buffer space or more, which may be split between the transmit and receive buffers in several configurations.

3. **Frame construction**   The NIC receives data that has been packaged by the network layer protocol and encapsulates it in a frame that consists of its own data link–layer protocol header and footer. Depending on the size of the packet and the data link–layer protocol used, the NIC may also have to split the data into segments of the appropriate size for transmission over the network. Ethernet frames, for example, carry up to 1,500 bytes of data, while Token Ring frames can carry up to 4,500 bytes. For incoming traffic, the NIC reads the information in the data link–layer frame, verifies that the packet has been transmitted without error, and determines whether the packet should be passed up to the next layer in the networking stack. If so, the NIC strips off the outer frame and passes the enclosed data to the network layer protocol.

4. **Media access control**   The NIC is responsible for arbitrating the system's access to the shared network medium, using an appropriate *media access control (MAC)* mechanism. This is necessary to prevent multiple systems on the network from transmitting at the same time and losing data because of a packet collision. The MAC mechanism is the single most defining element of a data link–layer protocol. Ethernet's *Carrier Sense Multiple Access with Collision Detection (CSMA/CD)* system is radically different from the token-passing system used on Token Ring network's, but their basic functions are ultimately the same. (The MAC mechanism is not needed for incoming traffic.)

5. **Parallel/serial conversion**   The system bus connecting the NIC to the computer's main memory array transmits data 16 or 32 bits at a time in parallel fashion, while the NIC transmits and receives data from the network serially, that is, one bit at a time. The NIC is responsible for taking the parallel data transmission that it receives into its buffers and converting it to a serial bit stream for transmission out over the network medium. For incoming data from the network, the process is reversed.

NETWORK HARDWARE

6. **Data encoding/decoding**   The data generated by the computer in binary form must be encoded in a matter suitable for the network medium before it can be transmitted and incoming signals decoded on receipt. This and the following step are the physical layer processes implemented by the NIC. For a copper cable, the data is encoded into electrical impulses; for fiber-optic cable, the data is encoded into pulses of light. Other media may use radio waves, infrared, or other technologies. The encoding scheme is determined by the data link–layer protocol being used. For example, Ethernet uses Manchester encoding and Token Ring uses Differential Manchester.

7. **Data transmission/reception**   The NIC takes the data it has encoded, amplifies the signal to the appropriate amplitude, and transmits it over the network medium. This process is entirely physical and depends wholly on the nature of the signal used on the network medium.

> **Note** *For more information on the protocol-specific elements of the previous procedure, see Chapter 8 for more information about the Ethernet protocol, Chapter 9 for Token Ring and 100VG AnyLAN, and Chapter 10 for high-speed data link–layer protocols such as FDDI and ATM.*

The NIC also provides the data link–layer hardware (or MAC) address that is used to identify the system on the local network. Most data link–layer protocols, including all forms of Ethernet and Token Ring, rely on addresses that are hardcoded into the NIC by the manufacturer. In actuality, the MAC address identifies a particular network interface, not necessarily the whole system. In the case of a computer with two NICs installed and connected to two different networks, each NIC has its own MAC address that identifies it on the network to which it is attached.

Some older protocols, such as ArcNet, required the network administrator to set the hardware address manually on each NIC. If systems with duplicate addresses were on the network, communications problems resulted. Today, MAC addresses are assigned in two layers, much like IP addresses and domain names. The *IEEE (Institute of Electrical and Electronic Engineers)* maintains a registry of NIC manufacturers and assigns 3-byte address codes to them as needed. Manufacturers use these codes as the first three bytes of the 6-byte MAC address for each NIC they produce. Then, it is up to the manufacturer to see that the remaining three bytes are unique to each NIC they build.

> **Note** *The IEEE maintains a searchable database of manufacturer codes on the Web at http://standards.ieee.org/regauth/oui/index.html.*

NIC Features

In addition to the basic functionality described thus far, NICs can have a variety of other features, depending on the manufacturer, price point, and the type of computer in which the device is to be used. Some of these features are discussed in the following sections.

Full Duplex

Most of the data link–layer protocols that use twisted-pair cable separate the transmitted and received signals onto different wire pairs. Even when this is the case, however, the NIC typically operated in *half-duplex mode,* meaning that at any given time, it can be transmitting or receiving data, but not both simultaneously. NICs that can operate in *full-duplex mode* can transmit and receive at the same time, effectively doubling the throughput of the network (see Figure 3-2).

When a NIC is operating in full-duplex mode, it can transmit and receive data at any time, eliminating the need for a media access control mechanism. This also eliminates collisions, which increases the overall efficiency of the network. Running a full-duplex network requires more than just NICs that support this feature, however. The hub, switch, router, or other device to which each computer connects must also support full-duplex operation.

Full-duplex operation is a feature that is usually associated with Fast Ethernet. For more information on full-duplex networking, see Chapter 8.

Bus Mastering

Normally, when data is transmitted between the memory and an expansion card over the system bus, the processor functions as the middleman, reading data from the source and transmitting it to the destination. This uses processor clock cycles that could otherwise be running applications or performing other important tasks. An expansion card capable of bus mastering has a chipset that can take on the task of arbitrating access to the bus by that device, eliminating the need for the system processor to be involved in the transfer of data to and from memory. Bus mastering NICs enable the system to operate more efficiently because they conserve the processor clock cycles that would otherwise be expended in data transfers. Most of the bus mastering NICs on the

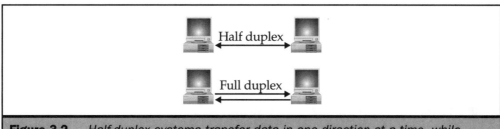

Figure 3-2.   *Half-duplex systems transfer data in one direction at a time, while full-duplex systems can transfer data in both directions simultaneously*

market use the PCI bus. This is one reason why a PCI NIC may be beneficial, even on a network that does not require the additional bus speed.

Parallel Tasking

Parallel Tasking is a feature that was developed by 3Com and, subsequently, implemented by other NIC manufacturers, using different names. The term describes a process by which the NIC can begin to transmit a packet over the network while it is still being transferred over the system bus. A NIC without this capability must wait until an entire packet is stored in its buffers before it can transmit.

3Com's next innovation is called *Parallel Tasking II*, which improves bus mastering communications over the PCI bus. Previously, a PCI NIC could transfer only 64 bytes at a time during a single bus master operation, which required dozens of operations to transfer each packet. Parallel Tasking II enables the NIC to stream up to an entire Ethernet packet's worth of data (1,518 bytes) during one single bus master operation.

Remote Wake-Up

Some of the PCI NICs available today support a remote wake-up feature than enables an administrator to power up the machine from a remote system on the network, to perform backups or other maintenance tasks. For this feature to function, the computer's motherboard must have a 3-pin remote wake-up connector and the administrator must be running a desktop management application that can transmit the remote wake-up packet to the workstation.

IEEE 802.1p

The 802.1p standard published by the IEEE defines a method for assigning priorities to network packets, so the data for specific types of applications can be transmitted on a timely basis. This enables streaming audio and video applications, for example, to transmit their data across the network in real time, without being affected by other traffic on the network. For priorities to be implemented, both the NIC and the operating system must support a standard like 802.1p. Also called *quality of service (QoS)*, this is relatively new technology, and other standards exist that provide similar services. For more information, see "Quality of Service" in Chapter 14.

Selecting a NIC

The selection of a NIC for a particular computer is based on several different factors:

- The data link–layer protocol used by the network
- The transmission speed of the network

- The type of interface that connects the NIC to the network
- The type of system bus into which you will install the NIC
- The hardware resources the NIC requires
- The electric power the NIC requires
- The role of the computer using the NIC: server versus workstation and home versus office
- The availability of appropriate drivers

The following sections examine these criteria and how they can affect the performance of the NIC and your network.

Protocol

The data link–layer protocol is the single most defining characteristic of a network interface adapter. The most popular protocol used at this layer is Ethernet, but NICs are also available that support Token Ring, FDDI, ATM, and others, as well as variations on these protocols. Other NIC characteristics, such as the bus type and hardware resources, relate only to the specific computer in which the device will be installed, but the protocol it uses is relevant to many other aspects of the network configuration.

All of the computers on the network must, of course, be using the same data link–layer protocol, and the selection of that protocol should be a decision made long before you're ready to purchase NICs. This is because all of the other network hardware, such as cables, hubs, and other devices, are also protocol specific. The NIC you select must also support the type of cable or other medium the network uses, as well as the transmission speed of the network. If, for example, you're running a Ethernet network, you can get NICs that support either the standard 10 Mbps speed, or 100 Mbps Fast Ethernet as well. You can also select Ethernet NICs that support the use of *unshielded twisted pair (UTP);* two types of coaxial, or fiber-optic cable; as well as various types of wireless transmissions. These are all aspects of the network configuration that you must consider before making NIC purchases.

Manufacturers and vendors of NICs typically categorize their products by protocol first because consumers are interested only in comparing products that use a specific protocol. The protocol is also the characteristic that has the greatest effect on the price of a NIC. Different protocols communicate over the network in different ways and require different types of NIC components. The price of a NIC is also affected by a protocol's popularity. Because the vast majority of protocols use Ethernet at the data link–layer, these NICs are typically the cheapest. Token Ring NICs are more expensive because fewer networks use that protocol; and relatively new technologies, such as ATM and Gigabit Ethernet, can command far higher prices for NICs and other hardware devices.

Transmission Speed

Some data link–layer protocols can run at different speeds, and the capability of a NIC to support these speeds can be an important part of selecting the correct product for your network. In some protocols, an increase in speed has been fully assimilated into the technology, while in others, the faster version is still an optional feature. The Token Ring protocol, for example, originally ran at 4 Mbps, but now virtually all Token Ring networks run at 16 Mbps, and it might be difficult to find a NIC that does not support the higher speed.

The higher-speed Ethernet protocols, by contrast, are relatively new. Fast Ethernet (running at 100 Mbps) is rapidly replacing traditional 10 Mbps Ethernet, but it is still an optional feature when it comes to network interface adapters. Virtually all Fast Ethernet NICs are combination devices that support both 10 and 100 Mbps operation, making it possible to gradually upgrade a traditional Ethernet network to Fast Ethernet. When the connection is established between the NIC and the hub, the devices negotiate the highest possible speed.

The popularity of Fast Ethernet has reached the point at which these dual-speed NICs are only slightly more expensive than the 10 Mbps devices; sometimes there is as little as $10 difference between the two. Eventually, all of the Ethernet NICs in production will support both speeds, and it will become difficult and expensive to buy cards that support only traditional 10 Mbps Ethernet. If you have even the remotest intention of upgrading your 10 Mbps Ethernet network to Fast Ethernet some time in the future, it is a good idea to make any NICs you purchase now dual-speed, so that you don't have to replace them later.

The 100VG AnyLAN standard, which was introduced at about the same time as Fast Ethernet, has failed to achieve a large market share, but it is still available. Combination NICs are on the market that support both standard Ethernet at 10 Mbps and 100VG AnyLAN at 100 Mbps. These tend to be a good deal more expensive than Ethernet/Fast Ethernet cards, however, because 100VG AnyLAN is substantially different from Ethernet and requires different components. An Ethernet/100VG AnyLAN NIC is essentially two separate adapters on a single card.

The latest Ethernet innovation, Gigabit Ethernet, runs at 1,000 Mbps. Manufacturers and dealers place this technology into a different category than traditional and Fast Ethernet for several reasons. First, because it is new, Gigabit Ethernet is still in the introductory stages of product development and marketing. This means relatively few products are on the market, and their prices are quite high. The current cost of a Gigabit Ethernet NIC can run anywhere from three to ten times the price of a typical Ethernet NIC, up to $700 or more. Second, its high-transmission speed makes Gigabit Ethernet a technology intended for use in backbone connections between high-end servers. Desktop systems do not as yet have a need for this much bandwidth. As a result, you are not likely to see combination NICs supporting Fast and Gigabit Ethernet in the near future.

Network Interface

The type of cable (or other medium) that forms the fabric of the network determines the network interface used on the NIC. The network cable type is typically selected at the same time as the data link–layer protocol, and the NICs you purchase must support that medium. Some data link–layer protocols support different types of cables, and NICs are available for each one, while other protocols are designed to use only one type of cable.

Ethernet supports more cabling options than any of the other commonly used data link–layer protocols. Most of the Ethernet networks installed today use *unshielded twisted-pair cable (UTP)*, which requires an RJ-45 jack on the NIC. However, NICs are also readily available with BNC and AUI connectors, for thin and thick Ethernet, respectively (see Figure 3-3). This is rather surprising because, while networks running thin or thick Ethernet are rare these days, the NICs that support these media are quite common. Because these three media all use electrical signals running over copper cable, the components of the NIC used to generate those signals are the same, regardless of the cable type. This makes it easy for manufacturers to produce combination devices with multiple jacks that support two or even all three cable types. The inclusion of multiple jacks on a NIC can add greatly to its cost, however, almost doubling it in many cases.

Note *Dual-speed Ethernet NICs with multiple jacks are common, but Fast Ethernet cannot run over coaxial cable of any type. Thus, on a NIC of this type, only the RJ-45 connector supports both 10 and 100 Mbps speeds. The AUI and/or BNC connectors run only at 10 Mbps. For more information on cables and connectors, see Chapter 4.*

The purchase of NICs with multiple jacks is justified when a network is going to be upgraded from coaxial to UTP cable at some future time. Considering that relatively

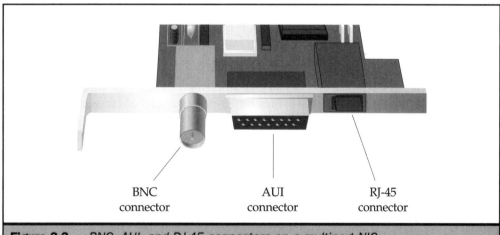

| BNC | AUI | RJ-45 |
| connector | connector | connector |

Figure 3-3.   *BNC, AUI, and RJ-45 connectors on a multiport NIC*

NETWORK HARDWARE

few coaxial networks are left, however, there is usually no good reason to spend the extra money for this type of combination NIC. One possible scenario when it might be justified, though, is when an organization is running a complex network that consists of both coaxial and UTP cable segments. Even if the coaxial cable is not going to be upgraded, it may be economically wise to purchase a large quantity of combination NICs, rather than smaller quantities of NICs supporting each type of media. This is because the prices of network adapter cards are often greatly discounted when purchased in multiple unit packs. As an example, the current prices for the 3Com Fast Etherlink 10/100 PCI NIC at one major vendor reflect a 10 percent discount for five units and almost a 40 percent discount for 100 units. In some cases, the discount may more than offset the additional cost for NICs with multiple jacks.

Ethernet also supports the use of *fiber-optic cable,* which is fundamentally different from the copper media, in that it carries data coded into light pulses rather than electric voltages. While there is a standard that defines the use of fiber-optic cable with 10 Mbps Ethernet, it is not often used. Fast Ethernet, however, can use fiber-optic cable to run at 100 Mbps over far longer distances than any copper medium. Because of these technological differences, fiber-optic Fast Ethernet NICs are not usually combined with other technologies.

Most of the Token Ring NICs on the market today use standard RJ-45 connectors for UTP cable, which is referred to as the *Type 3 cable system* in Token Ring parlance. Older Token Ring networks used the Type 1 cable system; NICs for this system have a DB9 connector like that used for a PC's serial ports.

The use of various types of cables and connectors on Ethernet and Token Ring networks can be attributed mostly to the fact that these are the oldest data link–layer protocols still in common use today. Ethernet, for example, has evolved from the use of coaxial cable to twisted pair, and the connectors have changed accordingly. Other protocols, like ATM, FDDI, and Gigabit Ethernet, are relatively new and the media they use have not yet evolved.

Bus Interface

The network interface adapter enables a PC to transmit data from the main system memory to a destination outside the computer, just as a parallel or serial port does. The data travels from the memory to the adapter across the system bus, in the same manner as with any other expansion card, like a graphics or audio adapter. The type of bus that the NIC uses to communicate with the computer can affect the performance of the network connection, but the selection of a bus type for the NIC is unique to each computer. In other words, you needn't use the same bus type for all of the NICs in your network workstations; one PC can use an ISA NIC, while others use PCI.

Integrated Systems Architecture (ISA) and *Peripheral Component Interconnect (PCI)* are the two bus types used in virtually all of the desktop computers sold today. Laptops and other portables use the PC Card bus (formerly known as the Personal Computer Memory Card International Association, or PCMCIA bus). Older systems use various other types of expansion buses, such as *VLB (VESA Local Bus), MCA (Micro Channel Architecture),* or *EISA (Extended Industry Standard Architecture).* Table 3-1 lists the characteristics of these buses and their respective throughput speeds.

Bottlenecks

The bus type selection can affect network performance if the selected bus is slow enough to cause a bottleneck in the network. A *bottleneck* occurs when one element of a network connection runs at a significantly slower speed than all of the others. This can cause the entire network to slow down to the speed of its weakest component, resulting in wasted bandwidth and needless expense.

As an exaggerated example, consider a network that consists of all top-of-the-line PCs with the fastest processors and hard drives available, connected by a Fast Ethernet network running at 100 Mbps. All of the workstations on the network have NICs that use the PCI bus except for the main database server, which has an ISA NIC. The PCI bus is twice as wide (32 bits as opposed to 16) runs at 1,066 Mbps, far faster than the 100 Mbps network itself, while the ISA bus runs at only 66.64 Mbps. The result of this is that the ISA NIC will probably be the slowest component in all of the workstation/ server connections, and will be a bottleneck that prevents the rest of the equipment from achieving its full potential.

The process of identifying actual bottlenecks is rarely this clean-cut. Just because a network protocol runs at 100 Mbps doesn't mean that data is continuously traveling over the cable at that speed, and the throughput of a particular bus type is not indicative of that actual throughput rate for the data generated by the system. However, it is a good idea to use common sense when purchasing NICs and to try to maximize the performance of your network.

Bus Type	Bus Width	Bus Speed	Theoretical Maximum Throughput
ISA	16 bits	8.33 MHz	66.64 Mbps (8.33 MBps)
MCA	32 bits	10 MHz	320 Mbps (40 MBps)
EISA	32 bits	8.33 MHz	266.56 Mbps (33.32 MBps)
VLB	32 bits	33.33 MHz	1,066.56 Mbps (133.33 MBps)
PCI	32 bits	33.33 MHz	1,066.56 Mbps (133.33 MBps)

Table 3-1.   *PC Bus Types, Widths, and Speeds*

NETWORK HARDWARE

ISA or PCI?

Although you may have to deal with the older bus types if you are using legacy PCs on your network, the choice for most desktop systems manufactured after about 1995 is between ISA and PCI. For a traditional Ethernet network running at 10 Mbps or a Token Ring network running at 4 or 16 Mbps, an ISA NIC is more than sufficient. In fact, ISA NICs can be perfectly serviceable on 100 Mbps networks as well, at least for workstations, because the average network user does not require anything approaching 100 Mbps of bandwidth on a continuous basis. The main reason for the ISA NIC being the bottleneck in the scenario described earlier is that it is installed in the server. A server PC that is handling data requests generated by dozens or hundreds of workstations simultaneously naturally requires more bandwidth than any single workstation. In a server, therefore, the use of the fastest bus available (usually PCI) is nearly always recommended.

Note   *If you are working with older PCs, you should be able to find a few EISA NICs still on the market, but MCA and VLB have all but disappeared. Fortunately, most of the systems that use these bus types support ISA as well, so you should be able to make them into functional workstations.*

The introduction of Fast Ethernet has led to an increasing number of PCI NICs on the market, to the point where they are usually not much more expensive, and may even be cheaper in some cases, than ISA NICs. However, there is another element to the bus type decision that you must consider, and that is the availability of expansion bus slots in your computers.

Obviously, to install a network interface card into a PC, it must have a free slot in its expansion bus. PCs have varying numbers of PCI and ISA slots, and the hardware configuration of the machine determines how many of those slots are free. Today's full-featured computers often have peripheral devices installed that occupy many of the bus slots, such as audio adapters and SCSI adapters. Of particular concern to the network administrator are DVD-equipped machines, which often contain MPEG decoder cards that occupy a slot, but do not protrude out the back of the computer. This means that simply looking at the outside of a system may not be sufficient to determine how many slots are available. You must open the machine to check for free slots and to determine which types of slots are available.

Administrators of large networks often purchase relatively inexpensive workstations that do not have all the state-of-the-art features found in many home systems, which may leave more slots free for additional components like a NIC. In addition, PCs targeted at the corporate market are more likely to have peripheral devices like audio and video adapters integrated into the motherboard, which also can leave more slots free. However, this type of machine may also use a slimline or low-profile case design that reduces the number of slots to minimize the computer's footprint.

Wherever possible, the selection of the bus type for the NIC should be based on the network bandwidth requirements of the user and not on the type of bus slot that the computer has free. Sometimes, though, you may have no other choice than to put an ISA NIC in a computer that could benefit from a PCI card or to install a PCI NIC in a computer that doesn't require the additional performance, but that has no ISA slots free. The latter situation, which only incurs an extra expense, is certainly less serious than the former, which can negatively affect the performance of the network.

Integrated Adapters

As mentioned earlier, some PCs, and particularly those intended for the corporate market, may have peripheral devices integrated into the motherboard. One of these devices may be the network interface adapter. Because this device is not a separate card, it cannot rightfully be called a NIC, but it does perform exactly the same function as a network adapter that installs into the system's expansion bus.

Although they reduce the distance the signals have to travel to reach the adapter and avoid the electrical interference that occurs during a bus transfer, the problem with integrated network adapters is that they are not upgradable. When 10 Mbps Ethernet was the only Ethernet game in town, integrating a 10BaseT network adapter onto the motherboard was a safe and practical alternative. However, the introduction of Fast Ethernet has complicated things by providing multiple cabling options, even for UTP cable, such as 100BaseTX and 100BaseT4. An integrated, dual-speed 10BaseT/100BaseTX adapter would be suitable for most consumers, but the industry has, instead, backed away from providing integrated network capabilities in desktop systems at all.

A system that has an integrated network adapter is under no obligation to use it. You can nearly always disable the adapter through the system BIOS, by manipulating a switch on the motherboard, or simply by installing a NIC into a bus slot. You might find a deal on workstations with the wrong type of integrated network adapter that is good enough to be worth buying NICs for the computers as well.

Portable Systems

Network interface adapters for laptops and other portable systems all take the form of PC Cards, so there is no choice of bus type for these machines. However, there is a choice between PC Card NICs that support CardBus and those that do not. *CardBus* is an improved version of the PC Card bus that doubles the bandwidth from 16 to 32 bits and provides speeds up to 33 MHz, which yields performance comparable to the PCI bus on desktop systems. If the computer supports CardBus and your network is running at 100 Mbps or faster, it is usually a good idea to buy a CardBus NIC.

Hardware Resource Requirements

In addition to a bus slot, a computer must have the appropriate hardware resources free to support a NIC. A network interface adapter requires a free *interrupt request line (IRQ)* and usually either an I/O port address, a memory address, or both. When evaluating NICs, you must take into account both the resource requirements of the NIC and the resources available on the computer.

On a PC with a lot of peripheral devices already installed, most of the IRQs may already be in use, and adding a NIC may be difficult. This is because a NIC may only be able to use a select few of the system's IRQs; and if all of those IRQs are occupied, the card cannot function. Two devices configured to use the same resource will conflict, often causing both to malfunction. To free up one of the IRQs usable by the NIC, you may have to reconfigure another device to use a different IRQ. Thus, you have to consider not only the number of available IRQs on the computer, but also which ones are available. The same is true for the other resources required by the card.

Many older NICs supported only two or three IRQs and other resources, and configuring the devices in the computer was a manual, trial-and-error process. System administrators could spend hours trying different combinations of hardware settings for the components in a single computer before finding one that enabled all of the devices to function simultaneously. Today, however, NICs are generally more flexible and support a wider range of resource settings. In addition, the BIOS and the operating system of a modern PC have features that simplify the process of configuring peripheral devices to work together.

Plug and Play, when it functions properly, eliminates the need to worry about hardware resource configuration for peripheral devices. When a system has a BIOS, an operating system, and hardware that all support the Plug and Play standard, the computer assigns hardware resources to each device dynamically when the system starts. When Plug and Play is not supported for a particular device like a NIC, operating systems like Windows 9*x*, NT, and 2000 provide tools that can identify the free resources in the machine and indicate whether the NIC's current configuration conflicts with any other devices in the system.

Thus, when selecting NICs, you should be conscious of the hardware resources in use on the computers that will use them. A computer with a lot of installed peripherals may be unable to support an additional card at all, without removing one of the existing components. In other cases, you may have to reconfigure other devices to support the addition of a NIC. Most NIC manufacturers publish specification sheets (often available on their Web sites) that list the hardware resources their NICs can use. By comparing this information to the current configuration of a PC, you can determine whether the computer has the resources to support the NIC.

Power Requirements

The power supplies in today's computers usually supply more than enough voltage to support a full load of expansion cards and other internal peripherals. However, if you're running a system with a large number of internal devices, such as hard disk, CD-ROM, or other drives, you may want to compare the power load incurred by these devices with the voltage furnished by the computer's power supply before you install a NIC or other device. Because the power drain of mechanical drives varies depending on how often and how heavily they're used, a system putting out insufficient power to support its hardware load may experience intermittent problems that are difficult to diagnose. What may seem to be a faulty drive may, in fact, be the effect of an insufficient power supply for the hardware.

Server Versus Workstation NICs

The NICs in servers and workstations perform the same functions, and yet there are cards on the market that are targeted specifically for use in servers. Some of these NICs use protocols, like Gigabit Ethernet, that are intended only for servers because their cost and capabilities make them impractical for use in desktop workstations. Others, however, are NICs that use standard protocols, like Ethernet and Fast Ethernet, but that contain additional features to make them more useful in servers. Naturally, these extra features drive the price of the NIC up considerably, and it is up to you to decide whether they are worth the extra expense. Because the basic functionality of all NICs is the same, there is no reason you can't use a standard NIC in a server.

The following sections examine some of the additional capabilities included in the server NICs marketed by various manufacturers. These features often have different names trademarked by their makers, and they may not function in exactly the same way, but the general principles are the same.

Multiport NICs

Servers must often be connected to two or more networks simultaneously, either to service clients on both networks or route traffic between them. To do this using standard NICs, you must install multiple cards in the computer, which raises problems of slot, power, and hardware resource availability. Several manufacturers have NICs available that are designed for servers like these, which have two or more RJ-45 ports on them, to support multiple network connections. These devices are essentially two (or more) network interface adapters, on a single card, that are able to use the hardware resources of the computer more effectively than separate cards. Multiport NICs also facilitate the implementation of other server-specific features, such as load balancing and fault tolerance.

Load Balancing

Because a server must support multiple clients, it is often the location of network bottlenecks. A single system running at 100 Mbps cannot conceivably keep up with dozens of clients, all requesting data at the same speed simultaneously. However, client systems usually do not all access the server at the same time, which is what makes LAN communications practical. When a network gets to the point at which the number of clients accessing a particular server at the same time gets too large, the server becomes a bottleneck and the performance of the client systems degrades as a result.

NETWORK HARDWARE

The traditional solution to this problem is to install another NIC into the server and divide the network into two segments. Half of the clients connect to one server NIC and half to the other, thus lessening the amount of traffic passing through each NIC. This process sounds easier than it is, however. The task requires that you take the server offline to install the new NIC, reassign IP addresses (on a TCP/IP network) for the new subnet, and possibly migrate clients from one segment to the other to properly balance the traffic load. If the network traffic continues to grow, the entire process must be performed again.

Several manufacturers, like Intel and 3Com, have addressed this problem by creating NICs that can work together in a server to balance the network traffic load between them. After installing multiple NICs of the same type in a server and connecting them to a switch (or switches), you can configure the NICs to function as a group. Normally, individual NICs in one machine each have their own IP addresses, but the NICs in a load-balancing group share one IP address, even though they retain their individual MAC addresses (see Figure 3-4). The group thus forms a *virtual NIC*, which can process the aggregate amount of traffic support by the entire group combined. Different products support different numbers of NICs in a group. 3Com, for example, supports up to eight NICs, for a total bandwidth of 800 Mbps, while Intel supports up to four NICs and 400 Mbps. With this capability, administrators can compensate for increasing traffic on the network simply by installing another NIC in the server and adding it to the group.

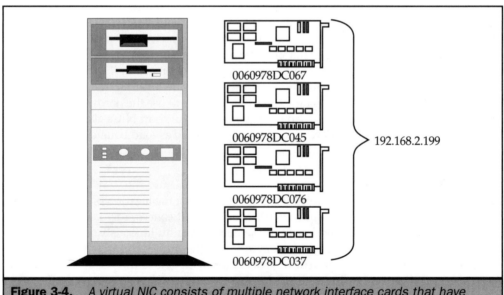

Figure 3-4. *A virtual NIC consists of multiple network interface cards that have individual hardware addresses but share a single IP address*

When the server transmits data to clients, the traffic is distributed evenly among the NICs in the group, based on the IP address of the client system. In most cases, a TCP connection between the server and a particular client is assigned to one NIC in the group, which is used for the duration of that connection. When a client has multiple connections to the server running simultaneously, it may use different NICs. Incoming traffic is treated differently by various load-balancing implementations. Because the server's incoming traffic consists largely of relatively small request messages, some products use one NIC in the group to process all of the incoming packets, while others distribute the incoming packets among the NICs in the group in a round-robin fashion.

Another form of load balancing, called *Link Aggregation* by Intel, can balance both incoming and outgoing traffic. Intel's standard load-balancing feature always uses one NIC for incoming traffic, even when the outgoing traffic is distributed among up to four NICs. Link Aggregation balances the load in both directions and supports full-duplex operation, for an aggregated bandwidth of up to 800 Mbps using Fast Ethernet and 8 Gbps using Gigabit Ethernet. This technology, however, requires hardware support in the switches, as well as the NICs, unlike standard load balancing, which can use any type or brand of switch.

Note *Currently, no standard exists for load balancing among server NICs; so, while different manufacturers may use implementations that appear similar, you cannot mix NICs from different makers in a server and expect them to work together in this way. Several vendors have gotten together to launch the IEEE 802.3ad Link Aggregation Task Force; but until a standard is developed and ratified for this technology (which is often a lengthy process), you must choose from among the proprietary implementations available today.*

Fault Tolerance

There is also a valuable byproduct of the load-balancing concept, and that is the fault tolerance provided by the NIC group. If one NIC should fail, the traffic is automatically distributed evenly among the remaining ones until it is replaced. Even if you don't use load balancing, you can install a redundant NIC in your servers that the system automatically uses if the primary connection fails for any reason, including a malfunction in the cable, hub, or switch to which it is connected.

Some products even enable you to use a more inexpensive NIC as a backup. For example, if you have a server with a Gigabit Ethernet connection to the network, it may not be worth the expense to install a second Gigabit Ethernet NIC into the server, just for fault tolerance purposes. However, it may be possible to use a relatively inexpensive Fast Ethernet card as a backup instead. In the event that the Gigabit Ethernet connection fails, the Fast Ethernet connection will take over and provide at least nominal service until you restore the higher-speed connection.

Another fault tolerance mechanism, called PCI Hot Plug capability, was developed by Compaq and is being implemented in many servers and NICs. This feature enables administrators to replace a malfunctioning NIC without powering the server down. Also called *hot swapping*, this PCI Hot Plug works in conjunction with the NIC's failover capability. When a NIC fails, the connection switches to a redundant NIC or another NIC in the same group. The administrator can then remove the malfunctioning device from the server while it is running and insert a new one. This eliminates any of the down time usually associated with a NIC failure.

Actual NIC hardware failures are not common occurrences; but for some networks, even the remotest chance of an outage that causes an interruption of service is unacceptable. In addition, these fault tolerance features can also protect against failures that are more common, such as severed cables or power failures to a switch or hub.

Remote Management

Other features often included in NICs intended for servers provide administrators with the ability to configure a NIC from a remote location and receive information about its status. In a case in which a hardware failure causes a server to switch to a backup NIC, for example, these features can generate an alert and send it to network administrators to inform them of the event. Many server NICs support standards for this type of interaction between network hardware and an administrative console application, such as the Simple Network Management Protocol (SNMP) and the Desktop Management Interface (DMI) 2.0.

Home and Office NICs

Arguably the most rapidly growing segment of the NIC market is the one for homes and small offices. Many families and small business owners, even those with only two or three computers, are beginning to see the advantages of networking their systems together. Most of the major NIC manufacturers now have a line of products targeted at these markets. The basic premise behind these product lines is to provide users that have little or no networking experience with an inexpensive yet functional NIC that is easy to install and run.

With the PCI bus and Plug and Play support built into the Windows operating systems, installation of a NIC is easier than it has ever been before. In many cases, all that's involved is simply inserting the card into a bus slot. The operating system (usually Windows 95 or 98) configures the card and installs the drivers. All that's left is to connect the computers to a hub (marketed as part of the same product line), and you have a basic network.

The NICs provided in these product lines don't have the advanced features found in server NICs, and may even lack some of the features directed at larger-scale networking operations, such as remote management. Their documentation is also simpler and reflects the type of user that is expected to be working with the card. However, in their basic functions the NICs are usually comparable to the other products targeted at the corporate market, for a substantially lower price.

Network Adapter Drivers

The final concern when evaluating NICs is the availability of drivers for the operating system that is running on the computer. In most cases, this is a nonissue, because all of the NICs on the market today include the various NDIS drivers required for the Windows operating systems, ODI drivers for Novell NetWare, and a packet driver that provides low-level access to basic NIC functions. In fact, operating systems usually include drivers for most of the major manufacturers' NICs. The only time you should be concerned about driver support is when you are working with very old NICs or with those by marginal manufacturers.

NETWORK HARDWARE

The
Complete
Reference

Upgrading
&
Troubleshooting
Networks

Chapter 4

Cabling a Network

Although there are networks that use radio transmissions and other wireless technologies to transmit data, the vast majority of local area networks use a cable as the network medium. Most of the cables used for data networking use a copper conductor to carry electrical signals; but *fiber-optic,* a spun glass cable that carries pulses of light, is an increasingly popular alternative.

Cabling issues have, in recent years, become separated from the typical network administrator's training and experience. Many veteran administrators have never pulled cable themselves and are less than familiar with the technology that forms the basis for the network. In many cases, the use of twisted-pair cable has resulted in telephone system contractors being responsible for the network cabling. Network consultants typically outsource all but the smallest cabling jobs to outside companies.

However, although the cabling represents only a small part of a network's total cost (as little as 6 percent), it has been estimated to be responsible for as much as 75 percent of network downtime. The cabling is also usually the longest lived element of a network. You may replace servers and other components more than once before you replace the cable. For these reasons, spending a bit extra on good quality cable, properly installed, is a worthwhile investment. This chapter examines the types of cables used for LANs, their composition, the connectors they use, and their installation processes.

Cable Properties

Data link–layer protocols are associated with specific cable types and include guidelines for the installation of the cable, such as maximum segment lengths. In some cases, such as Ethernet, you have a choice as to what kind of cable you want to use with the protocol, while in others you do not. Part of the process of evaluating and selecting a protocol involves an examination of the cable types and their suitability for your network site. For example, a connection between two adjacent buildings is better served by fiber-optic than copper, so with that requirement in mind you should proceed to evaluate the data link–layer protocols that support the use of fiber-optic cable.

Your cable installation may also be governed, in part, by the layout of the site and the local building codes. Cables generally are available in both nonplenum and plenum types. A *plenum* is a space within a building, created by the components of the building themselves, that is designed to provide ventilation, such as a space between floors or walls. Buildings that use plenums to move air usually do not have a ducted ventilation system. In most communities, to run cable through a plenum, you must use a plenum-rated cable that does not give off toxic gases when it burns because the air in the plenum is distributed throughout the building. The outer covering on a plenum cable is usually some sort of Teflon product, while nonplenum cables have a PVC (polyvinyl chloride) sheath, which does produce toxic gases when it burns.

Not surprisingly, plenum cable costs more than nonplenum, sometimes twice as much or more, and it is also less flexible. However, it is important to use the correct type of cable in any installation. If you violate the building codes, the local authorities can force you to remove the offending cable and possibly make you pay fines as well.

Cost is certainly an element that should affect your cable selection process, not only of the cable itself, but also of the ancillary components such as connectors and mounting hardware, the NICs for the computers, and the cable installation. The qualities of fiber-optic cable might make it seem an ideal choice for your entire LAN, but when you see the costs of purchasing, installing, and maintaining it, your opinion may change.

Finally, the quality of the cable itself is an important part of the evaluation and selection process. When you walk into your local computer center to buy a prefabricated 10BaseT cable, you won't have much of a selection, except for cable length. Vendors that provide a full cable selection, however (many of whom sell by mail order), have a variety of cable types that differ in their construction; their capabilities; and, of course, their prices.

Depending on the cable type, a good vendor may have both bulk cable and prefabricated cables. *Bulk cable* (that is, unfinished cable without connectors) should be available in various grades, in both plenum and nonplenum. The grade of the cable itself can depend on several features, including the following:

- **Conductor gauge** The gauge is the diameter of the actual conductor within a cable, measured using the American Wire Gauge (AWG) scale. The lower the AWG rating, the thicker the conductor. A 24 AWG cable, therefore, is smaller than a 22 AWG. A thicker conductor provides better conductivity and more resistance against attenuation.

- **Category rating** Some types of cables are assigned ratings by a standards body, like the EIA/TIA. Twisted-pair cable, for example, is given a category rating that defines its capabilities.

- **Shielded or unshielded** Some cables are available with casings that provide different levels of shielding against electromagnetic interference. The shielding usually takes the form of foil or copper braid, the latter of which provides better protection.

- **Solid or stranded conductor** A cable with a solid metal conductor provides better protection against attenuation, which means it can span longer distances. However, the solid conductor hampers the flexibility of the cable. If flexed or bent repeatedly, the conductor can break inside the cable. Solid conductor cables, therefore, should be used for permanent cable runs that will not be moved, such as those inside walls or ceilings. (Note that the cable can be flexed around corners and other obstacles during the installation; it is repeated flexing that can damage it.) Cables with conductors composed of multiple copper strands can be flexed repeatedly without breaking, but are subject to greater amounts of attenuation. Stranded cables, therefore, should be used for shorter runs that are likely to be moved, such as for patch cables running from wall plates to computers.

These features naturally affect the price of the cable. A lower gauge is more expensive than a higher one, a higher category is more expensive than a lower, shielded is more expensive than unshielded, and solid is more expensive than stranded. In addition to the cable itself, a good vendor should have all of the equipment you need to attach the appropriate connectors, including the components of the connectors and the tools needed to attach them.

Prefabricated cables have the connectors already attached and should be available in various lengths and colors, using cable with the features already listed, and with various grades of connectors. The highest quality prefabricated cables, for example, usually have a rubber boot around the connector that seals it to the cable end; prevents it from loosening or pulling out; protects the connector pins from bending; and reduces signal interference between the wires, called *crosstalk*. On lower-cost cables, the connector is simply attached to the end, without any extra protection.

Cabling Standards

Prior to 1991, the cabling used for LANs was specified by the manufacturers of specific networking products. This resulted in the incompatibilities that are common in proprietary systems, and the need was recognized for a standard that defined a cabling system that could support a multitude of different networking technologies. To address this need, the American National Standards Institute (ANSI), the Electronic Industry Association (EIA), and the Telecommunications Industry Association (TIA), along with a consortium of telecommunications companies, developed the ANSI/EIA/TIA-568-1991 Commercial Building Telecommunications Cabling Standard. This document was revised in 1995 and is now known as ANSI/TIA/EIA-T568-A.

ANSI/TIA/EIA-T568-A

- The *T568-A standard* defines a structured cabling system for voice and data communications in office environments that has a usable life span of at least ten years, will support products of multiple technology vendors, and uses any the following cable types for various applications:

- Unshielded twisted-pair (UTP)(100 ohm, 22 or 24 AWG)

- Shielded twisted-pair (STP)(150 ohm)

- Multimode optical fiber (62.5/125 μm)

- Singlemode optical fiber (8.3/125 μm)

For each cable type, the standard defines the following elements:

- Cable characteristics and technical criteria that determine its performance level

- Topology and cable segment length specifications

- Connector specifications and pinouts

The document also includes specifications for the installation of the cable within the building space. Toward this end, the building is divided into the following subsystems:

- **Building entrance**   The location at which the building's internal cabling interfaces with outside cabling.

- **Equipment room**   The location of equipment that can provide the same functions as that in a telecommunications closet, but which may be more complex.

- **Telecommunications closet**   The location of localized telecommunications equipment, such as the interface between the horizontal cabling and the backbone.

- **Backbone cabling**   The cabling that connects the building's various equipment rooms, telecommunications closets, and the building entrance, as well as connections between buildings in a campus network environment.

- **Horizontal cabling**   The cabling and other hardware used to connect the telecommunications closet to the work area.

- **Work area**   The components used to connect the telecommunications outlet to the workstation.

Thus, the cable installation for a modern building might look something like the diagram shown in Figure 4-1. The connections to external telephone and other services arrive at the building entrance and lead to the equipment room, which contains the PBX, network servers, and other equipment. A backbone network connects the equipment room to various telecommunications closets throughout the building, that contain network interface equipment, such as switches, bridges, routers, or hubs. From the telecommunications closets, the horizontal cabling branches out into the work areas, terminating at wall plates. The work area then consists of the patch cables that connect the computers and other equipment to the wall plates.

This is, of course, a simplified and generalized plan. The T568-A standard, in coordination with other TIA/EIA standards, provides guidelines for the types of cabling within and between these subsystems that you can use to create a wiring plan customized to your site and your equipment. Some of these other standards are as follows:

- **TIA/EIA-569**   Commercial Building Standard for Telecommunications Pathways and Spaces

- **TIA/EIA-606**   Administration Standard for the Telecommunications Infrastructure of Commercial Buildings

- **TIA/EIA-607**   Ground and Bonding Requirements for Telecommunications in Commercial Buildings

NETWORK HARDWARE

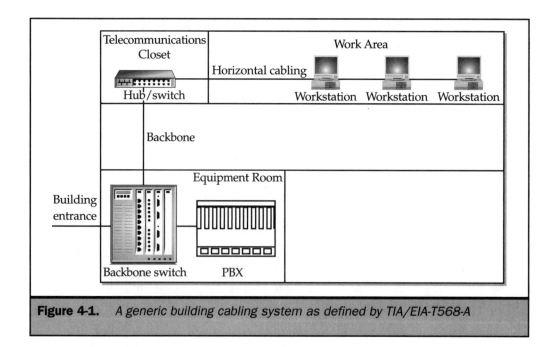

Figure 4-1. *A generic building cabling system as defined by TIA/EIA-T568-A*

Contractors you hire to perform an office cable installation should be familiar with these standards and should be willing to certify that their work conforms to the guidelines they contain.

ISO 11801E 1995

In addition to ANSI/TIA/EIA-T568-A, which defines cabling specifications used in the United States, the International Organization for Standardization (ISO) has published the ISO 11801E 1995 standard, which is the cabling standard most often used in Europe. Based on T568-A, this standard extends the cable types to include 100 ohm STP and 120 ohm cabling, which are more popular in France and other European countries.

Data Link–Layer Protocol Standards

The protocols traditionally associated with the data link–layer of the OSI reference model, such as Ethernet, Token Ring, and FDDI, also overlap into the physical layer in that they contain specifications for the network cabling. Thus, Ethernet and Token Ring standards, like those produced by the IEEE 802 working group and the ANSI X3T9.5 standard that defines FDDI, can also be said to be cabling standards. However, these documents do not go as deeply into the details of the cable properties and enterprise cable system design as T568-A.

Coaxial Cable

The first commercially viable LAN technologies introduced in the 1970s used coaxial cable as the network medium. *Coaxial cable* is named for the two conductors that share the same axis running through the cable's center. Many types of copper cable have two separate conductors, such as a standard electrical cord; but in most of these, the two conductors run side by side within an insulating sheath that protects and separates them. A coaxial cable, on the other hand, is round, with a copper core at its center that forms the first conductor. It is this core that carries the actual signals. A layer of dielectric foam insulation surrounds the core, separating it from the second conductor, which is made of braided wire mesh and functions as a ground. As with any electrical cable, the signal conductor and the ground must always be separated or a short will occur, producing noise on the cable. This entire assembly is then enclosed within an insulating sheath (see Figure 4-2).

Note   *Coaxial cables can have either a solid or a stranded copper core, and their designations reflect this difference. A /U indicates a solid core, while an A/U indicates a stranded one. Thin Ethernet, therefore, can use either an RG-58/U or an RG-58A/U cable.*

Several types of coaxial cables are used for networking; they have different properties, even if they are similar in appearance. Table 4-1 lists the various types of coaxial cable. Data link–layer protocols call for specific types of cable, the properties of which determine the guidelines and limitations for the cable installation. The cable's attenuation, for example, determines how long a cable segment can be. *Attenuation* is the rate at which a signal degrades as it travels along the cable. The Attenuation column in the table specifies how much of a 100 MHz signal's strength (in decibels) is lost for every hundred feet of cable. A lower value indicates less signal loss, meaning the cable can span a longer distance before the signal becomes unviable.

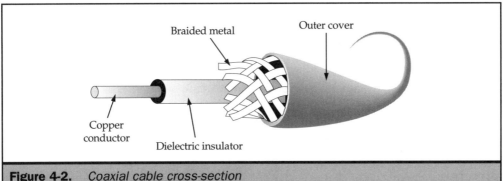

Figure 4-2.   *Coaxial cable cross-section*

Cable Designation	Cable Diameter	Impedance	Attenuation (dB/100'@ 100 MHz)	Connectors Used	Protocols Supported
RG-8/U	.405 inches	50 ohms	1.9	N	Thick Ethernet
RG-58/U or RG-58A/U	.195 inches	50 ohms	4.5	BNC	Thin Ethernet
RG-62A/U	.242 inches	93 ohms	2.7	BNC	ARCNET
RG-59/U	.242 inches	75 ohms	3.4	F	Cable TV

Table 4-1.   *Coaxial Cable Specifications*

The thickness of the cable also has a great effect on the nature of the installation. The layers of copper and foam insulation inside coaxial cable form a solid mass, unlike twisted-pair cables, for example, which contain separate wires and air space between and around them. Thus, coaxial cable is relatively heavy and relatively inflexible; and the thicker the cable, the heavier and more inflexible it is. This inflexibility makes the cable difficult to install and to conceal.

Coaxial networks are cabled using a bus topology, in which the cable forms a segment with two ends and computers connected along its length. Each signal transmitted on the cable by a workstation travels on the bus in both directions to all of the other computers and, eventually, to the two cable ends. Each end of the bus must have a terminating resistor on it that removes the signals it receives by nullifying the voltages. Without terminators, the signals can reach the end of the cable and reflect back, causing data corruption.

Compared to other cable types, coaxial is also relatively inefficient for data networking. An Ethernet network constructed with coaxial cable is limited to a speed of 10 Mbps. There is no upgrade path to any faster technology as with twisted-pair cable and Fast Ethernet. While you may encounter coaxial cable in networks that were installed years ago, virtually no new Ethernet LANs are being installed with it today. The following sections examine the applications for the various cable types, as well as the restrictions and advantages imposed by the cable itself.

Thick Ethernet

RG-8/U cable, when it is available at all, is usually referred to as *thick Ethernet trunk cable*, because that is its primary use. The RG-8/U cable used for thick Ethernet networks has the least amount of attenuation of the coaxial cables, due in no small part to its being much thicker than the other types. This is why a thick Ethernet network can have cable segments up to 500 meters long, while thin Ethernet is limited to 185 meters.

RG-8/U cable, at .405 inches in diameter, is similar in size to a garden hose, but much heavier and less flexible, which makes it difficult to bend around corners. For these reasons, the cable is typically installed along the floor of the site. The Ethernet specification calls for separate *Attachment Unit Interface (AUI)* cables that connect the NIC in each computer to the RG-8/U cable. By contrast, the RG-58A/U cable used by thin Ethernet is thinner, lighter, and flexible enough to run directly to the NIC. RG-8/U is also far more expensive than the other coaxial cable types, which today may be partially due to its scarcity. One vendor currently sells a 500 foot spool of nonplenum RG-8U cable for $399, as opposed to $129 for the same length of RG-58A/U (thin Ethernet). Plenum cable is even worse: $1,049 for 500 feet of RG-8/U, as opposed to $259 for RG-58A/U.

Thick Ethernet cable is usually yellow in color and is marked every 2.5 meters for the taps to which the workstations connect. To connect a workstation to the cable, you apply what is known as a vampire tap. A *vampire tap* is a clamp that you connect to the cable after drilling a hole in the sheath. It has metal "fangs" that penetrate into the core to send and receive signals (see Figure 4-3). The vampire tap also includes the transceiver (external to the computer on a thick Ethernet network), which connects to the NIC with an AUI cable that has 15-pin D-shell connectors at both ends.

Note *The fact that AUI cables can be up to 50 meters long is a major factor in planning a network layout. In most cases, a thick Ethernet trunk can run through a room along one wall, and all of the computers can connect to it.*

Because of this connection method, there is no need for breaks in the thick Ethernet cable for every workstation. In fact, the Ethernet specification recommends using a single, unbroken cable segment whenever possible and even supplies the ideal places where breaks should be located, if they have to exist (see "Thick Ethernet" in Chapter 8). When you do have breaks in a thick Ethernet cable, you use connectors, known as *N-connectors*, to join the ends. You also use special N-connectors with resistors in them to terminate the bus at both ends (see Figure 4-4).

As a result of inconveniences, such as its expense and rigidity, and despite its better performance than thin Ethernet, thick Ethernet is never used for new Ethernet installations anymore and is rarely seen even on legacy networks.

Thin Ethernet

The main advantage of the RG-58 cable used for thin Ethernet networks over RG-8 is its relative flexibility, which simplifies the installation process and makes it possible to run the cable directly to the computer, rather than using a separate AUI cable. Compared to twisted-pair, however, thin Ethernet is still ungainly and difficult to conceal because every workstation must have two cables connected to its NIC using a T fitting. Instead

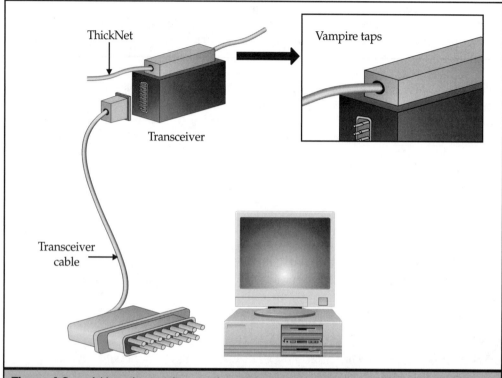

Figure 4-3.   *A Vampire tap/transceiver unit used to connect an AUI cable to a thick Ethernet trunk*

of neat wall plates with jacks for patch cables, an internal thin Ethernet installation had two thick, semirigid cables protruding from the wall for every computer.

As a result of this, the bus is actually broken into separate lengths of cable that connect each computer to the next, unlike a thick Ethernet bus, which ideally is one long cable

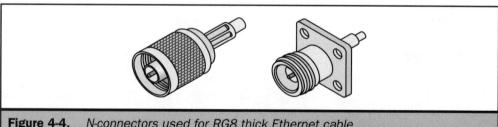

Figure 4-4.   *N-connectors used for RG8 thick Ethernet cable*

segment pierced with taps along its length. This makes a big difference in the functionality of the network because if one of the two connections to each computer is broken for any reason, the bus is severed. When this happens, network communications fail between systems on different sides of the break, and the lack of termination jeopardizes all of the network's traffic.

RG-58 cable uses BNC (Bayonet-Neill-Concelman) connectors to connect to the T and to connect the T to the NIC in the computer (see Figure 4-5). Even at the height of its popularity, thin Ethernet cable was typically purchased in bulk and the connectors attached by the installer or administrator. The process of attaching a BNC connector involves stripping the insulation off the cable end to expose both the copper core and the ground; applying the connector as separate components (a socket that the cable threads through and a post that slips over the core); and then compressing the socket so it grips the cable and holds the post in place, using a pliers-like tool called a *crimper* (see Figure 4-6).

Attaching BNC connectors properly is a skill that is rarely taught in formal education and that requires some practice to master. Connectors that are not tightly crimped are easily pulled off the cable, or worse, loosened so that the electrical connection is partially severed. The result of this is a network with uneven performance and occasional outages that are difficult to track down without the proper cable-testing equipment. Largely because of faulty connections like these, thin Ethernet sometimes gained a reputation for being quirky and, at times, unreliable.

RG-58 cable is much cheaper than RG-8 and is available in more varieties, but thin Ethernet is still an all-but-dead technology. The bus topology, relatively difficult installation, and limited speed of coaxial cables has made them impractical for today's LANs.

ARCNET

The *Attached Resource Computing Network (ARCNET)* is the only other major LAN technology that used coaxial cable. Although similar in appearance to thin Ethernet,

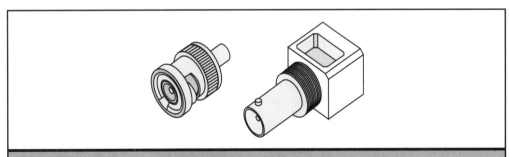

Figure 4-5.   *BNC connectors used on thin Ethernet networks*

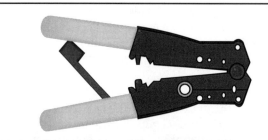

Figure 4-6. *A crimper tool used to attach cable connectors*

the cable used in ARCNET networks is 93 ohm RG-62A/U, and the two are not interchangeable. ARCNET is a token-passing network that runs at only 2.5 Mbps and can use a mixture of star and bus technologies. ARCNET products are no longer available, but at one time this was a reasonably serviceable and very inexpensive networking solution.

Cable Television

Just because coaxial cable is hardly ever used for LANs anymore does not mean that it has totally outlived its usefulness. Antennas, radios, and particularly the cable television industry still use it extensively. The cable delivering TV service to your home is RG-59 75 ohm coaxial, used in this case for broadband rather than baseband transmission (meaning that the single cable carries multiple, discrete signals simultaneously). This cable is also similar in appearance to thin Ethernet, but it has different properties and uses different connectors. The F connector used for cable TV connections screws into the jack, while BNC connectors use a bayonet lock coupling.

Many cable TV providers use this same coaxial cable to supply Internet access to subscribers, as well as television signals. In these installations, the coaxial cable connects to a cable modem, which then is connected to a computer using a 10BaseT Ethernet cable. However, while the coaxial cable may be part of an Ethernet network, do not confuse it with thin Ethernet, which uses a different type of coaxial cable and uses baseband transmissions only.

Twisted-Pair Cable

Twisted-pair cable is the current standard for LAN communications. When compared to coaxial, it is easier to install, suitable for many different applications, and provides far better performance. Perhaps the biggest advantage of twisted-pair cable, however, is that it is already used in countless telephone system installations throughout the world. This means that a great many contractors are familiar with the installation procedures and that in new construction, it is possible to install the LAN cables at the same time as the telephone cables.

Unlike coaxial cable, which has only one signal-carrying conductor and one ground, the twisted-pair cable used in most data networks has up to four pairs of insulated copper wires within a single sheath. Each wire pair is twisted with a different number of twists per inch to avoid electromagnetic interference from the other pairs and from outside sources (see Figure 4-7).

Each pair of wires in a twisted-pair cable is color-coded, using colors defined in the TIA/EIA-T568-A standard, which are as follows:

- **Pair 1**   Solid blue/white with blue stripe
- **Pair 2**   Solid orange/white with orange stripe
- **Pair 3**   Solid green/white with green stripe
- **Pair 4**   Solid brown/white with brown stripe

Unshielded Twisted-Pair (UTP)

The outer sheathing of a twisted-pair cable can either be relatively thin, as in *unshielded twisted-pair (UTP)* cable, or thick, as in *shielded twisted-pair (STP)*. UTP cable is the more commonly used of the two; most office Ethernet networks are more than adequately served by UTP cable. The UTP cable itself uses 22 or 24 AWH copper conductors and has an impedance of 100 ohms. The insulation can be plenum or nonplenum.

Beyond these specifications, The TIA/EIA-T568-A standard defines levels of performance for UTP cable that are referred to as categories. A higher category rating means that a cable is more efficient and able to transmit data at greater speeds. The major difference between the different cable categories is the tightness of each wire

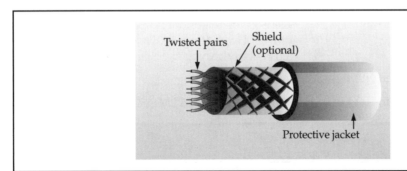

Figure 4-7.   *Twisted-pair cable cross section*

NETWORK HARDWARE

pair's twisting. Table 4-2 lists the categories defined by the T568-A standard, their speed ratings, and their applications.

Note   *The TIA/EIA-T568-A standard recognizes Categories 3, 4, and 5, from Table 4-2, as viable choices for a telecommunications network.*

Category 3 cable is traditionally used for telephone system installations; and this is also suitable for 10BaseT Ethernet networks, which run at 10 Mbps. Category 3 is not suitable for the 100 Mbps speed used by Fast Ethernet, except in the case of 100BaseT4, which is specifically designed to run on Category 3 cable. 100BaseT4 (and also the marginally successful 100VG-AnyLAN protocol) are only able to function on this cable because they use all four of the wire pairs to carry data, while the standard technologies use only two pairs.

Category 4 cable provides a marginal increase in performance over Category 3 and was, for a time, used in Token Ring networks. Most of the UTP cable installed for LANs today is Category 5, however, because it provides a substantial performance increase, supporting transmissions at up to 100 MHz. Even if they are only going to be running 10BaseT today, most administrators choose to install Category 5 cable in anticipation of an upgrade to Fast Ethernet or another high-speed technology in the future.

Category	Bandwidth	Applications
1	Up to 0 MHz	Voice-grade telephone; POTS (Plain Old Telephone System); alarm systems
2	Up to 1 MHz	Voice-grade telephone; IBM minicomputer and mainframe terminals; ARCNET; LocalTalk
3	Up to 16 MHz	Voice-grade telephone; 10BaseT Ethernet; 4 Mbps Token Ring; 100BaseT4; 100VG-AnyLAN
4	Up to 20 MHz	16 Mbps Token Ring
5	Up to 100 MHz	100BaseTX; OC-3 (ATM); SONet

Table 4-2.   *TIA/EIA Category Ratings for UTP Cable*

Although the TIA/EIA category ratings are primarily used in relation to the cable itself, the other components that comprise the network medium are rated as well. To build a cabling system that is completely compliant with the Category 5 rating, for example, all connectors, wall plates, patch panels, and other components must also be rated Category 5.

Post-Category 5 Standards

While Category 5 cable is sufficient for use on 100 Mbps networks such as Fast Ethernet, technology continues to advance; and Gigabit Ethernet products are now available, running at 1 Gbps (1,000 Mbps). To accommodate these ultra-high speeds, UTP cable ratings have continued to advance as well. However, the process by which the TIA/EIA standards are defined and ratified is (much) slower than the pace of technology, so while some cable products on the market exceed the current Category 5 specifications, their ratings have not been officially recognized by the standards body.

A company called Anixter, Inc., which played a prominent part in the development of the TIA/EIA standards, maintains its own cable ratings, in which it refers to *levels*, as opposed to categories. Table 4-3 lists the Anixter levels that go beyond the current Category 5 rating.

Level 5 doubles the bandwidth of the Category 5 specification to 200 MHz, to conform to the ISO 11801 international standard. This cable supports throughput of up to 1.2 Gbps, which makes it suitable for Gigabit Ethernet communications. Products supporting this standard are currently being called Category 5 Enhanced or Category 5E, among other names. Level 6 increases the bandwidth of the cable to 350 MHz and Level 7 increases it to 400 MHz. Cables are now on the market that use these levels to rate their performance.

The TIA/EIA is also working on its own extensions to the standard, which probably will not be equivalent to the Anixter levels. This Category 5E or Category 5 Enhanced rating includes testing for *near-end crosstalk (NEXT), far-end crosstalk (FEXT),*

Level	Bandwidth
Level 5	200 MHz
Level 6	350 MHz
Level 7	400 MHz

Table 4-3.   *Anixter Post-Category 5 UTP Cable Ratings*

NETWORK HARDWARE

and *return loss (RL)*. Category 6 is intended to double the current bandwidth of Category 5 to 200 MHz and Category 7 (which is only in the early stages of development) increases it to 750 MHz. Presently, no products are available conforming to these specifications.

Connector Pinouts

Twisted-pair cables use RJ-45 modular connectors at both ends (see Figure 4-8). An RJ-45 (RJ is the acronym for *Registered Jack*) is an 8-pin version of the 4-pin RJ-11 connector used on standard satin telephone cables. The pinouts for the connector, which are also defined in the TIA/EIA-T568-A standard, are shown on the left in Figure 4-9, and have come to be known as the 568A pin assignments. However, other standards that predate TIA/EIA-T568-A provide alternate connector pinouts.

The USOC standard (as shown on the right in Figure 4-10) was the traditional pinout originated for voice communications in the U.S., but this configuration is not suitable for data because, while pins 3 and 6 do connect to a single-wire pair, pins 1 and 2 are connected to separate pairs. AT&T discovered this shortcoming when it began doing research into computer networks that would run over the existing telecommunications infrastructure. AT&T published its own standard, called 258A, in 1985, which defined a new pinout in which the proper pins used the same wire pairs. The TIA/EIA, which was established in 1985 after the breakup of AT&T, then published this standard as an adjunct to TIA/EIA-T568-A in 1995, giving it the name T568-B (as shown on the left in Figure 4-10). Thus, while the pinout now known as 568B would seem to be newer than 568A, it is actually older. Pinout 568B began to be used widely in the U.S. before the TIA/EIA-T568-A standard was even published.

As you can see in Figure 4-10, the USOC standard uses a different layout for the wire pairs, while the 568A and 568B pinouts are identical except that the green and orange wire pairs are transposed. Thus, the two standards are functionally identical; neither one offers a performance advantage over the other, as long as both ends of the cable use the same pinout. Prefabricated cables are available that conform to either one of these standards. USOC cables are available as well, but under no circumstances should you use these on a LAN or other data network.

In most cases, twisted-pair cable is wired straight through, meaning that each of the pins on one connector is wired to its corresponding pin on the other connector. On a typical network, however, computers use separate wire pairs for transmitting and receiving data. For two machines to communicate, the transmitted signal generated at each computer must be delivered to the receive pins on the other, meaning that a

Figure 4-8. *An RJ-45 connector*

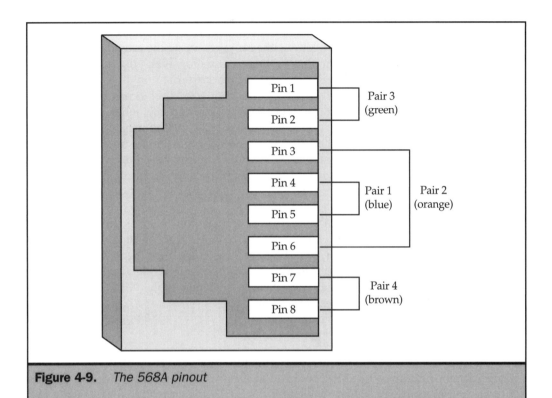

Figure 4-9.   *The 568A pinout*

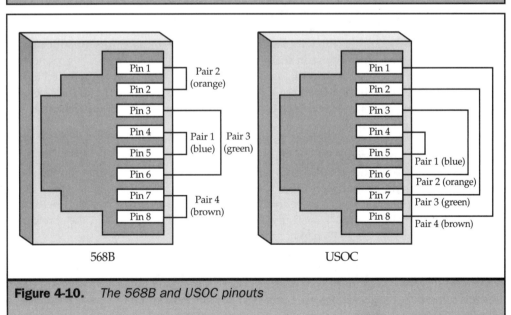

Figure 4-10.   *The 568B and USOC pinouts*

crossover must occur between the transmit and receive wire pairs. The cables are wired straight through because the hub is responsible for performing the crossover. If you want to connect one computer to another without a hub, however, you must use a *crossover cable,* in which the appropriate wire pairs are crossed.

Because each pin on a straight-through cable is connected to the corresponding pin at the other end, it doesn't matter what colors the wires are. So, when purchasing prefabricated cables, either the 568A or 568B pinouts will function properly. The time when you must make a conscious decision to use one standard or the other is when you install bulk cable (or have it installed). You must connect the same colors on each end of the cable to the same pins, so you get a straight-through connection. Selecting one standard and sticking to it is the best way to avoid confusion that can result in nonfunctioning connections.

Attaching the connectors to a cable requires a crimper tool, such as the one used for coaxial cable, except the process is complicated by having eight conductors to deal with, instead of only two. However, prefabricated twisted-pair cables are much more readily available than prefabricated thin Ethernet cables. A network administrator that is not handy with a crimper can easily purchase twisted-pair cables with connectors attached, in a wide variety of grades, lengths, and colors.

Shielded Twisted-Pair (STP)

STP is 150 ohm cable containing additional shielding that protects signals against the electromagnetic interference (EMI) produced by electric motors, power lines, and other sources. Used primarily in Token Ring networks, STP is also intended for installations where UTP cable would provide insufficient protection against interference.

The shielding in STP cable is not just an additional layer of inert insulation, as many people believe. Rather, the wires within the cable are encased in a metallic sheath that is as conductive as the copper in the wires. This sheath, when properly grounded, converts ambient noise into a current, just like an antenna. This current is carried to the wires within, where it creates an equal and opposite current flowing in the twisted pairs. The opposite currents cancel each other out, resulting in no noise to disturb the signals passing over the wires.

This balance between the opposite currents is delicate. If they are not exactly equal, the current can be interpreted as noise and can disturb the signals being transmitted over the cable. To keep the shield currents balanced, the entire end-to-end connection must be shielded and properly grounded. This means that all of the components involved in the connection, such as connectors and wall plates, must also be shielded. It is also vital to install the cable correctly, so it is grounded properly and the shielding is not ripped or otherwise disturbed at any point.

The shielding in an STP cable can be of two types, foil and braided metal. The metal braid is a more effective shield, but it adds weight, size, and expense to the cable. Foil-shielded cable, sometimes referred to as *screened twisted-pair (ScTP)* or *foil twisted-pair (FTP)*, is thinner, lighter, and cheaper, but is also less effective and more easily damaged.

In both cases, the installation is difficult when compared to UTP because the installers must be careful not to flex and bend the cable too much, or they could risk damaging the shielding. The cable may also suffer from increased attenuation and other problems because the effectiveness of the shielding is highly dependent on a multitude of factors, including the composition and thickness of the shielding, the type and location of the EMI in the area, and the nature of the grounding structure.

The properties of the STP cable itself were defined by IBM during the development of the Token Ring protocol. These STP cable types are as follows:

- **Type 1A**   Two pairs of 22 AWG wires, each pair wrapped in foil, with a shield layer (foil or braid) around both pairs, and an outer sheath of either PVC or plenum-rated material.

- **Type 2A**   Two pairs of 22 AWG wires, each pair wrapped in foil, with a shield layer (foil or braid) around both pairs, plus four additional pairs of 22 AWG wires for voice communications, within an outer sheath of either PVC or plenum-rated material.

- **Type 6A**   Two pairs of 22 AWG wires, with a shield layer (foil or braid) around both pairs, and an outer sheath of either PVC or plenum-rated material.

- **Type 9A**   Two pairs of 26 AWG wires, with a shield layer (foil or braid) around both pairs, and an outer sheath of either PVC or plenum-rated material.

Note   *The TIA/EIA-T568-A standard recognizes only two of these STP cable types: Type 1A, for use in backbones and horizontal wiring, and Type 6A, for patch cables.*

Token Ring networks running on STP use large, proprietary connectors called IBM Data Connectors (IDCs). However, due to the bulkiness of the cable and the difficult installation process, most of today's Token Ring networks run on standard 4-pair UTP cable instead of STP.

Fiber-Optic Cable

Fiber-optic cable is completely different from all of the other cables covered thus far in this chapter because it is not based on electrical signals transmitted through copper conductors. Instead, fiber-optic cable uses pulses of light to transmit the binary signals generated by computers. Because fiber-optic cable uses light (photons) instead of electricity, nearly all of the problems inherent in copper cable, such as electromagnetic interference, crosstalk, and the need for grounding, are completely eliminated. In addition, attenuation is reduced enormously, enabling fiber-optic links to span much greater distances than copper—up to 120 kilometers.

Fiber-optic cable is ideal for use in network backbones, and especially for connections between buildings, because it is immune to moisture and other outdoor conditions. Fiber cable is also inherently more secure than copper because it does not radiate detectable electromagnetic energy like copper, and it is extremely difficult to tap.

The drawbacks of fiber-optic mainly center around its installation and maintenance costs, which are usually thought of as being much higher than those for copper media. What used to be a great difference, however, has come closer to evening out in recent years. The fiber-optic medium itself is at this point only slightly more expensive than Category 5 UTP. Even so, the use of fiber does present some problems, such as in the installation process. Pulling the cable is basically the same as with copper, but attaching the connectors requires completely different tools and techniques; you can essentially throw everything you may have learned about electric wiring out the window.

Fiber-optic has been around for a long time; even the early 10 Mbps Ethernet standards supported its use, calling it FOIRL, and later 10BaseF. Fiber-optic came into its own, however, as a high-speed LAN technology, and today virtually all of the data link–layer protocols currently in use support it in some form, including the following:

- Fast Ethernet (100BaseFX)
- Gigabit Ethernet (1000BaseFX)
- Token Ring
- Fiber Distributed Data Interface (FDDI)
- 100VG-AnyLAN
- Asynchronous Transfer Mode
- Fibre Channel

As with copper, fiber-optic cable is typically installed using a star or a ring topology, although the FDDI protocol has popularized the *double ring*, which consists of two redundant rings with traffic traveling in opposite directions, for fault-tolerance purposes.

Fiber-Optic Cable Construction

A fiber-optic cable consists of a core made of glass or plastic, and a cladding that surrounds the core; then a plastic spacer layer; a layer of Kevlar fiber for protection; and an outer sheath of Teflon or PVC, as shown in Figure 4-11. The relationship between the core and the cladding enables fiber-optic cable to carry signals such long distances. The transparent qualities of the core are slightly greater than those of the cladding, which makes the inside surface of the cladding reflective. As the light pulses travel through the core, they reflect back and forth off of the cladding. This reflection enables you to bend the cable around corners and still have the signals pass through it without obstruction.

There are two main types of fiber-optic cable, called *singlemode* and *multimode*, that differ in several ways. The most important difference is in the thicknesses of the core

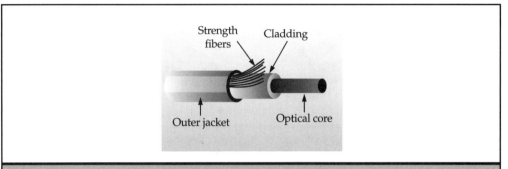

Strength fibers   Cladding

Outer jacket   Optical core

Figure 4-11. *Fiber-optic cable cross-section*

and the cladding. Singlemode fiber is typically rated at 8.3/125 microns and multimode fiber at 62.5/125 microns. These measurements refer to the thickness of the core and the thickness of the cladding and the core together. Light travels down the relatively thin core of singlemode cable without reflecting off of the cladding as much as in multimode fiber's thicker core. The signal carried by a singlemode cable is generated by a laser and consists of only a single wavelength, while multimode signals are generated by a light-emitting diode (LED) and carry multiple wavelengths. Together, these qualities enable singlemode cable to operate at higher bandwidths than multimode and traverse distances up to 50 times longer.

However, singlemode cable is much more expensive and has a relatively high bend radius compared to multimode, which makes it more difficult to work with. Most fiber-optic LANs use multimode cable, which, although inferior in performance to singlemode, is vastly superior to copper. Telephone and cable television companies tend to use singlemode fiber because they have to carry more data and span longer distances.

Fiber-Optic Connectors

The traditional connector used on fiber-optic cables is called an *ST (straight tip) connector*. It is a barrel-shaped connector with a bayonet locking system, as shown in Figure 4-12. A newer connector type, called the *SC (subscriber connector)*, is gaining in popularity, though. It has a square body and locks by simply pushing it into the socket.

Fiber-optic connectors can attach to the cable in several ways, using either a crimped compression fitting or an epoxy glue. Unlike the tools for crimping copper cables, a complete kit of which you can buy for under $100, a comparable fiber-optic toolkit costs well over $1,000.

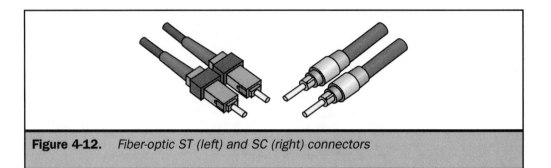

Figure 4-12.   *Fiber-optic ST (left) and SC (right) connectors*

Fiber-Optic Cable and Network Design

At this time, fiber-optic cable is primarily limited to backbones and is not often used for horizontal wiring because of its higher installation and maintenance costs. This technology has great potential in this area, however. Using fiber-optic cable imparts a freedom to the network designer that could never be realized with copper media. Because fiber-optic permits segment lengths much greater than UTP's 100 meters, having telecommunications closets containing switches or hubs scattered about a large installation is no longer necessary.

Instead, horizontal cable runs can extend all the way from wall plates down to a central equipment room that contains all of the network's patch panels, hubs, switches, routers, and other such devices. This is known as a *collapsed backbone*. Rather than traveling constantly to remote areas of the installation, the majority of the infrastructure maintenance can be performed at this one location.

Cable Installations

Installing network cable can be as simple as buying a few prefabricated cables at the computer center and tacking them to the baseboard, or as complicated as connecting a thousand workstations to a corporate backbone in a multifloored office building. As mentioned earlier in this chapter, cabling is a part of the LAN installation process that is frequently outsourced, not because it is especially difficult technically, but because it tends to be a dirty, time-consuming job. As with most professionals, however, cable installers with the proper tools, techniques, and experience can make the entire job look quick and easy.

While a relatively small network can be composed of all prefabricated cables, a good internal installation (that is, with the cables hidden from views in the walls and ceilings) is performed using bulk cable. The basic steps for this type of installation, assuming the use of a cable commonly found today, such as UTP or fiber-optic, are as follows:

1. Create a plan specifying the location of the wiring nexus where all of the cable runs will terminate and where each wall plate is to be located.

2. Starting at the nexus, pull the cables through the walls and ceilings to where each of workstations will be located.

3. Mount a wall plate near the site of each workstation and wire the cable end into the plate's connector.

4. At the nexus, mount a patch panel on the wall and "punch down" each of the cables to a connector in the panel.

5. Using the appropriate equipment, test each connection.

6. Using prefabricated patch cables, connect the ports on the patch panel to the appropriate hub and connect the computer to the jack in the wall plate.

Of course, this description simplifies the process greatly, so it is worth devoting some detail to the individual processes.

Creating a Plan

Planning is the single most important part of the entire network construction process. You must know the exact location for each cable drop, preferably marked on a floor plan, so that you can keep track of the various cables during the installation. Remember that in a large cable installation, you may have hundreds of identical cables passing through walls and ceiling; and unless you are organized, confusion is sure to result. Your plan must also be designed with the data link–layer protocol requirements, local building codes, and fire laws in mind, so that you are not forced to pull all your cables out later. Of course, depending on the physical layout of your site and the construction of your building, you may be in for a few surprises that cause you to change your plans in midstream, but this is why you left a 10 percent reserve in your budget, right?

Pulling Cables

The actual process of pulling cable begins at the server closet or data center where you have decided to locate your patch panel. A *patch panel*, also called a *punchdown block* (see Figure 4-13), is a wall-mounted frame containing jacks for all of the cables you intend to pull. This will be your wiring nexus and the starting point for all of your cable runs.

Bulk cable typically comes on a large spool. Locating this spool near the patch panel, you can start to strip cable off and pull it to the site of the first drop. How you do this depends on the construction of the building. In a modern office with hollow

Figure 4-13.   *A patch panel or punchdown block*

walls and a drop ceiling, you would typically run the cable through the ceiling to the approximate location of the drop, and then down through the wall to a hole you've cut for the wall plate.

Before you push that first cable end into the ceiling, however, be sure to label it. Most installers use adhesive labels of some kind and some sort of code representing that cable's ultimate location. You may also want to attach a pull string to the leading edge of the cable with tape. A *pull string* is simply a length of string or twine you pull along with the cable, so that if you later want to pull additional cable all or part of the way to that same location, you can attach it to the string and pull it through from the other end.

Another tool used by cable installers working inside drop ceilings is called a telpole. A *telpole* is a thin, telescoping pole, sometimes 10 or 15 feet long, with a clip on the end to hold a cable. With the pole in its closed state, you attach the leading cable end to it and then extend the pole inside the ceiling as far as it will reach. This tool is good for situations in which you have to pull cable by yourself because it prevents you from having to climb one ladder, throw the looped cable as far as possible inside the ceiling, and then climb another ladder across the room to retrieve it.

When you are pulling cable in a drop ceiling, you must push each cable down inside the wall to the location of the wall plate. Installers have another tool called a *fish tape*, which is similar to a plumber's snake with a clamp on the end to hold the cable. The tape is flexible enough (like a tape measure) to push the cable either down inside a wall from the ceiling or up from the floor. Once the cable segment has reached the location of the wall plate, you pull through an extra few yards for slack and cut the cable at the spool, remembering to number that end with the same code you put on the leading end.

You may encounter obstacles at any stage of this process. You may find that the tops of the walls are capped with wood or metal studs, or that they have horizontal barriers halfway down the wall. Inside a drop ceiling, you may have to route your cable around light fixtures or other sources of interference.

Mounting Hardware

Once you have your cable runs in place, it's time to terminate them at both ends by attaching them to the appropriate fixtures. At the workstation side, the cable usually terminates at a wall plate. A *wall plate* contains the jacks to which the cables are to be connected and is mounted flush with the wall, or sometimes is a box mounted on the wall surface. Wall plates are usually modular and can hold up to four jacks. You can install jacks of different types in the plate to support multiple voice and data connections as needed. Assuming a UTP installation, you attach the individual wires in the cable to the connectors in the jack (using the pinout standard you decided on earlier), and then snap it into the plate and screw the plate into the wall.

At the other end of the run, the cable connects to the patch panel you mounted. The patch panel performs the same function as the wall plate, except that it contains more jacks. The patch panel is not a hub; no communication occurs between the ports. It is simply a convenient way of keeping track of the cable runs. To connect a cable to a port in the patch panel, you lay the individual wires in the appropriate slots (using the same pinout as when you connected the cable to the wall plate) and use a punchdown tool (see Figure 4-14) to push them into the slots. The tool firmly seats the wire in the slot, making a connection, and cuts off the excess at the same time. Be sure to label the port in the patch panel so that you know the location of its terminus.

Testing Connections

Once you terminate both ends of a cable run, you should test the run to make sure it is functioning properly. You can do this by actually connecting a computer to the network

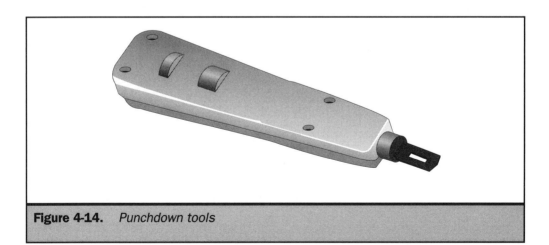

Figure 4-14. *Punchdown tools*

using the cable run, but professional installers use cable testing equipment that is easier and more accurate. See Chapter 30 for more information on cable testing tools.

Connecting Computers

At this point, you are ready to connect both ends of the cable run to the appropriate devices. Using patch cables that you have either purchased or made yourself by attaching connectors to bulk cable, you connect the wall plate to the NIC in a computer and the patch panel port to a hub, switch, or other device in the server closet or data center.

The Larger Picture

Even when covered in this detail, the process of installing the cable system can be considerably more complex than described here. This example covers only the installation of the horizontal cabling in one area. A large enterprise network can consist of many such horizontal cable installations, connected by a backbone that may have to run between the floors of a building or even between buildings.

Chapter 5

Repeaters, Hubs, and Bridges

R epeaters, hubs, and bridges are devices used to connect network cables at the bottom two layers of the OSI reference model. Depending on the capabilities of the device and the layer at which it operates, the result can be a network that spans longer distances, supports more computers, and provides increased bandwidth for each system on the network.

Repeaters

As a signal travels over a cable, it gradually weakens until it is no longer viable. The longer the cable, the weaker the signal gets. This weakening is called *attenuation,* and it is a problem that affects all types of cables to some degree. The effect of attenuation is dependent on the type of cable. Copper cable, for example, is much more prone to attenuation than fiber-optic. This is one reason why fiber-optic cable segments can be much longer than copper ones.

The standards on which computer networks are based define the minimum and maximum lengths for the cables connecting the computers. When you have to run a cable across a longer distance, you can use a device called a *repeater* to amplify the signal, enabling it to travel greater distances without attenuating to the point of being unreadable by the destination system. In its simplest form, a repeater is an electrical device that receives a signal through one cable connection, amplifies it, and transmits it out through another connection.

Because its function is purely electrical, this type of repeater functions at the network's physical layer only. The repeater cannot read the contents of the packets traveling over the network or even know that they are packets. The device simply amplifies the incoming electrical signals and passes them on. Repeaters are also incapable of performing any sort of filtration on the data traveling over the network. As a result, two cable segments joined by a repeater form a single collision domain.

On a modern network, it is rare to see a standalone repeater. In most cases, the repeating function is built into another device, such as a hub or a switch. On a network composed of coaxial cable, like a thin or thick Ethernet LAN, a standalone repeater enables you to extend the maximum bus length past 185 meters (for thin Ethernet) or 500 meters (for thick Ethernet). This type of repeater is a simple device consisting of a box with two coaxial connectors and a plug for a power source. Installation is simply a matter of connecting the two cable segments to the box.

Other factors limit the maximum distance a network signal can travel. On an Ethernet network, for example, a packet being transmitted by one computer must reach all the other computers on the local network before the last bit is transmitted. Therefore, you cannot extend a network segment without limit by adding multiple repeaters. A 10 Mbps Ethernet network can have up to five cable segments connected by four repeaters. Fast Ethernet networks are more limited, allowing a maximum of only two repeaters.

Hubs

A *hub* is a device that functions as the cabling nexus for a network that uses the star topology. Each computer has its own cable that connects to the central hub. The responsibility of the hub is to see to it that traffic arriving over any of its ports is propagated out of the other ports. Depending on the network medium, a hub will use electrical circuitry, optical components, or other technologies to split the incoming signal among the outgoing ports. A fiber-optic hub, for example, actually uses mirrors to split the light impulses.

The hub itself it a box, either freestanding or rack-mounted, with a number of ports to which the cables connect. The ports can be the standard RJ-45 connectors used by twisted-pair networks, ST connectors for fiber-optic cable, or any other type of connector used on a star network.

The term *hub* is used in reference to Ethernet networks; the equivalent device on a Token Ring network is called a *multistation access unit*. The internal functions of the two devices are different, but they serve the same basic purpose: to connect a collection of computers into a single collision domain.

Passive Hubs

Unlike repeaters, many different types of hubs exist with different capabilities. At its simplest, a hub supplies cable connections by passing all the signals entering the device through any port out through all the other ports. This is known as a *passive hub* because it operates only at the physical layer, has no intelligence, and makes no modifications to the signal. This type of hub is almost never used on networks today.

Repeating Hubs

The hubs used on today's networks, at the very minimum, supply repeating functionality by amplifying the signals as they propagate them to the other ports. In fact, these hubs are sometimes referred to as *multiport repeaters*. Unlike a passive hub, a repeating (or active) hub requires a power source to boost the signal. The device still operates at the physical layer, however, because it deals only with the raw signals traveling over the cables.

Some hubs go beyond repeating and can repair and retime the signals as well, to synchronize the transmissions through the outgoing ports. These hubs use a technique called *store and forward*, which involves actually reading the contents of the packets to retransmit them over individual ports as needed. A hub with these capabilities can lower the network performance for the systems connected to it because of processing delays but, at the same time, packet loss is diminished and the number of collisions reduced.

For a small workgroup network, such as that used in a home or small business, you can purchase a basic 10 Mbps Ethernet repeating hub with up to eight ports for less than $100. This device will connect all your computers into a single collision domain. Because the device is functioning as a repeater, each of the cables connecting the hub to a computer can be the maximum length allowed by the protocol standard. For Ethernet running on unshielded twisted-pair (UTP) cable, the maximum length is 100 meters.

Using multiple hubs on a network is possible, by connecting them together to form a star-bus or a branching tree network, as shown in Figure 5-1. When you do this using standard repeating hubs, all the computers remain in the same collision domain, and you must observe the configuration guidelines for the data link–layer protocol used on the network. Just as with the standalone repeaters discussed earlier in this chapter, the path between any two machines on a 10 Mbps Ethernet network cannot include more than four repeaters (hubs).

For example, if you have a small 10BaseT workgroup network that eventually outgrows your existing hub, you can add another one by connecting it to the uplink port found on most Ethernet hubs. All the computers will still be in the same collision domain and they can receive all the packets transmitted over the network. This growth can continue until you have a maximum of four hubs. If your network grows even more, you can replace your hubs with models having a greater number of ports, or you can split the network into two LANs (or collision domains) by using a different type of device, such as a bridge, router, or switch.

Note *For more information on the uplink port and the internal functioning of hubs, see "Hub Configurations," later in this chapter.*

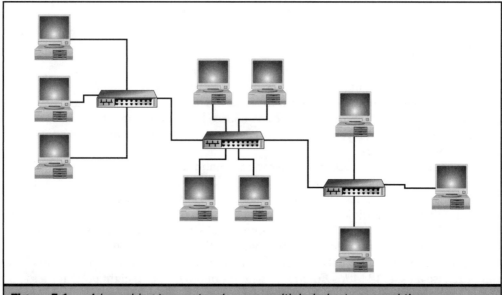

Figure 5-1. *A branching tree network uses multiple hubs to expand the collision domain*

Token Ring MSAUs

Token Ring networks use hubs as well, although they call them *multistation access units,* or *MAUs.* While a MAU, to all external appearances, performs the same function as an Ethernet hub, its internal workings are quite different. Instead of passing incoming traffic to the other ports in parallel, as in an Ethernet hub, a MAU transmits packets through each port serially, one at a time. After transmitting a packet to a workstation, the MAU waits until that packet returns through the same port before it transmits it out the next port. This forms the logical ring topology from which the protocol gets its name.

MAUs also contain switches that enable specific ports to be excluded from the ring, in the event of a failure of some kind. This prevents a malfunctioning workstation from disturbing the functionality of the entire ring.

Intelligent Hubs

Intelligent hubs are units that have some form of integrated management capability. A *basic repeating hub* is essentially an electrical device that propagates incoming packets to all available ports without discrimination. Intelligent hubs do the same thing, but they also monitor the operation of each port. The management capabilities vary widely between products, but many intelligent hubs use the Simple Network Management Protocol (SNMP) to send information to a centralized network management console, like Hewlett-Packard's OpenView. Other devices might use a terminal directly connected to the hub or an HTML interface you can access from a Web browser anywhere on the network.

The object of the management capability is to provide the network administrator with a centralized source of information about the hubs and the systems connected to them. This eliminates the need for the staff supporting a large network to go running to each wiring closet looking for the hub or system causing a problem. The management console typically displays a graphical model of the network and alerts the administrator when a problem or failure occurs on any system connected to the hub.

On smaller networks, this capability isn't needed; but when you're managing an enterprise network with hundreds or thousands of nodes, a technology that can tell you exactly which one of the hub ports is malfunctioning can be helpful. The degree of intelligence built into a hub varies greatly with the product. Many hybrid devices are on the market today that have sufficient intelligence to go beyond the definition of a hub and provide bridging, switching, or routing functions as well.

Hub Configurations

Hubs are available in a wide variety of sizes and with many different features, ranging from small, simple devices designed to service a handful of computers to huge rack-mounted affairs for large enterprise networks. The range of hub designs fall into three categories, as follows:

- Standalone hubs

- Stackable hubs
- Modular hubs

Standalone Hubs

A *standalone hub* is a small box about the size of a paperback book that has anywhere from 4 to 16 ports in it. As the name implies, the device is freestanding, has its own power cable, and can easily fit on or under a desk. Four- or five-port *minihubs* are good for home and small workgroup networks, or for providing quick, ad hoc expansions to a larger network. Larger units can support more connections and may have LEDs that indicate the presence of a link pulse signal on the connected cable and, possibly, the occurrence of a collision on the network.

Despite the name, a standalone hub usually has some mechanism for connecting with other hubs to expand the network within the same collision domain. The following sections examine how the most common mechanisms are used for this purpose.

THE UPLINK PORT   The cables used on a twisted-pair network are wired *straight through,* meaning that each of the eight pins on the RJ-45 connector on one end of the cable is wired to the corresponding pin on the other end. For a UTP connection between two computers to function, however, the transmit circuits on each system must be connected to the receive circuits on the other. Therefore, a *crossover* must exist somewhere in the connection and, traditionally, this occurs in the hub. The pins in each of a hub's ports are connected to those of every other port using crossover circuits that transpose the transport data (TD) and receive data (RD) signals.

| Note | *For more information on network cabling and signal crossovers, see Chapter 4.* |

Many hubs have a port that bypasses the crossover circuit, which you can use to connect to another hub. This port is typically labeled *uplink* and may or may not have a switch that enables you to specify whether the port should be crossed over or wired straight through. If you have more than one hub on your system, you connect them using the uplink port (on one hub only). Otherwise, both hubs would perform the crossover, and the circuits between a machine connected to one hub and a machine connected to the other would be the equivalent of a straight through connection. If a hub does not have an uplink port, you can still connect it to another hub using a standard port and a *crossover cable,* which is a cable that has the transmit pins on both ends wired directly to the receive pins on the other end.

You typically use the uplink port to connect hubs when they're located some distance away from each other and you want to use the same cable medium throughout the network. When you are evaluating hubs, being aware of just how many hub ports are available for workstation connections is important. A device advertised as an eight-port hub may have seven standard ports and one unswitched uplink port, leaving only seven connections for computers. No matter what the size of the network, purchasing hubs with a few ports more than you need—for expansion purposes—is always a good idea.

BACKBONE CONNECTIONS   Some standalone hubs have an *attachment unit interface (AUI)* port you can use to create a *backbone,* that is, a separate network segment that carries the traffic between hubs. Many inexpensive 10BaseT hubs, for example, have a BNC connector on them that you can use to connect the hub to a thin Ethernet coaxial cable segment, although the AUI connector may also support thick Ethernet, fiber-optic cable, or any other medium. Thin Ethernet is rarely used now in new network installations, and this method is not possible on Fast Ethernet networks (because coaxial cable is limited to speeds of 10 Mbps), but it illustrates the principle well.

Note   *This is only a basic example of the backbone concept, in which a dedicated network segment is used to connect individual segments or LANs. Larger networks, and even huge ones like the Internet, use backbones (often running at high speeds) to provide more efficient internetwork traffic paths.*

When you have several 10BaseT Ethernet hubs connected using their uplink ports, each length of cable is a separate segment. Because the Ethernet guidelines allow the path from one system to another to travel across only five segments, connected by four repeaters, you are limited to four hubs on any particular LAN. When you connect the hubs using a thin Ethernet bus, as shown in Figure 5-2, only one segment is added to the equation. The path between two systems involves, at most, three segments because the data travels over the bus to all the hubs at the same time.

As you expand this type of network further, you may run into another Ethernet limitation not yet mentioned. The bus connecting the hubs is called a *mixing segment* because it has more than two devices connected to it. A segment that connects only two devices, such as the UTP cable connecting hubs through the uplink port, is called a *link segment.* Of the five segments permitted on a 10BaseT LAN, only three of these can be mixing segments. This guideline, stating that you can connect up to five segments using four repeaters and that no more than three of the segments can be mixing segments, is known as the *Ethernet 5-4-3 rule.*

Note   *For more information on Ethernet cabling guidelines, see Chapter 8.*

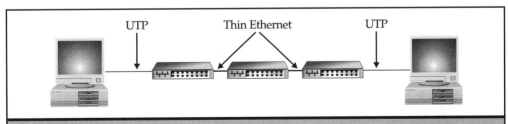

Figure 5-2.   *Because the two lengths of thin Ethernet coaxial cable in this illustration form a single bus, the path between the two workstations consists of three segments, not four*

Stackable Hubs

As you move up the scale of hub size and complexity (as well as expense), you find units called *stackable hubs* that provide greater expandability. As the name implies, these hubs have cases designed to stack one on top of the other, but this is not the only difference. Unlike standalone hubs, which can be located in different rooms or floors and still connected together, stackable hubs are typically located in a data center or wiring closet and are connected together with short cables.

When you connect stackable hubs together, they form what is functionally a single larger hub. The cables connecting the units do not form separate segments, so you can have more than four hubs interconnected. In addition, these devices can share their capabilities. A single intelligent hub unit can manage its own ports, as well as those of all the other units in the array.

Stackable hubs have their own power supplies and can function independently, thus providing a much more expandable environment than standalone hubs. You can start with a single unit, without incurring the major expense of a chassis (as used by modular hubs), and connect additional units as the network grows.

Modular Hubs

Modular hubs are designed to support the largest networks, and provide the greatest amount of expandability and flexibility. A modular hub consists of a chassis (sometimes called a *card cage*) that is nearly always rack-mounted and contains several slots into which you plug individual communications modules. The chassis provides a common power source for all the modules, as well as a backplane that enables them to communicate with each other. The modules contain the ports to which you connect the computer cables. When you plug multiple modules into the chassis, they become, in effect, a single large hub.

Modular hubs nearly always include management capabilities and are extremely flexible because you can insert modules supporting different technologies into the same chassis. By using various modules, you can mix media like 100BaseTX and 100BaseFX in the same hub; mix protocols, such as Ethernet and Token Ring; or insert cards that provide bridging, switching, or routing capabilities. As you might imagine, module hubs are the most expensive type and are intended for large, permanent network installations.

Note   *In some cases, the dividing line between stackable and modular hub products becomes rather indistinct. Stackable hubs exist with expansion slots that accept modules providing additional ports, management capabilities, or even support for other media, such as a fiber-optic backbone.*

Selecting a Hub

When evaluating hubs for your network, planning for future upgrades and expansion is arguably the most important element of your decision. You should always purchase a hub with a few more ports than you need, remembering that you may eventually want to connect printers, as well as workstations, directly to the hub. In addition, you should have a plan for how you are going to expand your network beyond the limits of a single hub.

Planning for Network Growth

For small networks, standalone hubs are sufficient, and you can expand your network by connecting another hub to the uplink port (or to a standard port using a crossover cable). This is also a good solution if you want to place hubs at different locations because the cable connecting the two hubs can be up to ten meters long on a UTP Ethernet network. You must, however, be conscious of the limits on the number of repeaters imposed by the Ethernet standards. Four 10BaseT hubs and two Class II 100BaseT hubs are all that are permitted on an Ethernet LAN. If you suspect your network may grow larger than this arrangement can support, you may be better served by purchasing a stackable hub that you can expand later.

Stackable hubs are an excellent choice for mid-sized networks because they can provide much of the flexibility of modular systems with a relatively small initial investment. You can purchase one unit to start and later add more to provide additional ports or more features, like network management or support for other protocols.

Because stackable hubs connect to form a single unit, you needn't worry about the Ethernet repeater limits unless you have several hub arrays in different locations. But be aware that stackable hub products are not infinitely expandable. Make sure you find out the maximum number of units you can interconnect because this differs greatly between products.

Stackable hubs use short cables to connect to each other, so all the units must be together, typically in a wiring closet or other safe location. This type of arrangement requires more planning than standalone hubs, which you can deploy at will anywhere on the network where you need additional ports. You should choose a central location for the stacked hubs that is roughly equidistant from all the workstations to which you will connect it and make sure the hubs have a reliable source of power. Remember, if the hubs go down, the network goes down, even if the PCs are protected by uninterruptible power supplies (UPSes).

Modular hubs require the most planning of all and the greatest initial expense because you have to purchase a chassis, as well as the cards containing the ports that will be mounted in it. Investing in modular hubs is usually a long-term commitment

NETWORK HARDWARE

because they are best suited to large networks that require the greatest amount of flexibility and expandability. The assumption is that your network will grow extensively over time and may require a variety of different technologies to keep up with that growth. Consider scenarios like the possibility of your company merging with another company and having to combine disparate network types. You would want to buy modular hubs from a reputable vendor that has all the features you may need in the next five years and that also would be around in five years.

Moving stackable hubs to a different location is easy (although the network cables may be another story), but modular hubs are usually permanently mounted in a data center or large wiring closet. Some modular products include additional fault-tolerance features like redundant fans, power supplies, and backup battery power, as well as the capability to hot swap modules in the event of a malfunction.

Planning for Network Upgrades

The other primary concern when it comes to hub purchases today is the question of whether you will be performing a speed upgrade to your network in the near future. For example, if you're currently running 10BaseT, you may want to upgrade at least some of your workstations to Fast Ethernet at a certain point.

Ethernet hubs can support 10BaseT, Fast Ethernet, or both. Unlike network interface cards, not every Fast Ethernet hub is capable of running at 10 Mbps and 100 Mbps. If you opt for single-speed hubs, you need to have separate network segments for the two speeds and two NICs in systems that must be accessible to both. On a dual- speed hub, each port auto-negotiates the best possible speed with the workstation connected to it.

Dual-speed hubs work by maintaining a separate logical segment within the unit for each speed and may use a two-port switch to pass data between the segments (so that only the data destined for the other segment gets passed to that segment). In some stackable hub arrangements, the switch is built into one "master" hub that can service all the other "client" hubs in the stack. This saves you money by making it possible to switch between the segments on interconnected hubs without having to pay for redundant switching circuitry in each unit.

Dual-speed hubs also simplify the migration path between standard and Fast Ethernet. No need exists for two NICs in servers and other shared systems because the hub provides a path between the two network segments. You also needn't change any of your workstation NICs to install the hub. Once the device is in place, your 10BaseT systems continue to function normally. At any subsequent time, you can replace a workstation's 10BaseT NIC with a 100BaseT model. When you boot the workstation, the new NIC connects with the hub at 100 Mbps and is added to the high-speed segment.

Not surprisingly, dual-speed hubs are significantly more expensive than the single-speed variety. Depending on where in the migration process you are when you buy the hubs, you may find sticking with single-speed units more economical. for example, if a large part of your network is already running Fast Ethernet and you have only a few 10 Mbps workstations left, spending a lot of extra money on dual-speed hubs is probably not worth the expense when you could spend a long weekend upgrading the remaining systems to Fast Ethernet instead. If, however, you are still running 10BaseT throughout the network and your migration to Fast Ethernet is still in the planning stages, then dual-speed hubs can be an ideal solution.

Bridges

A *bridge* is another device used to connect LAN cable segments together, but unlike hubs, bridges operate at the data link layer of the OSI model and are selective about the packets that pass through them. Repeaters and hubs are designed to propagate all the network traffic they receive to all of the connected cable segments.

A bridge has two or more ports connected to different cable segments and operates in *promiscuous mode*, meaning that it receives all of the packets transmitted on the connected segments. As each packet enters the bridge, the device reads the destination address in the data link–layer protocol header and, if the packet is destined for a system on another segment, forwards the packet to that segment. If the packet is destined for a system on the local segment, the bridge discards the packet, as it has already reached its destination. This process is called *packet filtering*.

As with a hub or repeater, the bridge makes no changes in the packet whatsoever and is completely unconscious of the contents within the data link–layer frame. As a result, you don't have to consider the protocols running at the network layer and above at all when evaluating or installing bridges.

In this manner, the bridge reduces the amount of excess traffic on the network by not propagating packets needlessly. Broadcast messages are forwarded to all of the connected segments, making it possible to use protocols that rely on broadcasts like NetBEUI without manual system configuration. Unlike a repeater, however, a bridge does not relay data to the connected segments until it has received the entire packet. Because of this, two systems on bridged segments can transmit simultaneously without incurring a collision. Thus, a bridge connects network segments in such a way as to keep them in the same broadcast domain, but in different collision domains.

If, for example, you have a LAN that is experiencing diminished performance due to high levels of traffic, you can split it into two segments by inserting a bridge at the midpoint. This will keep the local traffic generated on each segment local and still permit broadcasts and other traffic intended for the other segment to pass through. Bridges also provide the same repeating functions as a hub, enabling you to extend the cable length accordingly.

Bridges are available in three basic types, as follows:

- ■ **Local** A local bridge provides packet filtering and repeating services for network segments of the same type. This type of device is also called a *MAC-layer bridge* because the data arriving at the bridge only has to travel up the protocol stack as high as the media access control, or MAC, sublayer (that is, the lower of the two sublayers that comprise the data link layer, the other being the logical link control,

NETWORK HARDWARE

or LLC, sublayer). This is the simplest type of bridge because no need exists for packet translation or buffering. The device simply propagates the incoming packets to the appropriate ports or discards them.

■ **Translation**   A translation bridge provides the same functions as a local bridge, except that it connects segments running at different speeds or using different protocols. You can, for example, use a translation bridge to connect Ethernet to Token Ring, 10BaseT to 100BaseT, or 100BaseTX to 100BaseT4. In this type of bridge, the incoming packets travel up the protocol stack to the MAC sublayer, where they are stripped of their data link protocol headers and passed to the LLC sublayer. The data is then encapsulated by the appropriate protocol for each of the ports over which the bridge will transmit the outgoing packets. This translation adds a measure of complexity (and expense) to the bridge itself and a delay to the propagation of data over the entire network, but it remains an effective solution for joining disparate networks together into a single broadcast domain.

■ **Remote**   A remote bridge connects network segments at different locations, using a wide area network (WAN) link such as a modem or leased line. WAN links are usually slower and more expensive than LAN connections and a bridge conserves bandwidth by minimizing the amount of traffic passing over the link while giving both segments full access to the network. Because of the difference in speed between the local and wide area links, a remote bridge usually has an internal buffer it uses to store the data it receives from the LAN while it is waiting for transmission to the remote site.

Note   *On most networks constructed today, bridging has largely been replaced by routing and switching technologies, which provide a more comprehensive service at what has become a competitive price. For more information on routers and switches, see Chapter 6.*

Transparent Bridging

To filter the packets reaching it effectively, a bridge has to know which systems are located on which network segments, so it can determine which packets to forward and which to discard. The bridge stores this information in an address table that is internal to the unit. Originally, network administrators had to create the address table for a bridge manually, but today's bridges compile the address table automatically, a process called *transparent bridging*.

As soon as a transparent bridge (also known as a *learning bridge*) is connected to the network segments, it begins to compile its address table. By reading the source addresses in the arriving packets and noting which interface they arrived over, the bridge can build a table of node addresses for each segment connected to it.

To illustrate, imagine a network composed of three segments (A, B, and C), all connected to a local bridge, as shown in Figure 5-3. When the bridge is first activated,

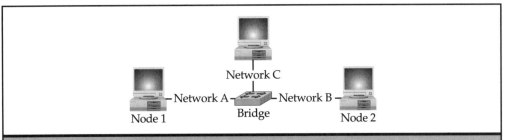

Figure 5-3.   *A transparent bridge forwards packets based on address tables it compiles from previously transmitted packets*

it receives a packet from Node 1 over the interface to Network A that is destined for Node 2 on Network B. Because the bridge now knows Node 1 is located on Network A, it creates an entry in its table for Network A that contains Node 1's MAC address.

At this time, the bridge has no information about Node 2 and the segment on which it's located, so it transmits the packet out to Networks B and C, that is, all of the connected segments except the one from which the packet arrived. This is the default behavior of a bridge whenever it receives a packet destined for a system not in its tables; it transmits the packet over all of the other segments to ensure that it reaches its destination.

Once Node 2 receives the packet, it transmits a reply to Node 1. Because Node 2 is located on Network B, its reply packet arrives at the bridge over a different interface. Now the bridge can add an entry to its table for Network B containing Node 2's address. On examining the packet, the bridge looks for the destination address in its tables and discovers that the address belongs to Node 1, on Network A. The bridge then transmits the packet over the interface to Node A only.

From this point on, when any other system on Network A transmits a packet to Node 1, the bridge knows to discard it because there is no need to pass it along to the other segments. However, the bridge still uses those packets to add the transmitting stations to its address table for Network A.

Eventually, the bridge will have address table entries for all of the nodes on the network and it can direct all of the incoming packets to the appropriate outgoing ports.

Note   *One of the statistics often cited in the specifications for specific bridge products is the number of addresses the device can store in its table. Usually, the amount of storage space is far more than virtually anyone would need, but it's good to make sure the product you purchase can support your network properly.*

Bridge Loops

When the segments of a network are connected using bridges, the failure or malfunction of a bridge can be catastrophic. For this reason, administrators often connect network segments with redundant bridges, to ensure that every node can access the entire network, even if a bridge should fail.

NETWORK HARDWARE

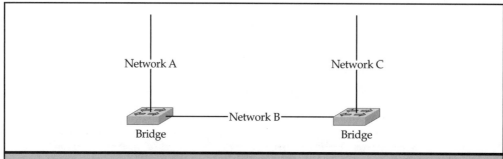

Figure 5-4. *When each segment is connected to the others using one bridge, a single point of failure is created*

In Figure 5-4, three segments are connected by two bridges. If one of the bridges fails, then one of the segments is cut off from the rest of the network. To remedy this problem and to provide fault tolerance, you can add a third bridge connecting the two end segments, as shown in Figure 5-5. This way, each system always has two possible paths to the other segments.

Installing redundant bridges is a good idea, but it also produces what can be a serious problem. When a computer (Node 1) is located on a segment connected to two bridges, as shown in Figure 5-6, both of the bridges will receive the first packet the system transmits and add the machine's address to their tables for that segment, Network A. Both bridges will then transmit the same packet onto the other segment, Network B. As a result, each bridge will then receive the packet forwarded by the other bridge. The packet headers will still show the address of Node 1 as the source, but both bridges will have received the packet over the Network B interface. As a result, the bridges may (or may not) modify their address tables to show Node 1 as being on Network B, not A. If this occurs, any

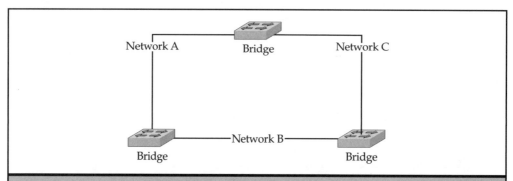

Figure 5-5. *Connecting each segment to two bridges provides fault tolerance*

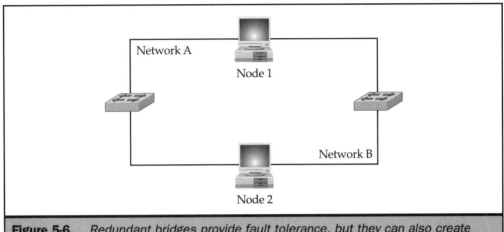

Figure 5-6.   *Redundant bridges provide fault tolerance, but they can also create bridging loops and broadcast storms*

subsequent transmissions from Node 2 on Network B that are directed to Node 1 will be dropped because the bridges think Node 1 is on Network B, when it is, in fact, on A.

The result of this occurrence is lost data because the bridges are improperly dropping frames and degradation of network performance. Eventually, the incorrect entries in the bridges' address tables will expire or be modified but, in the interim, Node 1 is cut off from the systems on the other network segments.

If this problem is not bad enough, what happens when Node 1 transmits a broadcast message is worse. Each of the bridges forward the packet to Network B, where it is received by the other bridge, which forwards it again. Because bridges always forward broadcast packets without filtering them, multiple copies of the same message circulate endlessly between the two segments, constantly being forwarded by both bridges. This is called a *broadcast storm* and it can effectively prevent all other traffic on the network from reaching its destination.

The Spanning Tree Algorithm

To address the problem of endless loops and broadcast storms on networks with redundant bridging, the Digital Equipment Corporation devised the *spanning tree algorithm (SPA)*, which preserves the fault tolerance provided by the additional bridges, while preventing the endless loops. SPA was later revised by the Institute of Electrical and Electronic Engineers (IEEE) and standardized as the 802.1d specification.

The spanning tree algorithm works by selecting one bridge for each network segment that has multiple bridges available. This designated bridge takes care of all of the packet filtering and forwarding tasks for the segment, while the others remain idle, but stand ready to take over should the designated bridge fail.

During this selection process, each bridge is assigned a unique identifier (using one of the bridge's MAC addresses, plus a priority value) as is each individual port on each bridge (using the port's MAC address). Each port is also associated with a path cost, that specifies the cost of transmitting a packet onto the LAN using that port. Path costs typically can be specified by an administrator when a reason exists to prefer one port over another, or left to default values.

Once all the components have been identified, the bridge with the lowest identifier becomes the *root bridge* for the entire network. Each of the other bridges then determines which of its ports can reach the root bridge with the lowest cost (called the *root path cost*) and designates it as the root port for that bridge.

Finally, for each network segment, a *designated bridge* is selected, as well as a *designated port* on that bridge. Only the designated port on the designated bridge is permitted to filter and forward the packets for that network segment. The other (redundant) bridges on that segment remain operative—in case the designated bridge should fail—but are inactive until they are needed. Now that only one bridge is operating on each segment, packets can be forwarded without loops forming.

To perform these calculations, bridges must exchange messages among themselves, using a message format defined in the 802.1d standard (see Figure 5-7). These messages are called *bridge protocol data units (BPDUs)* and contain the following fields:

- **Protocol Identifier (2 bytes)**   Always contains the value 0
- **Version (1 byte)**   Always contains the value 0
- **Message Type (1 byte)**   Always contains the value 0
- **Flags (1 byte)**   Contains two 1-bit flags, using the following values:
  - **Bit 1**   Topology change—indicates the message is being sent to signal a change in the network topology
  - **Bit 2**   Topology change acknowledgment—used to acknowledge receipt of a message with the topology change bit set
- **Root ID (8 bytes)**   Identifies the root bridge by specifying its 2-byte priority value followed by its 6-byte MAC address
- **Root Path Cost (4 bytes)**   Specifies the cost of the path from the bridge sending the BPDU message to the root bridge
- **Bridge ID (8 bytes)**   Identifies the bridge sending the message by specifying its 2-byte priority value followed by its 6-byte MAC address
- **Port ID (2 bytes)**   Identifies the port over which the message is being sent
- **Message Age (2 bytes)**   Specifies the elapsed time since the root bridge transmitted the message that triggered the generation of this message
- **Maximum Age (2 bytes)**   Specifies the age at which this message should be deleted

- **Hello Time (2 bytes)** Specifies the time interval between root bridge configuration messages
- **Forward Delay (2 bytes)** Specifies the time interval bridges should wait to complete the spanning tree algorithm after a change in the network topology. Premature state transitions can cause loops to form if all the bridges have not completed the algorithm.

NETWORK HARDWARE

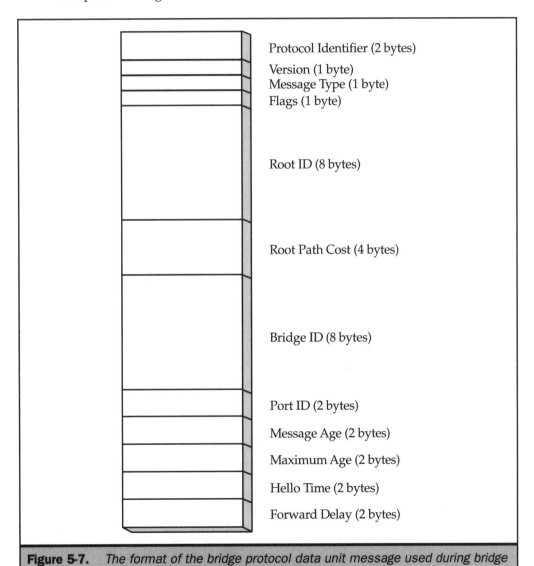

Figure 5-7. The format of the bridge protocol data unit message used during bridge spanning tree algorithm computations

BPDU messages are encapsulated with standard data link–layer protocol frames using the SAP value 01000010 and addressed to the "all bridges" multicast address. Bridges generate the messages autonomously, but they do not forward them to other networks. All BPDUs are exchanged by the bridges on the network segments to which they are directly connected.

As with the learning process, the spanning tree algorithm begins as soon as the bridges are connected to the network and powered up. Initially, each bridge assumes it will be the root bridge and uses a path cost of 0; but as the bridge receives BPDU messages from the other bridges on the segment, it compares the information in the messages and determines which bridge is better suited to performing the bridging tasks for the segment. The algorithm for making this determination is based on the values for the following criteria, in order:

- Root ID
- Root path cost
- Bridge ID
- Port ID

For each criterion, a lower value is better than a higher one. If a bridge receives a BPDU message with better values than those in its own messages, it stops transmitting BPDUs over the port through which it arrived, in effect, relinquishing its duties to the bridge better suited for the job. The bridge also uses the values in that incoming BPDU to recalculate the fields of the messages it will send through the other ports.

Note   *The spanning tree algorithm must complete before the bridges begin forwarding any network traffic. Depending on the bridge implementation, the algorithm might even be completed before the bridges begin compiling their address tables.*

Once the spanning tree algorithm has designated a bridge for each network segment, it must also continue to monitor the network so that the process can begin again when a bridge fails or goes offline. All of the bridges on the network store the BPDUs they've received from the other bridges and track their ages. Once a message exceeds the maximum allowable age, it is discarded and the spanning tree message exchanges begin again.

In addition, at periodic intervals (specified by the value of the hello time field), the root bridge transmits a new BPDU with a message age value of 0. This causes the other bridges on the network to follow suit. If one of the bridges on a network segment fails to transmit BPDU messages, the other bridges perform the entire algorithm again to select a new designated bridge for the segment. A 4-byte topology change message signals the other bridges to begin the algorithm again. This message consists of only the Protocol Identifier, Version, and Message Type fields from the BPDU format, with the first two fields having a value of 0 and the Message Type field having a value of 128.

Load Sharing Bridges

In the case of remote bridges that connect network segments using WAN links, it makes no sense to pay for a redundant leased line or other expensive telecommunications link and to allow it to remain unused as a result of the spanning tree algorithm. To address this problem, load sharing bridges are on the market that can use the backup WAN link to carry data without causing bringing loops.

Source Route Bridging

Source route bridging is an alternative to transparent bridging that was developed by IBM for use on multisegment Token Ring networks and is standardized in IEEE 802.5. On a network that uses transparent bridging, the path a packet takes to a destination on another segment is determined by the designated bridges selected by the spanning tree algorithm. In *source route bridging*, the path to the destination system is determined by the workstation and contained in each individual packet.

To discover the possible routes through the network to a given destination, a Token Ring system transmits an *All Rings Broadcast (ARB)* frame that all the bridges forward to all connected rings. As each bridge processes the frame, it adds its *route designator (RD)*, identifying the bridge and port, to the packet. By reading the list of RDs, bridges prevent loops by not sending the packet to the same bridge twice.

If more than one route exists to the destination system, multiple ARBs will arrive there, containing information about the various routes they took. The destination system then transmits a reply to each of the ARBs it receives, using the list of RDs to route the packet back to the sender.

When the original sender of the ARBs receives the responses, it selects one of the routes to the destination as the best one, based on one or more of the following criteria:

- The amount of time required for the explorer frame to return to the sender.
- The number of hops between the source and the destination.
- The size of the frame the system can use.

After selecting one of the routes, the system generates its data packets and includes the routing information in the Token Ring frame header.

The format for the ARB packet and for a data packet containing routing information is the same as a standard IEEE 802.5 frame, except that the first bit of the source address field, called the *routing information indicator (RII)* bit, is set to a value of 1, indicating that the packet contains routing information. The routing information itself, which is nothing more than a list of the bridges the packet will use when traveling through the network, is carried the *routing information field (RIF)* that appears as part of the information field, just after the frame's source address field (see Figure 5-8).

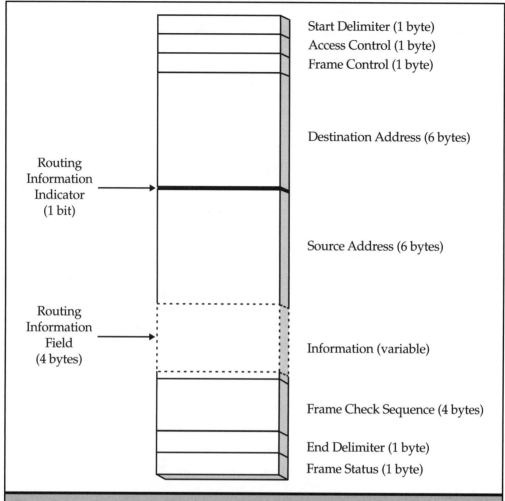

Routing Information Indicator (1 bit)

Routing Information Field (4 bytes)

Start Delimiter (1 byte)
Access Control (1 byte)
Frame Control (1 byte)

Destination Address (6 bytes)

Source Address (6 bytes)

Information (variable)

Frame Check Sequence (4 bytes)

End Delimiter (1 byte)
Frame Status (1 byte)

Figure 5-8.   *The routing information indicator and the routing information field used in source bridge routing are carried within standard Token Ring frames*

The RIF consists of a 2-byte routing control section and a number of 2-byte route designator sections, as shown in Figure 5-9. The routing control section contains the following fields:

- **Broadcast indicators (3 bits)**   Specifies the type of routing to be used by the frame, according to the following values:
    - **000 – Non-broadcast**   Indicates that the packet contains a specific route to the destination in the route designator sections of the RIF field

- **100 – All routes broadcast**   Indicates that the packet should be routed through all the bridges on the network (without traversing the same bridge twice) and that each bridge should add a route designator section to the RIF field identifying the bridge and the port onto which it is being forwarded.

- **110 – Single route broadcast**   Indicates that the packet should be routed only through the bridges designated by the spanning tree algorithm and that each bridge should add a route designator section to the RIF field identifying the bridge and the port onto which it is being forwarded.

- **Length (5 bits)**   Indicates the total length of the RIF field, from 2 to 30 bytes.

- **Direction bit (1 bit)**   Specifies the direction in which the packet is traveling. The value of this bit indicates whether the transmitting node should read the route designator sections in the RIF field from left to right (0) or right to left (1).

- **Largest frame (3 bits)**   Indicates the largest frame size that can be accommodated by the route, called the maximum transfer unit (MTU). Initially set by the transmitting system, a bridge lowers this value if it forwards the packet onto a segment that only supports smaller frames. The permitted values are as follows:

  - **000**   Indicates a MAC MTU of 552 bytes
  - **001**   Indicates a MAC MTU of 1,064 bytes
  - **010**   Indicates a MAC MTU of 2,088 bytes
  - **011**   Indicates a MAC MTU of 4,136 bytes
  - **100**   Indicates a MAC MTU of 8,232 bytes

- **Unused (4 bits)**

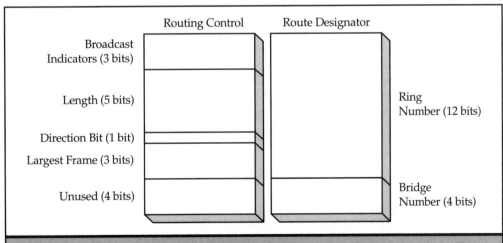

Figure 5-9.   *The Routing Information Field identifies the bridges the packet will use when traveling across the network*

The IBM standard for source route bridging originally specified a maximum of 8 route designator sections in a single packet, but the IEEE 802.5 standard allows up to 14. Most bridge manufacturers have adhered to the IBM standard; in this respect, however, newer IBM bridge implementations support up to 14 RDs. Each of the route designator sections in the RIF consist of the following two fields:

- **Ring number (12 bits)**   Uniquely identifies the network segment (ring).
- **Bridge number (4 bits)**   Identifies a specific bridge on the network, using a value that only has to be unique among the bridges connected to the network segment (ring).

Source route bridging is a relatively inefficient method because it relies heavily on broadcast transmissions that are propagated throughout all the segments on the network. Each workstation must maintain its own routing information to each of the systems with which it communicates. This can result in a large number of ARB frames being processed by a destination system before it even sees the first byte of application data.

Bridging Ethernet and Token Ring Networks

Generally speaking, Ethernet networks use transparent bridging and Token Ring networks use source route bridging. So what happens when you want to connect an Ethernet segment to a Token Ring using a bridge? The answer is complicated, both because the task presents a number of significant obstacles and because a well-defined standard providing a solution does not yet exist.

Some of the fundamental incompatibilities of the two data link–layer protocols are as follows:

- **Bit ordering**   Ethernet systems consider the first bit of a MAC address to be the low-order bit, while Token Ring systems treat the first bit as the high-order bit.
- **MTU sizes**   Ethernet frames have a maximum transfer unit size of 1,500 bytes, while Token Ring frames can be much larger. Bridges are not capable of fragmenting packets for transfer over a segment with a lower MTU and then reassembling them at the destination, as routers are. A too-large packet arriving at a bridge to a segment with a smaller MTU can only be discarded.
- **Exclusive Token Ring features**   Token Ring networks use frame status bits, priority indicators, and other features that have no equivalent in Ethernet.

In addition, the two bridging methods have their own incompatibilities. Transparent bridges neither understand the special function of the ARB messages used in source route bridging nor can they make use of the RIF field in Token Ring packets. Conversely, source route bridges do not understand the spanning tree algorithm messages generated by transparent bridges and they do not know what to do when they receive frames with no routing information.

Two primary methods exist for overcoming these incompatibilities, neither of which is an ideal solution. These methods are

- Translational bridging
- Source route transparent bridging

Translational Bridging

In *translation bridging,* a special bridge translates the data link–layer frames between the Ethernet and Token Ring formats. No standard at all exists for this process, so the methods used by individual product manufacturers can vary widely. Some compromise is needed in the translation process because no way exists to implement all the features fully in each of the protocols and to bridge methods to its counterpart. Some of the techniques used in various translational bridges to overcome the incompatibilities are described in the following paragraphs.

One of the basic functions of the bridge is to map the fields of the Ethernet frame onto the Token Ring frame and vice versa. The bridge reverses the bit order of the source and destination addresses for the packets passing across it and may, or may not, take action based on the values of a Token Ring packet's frame status, priority, reservation, and monitor bits. Bridges may simply discard these bits when translating from Token Ring to Ethernet and set predetermined values for them when translating from Ethernet to Token Ring.

To deal with the different MTU sizes of the network segments, a translation bridge can set the largest frame value in the Token Ring packets' RIF field to the MTU for the Ethernet network (1,500 bytes). As long as the Token Ring implementations on the workstations read this field and adjust their frame sizes accordingly, no problem should occur, but any frames larger than the MTU on the Ethernet segments will be dropped by the bridge connecting the two networks.

The biggest difference between the two types of bridging is that, on Ethernet networks, the routing information is stored in the bridges, while on Token Ring networks, it's stored at the workstations. For the translational bridge to support both network types, it must appear as a transparent bridge to the Ethernet side and a source route bridge to the Token Ring side.

To the Token Ring network, the translational bridge has a ring number and bridge number, just like a standard source route bridge. The ring number, however, represents the entire Ethernet domain, not just the segment connected to the bridge. As packets from the Token Ring network pass through the bridge, the information from their RIF fields is removed and cached in the bridge. From that point on, standard transparent bridging gets the packets to their destinations on the Ethernet network.

When a packet generated by an Ethernet workstation is destined for a system on the Token Ring network, the translational bridge looks up the system in its cache of RIF information and adds an RIF field to the packet containing a route to the network, if possible. If no route is available in the cache or if the packet is a broadcast or multicast, the bridge transmits it as a single-route broadcast.

Source Route Transparent Bridging

IBM has also come up with a proposed standard that combines the two primary bridging technologies, called *source route transparent (SRT)* bridging. This technology is standardized in Appendix C of the IEEE 802.1d document. SRT bridges can forward packets originating on either source route bridging or transparent bridging networks, using a spanning tree algorithm common to both. The standard spanning tree algorithm used by Token Ring networks for single-route broadcast messages is incompatible with the algorithm used by Ethernet, as defined in the 802.1d specification. This appendix reconciles the two.

SRT bridges use the value of the RII bit to determine whether a packet contains RIF information and, consequently, whether it should use source route or transparent bridging. The mixing of the two technologies is not perfect, however, and network administrators may find it easier to connect Ethernet and Token Ring segments with a switch or a router rather than either a translational or SRT bridge.

Chapter 6

Routers and Switches

R*outing* and *switching* are the basic concepts used to construct enterprise internetworks and that form the infrastructure of the ultimate internetwork, the Internet. This chapter examines how routers and switches connect networks and network segments, providing almost unlimited scalability.

Routers

In Chapter 5, you learned how devices called repeaters and bridges can connect network segments at the physical and data link layers of the OSI model, creating a larger LAN with a single collision domain. Repeaters and hubs are simple electrical devices that enlarge a network segment by amplifying signals. Bridging offers advantages over simply increasing the size of a LAN by adding hubs or repeaters, because bridges filter out packets that are not destined for systems on the other side of the network. Thus, unnecessary traffic is reduced, but broadcast messages are still propagated throughout the entire network.

The next step up in the network expansion process is to connect two completely separate LANs together at the network layer. This is the job of a router. Routers are more selective than bridges in the traffic they pass between the networks, and they are capable of intelligently selecting the most efficient path to a specific destination. Because they function at the network layer, routers can also connect dissimilar networks. You can, for example, connect an Ethernet network to a Token Ring one because packets entering a router are stripped of their data link–layer protocol headers as they pass up the protocol stack to the network layer, leaving *a protocol data unit (PDU)* encapsulated using whatever network-layer protocol is running (see Figure 6-1). After processing, the router then encapsulates the PDU in a new data link–layer header using whatever protocol is running on the other network to which the router is connected.

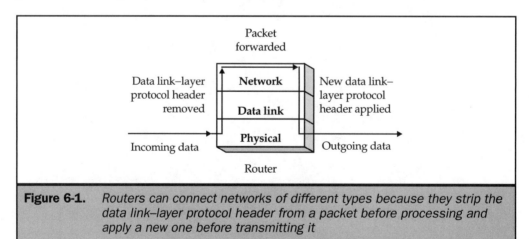

Figure 6-1.   *Routers can connect networks of different types because they strip the data link–layer protocol header from a packet before processing and apply a new one before transmitting it*

The general impression most people have of routers is that they are expensive, dedicated hardware devices used in large enterprise network installations. While this is certainly true in many cases, routing can also operate at a much smaller scale. If, for example, you use your home computer to dial into your system at work and access resources on the office network, your work computer is functioning as a router. In the same way, if you share an Internet connection with systems on a LAN, the machine connected to the Internet is a router. A router, therefore, can be either a hardware or a software entity, and it can range from the simple to the extraordinarily complex.

Routers are protocol specific; they must support the network-layer protocol used by each packet. By far, the most common network-layer protocol in use today is the *Internet Protocol* (*IP*), which is the basis for the Internet and for most private networks. In most cases, a reference to a router means an IP router. Some private networks, however, use Novell's *Internetwork Packet Exchange* (*IPX*) protocol at the network layer. A computer that is connected to two or more networks is said to be a *multihomed system*. Novell NetWare servers with two or more *network interface cards* (*NICs*) installed have always been able to function as IPX routers, and now the product includes multiprotocol routing software that supports IP as well. Multihomed Windows systems can function as routers, too. Windows NT and 2000 systems also have multiprotocol routing capabilities that support IP and IPX. Windows 95 and 98 systems can route IPX, but not IP. The NetBEUI protocol, strictly speaking, is not routable at all; but Windows NT, 2000, and 9*x* systems all support dial-up network access using NetBEUI.

Most of the routers used on large networks, though, are standalone devices that are essentially computers dedicated to a single function. Routers come in various sizes, from small units that connect a workgroup network to a backbone to large, modular, rack-mounted devices costing well into the six figures. However, while routers vary in their capabilities, such as the number of networks to which they connect, the protocols they support, and the amount of traffic they can handle, their basic functions are essentially the same.

Router Applications

Although the primary function of a router is to connect networks together and pass traffic between them, routers can fulfill several different roles in network designs. The type of router used for a specific function determines its size, cost, and capabilities. The simplest type of routing architecture is when a LAN must be connected to another LAN some distance away, using a *wide area network* (*WAN*) connection. A branch office for a large corporation, for example, might have a WAN connection to the corporate headquarters in another city (see Figure 6-2).

To make communications between the networks in the two offices possible, each must connect its LAN to a router, and the two routers are linked by the WAN connection. The WAN connection may take the form of a leased telephone line, an

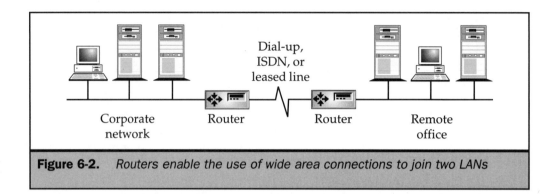

Dial-up,
ISDN, or
leased line

Corporate   Router   Router   Remote
network   office

Figure 6-2.   *Routers enable the use of wide area connections to join two LANs*

ISDN or DSL connection, or even a dial-up modem connection. The technology used to connect the two networks is irrelevant, as long as the routers in both offices are connected. Routers are required in this example because the LAN and WAN technologies are fundamentally incompatible. You can neither run an Ethernet connection between two cities nor can you use leased telephone lines to connect each workstation to the file server in the next room.

In a slightly more complicated arrangement, a site with a larger internetwork may have several LANs, each of which is connected to a backbone network using a router (see Figure 6-3). Here, routers are needed because one single LAN may be unable to support the number of workstations required. In addition, the individual LANs may be located in other parts of a building or in separate buildings on the same campus, and may require a different type of network to connect them. Connections between campus buildings, for example, require a network medium that is suitable for outdoor use, such as fiber-optic, while the LANs in each building can use more inexpensive copper cabling. Routers are available that can connect these different network types, no matter what protocols they use.

These two examples of router use are often combined. A large corporate internetwork using a backbone to connect multiple LANs will almost certainly want to be connected to the Internet. This means that another router is needed to support some type of WAN connection to an *Internet service provider* (*ISP*). Users anywhere on the corporate network can then access Internet services.

Both of these scenarios use routers to connect a relatively small number of networks, and they are dwarfed by the Internet, which is a routed internetwork comprised of thousands of LANs all over the world. To make it possible for packets to travel across this maze of routers with reasonable efficiency, a hierarchy of routers is leading from smaller, local ISPs to regional providers, which, in turn, get their service from large national services (see Figure 6-4). Traffic originating from a system using a small ISP travels up through this virtual tree to one of the main backbones, across the upper levels of the network, and back down again to the destination.

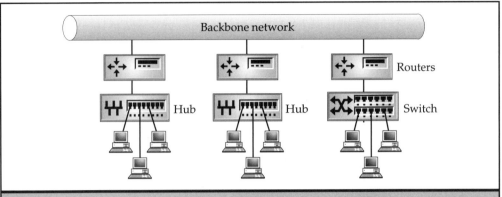

Figure 6-3. *Routers also can connect LANs to a backbone network*

You can see the route that packets take from your computer through the Internet to a specific destination by using the traceroute utility. Called *traceroute* on UNIX systems and *Tracert.exe* on Windows NT/2000/9x systems, this command-line utility takes the IP address or DNS name you specify and uses ICMP messages to display the names

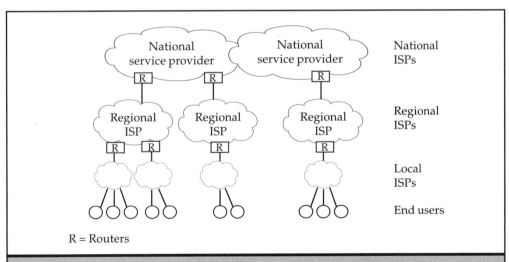

Figure 6-4. *The Internet uses a hierarchy of routers to forward traffic to any location*

and addresses of all the intermediate routers on the path to the destination. A typical traceroute display (here generated by a Windows 95 system) appears as follows:

```
Tracing route to zacker.com [192.41.15.74] over a maximum of 30 hops:
  1   213 ms    226 ms    230 ms   hil-qbu-pth-vty254.as.wcom.net [206.175.104.254]
  2   212 ms    208 ms    205 ms   hil-ppp2-fas2-1.wan.wcom.net [209.154.35.35]
  3   250 ms    263 ms    219 ms   205.156.214.145
  4   242 ms    218 ms    214 ms   hyt-core1-atm1-0-3.wan.wcom.net [205.156.223.134]
  5   290 ms    269 ms    263 ms   hyt-peer1-fdd4-0.wan.wcom.net [205.156.223.68]
  6   238 ms    369 ms    251 ms   hyt-mae-east-pos3-0.wan.wcom.net [205.156.223.98]
  7   392 ms    370 ms    448 ms   f0.iad0.verio.net [192.41.177.121]
  8   326 ms      *       239 ms   iad0.iad3.verio.net [129.250.2.178]
  9   498 ms    341 ms      *      iad3.dfw2.verio.net [129.250.2.209]
 10     *       342 ms    289 ms   dfw2.dfw3.verio.net [129.250.3.74]
 11   327 ms    389 ms    359 ms   dfw3.pvu1.verio.net [129.250.2.41]
 12   360 ms    376 ms    355 ms   pvu1.vwhpvu1.verio.net [129.250.16.118]
 13   372 ms    379 ms    325 ms   zacker.com [192.41.15.74]
Trace complete.
```

Router Functions

The basic function of a router is to evaluate each packet arriving on one of the networks to which it is connected and send it on to its destination through another network. The goal is for the router to select the network that provides the best path to the destination for each packet. A packet can pass through several different routers on the way to its destination. Each router on a packet's path is referred to as a *hop,* and the object is to get the packet where it's going with the smallest number of hops. On a private network, a packet may need three or four (or more) hops to get to its destination; on the Internet, a packet can easily pass through 20 or more routers along its path.

A router, by definition, is connected to two or more networks. The router has direct knowledge about those networks for the protocols that it supports. If, for example, a workstation on Network 1 (see Figure 6-5) transmits a packet to a system on Network 2, the router connecting Networks 1, 2, and 3 can directly determine which of the two networks (2 or 3) contains the destination system and forward the packet appropriately.

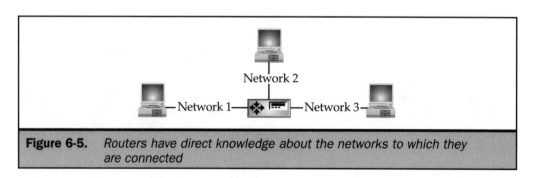

Figure 6-5. *Routers have direct knowledge about the networks to which they are connected*

Routing Tables

The router does this by maintaining a list of networks called a *routing table*. For computers to communicate over a network, each machine must have its own address. In addition to identifying the specific computer, however, its address must also identify the network on which it's located. On TCP/IP networks, for example, the standard 32-bit IP address consists of a network identifier and a host identifier. A routing table consists of entries that contain the network identifier for each connected network. When the router receives a packet addressed to a workstation on Network 3, it looks at the network identifier in the packet's destination address, compares it to the routing table, and forwards it to the network with the same identifier.

This is a rather simple task, as long as the router is connected to all of the LANs on the internetwork. When an internetwork is larger and uses multiple routers, however, no single router has direct knowledge of all of the LANs. In Figure 6-6, Router A is connected to Networks 1, 2, and 3 as before, and has the identifiers for those networks in its routing table, but it has no direct knowledge of Network 4, which is connected using another router.

How then does Router A know where to send packets that are addressed to a workstation on a distant network? The answer is that routers maintain information in their routing tables about other networks besides those to which they are directly attached. A routing table may contain information about many different networks. On a private internetwork, it is not uncommon for every router to have entries for all of the connected networks. On the Internet, however, so many networks and so many routers exist, that no single routing table can contain all of them and function efficiently. Thus, a router connected to the Internet sends packets to another router that it thinks has better information about the network to which the packet is ultimately destined.

WINDOWS ROUTING TABLES   Every computer on a TCP/IP network has a routing table, even if it is connected to only one network. At the very least, the routing table identifies the system's default gateway and instructs it how to handle traffic sent to the

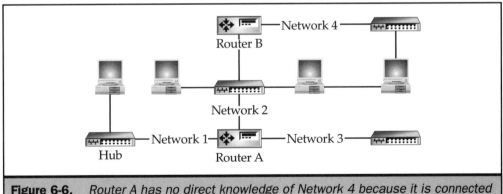

Figure 6-6.   *Router A has no direct knowledge of Network 4 because it is connected to a different router*

local network and the loopback network address (127.0.0.0). A typical routing table for a Windows NT, 2000, or 9x system appears as follows:

Network Address	Netmask	Gateway Address	Interface	Metric
0.0.0.0	0.0.0.0	192.168.2.100	192.168.2.5	1
127.0.0.0	255.0.0.0	127.0.0.1	127.0.0.1	1
192.168.2.0	255.255.255.0	192.168.2.5	192.168.2.5	1
192.168.2.5	255.255.255.255	127.0.0.1	127.0.0.1	1
192.168.2.255	255.255.255.255	192.168.2.5	192.168.2.5	1
224.0.0.0	224.0.0.0	192.168.2.5	192.168.2.5	1
255.255.255.255	255.255.255.255	192.168.2.5	0.0.0.0	1

To display the routing table on a Windows system and on most UNIX systems, type **netstat -nr** *at the command prompt.*

The entries in the table run horizontally. The function of the information in each column is as follows:

- **Network Address**   Specifies the network address for which routing information is to be provided. While most entries have network addresses in this field, it's also possible to supply routing information for a specific host address. This is called a *host route*.

- **Netmask**   Specifies the subnet mask used to determine which bits of the network address function as the network identifier.

- **Gateway Address**   Specifies the IP address of the gateway (router) that the system should use to send packets to the network address. When the entry is for a network to which the system is directly attached, this field contains the address of the system's network interface.

- **Interface**   Specifies the IP address of the network interface that the system should use to send traffic to the gateway address.

- **Metric**   Specifies the distance between the system and the destination network, usually in terms of the number of hops needed for traffic to reach the network address.

TCP/IP and Internet terminology often use the term gateway *synonymously with* router. *In general networking parlance, a gateway is an application-layer interface between networks that involves some form of high-level protocol translation, such as an e-mail gateway or a gateway between a LAN and a mainframe. When a Windows system refers to its default gateway, however, it is referring to a standard router, operating at the network layer.*

The system using this routing table has only one NIC, with the IP address 192.168.2.5. You can tell this from the fourth entry, which directs that address to the loopback adapter (127.0.0.1). The system is connected to a LAN with 192.168.2 as its network address. You can see from the third entry in the table that all traffic destined for this network uses the system's own NIC as the gateway because no router is needed to access systems on the local network. This is called a *direct route* because the destination address in the IP header represents the same machine as the destination address in the data link–layer protocol header. The 0.0.0.0 entry represents the system's default gateway, which it uses for traffic addressed to networks not listed in the table. This entry instructs the system to send this traffic over the NIC to 192.168.2.100, which is the IP address of the router that connects the network to the Internet.

If the system was connected to the Internet using a modem, both the Gateway and the Interface fields of the 0.0.0.0 entry would contain the address assigned to the modem connection by the server on the ISP's network. In this case, the modem functions as a network interface, just like a NIC, and has its own IP address.

The last three entries in the table define routes for broadcast and multicast messages. The "Assigned Numbers" RFC contains Class D network addresses that have been assigned to specific multicast groups, all of which fall in the 224.0.0.0 network. 255.255.255.255 is the standard broadcast address. The 192.168.2.255 entry is for broadcasts to the local network.

UNIX ROUTING TABLES   Other operating systems display the routing table slightly differently and may include other information, but the basic elements and functions of the table are the same. The following is a sample routing table from a System V–based UNIX system:

```
Destination        Gateway           Flags   Refcnt    Use        Interface
127.0.0.1          127.0.0.1         UH      1         298        lo0
default            192.168.2.76      UG      2         50360      le0
192.168.2.0        192.168.2.21      U       40        111379     le0
192.168.4.0        192.168.2.1       UG      4         5678       le0
192.168.5.0        192.168.2.1       UG      10        8765       le0
192.168.3.0        192.168.2.1       UG      2         1187       le0
```

The function of the columns in this table are as follows:

- **Destination**   Specifies the address of the network or host for which routing information is being provided.

- **Gateway**   Specifies the address of the gateway (router) that the system should use to send traffic to the specified network or host.

- **Flags**   Specify the special characteristics of each routing table entry, using the following values:
  - **U**   Indicates that the route is up and functioning.
  - **H**   Indicates that this is a route to a host rather than a network.
  - **G**   Indicates that the route uses a gateway to reach the specified network address (as opposed to being directly connected to that network).
  - **D**   Indicates that the entry was added to the table as a result of an ICMP redirect message.
- **Refcnt**   Specifies the number of times that the system has used the route to connect to another systm.
- **Use**   Specifies the number of packets transmitted by the system using this route.
- **Interface**   Identifies the network interface in the computer that the system should use to access the specified gateway.

Thus, in this table, you can see that the system is connected directly to the 192.168.2 network because the entry does not have a G flag, which indicates that the system needs a gateway to access the network. The value in the Gateway field is, therefore, the IP address of the computer's own network interface. The last three entries in the table are for other networks at the same site, which are accessible through the same router (192.168.2.1). The default entry specifies the address of a different router (in this case, one that provides access to the Internet) for all packets other than those destined for the networks listed elsewhere in the table.

Therefore, to return to the previous example, Router A has entries in its routing table for all of the LANs in the internetwork that specify how it should transmit packets to each of those networks. The entries for the networks to which the router is directly connected specify the interface that the router should use to access those networks, and the entries for distant networks specify the address of another router. When packets reach the specified router, the same process occurs again and the data may be transmitted to still another router. On the Internet, this process may be repeated dozens of times. No one router knows the complete path that a packet will take from source to destination; each one is only responsible for the next hop. In fact, when a file transfer or other operation consists of multiple packets, constantly changing network conditions may cause the individual packets to take different routes to the same destination.

ROUTING TABLE PARSING   Whether a system is functioning as a router or not, the responsibility of a network-layer protocol like IP is to determine where each packet should be transmitted next. The IP header in each packet contains the address of the system that is to be its ultimate destination but, before passing each packet down to the data link–layer protocol, IP uses the routing table to determine what the destination address should be for the packet's next hop. This is because a data link–layer protocol like Ethernet can only address a packet to a system on the local network, which may or may not be its final destination. To make this determination, IP reads the destination address for each packet it processes and searches for a matching entry in the routing table, using the following procedure:

1. IP first scans the routing table looking for a host route that exactly matches the destination address in the packet. If one exists, the packet is transmitted to the gateway specified in the routing table entry.

2. If no matching host route exists, IP uses the subnet mask to determine the network address for the packet and scans the routing table for an entry that matches that address. If IP finds a match, the packet is transmitted either to the specified gateway (if the system is not directly connected to the destination network) or out the specified network interface (if the destination is on the local network).

3. If no matching network address is in the routing table, IP scans for a default (or 0.0.0.0) route and transmits the packet to the specified gateway.

4. If no default route is in the table, IP returns a destination unreachable message to the source of the packet (either the application that generated it or the system that transmitted it).

Static and Dynamic Routing

The next logical question concerning the routing process is how do the entries get into the routing table? A system can generate entries for the default gateway, the local network, and the broadcast and multicast addresses because it possesses all of the information needed to create them. For networks to which the router is not directly connected, however, routing table entries must be created by an outside process. The two basic methods for creating entries in the routing table are called *static routing*, which is the manual creation of entries, and *dynamic routing*, which uses an external protocol to gather information about the network.

On a relatively small, stable network, static routing is a practical alternative because you only have to create the entries in your routers' tables once. Manually configuring the routing table on workstations isn't necessary because they typically have only one network interface and can access the entire network through one gateway. Routers, however, have multiple network interfaces and usually have access to multiple gateways. They must, therefore, know which route to use when trying to transmit to a specific network.

To create static entries in a computer's routing table, you use a program supplied with the operating system. The standard tool for this on UNIX and Windows systems is a character-based utility called *route* (in UNIX) or *Route.exe* (in Windows NT, 2000, or 9x). In some cases, graphical utilities are available that can perform the same task. A Windows NT Server 4.0 system with the Routing and Remote Access Server service installed, for example, enables you to create static routes using the interface shown in Figure 6-7. On a Novell NetWare server with the TCP/IP protocol installed, you can use either the Inetcfg.nlm or Tcpcon.nlm program to create static routes using a menu-based interface.

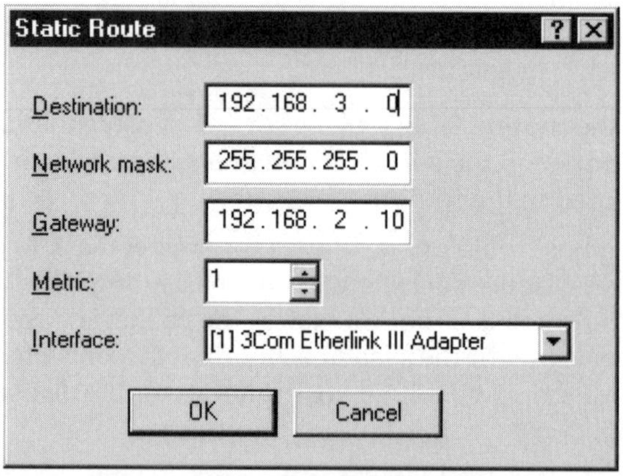

Figure 6-7. The Routing and Remote Access Server Manager program enables you to create static routes using a standard dialog box

Static routes created this way remain in the routing table until you manually change or remove them, and this can be a problem. If a gateway specified in a static route should fail, the system continues to send packets to it, to no avail. You must either repair the gateway or modify the static routes that reference it throughout the network before the systems can function normally again.

On larger networks, static routing becomes increasingly impractical, not only because of the sheer number of routing table entries involved, but also because network conditions can change too often and too quickly for administrators to keep the routing tables on every system current. Instead, these networks use dynamic routing, in which specialized routing protocols gather information about the other routers in the network and modify the routing tables accordingly. Once configured, dynamic routing needs little or no maintenance from network administrators because the protocols can create, modify, or destroy routing table entries as needed to accommodate changing network conditions. The Internet is totally dependent on dynamic routing because it is constantly mutating, and no manual process could possibly keep up with the changes.

Selecting the Most Efficient Route

Many internetworks, even relatively small ones, are designed with multiple routers that provide redundant paths to a given destination. Thus, while creating an internetwork that consists of several LANs joined in a series by routers would be possible, most use something approaching a mesh configuration instead, as shown in Figure 6-8. This way, if any one router should fail, all of the systems can still send traffic to any other system on any network.

When an internetwork is designed in this way, another important part of the routing process is selecting the best path to a given destination. The use of dynamic

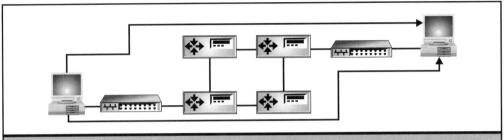

Figure 6-8. *By interconnecting routers, packets from one workstation can travel to a destination on another network by different routes*

NETWORK HARDWARE

routing on the network typically results in all possible routes to a given network being entered in the routing tables, each of which includes a metric that specifies how many hops are required to reach that network. Most of the time, the efficiency of a particular route is measured by the metric value because each hop involves processing by another router, which introduces a slight delay. When a router has to forward a packet to a network represented by multiple entries in the routing table, it chooses the one with the lower metric.

Discarding Packets

The goal of a router is to transmit packets to their destinations using the path that incurs the smallest number of hops, but routers also track the number of hops that packets take on the way to their destinations for another reason. When a malfunction or misconfiguration occurs in one or more routers, it is possible for packets to get caught in a router loop and be passed endlessly from one router to another.

To prevent this, the IP header contains a *Time-to-Live* (*TTL*) field that the source system gives a certain numerical value when a packet is created. (On Windows systems, the value is 128, by default.) As a packet travels through the network, each router that processes it decrements the value of this field by 1. If, for any reason, the packet passes through routers enough times to bring the value of this field down to 0, the last router removes it from the network and discards it. The router then returns an ICMP Time to Live Exceeded in Transit message to the source system to inform it of the problem.

Packet Fragmentation

Routers can connect networks of vastly different types, and the process of transferring datagrams from one data link–layer protocol to another can require more than simply stripping off one header and applying a new one. The biggest problem that can occur during this translation process is when one protocol supports frames that are larger than the other protocol.

If, for example, a router connects a Token Ring network to an Ethernet one, it may have to accept 4,500-byte datagrams from one network and then transmit them over a network that can carry only 1,500 byte datagrams. Routers determine the *maximum transfer unit (MTU)* of a particular network by querying the interface to that network. To make this possible, the router has to break up the datagram into fragments of the appropriate size and then encapsulate each fragment in the correct data link–layer protocol header. This fragmentation process may occur several times during a packet's journey from the source to its destination, depending on the number and types of networks involved.

For example, a packet originating on a Token Ring network may be divided into 1,500-byte fragments to accommodate a route through an Ethernet network, and then each of those smaller packets may themselves be divided into 512-byte fragments for transmission over the Internet. Note, however, that while routers fragment packets, they never defragment them. Even if the 576-byte datagrams are passed to an Ethernet network as they approach their destination, the router does not reassemble them back into 1,500-byte datagrams. All reassembly is performed at the network layer of the final destination system.

Note	*For more information on the IP fragmentation process, see "Fragmenting" in Chapter 11.*

Routing and ICMP

The Internet Control Message Protocol (ICMP) provides several important functions to routers and the systems that use them. Chief among these is the capability of routers to use ICMP messages to provide routing information to other routers. Routers send ICMP Redirect messages to source systems when they know of a better route than the system is currently using. If, for example, a workstation sends a packet to Router A, and Router A determines that the next hop should be to Router B, which is on the same network as the workstation, then Router A will use an ICMP message to inform the workstation that it should use Router B to access that destination instead. The workstation then modifies the entry in its routing table accordingly.

Routers also generate ICMP Destination Unreachable messages of various types when they are unable to forward packets. If a router receives a packet that is destined for a workstation on a locally attached network, and it can't deliver the packet because the workstation is offline, the router generates a Host Unreachable message and transmits it to the system that originated the packet. If the router is unable to forward the packet to another router that provides access to the destination, it generates a Network Unreachable message instead.

ICMP Router Solicitation and Advertisement messages enable workstations to discover the routers on the local network. A host system generates a Router Solicitation message and transmits it either as a broadcast or a multicast to the All Routers on This Subnet address (224.0.0.2). Routers receiving the message respond with Router Advertisement messages that the host system uses to update its routing table. The routers then generate periodic updates to inform the host of their continued operational status. Windows 2000 and Windows NT 4.0 with the Routing and Remote Access update installed can both update their routing tables with information from ICMP Router Advertisement messages. Support for these messages in hardware router implementations varies from product to product.

The ICMP Redirect and Router Solicitation/Advertisement messages do not constitute a routing protocol per se because they do not provide systems with information about the comparative efficiency of various routes. Routing table entries created or modified as a result of these messages are still considered to be static routes.

Note *For more information on ICMP messages, their formats, and their functions, see "ICMP" in Chapter 11.*

Routing Protocols

Routers that support dynamic routing use specialized protocols to exchange information about themselves with other routers on the network. Dynamic routing doesn't alter the actual routing process; it's just a different method of creating entries in the routing table. Two types of routing protocols exist: interior gateway protocols and exterior gateway protocols. Private internetworks typically use only *interior gateway protocols* because they have a relatively small number of routers and it is practical for all of them to exchange messages with each other.

On the Internet, the situation is different. Having every one of the Internet's thousands of routers exchange messages with every other router would be impossible. The amount of traffic involved would be enormous and the routers would have little time to do anything else. Instead, as is usual with the Internet, a two-level system was devised that splits the gigantic network into discrete units called *autonomous systems* (sometimes called *administrative domains,* or simply *domains*).

Autonomous systems (ASes) are usually private internetworks that are administered by a single authority, such as those run by corporations, educational institutions, and government agencies. The routers within an AS use an interior gateway protocol, such as the Routing Information Protocol (RIP) or the Open Shortest Path First (OSPF) protocol, to exchange routing information among themselves. At the edges of an AS are routers that communicate with the other ASes on the Internet, using an exterior gateway protocol (as shown in Figure 6-9), the most common of which on the Internet are the Border Gateway Protocol (BGP) and the Exterior Gateway Protocol (EGP).

Note *The term* exterior gateway protocol *is both a generic name for the routing protocols used between autonomous systems and the name of a specific protocol used between ASes. In the latter, the phrase is capitalized, in the former it is not.*

This way, packets traveling across the Internet are passed through routers that contain only the information needed to get them to the right AS. Once the packets arrive at the edge of the AS in which the destination is located, the routers there contain more specific information about the networks within the AS. The concept is much like the way that IP addresses and domain names are assigned on the Internet.

NETWORK HARDWARE

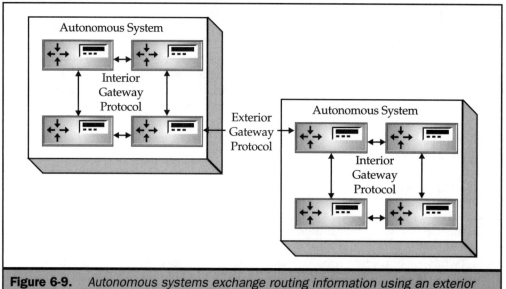

Figure 6-9.   *Autonomous systems exchange routing information using an exterior gateway protocol*

Outside entities track only the various network addresses or domains; the individual administrators of each network are responsible for maintaining the host addresses and host names within the network or domain.

The following sections examine the most common routing protocols in use today.

Routing Information Protocol

Routing Information Protocol (RIP) is the most commonly used of the interior gateway protocols, largely because it is supported by many operating systems and is easy to set up and use. In fact, RIP often requires no configuration at all. Originally conceived for Xerox Network Services (XNS) and included in Berkeley UNIX (BSD 4.2 and later versions), RIP takes the form of a daemon called *routed* (pronounced *rout-dee*) on most UNIX systems. Later standardized by the Internet Engineering Task Force (IETF) in 1988 as RFC 1058, the protocol has been implemented all but universally in hardware router products, as well as in the Windows NT, Windows 2000, and Novell NetWare operating systems. NetWare has long used RIP to exchange information about IPX routers, but now uses it for IP routing as well. The Windows NT and 2000 implementations also support both IP and IPX.

Routers that use RIP exchange request and reply messages using the User Datagram Protocol (UDP) and port 520, as specified in the "Assigned Numbers" RFC. When a router starts up, it sends an RIP request message to all of the other routers on the network using either a broadcast or a multicast transmission (depending on the RIP version). The other routers respond by transmitting their entire routing tables in RIP reply messages and repeat the advertisement every 30 seconds. Routers can also use RIP to request information on a specific route.

RIP always uses a hop count as the metric in a routing table entry and enforces a maximum hop count of 15. Networks or hosts more than 15 hops away are considered unreachable. This demonstrates that the protocol was designed for use on private internetworks and not the Internet because Internet routes often require more than 15 hops. This limitation on the number of hops is independent of the IP header's Time-to-Live field, although RIP routers generate the same ICMP Destination Unreachable messages when the maximum number of hops is exceeded.

RIP routing table entries also have a timeout value of three minutes. If an entry is not updated by an incoming RIP message for three minutes, the router increases its metric to 16, which for RIP is infinity. One minute later, the entry is purged from the table completely.

THE RIP MESSAGE FORMAT   RIP messages consist of a 4-byte header and one or more 20-byte routes. A single message can contain up to 25 routes, for a total UDP datagram size of 512 bytes (including the 8-byte UDP header). If more than 25 entries are in a routing table, the router generates additional messages until the entire table has been transmitted.

The format of the RIP message is shown in Figure 6-10. The functions of the header fields are as follows:

- **Command, 1 byte**   Specifies the function of the message, using the following values:
  - **1 – Request**   Requests transmission of the entire routing table or a specific route from all routers on the local network.
  - **2 – Reply**   Transmits routing table entries.
- **Version, 1 byte**   Specifies the version of RIP running on the system that generated the packet. Possible values are 1 and 2.
- **Unused, 2 bytes**

The functions of the fields in each 20-byte route are as follows:

- **Address family identifier, 2 bytes**   Identifies the network-layer protocol for which the message is carrying routing information. The value for IP is 2.
- **Unused, 2 bytes**
- **IP address, 4 bytes**   Specifies the address of a network or a host that is accessible through the router generating the message.
- **Unused, 4 bytes**
- **Unused, 4 bytes**
- **Metric, 4 bytes**   Specifies the number of hops between the system generating the message and the network or host identified by the IP address field value.

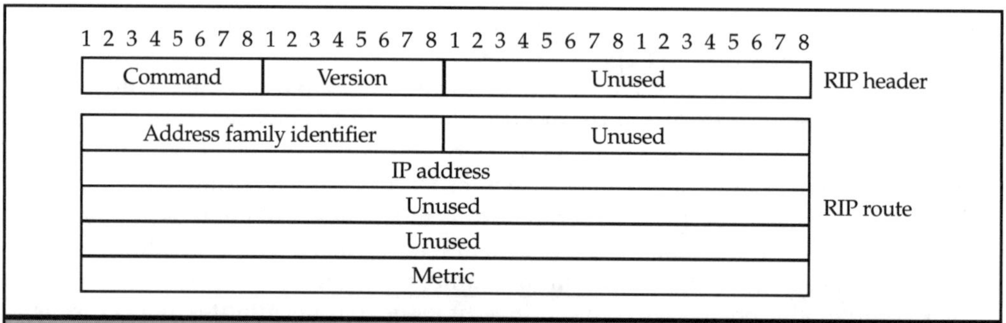

1 2 3 4 5 6 7 8 1 2 3 4 5 6 7 8 1 2 3 4 5 6 7 8 1 2 3 4 5 6 7 8

| Command | Version | Unused | RIP header |

Address family identifier	Unused	
IP address		
Unused		RIP route
Unused		
Metric		

Figure 6-10.   *The RIP header and route format*

RIP PROBLEMS   RIP is what is known as a *distance vector* routing protocol. This means that every router on the network advertises its routing table to its neighboring routers. Each router then examines the information supplied by the other routers, chooses the best route to each destination network, and adds it to its own routing table. Distance vector routing is relatively simple and reasonably efficient in terms of locating the best route to a given network. It has some fundamental problems, however. The process of updating the routing tables on all of a network's routers in response to a change in the network (such as the failure or addition of a router) is called *convergence*.

Distance vector protocols like RIP have a rather slow convergence rate because updates are generated by each router asynchronously, that is, without synchronization or acknowledgment. They are, therefore, prone to a condition known as *the count-to-infinity problem.* The count-to-infinity problem occurs when a router detects a failure in the network, modifies the appropriate entry in its routing table accordingly, and then has that entry updated by an advertisement from another router before it can broadcast it in its own advertisements. The routers then proceed to bounce their updates back and forth, increasing the metric for the same entry each time until it reaches infinity (16). The process eventually corrects itself, but the delay incurred each time a change occurs in the network slows down the entire routing process.

RIP is also widely criticized for the amount of broadcast traffic it produces. Every RIP router on an internetwork broadcasts its entire routing table every 30 seconds. Depending on the size of the network, this may involve several RIP messages per server. One advantage of the use of broadcasts, however, is that it is possible for systems to process the advertisement messages without advertising their own routing tables. This is called *silent RIP,* and it is more likely to be implemented in host systems that are not routers.

RIP also does not include a subnet mask with each route in an advertisement message. The protocol is designed for use with network addresses that conform to the IP address classes, which can be identified by the first three bits of the address. If the network address for a routing table entry fits the address classes, the protocol uses the subnet mask associated with its class. When this is not the case, the protocol uses the subnet mask of the network interface over which the RIP message was received. If this mask does not fit, the protocol assumes that the table entry contains a host route and uses a subnet mask of 255.255.255.255. These assumptions can cause traffic on certain types of networks, such a those that use variable-length subnets or disjointed subnets, to be forwarded incorrectly.

RIP also does not support any form of authentication for participating routers. A RIP router accepts and processes messages from any source, making it possible for the entire network's routing tables to be corrupted with incorrect information supplied (either accidentally or deliberately) by a rogue router.

RIP v2   Other interior gateway protocols, such as OSPF, were developed as a result of the shortcomings of the original RIP standard, but the RIP protocol itself was also upgraded. RIP version 2 was initially published as RFC 1388, proposed as a draft standard in RFC 1723, and finally ratified as an IETF standard and published in November 1998 as RFC 2453. The original Windows NT Server 4.0 release supports RIP v1, but the Routing and Remote Access Server (RRAS) update adds support for RIP v2, as defined in RFC 1723. The Windows 2000 server products also support RIP v2, as do many of the hardware routers on the market today.

RIP v2 addresses many of the problems inherent in version 1, including the following:

- **Broadcast traffic**   RIP v2 supports the use of multicast transmissions for router advertisements, as well as broadcasts. The "Assigned Numbers" RFC assigns RIP v2 routers a multicast address of 224.0.0.9. Transmissions sent to that address are processed only by the routers and do not affect other systems. The use of multicasts is optional on all RIP v2 routers; broadcasts are still supported. The only possible drawback to the use of multicasts is if the network contains systems that are using silent RIP and cannot monitor the multicast address for RIP traffic.

- **Subnet masks**   Unlike RIP v1, RIP v2 includes a subnet mask for every route it advertises. This makes it possible for the protocol to support networks that use variable-length or disjointed subnets.

- **Authentication**   RIP v2 supports the use of authentication, to ensure that incoming RIP messages originate from authorized routers. Windows NT's RRAS and Windows 2000 support the use of simple passwords only, but some hardware routers can use more advanced authentication mechanisms like Message Digest 5 (MD5) for this purpose.

THE RIP v2 MESSAGE FORMAT   The message format for RIP v2 is the same as that for RIP v1, except that the Version field has a value of 2, and the fields that were unused in the original format are now used to carry additional information. The format of the RIP v2 message is shown in Figure 6-11. The functions of the header fields are as follows:

- **Command, 1 byte**   Specifies the function of the message, using the following values:

  - **1 – Request**   Requests transmission of the entire routing table or a specific route from all routers on the local network.

  - **2 – Reply**   Transmits routing table entries.

- **Version, 1 byte**   Specifies the version of RIP running on the system that generated the packet. Possible values are 1 and 2.

- **Routing domain, 2 bytes**   Identifies the routing process for which this message is intended. By using various values in this field, administrators can create independent routing domains and separate the routing information in each one. The default value is 0.

The functions of the fields in each 20-byte route are as follows:

- **Address family identifier, 2 bytes**   Identifies the network-layer protocol for which the message is carrying routing information. The value for IP is 2.

- **Route tag, 2 bytes**   Contains a value that makes it possible to distinguish routes that have originated within the current autonomous system with those supplied by an exterior gateway protocol or a different autonomous system. Usually, the value is a number that uniquely identifies the autonomous system.

- **IP address, 4 bytes**   Specifies the address of a network or a host that is accessible through the router generating the message.

- **Subnet mask, 4 bytes**   Contains a mask that is used to distinguish the network identifier bits from the host identifier bits in the value of the IP address field.

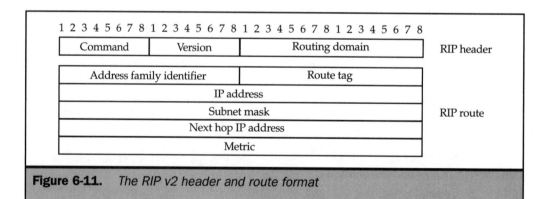

Figure 6-11.   *The RIP v2 header and route format*

- **Next hop IP address, 4 bytes**   Identifies the gateway that the router should use to send traffic to the network or host specified in the IP address field. In most cases, the router should use the gateway from which it received the route, but this field is intended to prevent the propagation of less than optimal routing information. A host route, for example, should instruct systems on the same network as the host to send traffic directly to the host, not to a router on the network, and this field can be used to provide that host address. In another example, when a router runs both OSPF and RIP, it may use RIP to propagate routing information that it obtained from OSPF, in which case the next hop IP address field may contain the address of the OSPF router that was the source of the information.
- **Metric, 4 bytes**   Specifies the number of hops between the system generating the message and the network or host identified by the IP address field value.

To provide authentication information, RIP v2 uses the first 20-byte route in a message, with the format shown in Figure 6-12. The functions of the fields are as follows:

- **Address family identifier, 2 bytes**   Contains the hexadecimal value FF FF, indicating that this route contains authentication data. RIP v1 routers do not recognize this value and, therefore, ignore the route.
- **Authentication type, 2 bytes**   Specifies the type of authentication the router is using. Simple password authentication uses a value of 2.
- **Password, 16 bytes**   Contains the authentication password, in a format specified by the value of the authentication type field.

Open Shortest Path First Protocol (OSPF)

Distance vector routing has a fundamental flaw: it bases its routing metrics solely on the number of hops between two networks. When an internetwork consists of multiple LANs in the same location, all connected using the same data link–layer protocol, the hop count is a valid indicator. When WAN links are involved, however, a single hop

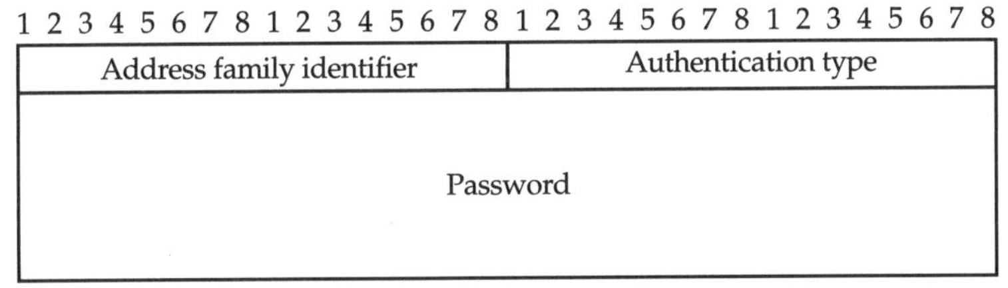

1 2 3 4 5 6 7 8	1 2 3 4 5 6 7 8	1 2 3 4 5 6 7 8	1 2 3 4 5 6 7 8
Address family identifier		Authentication type	
Password			

Figure 6-12.   *The RIP v2 authentication section*

can refer to routers in two adjacent rooms or a transatlantic link, and there is a vast difference in the time needed to traverse the two.

The alternative to distance vector routing is called *link state routing,* most commonly used in the Open Shortest Path First (OSPF) protocol. OSPF is an interior gateway protocol that was documented by the IETF in 1989 and published as RFC 1131. The current specification, which has been ratified as an IETF standard, was published in April 1998 as RFC 2328. Most router products now support OSPF in addition to RIP, including Windows NT's RRAS, Windows 2000, and Novell NetWare.

Unlike RIP and most other TCP/IP protocols, OSPF is not carried within a transport protocol like UDP or TCP. The OSPF messages are encapsulated directly in IP datagrams and addresses to other routers using port 89.

Link state routing, as implemented in OSPF, uses the Dijkstra algorithm to judge the efficiency of a route, based on several criteria, including the following:

- **Hop count**   While link state routing protocols still use the hop count to judge a route's efficiency, it is only part of the equation.

- **Transmission speed**   The speed at which the various links operate is an important part of a route's efficiency. Faster links obviously take precedence over slow ones.

- **Congestion delays**   Link state routing protocols consider the network congestion caused by the current traffic pattern when evaluating a route and bypass links that are overly congested.

- **Route cost**   The route cost is a metric assigned by the network administrator used to rate the relative usability of various routes. The cost can refer to the literal financial expense incurred by the link, or any other pertinent factor.

Link state routing is more complex than RIP and requires more processing by the router, but it judges the relative efficiency of routes more precisely and has a better convergence rate than RIP. OSPF also reduces the amount of bandwidth used by the routing protocol because it only transmits updates to other routers when changes in the network configuration take place, unlike RIP, which continually transmits the entire routing table.

Several of the advantages of OSPF are clearly the inspiration for the improvements made in the RIP version 2 specification. For example, all OSPF routes include a subnet mask and OSPF messages are all authenticated by the receiving router before they are processed. The protocol can also use routing information obtained from outside sources, such as exterior gateway protocols. In addition, OSPF provides the capability to create discrete areas within an autonomous system that exchange routing information among themselves. Only certain routers, called *area border routers,* exchange information with other areas. This reduces the amount of network traffic generated by the routing protocol.

Unlike RIP, OSPF can maintain multiple routes to a specific destination. When two routes to a single network address have the same metric, OSPF balances the traffic load between them.

Version 2 of RIP, therefore, is comparable to OSPF in its features and is definitely the preferable alternative on a relatively small internetwork that does not have severe traffic problems. However, on an internetwork that relies heavily on WAN connections or has many routers with large routing tables that would generate a lot of network traffic, OSPF is the preferable alternative.

Switches

The traditional internetwork configuration uses multiple LANs connected by routers to form a network that is larger than would be possible with a single LAN. This is necessary because each LAN is based on a network medium that is shared by multiple computers, and there is a limit to the number of systems that can share the medium before the network is overwhelmed by traffic. Routers segregate the traffic on the individual LANs, forwarding only those packets addressed to systems on other LANs.

Routers have been around for decades, but a newer type of device, called a *LAN switch*, has revolutionized network design and made creating LANs of almost unlimited size possible. A *switch* is essentially a multiport bridging device in which each port is a separate network segment. Similar in appearance to a hub, a switch receives incoming traffic through its ports; but unlike a hub, which forwards the traffic out through all of its other ports, a switch forwards the traffic only to the single port needed to reach the destination (see Figure 6-13). If, for example, you have a small workgroup network with each computer connected to a port in the same switching hub, then each system has what amounts to a dedicated connection to every other system. No shared network medium exists, and consequently, no collisions or traffic congestion. As an added bonus, you also get increased security because, without a shared medium, an unauthorized workstation cannot monitor and capture the traffic not intended for it.

Switches operate at layer 2 of the OSI reference model, the data link layer, so consequently, they are used to create a single large network, instead of a series of smaller networks connected by routers. This also means that switches can support any network-layer protocol. Like transparent bridges, switches can learn the topology of a network and perform functions like forwarding and packet filtering. Some switches are also capable of full-duplex communications and automatic speed adjustment.

In the traditional arrangement for a larger internetwork, multiple LANs are connected to a backbone network with routers. The backbone network is a shared-medium LAN like all of the others, however, and must therefore carry all of the internetwork traffic generated by the horizontal networks. This is why the backbone network traditionally uses a faster protocol. On a switched network, workstations are

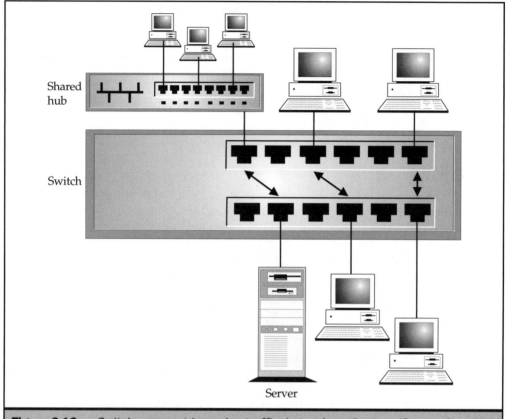

Figure 6-13.   *Switches repeat incoming traffic, but only to the specific port for which it is intended*

connected to individual workgroup switches, which in turn are connected to a single, high-performance switch, thus enabling any system on the network to open a dedicated connection to any other system (see Figure 6-14). This arrangement can be expanded further to include an intermediate layer of departmental switches as well. Servers accessed by all users can then be connected directly to a departmental switch or to the top-level switch, for better performance.

Replacing hubs with switches is an excellent way to improve the performance of a network without changing protocols or modifying individual workstations. Even a standard Ethernet network exhibits a dramatic improvement when each workstation is given a full 10 Mbps of bandwidth, rather than sharing it with 20 or 30 other systems. Full-duplex switches can double the effective bandwidth to 20 Mbps. While most of the LAN switches on the market are designed for Ethernet (and Fast Ethernet) networks, Token Ring and FDDI switches are available.

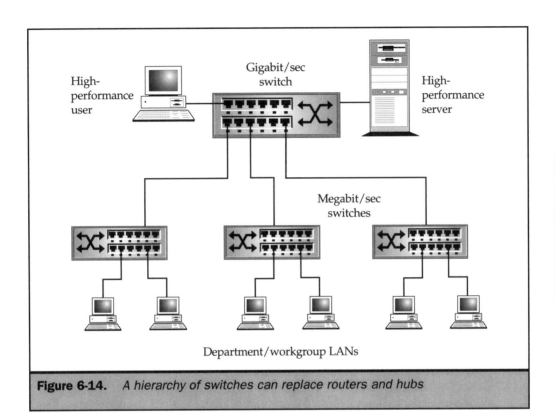

Figure 6-14. *A hierarchy of switches can replace routers and hubs*

Note

Asynchronous Transfer Mode (ATM) networks also rely on switching, but ATM is a connection-oriented, circuit-switched networking technology, and its switches are not interchangeable with those made for standard LANs.

While a fully switched network provides an ideal level of performance, switches are far more expensive than standard repeating hubs, and most networks combine these two technologies to reach a happy medium. You can, for example, connect standard hubs to the ports of a switch and share the bandwidth of a switched connection among a handful of machines, rather than several dozen.

Switch Types

There are two basic types of switching: cut-through and store-and-forward. A *cut-through switch* reads only the MAC address of an incoming packet, looks up the address in its forwarding table, and immediately begins to transmit it out through the port providing access to the destination without any additional processing, such as error checking, and before the entire packet is even received. This type of switch is relatively inexpensive and more commonly used at the workgroup or department level, where the lack of error checking will not affect the performance of the entire network. The immediate forwarding of incoming packets reduces the latency (that is, the delay) that results from error checking and other processing. If the destination port is in use, however, the switch buffers incoming data in memory, incurring a latency delay anyway, without the added benefit of error checking.

A *store-and-forward switch*, as the name implies, stores an entire incoming packet in buffer memory before forwarding it out the destination port. While in memory, the switch checks the packet for CRC errors and other conditions, such as runts, giants, and jabber. The switch immediately discards any packets with errors; those without errors are forwarded out through the correct port. These switching methods are not necessarily exclusive of each other. Some switches can work in cut-through mode until a pre-set error threshold is reached, and then switch to store-and-forward operation. Once the errors drop below the threshold, the switch reverts back to cut-through mode.

Note   *For more information on runts, giants, jabber, and other transmission problems, see Chapter 8.*

LAN switches implement these functions using one of three hardware configurations. *Matrix switching*, also called *crossbar switching*, uses a grid of input and output connections, such as that shown in Figure 6-15. Data entering through any port's input can be forwarded to any port for output. Because this solution is hardware based, there is no CPU or software involvement in the switching process. In cases where data can't be forwarded immediately, the switch buffers it until the output port is unblocked.

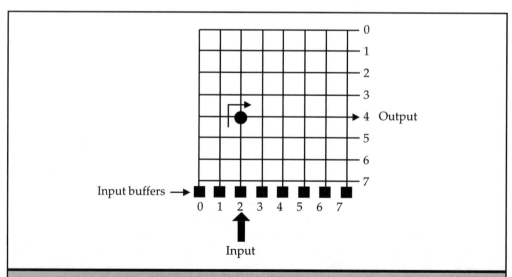

Figure 6-15.   *Matrix switching uses a grid of input and output circuits*

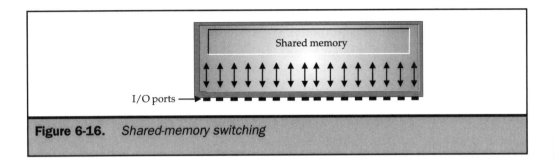

Figure 6-16.   *Shared-memory switching*

In a *shared-memory switch*, all incoming data is stored in a memory buffer that is shared by all of the switch's ports and then forwarded to an output port (see Figure 6-16). A more commonly used technology (shown in Figure 6-17), called *bus-architecture switching*, forwards all traffic across a common bus, using time-division multiplexing to ensure that each port has equal access to the bus. In this model, each port has its own individual buffer and is controlled by an ASIC (application-specific integrated circuit).

Switches are available for any size network, from inexpensive workgroup switches designed for small office networks to modular units with much higher prices.

Routing Versus Switching

The question of whether to route or switch on a network is a difficult one. Switching is faster and cheaper than routing, but it raises some problems in most network configurations. By using switches, you eliminate subnets and create a single flat network segment that hosts all of your computers. Any two systems can communicate using a dedicated link that is essentially a temporary two-node network. The problems arise when workstations generate broadcast messages. Because a switched network forms a single collision domain, broadcast messages are propagated throughout the whole network and every system must process them, which can waste enormous amounts of bandwidth.

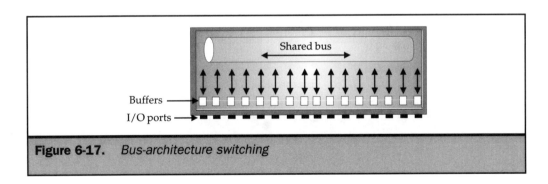

Figure 6-17.   *Bus-architecture switching*

One of the advantages of creating multiple LANs and connecting them with routers is that broadcasts are limited to the individual networks. Routers also provide security by limiting transmissions to a single subnet. To avoid the wasted bandwidth caused by broadcasts, implementing certain routing concepts on switched networks has been necessary. This has led to a number of new technologies that integrate routing and switching to varying degrees. Some of these technologies are examined in the following sections.

Virtual LANs

A *virtual LAN* or *VLAN* is a group of systems on a switched network that functions as a subnet and communicates with other VLANs through routers. The physical network is still switched, however; the VLANs exist as an overlay to the switching fabric, as shown in Figure 6-18. Network administrators create VLANs by specifying the MAC, port, or IP addresses of the systems that are to be part of each subnet. Messages that are broadcast on a VLAN are limited to the subnet, just as in a routed network. Because VLANs are independent of the physical network, the systems in a particular subnet can be located anywhere, and a single system can even be a member of more than one VNET.

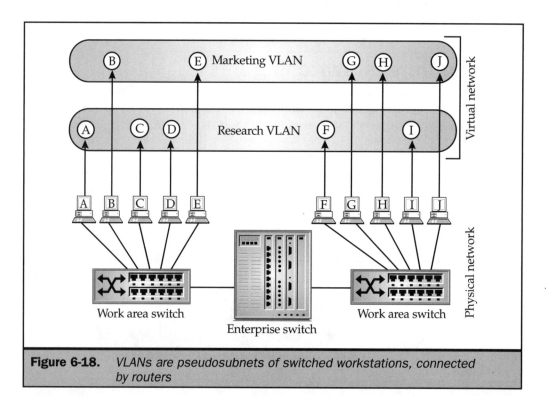

Figure 6-18.   *VLANs are pseudosubnets of switched workstations, connected by routers*

Despite the fact that all of the computers are connected by switches, routers are still necessary for systems in different VLANs to communicate. VLANs that are based solely on layer-2 technology, such as those that use port configuration or MAC addresses to define the member systems, must have a port dedicated to a router connection. In this type of VLAN, the network administrator either selects certain switch ports to designate the members of a VLAN or creates a list of the workstations' MAC addresses.

Because of the additional processing involved, routing is slower than switching. This particular arrangement is sometimes referred to as "switch where you can, route where you must," because routing is only used for communication between VLANs; all communication within a VLAN is switched. This is an efficient arrangement, as long as the majority of the network traffic (70 percent to 80 percent) is between systems in the same VLAN. Communication speed within a VLAN is maximized, at the expense of the inter-VLAN communication. When too much traffic occurs between systems in different subnets, the routing slows down the process too much and the speed of the switches is largely wasted.

Layer-3 Switching

Layer-3 switching also uses VLANs, but it mixes routing and switching functions to make communication between VLANs more efficient. This technology is known by several different names—depending on the vendor of the equipment—including *IP switching, multilayer routing, cut-through routing,* and *Fast IP.* The essence of the concept is described as "route once, switch afterward." A router is still required to establish connections between systems in different VLANs; but once the connection has been established, subsequent traffic travels over the layer-2 switching fabric, which is much faster.

Most of the hardware devices called layer-3 switches that are being produced by the major manufacturers combine the functions of a switch and a router into one unit. The device is capable of performing all of a router's standard functions, but is also able to transmit data using high-speed switches, all at a substantially lower cost than a standard router. Layer-3 switches are optimized for use on LAN and MAN (metropolitan area network) connections, not WANs.

Layer-3 switching has not yet matured to the point at which vendors are manufacturing completely interoperable solutions, but this technology could potentially represent the ideal upgrade path for internetworks that are now based on routers and repeating hubs. By replacing the routers that connect workgroup or department networks to the backbone with layer-3 switches, you retain all of the router functionality, while increasing the overall speed at which data is forwarded. Eventually, by moving workstation connections from repeating hubs to layer-2 switches, you can migrate to a network with no shared media at all, except for wide area links, still connected with traditional routers.

The
Complete
Reference

Upgrading
&
Troubleshooting
Networks

Chapter 7

Wide Area Networks

The physical- and data link–layer protocols used to build local area networks (LANs) are quite efficient over relatively short distances. Even for campus connections between buildings, fiber-optic solutions enable you to use a LAN protocol such as Ethernet or FDDI throughout your whole internetwork. However, when you want to make a connection over a long distance, you move into an entirely different world of protocols called *wide area network (WAN) protocols*. A WAN is a communications link that spans a long distance and connects two or more LANs together.

WAN connections enable you to connect networks in different cities or countries, enabling users to access resources at remote locations. Many companies use WAN links between office locations to exchange e-mail, groupware, and database information, or even just to access files and printers on remote servers. Banks and airlines, for example, must be in continual communication with all of their branch offices to keep their databases updated, but WAN connections can also function on a much smaller scale, such as a system that periodically dials in to a remote network to send and retrieve the latest e-mail messages.

WAN Connections

A WAN connection requires a router or a bridge at each end to provide the interface to the individual LANs, as shown in Figure 7-1. This minimizes the amount of traffic that passes across the link. *Remote link bridges* connect LANs running the same data link–layer protocol at different locations using an analog or digital WAN link. The bridges prevent unnecessary traffic from traversing the link by filtering packets according to their data link–layer MAC addresses. However, bridges do pass broadcast traffic across the WAN link. Depending on the speed of the link and applications for which it is intended, this may be a waste of bandwidth.

If the WAN link is intended only for highly specific uses, such as e-mail access, then data link–layer bridges can be wasteful, because they provide less control over the traffic that is permitted to pass over the link. Routers, on the other hand, keep the two LANs completely separate. No broadcasts are passed over the WAN link, and administrators can exercise greater control over the traffic passing between the LANs. In addition, routers also enable you to use different data link–layer protocols on each of the LANs, because they operate at the network layer of the OSI model.

While bridges are always separate units, the routers used to connect two networks with a WAN link can take the form of either a computer or a dedicated hardware device. When a remote user connects to a host PC with a dial-up modem connection and accesses other systems on the network, the host PC is functioning as a router. For technologies other than dial-up connections, however, most sites use dedicated routers. The router or bridge located at each terminus of the WAN link is connected to the local LAN and to whatever hardware is used to make the physical-layer connection to the WAN, such as a modem, CSU/DSU, or NT1.

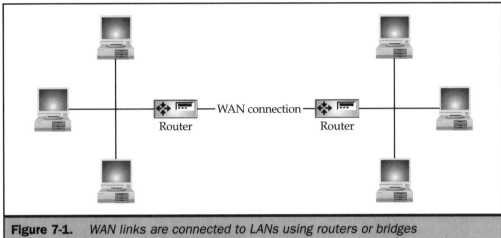

Figure 7-1.   *WAN links are connected to LANs using routers or bridges*

Selecting a WAN Technology

The selection of a WAN connection for a specific purpose is generally a tradeoff between speed and expense. LAN protocols routinely run at anywhere from 10 to 100 Mbps or more, but WAN connections running at this speed are out of reach for most organizations. Prices depend on the technology used, but as an example, a leased T1 line running at 1.544 Mbps will generally cost several thousand dollars a month in the U.S., depending on the distance between the sites. Other services offer more or less bandwidth, at higher and lower prices. The cost is also dependent on the location of the sites. In Europe, for example, leased lines are rarely used and are astronomically expensive (one quote for a short-distance T1 link in France in 1996 was over $35,000 per month!), but ISDN is much more prevalent than in the U.S. and quite reasonable. WAN links, therefore, are almost always slower than the networks that they connect, so it's important to determine just how much bandwidth you'll need as you design your network.

It often is not practical to use a WAN link in the same way that you would use a LAN connection. You might have to limit the amount of traffic that passes over the link or schedule certain tasks that require WAN communications to run at off-peak hours. For example, database replication tasks can easily monopolize a WAN link for extended periods of time, delaying normal user activities. Many applications that require periodic data replication, including directory services such as Active Directory, Windows NT domains, and NDS, enable you to specify when these activities should take place.

Before you select a WAN technology, you should consider the applications for which it will be used. Different functions require different amounts of bandwidth, and different types as well. E-mail, for example, not only requires relatively little bandwidth, but also is intermittent in its traffic. High-end applications, such as full-motion video, not only require enormous amounts of bandwidth, but also require that the bandwidth be continuously available, to avoid dropouts in service. The needs of most organizations fall somewhere between these two extremes, but it is important to remember that the continuity of the bandwidth can sometimes be as important as the transmission rate.

Table 7-1 lists some of the most common WAN applications and the approximate amount of bandwidth they require. When you examine these figures, remember to consider the number of people using the application. A hundred users querying a database at another site can use as much bandwidth as a single full-motion video stream.

Table 7-2 lists the most popular technologies used for WAN connections and their transmission speeds. Here, it is important to consider the nature of the link as well as its speed. A leased line, such as a T1, provides a permanent, dedicated, digital link between two points running at a fixed bandwidth. You pay for all of the bandwidth, 24 hours a day, whether you are using it or not, and that bandwidth cannot be exceeded. Basic rate ISDN also provides a digital link with a fixed bandwidth, but it is not permanent. You can dial in to various destinations without modifying the equipment,

Application	Transmission Rate
Personal communications	300 to 9,600 bps or higher
E-mail transmission	2,400 to 9,600 bps or higher
Remote-control program	9,600 bps to 56 Kbps or higher
Digitized voice phone call	64 Kbps
Database text query	Up to 1 Mbps
Digital audio	1 to 2 Mbps
Access image	1 to 8 Mbps
Compressed video	2 to 10 Mbps
Medical transmission	Up to 50 Mbps
Document imaging	10 to 100 Mbps
Scientific imaging	Up to 1 Gbps
Full-motion video	1 to 2 Gbps

Table 7-1.   *WAN Applications and Their Approximate Required Bandwidth*

Connection Type	Transmission Rate
Dial-up modem connection	Up to 56 Kbps (53 Kbps in U.S., by FCC restriction)
X.25	64 Kbps to 2 Mbps
Integrated Service Digital Network (ISDN)	Up to 128 Kbps or 1.544 Mbps
Fractional T1	64 Kbps
T1	1.544 Mbps
T3	44.736 Mbps
Frame relay	56 Kbps to 44.736 Mbps
Digital Subscriber Line (DSL)	Up to 51.84 Mbps
Synchronous Optical Network (SONET)	51.9 Mbps to 2.5 Gbps
Asynchronous Transfer Mode (ATM)	25 Mbps to 2.46 Gbps

Table 7-2. *WAN Technologies and Their Transmission Rates*

just as with a standard telephone line, and disconnect when the link is not in use. This can save money if there is a per-minute charge for the service, which is often the case.

The transmission rates listed in this table represent the maximum rated throughput for these technologies and, for a variety of reasons, usually do not necessarily reflect the actual throughput realized by applications using them. In the real world, the throughput is generally lower.

Some other WAN technologies provide *bandwidth on demand*, meaning that the capacity of the connection increases with your needs. Sometimes, as with frame relay, this process is automatic. A sudden burst of heavy traffic is immediately accommodated by the connection, and although there will probably be an additional charge, the application is served. In other cases, you might have to request additional bandwidth from the service provider as you notice a trend of increasing utilization, but this is still likely to be preferable to installing another leased line or taking other permanent action to accommodate what may be a temporary condition.

NETWORK HARDWARE

Suppose, for example, a large accounting firm experiences a dramatic increase in WAN bandwidth utilization each year during tax season, only to have it die down again after April 15. Installing additional leased lines just for a few months would be totally impractical because of their high installation and equipment fees. On the other hand, a frame-relay connection or even primary rate ISDN can be configured to accommodate temporarily increased bandwidth requirements and then revert back to the original service as needed.

The following sections examine some of the technologies that are most commonly used for WAN connectivity.

Dial-Up Connections

A WAN connection does not necessarily require a major investment in hardware and installation fees. A standard asynchronous modem connection using dial-up telephone lines to connect to an Internet service provider (ISP) is technically a wide area link, and for some purposes, this is all that is needed. For example, a user working at home or on the road can dial in to a server at the office and connect to the LAN to access e-mail and other network resources. In the same way, a dial-up connection may be sufficient for a small branch office to connect to the corporate headquarters for the same purposes. The connection can be scheduled to occur at regular intervals or to connect to the network whenever a user requests a remote resource.

The speed of a dial-up modem link like this is limited to 33.6 Kbps unless one side of the link uses a digital connection, in which case the maximum possible speed is 56 Kbps (for digital-to-analog traffic only; analog-to-digital traffic is limited to 31.2 Kbps). However, in the U.S. and Canada, the Federal Communications Commission imposes a 53 Kbps limit on transmission speed over standard telephone lines. In most cases, only ISPs and large corporations use the digital equipment necessary to operate at the higher speed. On a smaller scale, the increase in speed often isn't great enough to justify the expense. Analog modem communications are also dependent on the quality of the lines involved. Most telephone companies certify their lines for voice communications only, and will not perform repairs to improve the quality of data connections. As a result, it is rare for a dial-up connection to achieve a full 53 Kbps throughput.

In most cases, a dial-up WAN connection uses a computer as a router, although there are standalone devices that perform the same function. The most basic arrangement uses the connection for remote network access and involves a standard modem-equipped workstation running Windows NT, 2000, or 9*x*. The workstation is connected to a LAN and configured to function as a dial-up server. A remote user, also running a Windows operating system, dials in to the modem, connects to the workstation, and accesses the network through the workstation's LAN connection. The remote system can be running an e-mail client, a Web browser, or another application designed to access network resources, or simply access the file system on network servers.

A computer can also host multiple dial-up connections, with the right software and equipment. Windows 9*x* and Windows NT Workstation, for example, can host only a single remote user, but Windows NT Server can host up to 256 remote users simultaneously. There is a variety of hardware products available that enable a single computer to host a large number of modems. For remote access on a larger scale, the dedicated hardware platforms used by service providers and large corporations can split a single leased line, such as a T1 or T3, into separate channels supporting multiple dial-up or other connections. The process of splitting a single connection into multiple discrete channels is called *multiplexing.*

In addition to linking a single computer to a network, dial-up connections can connect two networks at remote locations. The Routing and Remote Access service for Windows NT Server, for example, enables you to configure a connection for *dial-on-demand.* When a user on one LAN performs an operation that requires access to the other LAN, the server automatically dials in to a server on the other network, establishes the connection, and begins routing traffic. When the link remains idle for a preset period of time, the connection terminates. There are also standalone routers that perform in the same way, enabling users to connect to a remote LAN or the Internet as needed. This arrangement minimizes the connection time, thus reducing the telephone charges, and provides WAN access to users without having to establish the connection manually. The only evidence that the requested resource is at a remote location is the delay incurred while the modem dials and connects.

Inverse Multiplexing

Some sites also use dial-up connections as backups, to provide access to a remote network in the event that a leased line or other technology fails, or to augment the bandwidth of a leased line during periods of high traffic. The process of combining the bandwidth of multiple connections into a single conduit is called *inverse multiplexing* (see Figure 7-2). Basic rate ISDN connections routinely use inverse multiplexing to combine two 64 Kbps B-channels into a single 128 Kbps channel, and there are routers

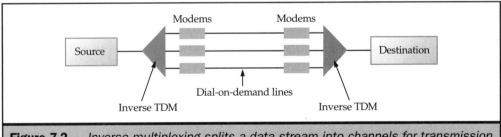

Figure 7-2.   *Inverse multiplexing splits a data stream into channels for transmission across separate media*

that can combine the bandwidth of leased lines, as well. More recently, however, inverse multiplexing has been introduced in lower-end products intended for home and small business users.

Windows 98, NT, and 2000, for example, all include a feature called *multilink* that enables you to combine the bandwidth of multiple modems to form a single higher-speed connection. However, as with all inverse multiplexing arrangements, the implementation at one end of the connection that separates the signal into multiple channels for transmission over separate connections must be matched by an equivalent process at the other end that combines the connections back into a single signal. This means that if you want to use this feature to connect to the Internet, for example, you must find an ISP that supports it on the server end.

Some of the router products with inverse multiplexing features also have the capability to open additional dial-up connections automatically when traffic passing over the link reaches a certain threshold. This feature goes by different names, such as channel aggregation, bonding, and (amusingly) rubber bandwidth.

Leased Lines

A *leased line* is a dedicated, permanent connection between two sites that runs through the telephone network. The line is said to be *dedicated* because the connection is active 24 hours a day and does not compete for bandwidth with any other processes. The line is *permanent* because there are no telephone numbers or dialing involved in the connection, nor is it possible to connect to a different location without modifying the hardware.

You install a leased line by contacting a telephone service provider, either local or long-distance, and agreeing to a contract that specifies a line granting a specific amount of bandwidth between two locations, for a specified cost. The price typically involves an installation fee, hardware costs, and a monthly subscription fee, and depends both on the bandwidth of the line and the distance between the two sites being connected.

The advantages of a leased line are that the connection delivers the specified bandwidth at all times, and the line is as inherently secure as any telephone line, because it is private. While the service functions as a dedicated line between the two connected sites, there is not really a dedicated physical connection, such as a separate wire running the entire distance. A dedicated line is installed between each of the two sites and the service provider's nearest point of presence, but from there, the connection uses the provider's standard switching facilities to make the connection. The provider guarantees that its facilities can provide a specific bandwidth and quality of service.

Leased-Line Hardware

Leased lines can be analog or digital, but digital lines are more common. An analog line is simply a normal telephone line that is continuously open. Modems are required at both ends to convert the digital signals of the data network to analog form for transmission, and back to digital at the other end. In some cases, the line may have a greater service quality than a standard voice telephone line. This type of leased line is relatively rare, because unless the connection is continuously transmitting data, it is often cheaper to use a dial-up connection with some form of dial-on-demand technology, so that you are not paying for the connection during nonproduction hours.

Digital leased lines are more common, because no analog-to-digital translation is required for data network connections, and the signal quality of a digital line is usually superior to that of an analog line, whether leased or dial-up. Digital lines are available at several bandwidths, the most common of which is called a *T1*. Running at 1.544 Mbps, a T1 is a digital link that can be used as a single data pipe or multiplexed into 24 channels of 64 Kbps each. The channels can each carry independent voice or data transmissions. Many service providers enable you to lease one or more of these 64 Kbps channels, which is called *fractional T1* service, to provide exactly the amount of bandwidth you need. This service also lets you ramp up the bandwidth by adding additional 64 Kbps channels as needed. The next step up in bandwidth is a *T3* connection, used mostly by ISPs and other service providers, which runs at 44.736 Mbps, the equivalent of 28 T1 lines. If anyone's interested, a *T4* runs at 274.176 Mbps.

A T1 line requires two twisted pairs of wires, and originally the line was *conditioned*, meaning that a repeater was installed 3,000 feet from each endpoint and every 6,000 feet in between. Today, however, a signaling scheme called *High-rate Digital Subscriber Line (HDSL)* makes it possible to transmit digital signals at T1 speeds over longer distances without the need for repeating hardware.

The hardware required at each end of a digital leased line is called a *channel service unit/data service unit (CSU/DSU)*, which is actually two devices that are usually combined into a single unit. The CSU provides the terminus for the digital link and keeps the connection active even when the connected bridge, router, private branch exchange (PBX), or other device isn't actually using it. The CSU also provides testing and diagnostic functions for the line. The DSU is the device that converts the signals it receives from the bridge, router, or PBX to the bipolar digital signals carried by the line. In appearance, a CSU/DSU looks something like a modem, and as a result, they are sometimes incorrectly called digital modems. (In fact, just about any device used to connect a computer or network to a telephone or Internet service is incorrectly called a modem, including ISDN and cable network equipment.) A single, basic CSU/DSU unit costs somewhere in the neighborhood of $1,000, but identical units are required at each end of the connection.

The CSU/DSU is connected to the leased line on one side using an RJ connector, and to a device (or devices) on the other side that provides the interface to the local network (see Figure 7-3), using a V.35 or RS-232 connector. This interface can be a bridge or a router for data networking, or a PBX for voice services. The line can be either *unchanneled*, meaning that it is used as a single data pipe, or *channeled*, meaning that a multiplexor is located in between the CSU/DSU and the interface, to break up the line into separate channels for multiple uses.

Digital leased lines use *time division multiplexing (TDM)* to create the individual channels, in which the entire data stream is divided into time segments that are

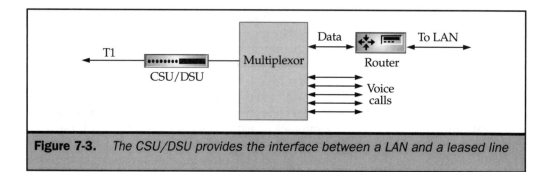

Figure 7-3. *The CSU/DSU provides the interface between a LAN and a leased line*

allocated to each channel in turn (see Figure 7-4). Each time division is dedicated to a particular channel, whether it is used or not. Thus, when one of the 64 Kbps voice lines that are part of a T1 is idle, that bandwidth is wasted, no matter how busy the other channels are.

Leased-Line Applications

T1s and other leased lines are used for several different purposes. Organizations with offices in several locations can use leased lines to build a *private network* for both voice and data traffic. With such a network in place, users can access network resources in any of the sites at will, and telephone calls can be transferred to users in the different offices. The problem with building a network in this manner is that it requires a mesh topology of leased lines—that is, a separate leased line connecting each office to every other office—to be reliable. An organization with four sites, for example, would need 6 leased lines, as shown in Figure 7-5, and eight sites would require 28 leased lines! It would be possible for the sites to be connected in series, using seven links to connect eight sites, but then the failure of any one link or router would split the network in two.

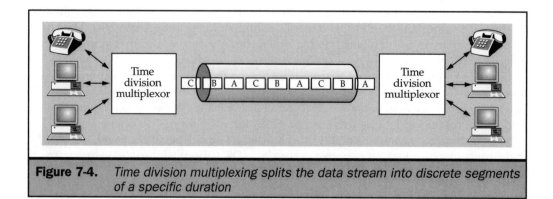

Figure 7-4. *Time division multiplexing splits the data stream into discrete segments of a specific duration*

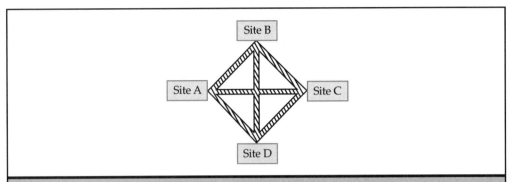

Figure 7-5. *A private WAN that uses leased lines requires a separate connection between every two sites*

This type of network can provide excellent and secure performance, but it can be abominably expensive. The monthly cost of a T1 line depends on the length of the connection. A short hop within a metropolitan area can cost in the area of $1,500 per month, while a long-distance connection running coast to coast in the U.S. can be $20,000 per month or more, and these prices do not include the installation and equipment fees. Thus, if an organization has eight sites scattered around the country, the monthly bill for the leased lines could reach $250,000 or more.

One alternative to a private network of this type would be to use leased lines at each site to connect to a public carrier network using a technology such as frame relay or ATM to provide the required bandwidth. Each site would require only a single leased line to a local service provider, instead of a separate line to each site. For more information on this alternative, see "Packet Switching Services," later in this chapter.

These days, most organizations use a less expensive technology to create WAN links between their various offices. However, leased lines are commonly used for connections to ISPs. A single T1 connection to the Internet can service the needs of hundreds of average users simultaneously.

ISDN and DSL

Integrated Service Digital Network (ISDN) and *Digital Subscriber Line (DSL)* links are both services that utilize the existing copper telephone cable at an installation, called *POTS (Plain Old Telephone Service)*, to carry data at much higher transmission rates. In both cases, the site must be relatively close to the telephone company's nearest *point of presence (POP)*, a location containing telephone switching equipment. Basic rate ISDN, for example, requires a location no farther than 18,000 feet (3.4 miles) from the POP; DSL distances vary with the data rate. ISDN and DSL are sometimes called *last-mile technologies,* because they are designed to get data from the user site to the POP at high speed.

The copper cable running from the POP to the individual user site is traditionally the weakest link in the phone system. Once a signal reaches the POP, it moves through the telephone company's switches at high speed. By eliminating the bottlenecks at both ends of the link, traffic can maintain that speed from end to end. While these technologies are currently being marketed primarily as Internet connectivity solutions for home users, they both are usable for office-to-office WAN connections as well.

ISDN

ISDN is a digital point-to-point telephone system that has been around for over a decade, but that has not been adopted as widely in the U.S. as its proponents had hoped. Originally, ISDN was to completely replace the current phone system with all-digital service, but it is now positioned as an alternative technology for home users who require high-bandwidth network connections and for links between business networks. In this country, ISDN technology has garnered a reputation for being overly complicated, difficult to install, and not particularly reliable; and to some extent, this reputation is justified. Up until a very few years go, inquiries to most local phone companies about ISDN service would be met only with puzzlement, and horror stories about installation difficulties were common. The situation has now improved somewhat, and many ISPs offer a turnkey service for home users, in which the ISP handles the entire ISDN installation process, including the negotiations with the telephone company. For business use, ISDN is not commonly used in North America, but it is a popular solution in Europe.

ISDN is a digital service that can provide a good deal more bandwidth than standard telephone service; but unlike a leased line, it is not permanent. ISDN devices dial a number to establish a connection, like a standard telephone, meaning that users can connect to different sites as needed. For this reason, ISDN is known as a *circuit-switching service,* because it creates a temporary point-to-point circuit between two sites. For the home or business user connecting to the Internet, this means that you can change ISPs without any modifications by the telephone company. For organizations using ISDN for WAN connections between offices, this means that you can dial in to different office networks when you need access to their resources, rather than maintain a separate connection to each site.

This impermanence also means that, in many cases, you only pay for the bandwidth you use. Most ISDN service agreements include a per-minute charge, as well as installation fees and monthly subscriber fees. Unlike a leased line, you can disconnect an ISDN WAN link during off hours. For home users wanting an Internet access solution, the per-minute charges make ISDN a rather costly alternative when compared to other options available today. However, for business use, a PRI ISDN connection can, in many cases, be far cheaper than a leased line and provide virtually the same service.

Unlike a modem connection using standard dial-up telephone lines, however, ISDN connections are nearly instantaneous because they're digital, like the computer network, and no analog-to-digital conversion is required. ISDN can carry different kinds of traffic, such as voice, fax, and data; but for these purposes, special hardware is required to convert the analog signals of the device into the digital format. This is exactly the opposite of the traditional arrangement, where digital signals are converted to analog format by a modem. Multiple devices can utilize the same channel using TDM to split the bandwidth. This side of the technology has not caught on; a few vendors sell ISDN phones and other devices, but not nearly as many as those who sell the ISDN terminal adapter used to connect to a computer or router.

ISDN Services

There are two main types of ISDN service, which are based on units of bandwidth called *B channels,* running at 64 Kbps, and *D channels,* running at 16 or 64 Kbps. B channels carry voice and data traffic, and D channels carry control traffic only. The service types are as follows:

- **BRI (Basic Rate Interface)**   Also called *2B+D,* because it consists of two 64 Kbps B channels and one 16 Kbps D channel. BRI is targeted primarily at home users for connections to business networks or the Internet.

- **PRI (Primary Rate Interface)**   Consists of up to 23 B channels and one 64 Kbps D channel, for a total bandwidth equivalent to a T1 leased line. PRI is aimed more at the business community, as an alternative to leased lines that can provide the same bandwidth and signal quality with greater flexibility.

Note
Another type of service, called Broadband ISDN (B-ISDN), *is not directly comparable to BRI and PRI, because it defines a cell-switching service that uses SONET at the physical layer and ATM at the data link layer to carry voice, data, and video traffic at speeds in excess of 155 Mbps.*

One of the primary advantages of ISDN is the ability to combine the bandwidth of multiple channels as needed, using inverse multiplexing. Each B channel has its own separate ten-digit number; so for the home user, one of the B channels of the BRI service can carry voice traffic while the other B channel is used for data, or both B channels can be combined to form a single 128 Kbps connection to the Internet or to a private network. The PRI service can combine any number of the B channels in any combination, to form connections of various bandwidths.

In addition, the ISDN service supports bandwidth-on-demand, which can supplement a connection with additional B channels to support a temporary increase in bandwidth requirements. Depending on the equipment used, it's possible to add bandwidth according to a predetermined schedule of usage needs or to dynamically augment a connection when the traffic rises above a particular level. Because you only pay for the channels that are currently in use, an ISDN connection can be far more economical than a leased line, which you must pay for whether it's being used or not.

ISDN Communications

The ISDN B channels carry user traffic only, whether in the form of voice or data. The D channel is responsible for carrying all of the control traffic needed to establish and terminate connections between sites. The traffic on these channels consists of protocols that span the bottom three layers of the OSI reference model. The physical layer establishes a circuit-switched connection between the user equipment and the telephone company's switching office that operates at 64 Kbps and also provides diagnostic functions like loopback testing and signal monitoring. This layer is also responsible for the multiplexing that enables devices to share the same channel.

At the data link layer, bridges and PBXs using an ISDN connection employ the *LAPD (Link Access Procedure for D Channel)* protocol, as defined by the International Telecommunications Union (ITU-T) documents Q.920 through Q.923, to provide frame-relay and frame-switching services. This protocol (which is similar to the LAP-B protocol used by X.25) uses the address information provided by the ISDN equipment to create virtual paths through the switching fabric of the telephone company's network to the intended destination. The end result is a private network connection much like that of a leased line.

The network layer is responsible for the establishment, maintenance, and termination of connections between ISDN devices. Unlike leased lines and similar technologies, which maintain a permanently open connection, ISDN must use a handshake procedure to establish a connection between two points. The process of establishing an ISDN connection involves messages exchanged between three entities: the caller, the switch (at the POP), and the receiver. As usual, network-layer messages are encapsulated within data link–layer protocol frames. The connection procedure is as follows:

1. The caller transmits a SETUP message to the switch.

2. If the SETUP message is acceptable, the switch returns a CALL PROC (call proceeding) message to the caller and forwards the SETUP message to the receiver.

3. If the receiver accepts the SETUP message, it rings the phone (either literally or figuratively) and sends an ALERTING message back to the switch, which forwards it to the caller.

4. When the receiver answers the call (again, either literally or figuratively), it sends a CONNECT message to the switch, which forwards it to the caller.

5. The caller then sends a CONNECT ACK (connection acknowledgment) message to the switch, which forwards it to the receiver. The connection is now established.

ISDN Hardware

ISDN does not require any modifications to the standard copper telephone wiring. As long as your site is within 18,000 feet of a POP, you can convert an existing telephone line to ISDN just by adding the appropriate hardware at each end. The telephone company uses special data-encoding schemes (*2B1Q* in North America and *4B3T* in Europe) to provide higher data transmission rates over the standard cable. All ISDN installations must have a device called an *NT1 (Network Termination 1)* connected to the telephone line at each end (see Figure 7-6). The service from the telephone company provides what is known as a *U interface* operating over one twisted pair of wires. The NT1 connects to the U interface and converts the signals to the four-wire *S/T interface* used by ISDN terminal equipment (that is, the devices that use the connection).

In some cases, the S/T interface can use six or eight wires, with the additional wires providing emergency power to telephones in the event that local power fails. Power may also be delivered through the standard four wires in some instances.

In North America, it is up to the consumer to provide the NT1, which is available in several forms as a commercial product. In Europe and Japan, where ISDN is much more prevalent, the NT1 is owned and provided by the telephone company; users only

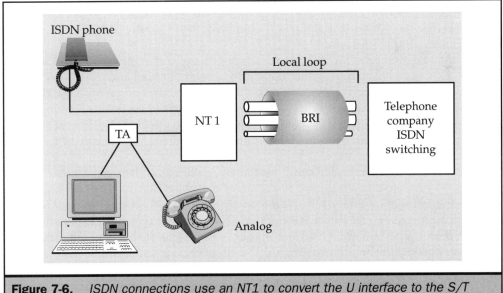

Figure 7-6.   *ISDN connections use an NT1 to convert the U interface to the S/T interface*

have to provide the terminal equipment. For the BRI service, a separate NT1 is required if you are going to use more than one type of terminal equipment, such as a terminal adapter for a computer and an ISDN phone. If the service is going to be used only for data networking, as is often the case in this country, there are single devices available that combine the NT1 with a terminal adapter. These combination devices can take the form of an expansion card for a PC, or a separate device, similar in appearance to a modem. Once again, the units that are often called "ISDN modems" are technically not modems at all, because they do not convert signals between analog and digital formats.

Devices that connect directly to the S/T interface, such as ISDN phones and ISDN fax machines, are referred to as *terminal equipment 1 (TE1)*. Devices that are not ISDN capable, such as standard analog phones and fax machines, are called *terminal equipment 2 (TE2)*. To connect a TE2 device to the S/T interface, you must have an intervening *terminal adapter (TA)*. You can connect up to seven devices to an NT1, both TE1 and TE2.

DSL

Digital Subscriber Line (DSL), or sometimes *xDSL*, is a collective term for a group of related technologies that provide a WAN service that is somewhat similar to ISDN, but at much higher speeds. Like ISDN, DSL uses standard telephone wiring to transmit data from a user site to a telephone company POP using a private point-to-point connection. From there, signals travel through the telephone company's standard switching equipment to another DSL connection at the destination. Also like ISDN, the distance between the site and the POP is limited; the faster the transmission rate, the shorter the operable distance.

The transmission rates for DSL services vary greatly, and many of the services function *asymmetrically*, meaning that they have different upload and download speeds. This speed variance occurs because the bundle of wires at the POP is more susceptible to a type of interference called *near-end crosstalk* when data is arriving from the user site than when it is being transmitted out to the user site. The increased attenuation resulting from the crosstalk requires that the transmission rate be lower when traveling in that direction.

DSL is relatively new, and is being promoted heavily as an Internet access solution. Asymmetrical operation is not much of a problem for this application, because the average Internet users download far more data than they upload. For WAN connections, however, symmetrical services are preferable. DSL differs from ISDN in that it is permanent; it has no numbers assigned to the connections, and has no session-establishment procedures. The connection is continuously active and private, much like that of a leased line. In addition, the relatively low prices and high transmission rates of the DSL service give it the potential to eclipse ISDN and leased-line technologies in the coming years.

Standard telephone communications only use a small amount of the bandwidth provided by the POTS cable. DSL works by utilizing frequencies above the standard telephone bandwidth (300 to 3,200 Hz) and by using advanced signal encoding methods to transmit data at higher rates of speed. Some of the DSL services use only frequencies that are out of the range of standard voice communications, which makes it possible for the line to be used for normal voice traffic while it is carrying digital data. In other words, imagine a high-speed Internet connection that enables you to talk on the phone while you're surfing the Web, all using a single standard telephone line.

The various DSL services have abbreviations with different first letters, which is why the technology is sometimes called *x*DSL, with the *x* acting as a placeholder. These services and their properties are shown in Table 7-3.

Note   *E1 is the European leased-line standard that is comparable to the North American T1, except that E1 runs at 2.048 Mbps.*

Service	Transmission Rate	Link Length	Simultaneous Voice Capability	Applications
HDSL (High-rate Digital Subscriber Line)	1.544 Mbps full duplex (2 wire pairs) or 2.048 Mbps full duplex (3 wire pairs)	12,000 to 15,000 feet, more with repeaters	No	T1/E1 substitute for Internet connections, LAN and PBX interconnections, and frame-relay traffic aggregation
SDSL (Symmetrical Digital Subscriber Line)	1.544 Mbps full duplex or 2.048 Mbps full duplex (1 wire pair)	10,000 feet	Yes	T1/E1 substitute for Internet connections, LAN and PBX interconnections, and frame-relay traffic aggregation
ADSL (Asymmetrical Digital Subscriber Line)	1.544 to 8.448 Mbps downstream; 640 Kbps to 1.544 Mbps upstream	10,000 to 18,000 feet, depending on speed	Yes	Internet/intranet access, remote LAN access, virtual private networking, video-on-demand, and voice-over-IP

Table 7-3.   *DSL Services and Their Properties*

NETWORK HARDWARE

Service	Transmission Rate	Link Length	Simultaneous Voice Capability	Applications
RADSL (Rate-Adaptive Digital Subscriber Line)	1.544 to 8.448 Mbps downstream; 640 Kbps to 1.544 Mbps upstream	10,000 to 18,000 feet	Yes	Same as ADSL, except that the transmission speed is dynamically adjusted to accommodate the link length and signal quality
ADSL Lite	Up to 1 Mbps downstream; up to 512 Kbps upstream	18,000 feet	Yes	Internet/intranet access, remote LAN access, IP telephony, and videoconferencing
VDSL (Very-high-rate Digital Subscriber Line)	12.96 to 51.84 Mbps downstream; 1.6 to 2.3 Mbps upstream	1,000 to 4,500 feet, depending on speed	Yes	Multimedia Internet access and high-definition television delivery
ISDL (ISDN Digital Subscriber Line)	Up to 144 Kbps full duplex	18,000 feet, more with repeaters	No	Internet/intranet access, remote LAN access, IP telephony, and videoconferencing

Table 7-3. *DSL Services and Their Properties* (continued)

The hardware required for a DSL connection is a standard POTS line and a DSL modem at both ends of the link. For services that provide simultaneous voice and data traffic, a POTS splitter is needed to separate the lower frequencies used by voice traffic from the higher frequencies used by the DSL service. In addition, the telephone line cannot use *loading coils*, inductors that extend the range of the POTS line at the expense of the higher frequencies that DSL uses to transmit data.

At this point, the two most commonly used DSL services are HDSL and ADSL. Telephone companies are using HDSL for their own feeder lines, and it can fulfill the same functions as the T1 and E1. For home users, however, ADSL is being marketed as an Internet access solution. The technology is still developing, though, as evidenced by the fact that two competing encoding schemes currently are in use. One is called *DMT (discrete multitone)*, which splits the available frequency range into 256 channels of 4.3125 KHz each, and the other is called *CAP (carrierless amplitude and phase)*, which uses a single channel and a modulation technique called *QAM (quadrature amplitude modulation)*. As with the competing 56 Kbps modem standards of a few years ago, the only real concern for the user is that both ends of the link are using the same technology. Many of the service providers offering ADSL Internet access supply the necessary modem (for sale or lease), so that you are certain of having compatible devices at either end.

The asymmetrical DSL services are suitable for Internet access, but they are not practical for LAN-to-LAN connections. The symmetrical services have the potential for being an excellent alternative to leased lines in the business world, but it remains to be seen whether the technology will gain wide acceptance. Remember that ISDN, too, was originally touted as the technology that would revolutionize the telecommunications industry, and that coup has not yet occurred.

Packet-Switching Services

A *packet-switching service* transmits data between two points by routing packets through the switching network owned by a carrier such as AT&T, MCI, Sprint, or another telephone company. The end result is a high-bandwidth connection similar in performance to a leased line, but the advantage of this type of service is that a single WAN connection at a network site can provide access to multiple remote sites, simply by using different routes through the network. Frame relay and ATM are the two most popular packet-switching services used today. Frame relay is based on variable-length packets called frames, while ATM uses 53-byte cells instead.

The packet-switching service consists of a network of high-speed connections that is sometimes referred to as a *cloud*. Once data arrives at the cloud, the service can route it to a specific destination at high speeds. It is up to the consumers to get their data to the nearest POP connected to the cloud, after which all switching is performed by the carrier. Therefore, an organization setting up WAN connections between remote sites installs a link to an *edge switch* at a local POP using whatever technology provides suitable performance. This local link can take the form of a leased line, ISDN, DSL, or even a dial-up connection. Once the data arrives at the edge switch, it is transmitted through the cloud to an edge switch at another POP, where it is routed on to a private link connecting the cloud to the destination site (see Figure 7-7).

As mentioned earlier, an organization with eight offices scattered around the country needs 28 leased lines to interconnect all of the sites, some of which have to span long distances. In this arrangement, the organization does all of its own switching. Using a packet-switching service instead requires one leased line connecting each site to the service's local POP. Eight leased lines is far cheaper than 28, especially when they span relatively short distances. To get the data where it's going, the carrier programs *virtual circuits (VCs)* from the POP used by each site to each of the seven other POPs. Thus, there are still 28 routes connecting each location to every other location, but the service maintains them, and the client only pays for the bandwidth used.

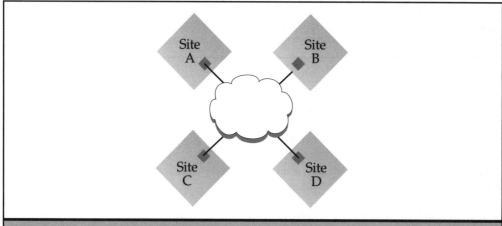

Figure 7-7.   *Packet-switching networks use a network cloud to route data between remote sites*

Unlike a leased line, however, a packet-switching service naturally shares its network among many users. The link between two sites is not permanently assigned a specific bandwidth. In some instances, this can be a drawback, because your links are competing with those of other clients for the same bandwidth. However, you can now contract for a specific bandwidth over a frame-relay network, and ATM is built around a QoS feature that allocates bandwidth for certain types of traffic. In addition, these technologies enable you to alter the bandwidth allotted to your links. Unlike a leased line with a specific bandwidth that you can't exceed, and which you pay for whether you're using it or not, you contract with a packet-switching service to provide a certain amount of bandwidth, which you can exceed during periods of heavy traffic (possibly with an additional charge), and which you increase as your network grows.

Frame Relay

Frame relay has come to be one of the most popular WAN technologies used today, because it provides the high-speed transmissions of leased lines with greater flexibility and lower costs. Frame-relay service operates at the data link layer of the OSI reference model and runs at bandwidths from 56 Kbps to 44.736 Mbps (T3 speed). You negotiate a *committed information rate (CIR)* with a carrier that guarantees you a specific amount of bandwidth, even though you are sharing the network medium with other users. It is possible to exceed the CIR, however, during periods of heavy use, called *bursts*. A burst can be a momentary increase in traffic or a temporary increase of longer duration. Usually, bursts up to a certain bandwidth or duration carry no extra charge, but eventually, additional charges will accrue.

The contract with the service provider also includes a *committed burst information rate (CBIR),* which specifies the maximum bandwidth that is guaranteed to be available during bursts. If you exceed the CBIR, there is a chance that data will be lost. The additional bandwidth provided during a burst may be "borrowed" from your other virtual circuits that aren't operating at full capacity, or even from other clients' circuits. One of the primary advantages of frame relay is that the carrier can dynamically allocate bandwidth to its client connections as needed. In many cases, it is the leased line to the carrier's nearest POP that is the factor limiting bandwidth.

Frame-Relay Hardware

Each site connected to a frame-relay cloud must have a *frame-relay access device (FRAD),* which functions as the interface between the local network and the leased line (or other connection) to the cloud (see Figure 7-8). The FRAD is something like a router, in that it operates at the network layer. The FRAD accepts packets from the LAN that are destined for other networks, strips off the data link–layer protocol header, and packages the datagrams in frames for transmission through the cloud. In the same way, the FRAD processes frames arriving through the cloud and packages them for transmission over the LAN. The difference between a FRAD and a standard router, however, is that the FRAD

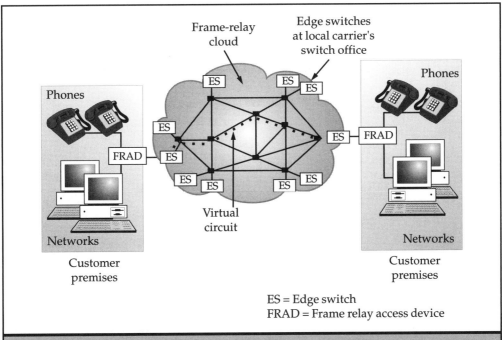

Figure 7-8. *Frame-relay connections use a FRAD to connect a LAN to the cloud*

takes no part in the routing of packets through the cloud; it simply forwards all of the packets from the LAN to the edge switch at the carrier's POP.

The only other hardware element involved in a frame-relay installation is the connection to the nearest POP. In frame relay, the leased line is the most commonly used type of connection. When selecting a carrier, it is important to consider the locations of their POPs in relation to the sites that you want to connect, because the cost of the leased lines (which is not included in the frame-relay contract) depends on their length. The large long-distance carriers usually have the most POPs, scattered over the widest areas, but it is also possible to use different carriers for your sites and create frame-relay links between them.

When installing leased lines, it is important to take into account the number of virtual circuits that will run from the FRAD to your various sites. Unlike the private network composed of separate leased lines to every site, the single leased-line connection between the FRAD and the carrier's edge server will carry all of the WAN data to and from the local network. Multiple VCs will be running from the edge server through the cloud to the other sites, and the leased line from the FRAD will essentially multiplex the traffic from all of those VCs to the LAN, as shown in Figure 7-9. Thus, if you are connecting eight remote sites together with frame-relay WAN links, the leased line at each location should be capable of handling the combined bandwidth of all seven VCs to the other locations.

In most cases, the actual traffic moving across a WAN link does not utilize all of the bandwidth allotted to it at all times. Therefore, it may be possible to create a serviceable WAN by contracting for T1-speed VCs between all eight offices and using T1 leased lines to connect all of the sites to the cloud. Be aware, however, that the leased lines are the only elements of the WAN that are not flexible in their bandwidth. If you find that your WAN

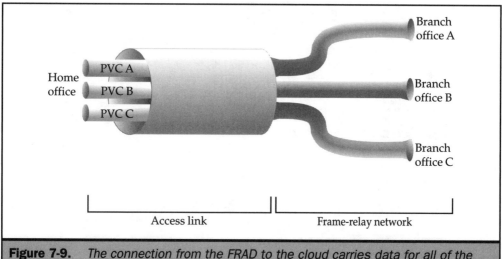

Figure 7-9. *The connection from the FRAD to the cloud carries data for all of the virtual circuits*

NETWORK HARDWARE

traffic exceeds the capacity of the leased line, the only recourse is to augment its bandwidth by installing another connection. This does not necessarily mean installing another T1, however. You can augment to the bandwidth connecting the FRAD to the edge server by adding a fractional T1 or even a dial-up connection that activates during periods of high traffic.

Virtual Circuits

The virtual circuits that are the basis for frame-relay communications come in two types: *permanent virtual circuits (PVCs)* and *switched virtual circuits (SVCs)*. PVCs are routes through the carrier's cloud that are used for the WAN connections between client sites. Unlike standard internetwork routing, PVCs are not dynamic. The frame-relay carrier creates a route through its cloud for a connection between sites, assigns it a unique 10-bit number called a *data link connection identifier (DLCI)*, and programs it into its switches. Programming a FRAD consists of providing it with the DLCIs for all of the PVCs leading to other FRADS. DLCIs are locally significant only; each FRAD has its own DLCI for a particular virtual circuit. Frames passing between two sites always take the same route through the cloud and use the DLCI as a data link–layer address. This is one of the reasons why frame relay is so fast; there is no need to dynamically route the packets through the cloud or establish a new connection before transmitting data.

Each PVC can have its own CIR and CBIR, and despite the description of the VC as permanent, the carrier can modify the route within a matter of hours if one of the sites moves. It is also possible to have the carrier create a PVC for temporary use, such as for a meeting in which a special videoconferencing session is required.

Although it was originally created for data transfers, you can also use frame relay to carry other types of traffic, such as voice or video. This capability is starting to become more popular, but the use of PVCs makes it difficult to implement practically. To set up a voice call or a videoconference between two sites, there has to be a virtual circuit between them. This is easy if the communications are between two of an organization's own sites, which are already connected by a PVC; but to conference with a client or other outside user requires a call to the carrier to set up a new PVC, which can take hours or days. To make applications of this type more practical, carriers are beginning to implement SVCs, as defined in the ITU-T Q.933 document, which are temporary routes through a cloud that are created dynamically as needed.

Frame-Relay Messaging

Frame relay uses two protocols at the data link layer: LAPD for control traffic, and *LAPF (Link Access Procedure for Frame-mode Bearer Services)* for the transfer of user data. The LAPD protocol, the same one used by ISDN (ITU-T Q.921), is used to establish VCs and prepare for the transmission of data. LAPF is used to carry data and for other processes, such as multiplexing and demultiplexing, error detection, and flow control.

The format of the frame used to carry data across a frame-relay cloud is shown in Figure 7-10. The functions of the fields are as follows:

- **Flag, 1 byte**   Contains the binary value 01111110 (or 7E in hexadecimal form) that serves as a delimiter for the frame.

- **Link Info, 2 bytes**   Contains the frame's address and control fields, as follows:

  - **Upper DLCI, 6 bits**   Contains the first 6 bits of the 10-bit DLCI identifying the virtual circuit that the frame will use to reach its destination.

  - **C/R (Command/Response), 1 bit**   Undefined.

  - **EA (Extended Address), 1 bit**   Indicates whether the current byte contains the last bit of the DLCI. The eighth bit of every byte in the Link Info field is an EA bit. When the frames use standard 10-bit DLCIs, the value of this bit will always be 0.

  - **Lower DLCI, 4 bits**   Contains last 4 bits of the 10-bit DLCI identifying the virtual circuit that the frame will use to reach its destination.

  - **FECN (Forward Explicit Congestion Notification), 1 bit**   Indicates that network congestion was encountered in the direction from source to destination.

  - **BECN (Backward Explicit Congestion Notification), 1 bit**   Indicates that network congestion was encountered in the direction from destination to source.

  - **DE (Discard Eligibility), 1 bit**   Indicates that a frame is of lesser importance than the other frames being transmitted and that it can be discarded in the event of network congestion.

  - **EA (Extended Address), 1 bit**   Indicates whether the current byte contains the last bit of the DLCI. When the frames use standard 10-bit DLCIs, the value of this bit will always be 1. The EA field is intended to support the future expansion of frame-relay clouds in which DLCIs longer than 10 bits are needed.

- **Information, variable**   Contains a protocol data unit (PDU) generated by a network-layer protocol, such as an IP datagram. The frame-relay protocols do not modify the contents of this field in any way.

- **FCS (Frame Check Sequence), 2 bytes**   Contains a value computed by the source FRAD that is checked at each switch during the frame's journey through the cloud. Frames in which this value does not match the newly computed value are silently discarded. Detection of the missing frame and retransmission are left to the upper-layer protocols at the end systems.

- **Flag, 1 byte**   Contains the binary value 01111110 (or 7E in hexadecimal form) that serves as a delimiter for the frame.

NETWORK HARDWARE

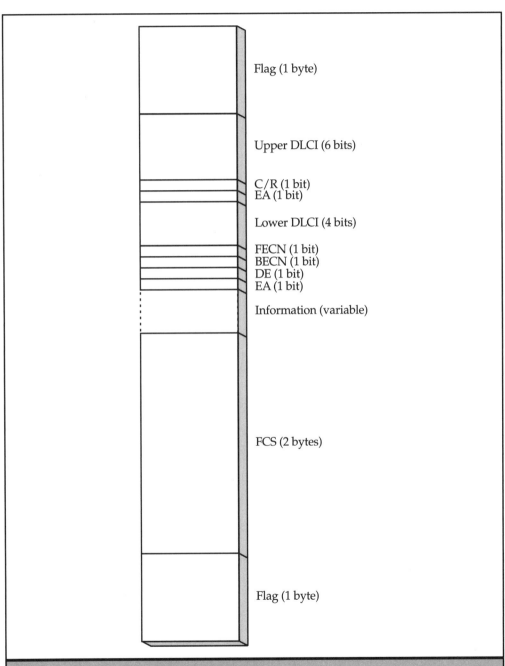

Flag (1 byte)

Upper DLCI (6 bits)

C/R (1 bit)
EA (1 bit)

Lower DLCI (4 bits)

FECN (1 bit)
BECN (1 bit)
DE (1 bit)
EA (1 bit)

Information (variable)

FCS (2 bytes)

Flag (1 byte)

Figure 7-10.   *The frame-relay frame format*

ATM

Asynchronous Transfer Mode differs from frame relay in that it uses uniformly sized cells instead of variable-length frames. This makes it easier to regulate and meter the bandwidth passing over a connection. ATM can also be a complete, high-speed, end-to-end communications solution for data, voice, and video traffic. Unlike frame relay, which you can only use for WAN links, ATM can be a LAN as well as a WAN protocol—meaning that the same cells generated by a workstation can travel to a switch that connects the LAN to an ATM carrier service, through the carrier's ATM cloud, and then to a workstation on the destination network. At no point do the cells have to reach higher than the data link layer of an intermediate system, and transmission speeds through the cloud can reach as high as 2.46 Gbps.

This dramatic potential has not been realized in the real world on a large scale, however. ATM is being used as a high-speed backbone protocol and for WAN connections, but the 25 Mbps ATM LAN solution intended for desktop use has been eclipsed by Fast Ethernet, which runs at 100 Mbps and is far more familiar to the majority of network administrators.

Note *For basic information on the ATM architecture and cell format, see Chapter 10.*

You can use an ATM packet-switching service for your WAN links in roughly the same way as you would use frame relay, by installing a router at your sites and connecting them to the carrier's POPs using leased lines. This process transmits the LAN data to the POP first and then repackages it into cells. It's also possible, however, to install an ATM switch at each remote site, either as part of an ATM backbone or as a separate device providing an interface to the carrier's network (see Figure 7-11). This way, the LAN data is converted to ATM cells at each site before it is transmitted over the WAN.

Like frame relay, ATM supports both PVCs and SVCs; but ATM was designed from the beginning to support voice and video using SVCs, while in frame relay, PVCs and SVCs were a later addition. It is expected that the need to transmit alternative data types like voice and video will become more prevalent in the future, and if this happens, ATM will have an advantage over frame relay because of its greater speed and manageability. However, at this time, frame relay provides a more economical WAN solution running at speeds that are sufficient for standard data networking tasks.

NETWORK HARDWARE

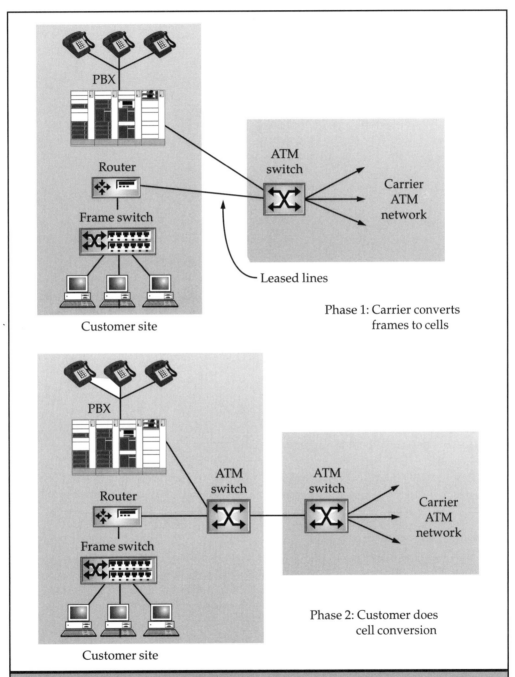

Figure 7-11. *The conversion of LAN data into ATM cells can occur at either the LAN site or the ATM carrier's site*

The Complete Reference

Upgrading & Troubleshooting Networks

Part III

Network Protocols

The Complete Reference

Upgrading & Troubleshooting Networks

Chapter 8

Ethernet

Ethernet is the data link–layer protocol used by the vast majority of the local area networks operating today. In the course of more than 20 years, several different versions of the Ethernet standard have existed, the most recent of which provide dramatic speed increases over the original protocol. Because all the Ethernet variants operate using the same basic principles and because the high-speed Ethernet technologies were designed with backward compatibility in mind, upgrading a standard 10 Mbps network to 100 Mbps or more is relatively easy. This is marked contrast to other high-speed technologies like FDDI and ATM that can require extensive infrastructure modifications, such as new cabling, as well as training and acclimation for the personnel supporting the new technology.

This chapter examines the fundamental Ethernet mechanisms and how they provide a unified interface between the physical layer and multiple protocols operating at the network layer. Then, you learn how newer technologies like Fast Ethernet and Gigabit Ethernet improve on the older standards and provide sufficient bandwidth for the needs of virtually any network application. Finally, there will be a discussion of upgrade strategies and real-world troubleshooting techniques to help you improve the performance of your own network.

Ethernet Defined

The Ethernet protocol provides a unified interface to the network medium that enables an operating system to transmit and receive multiple network-layer protocols simultaneously. Like most data link–layer protocols, Ethernet is, in technical terms, connectionless and unreliable. Ethernet makes its best effort to transmit data to the appointed destination, but no mechanism exists to guarantee a successful delivery. Providing this type of service is left up to the protocols operating at the higher layers of the OSI model, depending on whether the data warrants it.

Note   *In this context, the term "unreliable" means only that the protocol lacks a means of acknowledging that packets have been successfully received. For more information on protocol-related technical terms like "connectionless" and "unreliable," see Chapter 2.*

The Ethernet specifications define the protocol as consisting of three essential components:

- A series of physical-layer guidelines that specify the cable types and wiring restrictions for Ethernet networks

- A frame format the defines the order and functions of the bits transmitted in a Ethernet packet

- A media access control (MAC) mechanism called Carrier Sense Multiple Access with Collision Detection

From a product perspective, the Ethernet protocol is realized as the network interface cards you install in your computers, the network adapter drivers the operating system uses to communicate with the NICs, and the hubs you use to connect the computers together. When you purchase NICs and hubs, you must be sure they all support the same Ethernet standards for them to be able to work together.

Ethernet Standards

As it was first designed in the 1970s, Ethernet carried data over a baseband connection using coaxial cable running at 10 Mbps (megabits per second) and a signaling system called Manchester Encoding. This eventually came to be known as *thick Ethernet* because the cable itself was approximately one centimeter wide, about the thickness of a garden hose (indeed, its color and rigidity led to its being called "frozen yellow garden hose"). The first Ethernet standard was published in 1980 by a consortium of companies including DEC, Intel, and Xerox, giving rise to the acronym DIX.

Ethernet II

The DIX Ethernet II standard was published in 1982 and expanded the physical-layer options to include a thinner type of coaxial cable, which came to be called *thin Ethernet, ThinNet,* or *Cheapernet,* because it was less expensive than the original thick coaxial cable.

IEEE 802.3

During this time, a desire arose to build an international standard around the Ethernet protocol, but Xerox had trademarked the name Ethernet and building an international standard around a technology wholly controlled by a private company made no sense. As a result, a working group was formed in 1980 by a standards-making body called the Institute of Electrical and Electronics Engineers (IEEE) for the purpose of developing an "Ethernet-like" standard. This group was given a designation of IEEE 802.3 and the resulting standard, published in 1985, was called the "IEEE 802.3 Carrier Sense Multiple Access with Collision Detection (CSMA/CD) Access Method and Physical Layer Specifications." With a few minor differences, this document defined an Ethernet network under another name and, to this day, the products we refer to as Ethernet actually conform to the IEEE 802.3 standard.

While the Ethernet II standard treats the data link layer as a single entity, the IEEE standards divide the layer into two sublayers, called *logical link control (LLC)* and *media access control (MAC)*. The logical link control layer isolates the functions that occur beneath it from those above it, and is defined by a separate standard: IEEE 802.2. The IEEE committee uses the same abstraction layer with the network types defined by other 802 standards, such as the 802.5 Token Ring network. The media access control layer defines the mechanism by which Ethernet systems arbitrate access to the network medium, as discussed in the forthcoming section "CSMA/CD."

By 1990, the IEEE 802.3 standard had been developed further and now included other physical-layer options that abandoned coaxial cable entirely in favor of the twisted-pair cable commonly used in telephone installations and fiber-optic cable. Because it is easy to work with, inexpensive, and reliable, twisted-pair (or 10BaseT) Ethernet quickly became the most popular medium for this protocol. Most of the Ethernet networks installed today use twisted-pair cable, which continues to be supported by the new, higher-speed standards. Fiber-optic technology enables network connections to span far longer distances than copper and is immune from electromagnetic interference.

The differences between the IEEE 802.3 standard and the DIX Ethernet II standard are listed in the following table:

	IEEE 802.3	**DIX Ethernet II**
Physical-Layer Options	Coaxial, UTP, fiber-optic	Coaxial only
Bits 13–14 of the Frame Header	Length of the data field	Ethertype
External Transceiver Test	SQE Test	Collision presence test (Heartbeat)

The Fast Ethernet standard was published as IEEE 802.3u in 1995 and increases the speed of the network tenfold, to 100 Mbps, using either twisted-pair or fiber-optic cable. The newest Ethernet variant, called Gigabit Ethernet, is defined in IEEE 802.3z and increases the network speed by another ten times to 1,000 Mbps, or 1 Gbps.

CSMA/CD

The most definitive property of an Ethernet network is its media access control mechanism, which is called *Carrier Sense Multiple Access with Collision Detection,* or CSMA/CD. Like any MAC method, CSMA/CD enables the computers on the network to share a single baseband medium without data loss. There are no priorities on an Ethernet network, as far as media access is concerned; the protocol is designed so that every node has equal access rights to the network medium.

When a node on an Ethernet network wants to transmit data, it first monitors the network medium to see if it is currently in use. This is the *carrier sense* phase of the process. If the node detects traffic on the network, it pauses for a short interval and then listens to the network again. Once the network is clear, any of the nodes on the network may use it to transmit their data. This is the *multiple access* phase. This mechanism in itself arbitrates access to the medium, but it is not without fault.

It is entirely possible for two (or more) systems to detect a clear network and then transmit their data at nearly the same moment. This results in what the IEEE specifications call a *signal quality error (SQE)* or, as the condition is more commonly known, a *collision.* Collisions occur when one system transmits data and another system performs its carrier sense in the brief interval before the first bit in the transmitted packet reaches it (see Figure 8-1). This interval is known as the *contention time* or *slot time,* because each of the systems involved believes it has begun to transmit first. Every

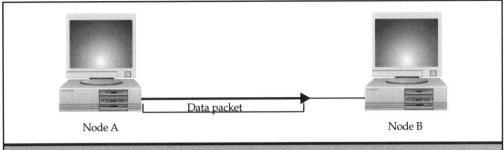

Figure 8-1. *Node A has begun to transmit its data, but since the beginning of the packet has not yet reached Node B, Node B senses the network as being clear. If Node B begins to transmit at this moment, a collision will occur*

node on the network is, therefore, always in one of three possible states: transmission, contention, or idle.

When packets from two different nodes collide, an abnormal condition is created on the cable that travels on toward both systems. On a coaxial network, the voltage level spike to the point at which it is the same or greater than the combined levels of the two transmitters (+/− 0.85v). On a twisted-pair or fiber-optic network, the anomaly takes the form of signal activity on both the transmit and receive circuits at the same time.

When each transmitting system detects the abnormality, it recognizes that a collision has taken place, immediately stops sending data, and begins taking action to correct the problem. This is the *collision detection* phase of the process. Because the packets that collided are considered corrupted, both the systems involved transmit a *jam pattern* to the rest of the network that fills the entire cable with voltage, informing the other systems on the network of the collision and preventing them from transmitting.

The jam pattern is a sequence of 32 bits that can have any value, as long as it does not equal the value of the cyclical redundancy check (CRC) field in the damaged packet. A system receiving an Ethernet packet uses the CRC field (or *checksum*) to determine if the data in the packet has been received without error. As long as the jam pattern differs from the correct CRC value, all receiving nodes will discard the packet. In most cases, network adapters simply transmit 32 bits with the value 1. The odds of this also being the value of the CRC for the packet are 1 in 2^{32}, in other words, not likely.

After transmitting the jam pattern, the nodes involved in the collision both reschedule their transmissions, using a randomized delay interval they calculate with an algorithm that uses their MAC addresses as a unique factor. This process is called *backing off*. Because both nodes perform their own independent backoff calculations, the chances of them both retransmitting at the same time are substantially diminished. This is a possibility, however, and if another collision occurs between the same two nodes, they both increase the possible length of their delay intervals and back off again.

As the number of possible values for the backoff interval increases, the probability of the systems again selecting the same interval diminishes. The Ethernet specifications call this process *truncated binary exponential backoff* (or *truncated BEB*). An Ethernet system will attempt to transmit a packet as many as 16 times and, if a collision results each time, the packet is discarded.

Collisions

Every system on an Ethernet network uses this MAC mechanism for every packet it transmits, so the entire process obviously occurs quickly. Most of the collisions that occur on a typical Ethernet network are resolved in microseconds (millionths of a second). The most important thing to understand when it comes to Ethernet media arbitration is that *packet collisions are natural and expected occurrences on this type of network, and they do not necessarily signify a problem.* If you use some type of network monitoring tool to analyze the traffic on an Ethernet network, you will see that a certain number of collisions always occur.

The type of packet collision described here is normal and expected, but there is a different type, called a "late collision," that signifies a serious network problem. See the next section, "Late Collisions," for more information.

Packet collisions only become a problem when there are too many of them and significant network delays begin to accumulate. The combination of the backoff intervals and the retransmission of the packets themselves (sometimes more than once) incurs delays that are multiplied by the number of packets transmitted by each computer and by the number of computers on the network.

The fundamental fault of the CSMA/CD mechanism is that the more traffic there is on the network, the more collisions there are likely to be. The utilization of a network is based on the number of systems connected to it and the amount of data they send and receive over the network. When expressed as a percentage, the network utilization represents the proportion of the time the network is actually in use, that is, the amount of time data is actually in transit. On an average Ethernet network, the utilization is likely to be somewhere in the 30 to 40 percent range. When the utilization increases to approximately 80 percent, the number of collisions increases to the point at which the performance of the network noticeably degrades. In the most extreme case, known as a *collapse,* the network is so heavily trafficked, it is almost perpetually in a state of contention, that is, waiting for collisions to be resolved. This condition can conceivably be caused by the coincidental occurrence of repeated collisions, but it is more likely to result from a malfunctioning network interface that is continuously transmitting bad frames without pausing for carrier sense or collision detection. An adapter in this state is said to be jabbering.

> **Note** *Data link–layer protocols that use a token-passing media-access control mechanism, like Token Ring and FDDI, are not subject to performance degradation cause by high-network traffic levels. This is because these protocols use a mechanism in which only one system on the network is permitted to transmit at any one time. On networks like these, collisions are not normal occurrences and can be a signal of a serious problem.*

Because of the possible performance degradation at high traffic levels, planning the expansion of Ethernet networks carefully is important, to prevent the network utilization from getting too high. When traffic levels become excessive, the use of switches or other connecting devices that separate a network into multiple collision domains is preferable to expansion using simple repeating hubs that propagate all the incoming traffic to the entire network.

> **Note** *For more information on expanding a network in this way, see Chapter 6.*

Late Collisions

The physical-layer specifications for the Ethernet protocol are designed so that the first 64 bytes of every packet transmission completely fill the entire aggregate length of cable in the collision domain. Thus, by the time a node has transmitted the first 64 bytes of a packet, every other node on the network has received at least the first bit of that packet. At this point, the other nodes will not transmit their own data because their carrier sense mechanism has detected traffic on the network.

It is essential for the first bit of each transmitted packet to arrive at every node on the network before the last bit leaves the sender. This is because the transmitting system can only detect a collision while it is still transmitting data. Once the last bit has left the sending node, the sender considers the transmission to have completed successfully and erases the packet from the memory buffer. To ensure this occurs, every packet transmitted on an Ethernet network must be at least 64 bytes in length, even if the sending system has to pad it with useless (0) bits to reach that length.

If a collision should occur after the last bit has left the sending node, it is called a *late collision*, or sometimes an *out-of-window collision* (see Figure 8-2). (To distinguish the two types of collisions, the normally occurring type is sometimes called an *early collision*.) Because the sending system has no way of detecting a late collision, it considers the packet to have been transmitted successfully. Any data lost as a result of a late transmission cannot be retransmitted by a data link–layer process. It is up to the protocols operating at higher layers of the OSI model to detect the data loss and to use their own mechanisms to force a retransmission. This process can take up to 100 times longer than an Ethernet retransmission, which is one reason why this type of collision is a problem.

Late collisions can result from several different causes. If a network interface should malfunction and transmit a packet less than 64 bytes long (called a *runt*), the last bit

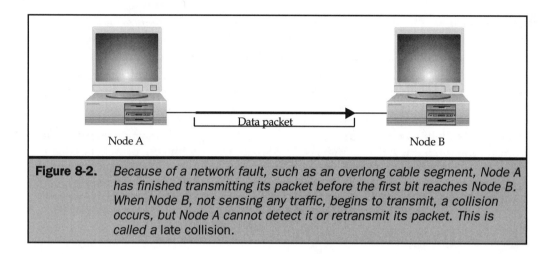

Figure 8-2.   *Because of a network fault, such as an overlong cable segment, Node A has finished transmitting its packet before the first bit reaches Node B. When Node B, not sensing any traffic, begins to transmit, a collision occurs, but Node A cannot detect it or retransmit its packet. This is called a* late collision.

could leave the sender before the packet has fully propagated around the net. In other cases, a NIC's carrier sense mechanism might fail, causing it to transmit at the wrong time.

Another possible cause is a network that does not fall within the Ethernet cabling guidelines. If cable segments are too long or if there are too many repeaters on the network, the signal propagation delay can increase beyond the 600 nanoseconds specified in the Ethernet specification as the maximum time allowed for a transmission between two systems.

Late collisions are not an ordinary occurrence on an Ethernet network. They are, rather, a sign that a serious problem exists that should be addressed immediately.

The Capture Effect

The existence of collisions as a regular occurrence on Ethernet networks can have deep and complex repercussions on the way in which the network operates. Theoretically, every system on an Ethernet network has equal access to the network medium at any given time. In practice, however, this has been found not to be so at certain times. When two nodes with a series of packets to transmit experience a collision, it is possible for one of the two to monopolize the network medium for the duration of its transmissions. This is known as the *capture effect*.

After the first collision, one of the two nodes wins the contention and successfully retransmits its packet. This system then proceeds to try to transmit the second packet in its sequence, while the other node is still trying to transmit its first. If a second collision occurs, one system backs off for the first time, while the other performs its second backoff using the truncated BEB mechanism. Statistically, the second system is more likely to lose this contention because it is selecting a backoff interval from a larger group of delay periods.

For a simplified example, the first system selects a backoff interval of either 1 or 2 milliseconds because it is backing off for the first time. However, the system backing off for the second time must select 1, 2, 3, or 4 seconds because the truncated BEB mechanism expands the pool of possible intervals with each successive backoff. The laws of probability dictate that the second system is likely to select a longer backoff interval than the first and lose the second contention. If the same system loses the second contention as well, then its pool of possible backoff intervals will increase even more, as will the likelihood of its losing yet another contention.

Thus, the first system, because it is continually transmitting new packets for the first time, has captured the network medium and prevented the second system from transmitting.

The ramifications of the capture effect on the network are, in most cases, not even detectable. The likelihood of this phenomenon occurring to the degree that it has a palpable effect on network performance is minimal, but the theory behind the capture effect is an excellent illustration of how complex the system interactions can be on a network. To the members of the IEEE 802 committee, however, the problem was worth exploring. They convened a working group (IEEE 802.3w) to develop a specification for an alternate backoff algorithm called the *Binary Logarithmic Arbitration Method (BLAM)*.

BLAM resolves the capture effect problem by incrementing the collision counters on every network node symmetrically. Whenever a collision occurs, all the systems on the network modify their backoff interval selection algorithm in the same way, unlike the truncated BEB method, which is asymmetrical. This and other modifications resulted in an adequate solution to the problem, but the committee eventually decided to disband the group and declined to submit the BLAM document for standardization.

This decision was as much political as it was technical. The committee felt that an actual occurrence of the capture effect problem was only a remote possibility to begin with and that updating the Ethernet standard to address it implied that the problem was more serious than it actually was. In addition, the increasing popularity of switched and full-duplex Ethernet solutions had largely rendered the issue moot.

Full-Duplex Ethernet

The CSMA/CD media access control mechanism is the defining element of the Ethernet protocol, but it is also the source of many of its limitations. The fundamental shortcoming of the Ethernet protocol is that data can travel only in one direction at a time. This is known as *half-duplex* operation. With special hardware, it is also possible to run Ethernet connections in *full-duplex* mode, meaning that the device can transmit and receive data simultaneously.

Full-duplex Ethernet is possible only on link segments that have separate channels for the communications in each direction. This means that twisted-pair and fiber-optic are supported in both regular and Fast Ethernet, but not coaxial cable. Because both of the systems in a full-duplex link can transmit and receive data at the same time, there is no possibility of collisions occurring. Because no collisions occur, the cabling restrictions intended to support the collision detection mechanism are not needed.

This is a particularly important point on a Fast Ethernet network using fiber-optic cable because the collision detection mechanism is responsible for its relatively short maximum segment lengths. While a half-duplex 100BaseFX link between two devices can only be a maximum of 412 meters long, the same link operating in full-duplex mode can be up to 2,000 meters long because it is restricted only by the strength of the signal. The signal attenuation on twisted-pair networks, however (that is, the tendency of the signal to weaken as it travels over the medium), makes them still subject to the 100-meter segment length restriction.

Full-duplex Ethernet capabilities are usually provided in Fast Ethernet switches or multiport bridges. This is because the device functioning as the network's hub must have the capability to buffer frames if the link to a destination device is currently in use. Simple repeating hubs are usually not designed with this capability. Running standard Ethernet 10BaseT and fiber-optic links in full-duplex mode is also possible, but this is generally not a practical solution. If you are going to upgrade your hardware to full duplex, why not go to Fast Ethernet as well?

Physical-Layer Guidelines

The Ethernet specifications define not only the types of cable you can use with the protocol, but also the installation guidelines for the cable, such as the maximum length of cable segments and the number of hubs or repeaters permitted. As explained earlier, the configuration of the physical-layer medium is a crucial element of the CSMA/CD media access control mechanism. If the overall distance between two systems on the network is too long, diminished performance can result, which is quite difficult to diagnose and troubleshoot.

Standard 10 Mbps Ethernet can run on four different media configurations, as shown in Table 8-1. The cabling guidelines vary for each of the media to compensate for the performance characteristics of the different cable types.

Note	*The designations used to describe the various Ethernet physical-layer options are based on a shorthand that describes the basic properties of the network. For example, thick Ethernet is known as 10Base5 because it runs at 10 Mbps, uses baseband communications, and has a maximum possible segment length of 500 (5 × 100) meters. This Ethernet differs only in that it uses a thinner cable with a maximum segment length of 185 meters (which is rounded up to 200 for the sake of the abbreviation). The T in 10BaseT specifies that the network uses twisted-pair cable instead of coaxial, and the F in 10BaseF for fiber-optic. The Fast Ethernet standard uses the same type of designations for the four physical-layer configurations it supports, as discussed in "Fast Ethernet," later in this chapter.*

Thick Ethernet

Thick Ethernet, or *ThickNet*, uses RG8 coaxial cable in a bus topology to connect up to 100 nodes to a single segment no more than 500 meters long. Both ends of the bus must

	Thick Ethernet	Thin Ethernet	Twisted-Pair	Fiber-Optic
Designation	10Base5	10Base2	10BaseT	10BaseFL
Maximum Segment Length	500 meters	185 meters	100 meters	1,000/2,000 meters
Maximum Nodes per Cable Segment	100	30	2	2
Cable Type	RG8 coaxial	RG58 coaxial	Category 3 unshielded twisted-pair	62.5/125 multimode fiber
Connector Type	N	BNC	RJ-45	ST

Table 8-1. *Physical-Layer Options for Standard Ethernet*

be terminated with a 50 ohm resistor and the cable should be grounded in one (and only one) place. Although it is hardly ever used anymore, the components of a ThickNet network are a good illustration of the various elements involved in the physical layer of an Ethernet network.

Note *The maximum of 100 nodes on a ThickNet cable segment (and 30 nodes on a ThinNet segment) is based on the number of MAUs present on the network. Because repeaters include their own MAUs, they count toward the maximum.*

The coaxial cable segment should, whenever possible, be a single unbroken length of cable or at least be pieced together from the same spool or cable lot using N connectors. There should be as few breaks as possible in the cable; and if you must use cable from different lots, the individual pieces should be 23.4, 70.2, or 117 meters long, to minimize the signal reflections that may occur.

Unlike all the other Ethernet physical-layer options, the ThickNet cable does not run directly to the network interface card in the PC. This is because the coaxial cable itself is large, heavy, and comparatively inflexible. Instead, the NIC is connected to the cable with another cable, called the *attachment unit interface (AUI)* cable (see Figure 8-3). The AUI cable has 15-pin D-shell connectors at both ends, one of which plugs directly into the NIC, and the other into a *medium attachment unit (MAU)*. The MAU connects to the coaxial cable, using a device called the *medium dependent interface (MDI)* that clamps to the cable and makes an electrical connection through holes but into the insulating

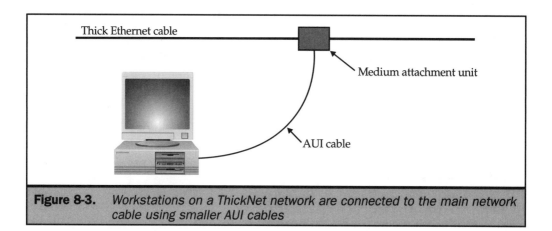

Figure 8-3.   *Workstations on a ThickNet network are connected to the main network cable using smaller AUI cables*

sheath. Because of the fang-like appearance of the connector, this device is commonly referred to as a *vampire tap*.

> **Note**   *The DIX Ethernet standard, if nothing else, should be remembered for using more sensible names for many of the various Ethernet elements, such as "collision" rather than "signal quality error." The DIX Ethernet name for the medium attachment unit is the* transceiver *(because it both transmits and receives) and its name for the attachment unit interface is the* transceiver cable.

Each standard AUI cable on a ThickNet network can be up to 50 meters long, which provides for an added degree of flexibility for the installation. Standard AUI cables are the same thickness as the thick Ethernet coaxial and similarly hard to work with; there are also thinner and more flexible "office grade" AUI cables, but these are limited to a maximum length of 12.5 meters.

The 500-meter maximum length for the ThickNet cable makes it possible to connect systems at comparatively long distances and provides excellent protection against interference and attenuation. Unfortunately, the cable is difficult to work with and even harder to hide. Virtually no new ThickNet networks are being installed today. Sites that require long cable segments or better insulation are now more likely to use fiber-optic, which exceeds the performance of thick Ethernet in almost every way. In addition, coaxial cable (both thick and thin) is limited to the 10 Mbps speed of the standard Ethernet specification.

Thin Ethernet

Thin Ethernet, or *ThinNet*, is similar in functionality to ThickNet, except that the cable itself is RG58 coaxial, about 5 millimeters in diameter, and much more flexible. For ThinNet (and all other Ethernet physical-layer options except ThickNet), the MAU (transceiver) is integrated into the network interface card and no AUI cable is needed.

Note *Some NICs contain both AUI connectors for ThickNet and BNC or RJ-45 connectors for ThinNet or 10BaseT. Although this type of card contains an on-board MAU, the circuit to the AUI connector bypasses it, so you must use a standard external MAU for ThickNet connections.*

ThinNet uses BNC (Bayonet-Neill-Concelman) connectors and a fitting called a *T-connector* that attaches to the network card in the PC. You create the network bus by running a cable to one end of the T-connector and then using another cable on the other end to connect to the next system (see Figure 8-4). The two systems at the ends of the bus must have a 50-ohm resistor on one end of their Ts to terminate the bus and one end (only) should be grounded.

Caution *The T-connectors on an Ethernet network must be directly connected to the network interface cards in the computers. Having a length of cable joining the T-connector to the computer is not permitted. The Ethernet standard calls for the distance from the MDI (built into the NIC) to the coaxial cable to be no more than 4 centimeters. Exceeding this length can cause signal reflections that damage packets, forcing them to be retransmitted by the higher-layer protocols. If you use these illegal "stub" cables, your network may seem to function properly, but the constant need for retransmissions can seriously degrade the performance of the network.*

Because the cable is thinner, ThinNet is more prone to interference and attenuation, and is, therefore, limited to a segment length of 185 meters and a maximum of 30 nodes. Each piece of cable forming the segment must be at least 0.5 meters long.

Thin Ethernet is easier to work with than the thick variety and it rapidly became the medium of choice for business Ethernet LANs. Both thick and thin Ethernet suffer from a failing common to all bus networks, however. If there is a break or a faulty connection anywhere on the bus, then the network is effectively split into two segments that cannot access each other. This is similar to the "Christmas light effect," where one blown bulb causes an entire string of lights to fail.

This is not an uncommon occurrence because the BNC connectors used to attach the cables together are notoriously sensitive to improper treatment. An accidental tug or a person tripping over one of the two cables connected to each machine can easily weaken the connection and cause intermittent transmission problems that are difficult to isolate and diagnose.

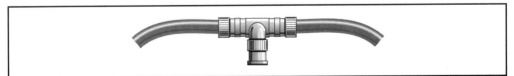

Figure 8-4. *Thin Ethernet networks use T-connectors to form a single cable segment connecting up to 30 computers in a bus topology*

Note however, that for this to occur, the problem must be in the cable or one of the T-connectors, not in the computer. You can safely shut off a system that lies in the middle of the bus without disturbing network communications between the other systems.

Twisted-Pair Ethernet

Most of the Ethernet networks today use *unshielded twisted-pair (UTP) cable,* also known as *10BaseT,* which solves several of the problems that plague coaxial cables. Among other things, UTP Ethernet networks are

- **Easily hidden** UTP cables can be installed inside walls, floors, and ceilings with standard wall plates providing access to the network. Only a single, thin cable has to run to the computer.

- **Fault tolerant** UTP networks use a star topology in which each computer has its own dedicated cable run to the hub. A break in a cable or a loose connection affects only the single machine to which it is connected.

- **Upgradable** A UTP cable installation running 10 Mbps Ethernet now can be upgraded to 100 Mbps Fast Ethernet, or possibly even Gigabit Ethernet, at a later time.

Unshielded twisted-pair cable consists of four pairs of wires in a single sheath, with each pair twisted together at regular intervals to protect against crosstalk and 8-pin RJ-45 connectors at both ends. Standard Ethernet uses only two of the four pairs, however, one pair for transmitting data signals (TD) and one for receiving them (RD), with one wire in each pair having a positive polarity and one a negative. The pin assignments for the connectors are shown in Table 8-2.

Pin	Pair	Polarity	Signal	Designation
1	1	Positive	Transmit	TD+
2	1	Negative	Transmit	TD–
3	2	Positive	Receive	RD+
4	3		Unused	
5	3		Unused	
6	2	Negative	Receive Data	RD–
7	4		Unused	
8	4		Unused	

Table 8-2.   *RJ-45 Pin Assignments for 10BaseT Networks*

Unlike coaxial networks, 10BaseT calls for the use of a *hub*, which is a device that functions both as a wiring nexus and as a signal repeater, to which each of the nodes on the network has an individual connection (see Figure 8-5). The maximum length for each cable segment is 100 meters but, because there is always an intervening hub, the total distance between two nodes can be as much as 200 meters.

UTP cables are typically wired *straight through*, meaning the wire for each pin is connected to the corresponding pin at the other end of the cable. For two nodes to communicate, however, the TD signals generated by each machine must be delivered to the RD connections in the other machine. In most cases, this is accomplished by a crossover circuit within the hub. You can connect two computers directly together without a hub by using a *crossover cable*, though, which connects the TD signals at each end to the RD signals at the other end.

 For more information on network cables and their installation, see Chapter 4. For more information on hubs and repeaters, see Chapter 5.

Fiber-Optic Ethernet

Fiber-optic cable is a radical departure from the copper-based physical-layer options discussed so far. Because it uses pulses of light instead of electric current, fiber-optic is immune to electromagnetic interference and is much more resistant to attenuation than copper. As a result, fiber-optic cable can span much longer distances and, because of

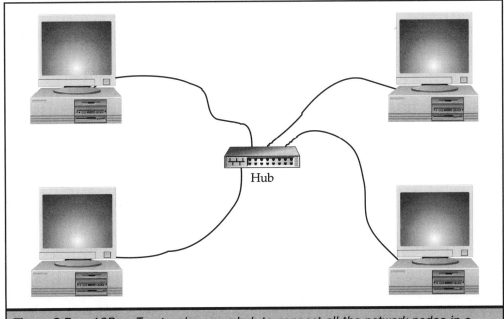

Figure 8-5. *10BaseT networks use a hub to connect all the network nodes in a star topology*

the electric isolation it provides, it is suitable for network links between buildings. Fiber-optic cable is an excellent medium for data communications; but installing and maintaining it is somewhat more expensive than copper, and it requires completely different tools and skills.

The network medium itself is two strands of 62.5/125 multimode fiber cable with one strand used to transmit and one to receive.

Two main fiber-optic standards exist for 10 Mbps Ethernet: the original FOIRL standard and 10BaseF, which defines three different fiber-optic configurations called 10BaseFL, 10BaseFB, and 10BaseFP. Of all these standards, 10BaseFL was the most popular, but running fiber-optic cable at 10 Mbps is a criminal underuse of the medium. Now that 100 Mbps data link–layer protocols, like Fast Ethernet and FDDI, run on the same fiber-optic cable, there is no reason to use any of these slower solutions in a new installation.

FOIRL   The original fiber-optic standard for Ethernet from the early 1980s was called the *Fiber-Optic Inter-Repeater Link (FOIRL)* and was designed to function as a link between two repeaters up to 1,000 meters away. Intended for use in campus networks, FOIRL can join two distant networks, particularly those in adjacent buildings, using a fiber-optic cable.

10BaseFL   The 10BaseF standard was developed by the IEEE 802.3 committee to provide a greater variety of fiber-optic alternatives for Ethernet networks. Designed with backward compatibility in mind, 10BaseFL is the IEEE counterpart to FOIRL, increases the maximum length of a fiber-optic link to 2,000 meters, and permits connections between two repeaters, two computers, or a computer and a repeater.

 If you are using any old FOIRL hardware on a 10BaseFL network, you should limit the maximum segment length to 1,000 meters.

As in all of the 10BaseF specifications, a computer connects to the network using an external fiber-optic MAU (or FOMAU) and an AUI cable up to 25 meters long. The other end of the cable connects to a fiber-optic repeating hub that provides the same basic functions as a hub for copper segments.

10BaseFB   10BaseFB is intended as a backbone cabling solution that connects hubs over distances up to 2,000 meters. By using synchronous signaling 10BaseFB hubs, you can safely exceed the number of repeaters permitted on an Ethernet network.

The other Ethernet standards used for links between repeaters (such as 10BaseFL and 10BaseT) keep their connections active through the use of an idle signal that is asynchronous with the normal packet transmissions. 10BaseFB's 2.5 MHz square wave idle signal, on the other hand, uses the same clock as the packet transmissions and, therefore, is said to be synchronous with them. Because the receiver of a communication is continuously locked to the transmitter's signal, no bits are stripped off at the beginning of the packet by the asynchronous squelching circuit in the receiver's MAU (transceiver).

Synchronous signaling means the *inter-packet gap* (that is, the brief interval between packets traveling over the network) is not varied nearly as much by a 10BaseFB repeater as it can be by other repeater types. A standard repeater can shrink the inter-packet gap by as much as 8 bits, while with a synchronous signaling repeater that variability is reduced to only 2 bits. Because of this reduction in the input to output variability, there can be up to 12 10BaseFB hubs on the transmission path between two nodes, rather than the normal Ethernet maximum of 4.

10BaseFB also has a remote data link–layer diagnostics capability, provided by a special RF (remote fault) signal that a hub uses in place of the standard idle signal when it detects a problem. This ensures that the hubs on both sides of a transmission are aware when a fault occurs. Without the RF signal, a cable or interface problem that disrupts communications on one of the two fiber strands will be undetected by the hub that transmits data using that strand. The transmitting hub will send its data and receive nothing in return but the idle signal. The other hub will detect the fault, however, because it receives neither data nor the idle signal from the other end of the link. When this happens, the hub realizing the problem changes its idle signal to the RF signal, informing the other hub of the problem.

Because 10BaseFB is used only for backbone connections between hubs, there is no need for external MAUs or AUI cables, and hubs can connect directly together using standard fiber-optic cable.

10BaseFB is an excellent long-distance backbone technology, but it suffers from the same 10 Mbps speed limitation as all of the 10BaseF standards. By replacing the hubs, it is possible to upgrade a 10BaseFB connection to 100BaseFX and gain a tenfold speed increase.

Note   *For more information on upgrading Ethernet networks to Fast Ethernet, see "Upgrading an Ethernet Network," later in this chapter.*

10BaseFP   10BaseFP defines a fiber network that uses a passive (that is, nonrepeating) star coupler to connect up to 33 workstations with segments up to 500 meters long. Intended as the 10BaseF element that would deliver fiber-optic to the desktop, this part of the specification was never adopted in a big way. A few products are still available, but the market for this technology, if it ever really existed, is all but gone.

Cabling Guidelines

In addition to the minimum and maximum segment lengths for the various types of Ethernet media, the standards also impose limits on the number of repeaters you can use in a single collision domain. This is necessary to ensure that every packet transmitted by an Ethernet node begins to reach its destination before the last bit leaves the sender. If the distance traveled by a packet is too long, the sender is unable to detect collisions reliably and data loss can occur.

LINK SEGMENTS AND MIXING SEGMENTS   When defining the limits on the number of repeaters allowed on the network, the Ethernet standards distinguish between two types of cable segments, called link segments and mixing segments. A *link segment* is a length of cable that joins only two nodes, while a *mixing segment* joins more than two.

In the real world, this distinction has largely disappeared because the vast majority of Ethernet networks use only link segments. All twisted-pair networks, for example, use only link segments because each node has its own dedicated cable leading to the hub. The same is true of 10BaseFL and 10BaseFB. The only types of Ethernet networks that employ mixing segments are the coaxial-based media, thick Ethernet and thin Ethernet, and 10BaseFP, which uses a hub that is passive and provides no repeater function. Because all three of these network types are seldom used today except on legacy installations, you can consider most Ethernet networks as composed only of link segments.

THE 5-4-3 RULE   The Ethernet standard states that, in a single Ethernet collision domain, the route taken between any two nodes on the network can consist of no more than *five* cable segments, joined by *four* repeaters, and only *three* of the segments can be mixing segments. This is known as the *Ethernet 5-4-3 rule*. This rule is manifested in different ways, depending on the type of cable used for the network medium.

Note	*A collision domain is defined as a network configuration on which two nodes transmitting data at the same time will cause a collision. The use of switches or intelligent hubs, instead of standard repeaters, does not extend the collision domain and does not fall under the Ethernet 5-4-3 rule. If you have a network that has reached its maximum size because of this rule, you should consider using a switch or similar device to create separate collision domains. See Chapters 5 and 6 for more information.*

On a coaxial network, whether it is thick or thin Ethernet, you can have five cable segments joined by four repeaters. On a coaxial network, a repeater has only two ports and does nothing but amplify the signal as it travels over the cable. A segment is the length of cable between two repeaters, even though in the case of thin Ethernet the segment can consist of many separate lengths of cable. This rule means the overall length of a thick Ethernet bus (called the *maximum collision domain diameter*) can be 2,500 meters (500 × 5) while a thin Ethernet bus can be up to 925 meters (185 × 5).

On either of these networks, however, only three of the cable segments can actually have nodes connected to them (see Figure 8-6). Thus, you can use the two link segments to join mixing segments located at some distance from each other, but you cannot populate them with computers or other devices.

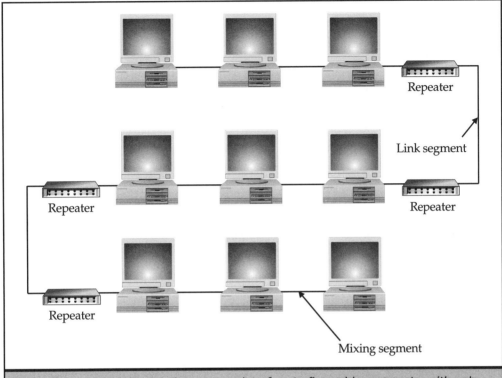

Figure 8-6. *Coaxial networks can consist of up to five cable segments, with only three of the five connected to computers or other devices*

On a UTP network, the situation is different. Because the repeaters on this type of network are actually multiport hubs, every cable segment connecting a node to the hub is a link segment. You can, therefore, have four hubs in a collision domain that are connected to each other and each of which can be connected to as many nodes as the hub can support (see Figure 8-7). Because data traveling from one node to any other node passes through only four hubs and because all the segments are link segments, the network is in compliance with the Ethernet standard.

One potentially complicating factor to this arrangement is when you connect 10BaseT hubs using thin Ethernet coaxial cable. Many of these hubs include BNC connectors that enable you to use a bus to chain multiple hubs together. When you do this with more than two hubs connected by a single coaxial segment, you are actually creating a mixing segment and you must count this toward the maximum of three mixing segments permitted on the network.

On a network that uses coaxial cable only to connect 10BaseT hubs together, this won't be a problem because you can't have more than one mixing segment when you

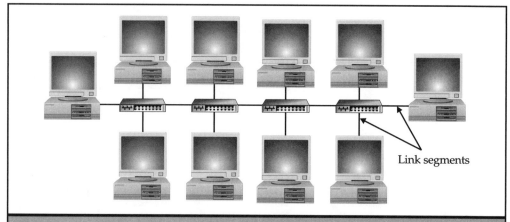

Link segments

Figure 8-7.   *Twisted-pair networks use link segments to connect to the computers, making it possible to have four populated hubs*

only have four hubs. If part of your network uses coaxial cable (either thick or thin Ethernet) to connect to nodes on its own mixing segments, however, you must count the bus connecting the 10BaseT hubs as one of the maximum of three allowed by the standard.

The 10BaseF specifications include some modifications to the 5-4-3 rule. When five cable segments are present on a 10BaseF network connected by four repeaters, FOIRL, 10BaseFL, and 10BaseFB segments can be no more than 500 meters long. 10BaseFP segments can be no more than 300 meters long.

When four cable segments are connected by three repeaters, FOIRL, 10BaseFL, and 10BaseFB segments can be no more than 1,000 meters long and 10BaseFP segments can be no more than 700 meters long. Cable segments connecting a node to a repeater can be no more than 400 meters for 10BaseFL and 300 meters for 10BaseFP. Also, there is no limitation to the number of mixing segments when there are only a total of four cable segments on the network.

ETHERNET TIMING CALCULATIONS   The 5-4-3 rule is a general guideline that is usually accurate enough to ensure your network will perform properly. However, it is also possible to assess the compliance of a network with the Ethernet cabling specifications more precisely by calculating the round trip signal delay time and the interframe gap shrinkage for the worst case path through your network.

The *round trip signal delay time* is the amount of time it takes a bit to travel from one node to the most distant node on the network and back again. The *interframe gap shrinkage* is the amount the normal 96-bit delay between packets is reduced by network conditions, such as the time required for repeaters to reconstruct a signal before sending it on its way.

In most cases, these calculations are unnecessary; as long as you comply with the 5-4-3 rule, your network should function properly. If you are planning to expand a complex network to the point at which it pushes the limits of the Ethernet guidelines, however, it might be a good idea to get a precise measurement to ensure that everything functions as it should. If you end up with a severe late collision problem that requires an expensive network upgrade to remedy, your boss isn't likely to want to hear about the 5-4-3 rule.

Note *Calculating the round trip signal delay time and the interframe gap shrinkage for your network is not part of a remedy for excessive numbers of early collisions. The collisions that result from networks not in compliance with these Ethernet specifications are late collisions, which do not register on elementary tools like Windows NT's Performance Monitor and NetWare's Monitor.nlm. You must use a high-end protocol analyzer tool like Fluke's LANMeter to detect late collisions at the data link–layer level.*

FINDING THE WORST CASE PATH   The *worst case path* is the route data takes when traveling between the two most distant nodes on the network, both in terms of segment length and number of repeaters. On a relatively simple network, you can find the worst case path by choosing the two nodes on the two outermost network segments that have either the longest link segments connecting them to the repeater or are at the far ends of the cable bus, as shown in Figure 8-8.

On more complex networks using various types of cable segments, you may have to select several paths to test your network. In addition, you may have to account for additional distance provided by AUI cables and the variations caused by having different cable segment types at the left and right ends of the path.

If your network is well documented, then you should have a schematic containing the precise distances of all your cable runs. You need these figures to make your

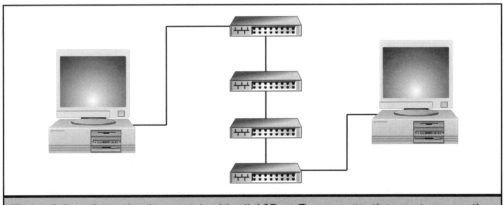

Figure 8-8.   *On a simple network with all 10BaseT segments, the worst case path runs between the nodes with the longest cables on both end segments*

calculations. If you don't have a schematic, then determining the exact distances may be the most difficult part of the whole process. A cable tester can help you measure the distance of a particular cable run, or you can measure the cable lengths manually by estimating the distances between drops. If you do this, you should err on the side of caution and include an additional distance factor to account for possible errors. Alternatively, you can simply use the maximum allowable cable distances for the various cable segments, as long as you are sure the cable runs do not exceed the Ethernet standard's maximum segment length specifications.

Once you have determined the worst case path (or paths) you will use for your calculations, a good idea is to create a simple diagram of each path with the cable distances involved, as shown in Figure 8-9. Each path will have left and right end segments and may have one or more middle segments. You will then perform your calculations on the individual segments and combine the results to test the entire path.

CALCULATING THE ROUND TRIP SIGNAL DELAY TIME   To determine whether the most distant nodes on your network are capable of properly sensing collisions from each other, you determine the total path delay by using the segment delay values in Table 8-3 to calculate the delay for each segment in the path and then adding them together. The table contains base and maximum bit-time values for each of the Ethernet cable types. There are separate values for the segment at the left and right ends of your worst case path, while all the segments in the middle use the same value. A *bit time* is the amount of time required to send one bit of data over the network.

To calculate the delay for a particular segment, use the following formula:

```
segment delay = (segment length * round trip delay/meter) + segment base
```

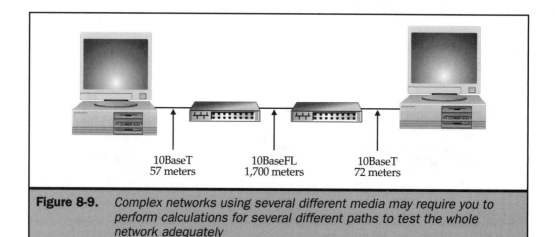

Figure 8-9.   *Complex networks using several different media may require you to perform calculations for several different paths to test the whole network adequately*

Cable Type	Maximum Length (Meters)	Left End Base	Middle Segment Base	Right End Base	Round Trip Delay/Meter
10Base5	500	11.75	46.5	169.5	0.0866
10Base2	185	11.75	46.5	169.5	0.1026
10BaseT	100	15.25	42	165	0.113
FOIRL	1,000	7.75	29	152	0.1
10BaseFL	2,000	12.25	33.5	156.5	0.1
10BaseFB	2,000	End connections not supported	24	End connections not supported	0.1
10BaseFP	1,000	11.25	61	183.5	0.1
Excess AUI	48	0	0	0	0.1026

Table 8-3. *Round Trip Delay Values for Ethernet Cable Types (in Bit Times)*

Thus, for a 50-meter 10BaseT segment at the left end of your worst case path, you would multiply 50×0.113 (the round trip delay/meter for 10BaseT) and add 15.25 (the base delay for a left-end 10BaseT segment) to get 20.9.

```
(50 * 0.113) + 15.25 = 20.9
```

If you want to use the delay for the maximum segment size permitted for each cable type, rather than measure the actual lengths of your network segments, then you can use the values in Table 8-4, which displays the results of the formula using the maximum segment length.

When you have calculated the delay values for all the segments on your network, you add them together and include an additional 5 bit times for a margin of error. This provides you with the total round trip signal delay time for the worst case path on your network. If this figure is less than or equal to 575, then your network conforms to the Ethernet specifications for this parameter. The value of 575 is derived from the 64 bytes (512 bits minus 1) required to fill the entire length of cable in the collision domain, plus the 64 bits that form the preamble and start of frame delimiter in the Ethernet frame. If the delay time is less than 575 bit times, this means the node at one end of the worst case path will be unable to send more than 511 bits of the frame plus the preamble and start of frame delimiter before it is notified of a collision.

NETWORK PROTOCOLS

Cable Type	Maximum Length (Meters)	Left End Maximum	Middle Segment Maximum	Right End Maximum
10Base5	500	55.05	89.8	212.8
10Base2	185	30.731	65.48	188.48
10BaseT	100	26.55	53.3	176.3
FOIRL	1,000	107.75	129	252
10BaseFL	2,000	212.25	233.5	356.5
10BaseFB	2,000	Not supported	224	Not supported
10BaseFP	1,000	111.25	161	284
External AUI	48	4.88	4.88	4.88

Table 8-4.   *Round Trip Delay Values for Maximum Ethernet Segment Lengths*

Because the delay values for the left and right end segments are different, you must perform these calculations twice if your network uses a different cable type at each end. After calculating the total delay in one direction, reverse the path and perform the same calculations using the other end as the left segment.

If your network uses thick Ethernet or 10BaseF segments with separate AUI cables connecting nodes to the network, you must figure these cable lengths into your calculations. The values for the standard cable types in Table 8-4 include a two-meter allowance for the total length of the AUI connections inside repeaters and network interfaces, but you can use the values shown in the External AUI row of the table to calculate the additional delay for AUI cables. Table 8-4 also includes External AUI values for the maximum allowable AUI cable length, if you want to use this figure instead of measuring your cables. Once you determine the delay time for all the AUI cables in your path, you add it to the total for the rest of the network and compare it to the 575 bit-time maximum delay.

CALCULATING THE INTERFRAME GAP SHRINKAGE   The interframe gap shrinkage test ensures that a sufficient delay exists between packet transmissions to make certain the network interfaces have sufficient time to cycle between transmit mode and receive mode. If the variable timing delays in the network components and the signal reconstruction delays in the repeaters cause this gap to become too small, the frames may arrive too quickly and overwhelm the interface of the receiving node.

The interframe gap of 9.6 microseconds specified by the Ethernet standard was ratified almost 20 years ago and the technology used to design and manufacture network interface cards has certainly advanced considerably since then. Many of the NICs manufactured today require a good deal less than 9.6 microseconds to cycle between modes. Some of them even deliberately use shorter interframe gaps to speed network transmissions. When all the NICs on a network have this capability, no problem should occur; but if you use cards like these on a network along with older network interfaces, you may find the older devices cannot keep up with the new ones.

To calculate the interframe gap shrinkage, you use the same worst case path through the network you used in the round trip signal delay time, except that only the transmitting segment and the middle segments are pertinent here. This is because the shrinkage values for the transmitting and middle segments include the repeaters to which they deliver the packets. The final segment leading to the destination node begins after the last repeater in the path and does not contribute any more shrinkage. The interframe gap shrinkage values for the various Ethernet cable types in both transmitting and middle segments are shown in Table 8-5.

The interframe gap shrinkage for the entire network is the sum of the values from the table for transmitting segment, plus all of the middle segments. If the total is less than 49 bit times, then the network passes the test. If your worst case path uses different cable types at both ends, then you should calculate the shrinkage twice, using first the value for one end and then the value for the other. The highest total of the two should be considered the interframe gap shrinkage measurement for the network.

Exceeding Ethernet Cabling Specifications

The Ethernet specifications have a certain amount of leeway built into them that makes it possible to exceed the cabling limitations, within reason. If a network has an extra repeater or a cable that's too long, it will probably continue to function without

Cable Type	Transmitting Segment	Middle Segment
10Base5, 10Base2	16	11
10BaseT, FOIRL, 10BaseFL	10.5	8
10BaseFB	End connections not supported	2
10BaseFP	11	8

Table 8-5. *Interframe Gap Shrinkage for Ethernet Cable Types in Bit Times*

causing the late collisions that occur when the specifications are grossly exceeded. You can see how this is so by calculating the actual amount of copper cable filled by an Ethernet signal.

Electrical signals passing through a copper cable travel at approximately 200,000,000 meters/second (2/3 of the speed of light). Ethernet transmits at 10 Mbps, or 10,000,000 bits/second. By dividing 200,000,000 by 10,000,000, you arrive at a figure of 20 meters of cable for every transmitted bit. Thus, the smallest possible Ethernet frame, which is 512 bits (64 bytes) long, occupies 10,240 meters of copper cable.

If you take the longest possible length of copper cable permitted by the Ethernet standards, a 500-meter thick Ethernet segment, you can see that the entire 500 meters would be filled by only 25 bits of data (at 20 meters/bit). Two nodes at the far ends of the segment would have a round trip distance of 1,000 meters.

When one of the two nodes transmits, a collision can only occur if the other node also begins transmitting before the signal reaches it. If you grant that the second node begins transmitting at the last possible moment before the first transmission reaches it, then the first node can send no more than 50 bits (occupying 1,000 meters of cable, 500 down and 500 back) before it detects the collision and ceases transmitting. Obviously, this 50 bits is well below the 512-bit barrier that separates early from late collisions.

Of course, this example involves only one segment; but even if you extend a thick Ethernet network to its maximum collision domain diameter—five segments of 500 meters each, or 2,500 meters—a node would still only transmit 250 bits (occupying 5,000 meters of cable, 2,500 down and 2,500 back) before detecting a collision.

Thus, you can see that the Ethernet specifications for the round trip signal delay time are fully twice as strict as they need to be in the case of a thick Ethernet network. For the other copper media, thin Ethernet and 10BaseT, the specifications are even more lax because the maximum segment lengths are smaller, while the signaling speed remains the same. For a full-length five-segment 10BaseT network, only 500 meters long, the specification is ten times stricter than it needs to be.

This is not to say that you can safely double the maximum cable lengths on your network across the board or install a dozen repeaters (although it is possible to safely lengthen the segments on a 10BaseT network up to 150 meters if you use category 5 UTP cable instead of category 3). Other factors can affect the conditions on your network to bring it closer to the limits defined by the specifications. In fact, the signal timing is not as much of a restricting factor on 10 Mbps Ethernet installations as is the signal strength. The weakening of the signal due to attenuation is far more likely to cause performance problems on an overextended network than are excess signal delay times. The point here is to demonstrate that the designers of the Ethernet protocol built a safety factor into the network from the beginning, perhaps partially explaining why it works so well 20 years later.

The Ethernet Frame

The *Ethernet frame* is the sequence of bits that begins and ends every Ethernet packet transmitted over the network. The frame consists of a header and footer that surround and encapsulate the data generated by the protocols operating at higher layers of the OSI model. The information in the header and footer specifies the addresses of the system sending the packet and the system that is to receive it, and also performs several other functions that are important to the ultimate delivery of the packet.

The IEEE 802.3 Frame

The basic Ethernet frame format, as defined by the IEEE 802.3 standard, appears as shown in Figure 8-10. The functions of the individual fields are as follows:

PREAMBLE AND START OF FRAME DELIMITER (SFD)   The preamble consists of 7 bytes of alternating 0's and 1's, which the systems on the network use to synchronize their clocks and then discard. The Manchester encoding scheme Ethernet uses requires the clocks on communicating systems to be in synch, so that they both agree on how long a bit time is. Systems in idle mode (that is, not currently transmitting and not in the process of rectifying a collision) are incapable of receiving any data until they use the signals generated by the alternating bit values of the preamble to prepare for the forthcoming data transmission.

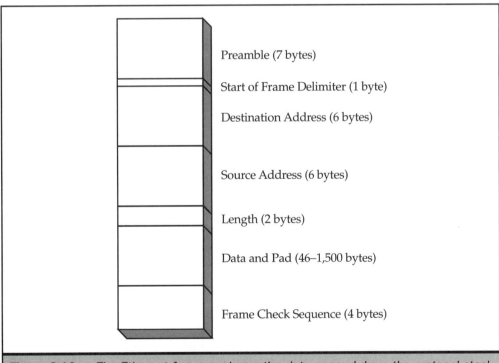

Preamble (7 bytes)

Start of Frame Delimiter (1 byte)

Destination Address (6 bytes)

Source Address (6 bytes)

Length (2 bytes)

Data and Pad (46–1,500 bytes)

Frame Check Sequence (4 bytes)

Figure 8-10.   *The Ethernet frame encloses the data passed down the protocol stack from the network layer and prepares it for transmission*

For more information on Manchester encoding and the signaling that occurs at the physical layer, see Chapter 2.

By the time the 7 bytes of the preamble have been transmitted, the receiving system has synchronized its clock with that of the sender, but the receiver is also unaware of how much of the 7 bytes have elapsed before it fell into synch. (Most of the adapters made today are designed to synch up within 11 bit times, but this is not an absolutely reliable figure.) To signal the commencement of the actual packet transmission, the sender transmits a 1-byte start of frame delimiter, which continues the alternating 0's and 1's, except for the last two bits, which are both 1's. This is the signal to the receiver that any data following is part of a packet and should be read into the network adapter's memory buffer for processing.

DESTINATION ADDRESS AND SOURCE ADDRESS   *Addressing* is the most basic function of the Ethernet frame. Because the frame can be said to form an envelope for the network-layer data carried inside it, it is only fitting that the envelope have an address. The addresses the Ethernet protocol uses to identify the systems on the network are 6 bytes long and hardcoded into the network interface adapters in each machine. These addresses are referred to as *hardware addresses* or *MAC addresses*. The hardware address on every Ethernet adapter made is unique. The IEEE assigns 3-byte prefixes to NIC manufacturers that it calls *organizationally unique identifiers (OUIs)* and the manufacturers themselves supply the remaining 3 bytes.

The destination address field identifies the system to which the packet is being sent. The address may identify the ultimate destination of the packet if it's on the local network, or the address may belong to a device that provides access to another network, such as a router. Addresses at the data link layer always identify the packet's next stop on the local network. It is up to the network layer to control end-to-end transmission and to provide the address of the packet's ultimate destination.

For more information on the interaction between data link–layer addresses and network-layer addresses, see "ARP" in Chapter 11.

Every node on an Ethernet network reads the destination address from the header of every packet transmitted by every system on the network, to determine if the header contains its own address. A system reading the frame header and recognizing its own address then reads the entire packet into its memory buffers and processes it accordingly. A destination address of all 1's signifies that the packet is a *broadcast,* meaning it is intended for all of the systems on the network. Certain addresses can also be designated as *multicast* addresses by the networking software on the system. A multicast address identifies a group of systems on the network, all of which are to receive certain messages.

The source address field contains the 6-byte MAC address of the system sending the packet.

When transmitting a packet, it is the network adapter driver on the system that generates the values for the destination address and source address fields.

LENGTH   The length field in an 802.3 frame is 2 bytes long and specifies how much data is being carried as the packet's payload in bytes. This figure includes only the actual upper-layer data in the packet. It does not include the frame fields from the header or footer or any padding that might have been added to the data field to reach the minimum size for an Ethernet packet (64 bytes). The maximum size for an Ethernet packet, including the frame, is 1,518 bytes. Because the frame consists of 18 bytes, the maximum value for the length field is 1,500.

 The frame format for the Ethernet II standard uses this field for a different purpose. See "The Ethernet II Frame," later in this chapter, for more information.

DATA AND PAD   The data field contains the payload of the packet, that is, the "contents" of the envelope. As passed down from the network-layer protocol, the data will include an original message generated by an upper-layer application or process, plus any header information added by the protocols in the intervening layers. In addition, an 802.3 packet will contain the 3-byte logical link control header in the data field as well.

For example, a packet containing an Internet host name to be resolved into an IP address by a DNS server consists of the original DNS message, a header applied by the UDP protocol at the transport layer, a header applied by the IP protocol at the network layer, and the LLC header. Although these three additional headers are not a part of the original message, to the Ethernet protocol they are just payload that is carried in the data field like any other information. Just as postal workers are not concerned with the contents of the mail they carry, the Ethernet protocol has no knowledge of the contents within the envelope.

The entire Ethernet packet (excluding the preamble and the start of frame delimiter) must be a minimum of 64 bytes in length, for the protocol's collision detection mechanism to function. Therefore, subtracting 18 bytes for the frame, the data field must be at least 46 bytes long. If the payload passed down from the network-layer protocol is too short, then the Ethernet adapter adds a string of meaningless bits to pad the data field out to the requisite length.

The maximum allowable length for an Ethernet packet is 1,518 bytes, meaning the data field can be no larger than 1,500 bytes (including the LLC header).

FRAME CHECK SEQUENCE (FCS)   The last 4 bytes of the frame, following the data field (and the pad, if any), carry a checksum value the receiving node uses to determine if the packet has arrived intact. Just before transmission, the network adapter at the sending node computes a cyclical redundancy check (CRC) on all of the packet's other fields (except for the preamble and the start of frame delimiter) using an algorithm called the AUTODIN II polynomial. The value of the CRC is uniquely based on the data used to compute it.

When the packet arrives at its destination, the network adapter in the receiving system reads the contents of the frame and performs the same computation. By comparing the newly computed value with the one in the FCS field, the system can verify that none of the packet's bit values have changed. If the values match, the system accepts the packet and writes it to the memory buffers for processing. If the values don't match, the system declares an *alignment error* and discards the frame. The system will also discard the frame if the number of bits in the packet is not a multiple of 8. Once a frame is discarded, it is up to the higher-layer protocols to recognize its absence and arrange for retransmission.

The Ethernet II Frame

The function of the 2-byte field following the source address is different in the frame formats of the two predominant Ethernet standards. While the 802.3 frame uses this field to specify the length of the data in the packet, the Ethernet II standard uses it to specify the frame type, also called the *Ethertype*. The Ethertype specifies the memory buffer in which the frame should be stored. The location of the memory buffer specified in this field identifies the network-layer protocol for which the data carried in the frame is intended.

This is a crucial element of every protocol operating in the data link, network, and transport layers of a system's networking stack. The data in the packet must be delivered not only to the proper system on the network, but also to the proper application or process on that system. Because the destination computer can be running multiple protocols at the network layer at the same time, such as IP, NetBEUI, and IPX, the Ethertype field informs the Ethernet adapter driver which of these protocols should receive the data.

When a system reads the header of an Ethernet packet, the only way to tell an Ethernet II frame from an 802.3 frame is by the value of the length/Ethertype field. Because the value of the 802.3 length field can be no higher than 1,500 (0x05DC, in hexadecimal notation), the Ethertype values assigned to the developers of the various network-layer protocols are all higher than 1,500.

Xerox continues to function as the registrar of the Ethertype assignments. Some of the possible values for the Ethertype field are shown in Table 8-6.

The Logical Link Control Sublayer

As mentioned earlier, the IEEE splits the functionality of the data link layer into two sublayers: media access control (MAC) and logical layer control (LLC). On an Ethernet network, the MAC sublayer includes elements of the 802.3 standard: the physical-layer specifications, the CSMA/CD mechanism, and the 802.3 frame. The functions of the LLC sublayer are defined in the 802.2 standard, which is also used with the other 802 MAC standards.

Ethertype	Protocol	Ethertype	Protocol
0600	Xerox NS IDP	6002	DEC MOP (Remote Console)
0800	Internet Protocol (IP)	6003	DECNET Phase 4
0801	X.75	6004	DEC LAT
0802	NBS	6005	DEC
0803	ECMA	6006	DEC
0804	Chaosnet	8005	HP Probe
0805	X.25 Packet (Level 3)	8010	Excelan
0806	Address Resolution Protocol (ARP)	8035	Reverse ARP
0807	XNS Compatibility	8038	DEC LANBridge
1000	Berkeley Trailer	809B	AppleTalk
5208	BBN Simnet	80F3	AppleTalk ARP
6001	DEC MOP (Dump/Load)	8137	NetWare IPX/SPX

Table 8-6.   *Ethertype Values for Network-Layer Protocols (in Hexadecimal Notation)*

NETWORK PROTOCOLS

The LLC sublayer is capable of providing a variety of communications services to network-layer protocols, including the following:

- **Unacknowledged connectionless service**   A simple service that provides no flow control or error control, and does not guarantee accurate delivery of data.

- **Connection-oriented service**   A fully reliable service that guarantees accurate data delivery by establishing a connection with the destination before transmitting data, and by using error and flow control mechanisms.

- **Acknowledged connectionless service**   A midrange service that uses acknowledgement messages to provide reliable delivery, but which does not establish a connection before transmitting data.

On a transmitting system, the data passed down from the network-layer protocol is encapsulated first by the LLC sublayer in what the standard calls a *protocol data unit (PDU)*. Then the PDU is passed down to the MAC sublayer, where it is encapsulated again in a header and footer, at which point it can technically be called a *frame*. In an Ethernet packet, this means the data field of the 802.3 frame contains a 3-byte LLC header, in addition to the network-layer data, thus reducing the maximum amount of data in each packet from 1,500 to 1,497 bytes.

The LLC header consists of three fields (see Figure 8-11), the functions of which are described in the following sections:

DSAP AND SSAP   The Destination Service Access Point (DSAP) field identifies a location in the memory buffers on the destination system where the data in the packet should be stored. The Source Service Access Point (SSAP) field does the same for the source of the packet data on the transmitting system. Both of these 1-byte fields use values assigned by the IEEE, which functions as the registrar for the protocol. Some of the possible values are shown in Table 8-7.

In an Ethernet SNAP packet, the value for both the DSAP and SSAP fields is 170 (or 0xAA, in hexadecimal form). This value indicates that the contents of the logical link control PDU begins with a Sub-Network Access Protocol (SNAP) header. The SNAP header provides the same functionality as the Ethertype field to the 802.3 frame.

CONTROL   The control field of the LLC header specifies the type of service needed for the data in the PDU and the function of the packet. Depending on which of the services is required, the control field can be either 1 or 2 bytes long. In an Ethernet SNAP frame, for example, the LLC uses the unacknowledged, connectionless service, which has a 1-byte control field value using what the standard calls the *unnumbered format*. The value for the control field is 3, which is defined as an *unnumbered information frame*—that is, a frame containing data. Unnumbered information frames are quite simple and signify either that the packet contains a noncritical message or that a higher-layer protocol is somehow guaranteeing delivery and providing other high-level services.

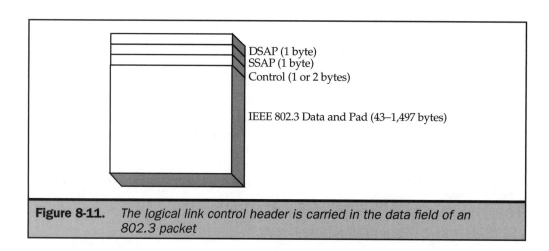

DSAP (1 byte)
SSAP (1 byte)
Control (1 or 2 bytes)

IEEE 802.3 Data and Pad (43–1,497 bytes)

Figure 8-11.   *The logical link control header is carried in the data field of an 802.3 packet*

DSAP/SSAP Value	Description
0	Null LSAP
2	Indiv LLC Sublayer Mgt
3	Group LLC Sublayer Mgt
4	SNA Path Control
6	Reserved (DOD IP)
14	PROWAY-LAN
78	EIA-RS 511
94	ISI IP
142	PROWAY-LAN
170	SNAP
254	ISO CLNS IS 8473
255	Global DSAP

Table 8-7.   *IEEE DSAP and SSAP Values*

The other two types of control field (which are 2 bytes each) are the *information format* and the *supervisory format*. The three control field formats are distinguished by their first bits, as follows:

- The information format begins with a 0 bit.
- The supervisory format begins with a 1 bit and a 0 bit.
- The unnumbered format begins with two 1 bits.

The remainder of the bits specify the precise function of the PDU. In a more complex exchange involving the connection-oriented service, unnumbered frames contain commands, such as those used to establish a connection with the other system and terminate it at the end of the transmission. The commands transmitted in unnumbered frames are as follows:

- **UI (Unnumbered Information)**   Used to send data frames by the unacknowledged, connectionless service
- **XID (Exchange Identification)**   Used as both a command and a response in the connection-oriented and connectionless services

- **TEST** Used as both a command and a response when performing an LLC loopback test

- **FRMR (Frame Reject)** Used as a response when a protocol violation occurs

- **SABME (Set Asynchronous Balanced Mode Extended)** Used to request that a connection be established

- **UA (Unnumbered Acknowledgment)** Used as the positive response to the SABME message

- **DM (Disconnect Mode)** Used as a negative response to the SABME message

- **DISC (Disconnect)** Used to request that a connection be closed; a response of either UA or DM is expected

Information frames contain the actual data transmitted during connection-oriented and acknowledged connectionless sessions, as well as the acknowledgment messages returned by the receiving system. Only two types of messages are sent in information frames: N(S) and N(R) for the send and receive packets, respectively. Both systems track the sequence numbers of the frames they receive. An N(S) message enables the receiver to know how many packets in the sequence have been sent and the N(R) message enables the sender to know what packet in the sequence it expects to receive.

Supervisory frames are used only by the connection-oriented service and provide connection maintenance in the form of flow control and error-correction services. The types of supervisory messages are as follows:

- **RR (Receiver Ready)** Used to inform the sender that the receiver is ready for the next frame and to keep a connection alive.

- **RNR (Receiver Not Ready)** Used to instruct the sender not to send any more packets until the receiver transmits an RR message.

- **REJ (Frame Reject)** Used to inform the sender of an error and request retransmission of all frames sent after a certain point.

LLC APPLICATIONS In some cases, the LLC frame plays only a minor role in the network communications process. On a network running TCP/IP along with other protocols, for example, the only function of LLC may be to enable 802.3 frames to contain a SNAP header, which specifies the network-layer protocol the frame should go to, just like the Ethertype. In this scenario, the LLC PDUs all use the unnumbered information format. Other high-level protocols, however, require more extensive services from LLC. NetBIOS sessions, for example, and several of the NetWare protocols, use LLC's connection-oriented services more extensively.

The SNAP Header

Because the IEEE 802.3 frame header does not have an Ethertype field, it would normally be impossible for a receiving system to determine which network-layer protocol should receive the incoming data. This would not be a problem if you ran only one network-layer protocol; but with multiple protocols installed, it becomes a serious problem. 802.3 packets address this problem by using yet another protocol within the LLC PDU, called the *Sub-Network Access Protocol (SNAP)*.

The SNAP header is 5 bytes long and found directly after the LLC header in the data field of a 802.3 frame, as shown in Figure 8-12. The functions of the fields are as follows:

ORGANIZATION CODE   The organization code, or vendor code, is a 3-byte field that takes the same value as the first 3 bytes of the source address in the 802.3 header.

LOCAL CODE   The local code is a 2-byte field that is the functional equivalent of the Ethertype field in the Ethernet II header, using the same values as assigned by Xerox.

 Many, if not all, of the registered values for the NIC hardware address prefixes, the Ethertype field, and the DSAP/SSAP fields are listed in the "Assigned Numbers" document published as a Request for Comment (RFC) by the Internet Engineering Task Force (IETF). The current version number for this document is RFC1700 and is available at http://andrew2.andrew.cmu.edu/rfc/rfc1700.html.

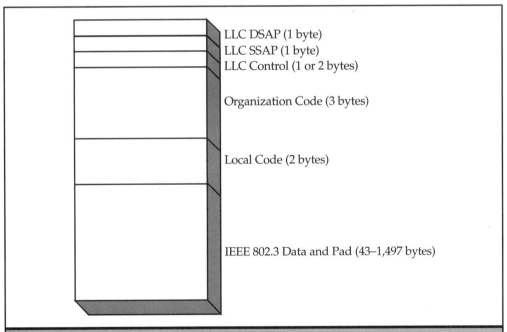

LLC DSAP (1 byte)
LLC SSAP (1 byte)
LLC Control (1 or 2 bytes)

Organization Code (3 bytes)

Local Code (2 bytes)

IEEE 802.3 Data and Pad (43–1,497 bytes)

Figure 8-12.   *The SNAP header is carried with an LLC protocol data unit and provides the same functionality as the Ethertype field*

NETWORK PROTOCOLS

Fast Ethernet

The IEEE 802.3u specification, ratified in 1995, defines what is commonly known as Fast Ethernet or 100BaseT, a data link–layer protocol running at 100 Mbps, ten times the speed of the original Ethernet protocol. Fast Ethernet is rapidly becoming the industry standard for new LAN installations, largely because it improves network performance so much while changing so little.

Fast Ethernet leaves two of the three defining elements of an Ethernet network unchanged. The new protocol uses the same frame format as IEEE 802.3 and the same CSMA/CD media access control mechanism. The changes that enable the increase in speed are in several elements of the physical-layer configuration, including the types of cable used, the length of segments, and the number of hubs allowed.

Physical-Layer Options

Coaxial cable is gone from the standard; Fast Ethernet runs only on UTP or fiber-optic cable (although shielded twisted-pair [STP] is an option as well). The physical-layer options defined in the standard are intended to provide the most flexible possible installation parameters. Virtually every aspect of the Fast Ethernet protocol is designed to facilitate upgrades from earlier technologies and, particularly, from 10BaseT. In many cases, existing UTP networks can upgrade to Fast Ethernet without pulling new cable. The only exception to this would be in the case of a network that spanned longer distances than Fast Ethernet can support with copper cabling. See "Upgrading an Ethernet Network," later in this chapter, for more information on the upgrade process.

Fast Ethernet defines three physical-layer configurations, as shown in Table 8-8.

In addition to the connectors shown for each of the cable types, the Fast Ethernet standard describes a *medium independent interface (MII)* that uses a 40-pin D-shell connector. Taking from the design of the original thick Ethernet standard, the MII connects to an external transceiver called a *physical-layer device (PHY)*, which, in turn,

	100BaseTX	100BaseT4	100BaseFX
Maximum Segment Length	100 meters	100 meters	412 meters
Cable Type	Category 5 UTP or Type 1 STP (two wire pairs)	Category 3 UTP (four wire pairs)	62.5/125 multimode fiber
Connector Type	RJ-45	RJ-45	SC, MIC, or ST

Table 8-8.   *IEEE 802.3u Physical-Layer Configurations*

connects to the network medium. The MII makes it possible to build devices such as hubs and computers that have integrated Fast Ethernet adapters, but are not committed to a particular media type. By supplying different PHY units, you can connect the device to a Fast Ethernet network using any supported cable type. Some PHY devices connect directly to the MII, while others use a cable not unlike the AUI cable arrangement in thick Ethernet. If this is the case, the MII cable can be no more than 0.5 meters long.

Most of the Fast Ethernet hardware on the market today uses internal transceivers and does not need an MII connector or cable, but a few products do take advantage of this interface.

100BaseTX

Using standards for physical media developed by ANSI (the American National Standards Institute), 100BaseTX and its fiber-optic counterpart 100BaseFX are known collectively as 100BaseX; they provide the core physical-layer guidelines for new cable installations. Like 10BaseT, 100BaseTX calls for the use of unshielded twisted-pair cable segments up to 100 meters in length. The only difference from a 10BaseT segment is in the quality and capabilities of the cable itself.

100BaseTX is based on the ANSI TP-PMD specification and calls for the use of category 5 UTP cable for all network segments. The ratings for UTP cable are defined by the TIA/EIA (Telecommunications Industry Association/Electronic Industry Association), and are shown in Table 4-2 in Chapter 4.

As you can see, the category 5 cable specification provides the potential for much greater bandwidth than the category 3 cable specified for 10BaseT networks. As an alternative, using Type 1 shielded twisted-pair cable (STP) is also possible for installations where the operating environment present a greater danger of electromagnetic interference.

For the sake of compatibility, 100BaseTX (as well as 100BaseT4) uses the same type of RJ-45 connectors as 10BaseT and the pin assignments are also the same (see Table 8-2). The pin assignments are the one area in which the cable specifications differ from ANSI TP-PMD, to maintain backward compatibility with 10BaseT networks.

100BaseT4

100BaseT4 is intended for use on networks that already have UTP cable installed, but the cable is not rated as category 5. The 10BaseT specification allows for the use of standard voice-grade (category 3) cable and a great many networks are already wired for 10BaseT Ethernet (or even for telephone systems). 100BaseT4 runs at 100 Mbps on category 3 cable by using all four pairs of wires in the cable, instead of just two, as 10BaseT and 100BaseTX do.

The transmit and receive data pair in a 100BaseT4 circuit are the same as that of 100BaseTX (and 10BaseT). The remaining four wires function as bidirectional pairs. The pin assignments for the RJ-45 connectors in a 100BaseT4 network are shown in Table 8-9.

Pin	Pair	Polarity	Signal	Designation
1	1	Positive	Transmit	TX_D1+
2	1	Negative	Transmit	TX_D1−
3	2	Positive	Receive	RX_D2+
4	3	Positive	Bidirectional	BI_D3+
5	3	Negative	Bidirectional	BI_D3−
6	2	Negative	Receive Data	RX_D2−
7	4	Positive	Bidirectional	BI_D4+
8	4	Negative	Bidirectional	BI_D4−

Table 8-9.   *RJ-45 Pin Assignments for 100BaseT4 Networks*

As on a 10BaseT network, the transmit-and-receive pairs must be crossed over for traffic to flow. The crossover circuits in a Fast Ethernet hub connect the transmit pair to the receive pair, as always. In a 100BaseT4 hub, the two bidirectional pairs are crossed as well, so that pair 3 connects to pair 4, and vice versa.

100BaseFX

The 100BaseFX specification calls for exactly the same hardware as the 10BaseFL specification, except the maximum length of a cable segment can be no more than 412 meters. As with the other Fast Ethernet physical-layer options, the medium is capable of transmitting a signal over longer distances, but the limitation is imposed to ensure the proper operation of the collision detection mechanism.

Cable Length Restrictions

Because the network is operating at ten times the speed, Fast Ethernet cable installations are more restricted than standard Ethernet. In effect, the Fast Ethernet standard uses up a good deal of the latitude built into the original Ethernet standards to achieve greater performance levels. In 10 Mbps Ethernet, the signal timing specifications are at least twice as strict as they have to be for systems to detect early collisions properly on the network. The lengths of the network segments are dictated more by the need to maintain the signal strength than the signal timing.

On 100BaseT networks, however, signal strength is not as much of an issue as signal timing. The CSMA/CD mechanism on a Fast Ethernet network functions exactly like that of a 10 Mbps Ethernet network and the packets are the same size, but they travel over the medium at ten times the speed. Because the collision detection mechanism is the same, a system still must be able to detect the presence of a collision before the slot time expires (that is, before it transmits 512 bytes of data). Because the traffic is moving faster, though, the duration of that slot time is reduced and the maximum length of the network must be reduced as well to sense collisions accurately. For this reason, the maximum overall length of a 100BaseTX network is approximately 210 meters. This is a figure you should observe much more stringently than the 500 meter maximum for a 10BaseT network.

> **Tip** *When you plan your network, be sure to remain conscious that the 100-meter maximum cable segment length specification in the Fast Ethernet standard includes the entire length of cable connecting a computer to the hub. If you have an internal cable installation that terminates in wall plates at the computer site and a patch panel at the hub site, then you must include the lengths of the patch cables connecting the wall plate to the computer and the patch panel to the hub in your total measurement. The specification recommends that the maximum length for an internal cable segment be 90 meters, leaving 10 meters for the patch cables.*

Hub Configurations

Because the maximum length for a 100BaseTX segment is 100 meters, the same as that for 10BaseT, the restrictions on the overall length of the network are found in the configuration of the repeating hubs used to connect the segments. The Fast Ethernet standard describes two types of hubs for all 100BaseT networks: Class I and Class II. Every Fast Ethernet hub must have a circled Roman numeral I or II identifying its class.

Class I hubs are intended to support cable segments with different types of signaling. 100BaseTX and 100BaseFX use the same signaling type, while 100BaseT4 is different (because of the presence of the two bidirectional pairs). A Class I hub contains circuitry that translates incoming 100BaseTX, 100BaseFX, and 100BaseT4 signals to a common digital format and then translates them again to the appropriate signal for each outgoing hub port. These translation activities cause the hub to produce comparatively long timing delays, so you can only have one Class I hub on the path between any two nodes on the network.

Class II hubs can only support cable segments of the same signaling type. Because no translation is involved, the hub passes the incoming data rapidly to the outgoing ports. Because the timing delays are shorter, you can have up to two Class II hubs on the path between two network nodes, but all the segments must use the same signaling type. This means a Class II hub can support either 100BaseTX and 100BaseFX together, or 100BaseT4 alone.

Additional segment length restrictions are also based on the combination of segments and hubs used on the network. The more complex the network configuration gets, the shorter its maximum collision domain diameter can be. These restrictions are summarized in the Table 8-10.

NETWORK PROTOCOLS

	One Class I Hub	One Class II Hub	Two Class II Hubs
All Copper Segments (100BaseTX or 100BaseT4)	200 meters	200 meters	205 meters
All Fiber Segments (100BaseFX)	272 meters	320 meters	228 meters
One 100BaseT4 Segment and One 100BaseFX Segment	231 meters	Not applicable	Not applicable
One 100BaseTX Segment and One 100BaseFX Segment	260.8 meters	308.8 meters	216.2 meters

Table 8-10. *Fast Ethernet Multisegment Configuration Guidelines*

Note that a network configuration that uses two Class II hubs actually uses three lengths of cable to establish the longest connection between two nodes: two cables to connect the nodes to their respective hubs, and one cable to connect the two hubs together. For example, the assumption of the standard is that the additional 5 meters added to the length limit for an all-copper network will account for the cable connecting the two hubs (see Figure 8-13); but in practice, the three cables can be of any length as long as their total length does not exceed 205 meters.

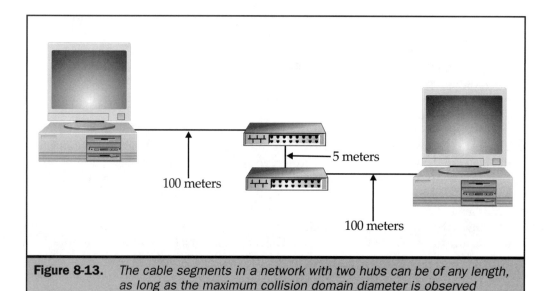

Figure 8-13. *The cable segments in a network with two hubs can be of any length, as long as the maximum collision domain diameter is observed*

What these restrictions mean is that the only fiber segment that can be 412 meters long is one that connects two computers directly together. Once you add a hub to the network, the total distance between computers drops drastically. This largely negates one of the major benefits of using fiber-optic cable. You saw earlier in this chapter that the original Ethernet standards allow for fiber-optic segments up to 2 kilometers (2,000 meters) long. The closer tolerances of the collision detection mechanism on a Fast Ethernet network makes it impossible to duplicate the collision domain diameter of standards like 10BaseFL. Considering that other high-speed protocols like FDDI use the same type of cable and can support distances up to 200 kilometers, Fast Ethernet might not be the optimal fiber-optic solution.

Fast Ethernet Timing Calculations

As with the original Ethernet standards, these cabling guidelines are no more than rules of thumb that provide general size limitations for a Fast Ethernet network. Making more precise calculations to determine if your network is fully compliant with the specifications is also possible. For Fast Ethernet, these calculations consist only of determining the round trip delay time for the network. No interframe gap shrinkage calculation exists for Fast Ethernet because the limited number of repeaters allowed on the network all but eliminates this as a possible problem.

CALCULATING THE ROUND TRIP DELAY TIME   The process of calculating the round trip delay time begins with determining the worst case path through your network, just as in the calculations for standard Ethernet networks. As before, if you have different types of cable segments on your network, you may have more than one path to calculate. There is no need to perform separate calculations for each direction of a complex path, however, because the formula makes no distinction between the order of the segments.

The round trip delay time consists of a delay per meter measurement for the specific type of cable your network uses, plus an additional delay constant for each node and repeater on the path. Table 8-11 lists the delay factors for the various network components.

To calculate the round trip delay time for the worst case path through your network, you multiply the lengths of your various cable segments by the delay factors listed in the table and add them together, along with the appropriate factors for the nodes and hubs and a safety buffer of 4 bit times. If the total is less than 512, then the path is compliant with the Fast Ethernet standard. Thus, the calculations for the network shown in Figure 8-14 would be as follows:

```
(150 meters * 1.112 bit times/meter) + 100 bit times + (2 * 92 bit
times) + 4 bit times = 454.8 bit times
```

150 meters of category 5 cable multiplied by a delay factor of 1.112 bit times per meter yield a delay of 166.8 bit times, plus 100 bit times for two 100BaseTX nodes, two hubs

Component	Delay (in Bit Times)
Category 3 UTP cable segment	1.14/meter
Category 4 UTP cable segment	1.14/meter
Category 5 UTP cable segment	1.112/meter
STP cable segment	1.112/meter
Fiber-optic cable segment	1.0/meter
Two 100BaseTX/100BaseFX nodes	100
Two 100BaseT4 nodes	138
One 100BaseTX/100BaseFX node and one 100BaseT4 node	127
Class I hub	140
Class II 100BaseTX/100BaseFX hub	92
Class II 100BaseT4 hub	67

Table 8-11. *Delay Times for Fast Ethernet Network Components*

at 92 bit times each, and an extra 4 for safety yields a total round trip delay time of 454.8 bit times, well within the 512 limit.

As with the calculations for standard Ethernet networks, you may be able to avoid having to measure your cable segments by using the maximum permitted segment length in your calculations. Only if the result of this calculation exceeds the specification do you have to consider the actual lengths of your cables.

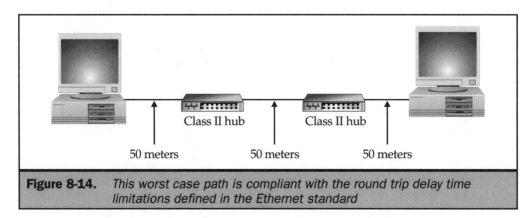

Figure 8-14. *This worst case path is compliant with the round trip delay time limitations defined in the Ethernet standard*

CALCULATING CABLE DELAY VALUES The delay values for the cable types shown in Table 8-12 are general estimations based only on the cable's rating. If you want to achieve even greater accuracy in your calculations and you have the necessary specifications from the cable manufacturer, you can also compute the rate of delay for your specific cables.

To do this, you must find out the cable's speed relative to the speed of light, usually referred to as the *Nominal Velocity of Propagation (NVP)* in the specifications for the cable. Once you have this figure, you can use the values in Table 8-11 to determine the delay factor of your cable in bit times/meter. Use this figure in place of the more general delay factors supplied in Table 8-12.

Note | *Some manufacturers furnish the NVP as a percentage, in which case you divide the percentage by 100 and find the corresponding value in the table's NVP column.*

NETWORK PROTOCOLS

NVP	Nanoseconds/ Meter	Bit Times/ Meter	NVP	Nanoseconds/ Meter	Bit Times/ Meter
0.4	8.34	0.834	0.62	5.38	0.538
0.5	6.67	0.667	0.63	5.29	0.529
0.51	6.54	0.654	0.64	5.21	0.521
0.52	6.41	0.641	0.65	5.13	0.513
0.53	6.29	0.629	0.654	5.10	0.510
0.54	6.18	0.618	0.66	5.05	0.505
0.55	6.06	0.606	0.666	5.01	0.501
0.56	5.96	0.596	0.67	4.98	0.498
0.57	5.85	0.585	0.68	4.91	0.491
0.58	5.75	0.575	0.69	4.83	0.483
0.5852	5.70	0.570	0.7	4.77	0.477
0.59	5.65	0.565	0.8	4.17	0.417
0.6	5.56	0.556	0.9	3.71	0.371
0.61	5.47	0.547			

Table 8-12. *Nominal Velocity of Propagation (NVP) Figures and Their Equivalent Delay Times*

Autonegotiation

Virtually all of the Fast Ethernet adapters on the market today are dual-speed devices, meaning that they can operate at either 10 or 100 Mbps. This helps simplify the process of upgrading a 10BaseT network to Fast Ethernet. The Fast Ethernet standard also defines an autonegotiation system that enables a dual-speed device to sense the capabilities of the network to which it is connected and to adjust its speed accordingly. The autonegotiation mechanism in Fast Ethernet is based on *fast link pulse (FLP)* signals, which are themselves a variation on the *normal link pulse (NLP)* signals used by 10BaseT and 10BaseFL networks.

Standard Ethernet networks use NLP signals to verify the integrity of a link between two devices. Fast Ethernet devices capable of multiple speeds transmit FLP signals instead, which include a 16-bit data packet within a burst of link pulses, producing what is called an *FLP burst*. The data packet contains a *link code word (LCW)* with two fields: the *selector field* and the *technology ability* field. Together, these fields identify the capabilities of the transmitting device, such as its maximum speed and whether it is capable of full-duplex communications.

Because the FLP burst has the same duration (2 nanoseconds) and interval (16.8 nanoseconds) as an NLP burst, a standard Ethernet system can simply ignore the LCW and treat the transmission as a normal link integrity test. When it responds to the sender, the multiple-speed system sets itself to operate at 10BaseT speed, using a technique called *parallel detection*. This same method applies also to Fast Ethernet devices incapable of multiple speeds.

When two Fast Ethernet devices capable of operating at multiple speeds autonegotiate, they determine the best performance level they have in common and configure themselves accordingly. The systems use the following list of priorities when comparing their capabilities, with full-duplex 100BaseTX providing the best performance and half-duplex 10BaseT providing the worst:

1. 100BaseTX (full-duplex)

2. 100BaseT4

3. 100BaseTX

4. 10BaseT (full-duplex)

5. 10BaseT

The benefit of autonegotiation is that it permits administrators to upgrade a network gradually to Fast Ethernet with a minimum of reconfiguration, If, for example, you have 10/100 dual-speed NICs in all your workstations, you can run normally at 10 Mbps using 10BaseT hubs. Later, you can replace the hubs with models supporting Fast Ethernet and the NICs will automatically reconfigure themselves to operate at the higher speed during the next system reboot. No manual configuration at the workstation is necessary.

Upgrading an Ethernet Network

The two most typical upgrades performed on an Ethernet network are the addition of new computers and the migration to Fast Ethernet. The following sections examine the procedures involved for these upgrades and present some of the more common problems you may encounter.

Adding Workstations

For the most part, the addition of new workstations on an Ethernet network is purely a mechanical exercise. Depending on the network medium, you do one of the following:

- On a thick Ethernet network, attach new vampire taps to the coaxial cable and connect them to the computers with an external MAU (transceiver) and an AUI cable.

- On a thin Ethernet network, connect a new length of coaxial cable to the T-connector of one of the existing workstations and to the T-connector of the new workstation, and then connect the old cable to the other end of the T-connector on the new workstation.

- On a UTP or fiber-optic network, plug one end of a new cable into a free port on the hub and the other end into the new computer. For an internal cable installation, you may have to use patch cables to connect the hub to a port on the patch panel and the computer to the wall plate corresponding to the port on the patch panel.

When difficulties arise, this is usually because you have reached the maximum number of nodes permitted on a coaxial segment, run out of ports on your hub, or exceeded the segment length restrictions for the cable type. In some cases, you can work around these problems without major renovations; but if you're approaching the limits of your network configuration, it may be time to consider a more comprehensive upgrade.

Bus Network Expansion

When adding workstations to a thick or thin Ethernet network, the primary danger is that you will have too many nodes on the cable segment. You learned earlier in this chapter that the Ethernet cabling specifications have a built-in buffer, which usually enables you to exceed the configuration guidelines to some degree. As long as your maximum segment lengths comply with the specifications, having as many as 110 nodes on a thick Ethernet segment or 35 nodes on thin Ethernet (instead of 100 and 30, respectively) should not be a problem.

Exceeding the maximum segment length is a problem limited primarily to thin Ethernet networks because every workstation you add means attaching another length of cable. On thick Ethernet networks, you are only adding more taps to the already-installed cable. Again, if you find that the new additions bring your thin Ethernet segment to 210 or 220 meters, the network should continue to function normally, as long as you have 30 nodes or less. Exceeding both the maximum length and maximum number of nodes is not recommended, as this compounds the risk of malfunctions significantly.

If your expansion sends you well over the maximum recommended segment length, you can add a repeater at some point near the middle of the cable to prevent the attenuation that is the primary source of problems on overlong coaxial networks. If you do have to add a repeater, you must consider also the guideline governing the maximum number of repeaters allowed on your network. Again, you can probably get away with one too many repeaters, as long as your network is compliant in every other way. Only when you exceed the specifications in two dimensions should you begin to worry.

When you add more nodes to a coaxial network, observing the guidelines regarding the minimum amount of cable required between workstations is important. In fact, it is less dangerous to exceed the segment length than to save length by placing the node connection too close together. On a thick Ethernet network, the coaxial cable is usually marked with black stripes every 2.5 meters. This is the minimum safe distance between cable taps. On a thin Ethernet network, every length of coaxial cable must be at least 0.5 meters long. This is usually not a problem; but even if you have two computers arranged back to back so that they are nearly touching, you should use a piece of cable at least a meter long to be safe.

Star Network Expansion

Adding nodes to your twisted-pair Ethernet network couldn't be easier, as long as you have the hub ports and cable drops you need. However, when you run short of either of these things, there are sometimes relatively easy solutions.

On a 10BaseT network, you can add a minihub to a location that has run short of cable drops or when you run out of ports on your other hubs. Just as on a coaxial network, if you have one too many hubs on your worst case path through the network, this will probably not be a problem. Also, remember that because 10BaseT hubs also function as repeaters, you can use a minihub to connect a workstation more than 100 meters away from your main hub.

Fast Ethernet networks, however, are a different matter entirely. The tolerances built into the Fast Ethernet specifications are much tighter than those for standard Ethernet. Exceeding the recommended cable lengths, and especially the maximum number of repeaters, is strongly discouraged.

For either standard or Fast Ethernet, when you expand beyond the point at which you can add more nodes, you must consider splitting the collision domain in two. To do this, you add a device that filters the network traffic that passes through it, such as a switching hub. Unlike repeating hubs, which are purely electrical devices that manage and amplify all the signals they receive indiscriminately, switches actually read the headers of the packets and propagate incoming traffic only to the ports for which it is destined.

For more information on expanding your network with switches, see Chapter 6.

Upgrading to Fast Ethernet

Because Fast Ethernet is so similar to standard Ethernet, upgrading networks from 10 to 100 Mbps can often be quite easy. The key to simplifying the procedure in a production environment is the use of the dual-speed devices available today. Originally, Fast Ethernet devices were all single speed and you had to have separate hubs for the 10BaseT and 100BaseT workstations.

In addition, any servers you wanted accessible at both speeds had to have separate 10 and 100 Mbps NICs in them. Each NIC was connected to the appropriate speed hub along with the workstations running at that speed. Upgrading a workstation to Fast Ethernet meant installing a new NIC into the computer and plugging the other end of the cable into the other hub.

Upgrading NICs and Hubs

Today, virtually all Fast Ethernet NICs are dual-speed, and many dual-speed hubs are available as well. This provides the network administrator with complete flexibility over the upgrade process. When faced with economic or scheduling constraints, you can gradually upgrade the network to Fast Ethernet, at any desired pace.

If you are running 10BaseT and have even the remotest plans of upgrading to Fast Ethernet in the future, you should install 10/100 NICs in all your new workstations and think about replacing the old NICs as time permits. Dual-speed NICs are only slightly more expensive than 10BaseT-only cards, particularly when bought in bulk. In fact, as Fast Ethernet becomes more ubiquitous, it is likely that 10BaseT cards will eventually be rarer and more expensive than dual-speed NICs.

The other half of the equation is the Fast Ethernet hub. If you purchase Fast Ethernet–only hubs, you should either wait until all of your dual-speed NICs are installed to deploy them or plan on maintaining your 10BaseT hubs for the standard Ethernet workstations until they are upgraded. As you upgrade a workstation to a Fast Ethernet NIC, you will also have to plug into the new hub.

If, however, you buy dual-speed hubs, you can replace the old hubs completely and plug all of your workstations in, regardless of speed. The Fast Ethernet autonegotiation mechanism enables each NIC and hub port to function at the fastest possible speed. As you upgrade the workstation NICs, they will automatically negotiate the higher speed, without any adjustments at the hub end.

Upgrading the Cable Plant

In most cases, Fast Ethernet is designed to use the UTP cable already installed at a site. If you have category 3 or 4 cable installed, you can run 100BaseT4; with category 5 cable, you can run 100BaseTX. 100BaseT4 and 100BaseTX require different NICs and hubs, so be sure that you purchase the correct hardware for your network.

On a relatively simple network, migrating to Fast Ethernet can be as easy as replacing the NICs and hubs, with no modifications to the cable installation. Because the maximum segment length is the same (100 meters), there should be no problem with the locations of your hubs relative to the workstations. However, the big additional restriction in the Fast Ethernet standard is the limitation on the number of hubs.

If you have a network in which the paths between workstations routinely run through three or four hubs, then you need to rethink your network architecture to use Fast Ethernet because the maximum of two Class II hubs is a restriction you should not ignore. To remain within the Fast Ethernet guidelines, you must eliminate some of the hops on your network paths. You do this by dividing the network into two or more collision domains, so no more than two hops are in any path between two workstations, using a switching hub or a device operating higher in the OSI model, such as a router. (Remember, mixing cable types using Class I hubs limits you to only one hop.)

Dividing a network into multiple collision domains is easier when the hubs are all located in the same place, such as a data center or wiring closet. If you have a more informal network with ad hoc upgrades in the form of minihubs scattered about in different locations, you may have a difficult time making the network compliant with the Fast Ethernet specifications.

Ethernet Troubleshooting

Troubleshooting an Ethernet network often means dealing with a problem in the physical layer, such as a faulty cable or connection, or possibly a malfunctioning NIC or hub. When a network connection completely fails, you should immediately start examining the cabling and other hardware for faults. If you find that the performance of the network is degrading, however, or if a problem is affecting specific workstations, you can sometimes get an idea of what is going wrong by examining the Ethernet errors occurring on the network.

Ethernet Errors

Following are some of the errors that can occur on an Ethernet network. Some are relatively common, while others are rare. Detecting these errors usually requires special tools designed to analyze network traffic. Basic software applications like Windows NT's Network Monitor and NetWare's Monitor.nlm can detect some of these conditions, such as the number of early collisions and FCS errors. Others, like late collisions, are much more difficult to detect and may require high-end software or hardware tools to diagnose.

■ **Early collisions** Strictly speaking, not an error, because collisions occur normally on an Ethernet network; but too many collisions (more than approximately 5 percent of the total packets) is a sign that network traffic is approaching critical levels. It is a good idea to keep a record of the number of collisions occurring on the network at regular intervals (such as weekly). If you notice a marked increase in the number of collisions, you might consider trying to decrease the amount of traffic, either by splitting the network into two collision domains or moving some of the nodes to another network.

- **Late collisions**   Late collisions are always a cause for concern and are difficult to detect. They usually indicate that data is taking too long to traverse the network, either because the cable segments are too long or there are too many repeaters. A NIC with a malfunctioning carrier sense mechanism could also be at fault. Network analyzer products that can track late collisions can be extremely expensive, but are well worth the investment for a large enterprise network. Because late collisions force lost packets to be retransmitted by higher-layer protocols, you can sometimes detect a trend of network-layer retransmissions (by the IP protocol, for example) caused by late collisions, using a basic protocol analyzer like Network Monitor.

- **Runts**   A *runt* is a packet less than 64 bytes long, caused either by a malfunctioning NIC or hub port, or by a node that ceases transmitting in the middle of a packet because of a detected collision. A certain number of runt packets occur naturally as a result of normal collisions, but a condition where more runts occur than collisions indicates a faulty hardware device.

- **Giants**   A *giant* is a packet that is larger than the Ethernet maximum of 1,518 bytes. The problem is usually caused by a NIC that is *jabbering*, or transmitting improperly or continuously, or (less likely) by the corruption of the header's length indicator during transmission. Giants never occur normally. They are an indication of a malfunctioning hardware device or a cable fault.

- **Alignment errors**   A packet that contains a *partial byte* (that is, a packet with a size in bits that is not a multiple of 8) is said to be *misaligned*. This can be the result of an error in the formation of the packet (in the originating NIC) or evidence of corruption occurring during the packet's transmission. Most misaligned packets also have CRC errors.

- **CRC errors**   A packet in which the frame check sequence generated at the transmitting node does not equal the value computed at the destination is said to have experienced a CRC error. The problem can be caused by data corruption occurring during transmission (because of a faulty cable or other connecting device) or conceivably by a malfunction in the FCS computation mechanism in either the sending or receiving node.

- **Broadcast storms**   When a malformed broadcast transmission causes the other nodes on the network to generate their own broadcasts for a total traffic rate of 126 packets per second or more, the result is a self-sustaining condition, known as a *broadcast storm*. Because broadcast transmissions are processed before other frames, the storm effectively prevents any other data from being successfully transmitted.

NETWORK PROTOCOLS

Isolating the Problem

Whenever you exceed any of the Ethernet specifications (or the specifications for any protocol, for that matter), the place where you're pushing the envelope should be the first place you check when a problem arises. If you have exceeded the maximum length for a segment, for example, try to eliminate some of the excess length to see if the problem continues. On a thin Ethernet network, this usually means cross-cabling to eliminate some of the workstations from the segment. On a UTP network, connect the same computer to the same hub port using a shorter cable run.

If you have too many workstations running on a coaxial bus (thick or thin Ethernet), you can determine if overpopulation is the problem simply by shutting down some of the machines.

Excessive repeater hops on a UTP network is a condition that you can test for by checking to see if problems occur more often on paths with a larger number of hops. You can also try to cross-cable the hubs to eliminate some of the hops from a particular path. This is relatively easy to do in an environment in which all the hubs are located in the same wiring closet or data center, but if the hubs are scattered all over the site, you may have to disconnect some of the hubs temporarily to reduce the size of the collision domain to perform your tests. The same is true of a coaxial network on which the primary function of the repeaters is to extend the collision domain diameter. You may have to disconnect the cable from each of the repeaters in turn (remembering to terminate the bus properly each time) to isolate the problem.

Reducing the size of the collision domain is also a good way to narrow down the location of a cable fault. In a UTP network, the star topology means that a cable break will only affect one system. On a coaxial network using a bus topology, however, a single cable fault can bring down the entire network. On a multisegment network, terminating the bus at each repeater in turn can tell you which segment has the fault.

A better, albeit more expensive method, for locating cable problems is to use an electronic cable tester. These devices can pinpoint the exact location of the fault. For more information on network testing and diagnostic products, see Chapter 30.

The
Complete
Reference

Upgrading
&
Troubleshooting
Networks

Chapter 9

Token Ring and 100VG AnyLAN

Although the vast majority of local area networks use one of the Ethernet variants to connect desktop workstations, other data link–layer protocols provide their own unique advantages. Chief among these advantages is the use of media access control mechanisms other than CSMA/CD. 100VG-AnyLAN and Token Ring are both viable LAN protocols that approach the problem of sharing a network cable in different ways.

Token Ring

Token Ring is the traditional alternative to the Ethernet protocol at the data link layer. The supporters of Token Ring are stalwart and, while it is not likely ever to overtake Ethernet in popularity, it is far from being out of the race. Token Ring was originally developed by IBM and later standardized in the IEEE 802.5 document, so, like Ethernet, slightly divergent standards exist. The products on the market today, however, usually conform to the IEEE specifications.

The biggest difference between Token Ring and Ethernet is the media access control mechanism. To transmit its data, a workstation must be the holder of the *token*, a special packet circulated to each node on the network in turn. Only the system in possession of the token can transmit, after which it passes the token to the next system. This eliminates all possibility of collisions in a properly functioning network, as well as the need for a collision detection mechanism.

Token Ring is also faster than standard Ethernet. Although the technology originally ran at 4 Mbps, most implementations now run at 16 Mbps. A Fast Token Ring standard also exists that pushes the speed to 100 Mbps, making it the equal of Fast Ethernet in this respect.

The Token Ring Physical Layer

As the name implies, the nodes on a Token Ring network are connected in a ring topology. This is, in essence, a bus with the two ends connected to each other, so that systems can pass data to the next node on the network until it arrives back at its source. This is exactly how the protocol functions; the system that transmits a packet is also responsible for removing it from the network after it has traversed the ring.

This ring, however, is logical, not physical. That is, the network, to all appearances, takes the form of a star topology, with the workstations connected to a central hub called a *multistation access unit* (*MAU*, or sometimes *MSAU*). The *logical ring* (sometimes called a *collapsed ring*) is actually a function of the MAU, which accepts packets transmitted by one system and directs them out each successive port in turn, waiting for them to return over the same cable before proceeding to the next port (see Figure 9-1). In this arrangement, therefore, the transmit and receive circuits in each workstation are actually separate ports that just happen to use the same cable because the system always transmits data to the next downstream system and receives data from the next upstream.

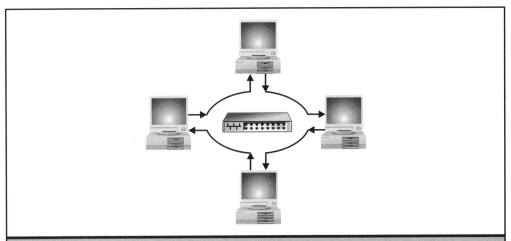

Figure 9-1. *Token Ring networks appear to use a star topology, but data travels in the form of a ring*

Cable Types

The original IBM Token Ring implementations used a proprietary cable system designed by IBM, which they referred to as their Type 1, or the IBM Cabling System (ICS). The MAU ports use proprietary connectors called IBM Data Connectors (IDCs) or Universal Data Connectors (UDCs), and network interface cards use DB9 connectors. A cable with IDCs at each end, used to connect MAUs together, is called a *patch cable;* while a cable with one IDC and one DB9, used to connect a workstation to the MAU, is called a *lobe cable.*

Note   *See "Shielded Twisted-Pair" in Chapter 4 for for information about the cable used for Token Ring networks.*

The Type 3 cabling system uses standard unshielded twisted-pair (UTP)—with category 5 cable recommended—and has largely supplanted Type 1. Like Ethernet, Token Ring uses only two of the wire pairs in the cable, one pair to transmit data and one to receive it. Type 3 cable systems use standard RJ-45 connectors for both the patch cables and the lobe cables. The signaling system used by Token Ring networks at the physical layer is different, however. Token Ring uses Differential Manchester signaling, while Ethernet uses Manchester.

Note   *For more information on the cables used for Token Ring networks and physical-layer signaling, see Chapter 4.*

Type 1 cable is thick and relatively inflexible when compared to Type 3, and the IDC connectors are large, making internal cable installations difficult. Type 1 cable can span longer distances than Type 3, however. Table 9-1 lists the general cabling guidelines for a Token Ring network.

Note *The physical-layer standards for Token Ring networks are not as precisely specified as those for Ethernet. In fact, the IEEE 802.5 standard is quite a brief document that contains no physical-layer specifications at all. The cable types and wiring standards for Token Ring are derived from the practices used in products manufactured by IBM, the original developer and supporter of the Token Ring protocol. As a result, products made by other manufacturers may differ in their recommendations for physical-layer elements like cable lengths and the maximum number of workstations allowed on a network.*

Token Ring NICs

The network interface cards for Token Ring systems are similar to Ethernet NICs in appearance. Most of the cards on the market today use RJ-45 connectors for UTP cable, although DB9 connectors are also available and the internal connectors support all of the major system buses, including PCI and ISA. Every Token Ring adapter has a VLSI (Very Large Scale Integration) chipset that consists of five separate CPUs, each of which has its own separate executable code, data storage area, and memory space. Each CPU corresponds to a particular state or function of the adapter.

Token Ring MAUs

To maintain the ring topology, all of the MAUs on a Token Ring network must be interconnected using the Ring In and Ring Out ports intended for this purpose. Figure 9-2 illustrates how the MAUs themselves are cabled in a ring that is extended by the lobe cables connecting each of the workstations.

	Type 1 Cable	Type 3 Cable
Maximum Lobe Cable Length	300 meters	150 meters
Maximum Number of Workstations	260	72
Maximum Ring Length at 16 Mbps	160 meters	60 meters
Maximum Ring Length at 4 Mbps	360 meters	150 meters
Maximum 8-Port MAUs	32	9

Table 9-1. *Token Ring Cabling Guidelines*

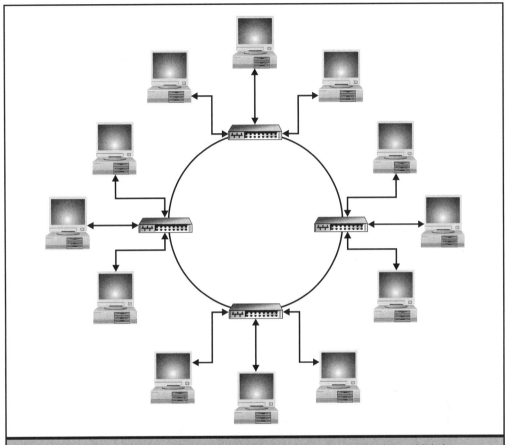

Figure 9-2. *The MAUs in a Token Ring network form the basic ring, which is extended with each workstation added to the network*

Token Ring MAUs (not to be confused with the Ethernet MAU, or medium access unit) are quite different from Ethernet hubs in several ways. First, the typical MAU is a *passive device,* meaning that it does not function as a repeater. The cabling guidelines for Token Ring networks are based on the use of passive MAUs. Repeating MAUs are on the market, however, that enable you to extend the network cable lengths beyond the published standards.

Second, the ports on all MAUs remain in a loopback state until they are initialized by the workstation connected to them. In the *loopback state,* the MAU passes signals it receives from the previous port directly to the next port without sending them out over the lobe cable. When the workstation boots, it transmits what is known as a *phantom voltage* to the MAU. Phantom voltage does not carry data, it just informs the MAU of the presence of the workstation, causing the MAU to add it to the ring. Because of the need for this initialization process, it is impossible to connect two Token Ring networks together without a MAU, as you can with Ethernet.

Finally, MAUs always have two ports for connecting to the other MAUs in the network. Ethernet systems using a star topology connect their hubs in a branching tree configuration, in which one hub can be connected to several others, each of which, in turn, is connected to other hubs, as shown in Figure 9-3. Token Ring MAUs are always connected in a ring, with the Ring In port connected to the next upstream MAU and the Ring Out port to the next downstream MAU. Even if your network only has two MAUs, you must connect the Ring In port on each one to the Ring Out port on the other using two patch cables.

The connections between Token Ring MAUs are redundant. That is, if a cable or connector failure causes a break between two of the MAUs, the adjacent MAUs will transmit any data reaching them back in the other direction, so the packets will always reach all of the workstations connected to the network. The Token Ring standards use a specification called the *adjusted ring length (ARL)* to determine the total length of the data path in the event of this type of failure.

Calculating the ARL

To calculate the ARL for a network, you take the sum of all the patch cable lengths between wiring closets minus the length of the shortest patch cable connecting two wiring closets and make the following adjustments:

- Add 3 meters for every punch-down connection involved in the path between two MAUs.

- Add 30 meters for every surge protector used on the network.

- Add 16 meters for every 8-port MAU.

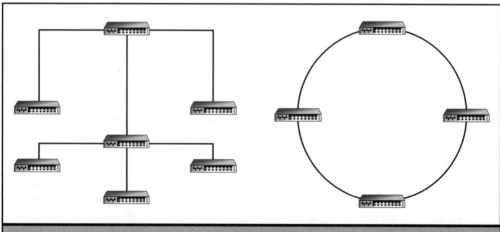

Figure 9-3. *Ethernet hubs (at left) are connected using a branching tree arrangement, while Token Ring MAUs (at right) are connected in a ring*

Because MAUs are often stored in wiring closets, the standard refers to the number of wiring closets used on the network to refer to MAUs more than 3 meters apart. Whether the MAUs are physically located in different closets is not relevant; any two MAUs connected by a cable more than 3 meters long are said to be in different wiring closets. Patch cables shorter than 3 meters should not be included in the ARL calculations.

Thus, the ARL is essentially the longest possible path (also called the *worst case distance*) between two MAUs on the network. The total ARL multiplied by 2 should not exceed 366 meters for the network to be within specifications. The ARL plus twice the length of the longest lobe cable is known as the *worst case maximum adapter signal drive distance* for the network.

All of the ring lengths discussed in reference to Token Ring networks refer to passive MAU networks. Unlike an Ethernet hub, a Token Ring MAU does not necessarily function as a repeater. When you use active MAUs that include signal-repeating capabilities, the cables can be much longer, depending on the capabilities of the individual MAU.

Calculating the Maximum Main Ring Distance

The *main ring distance* is the total length of all the MAU-MAU connections on the network. The maximum main ring distance is determined by the number of MAUs on the network and the number of wiring closets used for the MAUs. Tables 9-2 through 9-5 list the maximum main ring distances for networks using Type 1 and Type 3 cable, running at 4 Mbps and 16 Mbps.

	1 WC	2 WC	3 WC	4 WC	5 WC
1 MAU	427/130				
2 MAU	416/216	410/124			
3 MAU	406/123	399/121	402/122		
4 MAU	396/120	389/118	382/116	375/114	
5 MAU	385/117	378/115	371/113	364/110	357/108
6 MAU	375/114	368/112	361/110	354/107	347/105
7 MAU	364/110	357/108	350/106	343/104	336/102
8 MAU	364/110	347/105	340/103	333/101	326/99

Table 9-2.   *Maximum Main Ring Distances for Type 1 Cable Running at 16 Mbps (in Feet and Meters)*

NETWORK PROTOCOLS

	1 WC	2 WC	3 WC	4 WC	5 WC
1 MAU	1220/371				
2 MAU	1190/362	1170/356			
3 MAU	1160/353	1140/347	1120/341		
4 MAU	1130/344	1110/338	1090/332	1070/326	
5 MAU	1100/335	1080/329	1060/323	1040/316	1010/310
6 MAU	1070/326	1050/320	1030/313	1010/307	990/301
7 MAU	1040/316	1020/310	1000/304	980/298	960/292
8 MAU	1010/307	990/301	970/295	950/289	930/283

Table 9-3. *Maximum Main Ring Distances for Type 1 Cable Running at 4 Mbps (in Feet and Meters)*

	1 WC	2 WC	3 WC	4 WC	5 WC
1 MAU	210/64				
2 MAU	205/62	202/61			
3 MAU	200/61	197/60	195/59		
4 MAU	195/59	193/58	190/57	168/56	
5 MAU	190/58	188/57	185/56	164/55	179/54
6 MAU	186/56	183/55	180/54	160/54	174/52
7 MAU	181/55	178/54	175/53	155/52	169/51
8 MAU	176/53	173/52	170/51	151/50	165/50

Table 9-4. *Maximum Main Ring Distances for Type 3 Cable Running at 16 Mbps (in Feet and Meters)*

	1 WC	2 WC	3 WC	4 WC	5 WC
1 MAU	500/150				
2 MAU	485/147	475/144			
3 MAU	470/143	460/140	450/137		
4 MAU	455/138	445/135	435/132	425/129	
5 MAU	440/134	430/131	420/128	410/124	400/121
6 MAU	425/129	415/126	405/123	395/120	385/117
7 MAU	410/124	400/121	390/118	380/115	370/112
8 MAU	395/120	385/117	375/114	365/111	355/108

Table 9-5.   *Maximum Main Ring Distances for Type 3 Cable Running at 4 Mbps (in Feet and Meters)*

Token Passing

Access to the network medium on a Token Ring network is arbitrated through the use of a 3-byte packet known as the *token*. When the network is idle, the workstations are said to be in *bit repeat mode*, awaiting an incoming transmission. The token circulates continuously around the ring, from node to node, until it reaches a workstation that has data to transmit. The workstation modifies a single *monitor setting bit* in the token to reflect that the network is busy and transmits it to the next station, followed immediately by its data packet.

The packet also circulates around the ring. Each node reads the destination address in the frame header and either writes the packet to its memory buffers for processing before transmitting it to the next node or just transmits it without processing. In this way, the packet reaches every node on the network until it arrives back at the workstation that originally sent it.

On receipt of the packet, the sending node compares the incoming data with the data it originally transmitted, to see if any errors occurred during transmission. If errors did occur, the station retransmits the packet. If not, the station removes the packet from the network and discards it, and then changes the monitor setting bit back to its free state and transmits it. The process is then repeated with each system having an equal chance to transmit.

Although it was not part of the original standard, most 16 Mbps Token Ring systems today include a feature called *early token release (ETR)*, which enables the transmitting system to send the "free" token immediately after the data packet (instead of the "busy" token before the data packet), without waiting for the data to traverse the network. This way, the next node on the network can receive the data packet, capture the free token, and transmit its own data packet, followed by another free token. This enables multiple data packets to exist on the network simultaneously, but there is still only one token. Early token release eliminates some of the latency on the network that occurs while systems wait for the free token to arrive.

Note   *Early token release is only possible on 16 Mbps Token Ring networks. Systems that use ETR can co-exist on the same network with systems that do not.*

Because only the system holding the token can transmit data, Token Ring networks do not experience collisions unless a serious malfunction occurs. This means that the network can operate up to its full capacity with no degradation of performance, as can happen in an Ethernet network. The token-passing system is also deterministic, which means that it can calculate the maximum amount of time that will elapse before a particular node can transmit.

Token Ring is not the only data link–layer protocol that uses token passing for its media access control method. FDDI uses token passing, as well as obsolete protocols like Arcnet. Using token passing in a ring topology isn't even necessary. The IEEE 802.4 document defined the specifications for a token-passing network that uses a bus topology.

System Insertion

Before it can join the ring, a workstation must complete a five-step insertion procedure that verifies the system's capability to function on the network (see Figure 9-4). The five steps are as follows:

1. **Media lobe check**   The media lobe check tests the network adapter's capability to transmit and receive data, and the cable's capability to carry the data to the MAU. With the MAU looping the incoming signal for the system right back out through the same cable, the workstation transmits a series of MAC LOBE MEDIA TEST frames to the broadcast address, with the system's own address as the source. Then, the system transmits a MAC DUPLICATION ADDRESS TEST frame with its own address as both the source and the destination. To proceed to the next step, the system must successfully transmit 2,047 lobe media test frames and one duplication address test frame. The testing sequence can only be repeated two times before the adapter is considered to have failed.

2. **Physical insertion** During the physical insertion process, the workstation sends a phantom voltage (a low-voltage DC signal invisible to any data signals on the cable) up the lobe cable to the MAU to trigger the relay that causes the MAU to add the system into the ring. After doing this, the workstation waits for a sign that an active monitor is present on the network, in the form of either an Active Monitor Present (AMP), Standby Monitor Present (SMP), or ring purge frame. If the system does not receive one of these within 18 seconds, it initiates a monitor contention process. If the contention process does not complete within one second, or if the workstation becomes the active monitor and initiates a ring purge that does not complete within one second, or if the workstation receives a MAC beacon or remove station frame, then the connection to the MAU fails to open and the insertion is unsuccessful.

3. **Address verification** The address verification procedure checks to see if another workstation on the ring has the same address. Because Token Ring supports locally administered addresses (LAAs), it is possible for this to occur. The system generates a series of MAC duplication address test frames like those in step 1, except that these are propagated over the entire network. If no other system is using the same address, then the test frames should come back with their ARI and FCI bits set to 0, at which time the system proceeds to the next step. If the system receives two test frames with the ARI and FCI bits set to 1, or if the test frames do not return within 18 seconds, the insertion fails and the workstation is removed from the ring.

4. **Ring poll participation** The system must successfully participate in a ring poll by receiving an AMP or SMP frame with the ARI and FCI bits set to 0, changing those bits to 1, and transmitting its own SMP frame. If the workstation does not receive an AMP or SMP frame within 18 seconds, the insertion fails and the workstation is removed from the ring.

5. **Request initialization** The workstation transmits four MAC request initialization frames to the functional address of the network's ring parameter server (C0 00 00 00 00 02). If the system receives the frames back with the ARI and FCI bits set to 0, indicating that there is no functioning ring parameter server, the system's network adapter uses its default values and the initialization (as well as the entire system insertion) is deemed successful. If the system receives one of its frames back with the ARI and FCI bits set to 1 (indicating that a ring parameter server has received the frame), it waits two seconds for a response. If there is no response, the system retries up to four times, after which the initialization fails and the workstation is removed from the ring.

NETWORK PROTOCOLS

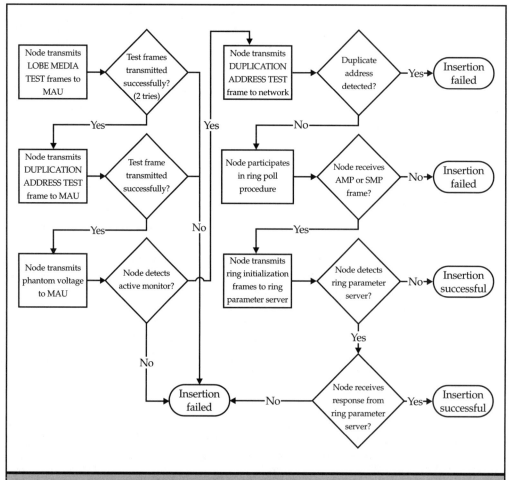

Figure 9-4. *The Token Ring workstation insertion procedure ensures that each system connected to the ring is functioning properly*

System States

During its normal functions, a Token Ring system enters three different operational states, which are as follows:

- **Repeat** While in the repeat state, the workstation transmits all the data arriving at the workstation through the receive port to the next downstream node. When the workstation has a packet of its own queued for transmission, it modifies the token bit in the frame's access control byte to a value of 1 and enters the transmit state. At the same time, the *token holding timer (THT)* that allows the system 8.9 ms of transmission time is reset to zero.

- **Transmit**   Once in the transmit state, the workstation transmits a single frame onto the network and releases the token. After successfully transmitting the frame, the workstation transmits *idle fill* (a sequence of 1's) until it returns to the repeat state. If the system receives a Beacon, Ring Purge, or Claim Token MAC frame while it is transmitting, it interrupts the transmission and sends an abort delimiter frame to clear the ring.

- **Stripping**   At the same time that a workstation's transmit port is in the transmit state, its receive port is in the stripping state. As the transmitted data returns to the workstation after traversing the ring, the system strips it from the network, so that it will not circulate endlessly. Once the system detects the end delimiter field on the receive port, it knows that the frame has been completely stripped and returns to the repeat state. If the 8.9 ms THT expires before the end delimiter arrives, the system records a *lost frame error* for later transmission in a *soft error report frame* before returning to the repeat state.

Token Ring Monitors

Every Token Ring network has a system that functions as the *active monitor* that is responsible for ensuring the proper performance of the network. The active monitor does not have any special programming or hardware, it is simply elected to the role by a process called *monitor contention*. All of the other systems on the network then function as *standby monitors*, should the system functioning as the active monitor fail. The functions of the active monitor are as follows:

- **Transmit Active Monitor Present frames**   Every seven seconds, the active monitor (AM) transmits an Active Monitor Present MAC frame that initiates the ring polling process.

- **Monitor ring polling**   The AM must receive either an Active Monitor Present or Standby Monitor Present frame from the node immediately upstream of it within seven seconds of initiating a ring polling procedure. If the required frame does not arrive, the AM records a ring polling error.

- **Provide master clocking**   The AM generates a master clock signal that the other workstations on the network use to synchronize their clocks. This ensures that all the systems on the network know when each transmitted bit begins and ends. This also reduces network *jitter*, the small amount of phase shift that tends to occur on the network as the nodes repeat the transmitted data.

- **Provide a latency buffer**   In the case of a small ring, it is possible for a workstation to begin transmitting a token frame and to receive the first bits back on its receive port before it has finished transmitting. The AM prevents this by introducing a propagation delay of at least 24 bits (called a *latency buffer*), which ensures that the token circulates around the network properly.

■ **Monitor the token-passing process**   The active monitor must receive a good token every 10 milliseconds, which ensures that the token-passing mechanism is functioning properly. If a workstation raises the token priority and fails to lower it, or fails to completely strip its packet from the ring, the AM detects the problem and remedies it by purging the ring and generating a new token. Every node, on receiving a Ring Purge MAC frame from the AM, stops what it's doing, resets its timers, and enters bit repeat mode, in preparation for the receipt of a new packet.

Ring Polling

Ring polling is the process by which each node on a Token Ring network identifies its nearest active upstream neighbor (NAUN). The workstations use this information during the beaconing process to isolate the location of a network fault.

The ring polling process is initiated by the active monitor when it transmits an Active Monitor Present (AMP) MAC frame. This frame contains an Address Recognized (ARI) bit and a Frame Copied (FCI) bit, both of which have a value of 0. The first system downstream of the AM receives the frame and changes the ARI and FCI bits to 1. The receiving system also records the address of the sending system as its NAUN. This is because the first station that receives an AMP frame always changes the values of those two bits. Therefore, the system receiving a frame with zero-valued ARI and FCI bits knows the sender is its nearest active upstream neighbor.

After recording the address of its NAUN, the system then generates a MAC frame of the same type, except it is a Standby Monitor Present (SMP) instead of an Active Monitor Present. The system queues the SMP frame for transmission with a delay of 20 milliseconds, to give other systems a chance to send data. Without the delay, the ring would likely be clogged with ring polling traffic, preventing the timely transmission of data packets.

After queuing the SMP frame, the system repeats the original AMP frame to the next system downstream. Because the ARI and FCI bits now have a value of 1, no further action is taken by any of the downstream systems except to pass the frame around the ring until it returns back to the active monitor, which strips it from the network.

When the 20-millisecond delay expires, the second system transmits the SMP packet and the entire process repeats with the next system downstream. Eventually, each system on the network will generate an SMP or AMP frame that identifies it as the NAUN of the next system downstream. When the active monitor receives an SMP packet with 0 values for the ARI and FCI bits, it knows the polling process has been completed.

The entire operation must take no more than seven seconds or the AM records a ring poll error before initiating the whole process again. If any system on the network fails to receive an AMP packet for a 15-second interval, it assumes that the active monitor is not functioning properly and initiates the contention process that elects a new AM.

Beaconing

When a station on a Token Ring network fails to detect a signal on its receive port, it assumes that there is a fault in the network and initiates a process called *beaconing*. The system broadcasts MAC beacon frames to the entire network every 20 milliseconds (without capturing a token) until the receive signal commences again. Each station transmitting beacon frames is saying, in essence, that a problem exists with its nearest active upstream neighbor because it is not receiving a signal. If the NAUN begins beaconing also, this indicates that the problem lies farther upstream. By noting which stations on the network are beaconing, it is possible to isolate the malfunctioning system or cable segment. There are four types of MAC beacon frames, as follows:

- **Set Recovery Mode (Priority 1)**   The Set Recovery Mode frame is almost never seen because it is not transmitted by a system's Token Ring adapter. This frame is used only during a recovery process initiated by an attached network management product.

- **Signal Loss (Priority 2)**   The Signal Loss frame is generated when a monitor contention process fails due to a timeout and the system enters the contention transmit mode due to a failure to receive any signal from the active monitor. The presence of this frame on the network usually indicates that a cable break or a hardware failure has occurred.

- **Streaming Signal, Not Claim Token (Priority 3)**   The Streaming Signal, Not Claim Token frame is generated when a monitor contention process fails due to a timeout and the system has received no MAC Claim Token frames during the contention period. The system has received a clock signal from the active monitor, however, or the Signal Loss frame would have been generated instead.

- **Streaming Signal, Claim Token (Priority 4)**   The Streaming Signal, Claim Token frame is generated when a monitor contention process fails due to a timeout and the system has received MAC Claim Token frames during the contention period. This frame is usually an indication of a transient problem caused by a cable that is too long or by signal interference caused by environmental noise.

When a system suspects that it may be the cause of the network problem resulting in beaconing, it removes itself from the ring to see if the problem disappears. If the system transmits beacon frames for more than 26 seconds, it performs a *beacon transmit auto-removal test.* If the system receives 8 consecutive beacon frames that name it as the NAUN of a beaconing system downstream, it performs a *beacon receive auto-removal test.*

You can learn more about a Token Ring network problem by analyzing the packets transmitted during a beaconing event. For more information on protocol analysis and Token Ring beaconing, see Chapter 30.

Token Ring Frames

Four different types of frames are used on Token Ring networks, unlike Ethernet networks, which have one single frame format. The *data frame* is the only one that actually carries the data generated by upper-layer protocols, while the *command frame* performs ring maintenance and control procedures. The *token frame* is a separate construction used only to arbitrate media access and the *abort delimiter frame* is only used when certain types of errors occur.

The Data Frame

Token Ring *data frames* carry the information generated by the upper-layer protocols in a standard logical link control (LLC) protocol data unit (PDU), as defined in the IEEE 802.2 document. The fields that make up the frame format are shown in Figure 9-5; their functions are as follows:

- **Start Delimiter (SD), 1 byte**   The start delimiter signals the beginning of the frame by deliberately violating the rules of the Differential Manchester encoding system. The bit pattern used is JK0JK000, where the *J*s are encoding violations of the value 0 and the *K*s are encoding violations of the value 1.

- **Access Control (AC), 1 byte**   The access control byte uses the bit pattern PPPTMRRR, where the *P*s are three *priority bits* and the *R*s are three *reservation bits* used to prioritize the data transmitted on Token Ring networks. Token ring workstations can have priority levels from 0 to 7, where 7 is the highest priority. A system can only capture a free token and transmit data if that token has a priority lower than that of the workstation. When a node has a higher priority than that of the free token transmits, it can raise the priority of the token by modifying the priority bits in order to transmit further packets more quickly. When the token returns to the system that raised its priority, it can transmit another packet at the same priority or return the token to its previous priority and change it to the "free" state. A system denied the token because its priority is too low can modify the reservation bits to request a token with a lower priority. Of the remaining two bits in the AC field, the *T* represents the *token bit,* the value of which indicates whether the frame is a data/command (1) or a token (0) frame. The *M* represents the *monitor bit,* which is changed from 0 to 1 by the system on the network designated as the active monitor. Because the active monitor is the only system able to change the value of this bit, the assumption is, if the active monitor ever receives a packet with a value of 1 there, the packet has, for some reason, not been removed from the network by the transmitting node and it is incorrectly traversing the ring again.

- **Frame Control (FC), 1 byte**   The frame control byte uses the bit pattern TT00AAAA, where the *T*s specify whether the packet contains a data or a command frame. The third and fourth bits are unused and always have a value of 0. The *A*s represent *attention code bits* that identify a specific type of MAC frame that should be written immediately to the receiving system's express buffer.

- **Destination Address (DA), 6 bytes**   The destination address field identifies the intended recipient of the packet, using either the hardware address coded into the network interface card or a broadcast or multicast address.

- **Source Address (SA), 6 bytes**   The source address field address identifies the sender of the packet using the hardware address coded into the network interface card.

- **Information (INFO), variable**   In a data frame, the information field contains the *protocol data unit* passed down from a network-layer protocol, including a standard LLC header consisting of DSAP, SSAP, and control fields. The size of the information field can be up to 4,500 bytes and is limited by the *ring token holding time*, that is, the maximum length of time a workstation can hold on to the token.

- **Frame Check Sequence (FCS), 4 bytes**   The frame check sequence field contains the 4-byte result of the CRC computation calculated from the frame control, destination address, source address, and information fields, for the purpose of verifying the successful transmission of the packet. The CRC value is calculated by the sending node and stored in the FCS field. At the destination, the same calculation is performed again and compared to the stored results. A match indicates a successful transmission.

- **End Delimiter (ED), 1 byte**   The end delimiter field indicates the end of the packet by again violating the Differential Manchester signaling rules. The bit pattern is JK1JK1IE, where the *J*s and *K*s are encoding violations of 1's and 0's, respectively (as in the start delimiter field). The *I* is an *intermediate frame bit* that has a value of 1 if more packets in the current sequence are waiting to be transmitted. The *E* is an *error detection bit*, which a receiving system sets to 1 if it detects a CRC error in the transmission. This prevents the systems downstream from having to report the same error.

- **Frame Status (FS), 1 byte**   The frame status field uses the bit pattern AF00AF00, in which the *A* is the Address Recognized Indicator (ARI) and the *F* is the Frame Copied Indicator (FRI). The values for these bits are repeated because the frame status field is not included in the frame check sequence's CRC check. The ARI and FCI are both set to 0 by the sending workstation. If the receiving node recognizes the frame, it sets the ARI value to 1. If the receiving node can copy the frame to the adapter's buffer memory, it sets the FCI value to 1. Failure to modify the FCI bits is an indication the packet has failed the CRC check or has been damaged in some other way and must be retransmitted.

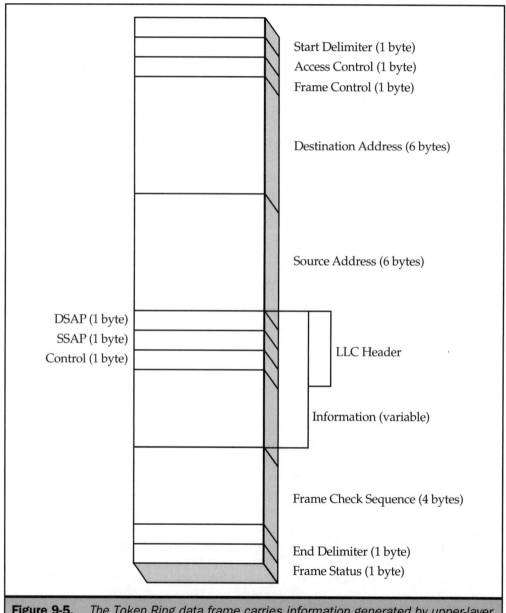

Start Delimiter (1 byte)
Access Control (1 byte)
Frame Control (1 byte)

Destination Address (6 bytes)

Source Address (6 bytes)

DSAP (1 byte)
SSAP (1 byte)
Control (1 byte)

LLC Header

Information (variable)

Frame Check Sequence (4 bytes)

End Delimiter (1 byte)
Frame Status (1 byte)

Figure 9-5.   *The Token Ring data frame carries information generated by upper-layer protocols*

The Token Ring specification lists a number of functional addresses that define specialized roles fulfilled by certain systems on the network. Using these addresses, it is possible for a node to send messages directly to the system performing a specific function, without having to know the machine's hardware address. The predefined addresses are as follows:

Active monitor	C0 00 00 00 00 01
Ring parameter server	C0 00 00 00 00 02
Ring error monitor	C0 00 00 00 00 08
Configuration report server	C0 00 00 00 00 10
Source route bridge	C0 00 00 00 01 00

The Command Frame

Command frames, also called *MAC frames*, differ from data frames only in the information field and sometimes the frame control field. MAC frames do not use an LLC header; instead, they contain a PDU consisting of two bytes that indicate the length of the control information to follow, a 2-byte major vector ID that specifies the control function of the frame, and a variable number of bytes containing the control information itself (see Figure 9-6).

MAC frames perform ring maintenance and control functions only. They never carry upper-layer data and they are never propagated to other collision domains by bridges, switches, or routers. Some of the most common functions are identified using only a 4-bit code in the frame control field, such as the following:

0010	Beacon
0011	Claim Token
0100	Ring Purge
0101	Active Monitor Present
0110	Standby Monitor Present

Some MAC frames with particular functions are processed by network adapters using a special memory area called the *express buffer*. This enables the node to process MAC frames containing important control commands at any time, even when it is busy receiving a large number of data frames.

The Token Frame

The *token frame* is extremely simple, consisting of only three 1-byte fields: the start delimiter, access control, and end delimiter fields (see Figure 9-7). The token bit in the access control field is always set to a value of one and the delimiter fields take the same form as in the data and command frames.

NETWORK PROTOCOLS

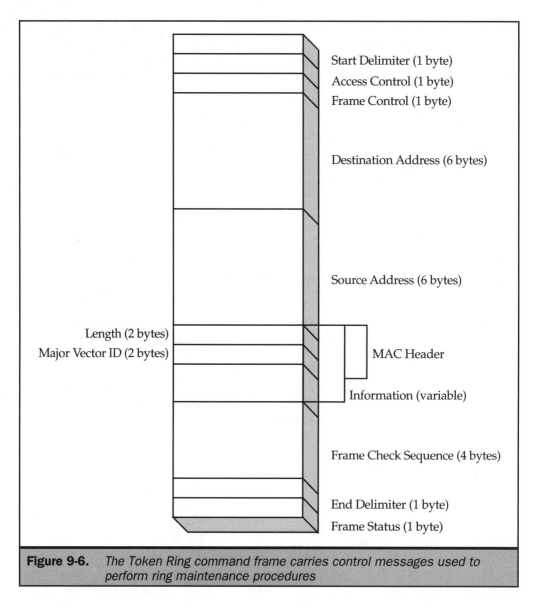

Figure 9-6.   *The Token Ring command frame carries control messages used to perform ring maintenance procedures*

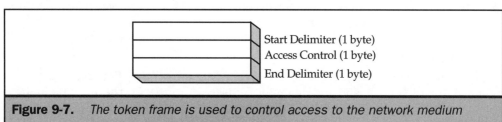

Figure 9-7.   *The token frame is used to control access to the network medium*

The Abort Delimiter Frame

The *abort delimiter frame* consists only of the start delimiter and the end delimiter fields, using the same format as the equivalent fields in the data and command frames (see Figure 9-8). This frame type is used primarily when an unusual event occurs, such as when the transmission of a packet is interrupted and ends prematurely. When this happens, the active monitor transmits an abort delimiter frame that flushes out the ring, removing all the improperly transmitted data and preparing it for the next transmission.

Token Ring Errors

The 802.5 standard defines a number of soft error types that systems on the network can report to the workstation functioning as the *ring error monitor* using MAC frames. When a Token Ring adapter detects a soft error, it begins a two-second countdown, during which it waits to see if other errors occur. After the two seconds, the system sends a soft error report message to the address of the ring error monitor (C0 00 00 00 00 08). The types of soft errors detectable by Token Ring systems are as follows:

- **Burst error**   A burst error occurs when a system detects five half-bit times (that is, three transmitted bits) that lack the click transition in the middle of the bit called for by the Differential Manchester encoding system. This type of error is typically caused by noise on the cable resulting from faulty hardware or some other environmental influence.

- **Line error**   A line error occurs when a workstation receives a frame that has an error detection bit (in the end delimiter field) with a value of 1, either because of a CRC error in the frame check sequence or because a bit violating the Differential Manchester encoding system was detected in any fields other than the start delimiter and end delimiter. A network with noise problems will typically have one line error for every ten burst errors.

- **Lost frame error**   A lost frame error occurs when a system transmits a frame and fails to receive it back within the 4 milliseconds allotted by the *return to repeat timer* (TRR). This error can be caused by excessive noise on the network.

- **Token error**   A token error occurs when the active monitor's 10 millisecond *valid transmission timer (TVX)* expires without the receipt of a frame, and the AM must generate a new token. This error can be caused by excessive noise on the network.

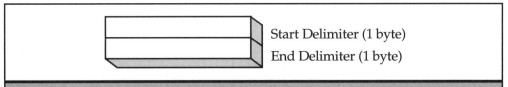

Start Delimiter (1 byte)

End Delimiter (1 byte)

Figure 9-8.   *The abort delimiter frame is used to clear the ring before the generation of a new token by the active monitor*

■ **Internal error**   An internal error occurs when a system detects a parity error during direct memory access (DMA) between the network adapter and the computer. The problem could be with the adapter's own memory or with the computer's memory. If you install the adapter in another system, the problem is with the card itself.

■ **Frequency error**   A frequency error occurs when a standby monitor system receives a signal that differs from the expected frequency by more than a given amount. This error may mean that the active monitor is not supplying a proper clock signal. Shut down the current active monitor to force a new contention process. If no more frequency errors occur, then the network adapter on the original active monitor system is malfunctioning.

■ **AC error**   An AC error occurs when a system receives two consecutive ring-polling frames with ARI and FCI bits set to 0, in which the first frame is an AMP or an SMP, and the second frame is an SMP. Because the nearest downstream neighbor to the system transmitting an AMP or SMP frame should modify those bits, no system should ever receive two unmodified frames in this order. This error means that the system immediately upstream from the computer experiencing the error is failing to modify the ARI and FCI bits properly, probably due to a malfunctioning network adapter.

■ **FC error**   An FC (Frame Copied) error occurs when a system receives a unicast MAC frame with the ARI bit set to 1, indicating either a noise problem or a duplicate address on the network.

■ **Abort delimiter transmitted error**   An abort delimiter transmitted error occurs whenever a network condition causes a workstation to stop transmitting in the middle of a frame and to generate an abort delimiter frame. This occurs when the transmitting system receives a token with an invalid end delimiter or receives a claim token, beacon, or ring purge frame when it is expecting the start delimiter of its own transmitted frame.

■ **Receive congestion error**   A receive congestion error occurs when a system receives a unicast frame, but has no available buffer space to store the packet because of its being overwhelmed by incoming frames.

Note	*The AC error is called an* isolating error, *because it points to a specific machine as the source of the problem. An error that does not indicate a specific source is called a* nonisolating error.

100VG-AnyLAN

100VG-AnyLAN is a 100 Mbps desktop networking protocol that is usually grouped with Fast Ethernet because the two were created at the same time and competed for the same market. However, this protocol cannot strictly be called an Ethernet variant because it does not use the CSMA/CD media access control mechanism.

100VG-AnyLAN is defined in the IEEE 802.12 specification, while all of the Ethernet variants are documented by the 802.3 working group. Originally touted by Hewlett-Packard and AT&T as a 100 Mbps UTP networking solution that is superior to Fast Ethernet, the market has not upheld that belief and, while some 100VG products are still available, Fast Ethernet has clearly become the dominant 100 Mbps networking technology.

As with Fast Ethernet, the intention behind the 100VG standard is to use existing 10BaseT cable installations and to provide a clear, gradual upgrade path to the faster technology. Originally intended to support all the same physical-layer options as Fast Ethernet, only the first 100VG cabling option has actually materialized, using all four wire pairs in a UTP cable rated category 3 or better. The maximum cable segment length is 100 meters for category 3 and 4 cables, and 200 meters for category 5. Up to 1,024 nodes are permitted on a single collision domain. 100VG-AnyLAN uses a technique called *quartet signaling* to use the four wire pairs in the cable.

100VG uses the same frame format as either 802.3 Ethernet or 802.5 Token Ring, making it possible for the traffic to coexist on a network with these other protocols. This is an essential point that provides a clear upgrade path from the older, slower technologies. As with Fast Ethernet, dual-speed NICs are available to make it possible to perform upgrades gradually, one component at a time.

A 10BaseT/100VG-AnyLAN NIC, however, is a substantially more complex device than a 10/100 Fast Ethernet card. While the similarity between standard and Fast Ethernet enables the adapter to use many of the same components for both protocols, 100VG is sufficiently different from 10BaseT to force the device to be essentially two network interface adapters on a single card, which share little else but the cable and bus connectors. This, and the relative lack of acceptance for 100VG-AnyLAN, has led the prices of the hardware to be substantially higher than those for Fast Ethernet.

The one area in which 100VG-AnyLAN differs most substantially from Ethernet is in its media access control mechanism. 100VG networks use a technique called *demand priority*, which eliminates the normally occurring collisions from the network and also provides a means to differentiate between normal and high-priority traffic. The introduction of priority levels is intended to support applications that require consistent streams of high bandwidth, such as real-time audio and video.

The 100VG-AnyLAN specification subdivides its functionality into several sublayers. Like the other IEEE 802 standards, the *logical link control (LLC)* sublayer is at the top of a node's data link layer's functionality, followed by the *media access control (MAC)* sublayer. On a repeater (hub), the *repeater media access control (RMAC)* sublayer is directly below the LLC. Beneath the MAC or RMAC sublayer, the specification calls for a physical medium–independent (PMI) sublayer, a medium-independent interface (MII), and a physical medium–dependent (PMD) sublayer. Finally, the medium-dependent interface provides the actual connection to the network medium. The following sections examine the activities at each of these layers.

NETWORK PROTOCOLS

The Logical Link Control Sublayer

The LLC-sublayer functionality is defined by the IEEE 802.2 standard and is the same as that used with 802.3 (Ethernet) and 802.5 (Token Ring) networks. For more information, see "The Logical Link Control Sublayer" section in Chapter 8.

The MAC and RMAC Sublayers

100VG's demand priority mechanism replaces the CSMA/CD mechanism in Ethernet and Fast Ethernet networks. Unlike most other MAC mechanisms, access to the medium on a demand priority network is controlled by the hub. Each node on the network, in its default state, transmits an *Idle_Up* signal to its hub, indicating that it is available to receive data. When a node has data to transmit, it sends either a *Request_Normal* or *Request_High* signal to the hub. The signal the node uses for each packet is determined by the upper-layer protocols, which assign priorities based on the application generating the data.

The hub continuously scans all of its ports in a round-robin fashion, waiting to receive request signals from the nodes. After each scan, the hub selects the node with the lowest port number that has a high-priority request pending and sends it the *Grant* signal, which is the permission for the node to transmit. After sending the *Grant* signal to the selected node, the hub sends the *Incoming* signal to all of the other ports, which informs the nodes of a possible transmission. As each node receives the incoming signal, it stops transmitting requests and awaits the incoming transmission.

When the hub receives the packet from the sending node, it reads the destination address from the frame header and sends the packet out the appropriate port. All the other ports receive the *Idle_Down* signal. After receiving either the data packet or the *Idle_Down* signal, the nodes return to their original state and begin transmitting either a request or an *Idle_Up* signal. The hub then processes the next high-priority request. When all the high-priority requests have been satisfied, the hub then permits the nodes to transmit normal priority traffic, in port number order. This exchange of signals is illustrated in Figure 9-9.

Note   *By default, a 100VG hub only transmits incoming packets out to the port (or ports) identified in the packet's destination address. This is known as operating in* private mode. *Configuring specific nodes to operate in* promiscuous mode *is possible, however, in which case they receive every packet transmitted over the network.*

The processing of high-priority requests first enables applications that require timely access to the network to receive it, but a mechanism also exists to protect normal priority traffic from excessive delays. If the time needed to process a normal priority request exceeds a specified interval, the request is upgraded to high priority.

On a network with multiple hubs, one *root hub* always exists, to which all the others are ultimately connected. When the root hub receives a request through a port to which another hub is connected, it enables the subordinate hub to perform its own port scan

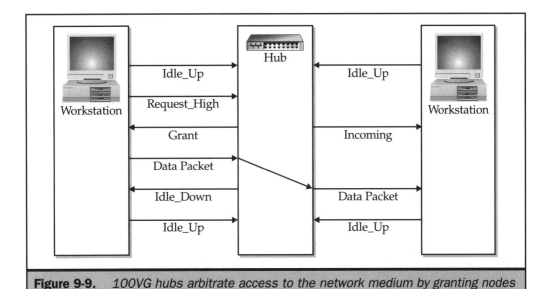

Figure 9-9. *100VG hubs arbitrate access to the network medium by granting nodes permission to transmit*

and process one request from each of its own ports. In this way, permission to access the media is propagated down the network tree and all nodes have an equal opportunity to transmit.

MAC Frame Preparation

In addition to controlling access to the network medium, the MAC sublayer also assembles the packet frame for transmission across the network. Four possible types of frames exist on a 100VG-AnyLAN network:

- 802.3
- 802.5
- Void
- Link training

802.3 AND 802.5 FRAMES   100VG-AnyLAN is capable of using either 802.3 (Ethernet) or 802.5 (Token Ring) frames, so that the 100VG protocol can coexist with the other network types during a gradual deployment process. Using both frame types at once is impossible, however. You must configure all of the hubs on the network to use one or the other frame type.

All 100VG frames are encapsulated within a Start of Stream field and an End of Stream field by the physical medium–independent sublayer, which informs the PMI sublayer on the receiving station when a packet is being sent and when the transmission is completed. Inside these fields, the 802.3 and 802.5 frames use the exact same formats defined in their respective specifications.

The MAC sublayer supplies the system's own hardware address for each packet's source address field and also performs the CRC calculations for the packet, storing them in the FCS field.

On incoming packets, the MAC sublayer performs the CRC calculations and compares the results with the contents of the FCS field. If the packet passes the frame check, the MAC sublayer strips off the two address and the FCS fields and passes the remaining data to the next layer.

VOID FRAMES   *Void frames* are generated only by repeaters when a node fails to transmit a packet within a given time period after the repeater has acknowledged it.

LINK TRAINING FRAMES   Every time a node is restarted or reconnected to the network, it initiates a link training procedure with its hub by transmitting a series of specialized link training packets. This procedure serves several purposes, as follows:

- **Connection testing**   For a node to connect to the network, it must exchange 24 consecutive training packets with the hub without corruption or loss. This ensures that the physical connection is viable and that the NIC and hub port are functioning properly.

- **Port configuration**   The data in the training packets specifies whether the node will use 802.3 or 802.5 frames, operate in private or promiscuous mode, and whether it is an end node (computer) or a repeater (hub).

- **Address registration**   The hub reads the node's hardware address from the training packets and adds to the table it maintains of all the connected nodes' addresses.

Training packets contain two-byte *requested configuration* and *allowed configuration* fields that enable nodes and repeaters to negotiate the port configuration settings for the connection. The training packets the node generates contain its settings in the requested configuration field and nothing in the allowed configuration field. The repeater, on receiving the packets, adds the settings it can provide to the allowed configuration field and transmits the packets back to the node.

The packets also contain between 594 and 675 bytes of padding in the data field, to ensure that the connection between the node and the repeater is functioning properly and can transmit data without error.

The Physical Medium–Independent Sublayer

As the name implies, the *physical medium–independent (PMI) sublayer* performs the same functions for all 100VG packets, regardless of the network medium. When the PMI sublayer receives a frame from the MAC sublayer, it prepares the data for transmission using a technique called *quartet signaling*. The quartet refers to the four pairs of wires in a UTP cable, all of which the protocol uses to transmit each packet. Quartet signaling includes four separate processes, as follows:

1. Each packet is divided into a sequence of 5-bit segments (called *quintets*) and assigned sequentially to four channels that represent the four wire pairs. Thus, the first, fifth, and ninth quintets will be transmitted over the first pair, the second, sixth, and tenth over the second pair, and so on.

2. The quintets are scrambled using a different algorithm for each channel, to randomize the bit patterns for each pair and eliminate strings of bits with equal values. Scrambling the data in this way minimizes the amount of interference and crosstalk on the cable.

3. The scrambled quintets are converted to sextets (6-bit units) using a process called *5B6B encoding*, which relies on a predefined table of equivalent 5-bit and 6-bit values. Because the sextets contain an equal number of 0's and 1's, the voltage on the cable remains even and errors (which take the form of more than three consecutive 0's or 1's) are more easily detected. The regular voltage transitions also enable the communicating stations to synchronize their clocks more accurately.

4. Finally, the preamble, start of frame, and end of frame fields are added to the encoded sextets and, if necessary, padding is added to the data field to bring it up to the minimum length.

The Medium-Independent Interface Sublayer

The *medium-independent interface (MII) sublayer* is a logical connection between the PMI and PMD layers. As with Fast Ethernet, the MII can also take the form of a physical hardware element that functions as a unified interface to any of the media supported by 100VG-AnyLAN.

The Physical Medium–Dependent Sublayer

The *physical medium–dependent (PMD) sublayer* is responsible for generating the actual electrical signals transmitted over the network cable. This includes the following functions:

■ **Link status control signal generation**   Nodes and repeaters exchange link status information using control tones transmitted over all four wire pairs in full-duplex mode (two pairs transmitting and two pairs receiving). Normal data transmissions are transmitted in half-duplex mode.

■ **Data stream signal conditioning**   The PMD sublayer uses a system called *NRZ* (non-return to zero) encoding to generate the signals transmitted over the cable. NRZ minimizes the effects of crosstalk and external noise that can damage packets during transmission

■ **Clock recovery**   NRZ encoding transmits one bit of data for every clock cycle, at 30 MHz per wire pair, for a total of 120 MHz. Because the 5B6B encoding scheme uses 6 bits to carry 5 bits of data, the net transmission rate is 100 MHz.

The Medium-Dependent Interface

The *medium-dependent interface (MDI)* is the actual hardware that provides access to the network medium, as realized in a network interface card or a hub.

Working with 100VG-AnyLAN

When compared to the success of Fast Ethernet products in the marketplace, 100VG-AnyLAN obviously has not been accepted as an industry standard, but some networks still use it. The problem is not so much one of performance, because 100VG certainly rivals Fast Ethernet in that respect, but, instead, of marketing and support.

Despite using the same physical-layer specifications and frame formats, 100VG-AnyLAN is sufficiently different from Ethernet to cause hesitation on the part of network administrators who have invested large amounts of time and money in learning to support CSMA/CD networks. Deploying a new 100VG-AnyLAN would not be a wise business decision at this point, but preserving an existing investment in this technology is still possible.

Mixing 100VG-AnyLAN and Fast Ethernet nodes on the same collision domain is impossible, but you can continue to use your existing 100VG segments and to add new Fast Ethernet systems, as long as you use a switch to create a separate collision domain. The most practical method for doing this is to install a modular switch into which you can plug transceivers supporting different data link–layer protocols.

Hewlett-Packard, for example (one of the original supporters of 100VG-AnyLAN), still has 100VG transceiver modules available for its AdvanceStack Switch 2000, which can also support standard, Fast, and Gigabit Ethernet segments, as well as FDDI and ATM. This arrangement provides your 100VG systems with full access to the rest of the network while enabling you to expand using any of these protocols, without making further investments in 100VG-AnyLAN technology.

It's probably only a matter of time before 100VG-AnyLAN is abandoned entirely and, at this time, you can think about replacing the transceiver and the NICs in your 100VG systems with Fast Ethernet or another technology. Switches of this type are an effective stopgap, but they are only a temporary solution to what has turned out to be an unsuccessful product.

Chapter 10

High-Speed Backbones

A *backbone* is essentially a network that connects other networks together, forming an internetwork. The standard model for an enterprise network is to have individual networks (sometimes called *horizontal networks*) servicing departments, or floors of a building, or even whole buildings. Each of the horizontal networks is then connected to a backbone network, using a router or switch, as shown in Figure 10-1. This enables a workstation on any of the networks to communicate with any other workstation.

Note *The terms* router *and* switch *describe different components, but for the purposes of this discussion, they are functionally the same in that they both provide an interface between networks. When the term router is used in this chapter, it should be understood that a switch is equally applicable. For more information on routers and switches and their functions, see Chapter 6.*

When two workstations on the same network communicate, the traffic stays on that local network. However, when the workstations are on different networks, the traffic goes through the router to the backbone and then to the destination network. Because the backbone is shared by all of the networks, it tends to carry a great deal of traffic. For this reason, the backbone typically runs at a higher speed than the local networks. Backbones may also have to traverse greater distances than local networks, so it is common for them to use fiber-optic cable, which can span much longer distances than copper.

At the time when the concept of the backbone network originated, the typical departmental LAN was relatively slow, running 10 Mbps Ethernet. The first backbones were thick Ethernet, selected because the thick coaxial cable could be installed in segments up to 500 meters long. These backbones ran at the same speed as the horizontal networks, however. To support all of the internetwork traffic, a distributed backbone running at a higher speed was needed. This led to the development of data link–layer protocols like *Fiber Distributed Data Interface (FDDI)*. FDDI runs at 100 Mbps, which is faster than anything else at the time, and it uses fiber-optic cable, which can span much greater distances than thick Ethernet.

Once Fast Ethernet products hit the market, the situation advanced by an order of magnitude. 100 Mbps horizontal networks became common, and an even faster backbone technology was needed. This led to the development of protocols like Asynchronous Transfer Mode (ATM) and Gigabit Ethernet.

Distributed and Collapsed Backbones

Two basic types of backbone networks are in general use: the distributed backbone and the collapsed backbone. In a *distributed backbone*, the backbone takes the form of a separate cable segment that runs throughout the enterprise and is connected to each of the horizontal networks using a router or switch. In a *collapsed backbone*, the hub on each of the horizontal networks is connected to a centrally located router or switch (see

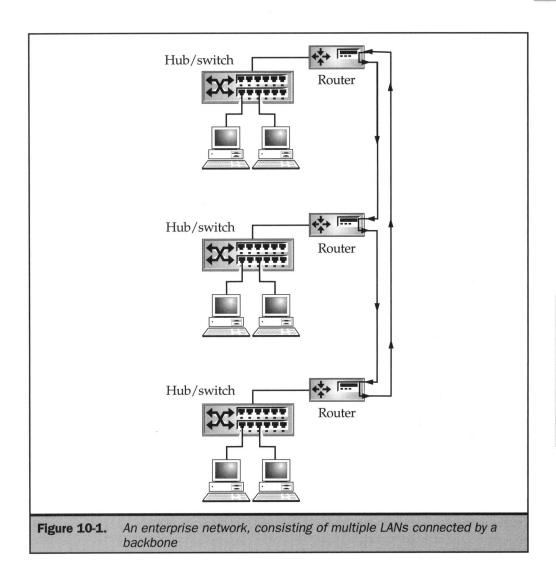

Figure 10-1.   *An enterprise network, consisting of multiple LANs connected by a backbone*

Figure 10-2). This router functions as the backbone for the entire internetwork, by passing traffic between the horizontal networks. This type of backbone uses no additional cable segment because the central router has individual modules for each network, connected by a backplane. The *backplane* is an internal communications bus that takes the place of the backbone cable segment in a distributed backbone network.

The advantage of a collapsed backbone is that internetwork traffic only has to pass through one router on the way to its destination, unlike a distributed backbone, which has separate routers connecting each network to the backbone. The disadvantage of a

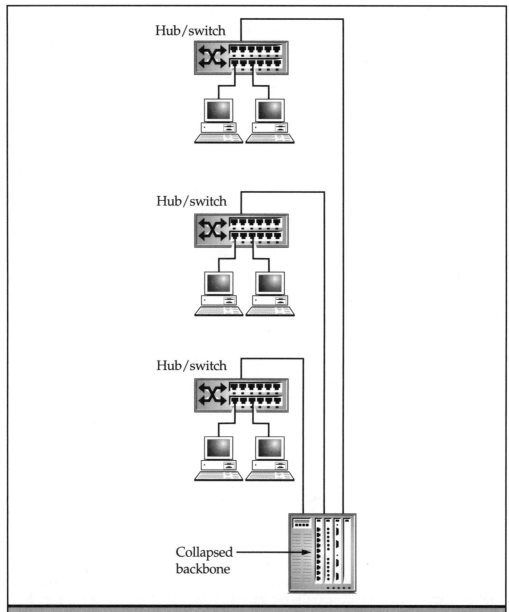

Hub/switch

Hub/switch

Hub/switch

Collapsed
backbone

Figure 10-2. *A collapsed backbone connects all of the LANs to a single router or switch*

collapsed backbone is that the hub on each network must connect to the central router with one cable segment. Depending on the layout of the site and the location of the router, this may be too long a distance for copper cable to run.

Because a collapsed backbone does not use a separate cable segment to connect the horizontal networks, it does not need its own protocol. Today's Fast Ethernet technology has made the collapsed backbone a practical solution. As an example, consider an enterprise that consists of horizontal networks running 100BaseTX and using modular hubs, which can connect different media types. While copper cable connects the individual workstations to the hub, a single 100BaseFX fiber-optic segment runs to the organization's data center, where a large multinetwork switch is installed. This switch routes the traffic between the networks, and the use of fiber-optic cable means that it can be located virtually anywhere in the building. The entire network runs at 100 Mbps, and no traffic has to pass through more than two networks to get from one workstation to another.

While this may be an ideal solution for a new network being constructed today, there are thousands of existing networks that still use 10 Mbps Ethernet or other relatively slow protocols on their horizontal networks, and can't easily adapt to the collapsed backbone concept. The horizontal networks might be using older media, such as Category 3 UTP or even thin Ethernet, and can't support the long cable runs to a central router. The horizontal networks might even be in separate buildings on a campus, in which case a collapsed backbone would require each building to have a cable run to the location of the router.

In cases like these, a distributed backbone is necessary. Each of the protocols discussed in this chapter is suitable for use as a backbone network, connecting individual horizontal networks. All of these protocols can conceivable be used for the horizontal networks as well, but in most cases they are not. Few networks today run fiber-optic cable to the desktop, and with Fast Ethernet able to run over copper at 100 Mbps, this is not likely to change until even more bandwidth than that is required.

FDDI

Appearing first in the late 1980s and defined in standards developed by the ANSI (American National Standards Institute) X3T9.5 committee, the *Fiber Distributed Data Interface (FDDI)* was the first 100 Mbps data link–layer protocol to achieve popular use. In 1995, the committee became known as X3T12. The FDDI standards have also been approved by the International Organization for Standardization (ISO).

At the time of FDDI's introduction, 10 Mbps thick and thin Ethernet were dominant LAN technologies, and FDDI represented a major step forward in speed. In addition, the use of fiber-optic cable provided dramatic increases in packet size, network segment size, and number of workstations supported. FDDI packets can carry up to 4,500 bytes of data (compared to 1,500 for Ethernet) and a network can consist of up to 100 kilometers of cable, supporting up to 500 workstations. These improvements, in combination with fiber-optic's resistance to the effects of electromagnetic interference, made it an excellent protocol for connecting distant workstations and networks, even those in different buildings. As a result, FDDI became known primarily as a backbone protocol, a role for which it is admirable suited.

Although it can run to the desktop, few networks use fiber-optic cable for this purpose because of its high hardware, installation, and maintenance costs. To address this problem, a standard was developed for running the same protocol over copper cable, called TP-PMD (Twisted Pair – Physical Media Dependent) or Copper Distributed Data Interface (CDDI), but this never achieved widespread acceptance.

Note	*For more information on fiber-optic cable and its properties, see Chapter 4.*

Because of its common use as a backbone protocol, products like bridges and routers that connect Ethernet networks to FDDI backbones are common. FDDI is completely different from Ethernet, and the two network types can only be connected using a device like a router that is designed to provide an interface between different networks. Today, the widespread acceptance of Fast Ethernet, which can run over the same fiber-optic cable, has resulted in a decline in the popularity of FDDI. A Fast Ethernet fiber network provides the same speed and comparable segment lengths and does not introduce a completely new frame format and media access control method onto the network. Therefore, fiber-optic Fast Ethernet segments can be joined using relatively inexpensive hubs, instead of routers.

FDDI Topology

FDDI is a token-passing protocol like Token Ring, that uses either a double-ring or a star topology. Unlike Token Ring, in which the network ring is logical and not physical, the original FDDI specification called for the systems to actually be cabled in a ring topology. In this case, it is a double ring, however. The *double ring,* also called a *trunk ring,* consists of two separate rings, a primary and a secondary, with traffic running in opposite directions to provide fault tolerance. The circumference of the double ring can be up to 100 km and workstations can be up to 2 km apart.

Workstations connected to both rings are called *dual attachment stations (DASs)*. If a cable should break or a workstation malfunction, traffic is diverted to the secondary ring, running in the opposite direction, enabling it to access any other system on the network using the secondary path. A properly functioning FDDI dual ring network and a wrapped ring are depicted in Figure 10-3.

An FDDI network operating in this state is called a *wrapped ring*. If a second cable break should occur, the network is then divided into two separate rings, and network communications are interrupted. A wrapped ring is inherently less efficient than the

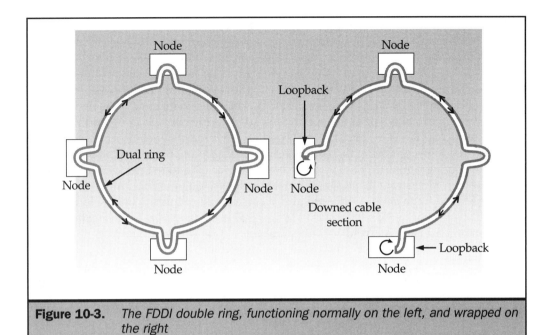

Figure 10-3. *The FDDI double ring, functioning normally on the left, and wrapped on the right*

fully functional double ring because of the additional distance that the traffic must travel and is, therefore, only a temporary measure until the fault is repaired.

FDDI can also use a star topology in which workstations are attached to a hub, called a *dual attachment concentrator (DAC)*. The hub can either standalone or be connected to a double ring, forming what is sometimes called a *dual ring of trees*. Workstations connected to the hub are *single-attachment stations (SASs)*; they are connected only to the primary ring and cannot take advantage of the secondary ring's wrapping capabilities. The FDDI specifications define four types of ports used to connect workstations to the network. These are as follows:

- **A** DAS connection to secondary ring
- **B** DAS connection to primary ring
- **M** DAC port for connection to an SAS
- **S** SAS connection to M port in a concentrator

DASes and DACs have both A and B ports to connect them to a double ring. Signals from the primary ring enter through the B port and exit from the A port, while the signals from the secondary ring enter through A and exit through B. An SAS has a single S port, which connects it to the primary ring only through an M port on a DAC.

The 500 workstation and 100 km network-length limitations are based on the use of DAS computers. An FDDI network composed only of SAS machines can be up to 200 km long and support up to 1,000 workstations.

DAS computers that are attached directly to the double ring function as repeaters; they regenerate the signals as they pass each packet along to the rest of the network. When a system is turned off, however, it does not pass the packets along and the network wraps, unless the station is equipped with a bypass switch. A *bypass switch*, implemented either as part of the network interface adapter or as a separate device, enables incoming signals to pass through the station and on to the rest of the network, but it does not regenerate them. On a fiber-optic network, this is the equivalent of opening a window to let the sunlight into a room instead of turning on an electric light. As with any network medium, however, the signal has a tendency to attenuate if it is not regenerated. If too many adjacent systems are not repeating the packets, the signals can weaken to the point at which stations can't read them.

The DAC functions much like a Token Ring MAU, in that it implements a logical ring while using a physical star topology. Connecting a DAC to a double ring extends the primary ring out to each connected workstation and back, as shown in Figure 10-4. Notice that while the DAC is connected to both the primary and secondary rings, the M ports connect only the primary ring to the workstations. Thus, while the DAC itself takes advantage of the double ring's fault tolerance, a break in the cable connecting a workstation to the DAC severs the workstation from the network. However, the DAC is capable of dynamically removing a malfunctioning station from the ring (again, like a Token Ring MAU), so that the problem affects only the single workstation and not the entire ring.

It is sometimes possible to connect a DAS to two DAC ports, to provide a standby link to the hub if the active link fails. This is called *dual homing*. However, this is different from connecting the DAS directly to the double ring, because both the A and B ports on the workstation are connected to M ports on the hub. M ports are connected only to the primary ring, so a dual-homed system simply has a backup connection to the primary ring, not a connection to both rings.

Cascading hubs are permitted on an FDDI network. This means that you can plug one DAC into an M port of another DAC to extend the network. There is no limit to the number of layers, as long as you observe the maximum number of workstations permitted on the ring. It is also possible to create a two-station ring by connecting the S ports on two SAS computers or by connecting an S port to either the A or B port of a DAS. Some FDDI adapters may require special configuration to do this.

In the case of a network that uses FDDI for all of its systems, administrators typically connect servers and other important computers directly to the double ring

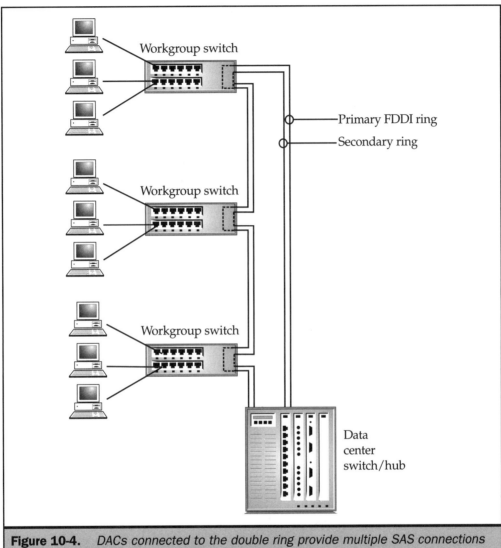

Primary FDDI ring
Secondary ring
Workgroup switch
Data center switch/hub

Figure 10-4. *DACs connected to the double ring provide multiple SAS connections*

as DASs, to avoid any downtime caused by cable faults. DACs are used for single-attachment connections to user workstations. When FDDI is used only for the backbone, connecting all of the systems as DASs is recommended.

NETWORK PROTOCOLS

FDDI Subsystems

The functionality of the FDDI protocol is broken down into four distinct layers, as follows:

- **Physical Media Dependent (PMD)**   Prepares data for transmission over a specific type of network medium.

- **Physical (PHY)**   Encodes and decodes the packet data into a format suitable for transmission over the network medium and is responsible for maintaining the clock synchronization on the ring.

- **Media Access Control (MAC)**   Constructs FDDI packets by applying the frame containing addressing, scheduling, and routing data, and then negotiates access to the network medium.

- **Station Management (SMT)**   Provides management functions for the FDDI ring, including insertion and removal of the workstation from the ring, fault detection and reconfiguration, neighbor identification, and statistics monitoring.

The FDDI standards consist of separate documents for each of these layers, as well as separate specifications for some of the options at certain layers. The operations performed at each layer are discussed in the following sections.

The FDDI standards, as with all ANSI and ISO standards, are not freely available, online or otherwise. You can purchase them, however, in either printed form or on CD-ROM, from the American National Standards Institute at http://www.ansi.org or from Global Engineering Documents at http://global.his.com.

The Physical Media Dependent Layer

The *Physical Media Dependent (PMD)* layer is responsible for the mechanics involved in transmitting data over a particular type of network medium. The FDDI standards define two physical layer options, as follows.

FIBER-OPTIC   The Fiber-PMD standards define the use of either singlemode or multimode fiber-optic cable, as well as the operating characteristics of the other components involved in producing the signal, including the optical power sources, photodetectors, transceivers, and medium interface connectors. For example, the optical power sources must be able to transmit a 25-microwatt signal, while the photodetectors must be capable of reading a 2 microwatt signal.

The original cable defined in the standard is 62.5/125 micron-graded index multimode fiber, although cables with other core and cladding diameters are allowed, such as 50/125, 80/125, and 100/140. You can also use singlemode fiber cable, as defined in the SMF-PMD standard, with a core diameter from 8 to 10 microns and a 125-micron cladding diameter. Singlemode fiber provides significantly less signal attenuation than multimode, enabling it to span longer distances; but it is also more expensive and less flexible, making it more difficult to install.

The 2 km maximum distance between FDDI stations cited earlier is for multimode fiber; with singlemode cable, runs of 40 to 60 km between workstations are possible. There is also a low-cost multimode fiber cable standard, called LCF-PMD, that allows only 500 meters between workstations. All of these fiber cables use the same wavelength (1300 nm), so it's possible to mix them on the same network, as long as you adhere to the cabling guidelines of the least capable cable in use.

TWISTED-PAIR   The TP-PMD standard, published in 1995 and sometimes called the Copper Distributed Data Interface (CDDI), calls for the use of either standard Category 5 unshielded twisted-pair (UTP) or Type 1 shielded twisted-pair (STP) cable. In both cases, the maximum distance for a cable run is 100 meters. Twisted-pair cable is typically used for SAS connections to concentrators, while the backbone uses fiber-optic. This makes it possible to use inexpensive copper cable for horizontal wiring to the workstations and retain the attributes of fiber-optic on the backbone without the need to bridge or route between FDDI and Ethernet. CDDI never gained wide acceptance in the marketplace, probably because of the introduction of Fast Ethernet soon after its introduction.

The Physical Layer

While the PMD layer defines the characteristics of specific media types, the PHY layer is implemented in the network interface adapter's chipset and provides a media-independent interface to the MAC layer above it. In the original FDDI standards, the PHY layer is responsible for the encoding and decoding of the packets constructed by the MAC layer into the signals that are transmitted over the cable. FDDI uses a signaling scheme called *NRZI 4B/5B (Non-Return to Zero Inverted)*, which is substantially more efficient than the Manchester and Different Manchester schemes used by Ethernet and Token Ring.

Note   *For more information on physical-layer signaling techniques, see Chapter 2.*

The TP-PMD standard, however, calls for a different signaling scheme, called MLT-3 (Multi-Level Transition), which uses three signal values instead of the two used by NRZI 4B/5B. Both of these schemes provide the signal needed to synchronize the clocks of the transmitting and receiving workstations.

The Media Access Control Layer

The MAC layer accepts protocol data units (PDUs) of up to 9,000 bytes from the network-layer protocol and constructs packets up to 4,500 bytes in size by encapsulating the data within an FDDI frame. This layer is also responsible for negotiating access to the network medium by claiming and generating tokens.

DATA FRAMES Most of the packets transmitted by an FDDI station are data frames. A data frame can carry network-layer protocol data, MAC data used in the token claiming and beaconing processes, or station management data.

FDDI frames contain information encoded into symbols. A symbol is a 5-bit binary string that the NRZI 4B/5B signaling scheme uses to transmit a 4-bit value. Thus, two symbols are equivalent to one byte. This encoding provides values for the 16 hexadecimal data symbols, eight control symbols that are used for special functions (some of which are defined in the frame format that follows), plus eight violation symbols that FDDI does not use. Table 10-1 lists the symbols used by FDDI and the 5-bit binary sequences used to represent them.

Symbol	5-Bit Binary Value
0 (binary 0000)	11110
1 (binary 0001)	01001
2 (binary 0010)	10100
3 (binary 0011)	10101
4 (binary 0100)	01010
5 (binary 0101)	01011
6 (binary 0110)	01110
7 (binary 0111)	01111
8 (binary 1000)	10010
9 (binary 1001)	10011
A (binary 1010)	10110
B (binary 1011)	10111
C (binary 1100)	11010
D (binary 1101)	11011
E (binary 1110)	11100
F (binary 1111)	11101
Q	00000

Table 10-1. *FDDI Symbol Values*

Symbol	5-Bit Binary Value
H	00100
I	11111
J	11000
K	10001
T	01101
R	00111
S	11001

Table 10-1. *FDDI Symbol Values* (continued)

The format of an FDDI data frame is shown in Figure 10-5. The functions of the frame fields are as follows:

- **Preamble (PA)** Contains a minimum of 16 symbols of idle, that is, alternating 0's and 1's, which the other systems on the network use to synchronize their clocks, after which they are discarded.

- **Starting Delimiter (SD), 1 byte** Contains the symbols J and K, which indicate the beginning of the frame.

- **Frame Control (FC), 1 byte** Contains two symbols that indicate what kind of data is found in the INFO field. Some of the most common values are as follows:

  - **40 – Void Frame**

  - **41, 4F – Station Management (SMT) Frame** Indicates that the INFO field contains an SMT Protocol Data Unit, which is composed of an SMT header and SMT information.

  - **C2, C3 – MAC Frame** Indicates that the frame is either a MAC Claim frame (C2) or a MAC Beacon frame (C3). These frames are used to recover from abnormal occurrences in the token-passing process, such as failure to receive a token or failure to receive any data at all.

  - **50, 51 – LLC Frame** Indicates that the INFO field contains a standard IEEE 802.2 LLC frame. FDDI packets carrying application data use logical link control (LLC) frames.

  - **60 – Implementer Frame**

  - **70 – Reserved Frame**

- **Destination Address (DA), 6 bytes**   Specifies the MAC address of the system on the network that will next receive the frame, or a group or broadcast address.

- **Source Address (SA), 6 bytes**   Specifies the MAC address of the system sending the packet.

- **Data (INFO), variable**   Contains network-layer protocol data, or an SMT header and data, or MAC data, depending on the function of the frame, as specified in the FC field.

- **Frame Check Sequence (FCS), 4 bytes**   Contains a cyclic redundancy check value, generated by the sending system, that will be recomputed at the destination and compared with this value to verify that the packet has not been damaged in transit.

- **Ending Delimiter (ED), 4 bits**   Contains a single T symbol indicating that the frame is complete.

- **End of Frame Sequence (FS), 12 bits**   Contains three indicators that can have either the value R (Reset) or S (Set). All three have the value R when the frame is first transmitted, and may be modified by intermediate systems when they retransmit the packet. The functions of the three indicators are as follows:

  - **E (Error)**   Indicates that the system has detected an error, either in the FCS or in the frame format. Any system receiving a frame with a value of S for this indicator immediately discards the frame.

  - **A (Acknowledge)**   Indicates that the system has determined that the frame's destination address applies to itself, either because the DA field contains the MAC address of the system or a broadcast address.

  - **C (Copy)**   Indicates that the system has successfully copied the contents of the frame into its buffers. Under normal conditions, the A and the C indicators are set together; a frame in which the A indicator is set and C is not indicates that the frame could not be copied to the system's buffers. This is most likely due to the system's having been overwhelmed with traffic.

TOKEN PASSING   FDDI uses token passing as its media access control (MAC) mechanism, like the Token Ring protocol. A special packet called a *token* circulates around the network, and only the system in possession of the token is permitted to transmit its data. The optional feature called *early token release* on a Token Ring network, in which a system transmits a new token immediately after it finishes transmitting its last packet, is standard on an FDDI network. FDDI systems can also transmit multiple

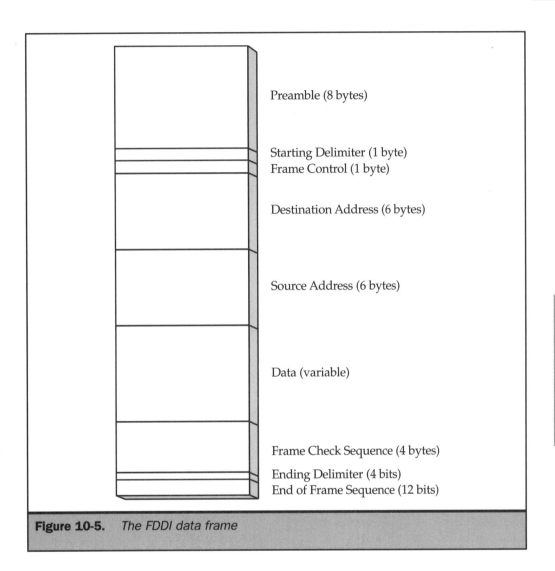

Preamble (8 bytes)

Starting Delimiter (1 byte)
Frame Control (1 byte)

Destination Address (6 bytes)

Source Address (6 bytes)

Data (variable)

Frame Check Sequence (4 bytes)

Ending Delimiter (4 bits)
End of Frame Sequence (12 bits)

Figure 10-5.   *The FDDI data frame*

NETWORK PROTOCOLS

packets before releasing the token to the next station. When a packet has traversed the entire ring and returned to the system that originally created it, that system removes the token from the ring to prevent it from circulating endlessly.

The format of the token frame is shown in Figure 10-6. The functions of the fields are as follows:

- **Preamble (PA)**   Contains a minimum of 16 symbols of idle, that is, alternating 0's and 1's, which the other systems on the network use to synchronize their clocks, after which they are discarded.

- **Starting Delimiter (SD), 1 byte**   Contains the symbols J and K, which indicate the beginning of the frame

- **Frame Control (FC), 1 byte**   Contains two symbols that indicate the function of the frame, using the following hexadecimal values:

  - **80**   Nonrestricted Token

  - **C0**   Restricted Token

- **Ending Delimiter (ED), 1 byte**   Contains two T symbols indicating that the frame is complete.

FDDI is a *deterministic* network protocol. By multiplying the number of systems on the network by the amount of time needed to transmit a packet, you can calculate the maximum amount of time it can take for a system to receive the token. This is called the *target token rotation time*. FDDI networks typically run in *asynchronous ring mode*, in which any system can transmit data when it receives the token. Some FDDI products can also run in *synchronous ring mode*, which enables administrators to allocate a portion of the network's total bandwidth to a system or group of systems. All of the other systems on the network run asynchronously and contend for the remaining bandwidth in the normal manner.

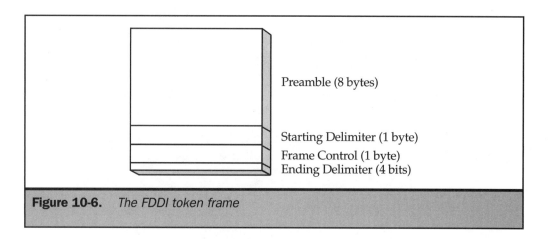

Preamble (8 bytes)

Starting Delimiter (1 byte)
Frame Control (1 byte)
Ending Delimiter (4 bits)

Figure 10-6.   *The FDDI token frame*

The Station Management Layer

Unlike Ethernet and most other data link–layer protocols, FDDI has network management and monitoring capabilities integrated into it and was designed around these capabilities. The SMT layer is responsible for ring maintenance and diagnostics operations on the network, such as

- Station initialization
- Station insertion and removal
- Connection management
- Configuration management
- Fault isolation and recovery
- Scheduling policies
- Statistics collection

A computer can contain more than one FDDI adapter, and each adapter has its own PMD, PHY, and MAC layer implementations, but there is only one SMT implementation for the entire system. SMT messages are carried within standard FDDI data frames with a value of 41 or 4F in the Frame Control field. In station management frames, the INFO field of the FDDI data frame contains an SMT PDU, which is composed of an SMT header and an SMT info field. The format of the SMT PDU is shown in Figure 10-7. The functions of the fields are as follows:

- **Frame Class, 1 byte**   Specifies the function of the message, using the following values:

    - **01 – Neighbor Information Frame (NIF)**   FDDI stations transmit periodic announcements of their MAC addresses, which enable the systems on the network to determine their *upstream neighbor addresses (UNA)* and their *downstream neighbor addresses (DNA)*. This is known as the *Neighbor Notification Protocol*. Network monitoring products can also use these messages to create a map of the FDDI ring.

    - **02 – Status Information Frame-Configuration (SIF-Cfg)**   Used to request and provide a system's configuration information for purposes of fault isolation, ring mapping, and statistics monitoring.

    - **03 – Status Information Frame-Operation (SIF-Opr)**   Used to request and provide a system's operation information for purposes of fault isolation, ring mapping, and statistics monitoring.

    - **04 – Echo Frame**   Used for SMT-to-SMT loopback testing between FDDI systems.

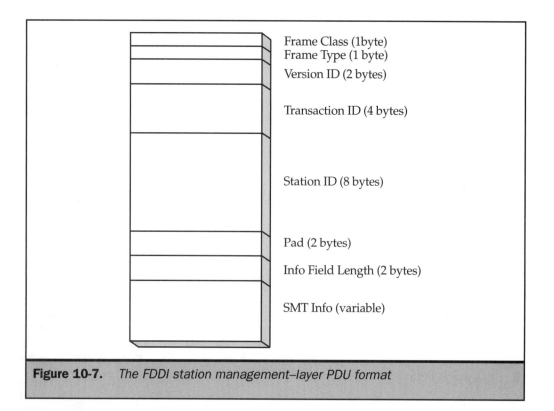

Frame Class (1byte)
Frame Type (1 byte)

Version ID (2 bytes)

Transaction ID (4 bytes)

Station ID (8 bytes)

Pad (2 bytes)

Info Field Length (2 bytes)

SMT Info (variable)

Figure 10-7. *The FDDI station management–layer PDU format*

- **05 – Resource Allocation Frame (RAF)**   Used to implement network policies, such as the allocation of synchronous bandwidth.

- **06 – Request Denied Frame (RDF)**   Used to deny a request issued by another station because of an unsupported Version ID value or a length error.

- **07 – Status Report Frame (SRF)**   Used to report a station's status to network administrators when specific conditions occur, much like an SNMP trap. Some of these conditions are as follows:

    - **Frame Error Condition**   Indicates the occurrence of an unusually high number of frame errors.

    - **LER Condition**   Indicates the occurrence of link errors on a port above a specified limit.

    - **Duplicate Address Condition**   Indicates that the system or its upstream neighbor is using a duplicate address.

- **Peer Wrap Condition**   Indicates that a DAS is operating in wrapped mode, in other words, that it is diverting data from the primary ring to the secondary due to a cable break or other error.

- **Hold Condition**   Indicates that the system is in a holding-prm or holding-sec state.

- **NotCopied Condition**   Indicates that the system's buffers are overwhelmed and that packets are being repeated without being copied into the buffers.

- **EB Error Condition**   Indicates the presence of an elasticity buffer error on any port.

- **MAC Path Change**   Indicates that the current path has changed for any of the system's MAC addresses.

- **Port Path Change**   Indicates that the current path has changed for any of the system's ports.

- **MAC Neighbor Change**   Indicates a change in either the upstream or downstream neighbor address.

- **Undesirable Connection**   Indicates the occurrence of an undesirable connection to the system.

- **08 – Parameter Management Frame-Get (PMF-Get)**   Provides the means to look at management information base (MIB) attributes on remote systems.

- **09 – Parameter Management Frame-Set (PMF-Set)**   Provides the means to set values for certain MIB attributes on remote systems.

  - **FF – Extended Service Frame (ESF)**   Intended for use when defining new SMT services.

- **Frame Type, 1 byte**   Indicates the type of message contained in the frame, using the following values:

  - **01**   Announcement

  - **02**   Request

  - **03**   Response

- **Version ID, 2 bytes**   Specifies the structure of the SMT Info field, using the following values:

  - **0001**   Indicates the use of a version lower than $7.x$

  - **0002**   Indicates the use of version $7.x$

- **Transaction ID, 4 bytes**   Contains a value used to associate request and response messages.

- **Station ID, 8 bytes**   contains a unique identifier for the station, consisting of two user-definable bytes and the 6-byte MAC address of the network interface adapter.

- **Pad, 2 bytes**   Contains two bytes with a value of 00 that bring the overall size of the header to 32 bytes.

- **Info Field Length, 2 bytes**   Specifies the length of the SMT Info field.

- **SMT Info, variable**   Contains one or more parameters, each of which is composed of the following subfields:

  - **Parameter Type, 2 bytes**   Specifies the function of the parameter. The first of the two bytes indicates the parameter's class, using the following values:

    - **00**   General parameters

    - **10**   SMT parameters

    - **20**   MAC parameters

    - **32**   PATH parameters

    - **40**   PORT parameters

  - **Parameter Length, 2 bytes**   Specifies the total length of the Resource Index and Parameter Value fields.

  - **Resource Index, 4 bytes**   Identifies the MAC, PATH, or PORT object that the parameter is describing.

  - **Parameter Value, variable**   Contains the actual parameter information.

An FDDI system uses SMT messages to insert itself into the ring when it is powered up. The procedure consists of several steps, in which it initializes the ring and tests the link to the network. Then, the system initiates its connection to the ring using a Claim Token, which determines whether a token already exists on the network. If a token frame already exists, the Claim Token configures it to include the newly initialized system in the token's path. If no token is detected, all of the systems on the network generate Claim Frames, which enable the systems to determine the value for the token rotation time and determine which system should generate the token.

Because of the SMT header's size and the number of functions performed by SMT messages, the control overhead on an FDDI network is high, relative to other protocols.

FDDI-II

FDDI-II is a newer standard that is designed to provide a better form of bandwidth allocation than the original FDDI standard's synchronous ring mode. FDDI-II is intended for networks that require dedicated bandwidth for real-time applications, such as streaming audio and video. FDDI-II is essentially a circuit-switching technology, in which the existing bandwidth can be divided into 16 discrete channels of varying capacities. A specific application can then be assigned a dedicated circuit between a client and a server, providing consistent, continuous bandwidth.

FDDI-II never captured a significant market, largely because the technology requires that all of the systems on the network be running FDDI-II equipment. If there are any standard FDDI stations on the ring, than all of the systems run in standard FDDI mode.

Gigabit Ethernet

When 100 Mbps networking technologies like FDDI were first introduced, most horizontal networks used 10 Mbps Ethernet. These new protocols were used primarily on backbones. Now that Fast Ethernet is rapidly overtaking the horizontal network market, a 100 Mbps backbone is, in many cases, insufficient to support the connections between switches that support multiple Fast Ethernet networks. Gigabit Ethernet was developed to be the next generation of Ethernet network, running at 1 Gbps, or 1,000 Mbps, ten times the speed of Fast Ethernet.

Although it is still a relatively new technology, Gigabit Ethernet is virtually assured of a place in the market because, like Fast Ethernet before it, it uses the same frame format, frame size, and media access control method as standard 10 Mbps Ethernet. Fast Ethernet has overtaken FDDI as the dominant 100 Mbps solution because it prevented network administrators from having to use a different protocol on the backbone. In the same way, Gigabit Ethernet prevents administrators from having to use a different protocol like ATM for their backbone.

To connect an ATM or FDDI network to an Ethernet network requires that the data be converted at the network layer from one frame format to another. Connecting two Ethernet networks together, even when they're running at different speeds, is a data link–layer operation because the frames remain unchanged. In addition, using Ethernet throughout your network eliminates the need to train administrators to work with a new protocol and purchase new testing and diagnostic equipment. The bottom line is that in most cases, it is possible to upgrade a Fast Ethernet backbone to Gigabit Ethernet without completely replacing hubs, switches, and cables. This is not to say, however, that some hardware upgrades will not be necessary. Hubs and switches will need modules supporting the new protocol, and networking monitoring and testing products may also have to be upgraded to support the higher speed.

Gigabit Ethernet Architecture

Gigabit Ethernet is defined in the 802.3z document published by the Institute of Electrical and Electronic Engineers (IEEE) in June, 1998. The same 802.3 working group is also responsible for the Ethernet and Fast Ethernet standards published earlier. IEEE 802.3 defines a network running at 1,000 Mbps in either half-duplex or full-duplex mode, over a variety of different network media. The frame used to encapsulate the packets is identical to that of 802.3 Ethernet, and the protocol uses the same Carrier Sense Multiple Access with Collision Detection (CSMA/CD) MAC mechanism as the other Ethernet incarnations.

As with standard and Fast Ethernet, the Gigabit Ethernet standard contains both physical and data link–layer elements, as shown in Figure 10-8. The data link–layer consists of the logical link control (LLC) and media access control (MAC) sublayers that are common to all of the IEEE 802 protocols. The LLC sublayer is identical to that used by the other Ethernet standards, as defined in the IEEE 802.2 document. The underlying concept of the MAC sublayer, the CSMA/CD mechanism, is fundamentally the same as on a standard Ethernet or Fast Ethernet network, but with a few changes in the way that it's implemented.

Media Access Control

Gigabit Ethernet is designed to support full-duplex operation as its primary signaling mode. When systems can transmit and receive data simultaneously, there is no need for a media access control mechanism like CSMA/CD. For systems on a 1000BaseX network to operate in half-duplex mode, however, some modifications to the CSMA/CD mechanism were necessary. Ethernet's collision-detection mechanism only works properly when collisions are detected while a packet is still being transmitted. Once the source system finishes transmitting a packet, the data is purged from its buffers and it is no longer possible to retransmit that packet in the event of a collision.

> **Note**   *For more information on the mechanics of the CSMA/CD MAC mechanism, see Chapter 8.*

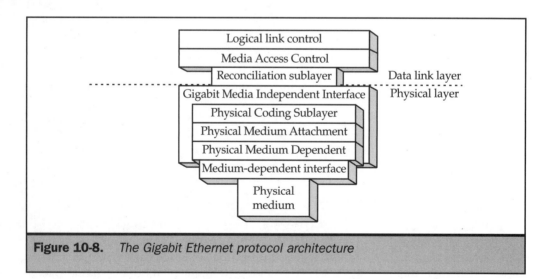

Figure 10-8.   *The Gigabit Ethernet protocol architecture*

When the speed at which systems transmit data increases, the amount of time available for a collision to be detected (called the *round-trip propagation delay*) decreases. When Fast Ethernet increased the speed of an Ethernet network by ten times, the standard compensated by reducing the maximum diameter of the network. This enabled the protocol to use the same 64-byte minimum packet size as the original Ethernet standard and still be able to detect collisions effectively.

Gigabit Ethernet increases the transmission speed another ten times, but reducing the maximum diameter of the network again was impractical because it would result in networks no longer than 20 meters or so. As a result, the 802.3z standard increases the size of the CSMA/CD carrier signal from 64 bytes to 512 bytes. This means that while the 64-byte minimum packet size is retained, the MAC sublayer of a Gigabit Ethernet system appends a carrier extension signal to small packets that pads them out to 512 bytes. This ensures that the minimum time required to transmit each packet is sufficient for the collision detection mechanism to operate properly, even on a network with the same diameter as Fast Ethernet.

The carrier extension bits are added to the Ethernet frame after the Frame Check Sequence, so that while they are a valid part of the frame for collision-detection purposes, the carrier extension bits are stripped away at the destination system before the FCS is computed and the results compared with the value in the packet. This padding, however, can greatly reduce the efficiency of the network. A small packet may consist of up to 448 bytes of padding (512 − 64), the result of which is a throughput only slightly faster than Fast Ethernet. To address this problem the 802.3z standard introduces a packet-bursting capability along with the carrier extension. *Packet bursting* works by transmitting several packets back to back until a 1,500-byte burst timer is reached. This compensates for the loss incurred by the carrier extension bits and brings the network back up to speed.

When Gigabit Ethernet is used for backbone networks (as it will be almost exclusively at first), full-duplex connections between switches and servers are the more practical choice. The additional expenditure is minimal, and aside from eliminating this collision-detection problem, it increases the theoretical throughput of the network to 2 Gbps.

The Gigabit Media Independent Interface

The interface between the data link and physical layers, called the *Gigabit Media Independent Interface (GMII)*, enables any of the physical-layer standards to use the MAC and LLC sublayers. The GMII is an extension of the Media Independent Interface (MII) in Fast Ethernet, that supports transmission speeds of 10, 100, and 1,000 Mbps and has separate 8-bit transmit and receive data paths, for full-duplex communications. The GMII also includes two signals that are readable by the MAC sublayer, called *carrier sense and collision detect*. One of the signals specifies that a carrier is present, and the other that a collision is currently occurring. These signals are carried to the data link layer by way of the *reconciliation sublayer* located between the GMII and the MAC sublayer.

The GMII is broken up into three sublayers of its own, which are as follows:

- Physical Coding Sublayer (PCS)
- Physical Medium Attachment (PMA)
- Physical Medium-Dependent (PMD)

The following sections discuss the functions performed at these sublayers.

The Physical Coding Sublayer

The Physical Coding Sublayer (PCS) is responsible for encoding and decoding the signals on the way to and from the PMA. The physical-layer options defined in the 802.3z document all use the 8B/10B coding system, which was adopted from the ANSI Fibre Channel standards. In this system, each 8-bit data symbol is represented by a 10-bit code. There are also codes that represent control symbols, such as those used in the MAC carrier extension mechanism. Each code is formed by breaking down the eight data bits into two groups consisting of the three most significant bits (y) and the five remaining bits (x). The code is then named using the following notation:

    /Dx,y/

where x and y equal the decimal values of the two groups. The control codes are named the same way, except that the letter D is replaced by a K, as follows:

    /Kx,y/

Note   *Fibre channel is a device interconnection standard that is designed to provide computers with high-speed (up to 800 Mbps) access over short distances to peripheral devices such as RAID arrays and other mass storage systems. Not a network in the traditional sense of the word, fibre channel nevertheless uses various technologies that are useful in network settings.*

The idea behind this type of coding is to minimize the occurrence of consecutive 1's and 0's, which make it difficult for systems to synchronize their clocks. To help do this, each of the code groups must be composed of one of the following:

- Five 0's and five 1's
- Six 0's and four 1's
- Six 1's and four 0's

Note   *The 1000BaseT physical-layer option does not use the 8B/10B coding system. See "1000BaseT," later in this chapter, for more information.*

The PCS is also responsible for generating the carrier sense and collision detect signals, and for managing the auto-negotiation process used to determine what speed the network interface card should use (10, 100, or 1,000 Mbps) and whether it should run in half-duplex or full-duplex mode.

The Physical Medium Attachment Sublayer

The Physical Medium Attachment (PMA) sublayer is responsible for converting the code groups generated by the PCS into a serialized form that can be transmitted over the network medium, and converting the serial bit stream arriving over the network into code groups for use by the upper layers.

The Physical Medium-Dependent Sublayer

The Physical Medium-Dependent (PMD) sublayer provides the interface between the coded signals generated by the PCS and the actual physical network medium. This is where the actual optical or electric signals that are transmitted over the cable are generated and passed onto the cable through the medium-dependent interface (MDI).

The Physical Layer

Collectively called 1000BaseX, there are three physical-layer options for Gigabit Ethernet defined in the 802.3z document, two for fiber-optic cable and one for copper. Another copper option is defined in a separate document, IEEE 802.3ab, which was ratified in June, 1999. These three physical-layer options in 802.3z were adopted from the ANSI X3T11 Fibre Channel specifications. The use of an existing standard for this crucial element of the technology has greatly accelerated the development process, both of the Gigabit Ethernet standards and of the hardware products. In general, 1000BaseX calls for the use of the same types of fiber-optic cables as FDDI and 100BaseFX (the Fast Ethernet fiber-optic standard), but at shorter distances. The longest possible Gigabit Ethernet segment, using singlemode fiber cable, is 5 kilometers.

Note *For its multimode cable options, the 802.3z standard pioneers the use of laser light sources at high speeds. Most fiber-optic applications use lasers only with singlemode cable, while the signals on multimode cables are produced by light-emitting diodes (LEDs). The jitter effect, which was a problem with previous efforts to use lasers with multimode cable, was resolved by redefining the properties of the laser transmitters used to generate the signals.*

Unlike standard and Fast Ethernet, the fiber-optic physical-layer standards for 1000BaseX are not based on the properties of specific cable types, but rather on the properties of the optical transceivers that generate the signal on the cable. Each of the fiber-optic standards supports several grades of cable, using short or long wavelength laser transmitters. The physical-layer options for 1000BaseX are described in the following sections.

1000BaseLX

1000BaseLX is intended for use in backbones spanning relatively long distances, using long wavelength laser transmissions in the 1,270 to 1,355 nanometer range with either multimode fiber cable within a building or singlemode fiber for longer links, such as those between buildings on a campus network. Multimode fiber cable with a core diameter of 50 or 62.5 microns supports links of up to 550 meters, while 9-micron singlemode fiber supports links of up to 5,000 meters (5 km). Both fiber types use standard SC connectors. The cable types supported by 1000BaseLX are shown in Table 10-2.

1000BaseSX

1000BaseSX uses short wavelength laser transmissions ranging from 770 to 860 nanometers and is intended for use on shorter backbones and horizontal wiring. This option is more economical than 1000BaseLX because it uses only the relatively inexpensive multimode fiber cable, in several grades, and the lasers that produce the short wavelength transmissions are the same as those commonly used in CD and CD-ROM players. As of this writing, most of the Gigabit Ethernet products on the market support the 1000BaseSX standard.

The cable types supported by 1000BaseSX are shown in Table 10-3.

1000BaseLH

1000BaseLH (LH stands for *Long Haul*) is neither a standard that has been ratified by the IEEE, nor is it in the process of being ratified. This is a physical-layer specification that has been developed by a group of hardware vendors, including 3Com and Cisco, that are seeking a longer-distance Gigabit Ethernet solution that is suitable for metropolitan area network (MAN) applications. Specific cable options have not been solidified yet, as there are several manufacturers working on different implementations. 3Com, for example, has defined two cable options, both using 9-micron singlemode fiber. One, with a wavelength of 1,310 nanometers, is rated for distances of 1 to 49 kilometers, and the other uses a 1,550 nm wavelength for distances of 50 to 100 km.

Cable Type	Core Diameter	Bandwidth	Maximum Link Length
Singlemode	9 microns	N/A	5,000 meters
Multimode	50 microns	400 MHz/km	550 meters
Multimode	50 microns	500 MHz/km	550 meters
Multimode	62.5 microns	500 MHz/km	550 meters

Table 10-2.   *1000BaseLX Cable Specifications*

Cable Type	Core Diameter	Bandwidth	Maximum Link Length
Multimode	50 microns	400 MHz/km	500 meters
Multimode	50 microns	500 MHz/km	550 meters
Multimode	62.5 microns	160 MHz/km	220 meters
Multimode	62.5 microns	200 MHz/km	275 meters

Table 10-3.   *1000BaseSX Cable Specifications*

1000BaseCX

There is only one standard for copper cabling in the original 802.3z document. 1000BaseCX is intended for links that span only short distances (under 25 meters), such as for connections within the same telecommunications closet or data center. These connections require the use of a special 150-ohm shielded copper cable. The standard specifically mentions that the use of UTP or IBM Type 1 STP is not recommended. 1000BaseCX is intended for equipment connections such as server clusters and links between switches, because it is less expensive and easier to install than fiber-optic. The connections are often located within a controlled environment that doesn't need the long lengths and resistance to interference provided by fiber. There has not been a great deal of interest from hardware manufacturers in producing 1000BaseCX equipment, presumably because of the limits of its market.

1000BaseT

Although it is not included in the 802.3z standard, one of the original goals of the Gigabit Ethernet development team was for it to run on standard Category 5 UTP cable and support connections up to 100 meters long. This enables existing Fast Ethernet networks to be upgraded to Gigabit Ethernet without pulling new cable or changing the network topology. 1000BaseT is defined in a separate document called 802.3ab, which was unanimously ratified by the IEEE in June, 1999.

To achieve these high speeds over copper, 1000BaseT modifies the way that the protocol uses the UTP cable. While designed to use the same cable installations as 100BaseTX, 1000BaseT uses all four of the wire pairs in the cable, while 100BaseTX uses only two pairs. This effectively doubles the throughput of 100BaseTX, but this still doesn't approach speeds of 1,000 Mbps. However, 1000BaseT also uses a different signaling scheme to transmit data over the cable than the other 1000BaseX standards. This makes it possible for each of the four wire pairs to carry 250 Mbps, for a total of 1,000 Mbps or 1 Gbps. This signaling scheme is called *Pulse Amplitude Modulation 5 (PAM-5)*.

While designed to run over standard Category 5 cable, as defined in the TIA/EIA standards, the 1000BaseX standard recommends that new 1000BaseT networks use at least Category 5E (or Enhanced Category 5) cable. Category 5E cable is tested for its resistance to return loss and equal-level far-end crosstalk (ELFEXT). As with Fast Ethernet, 1000BaseT NICs and other equipment are expected that can run at multiple speeds, either 100/1000 or 10/100/1000 Mbps, to facilitate gradual upgrades to Gigabit Ethernet. While networks that run Gigabit Ethernet to the desktop are unlikely to be common for some time, it will eventually happen, if history is any indicator. (Who imagined, ten years ago, that PCs would have processors running at 700 MHz and come with 13 gigabyte hard drives?)

Gigabit Ethernet Applications

Gigabit Ethernet seems like a simple way to increase a network to lightning-fast speeds, but there are several important issues to consider before you begin to upgrade your networks. The first issue, and the basis for all of the others, is that Gigabit Ethernet is still a new technology. Relatively few hardware products are supporting the standards on the market, and the prices of those that are available are high. As of this writing, 1000BaseSX network interface cards from the major manufacturers have street prices in the $600 to $700 range, while hubs and switches start at $1,000 and rise quickly into the stratosphere. Many more products will certainly be introduced as the technology matures, and prices will eventually come down, particularly when the 1000BaseT equipment hits the market; but you must decide if the benefit resulting from an upgrade is worth the expense.

Caution   *A number of Gigabit Ethernet products have been on the market since well before the standards for the technology were ratified by the IEEE. Although the fundamental elements of Gigabit Ethernet networking were stabilized long before the ratification and many of these products may be completely compliant with the standards, it is recommended that you check the manufacturer specifications carefully before making your purchases.*

The reason you must question the economic practicality of an upgrade to Gigabit Ethernet is that converting your backbone may not necessarily produce a remarkable increase in your network's performance. By increasing Ethernet throughput from 10 to 100, and now to 1,000 Mbps in less than five years, the networking technology has outpaced that of the computers on the network. Even the most efficient server PCs are not equipped to handle a traffic rate of 1,000 Mbps. SCSI adapters and system buses can easily be overwhelmed by the huge amount of I/O traffic that Gigabit Ethernet can provide. Therefore, while a Gigabit Ethernet backbone is useful for links between switches that connect multiple 100 Mbps networks, putting your servers directly on the backbone may not yield that much of a performance improvement.

Another issue with Gigabit Ethernet concerns the applications that make use of large amounts of bandwidth. Typical network activities, such as file and printer sharing and Web browsing, do not require a 1,000 Mbps network. Many of the applications that are expected to make use of this much bandwidth involve voice and video traffic, but Gigabit Ethernet is designed to be a data-only protocol. The 1,000 Mbps bandwidth is certainly sufficient to support these applications, but Gigabit Ethernet has no built-in mechanism to guarantee a certain amount of bandwidth to an application.

Voice and video require a continuous stream of bandwidth to function properly, and other technologies, such as ATM, are designed from the ground up to provide it. There are, however, other emerging quality-of-service standards that can conceivably be used with Gigabit Ethernet to provide sufficient continuous bandwidth, such as the Resource Reservation Protocol (RSVP) and the IEEE 802.1p packet prioritization standard. Therefore, it remains to be seen whether Gigabit Ethernet will be an adequate solution when users come to rely on high-speed LANs for critical communications using videoconferencing and other technologies.

ATM

Asynchronous Transfer Mode (ATM) has, since the early 1990s, been the holy grail of the networking industry. Fabled as the ultimate networking technology, ATM is designed to carry voice, data, and video over various network media, using a high-speed, cell-switched, connection-oriented, full-duplex, point-to-point protocol. Unfortunately, as with the holy grail, the quest is taking far longer than anyone expected and the ultimate goal continues to be elusive.

The theory behind ATM is perfectly sound. Instead of using variable-length frames like Ethernet and other protocols, all ATM traffic is broken down into 53-byte *cells*. By using data structures of a predetermined size, network traffic becomes more readily quantifiable, predictable, and manageable. With ATM, it's possible to guarantee that a certain quantity of data will be delivered within a given time. This makes the technology more suitable for a unified voice/data/video network than a nondeterministic protocol like Ethernet, no matter how fast it runs. In addition, ATM has *quality of service (QoS)* features built into the protocol that enable administrators to reserve a certain amount of bandwidth for a specific application.

ATM is both a LAN and WAN protocol, and is a radical departure from the other lower-layer protocols examined in this book. All ATM communication is point to point. There are no broadcasts, which means that switching, and not routing, is an integral part of this technology. ATM can also be deployed on public networks, as well as private ones. Public carriers can provide ATM services that enable clients to connect LANs at remote locations. On private networks, ATM implementations at various speeds can run throughout the network, from the backbone to the desktop.

The reality of the situation, however, is that the only place where ATM has found a healthy share of the market is in campus backbones for large enterprise networks. Approximately 20 percent of installed enterprise backbones run over ATM, largely because administrators find that its QoS capabilities and support for voice, data, and video make it a better performer than traditional LAN protocols.

ATM Architecture

Many of the familiar concepts of other protocols, such as media access control and variable-length frames, are not applicable to ATM. Because ATM does not share bandwidth among systems, there is no need for a MAC mechanism like CSMA/CD or token passing. Switches provide a dedicated connection to every device of the ATM network. Because all ATM transmissions are composed of fixed-length cells, the switching process is simpler and predictable. All ATM switching is hardware based because there is no need for software-managed flow control and other such technologies.

Note	*References to ATM systems and devices refer to switches and routers, as well as actual computers.*

The bandwidth delivered by an ATM network is also readily quantifiable, making it easier to designate the appropriate amount of bandwidth for a specific application. On an Ethernet network, for example, it may be necessary to provide much more bandwidth than is actually needed to ensure good performance from a videoconferencing application. This is because you must account for the bandwidth required for videoconferencing on top of the maximum bandwidth used by all other applications combined. The network, therefore, is designed to accommodate the peak traffic condition that occurs only a small fraction of the time. On an ATM network, bandwidth can be more precisely calculated.

Like Ethernet and Token Ring, ATM encompasses the physical- and data link–layers of the OSI reference model, but is itself divided into three layers (see Figure 10-9), which are as follows:

- Physical layer
- ATM layer
- ATM adaptation layer

The following sections examine the functions performed at each of these layers.

The Physical Layer

The ATM standards do not specify precise physical-layer technologies as most other data link–layer protocols do. This media independence is one of the guiding design principles behind the technology. ATM can run at various speeds over SONET (Synchronous Optical Network) and DS-3 (Digital Signal Level-3) connections, multimode fiber-optic cable, and shielded twisted-pair (STP) cable, among others. Speeds range from 25 Mbps for desktop connections to 2.46 Gbps, although the most common implementations run at 155 or 625 Mbps. It seems unlikely that the 25 Mbps

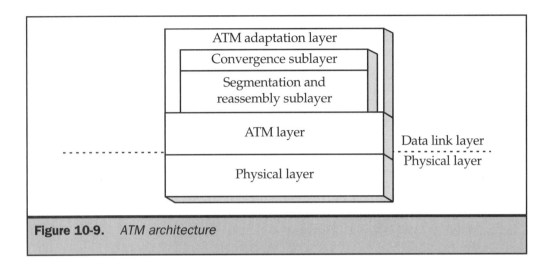

Figure 10-9.   *ATM architecture*

implementation will ever become popular on the desktop because Fast Ethernet provides four times the speed at far less cost. The higher speeds are commonly used for backbones and WAN connections.

Note   *SONET and DS-3 are telecommunications standards that define connections running at specific speeds and using certain signal formats. A DS-3 connection runs at 44.736 Mbps and is equivalent to a T3. SONET is a fiber-optic standard that defines a series of optical carrier (OC) standards that range from OC-1, operating at 51.84 Mbps, to OC-192 at 9,952 Mbps.*

The ATM physical layer itself is divided into two sublayers, called the *physical medium dependent (PMD)* sublayer and the *transmission convergence (TC)* sublayer. The PMD sublayer defines the actual medium used by the network, including the type of cable and other hardware, such as connectors, and the signaling scheme used. This sublayer is also responsible for maintaining the synchronization of all the clocks in the network systems, which it does by continuously transmitting and receiving clock bits from the other systems.

The TC sublayer is responsible for the following four functions:

- **Cell delineation**   Maintains the boundaries between cells, enabling systems to isolate cells within a bit stream.

- **Header error control (HEC) sequence generation and verification**   Ensures the validity of the data in the cells by checking the error-control code in the cell headers.

- **Cell rate decoupling**   Inserts or removes idle cells to synchronize the transmission rate to the capacity of the receiving system.

- **Transmission frame adaptation**   Packages cells into the appropriate frame for transmission over a particular network medium.

The ATM Layer

The ATM layer specifies the format of the cell, constructs the header, implements the error control mechanism, and creates and destroys virtual circuits. There are two versions of the cell header, one for the *User Network Interface (UNI)*, which is used for communications between user systems or between user systems and switches, and the *Network-to-Network Interface (NNI)*, which is used for communications between switches.

In each case, the 53 bytes of the cell are divided into a 5-byte header and a 48-byte payload. Compared to an Ethernet header, which is 18 bytes, the ATM header seems quite small, but remember that an Ethernet frame can carry up to 1,500 bytes of data. Thus, for a full-sized Ethernet frame, the header is less than 2 percent of the packet, while an ATM header is almost 10 percent of the cell. This makes ATM considerably less efficient than Ethernet, as far as the amount of control data transmitted across the wire is concerned.

The format of the ATM cell is shown in Figure 10-10. The functions of the fields are as follows:

- **Generic flow control (GFC), 4 bits**   Provides local functions in the UNI cell that are not currently used and are not included in the NNI cell.

- **Virtual path identifier (VPI), 8 bits**   Specifies the next destination of the cell on its path through the ATM network to its destination.

- **Virtual channel identifier (VCI), 16 bits**   Specifies the channel within the virtual path that the cell will use on its path through the ATM network to its destination.

- **Payload type indicator (PTI), 3 bits**   Specifies the nature of the data carried in the cell's payload, using the following bit values:

  - **Bit 1**   Specifies whether the cell contains user data or control data.

  - **Bit 2**   When the cell contains user data, specifies whether congestion is present on the network.

  - **Bit 3**   When the cell contains user data, specifies whether the payload contains the last segment of an AAL-5 PDU.

- **Cell loss priority (CLP), 1 bit**   Specifies a priority for the cell, which is used when a network is forced to discard cells because of congestion. A value of 0 indicates a high priority for the cell, while a value of 1 indicates that the cell may be discarded.

- **Header error control (EC), 8 bits**   Contains a code computed on the preceding four bits of the header, that is used to detect multiple-bit header errors and correct single-bit errors. This feature detects errors in the ATM header only; there is no error control of the payload at this layer.

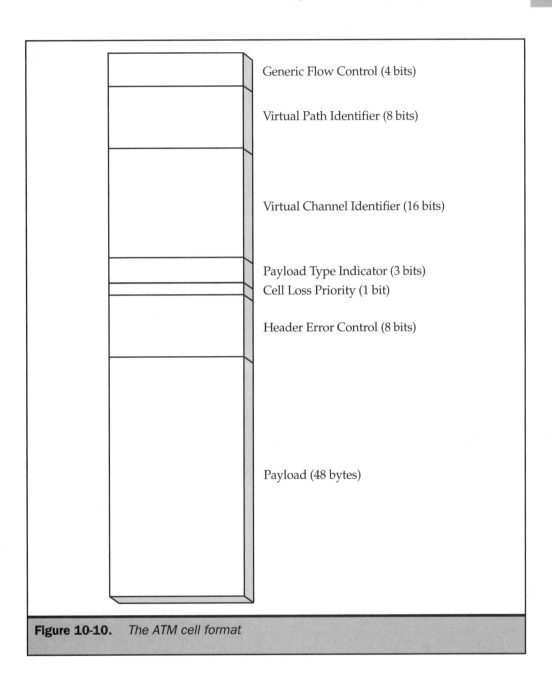

Figure 10-10. *The ATM cell format*

■ **Payload, 48 bytes** Contains the user, network, or management data to be transported in the cell.

The only difference between the UNI header and the NNI header is the GFC field, which is omitted from NNI cells. The four bits from the GFC field are, in this case, added to the VPI field, making it 12 bits long instead of 8.

VIRTUAL CIRCUITS   A connection between two ATM systems takes the form of a *virtual circuit (VC)*. ATM uses two types of virtual circuits: *permanent virtual circuits (PVCs)*, which network administrators manually create and which are always available, and *switched virtual circuits (SVCs)*, which systems dynamically create as needed and then terminate after use.

Establishing a VC through the network to a destination enables the transmission of cells through that circuit without extensive processing by intermediate systems along the way. A VC is composed of a *virtual path (VP)* and a *virtual channel (VC)*. A virtual path is a logical connection between two systems that is comprised of multiple virtual circuits, much as a cable between two points can contain multiple wires, each carrying a separate signal. Once a VP is established between two points, creating an additional VC for a new connection within that VP is a relatively simple matter.

In addition, managing the VP is an easy way of modifying the properties of all of the VCs it contains. When a switch fails, for example, the VP can be rerouted to use another path, and all of its VCs are rerouted with it. Every ATM cell header contains a virtual path identifier and a virtual channel identifier, which specify the VP that the cell is using and the VC within that VP.

ATM ADDRESSING   ATM networks have their own addresses for each device, in addition to any upper-layer addresses they might possess. The addresses are 20 bytes long and hierarchical, much like telephone numbers, enabling them to support extremely large networks. Unlike protocols that share network bandwidth, it isn't necessary to include source and destination addresses in each cell because ATM transmissions use dedicated point-to-point links. Instead, the addresses are used by the ATM switches to establish the VPIs and VCIs for a connection.

The ATM Adaptation Layer

The primary function of the *ATM adaptation layer (AAL)* is to prepare the data received from the network-layer protocol for transmission and segment it into 48-byte units that the ATM layer will package as cells by applying the header. The AAL consists of two sublayers, called the *convergence sublayer (CS)* and the *segmentation and reassembly sublayer (SAR)*. The CS prepares the network-layer data for segmentation by applying various fields that are specific to the type of service that will transmit the data, creating CS-PDUs (convergence sublayer protocol data units). The SAR then splits the CS-PDUs into segments of the appropriate size for packaging in cells.

Several AAL protocols are available at this sublayer, which provide different types of service to support various applications. The AAL protocols are as follows:

- **AAL-1**   A connection-oriented service intended for applications that require circuit emulation, such as voice and videoconferencing. This service requires clock synchronization, so a network medium that supports clocking, such as SONET, is required. For this service, the CS sublayer adds Sequence Number (SN) and Sequence Number Protection (SNP) fields to the data that enable the receiving system to assemble the cells in the proper order.

- **AAL-3/4**   Supports both connection-oriented and connectionless data transfers with cell-by-cell error-checking and multiplexing. The CS creates a PDU by adding a beginning/end tag to the data as a header and a length field as a footer. After the SAR layer splits the CS-PDU into cell-sized segments, it adds a CRC value to each segment for error-detection purposes.

- **AAL-5**   Also called *SEAL, the Simple and Efficient Adaptation Layer*, AAL-5 provides both connection-oriented and connectionless services, and is most commonly used for LAN traffic. The CS takes a block of network-layer data up to 64KB in size and adds a variable-length pad and an 8-byte trailer to it. The pad ensures that the data block falls on a cell boundary and the trailer includes a block length field and a CRC value for the entire PDU. The SAR then splits the PDU into 48-byte segments for packaging into cells. The third bit of the PTI field in the ATM header is then set to a value of 0 for all of the segments of the data block except the last one, in which it is set to 1.

ATM Drawbacks

There are serious drawbacks to consider before you even think about implementing ATM on a backbone (or any) network. The first is the cost: ATM hardware is much more expensive than that for Gigabit Ethernet or virtually any other high-speed protocol. ATM server NICs start at $600 to $800, and the prices for ATM switches run quickly into five and six figures.

Support

The other big problem is the cost and complexity of installing and supporting an ATM network. While a competent Ethernet LAN administrator should be able to install the components of a Gigabit Ethernet backbone with little trouble, an ATM backbone is a completely different story. ATM networks are a hybrid of telecommunications and data networking technologies. These are two separate types of networks, but in the

NETWORK PROTOCOLS

case of ATM, both can use the same cables and switches. An ATM backbone, therefore, may be connected not only to data networking components such as routers, switches, and servers, but also to PBXs and other telecommunications devices.

The fact that these two types of networks are traditionally separated means that the people who support them are often separated as well. People with the advanced knowledge of both disciplines needed to master the intricacies of ATM are relatively rare and therefore command high salaries. As a result, part of the danger in using ATM is that you are likely to be trusting your network to a technology that only one or two highly trained people in your company fully understand. In today's volatile job market, this is a bad thing.

LANE

Another problem with using ATM as a network backbone is the need to make it run with other protocols. Unless you use ATM throughout your network, including runs to the desktops, the backbone must connect individual LANs running Ethernet or other data link–layer protocols. This is a problem because ATM is a connection-oriented protocol and Ethernet and Token Ring are connectionless. Connection-oriented protocols have no broadcast capabilities, so there is no inherent means for a system on an Ethernet (or Token Ring) LAN to discover the address or even the existence of a server on the ATM backbone.

Originally, the solution to this problem was for network administrators to map PVCs between the ATM/Ethernet switches and the servers and other resources on the ATM network. This way, the switches provide the address needed for the Ethernet systems to communicate with the ATM systems. This is a functional solution, but it requires a good deal of administrative effort that grows with the number of systems on the ATM network.

In 1995, *LANE (LAN Emulation)* 1.0 was introduced, which eliminates the need for this manual PVC configuration. LANE automatically creates and deletes SVCs between switches and ATM network systems. This makes the backbone transparent to the Ethernet LANs create a virtual broadcast domain that includes the ATM systems. LANE 2.0, ratified in 1997, adds support for ATM's QoS classes and multicasting.

LANE, unfortunately, requires many different software modules to do its job, including the following:

- **LAN Emulation Client (LEC)**   A module on each ATM device that has both a LAN MAC address and an ATM address. These devices together form an *emulated LAN (ELAN)*. Ethernet systems contact the LECs on the switches joining the networks to discover the addresses of ATM systems. If the LEC is currently communicating with the requested ATM system, it furnishes the address to the Ethernet system. If not, the LEC contacts the LES and the BUS using the *LAN Emulation Address Resolution Protocol (LE_ARP)* to discover the address. Once the address is resolved, the LEC also performs data-forwarding services.

■ **LAN Emulation Server (LES)**   Maintains a database containing all of the addresses known to the LECs on an ELAN. All LECs have a *virtual channel connection (VCC)* to the LES that they use to request the addresses of specific systems on the ATM network. If the LES does not have the requested address in its database, it forwards the request to the other LECs on the network.

■ **Broadcast and Unknown Server (BUS)**   If the LES is unable to discover the proper address for the requested system, the BUS establishes VCCs to all of the LECs on the network and floods them with cells, which the LECs forward to the devices on the Ethernet LANs to which they are attached. The BUS also provides a broadcast emulation service by forwarding messages to all of the LECs on the network.

■ **LAN Emulation Configuration Server (LECS)**   Maintains a database of configuration information for each ELAN, coordinates the activities of the other modules, and inserts new clients into ELANs.

This is a lot of complex software just to make an ATM network visible to Ethernet or other LAN protocols, when a Gigabit Ethernet backbone can do same thing transparently. Many network administrators are staying away from ATM because it requires so much effort to perform what should be simple tasks. Many of the organizations that find ATM most suitable for their backbones are those that require support for voice and video, as well as data such as campus networks servicing hospitals and universities. Medical imaging and remote learning applications need the dedicated bandwidth that ATM can provide more efficiently than other technologies. However, if you're upgrading an existing Ethernet LAN, already have a telephone network installed, and high-bandwidth applications like videoconferencing are not in your organization's immediate future, then Gigabit Ethernet is probably a more practical and economical choice for you.

NETWORK PROTOCOLS

The
Complete
Reference

Upgrading
&
Troubleshooting
Networks

Chapter 11

TCP/IP

Since its inception in the 1970s, the TCP/IP protocol suite has evolved into the industry standard for data transfer protocols at the network and transport layers of the OSI model. In addition, the suite includes myriad other protocols that operate as low as the data link layer and as high as the application layer.

Operating systems tend to simplify the network protocol stack to make it more comprehensible to the average user. On a Windows workstation, for example, you install TCP/IP by selecting a single module called a *protocol,* but this process actually installs support for a whole family of protocols, of which the Transmission Control Protocol (TCP) and the Internet Protocol (IP) are only two. The alternatives to TCP/IP function in much the same way: the IPX protocol suite consists of multiple protocols derived from TCP/IP, and NetBEUI, although much simpler, relies on other protocols as well, such as Server Message Blocks (SMB), for many of its operations. Understanding how the individual TCP/IP protocols function and how they work together to provide communication services is an essential part of maintaining and troubleshooting a TCP/IP network.

TCP/IP Attributes

There are several reasons why TCP/IP has become the protocol suite of choice on the majority of data networks, not the least of which is that these are the protocols used on the Internet. TCP/IP was designed to support the fledgling Internet (then called the ARPANET) at a time before the introduction of the PC when interoperability between computing products made by different manufacturers was all but unheard of. The Internet was, and is, composed of many different types of computers and what was needed was a suite of protocols that would be common to all of them.

The main element that sets TCP/IP apart from the other suites of protocols that provide network and transport-layer services is its self-contained addressing mechanism. Every device on a TCP/IP network is assigned an IP address (or sometimes more than one) that uniquely identifies it to the other systems. Most of the PCs on networks today use Ethernet or Token Ring network interface adapters that have unique identifiers (MAC addresses) hardcoded into them, which makes the IP address redundant. Many other types of computers have identifiers assigned by network administrators, however, and no means exists to ensure that another system on a worldwide internetwork like the Internet does not use the same identifier.

Because IP addresses are registered by a centralized body, you can be certain that no two (properly configured) machines on the Internet have the same address. Because of this addressing, the TCP/IP protocols can support virtually any hardware or software platform in use today. The IPX protocols will always be associated primarily with Novell NetWare, and NetBEUI is now used almost exclusively on Microsoft Windows networks. TCP/IP, however, is truly universal in its platform interoperability, supported by all and dominated by none.

Another unique aspect of the TCP/IP protocols is the method by which they are designed, refined, and ratified. Rather than relying on an institutionalized standards-making body like the IEEE, the TCP/IP protocols are developed in a democratic manner by an ad hoc group of volunteers that communicate largely through the Internet itself. Anyone who is interested enough to contribute to the development of a protocol is welcome. In addition, the standards themselves are published by a body called the Internet Engineering Task Force (IETF) and are released to the public domain, making them accessible and reproducible by anyone. Standards like those published by the IEEE are available, but not freely. You have to pay hundreds of dollars to purchase an official copy of the IEEE 802.3 standards on which Ethernet is based. On the other hand, you can legally download any of the TCP/IP standards, called *Requests for Comment (RFCs)*, from the IETF's Web site at http://www.ietf.org or from any number of other Internet sites.

The TCP/IP protocols are also extremely scaleable. As evidence of this, consider that these protocols were designed at a time when the ARPANET was essentially an exclusive club for scientists and academics and no one in their wildest dreams imagined that the protocols they were creating would be used on a network the size of the Internet. The main factor limiting the growth of the Internet is the 32-bit size of the IP address space itself, and a new version of the IP protocol, called IPv6, is addressing that shortcoming with a 128-bit address space.

TCP/IP Architecture

TCP/IP is designed to support networks of almost any practical size. As a result, TCP/IP must be able to provide the services needed by the applications using it without being overly profligate in its expenditure of network bandwidth and other resources. For example, the NetBEUI protocol locates other systems by transmitting a broadcast message and expecting the desired system to respond. For this reason, NetBEUI is effective only on small networks comprised of a single broadcast domain. Imagine the state of the Internet today if every computer had to broadcast a message to all the millions of machines on the network each time it wanted to locate a single one! To accommodate the needs of specific applications and functions within those applications, TCP/IP uses multiple protocols in combination to provide the quality of service required for the task and no more.

The TCP/IP Protocol Stack

TCP/IP predates the OSI reference model, but its protocols break down into four layers that can be roughly equated to the seven-layer OSI stack, as shown in Figure 11-1.

On LANs, the link-layer functionality is not defined by a TCP/IP protocol, but by the standard data link–layer protocols like Ethernet and Token Ring. A TCP/IP protocol called the *Address Resolution Protocol (ARP)* exists, however, which systems use to reconcile the MAC address supplied by a network interface adapter with the IP address used at the network layer.

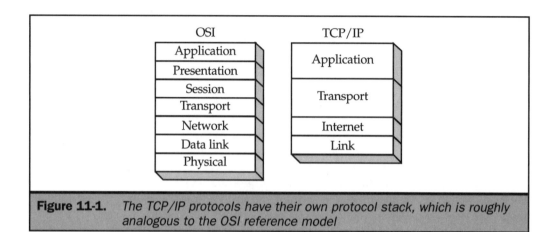

Figure 11-1.   *The TCP/IP protocols have their own protocol stack, which is roughly analogous to the OSI reference model*

The TCP/IP standards do define the two protocols most commonly used to establish link-layer communications using modems and other direct connections. These are the Point-to Point Protocol (PPP) and the Serial Line Internet Protocol (SLIP).

At the internet layer is the *Internet Protocol (IP)*, which is the primary carrier for all the protocols operating at the upper layers, and the *Internet Control Message Protocol (ICMP)*, which TCP/IP systems use for diagnostics and error reporting. IP, as a general carrier protocol, is connectionless and unreliable, because these services are supplied at the transport layer when required.

Two protocols operate at the transport layer: the Transmission Control Protocol (TCP) and the User Datagram Protocol (UDP). TCP is connection oriented and reliable, while UDP is connectionless and unreliable. An application uses one or the other, depending on its requirements and the services already provided for it.

The transport layer can in some ways be said to encompass the OSI session layer as well as the transport layer in the OSI model, but not in every case. Windows systems, for example, can use TCP/IP to carry the NetBIOS messages they use for their file and printer sharing activities, and NetBIOS still provides the same session-layer functionality as when a system uses NetBEUI or IPX instead of TCP/IP. This is just one illustration of how the layers of the TCP/IP protocol stack are roughly equivalent to those of the OSI model, but not definitively so. Both of these models are pedagogical and diagnostic tools more than they are guidelines for protocol development and deployment, and they do not hold up to strict definitions of the various layers' functions.

The application layer is the most difficult to define because the protocols operating there can be fully realized, self-contained applications in themselves, such as FTP, or mechanisms used by other applications to perform a service, such as the Domain Name System (DNS) and the Simple Mail Transfer Protocol (SMTP).

IP Addressing

The IP addresses used to identify systems on a TCP/IP network are the single most definitive feature of the protocol suite. The IP address is an absolute identifier of both the individual machine and the network on which it resides. Every IP datagram packet transmitted over a TCP/IP network contains the IP addresses of the source and destination systems in its header. While Ethernet and Token Ring systems have a unique hardware address coded into the network interface card, there is no inherent method to effectively route traffic to an individual system on a large network using this address.

A NIC's hardware address is composed of a prefix that identifies the manufacturer of the card and a node address that is unique among all the cards built by that manufacturer. The manufacturer prefix is useless, as far as routing traffic is concerned, because any one manufacturer's cards can be scattered around the network virtually at random. To deliver network packets to a specific machine, a master list of all of the systems on the network and their hardware addresses would be needed. On a network the size of the Internet, this would obviously be impractical. By identifying the network on which a system is located, IP addresses can be routed to the proper location using a relatively manageable list of network addresses, not a list of individual system addresses.

IP addresses are 32 bits long and are notated as four 8-bit decimal numbers separated by periods, as in 192.168.2 45. This is known as *dotted decimal notation*; each of the 8-bit numbers is sometimes called an *octet* or a *quad*. (These terms were originally used because there are computers for which the more common term *byte* does not equal 8 bits.) Because each quad is the decimal equivalent of an 8-bit binary number, their possible values are from 0 to 255. Thus, the full range of IP addresses is 0.0.0.0 to 255.255.255.255.

IP addresses do not represent computers per se; rather, they represent network interfaces. A computer with two network interface cards, or one NIC and a modem connection to a TCP/IP server, has two IP addresses. A system with two or more interfaces is said to be *multihomed*. If the interfaces are on different networks and the computer is configured to pass traffic between them, then the system is said to function as a *router*.

Note   *A router can be a standard computer with two network interfaces and software that provides routing capabilities, or it can be a dedicated hardware device designed specifically for routing network traffic. At times, the TCP/IP standards refer to routers of any kind as gateways, while standard networking terminology defines a gateway as being a device that routes traffic between networks that use different protocols.*

Every IP address contains bits that identify a network and bits that identify an interface (called a *host*) on that network. To reference a network, systems use just the network bits, replacing the host bits with zeroes. Routers use the network bits to forward packets to another router connected to the destination network, which then transmits the data to the destination host system.

Subnet Masking

IP addresses always dedicate some of the bits to the network identifier and some to the host identifier, but the number of bits used for each purpose is not always the same. Many common addresses use 24 bits for the network and eight for the host, but the split between the network and host bits can be anywhere in the address. To identify which bits are used for each purpose, every TCP/IP system has a subnet mask along with its IP address. A *subnet mask* is a 32-bit binary number in which the bits correspond to the IP address. A bit with a 1 value in the mask indicates that the corresponding bit in the IP address is part of the network identifier, while a 0 bit indicates that the corresponding address bit is part of the host identifier. As with an IP address, the subnet mask is expressed in dotted decimal notation, so although it may look like an IP address, the mask has a completely different function.

As an example, consider a system with the following TCP/IP configuration:

```
IP address: 192.168.2.45
Subnet mask: 255.255.255.0
```

In this case, the 192.168.2 portion of the IP address identifies the network, while the 45 identifies the host. When expressed in decimal form, this may appear confusing, but the binary equivalents are as follows:

```
IP address: 11000000 10101000 00000010 00101101
Subnet mask: 11111111 11111111 11111111 00000000
```

As you can see in this example, the dividing line between the network and host bits lies between the third and fourth quads. The dividing line need not fall between quads, however. A subnet mask of 255.255.240.0 allocates 12 bits for the host address because the binary equivalent of the mask is

```
11111111 11111111 11110000 00000000
```

The dividing line between the network and host bits can fall anywhere in the 32 bits of the mask, but you never see network bits mixed up with host bits. A clear line always separates the network bits on the left from the host bits on the right.

IP Address Registration

For IP addresses to uniquely identify the systems on the network, it is essential that no two interfaces be assigned the same address. On a private network, the administrators must ensure that every address is unique. They can do this by manually tracking the addresses assigned to their networks and hosts, or they can use a service like DHCP (the Dynamic Host Configuration Protocol) to assign the addresses automatically.

 For more information on DHCP and automatic IP address assignment and TCP/IP configuration, see Chapter 18.

On the Internet, however, this problem is considerably more complicated. With individual administrators controlling thousands of different networks, not only is it impractical to assume that they can get together and make sure that no addresses are duplicated, but no worldwide service exists that can assign addresses automatically. Instead, there must be a clearing house or registry for IP address assignments that ensures no addresses are duplicated.

Even this task is monumental, however, because literally millions of systems are connected to the Internet. In fact, such a registry exists; but instead of assigning individual host addresses to each system, it assigns network addresses to companies and organizations instead. The organization charged with registering network addresses for the Internet is called the *Internet Assigned Numbers Authority (IANA)*. After an organization obtains a network address, the IANA is solely responsible for assigning unique host addresses to the machines on that network.

This two-tier system of administration is one of the basic principles of the Internet. Domain name registration works the same way. NSI registers domain names and the individual administrators of those domains are responsible for assigning names to their hosts.

IP Address Classes

The IANA registers several different classes of network addresses, which differ only in their subnet masks, that is, the number of bits used to represent the network and the host. These address classes are summarized in Table 11-1.

The idea behind the different classes is to create networks of varying sizes suitable for different organizations and applications. A company building a relatively small network can register a Class C address that supports up to 254 systems, while larger organizations can use Class B or A addresses and create subnets out of them. You create subnets by "borrowing" some of the host bits and using them to create subnetwork identifiers, essentially networks within a network.

In practice, network addresses are not registered directly by the companies and organizations running the individual networks. Instead, companies in the business of providing Internet access, called *Internet service providers (ISPs)*, register multiple networks and supply blocks of addresses to clients as needed.

Class D addresses are not intended for allocation in blocks like the other classes. This part of the address space is allocated for multicast addresses. *Multicast addresses* represent groups of systems that have a common attribute, but that are not necessarily located in the same place or even administered by the same organization. The block of addresses designated as Class E is reserved for future use.

NETWORK PROTOCOLS

	Class A	Class B	Class C	Class D	Class E
Network Address Bits	8	16	24	N/A	N/A
Host Address Bits	24	16	8	N/A	N/A
Subnet Mask	255.0.0.0	255.255.0.0	255.255.255.0	N/A	N/A
Addresses Begin with: (Binary)	0	10	110	1110	1111
First Byte Values (Decimal)	0–127	128–191	192–223	224–239	240–255
Number of Networks	127	16,384	2,097,151	N/A	N/A
Number of Hosts	16,777,214	65,534	254	N/A	N/A

Table 11-1.   *IP Address Classes*

Unregistered IP Addresses

Address registration is designed for networks connected to the Internet with systems that must be accessible from other networks. For a private network that is not connected to the Internet, it is not necessary to register network addresses. In addition, most business networks connected to the Internet use some sort of firewall product to prevent intruders from accessing their systems. In nearly all cases, there is no real need for every system on a network to be directly accessible from the Internet, and there is a genuine danger in doing so. Many firewall products, therefore, isolate the systems on the network, making registered IP addresses unnecessary.

For a network that is completely isolated from the Internet, administrators can use any IP addresses they wish, as long as there are no duplicates on the same network. If any of the network's systems connect to the Internet by any means, however, there is potential for a conflict between an internal address and the system on the Internet for which the address was registered. If, for example, you happened to assign one of your network systems the same address as a Microsoft Web server, a user on your network attempting to access Microsoft's site may reach the internal machine with the same address instead.

To prevent these conflicts, the TCP/IP standards specify addresses intended for use on unregistered networks, as shown in Table 11-2. These addresses are not assigned to any registered network and can, therefore, be used by any organization, public or private.

Class A	10.0.0.0 through 10.255.255.255
Class B	172.16.0.0 through 172.31.255.255
Class C	192.168.0.0 through 192.168.255.255

Table 11-2. *Unregistered Network IP Addresses*

Using unregistered IP addresses not only simplifies the process of obtaining and assigning addresses to network systems, it also conserves the registered IP addresses for use by systems that actually need them for direct Internet communications. As with many design decisions in the computer field, no one expected at the time of its inception that the Internet would grow as enormous as it is now. The 32-bit address space for the IP protocol was thought to be big enough to support all future growth (as was the 640KB memory limitation in PCs).

The Internet has now reached the point, however, where addresses are nearly always obtained from third parties and not directly from NSI. In addition, the imminent proliferation of other communications devices that use IP addresses, such as palmtop computers and cellular phones, could result in a shortage of addresses in the near future. The IPv6 protocol, currently in development, is intended to address this shortage by expanding the address space from 32 bits to 128.

Special IP Addresses

Aside from the blocks of addresses designated for use by unregistered networks, there are other addresses not allocated to registered networks because they are intended for special purposes. These addresses as listed in Table 11-3.

The Internal Host Loopback Address

The *internal host loopback address* is a diagnostic tool that enables you to send traffic from a TCP/IP system back to itself, without actually leaving the computer. A system transmitting any packets with a Class A destination address with the value 127 as the first quad (typically, the address 127.0.0.1 is used) automatically diverts those packets to the machine's IP input queue. Because the packets never leave the system, the data link and physical-layer implementations are effectively removed from the loop, thus eliminating these protocols as the cause of any problems that may occur.

The loopback address is useful for testing client and server processes on the same machine. For example, when you supply the loopback address as a URL in a Web browser, the program accesses the default page on the Web server program running on the same machine.

NETWORK PROTOCOLS

Address	Example	Function
All bits zero	0.0.0.0	Addresses the current host on the current network, such as during a DHCP transaction before a workstation is assigned an IP address.
All bits one	255.255.255.255	Limited broadcast; addresses all the hosts on the local network.
Host bits all zero	192.168.2.0	Identifies a network
Host bits all one	192.168.2.255	Directed broadcast; addresses all the hosts on another network.
Network bits all zero	0.0.0.22	Addresses a specific host on the current network.
First quad 127	127.0.0.1	Internal host loopback address

Table 11-3.   *Special Purpose IP Addresses*

Subnetting

Theoretically, the IP addresses you assign to the systems on your network do not have to correlate exactly to the physical network segments; but in standard practice, it's a good idea if they do. Obviously, an organization that registers a Class B address does not have 65,534 nodes on a single network segment; they have an internetwork composed of many segments, joined by routers, switches, or other devices. To support a multisegment network with a single IP network address, you create subnets corresponding to the physical network segment.

A *subnet* is simply a subdivision of the network address that you create by taking some of the host identifier bits and using them as a subnet identifier. To do this, you modify the subnet mask on the machines to reflect the borrowed bits as part of the network identifier, instead of the host identifier.

For example, you can subnet a Class B network address by using the third quad, originally intended to be part of the host identifier, as a subnet identifier instead, as shown in Figure 11-2. By changing the subnet mask from 255.255.0.0 to 255.255.255.0, you divide the Class B address into 254 subnets of 254 hosts each. You then assign each of the physical segments on the network a different value for the third quad and number the individual systems using only the fourth quad. The result is that the routers on your network can use the value of the third quad to direct traffic to the appropriate segments.

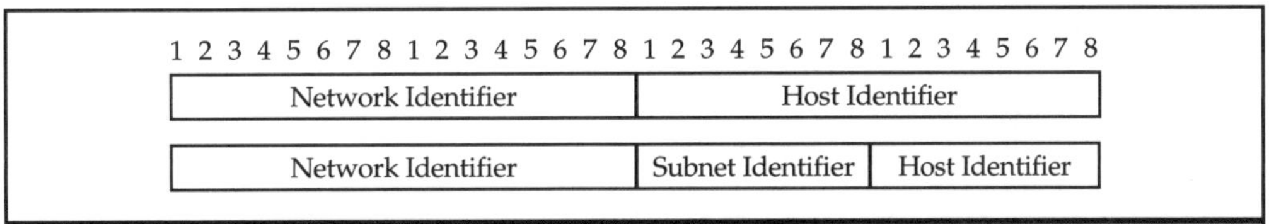

```
1 2 3 4 5 6 7 8 1 2 3 4 5 6 7 8 1 2 3 4 5 6 7 8 1 2 3 4 5 6 7 8
```

Network Identifier	Host Identifier

Network Identifier	Subnet Identifier	Host Identifier

Figure 11-2.   *The top example shows a standard Class B address, split into 16-bit network and host identifiers. In the bottom example, the address has been subnetted by borrowing eight of the host bits for use as a subnet identifier*

The subnet identifier is purely a theoretical construction. To routers and other network systems, an IP address consists only of network and host identifiers, with the subnet bits incorporated into the network identifier.

The previous example demonstrates the most basic type of subnetting, in which the boundaries of the subnet identifier fall between the quads. However, you can use any number of host bits for the subnet identifier and adjust the subnet mask and IP address accordingly. If, for example, you have a Class B address and decide to use 4 host bits for the subnet identifier, you would use a subnet mask with the following binary value:

```
11111111 11111111 11110000 00000000
```

The first 4 bits of the third quad are changed from 0's to 1's, to indicate that these bits are now part of the network identifier. The decimal equivalent of this number is 255.255.240.0, which is the value you would use for the subnet mask in the systems' TCP/IP configuration. By borrowing four bits in this way, you can create up to 14 subnets, consisting of 4,094 hosts each. The formula for determining the number of subnets and hosts is as follows:

```
2ˣ - 2
```
$$2^x - 2$$

where *x* equals the number of bits used for the subnet identifier. You subtract two to account for identifiers consisting of all zeroes and all ones, which are traditionally not used. For this example, therefore, you perform the following calculations:

$$2^4 - 2 = 14$$
$$2^{12} - 2 = 4{,}094$$

Some TCP/IP implementations are capable of using zero as a subnet identifier, but you should avoid this practice unless you are certain that all of your routers also support this feature.

To determine the IP addresses you assign to particular systems, you increment the 4 bits of the subnet identifier separately from the 12 bits of the host identifier and convert the results into decimal form. Thus, assuming a Class B network address of 172.16.0.0, the first IP address of the first subnet will have the following binary address:

```
10101100 00010000 00010000 00000001
```

The first two quads are the binary equivalents of 172 and 16. The third quad consists of the 4-bit subnet identifier, with the value 0001, and the first 4 bits of the 12-bit host identifier. Because this is the first address on this subnet, the value for the host identifier is 000000000001.

Although these 12 bits are incremented as a single unit, when converting the binary values to decimals, you treat each quad separately. Therefore, the value of the third quad is 16, and the value of the fourth quad is 1, yielding an IP address of 172.16.16.1. The last address in this subnet will have the following binary value:

```
10101100 00010000 00011111 11111110
```

which yields an IP address of 172.16.31.254.

For the next subnet, you increment the subnet identifier bits to 0010 and start again with 000000000001 as the first host in the new subnet. Thus, the first address in the second subnet is

```
10101100 00010000 00100000 00000001
```

or

```
172.16.32.1.
```

Proceeding in this way, you can create all 14 subnets, using the following address ranges:

```
172.16.16.1   -   172.16.31.25
172.16.32.1   -   172.16.47.25
172.16.48.1   -   172.16.63.25
172.16.64.1   -   172.16.79.25
172.16.80.1   -   172.16.95.25
172.16.96.1   -   172.16.111.25
172.16.112.1  -   172.16.127.25
172.16.128.1  -   172.16.143.25
```

```
172.16.144.1  -  172.16.159.25
172.16.160.1  -  172.16.175.25
172.16.176.1  -  172.16.191.25
172.16.192.1  -  172.16.207.25
172.16.208.1  -  172.16.223.25
172.16.224.1  -  172.16.239.25
```

Fortunately, manually computing the values for your IP addresses isn't necessary when you subnet the network in this way. Utilities are available that enable you to specify a network address and class, and then select the number of bits to be used for the subnet identifier. The program then supplies you with the IP addresses for the machines in the individual subnets.

A freeware IP Subnet Calculator utility is available for download at http://www.net3group.com/ipcalc.asp.

Ports and Sockets

The IP address makes it possible to route network traffic to a particular system, but once packets arrive at the computer and begin traveling up the protocol stack, they still must be directed to the appropriate application. This is the job of the transport-layer protocol, either TCP or UDP. To identify specific processes running on the computer, TCP and UDP use port numbers that are included in every TCP and UDP header. Typically, the port number identifies the application-layer protocol that generated the data carried in the packet.

For example, the IP header of a DNS query message contains the IP address of a DNS server in its Destination Address field. Once the packet has arrived at the destination, the system sees that port number 53 is specified in the UDP header's Destination Port field. The system then knows to pass the message to the service using port number 53, which is the DNS service.

The port number assignments for the TCP and UDP protocols are separate. Although not typical, it is possible for a service to use different port numbers for TCP and UDP, and for the same port number to be assigned to a different service for each protocol.

The port numbers assigned to specific services are also standardized by the Internet Assigned Numbers Authority (IANA) and published in the Assigned Numbers RFC (currently RFC 1700). Every TCP/IP system has a file called Services that lists the port numbers and the services to which they are assigned.

The combination of an IP address and a port number is known as a *socket*. The URL format calls for a socket to be notated with the IP address followed by the port number, separated by a colon, as in 192.168.2.45:80.

NETWORK PROTOCOLS

TCP/IP Naming

IP addresses are an efficient means of identifying networks and hosts; but when it comes to user interfaces, they are difficult to use and remember. Therefore, the Domain Name System (DNS) was devised to supply friendly names for TCP/IP systems. In a discussion of the network and transport-layer TCP/IP protocols, the most important information to remember about DNS names is that they have nothing to do with the actual transmission of data across the network.

Packets are addressed to their destinations using IP addresses only. Whenever a user supplies a DNS name in an application (such as a URL in a Web browser), the first thing the system does is initiate a transaction with a DNS server to resolve the name into an IP address. This occurs before the system transmits any traffic at all to the destination system. Once the system has discovered the IP address of the destination, it uses that address in the IP header to address future packets and the DNS name is out of the picture from this point.

The structure of DNS names and the functions of DNS servers are discussed more fully in Chapter 20.

TCP/IP Protocols

The following sections examine the major protocols that make up the TCP/IP suite. There are literally dozens of TCP/IP protocols and standards, but only a few are commonly used by the systems on a TCP/IP network. Other chapters in this book discuss some of the more specialized protocols in the TCP/IP suite, such as the protocols used by routers to exchange routing data (see Chapter 6) and the application-layer protocols used by specific services.

SLIP and PPP

The Serial Line Internet Protocol (SLIP) and the Point-to-Point Protocol (PPP) are unique among the TCP/IP protocols because they provide full data link–layer functionality. Systems connected to a LAN nearly always rely on one of the standard data link–layer protocols, like Ethernet and Token Ring, to control the actual connection to the network. This is because the systems are sharing a common medium and must have a MAC mechanism to regulate access to it.

SLIP and PPP are designed for use with modems and other direct connections in which there is no need for media access control. Because they connect only two systems, SLIP and PPP are called *end-to-end protocols*. In these cases, the TCP/IP protocols can define the workings of the entire protocol stack, except for the physical layer itself, which will rely on a standard like that for the RS-232 serial port interface to provide a connection to the modem.

In most cases, systems use SLIP or PPP to provide Internet or WAN connectivity, whether or not the system is connected to a LAN. Virtually every standalone PC that uses a modem to connect to an ISP for Internet access does so using a PPP connection, although a few system types still use SLIP. LANs also use SLIP or PPP connections in their routers to connect to an ISP to provide Internet access to the entire network or to connect to another LAN, forming a WAN connection. Although commonly associated with modem connections, other physical-layer technologies can also use SLIP and PPP, including leased lines, ISDN, frame relay, and ATM connections.

SLIP and PPP are connection-oriented protocols that provide a data link between two systems in the simplest sense of the term. They encapsulate IP datagrams for transport between computers, just as Ethernet and Token Ring do, but the frame they use is far simpler. This is because the protocols are not subject to the same problems as the LAN protocols. Because the link consists only of a connection between the two computers, there is no need for a medium access-control mechanism like CSMA/CD or token passing. Also, there is no problem with addressing the packets to a specific destination—because only two computers are involved in the connection, the data can only go to one place.

SLIP

SLIP was created in the early 1980s to provide the simplest possible solution for transmitting data over serial connections. No official standard defines the protocol, mainly because there is nothing much to standardize and interoperability is not a problem. There is an IETF document, however, called "A Nonstandard for Transmission of IP Datagrams over Serial Lines" (RFC 1055), that defines the functionality of the protocol.

The SLIP frame is simplicity itself. A single 1-byte field with the value c0 serves as an END delimiter, following every IP datagram transmitted over the link. The END character informs the receiving system that the packet currently being transmitted has ended. Some systems also precede each IP datagram with an END character. This way, if any line noise occurs between datagram transmissions, the receiving system treats it as a packet unto itself because it is delimited by two END characters (see Figure 11-3). When the upper-layer protocols attempt to process the noise "packet," they interpret it as gibberish and discard it.

If a datagram contains a byte with the value c0, the system alters it to the 2-byte string db dc before transmission, to avoid terminating the packet incorrectly. The db byte is referred to as the ESC character, which, when coupled with another character, serves a special purpose. If the datagram contains an actual ESC character as part of the data, the system substitutes the string db dd before transmission.

| END | Data | END | Noise | END | Data | END |

Figure 11-3.   *Data on a SLIP link can be surrounded by END characters to exclude line noise*

The ESC character defined by SLIP is not the equivalent of the ASCII ESC character.

SLIP Shortcomings

Because of its simplicity, SLIP is easy to implement and adds little overhead to data transmissions, but it also lacks features that could make it a more useful protocol. For example, SLIP lacks the capability to supply the IP address of each system to the other, meaning that both systems must be configured with the IP address of the other. SLIP also has no means of identifying the protocol it is carrying in its frame, which prevents it from multiplexing network-layer protocols (such as IP and NetBEUI) over a single connection. SLIP also has no error detection or correction capabilities, which leaves these tasks to the upper-layer protocols, causing greater delays than a data link–layer error-detection mechanism would.

Compressed SLIP (CSLIP)

When two systems communicate using SLIP, much of the control overhead contributed by the protocols at the network and transport layers becomes redundant, particularly in TCP connections. During the course of a typical SLIP connection, the two systems can exchange hundreds or thousands of packets with identical information in the network- and transport-layer protocol headers.

RFC 1144, "Compressing TCP/IP Headers for Low-Speed Serial Links," defines a mechanism by which the systems participating in a SLIP connection omit much of the redundant information from the headers, reducing the overhead from 40 bytes down to 5 bytes or less. This can speed up the performance of the connection considerably.

This type of header compression is also found in many PPP implementations, using the name of RFC 1144's author, as *Van Jacobson header compression*.

PPP

PPP was created as an alternative to SLIP that provides greater functionality, such as the capability to multiplex different network-layer protocols and support for various authentication protocols. Naturally, the cost of these additional features is a larger header, but PPP still only adds a maximum of 8 bytes to a packet (as compared to the 16 bytes needed for an Ethernet frame). Most of the connections to Internet service providers, whether by standalone systems or routers, use PPP because it enables the ISP to implement access control measures that protect their networks from intrusion by unauthorized users.

A typical PPP session consists of several connection establishment and termination procedures, using other protocols in addition to the PPP itself. These procedures are as follows:

■ **Connection establishment** The system initiating the connection uses the Link Control Protocol (LCP) to negotiate communication parameters that the two machines have in common.

- **Authentication**   Although not required, the system may use an authentication protocol such as PAP (the Password Authentication Protocol) or CHAP (the Challenge Handshake Authentication Protocol) to negotiate access to the other system.

- **Network-layer protocol connection establishment**   For each network-layer protocol that the systems use during the session, they perform a separate connection establishment procedure using a Network Control Protocol (NCP) such as IPCP (the Internet Protocol Control Protocol).

Unlike SLIP, PPP is standardized, but the specifications are divided among several different RFCs. The documents for each of the protocols are listed in Table 11-4.

The PPP Frame

RFC 1661 defines the basic frame used by the PPP protocol to encapsulate other protocols and transmit them to the destination. The frame is small, only 8 (or sometimes 10) bytes, and is illustrated in Figure 11-4.
The functions of the fields are as follows:

- **Flag (1 byte)**   Contains a hexadecimal value of 7e and functions as a packet delimiter, like SLIP's END character.

- **Address (1 byte)**   Contains a hexadecimal value of ff, indicating the packet is addressed to all stations.

- **Control (1 byte)**   Contains a hexadecimal value of 03, identifying the packet as containing an HDLC unnumbered information message.

Document	Title
RFC 1661	The Point-to-Point Protocol (PPP)
RFC 1662	PPP in HDLC-like Framing
RFC 1663	PPP Reliable Transmission
RFC 1332	The PPP Internet Protocol Control Protocol (IPCP)
RFC 1552	The PPP Internetworking Packet Exchange Control Protocol (IPXCP)
RFC 1334	PPP Authentication Protocols
RFC 1994	PPP Challenge Handshake Authentication Protocol (CHAP)
RFC 1989	PPP Link Quality Monitoring

Table 11-4.   *PPP and Related Standards*

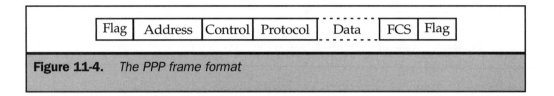

Figure 11-4.   *The PPP frame format*

- **Protocol (2 bytes)**   Contains a code identifying the protocol that generated the information in the data field. Code values in the 0xxx to 3xxx range are used to identify network-layer protocols, values from 4xxx to 7xxx identify low-volume network-layer protocols with no corresponding NCP, values from 8xxx to bxxx identify network-layer protocols with corresponding NCPs, and values from cxxx to fxxx identify link-layer control protocols like LCP and the authentication protocols. The permitted codes, specified in the TCP/IP "Assigned Numbers" document (currently RFC 1700), include the following:

  - **0021**   Uncompressed IP datagram (used when Van Jacobson compression is enabled)

  - **002b**   Novell IPX datagram

  - **002d**   IP datagrams with compressed IP and TCP headers (used when Van Jacobson compression is enabled)

  - **002f**   IP datagrams containing uncompressed TCP data (used when Van Jacobson compression is enabled)

  - **8021**   Internet Protocol Control Protocol (IPCP)

  - **802b**   Novell IPX Control Protocol (IPXIP)

  - **c021**   Link Control Protocol (LCP)

  - **c023**   Password Authentication Protocol (PAP)

  - **c223**   Challenge Handshake Authentication Protocol (CHAP)

- **Data and Pad (variable, up to 1,500 bytes)**   Contains the payload of the packet, up to a default maximum length (called the *maximum receive unit*, or *MRU*) of 1,500 bytes. The field may contain meaningless bytes to bring its size up to the MRU.

- **Frame Check Sequence (FCS)(2 or 4 bytes)**   Contains a CRC value calculated on the entire frame, excluding the flag and frame check sequence fields, for error-detection purposes.

- **Flag (1 byte)**   Contains the same value as the flag field at the beginning of the frame. When a system transmits two packets consecutively, one of the flag fields is omitted, as two would be mistaken as an empty frame.

Several of the fields in the PPP frame can be modified as a result of LCP negotiations between the two systems, such as the length of the protocol and FCS fields and the MRU for the data field. The systems can agree to use a 1-byte protocol field or a 4-byte FCS field.

The LCP Frame

PPP systems use LCP to negotiate their capabilities during the connection establishment process, so they can achieve the most efficient possible connection. LCP messages are carried within PPP frames and contain configuration options for the connection. Once the two systems agree on a configuration they can both support, the link establishment process continues. By specifying the parameters for the connection during the link establishment process, the systems don't have to include redundant information in the header of every data packet.

The LCP message format is shown in Figure 11-5. The functions of the individual fields are as follows:

- **Code (1 byte)**   Specifies the LCP message type, using the following codes:
    - **1**   Configure-Request
    - **2**   Configure-Ack
    - **3**   Configure-Nak
    - **4**   Configure-Reject
    - **5**   Terminate-Request
    - **6**   Terminate-Ack
    - **7**   Code Reject
    - **8**   Protocol-Reject
    - **9**   Echo-Request
    - **10** Echo-Reply
    - **11** Discard-Request
- **Identifier (1 byte)**   Contains a code used to associate the request and replies of a particular LCP transaction.

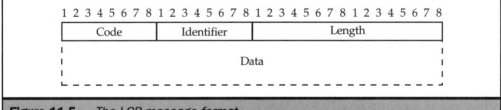

Figure 11-5.   *The LCP message format*

- **Length (2 bytes)**   Specifies the length of the LCP message, including the code, identifier, length, and data fields.
- **Data (variable)**   Contains multiple configuration options, each of which is composed of three subfields.

Each of the options in the LCP message's data field consists of the subfields shown in Figure 11-6. The functions of the subfields are as follows:

- **Type (1 byte)**   Specifies the option to be configured, using a code from the "Assigned Numbers" RFC, as follows:
  - **0**   Vendor Specific
  - **1**   Maximum Receive Unit
  - **2**   Async Control Character Map
  - **3**   Authentication Protocol
  - **4**   Quality Protocol
  - **5**   Magic Number
  - **6**   Reserved
  - **7**   Protocol Field Compression
  - **8**   Address and Control Field Compression
  - **9**   FCS Alternatives
  - **10** Self-Describing Pad
  - **11** Numbered Mode
  - **12** Multilink Procedure
  - **13** Callback
  - **14** Connect Time
  - **15** Compound Frames
  - **16** Nominal Data Encapsulation
  - **17** Multilink MRRU

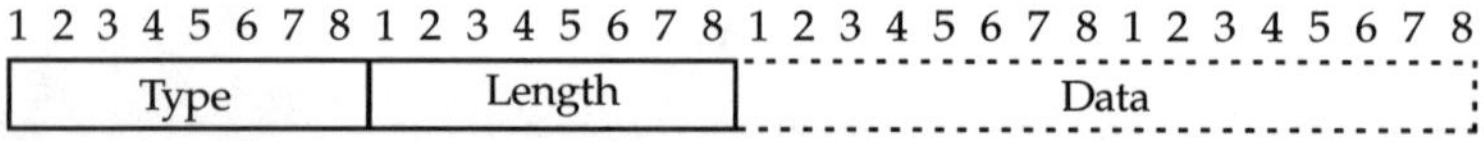

1 2 3 4 5 6 7 8 1 2 3 4 5 6 7 8 1 2 3 4 5 6 7 8 1 2 3 4 5 6 7 8

Type	Length	Data

Figure 11-6.   *The LCP option format*

- **18**   Multilink Short Sequence Number Header Format
- **19**   Multilink Endpoint Discriminator
- **20**   Proprietary
- **21**   DCE Identifier
- **Length (1 byte)**   Specifies the length of the LCP message, including the code, identifier, length, and data fields.
- **Data (variable)**   Contains information pertinent to the specific LCP message type, as indicated by the code field.

The LCP protocol is also designed to be extensible. By using a code value of 0, vendors can supply their own options without standardizing them with the IANA, as documented in RFC 2153, "PPP Vendor Extensions."

Authentication Protocols

PPP connections can optionally require authentication to prevent unauthorized access, using an external protocol agreed on during the exchange of LCP configuration messages and encapsulated within PPP frames. Two of the most popular authentication protocols— PAP and CHAP—are defined by TCP/IP specifications, but systems can also use other proprietary protocols developed by individual vendors.

THE PAP FRAME   PAP is the inherently weaker of the two protocols because it uses only a two-way handshake and transmits account names and passwords over the link in clear text. Systems generally use PAP only when they have no other authentication protocols in common. PAP packets have a value of c023 in the PPP header's protocol field and use a message format that is basically the same as LCP, except for the options. The functions of the message fields are as follows:

- **Code (1 byte)**   Specifies the type of PAP message, using the following values:
  - **1**   Authenticate Request
  - **2**   Authenticate Ack
  - **3**   Authenticate Nak
- **Identifier (1 byte)**   Contains a code used to associate the request and replies of a particular PAP transaction.
- **Length (2 bytes)**   Specifies the length of the PAP message, including the code, identifier, length, and data fields.
- **Data (variable)**   Contains a number of subfields, depending on the value in the code field, as follows:
  - **Peer ID Length (1 byte)**   Specifies the length of the peer ID field (Authenticate Request messages only).

- **Peer ID (variable)**   Specifies the account the destination computer will use to authenticate the source system (Authenticate Request messages only).

- **Password Length (1 byte)**   Specifies the length of the password field (Authenticate Request messages only).

- **Password (variable)**   Specifies the password associated with the account name in the peer ID field (Authenticate Request messages only).

- **Message Length (1 byte)**   Specifies the length of the message field (Authenticate Ack/Authenticate Nak messages only).

- **Message (variable)**   Contains a text message that will be displayed on the user interface describing the success or failure of the authentication procedure (Authenticate Ack and Authenticate Nak messages only).

THE CHAP FRAME   The CHAP protocol is considerably more secure than PAP because it uses a three-way handshake and never transmits account names and passwords in cleartext. CHAP packets have a value of c223 in the PPP header's protocol field and use a message format almost identical to PAP's. The functions of the message fields are as follows:

- **Code (1 byte)**   Specifies the type of CHAP message, using the following values:
  - **1**   Challenge
  - **2**   Response
  - **3**   Success
  - **4**   Failure
- **Identifier (1 byte)**   Contains a code used to associate the request and replies of a particular CHAP transaction.
- **Length (2 bytes)**   Specifies the length of the CHAP message, including the code, identifier, length, and data fields.
- **Data (variable)**   Contains a number of subfields, depending on the value of the code field, as follows:
  - **Value Size (1 byte)**   Specifies the length of the value field (Challenge and Response messages only).
  - **Value (variable)**   In a Challenge message, contains a unique byte string that the recipient uses along with the contents of the identifier field and an encryption "secret" to generate the value field for the Response message (Challenge and Response messages only).
  - **Name (variable)**   Contains a string that identifies the transmitting system (Challenge and Response messages only).

- **Message (variable)**   Contains a text message to be displayed on the user interface describing the success or failure of the authentication procedure (Success and Failure messages only).

The IPCP Frame

PPP systems use Network Control Protocols (NCPs) to negotiate connections for each of the network-layer protocols they will use during the session. Before a system can multiplex the traffic generated by different protocols over a single PPP connection, it must establish a connection for each protocol using the appropriate NCPs.

The *Internet Protocol Control Protocol (IPCP)*, which is the NCP for IP, is a good example of the protocol structure. The message format of the NCPs is nearly identical to that of LCP, except that it supports only values 1 through 7 for the code field (the link configuration, link termination, and code reject values) and uses different options in the data field. Like LCP, the messages are carried in PPP frames, but with a value of 8021 in the PPP header's protocol field.

The options that can be included in the data field of an IPCP message use the following values in the type field:

- **2 – IP Compression Protocol**   Specifies the protocol the system should use to compress IP headers, for which the only valid option is Van Jacobson compression.

- **3 – IP Address**   Used by the transmitting system to request a particular IP address or, if the value is 0.0.0.0, to request that the receiving system supply an address (replaces the type 1 IP Addresses option, which is no longer used).

PPP Connection Establishment

Once the physical-layer connection between the two systems has been established (through a modem handshake or other procedure), the PPP connection establishment process begins. The two systems pass through several distinct phases during the course of the session, as illustrated in Figure 11-7 and discussed in the following sections.

LINK DEAD   Both systems begin and end the session in the *link dead phase*, which indicates that no physical-layer connection exists between the two machines. On a typical session, an application on one system initiates the physical-layer connection by dialing the modem or using some other means. Once this connection is completed, the systems pass into the link establishment phase.

LINK ESTABLISHMENT   In the link establishment phase, the system initiating the connection transmits an LCP Configure Request message to the destination containing the options it would like to enable, such as the use of an authentication protocol, header compression, or a different MRU value. If the receiving system can support all the specified options, it replies a Configure Ack message containing the same option values, and this phase of the connection process is completed.

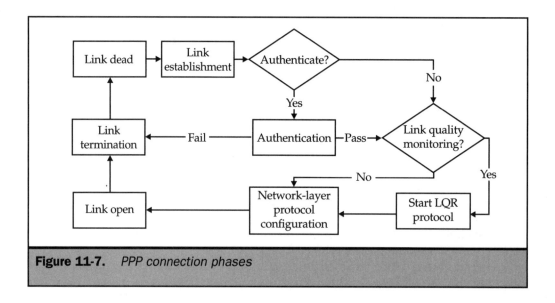

Figure 11-7.   *PPP connection phases*

If the receiving system recognizes the options in the request message, but cannot support the values for those options supplied by the sender (such as if the system supports authentication, but not with the protocol the sender has specified), it replies with a Configure Nak message containing the options with values it cannot support. With these options, the replying system supplies all the values it does support and also may include other options it would like to see enabled. Using this information, the connecting system generates another Configure Request message containing options it knows are supported, to which the receiver replies with a Configure Ack message.

If the receiving system fails to recognize any of the options in the request, it replies with a Configure Reject message containing only the unrecognized options. The sender then generates a new Configure Request message that does not contain the rejected options and the procedure continues as previously outlined. Eventually, the systems perform a successful request/acknowledgment exchange and the connection process moves on to the next phase.

AUTHENTICATION   The *authentication phase* of the connection process is optional and is triggered by the inclusion of the Authentication Protocol option in the LCP Configure Request message. During the LCP link establishment process, the two systems agree on an authentication protocol to use. Use of the PAP and CHAP protocols is common, but other proprietary protocols are available.

The message format and exchange procedures for the authentication phase are dictated by the selected protocol. In a PAP authentication, for example, the sending system transmits an Authenticate Request message containing an account name and password and the receiver replies with either an Authenticate Ack or Authenticate Nak message.

CHAP is inherently more secure than PAP and requires a more complex message exchange. The sending system transmits a Challenge message containing data that the receiver uses with its encryption key to compute a value it returns to the sender in a Response message. Depending on whether the value in the response matches the sender's own computations, it transmits a Success or Failure message.

A successful transaction causes the connection procedure to proceed to the next phase, but the effect of a failure is dictated by the implementation of the protocol. Some systems proceed directly to the link termination phase in the event of an authentication failure, while others might permit retries or limited network access to a help subsystem.

LINK QUALITY MONITORING   The use of a link quality monitoring protocol is also an optional element of the connection process, triggered by the inclusion of the Quality Protocol option in the LCP Configure Request message. Although the option enables the sending system to specify any protocol for this purpose, only one has been standardized, the Link Quality Report protocol. The negotiation process that occurs at this phase enables the systems to agree on an interval at which they should transmit messages containing link traffic and error statistics throughout the session.

NETWORK-LAYER PROTOCOL CONFIGURATION   Individual NCP negotiations are required for all of the network-layer protocols to be transmitted over the PPP connection. The structure of an NCP message exchange is similar to that of LCP, except the options carried in the Configure Request message are unique to the requirements of the protocol. During an IPCP exchange, for example, the systems inform each other of their IP addresses and agree on whether or not to use Van Jacobson header compression. Other protocols have their own individual needs that the systems negotiate as needed. NCP initialization and termination procedures can also occur at any other time during the connection.

LINK OPEN   Once the individual NCP exchanges are completed, the connection is fully established and the systems enter the *link open phase*. Network-layer protocol data can now travel over the link in either direction.

LINK TERMINATION   When a user ends the session, or as a result of other conditions such as a physical-layer disconnection, an authentication failure, or an inactivity timeout, the systems enter the *link termination phase.* To sever the link, one system transmits an LCP Terminate Request message, to which the other system replies with a Terminate Ack.

NCPs also support the Terminate Request and Terminate Ack messages, but they are intended for use while the PPP connection remains intact. In fact, the PPP connection can remain active even if all of the network-layer protocol connections have been terminated. It is unnecessary for systems to terminate the network-layer protocol connections before terminating the PPP connection.

ARP

The Address Resolution Protocol (ARP) occupies an unusual place in the TCP/IP suite because it defies all attempts at categorization. Unlike most of the other TCP/IP protocols, ARP messages are not carried within IP datagrams. A separate protocol identifier is defined in the "Assigned Numbers" document that data link–layer protocols use to indicate that they contain ARP messages. Because of this, there is some difference of opinion about the layer of the protocol stack to which ARP belongs. Some say ARP is a data link–layer protocol because it provides a service to IP, while others associate it with the network layer because its messages are carried within data link–layer protocols.

The function of the ARP protocol, as defined in RFC 826, "An Ethernet Address Resolution Protocol," is to reconcile the IP addresses used to identify systems at the upper layers with the hardware addresses at the data link layer. When it requests network resources, a TCP/IP application supplies the destination IP address used in the IP protocol header. The system may discover the IP address using a DNS or NetBIOS name resolution process, or it may use an address supplied by an operating system or application configuration parameter.

Data link–layer protocols like Ethernet, however, have no use for IP addresses and cannot read the contents of the IP datagram anyway. To transmit the packet to its destination, the data link–layer protocol must have the hardware address coded into the destination system's network interface adapter. ARP converts IP addresses into hardware addresses by broadcasting request packets containing the IP address on the local network and waiting for the holder of that IP address to respond with a reply containing the equivalent hardware address.

> **Note** *ARP was originally developed for use with DIX Ethernet networks, but has been generalized to allow its use with other data link–layer protocols.*

The biggest difference between IP addresses and hardware addresses is that IP is responsible for the delivery of the packet to its ultimate destination, while an Ethernet implementation is only concerned with delivery to the next stop on the journey. If the packet's destination is on the same network segment as the source, then the IP protocol uses ARP to resolve the IP address of the ultimate destination into a hardware address. If, however, the destination is located on another network, the IP protocol will not use ARP to resolve the ultimate destination address (that is, the destination address in the IP header). Instead, it will pass the IP address of the default gateway to the ARP protocol for address resolution.

This is because the data link protocol header must contain the hardware address of the next intermediate stop as its destination, which may well be a router or switch. It is up to that router or switch to forward the packet on the next leg of its journey.

Thus, in the course of a single internetwork transmission, many different machines may perform ARP resolutions on the same packet with different results.

ARP Message Format

ARP messages are carried directly within data link–layer frames, using 0806 as the EtherType value to identify the protocol being carried in the packet. There is one format for all of the ARP message types, which is illustrated in Figure 11-8.

The functions of the fields are as follows:

- **Hardware Type (2 bytes)**   Specifies the type of hardware addresses found in the Sender Hardware Address and Target Hardware Address fields. The hexadecimal value for Ethernet is 0001.

- **Protocol Type (2 bytes)**   Specifies the type of protocol addresses found in the Sender Protocol Address and Target Protocol Address fields. The hexadecimal value for IP addresses is 0800 (the same as the EtherType value for IP).

- **Hardware Size (1 byte)**   Specifies the size (in bytes) of the hardware addresses found in the Sender Hardware Address and Target Hardware Address fields. The value for Ethernet hardware addresses is 6.

- **Protocol Size (1 byte)**   Specifies the size (in bytes) of the protocol addresses found in the Sender Protocol Address and Target Protocol Address fields. The value for IP addresses is 4.

- **Opcode (2 bytes)**   Specifies the type of message contained in the packet, using the following values:
  - **1**   ARP Request
  - **2**   ARP Reply
  - **3**   RARP Request
  - **4**   RARP Reply

- Sender Hardware Address (length specified by the value of the Hardware Size field)   Specifies the hardware (e.g., Ethernet) address of the system sending the message, in both requests and replies.

- **Sender Protocol Address (length specified by the value of the Protocol Size field)**   Specifies the protocol (e.g., IP) address of the system sending the message, in both requests and replies.

- **Target Hardware Address (length specified by the value of the Hardware Size field)**   Left blank in request messages; in replies, contains the value of the Sender Hardware Address field in the associated request.

- **Target Protocol Address (length specified by the value of the Protocol Size field)**   Specifies the protocol (e.g., IP) address of the system to which the message is being sent, in both requests and replies.

```
1 2 3 4 5 6 7 8 1 2 3 4 5 6 7 8 1 2 3 4 5 6 7 8 1 2 3 4 5 6 7 8
```

Hardware Type		Protocol Type	
Hardware Size	Protocol Size	Op Code	
Sender Hardware Address			
Sender Hardware Address (cont'd)		Sender Protocol Address	
Sender Protocol Address (cont'd)		Target Hardware Address	
Target Hardware Address (cont'd)			
Target Protocol Address			

Figure 11-8.   *The ARP Message format*

Note   *The RARP Request and RARP Reply message types are not used in the course of standard TCP/IP network traffic. For more information on the Reverse Address Resolution Protocol (RARP), see Chapter 18.*

ARP Transactions

An ARP transaction occurs when the IP protocol in a TCP/IP system is ready to transmit a datagram over the network. The system knows its own hardware and IP addresses, as well as the IP address of the packet's intended destination. All it lacks is the hardware address of the system on the local network that is to receive the packet. The ARP message exchange proceeds according to the following steps:

1. The transmitting system generates an ARP Request packet containing its own addresses in the Sender Hardware Address and Sender Protocol Address fields (see the captured packet shown in Figure 11-9). The Target Protocol Address contains the IP address of the system on the local network that is to receive the datagram, while the Target Hardware Address is left blank. Some implementations insert a broadcast address or other value into the Target Hardware Address field of the ARP Request message, but this value is ignored by the recipient because this is the address the protocol is trying to ascertain.

2. The system transmits the ARP Request message as a broadcast to the local network, asking in effect, "who is using this IP address and what is your hardware address?"

3. Each TCP/IP system on the local network receives the ARP Request broadcast and examines the contents of the Target Protocol Address field. If the system does not use that address on one of its network interfaces, it silently discards the packet. If the system does use the address, it generates an ARP Reply message in response. The system uses the contents of the request message's Sender Hardware Address and Sender Protocol Address fields as the values

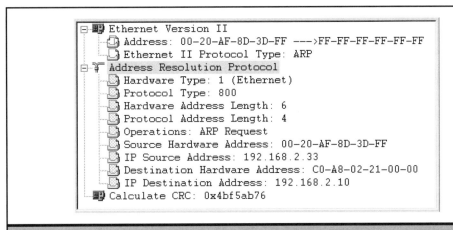

Figure 11-9. *The ARP Request message*

for its reply message's Target Hardware Address and Target Protocol Address fields. The system then inserts its own hardware address and IP address into the Sender Hardware Address and Sender Protocol Address fields, respectively (see Figure 11-10).

4. The system using the requested IP address transmits the reply message as a unicast back to the original sender. On receipt of the reply, the system that initiated the ARP exchange uses the contents of the Sender Hardware Address field as the Destination Address for the data link–layer transmission of the IP datagram.

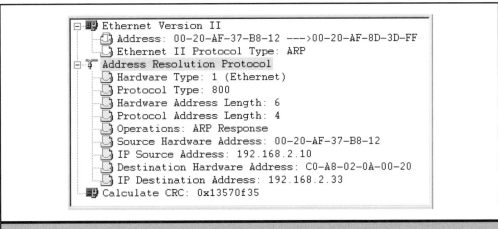

Figure 11-10. *The ARP Reply message*

NETWORK PROTOCOLS

ARP Caching

Because of its reliance on broadcast transmissions, ARP can generate a significant amount of network traffic. To lessen the burden of the protocol on the network, TCP/IP systems cache the hardware addresses discovered through ARP transactions in memory for a designated period of time. This way, a system transmitting a large string of datagrams to the same host doesn't have to generate individual ARP requests for each packet.

This is particularly helpful in an internetwork environment in which systems routinely transmit the majority of their packets to destinations on other networks. When a network segment has only a single router, all IP datagrams destined for other networks are sent through that router. When systems have the hardware address for that router in the ARP cache, they can transmit the majority of their datagrams without using ARP.

The amount of time that entries remain in the ARP cache varies with different TCP/IP implementations. Windows systems purge entries after two minutes when they are not used to transmit additional datagrams.

> **Tip**   *The Windows operating systems include a command-line utility called Arp.exe, which you can use to create entries manually in the ARP cache. Unlike dynamically created entries, manual ARP cache entries are permanent. If you have a stable network, you can reduce network traffic by adding ARP cache entries for the routers that provide access to other networks (and particularly to the Internet). Client applications (like Web browsers) are then able to access systems on other networks without generating repeated ARP request broadcasts.*

IP

The Internet Protocol (IP), as defined in RFC 791, is the primary carrier protocol for the TCP/IP suite. IP is essentially the envelope that carries the messages generated by most of the other TCP/IP protocols. Operating at the network layer of the OSI model, IP is a connectionless, unreliable protocol that performs several functions that are a critical part of getting packets from the source system to the destination. Among these functions are

- **Addressing**   Identifying the system that will be the ultimate recipient of the packet.

- **Packaging**   Encapsulating transport-layer data in datagrams for transmission to the destination.

- ■ **Fragmenting**   Splitting datagrams into sections small enough for transmission over a network.

- ■ **Routing**   Determining the path of the packet through the internetwork to the destination.

The following sections examine these functions in more detail.

Addressing

IP is the protocol responsible for the delivery of TCP/IP packets to their ultimate destination. It is vital to understand how this differs from the addressing performed by a data link–layer protocol like Ethernet or Token Ring. Data link–layer protocols are only aware of the machines on the local network segment. No matter where the packet finally ends up, the destination address in the data link–layer protocol header is always that of a machine on a local network.

If the ultimate destination of the packet is a system on another network segment, then the data link protocol address will point to a router that provides access to that segment. On receipt of the packet, the router strips off the data link–layer protocol header and generates a new one containing the address of the packet's next intermediate destination, called a *hop*. Thus, throughout the packet's journey, the data link protocol header will contain a different destination address for each hop.

The destination address in the IP header, however, always points to the final destination of the packet, regardless of the network on which it's located, and it never changes throughout the journey. IP is the first protocol in the stack (working up from the bottom) to be conscious of the packet's end-to-end journey from source to destination. Most of the protocol's functions revolve around the preparation of the transport-layer data for transmission across multiple networks to the destination.

Packaging

IP is also responsible for packaging transport-layer protocol data into structures called *datagrams* for its journey to the destination. During the journey, routers apply a new data link–layer protocol header to a datagram for each hop. Before reaching its final destination, a packet may pass through networks using several different data link–layer protocols, each of which requires a different header. The IP "envelope," on the other hand, remains intact throughout the entire journey, except for a few bits that are modified along the way, just as a mailing envelope is postmarked.

As it receives data from the transport-layer protocol, IP packages it into datagrams of a size suitable for transmission over the local network. A datagram (in most cases) consists of a 20-byte header plus the transport-layer data. The header is illustrated in Figure 11-11.

NETWORK PROTOCOLS

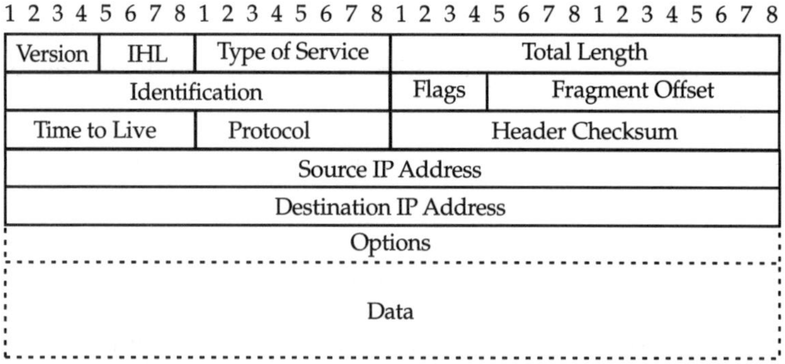

Figure 11-11.   *The IP header format*

The functions of the header fields are as follows:

- **Version, 4 bits**   Specifies the version of the IP protocol in use. The value for the current implementation is 4.

- **IHL (Internet Header Length), 4 bits**   Specifies the length of the IP header, in 32-bit words. When the header contains no optional fields, the value is 5.

- **TOS (Type of Service), 1 byte**   Bits 1 through 3 and 8 are unused. Bits 4 through 7 specify the service priority desired for the datagram, using the following values:

  - **0000**   Default
  - **0001**   Minimize Monetary Cost
  - **0010**   Maximize Reliability
  - **0100**   Maximize Throughput
  - **1000**   Minimize Delay
  - **1111**   Maximize Security

- **Total Length, 2 bytes**   Specifies the length of the datagram, including all the header fields and the data.

- **Identification, 2 bytes**   Contains a unique value for each datagram, used by the destination system to reassemble fragments.

- **Flags, 3 bits**   Contains bits used during the datagram fragmentation process, with the following values:

  - **Bit 1**   Not used

- **Bit 2 – Don't Fragment**   When set to a value of 1, prevents the datagram from being fragmented by any system.

- **Bit 3 – More Fragments**   When set to a value of 0, indicates that the last fragment of the datagram has been transmitted; when set to 1, indicates that fragments still await transmission.

- **Fragment Offset, 13 bits**   Specifies the location (in 8-byte units) of the current fragment in the datagram.

- **TTL (Time to Live), 1 byte**   Specifies the number of routers the datagram should be permitted to pass through on its way to the destination. Each router that processes the packet decrements this field by 1. Once the value reaches 0, the packet is discarded, whether or not it has reached the destination.

- **Protocol, 1 byte**   Identifies the protocol that generated the information in the data field, using values found in the "Assigned Numbers" RFC and the PROTOCOL file found on every TCP/IP system, some of which are as follows:

  - **1**   Internet Control Message Protocol (ICMP)

  - **2**   Internet Group Management Protocol (IGMP)

  - **3**   Gateway-to-Gateway Protocol (GGP)

  - **6**   Transmission Control Protocol (TCP)

  - **8**   Exterior Gateway Protocol (EGP)

  - **17**   User Datagram Protocol (UDP)

- **Header Checksum, 2 bytes**   Contains a checksum value computer in the IP header fields only, for error-detection purposes.

- **Source IP Address, 4 bytes**   Specifies the IP address of the system from which the datagram originated.

- **Destination IP Address, 4 bytes**   Specifies the IP address of the system that will be the ultimate recipient of the datagram.

- **Options (variable)**   Can contain any of 16 options defined in the "Assigned Numbers" RFC, as described later in this section.

- **Data (variable, up to the MTU for the connected network)**   Contains the payload of the datagram, consisting of data passed down from a transport-layer protocol.

Systems use the IP header options to carry additional information, either supplied by the sender or gathered as the packet travels to the destination. Each option is composed of the following fields (see Figure 11-12):

- **Option Type (1 byte)**   Contains a value identifying the option that consists of the following three subfields:

NETWORK PROTOCOLS

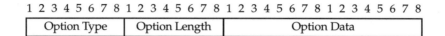

Figure 11-12. The IP Option Format

- **Copy Flag (1 bit)** When set to a value of 1, indicates the option should be copied to each of the fragments that comprise the datagram.
- **Option Class (2 bits)** Contains a code that identifies the option's basic function, using the following values:
  - **0** Control
  - **2** Debugging and measurement
- **Option Number (5 bits)** Contains a unique identifier for the option, as specified in the "Assigned Numbers" RFC.
- **Option Length (1 byte)** Specifies the total length of the option, including the Option Type, Option Length, and Option Data fields.
- **Option Data (Option Length minus 2)** Contains the option-specific information being carried to the destination.

Table 11-5 lists some of the options systems can insert into IP datagrams, the values for the option subfields, and the RFCs that define the option's function. The functions of the options are described in the following sections.

Copy Flag	Option Class	Option Number	Option Value	RFC	Option Name
0	0	0	0	RFC 791	End of Options List
0	0	1	1	RFC 791	No Operation
1	0	3	131	RFC 791	Loose Source Route
0	2	4	68	RFC 791	Time Stamp
0	0	7	7	RFC 791	Record Route
1	0	9	137	RFC 791	Strict Source Route

Table 11-5. IP Header Options

END OF OPTIONS LIST   Consisting only of an Option Type field with the value 0, this option marks the end of all the options in an IP header.

NO OPERATION   Consisting only of an Option Type field, systems can use this option to pad out the space between two other options, to force the following option to begin at the boundary between 32-bit words.

LOOSE SOURCE ROUTE AND STRICT SOURCE ROUTE   Systems use the Loose Source Route and Strict Source Route options to carry the IP addresses of routers the datagram must pass through on its way to the destination. When a system uses the Loose Source Route option, the datagram can pass through other routers in addition to those listed in the option. The Strict Source Route option defines the entire path of the datagram from the source to the destination.

TIME STAMP   This option is designed to hold timestamps generated by one or more systems processing the packet as it travels to its destination. The sending system may supply the IP addresses of the systems that are to add timestamps to the header, or enable the systems to save their IP addresses to the header along with the timestamps, or omit the IP addresses of the timestamping systems entirely. The size of the option is variable to accommodate multiple timestamps, but must be specified when the sender creates the datagram and cannot be enlarged en route to the destination.

RECORD ROUTE   This option provides the receiving system with a record of all the routers through which the datagram has passed during its journey to the destination. Each router adds its address to the option as it processes the packet.

Fragmenting

The size of the IP datagrams used to transmit the transport-layer data depends on the data link–layer protocol in use. Ethernet networks, for example, can carry datagrams up to 1,500 bytes in size, while Token Ring networks can support packets as large as 17,914. The system transmitting the datagram uses the *maximum transfer unit (MTU)* of the connected network, that is, the largest possible frame that can be transmitted using that data link–layer protocol, as one factor in determining how large each datagram should be.

During the course of its journey from the source to the destination, packets may encounter networks with different MTUs. As long as the MTU of each network is larger than the packet, the datagram is transmitted without a problem. If a packet is larger than the MTU of a network, however, it cannot be transmitted in its current form. When this occurs, the IP protocol in the router providing access to the network is responsible for splitting the datagram into fragments smaller than the MTU. The router then transmits each fragment in a separate packet with its own IP header.

Depending on the number and nature of the networks it passes through, a datagram may be fragmented more than once before it reaches the destination.

A system might split a datagram into fragments that are themselves too large for networks further along in the datagram's path. Another router, therefore, splits the fragments into still smaller fragments. Reassembly of a fragmented datagram takes place only at the destination system after it has received all of the packets containing the fragments, not at the intermediate routers.

Note	*Technically speaking, the datagram is defined as the unit of data, packaged by the source system, containing a specific value on the IP header's Identification field. When a router fragments a datagram, it uses the same Identification value for each new packet it creates, meaning the individual fragments are collectively known as a datagram. Referring to a single fragment as a datagram is incorrect use of the term.*

When a router receives a datagram that must be fragmented, it creates a series of new packets using the same value for the IP header's Identification field as the original datagram. The other fields of the header are the same as well, with three important exceptions, which are as follows:

■ The value of the Total Length field is changed to reflect the size of the fragment, instead of the size of the entire datagram.

■ Bit 3 of the Flags field, the More Fragments bit, is changed to a value of 1 to indicate that further fragments are to be transmitted, except in the case of the datagram's last fragment, in which this bit is set to a value of 0.

■ The value of the Fragment Offset field is changed to reflect each fragment's place in the datagram, based on the size of the fragments (which is, in turn, based on the MTU of the network across which the fragments are to be transmitted). The value for the first fragment is 0; the next is incremented by the size of the fragment, in bytes.

These changes to the IP header are needed for the fragments to be properly reassembled by the destination system. The router transmits the fragments like any other IP packets, and because IP is a connectionless protocol, the individual fragments may take different routes to the destination and arrive in a different order. The receiving system uses the More Fragments bit to determine when it should begin the reassembly process and the Fragment Offset field to assemble the fragments in the proper order.

Selecting the size of the fragments is left up to individual IP implementations. Typically, the size of each fragment is the MTU of the network over which it must be transmitted, minus the size of the data link and IP protocol headers, and rounded down to the nearest 8 bytes. Some systems, however, automatically create 576-byte fragments, as this is the default path MTU used by many routers.

Fragmentation is not desirable, but it is a necessary evil. Obviously, because fragmenting a datagram creates many packets out of one packet, it increases the control overhead incurred by the transmission process. Also, if one fragment of a datagram is lost or damaged, the entire datagram must be retransmitted. No means of reproducing and retransmitting a single fragment exists because the source system has no knowledge of the fragmentation performed by the intermediate routers. The IP implementation on the destination system does not pass the incoming data up to the transport layer until all the fragments have arrived and been reassembled. The transport-layer protocol must therefore detect the missing data and arrange for the retransmission of the datagram.

Routing

Because the IP protocol is responsible for the transmission of packets to their final destinations, IP determines the route the packets will take. A packet's route is the path it takes from one end system, the source, to another end system, the destination. The routers the packet passes through during the trip are called *intermediate systems*. The fundamental difference between end systems and intermediate systems is how high the packet data reaches in the protocol stack.

On the source computer, a request for access to a network resource begins at the application layer and wends its way down through the layers of the protocol stack, eventually arriving at the physical layer encapsulated in a packet, ready for transmission. When it reaches the destination, the reverse occurs, and the packet is passed up the stack to the application layer. On end systems, therefore, the entire protocol stack participates in the processing of the data. On intermediate systems, such as routers, the data arriving over the network is passed only as high as the network-layer protocol, which, in this case, is IP (see Figure 11-13).

IP strips off the data link–layer protocol header and, after determining where it should send the packet next, prepares it for packaging in a data link–layer protocol frame suitable for the outgoing network. This may involve using ARP to resolve the IP address of the packet's next stop into a hardware address and then furnishing that address to the data link–layer protocol.

Routing is a process that occurs one hop of a packet's journey at a time. The source system transmits the packet to its default gateway (router) and the router determines where to send the packet next. If the final destination is on a network segment to which the router is attached, it sends the packet there. If the destination is on another network, the router determines which of the other routers it should send the packet to, in order for it to reach its destination most efficiently. Thus, the next destination for the packet, identified by the destination address in the data link–layer protocol, may not be the same system as that specified in the IP header's Destination IP Address field.

Eventually, one of the routers will have access to the network on which the packet's final destination system is located, and will be able to send it directly to that machine. Using this method, the routing process is distributed among the network's routers. None of the computers involved in the process has complete knowledge of the packet's route through the network at any time. This distribution of labor makes huge networks like the Internet possible. No practical method exists for a single system to determine a viable path through the many thousands of routers on the Internet to a specific destination for each packet.

NETWORK PROTOCOLS

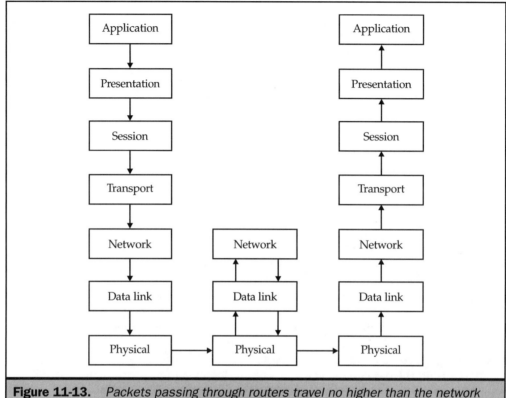

Figure 11-13.   *Packets passing through routers travel no higher than the network layer of the protocol stack*

The most complex part of the routing process is the manner in which the router determines where to send each packet next. Routers have direct knowledge only of the network segments to which they are connected. They have no means of unilaterally determining the best route to a particular destination. In most cases, routers gain knowledge about other networks by communicating with other routers using specialized protocols designed for this purpose, such as the Routing Information Protocol (RIP). Each router passes information about itself to the other routers on the networks to which it is connected, those routers update their neighboring routers, and so on.

Note   *For more information on routers, the routing process, and routing protocols, see Chapter 6.*

Regular updates from the neighboring routers enable each system to keep up with changing conditions on the network. If a router should go down, for example, its neighbors will detect its absence and spread the word that the router is unavailable.

The other routers will adjust their behavior as needed to ensure that their packets are not sent down a dead-end street.

Routing protocols enable each router to compile a table of networks with the information needed to send packets to that network. Essentially, the table says "send traffic to network *x*; use interface *y*," where *y* is one of the router's own network interfaces. Administrators can also manually configure routes through the network. This is called *static routing*, as opposed to protocol-based configuration, which is called *dynamic routing*.

On complex networks, there may be several viable routes from a source to a particular destination. Routers continually rate the possible paths through the network, so they can select the shortest, fastest, or easiest route for a packet.

ICMP

The Internet Control Message Protocol (ICMP) is a network-layer protocol that does not carry user data, although its messages are encapsulated in IP datagrams. ICMP fills two roles in the TCP/IP suite: it provides error-reporting functions, informing the sending system when a transmission cannot reach its destination, for example, and it carries query and response messages for diagnostic programs. The PING utility, for instance, which is included in every TCP/IP implementation, uses ICMP echo messages to determine if another system on the network can receive and send data.

The ICMP protocol, as defined in RFC 792, consists of messages carried in IP datagrams, with a value of 1 in the IP header's Protocol field and 0 in the Type of Service field. The ICMP message format is illustrated in Figure 11-14.

The ICMP message format consists of the following fields:

- **Type (1 byte)**   Contains a code identifying the basic function of the message.
- **Code (1 byte)**   Contains a secondary code identifying the function of the message within a specific type.
- **Checksum (2 bytes)**   Contains the results of a checksum computation on the entire ICMP message, including the Type, Code, Checksum, and Data fields (with a value of 0 in the Checksum field for computation purposes).
- **Data (variable)**   Contains information specific to the function of the message.

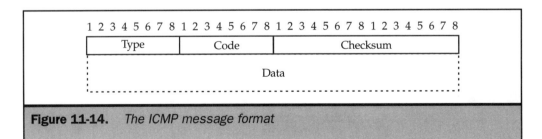

Figure 11-14.   *The ICMP message format*

The ICMP message types are listed in Table 11-6.

Type	Code	Query/Error	Function
0	0	Q	Echo Reply
3	0	E	Net Unreachable
3	1	E	Host Unreachable
3	2	E	Protocol Unreachable
3	3	E	Port Unreachable
3	4	E	Fragmentation Needed and Don't Fragment Was Set
3	5	E	Source Route Failed
3	6	E	Destination Network Unknown
3	7	E	Destination Host Unknown
3	8	E	Source Host Isolated
3	9	E	Communication with Destination Network is Administratively Prohibited
3	10	E	Communication with Destination Host is Administratively Prohibited
3	11	E	Destination Network Unreachable for Type of Service
3	12	E	Destination Host Unreachable for Type of Service
4	0	E	Source Quench
5	0	E	Redirect Datagram for the Network (or Subnet)
5	1	E	Redirect Datagram for the Host
5	2	E	Redirect Datagram for the Type of Service and Network
5	3	E	Redirect Datagram for the Type of Service and Host

Table 11-6.   *ICMP Message Types*

Type	Code	Query/Error	Function
8	0	Q	Echo Request
9	0	Q	Router Advertisement
10	0	Q	Router Solicitation
11	0	E	Time to Live Exceeded in Transit
11	1	E	Fragment Reassembly Time Exceeded
12	0	E	Pointer Indicates the Error
12	1	E	Missing a Required Option
12	2	E	Bad Length
13	0	Q	Timestamp
14	0	Q	Timestamp Reply
15	0	Q	Information Request
16	0	Q	Information Reply
17	0	Q	Address Mask Request
18	0	Q	Address Mask Reply
30	0	Q	Traceroute
31	0	E	Datagram Conversion Error
32	0	E	Mobile Host Redirect
33	0	Q	IPv6 Where-are-you
34	0	Q	IPv6 I-am-here
35	0	Q	Mobile Registration Request
36	0	Q	Mobile Registration Reply

Table 11-6. *ICMP Message Types* (continued)

ICMP Error Messages

Because of the way TCP/IP networks distribute routing chores among various systems, there is no way for either of the end systems involved in a transmission to know what has happened during a packet's journey. IP is a connectionless protocol, so no acknowledgment messages are returned to the sender at that level. When using a connection-oriented protocol at the transport layer, like TCP, the destination system acknowledges transmissions, but only for the packets it receives. If something happens during the transmission process that prevents the packet from reaching the destination, there is no way for IP or TCP to inform the sender about what happened.

ICMP error messages are designed to fill this void. When an intermediate system, such as a router, has trouble processing a packet, the router typically discards the packet, leaving the upper-layer protocols to detect the packet's absence and arrange for a retransmission. ICMP messages enable the router to inform the sender of the exact nature of the problem. Destination systems can also generate ICMP messages when a packet arrives successfully, but cannot be processed.

The Data field of an ICMP error message always contains the IP header of the datagram the system could not process, plus the first 8 bytes of the datagram's own Data field. In most cases, these 8 bytes contain a UDP header or the beginning of a TCP header, including the source and destination ports and the sequence number (in the case of TCP). This enables the system receiving the error message to isolate the exact time the error occurred and the transmission that caused it.

However, ICMP error messages are informational only. The system receiving them does not respond, nor does it necessarily take any action to correct the situation. The user or administrator may have to address the problem that is causing the failure.

In general, all TCP/IP systems are free to transmit ICMP error messages, except in certain specific situations. These exceptions are intended to prevent ICMP from generating too much traffic on the network by transmitting large numbers of identical messages. These exceptional situations are as follows:

- TCP/IP systems do not generate ICMP error messages in response to other ICMP error messages. Without this exception, it would be possible for two systems to bounce error messages back and forth between them endlessly. Systems can generate ICMP errors in response to ICMP queries, however.

- In the case of a fragmented datagram, a system only generates an ICMP error message for the first fragment.

- TCP/IP systems never generate ICMP error messages in response to broadcast or multicast transmissions, transmissions with a source IP address of 0.0.0.0, or transmissions addressed to the loopback address.

The following sections examine the most common types of ICMP error messages and their functions.

DESTINATION UNREACHABLE MESSAGES   Destination unreachable messages have a value of 3 in the ICMP Type field and any one of 13 values in the Code field. As the name implies, these messages indicate that a packet or the information in a packet could not be transmitted to its destination. The various messages specify exactly which component was unreachable and, in some cases, why. This type of message can be generated by a router when it cannot forward a packet to a certain network or to the destination system on one of the router's connected networks. Destination systems themselves can also generate these messages when they cannot deliver the contents of the packet to a specific protocol or host.

In most cases, the error is a result of some type of failure, either temporary or permanent, in a computer or the network medium. These errors could also possibly occur as a result of IP options that prevent the transmission of the packet, such as when datagrams must be fragmented for transmission over a specific network and the Don't Fragment flag in the IP header is set.

SOURCE QUENCH MESSAGES   The source quench message, with a Type value of 4 and a Code value of 0, functions as an elementary form of flow control by informing a transmitting system that it is sending packets too fast. When the receiver's buffers are in danger of being overfilled, the system can transmit a source quench message to the sender, which slows down its transmission rate as a result. The sender should continue to reduce the rate until it is no longer receiving the messages from the receiver.

This is a basic form of flow control that is reasonably effective for use between systems on the same network, but that generates too much additional traffic on routed internetworks. In most cases, this is unnecessary because TCP provides its own flow control mechanism.

REDIRECT MESSAGES   Redirect messages are generated only by routers, to inform hosts or other routers of better routes to a particular destination. In the network diagram shown in Figure 11-15, a host on Network A transmits a packet to another host on Network B and uses Router 1 as the destination of its first hop. After consulting its routing table, Router 1 determines that the packet should be sent to Router 2, but also realizes that Router 2 is located on the same network as the original transmitting host.

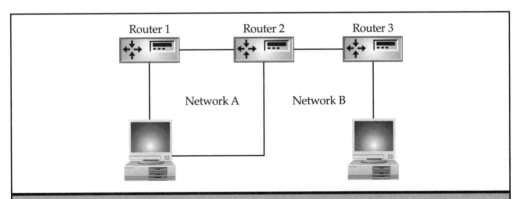

Figure 11-15.   *Packets transmitted to a host on another network can often take any one of multiple routes to the destination*

Because having the host send the packets intended for that destination directly to Router 2 would be more efficient, Router 1 sends a Redirect Datagram for the Network message (Type 5, Code 0) to the transmitting host after it forwards the original packet to Router 2. The redirect message contains the usual IP header and partial data information, as well as the IP address of the router the host should use for its future transmissions to that network.

In this example, the redirect message indicates that the host should use the other router for the packets it will transmit to all hosts on Network B in the future. The other redirect messages (with Codes 1 through 3) enable the router to specify an alternative router for transmissions to the specific host, to the specific host with the same Type of Service value, and to the entire network with the same Type of Service value.

TIME EXCEEDED MESSAGES   Time exceeded messages are used to inform a transmitting system that a packet has been discarded because a timeout has elapsed. The Time to Live Exceeded in Transit message (Type 11, Code 0) indicates that The Time-to-Live value in a packet's IP header has reached zero before arriving at the destination, forcing the router to discard it.

This message enables the TCP/IP Traceroute program to display the route through the network that packets take to a given destination. By transmitting a series of packets with incremented values in the Time-to-Live field, each successive router on the path to the destination discards a packet and returns an ICMP time exceeded message to the source.

| Note | *For more information on Traceroute, see Chapter 28.* |

The Fragment Reassembly Time Exceeded message (Code 1) indicates that a destination system has not received all the fragments of a specific datagram within the time limit specified by the host. As a result, the system must discard all the fragments it has received and return the error message to the sender.

ICMP Query Messages

ICMP query messages are not generated in response to other activities, as are the error messages. Systems use them for self-contained request/reply transactions in which one computer requests information from another, which responds with a reply containing that information.

Because they are not associated with other IP transmissions, ICMP queries do not contain datagram information in their Data fields. The data they do carry is specific to the function of the message. The following sections examine some of the more common ICMP query messages and their functions.

ECHO REQUESTS AND REPLIES   Echo Request and Echo Reply messages are the basis for the TCP/IP PING utility, which sends test messages to another host on the network to determine if it is capable of receiving and responding to messages. Each ping consists of an ICMP Echo Request message (Type 8, Code 0) that, in addition to the standard ICMP Type, Code, and Checksum fields, adds Identifier and Sequence Number fields the systems use to associate requests and replies. Packet captures of a typical request and reply exchange are shown in Figure 11-16 and Figure 11-17.

If the system receiving the message is functioning normally, it reverses the source and destination IP address fields in the IP header, changes the value of the ICMP Type field to 8 (Echo Reply), and recomputes the checksum before transmitting it back to the sender.

 For more information on Ping, see Chapter 28.

ROUTER SOLICITATIONS AND ADVERTISEMENTS   These messages make it possible for a host system to discover the addresses of the routers connected to the local network. Systems can use this information to configure the default gateway entry in their routing tables. When a host broadcasts or multicasts a Router Solicitation message (Type 10, Code 0), the routers on the network respond with Router Advertisement messages (Type 9, Code 0). Routers continue to advertise their availability at regular intervals (typically seven to ten minutes). A host may stop using a router as its default gateway if it fails to receive continued advertisements.

The Router Solicitation message consists only of the standard Type, Code, and Checksum fields, plus a 4-byte pad in the Data field. The Router Advertisement message format is shown in Figure 11-18.

NETWORK PROTOCOLS

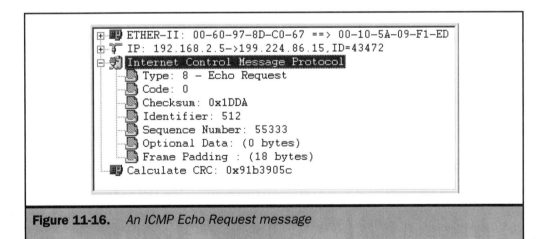

Figure 11-16. *An ICMP Echo Request message*

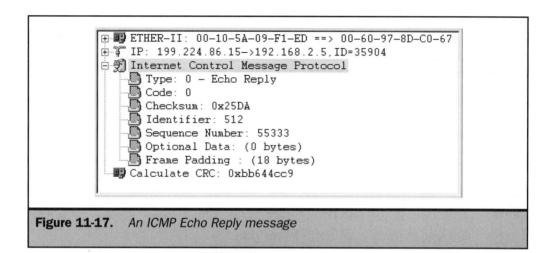

```
ETHER-II: 00-10-5A-09-F1-ED ==> 00-60-97-8D-C0-67
IP: 199.224.86.15->192.168.2.5,ID=35904
Internet Control Message Protocol
    Type: 0 - Echo Reply
    Code: 0
    Checksum: 0x25DA
    Identifier: 512
    Sequence Number: 55333
    Optional Data: (0 bytes)
    Frame Padding : (18 bytes)
Calculate CRC: 0xbb644cc9
```

Figure 11-17.   *An ICMP Echo Reply message*

The Router Advertisement message format contains the following additional fields:

■ **Number of Addresses (1 byte)**   Specifies the number of router addresses contained in the message. The format can support multiple addresses, each of which will have its own Router Address and Preference Level fields.

■ **Address Entry Size (1 byte)**   Specifies the number of 4-byte words devoted to each address in the message. The value is always 2.

■ **Lifetime (2 bytes)**   Specifies the time, in seconds, that can elapse between advertisements before a system assumes a router is no longer functioning. The default value is usually 1,800 seconds (0 minutes).

■ **Router Address (4 bytes)**   Specifies the IP address of the router generating the advertisement message.

■ **Preference Level (4 bytes)**   Contains a value specified by the network administrator that host systems can use to select one router over another.

1 2 3 4 5 6 7 8	1 2 3 4 5 6 7 8	1 2 3 4 5 6 7 8 1 2 3 4 5 6 7 8
Number of Addresses	Address Entry Size	Lifetime
Router Address		
Preference Level		

Figure 11-18.   *The Router Advertisement message format*

UDP

Two TCP/IP protocols operate at the transport layer: TCP and UDP. The *User Datagram Protocol (UDP)*, defined in RFC 768, is a connectionless, unreliable protocol that provides minimal transport service to application-layer protocols with a minimum of control overhead. Thus, UDP provides no packet acknowledgment or flow control services like TCP, although it does provide end-to-end checksum verification on the contents of the packet.

Although it provides a minimum of services of its own, UDP does function as a *pass-through protocol,* meaning that it provides applications with access to network-layer services, and vice versa. If, for example, a datagram containing UDP data cannot be delivered to the destination and a router returns an ICMP Destination Unreachable message, UDP always passes the ICMP message information up from the network layer to the application that generated the information in the original datagram. UDP also passes along any option information included in IP datagrams to the application layer and, in the opposite direction, information from applications that IP will use as values for the Time-to-Live and Type of Service header fields.

The nature of the UDP protocol makes it suitable only for brief transactions in which all the data to be sent to the destination fits into a single datagram. This is because no mechanism exists in UDP for splitting a data stream into segments and reassembling them, as in TCP. This does not mean that the datagram cannot be fragmented by IP in the course of transmission, however. This process is invisible to the transport layer, as the receiving system reassembles the fragments before passing the datagram up the stack.

In addition, because no packet acknowledgment exists in UDP, it is most often used for client/server transactions in which the client transmits a request and the server's reply message serves as an acknowledgment. If a system sends a request and no reply is forthcoming, the system assumes the destination system did not receive the message and retransmits. It is mostly TCP/IP support services like DNS and DHCP, services that don't carry actual user data, that use this type of transaction. Applications such as DHCP also use UDP when they have to send broadcast or multicast transmissions. Because the TCP protocol requires two systems to establish a connection before they transmit user data, it does not support broadcasts and multicasts.

The header for UDP messages (sometimes confusingly called datagrams, like IP messages) is small, only 8 bytes, as opposed to the 20 bytes of the TCP header. The format is illustrated in Figure 11-19.

The functions of the fields are as follows:

■ **Source Port Number (2 bytes)**   Identifies the port number of the process in the transmitting system that generated the data carried in the UDP datagram. In some cases, this may be an ephemeral port number selected by the client for this transaction.

NETWORK PROTOCOLS

```
1 2 3 4 5 6 7 8 1 2 3 4 5 6 7 8 1 2 3 4 5 6 7 8 1 2 3 4 5 6 7 8
```

Source Port Number	Destination Port Number
UDP Length	UDP Checksum

Figure 11-19.   *The UDP message format*

- **Destination Port Number (2 bytes)**   Identifies the port number of the process on the destination system that will receive the data carried in the UDP datagram. Well-known port numbers are listed in the "Assigned Numbers" RFC and in the SERVICES file on every TCP/IP system.

- **UDP Length (2 bytes)**   Specifies the length of the entire UDP message, including the header and data fields, in bytes.

- **UDP Checksum (2 bytes)**   Contains the results of a checksum computation computed from the UDP header and data, along with a pseudo-header comprised of the IP header's Source IP Address, Destination IP Address, and Protocol fields, plus the UDP Length field. This pseudo-header enables the UDP protocol at the receiving system to verify that the message has been delivered to the correct protocol on the correct destination system.

- **Data (variable, up to 65,507 bytes)**   Contains the information supplied by the application-layer protocol.

TCP

The Transmission Control Protocol (TCP) is the connection-oriented, reliable alternative to UDP, which accounts for the majority of the user data transmitted across a TCP/IP network, as well as for giving the protocol suite its name. TCP, as defined in RFC 793, provides applications with a full range of transport services, including packet acknowledgment, error detection and correction, and flow control.

TCP is intended for the transfer of relatively large amounts of data that will not fit into a single packet. The data often takes the form of complete files that must be split up into multiple datagrams for transmission. In TCP terminology, the data supplied to the transport layer is referred to as a *sequence,* and the protocol splits it into *segments* for transmission across the network. As with UDP, however, the segments are packaged in IP datagrams that may end up taking different routes to the destination. TCP, therefore, assigns sequence numbers to the segments, so the receiving system can reassemble them in the correct order.

Before any transfer of user data begins using TCP, the two systems exchange messages to establish a connection. This ensures that the receiver is operating and capable of receiving data. Once the connection is established and data transfer begins, the receiving system generates periodic acknowledgment messages. These messages inform the sender of lost packets and also provide the information used to control the rate of flow to the receiver.

The TCP Header

To provide these services, the header applied to TCP segments is necessarily larger than that for UDP. At 20 bytes (without options), it's the same size as the IP header. The header format is illustrated in Figure 11-20.

The functions of the fields are as follows:

- **Source Port (2 bytes)**   Identifies the port number of the process in the transmitting system that generated the data carried in the TCP segments. In some cases, this may be an ephemeral port number selected by the client for this transaction.

- **Destination Port (2 bytes)**   Identifies the port number of the process on the destination system that will receive the data carried in the TCP segments. Well-known port numbers are listed in the "Assigned Numbers" RFC and in the SERVICES file on every TCP/IP system.

- **Sequence Number (4 bytes)**   Specifies the location of the data in this segment in relation to the entire data sequence.

- **Acknowledgment Number (4 bytes)**   Specifies the sequence number of the next segment that the acknowledging system expects to receive from the sender. Active only when the ACK bit is set.

- **Data Offset (4 bits)**   Specifies the length, in 4-byte words, of the TCP header (which may contain options expanding it to as much as 60 bytes).

- **Reserved (6 bits)**   Unused.

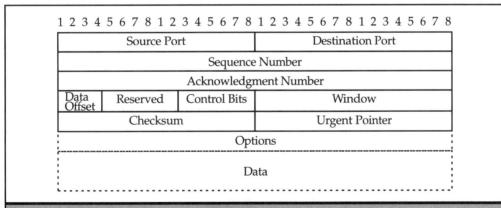

Figure 11-20.   *The TCP message format*

■ **Control Bits (6 bits)**   Contains six 1-bit flags that perform the following functions:

  ■ **URG**   Indicates that the sequence contains urgent data and activates the Urgent Pointer field.

  ■ **ACK**   Indicates that the message is an acknowledgment of previously transmitted data and activates the Acknowledgment number field.

  ■ **PSH**   Instructs the receiving system to push all the data in the current sequence to the application identified by the port number without waiting for the rest.

  ■ **RST**   Instructs the receiving system to discard all the segments in the sequence that have been transmitted thus far and resets the TCP connection.

  ■ **SYN**   Used during the connection establishment process to synchronize the sequence numbers in the source and destination systems.

  ■ **FIN**   Indicates to the other system that the data transmission has been completed and the connection is to be terminated.

■ **Window (2 bytes)**   Implements the TCP flow control mechanism by specifying the number of bytes the system can accept from the sender.

■ **Checksum (2 bytes)**   Contains a checksum computation computed from the TCP header; data; and a pseudo-header composed of the Source IP Address, Destination IP Address, Protocol fields from the packet's IP header, plus the length of the entire TCP message.

■ **Urgent Pointer (2 bytes)**   Activated by the URG bit, specifies the data in the sequence that should be treated by the receiver as urgent.

■ **Options (variable)**   May contain additional configuration parameters for the TCP connection, along with padding to fill the field to the nearest 4-byte boundary. The available options are as follows:

  ■ **Maximum Segment Size**   Specifies the size of the largest segments the current system can receive from the connected system.

  ■ **Window Scale Factor**   Used to double the size of the Window Size field from 2 to 4 bytes.

  ■ **Timestamp**   Used to carry timestamps in data packets that the receiving system returns in its acknowledgments, enabling the sender to measure the round trip time.

■ **Data (variable)**   May contain a segment of the information passed down from an application-layer protocol. In SYN, ACK, and FIN packets, this field is left empty.

Connection Establishment

Distinguishing TCP connections from the other types of connections commonly used in data networking is important. When you log on to a network, for example, you initiate a session that remains open until you log off. During that session, you may establish other connections to individual network resources like file servers that also remain open for extended lengths of time. TCP connections are much more transient, however, and typically remain open only for the duration of the data transmission. In addition, a system (or even a single application on that system) may open several TCP connections at once with the same destination.

As an example, consider a basic client/server transaction between a Web browser and a Web server. Whenever you type a URL in the browser, the program opens a TCP connection with the server to transfer the default HTML file that the browser uses to display the home page. The connection only lasts as long as it takes to transfer that one page. When the user clicks a hyperlink to open a new page, an entirely new TCP connection is needed.

The additional messages required for the establishment of the connection, plus the size of the header, add considerably to the control overhead incurred by a TCP connection. This is the main reason why TCP/IP has UDP as a low-overhead transport-layer alternative.

The communication process between the client and the server begins when the client generates its first TCP message, beginning the three-way handshake that establishes the connection between the two machines. This message contains no application data, it simply signals to the server that the client wishes to establish a connection. The SYN bit is set, and the system supplies a value in the Sequence Number field, called the *initial sequence number (ISN)* (see Figure 11-21). In this packet capture, the sequence number is 119841003.

The system uses a continuously incrementing algorithm to determine the ISN it will use for each connection. The constant cycling of the sequence numbers makes it highly unlikely that multiple connections using the same sequence numbers will occur between the same two sockets. The client system then transmits the message as a unicast to the destination system and enters the SYN-SENT state, indicating that it has transmitted its connection request and is waiting for a matching request from the destination system.

The server, at this time, is in the LISTEN state, meaning that it is waiting to receive a connection request from a client. When the server receives the message from the client, it replies with its own TCP control message. This message serves two functions: it acknowledges the receipt of the client's message, as indicated by the ACK bit, and initiates its own connection, as indicated by the SYN bit (see Figure 11-22). The server then enters the SYN-RECEIVED state, indicating that it has received a connection request, issued a request of its own, and is waiting for an acknowledgment from the other system. Both the ACK and SYN bits are necessary because TCP is a *full-duplex* protocol, meaning that a separate connection is actually running in each direction. Both connections must be individually established, maintained, and terminated. The server's message also contains a value in the Sequence Number field (116270), as well as a value in the Acknowledgment Number field (119841004).

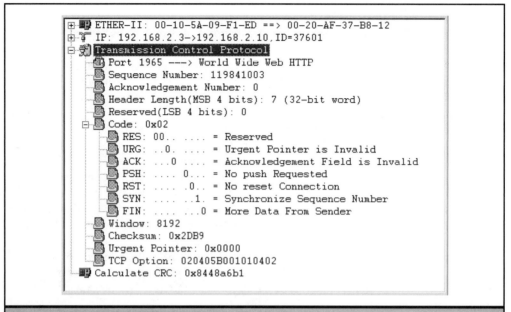

Figure 11-21.   *The client's SYN message initiates the connection establishment process*

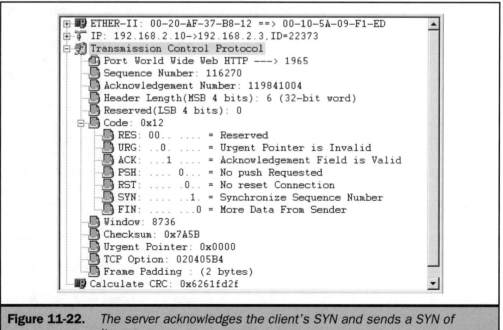

Figure 11-22.   *The server acknowledges the client's SYN and sends a SYN of its own*

Both systems maintain their own sequence numbers and are also conscious of the other system's sequence numbers. Notice that the server's value for the Acknowledgment Number field is the client's ISN plus one, indicating that the server expects the client's next packet to have this value for its sequence number. Later, when the systems actually begin to send application data, these sequence numbers enable a receiver to assemble the individual segments transmitted in separate packets into the original sequence.

Remember, although the two systems must establish a connection before they send application data, the TCP messages are still transmitted within IP datagrams and are subject to the same treatment as any other datagram. Thus, the connection is actually a virtual one, and the datagrams may take different routes to the destination and arrive in a different order from that in which they were sent.

After the client receives the server's message, it transmits its own ACK message (see Figure 11-23), acknowledging the server's SYN bit and completing the bidirectional connection establishment process. This message has a value of 119841004 as its sequence number, which is the value the server expects, and an acknowledgment number of 116271, which is the sequence number it expects to see in the server's next transmission. Both systems now enter the ESTABLISHED state, indicating that they are ready to transmit and receive application data.

NETWORK PROTOCOLS

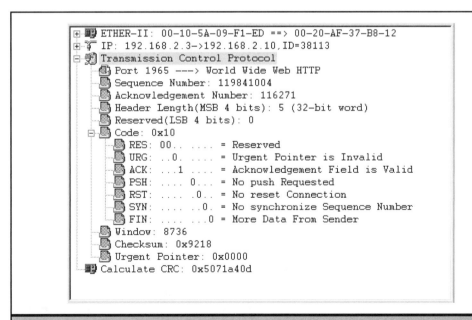

```
⊞ ▦ ETHER-II: 00-10-5A-09-F1-ED ==> 00-20-AF-37-B8-12
⊞ ▼ IP: 192.168.2.3->192.168.2.10,ID=38113
⊟ ▤ Transmission Control Protocol
    ▱ Port 1965 ---> World Wide Web HTTP
    ▨ Sequence Number: 119841004
    ▨ Acknowledgement Number: 116271
    ▨ Header Length(MSB 4 bits): 5 (32-bit word)
    ▨ Reserved(LSB 4 bits): 0
  ⊟ ▨ Code: 0x10
      ▨ RES: 00.. .... = Reserved
      ▨ URG: ..0. .... = Urgent Pointer is Invalid
      ▨ ACK: ...1 .... = Acknowledgement Field is Valid
      ▨ PSH: .... 0... = No push Requested
      ▨ RST: .... .0.. = No reset Connection
      ▨ SYN: .... ..0. = No synchronize Sequence Number
      ▨ FIN: .... ...0 = More Data From Sender
    ▨ Window: 8736
    ▨ Checksum: 0x9218
    ▨ Urgent Pointer: 0x0000
  ▦ Calculate CRC: 0x5071a40d
```

Figure 11-23.   *The client then acknowledges the server's SYN, and the connection is established in both directions*

Data Transfer

Once the TCP connection is established in both directions, the transmission of data can begin. The application-layer protocol determines whether the client or the server initiates the next exchange. In an FTP session, for example, the server sends a Ready message first. In an HTTP exchange, the client begins by sending the URL of the document it wants to receive.

The data to be sent is not packaged for transmission until the connection is established. This is because the systems use the SYN messages to inform the other system of the *maximum segment size (MSS)*. The MSS specifies the size of the largest segment each system is capable of receiving. The value of the MSS depends on the data link–layer protocol used to connect the two systems.

Each system supplies the other with an MSS value in the TCP message's Options field. As with the IP header, each option consists of multiple subfields, which for the Maximum Segment Size option, are as follows:

- **Kind (1 byte)**   Identifies the function of the option. For the Maximum Segment Size option, the value is 2.

- **Length (1 byte)**   Specifies the length of the entire option. For the Maximum Segment Size option, the value is 4.

- **Maximum Segment Size (2 bytes)**   Specifies the size (in bytes) of the largest data segment the system can receive.

In the client system's first TCP message, shown earlier in Figure 11-21, the value of the Options field is (in hexadecimal notation) 020405B001010402. The first 4 bytes of this value constitute the MSS option. The Kind value is 02; the Length is 04; and the MSS is 05B0, which in decimal form is 1,456 bytes. This works out to the maximum frame size for an Ethernet II network (1,500 bytes) minus 20 bytes for the IP header and 24 bytes for the TCP header (20 bytes plus 4 option bytes). The server's own SYN packet contains the same value for this option because these two computers were located on the same Ethernet network.

> **Note**   *The remaining 4 bytes in the Options field consist of 2 bytes of padding (0101) and the Kind (04) and Length (02) fields of the SACK-Permitted option, indicating that the system is capable of processing extended information as part of acknowledgment messages.*

When the two systems are located on different networks, their MSS values may also be different, and how the systems deal with this is left up to the individual TCP implementations. Some systems may just use the smaller of the two values, while others might revert to the default value of 536 bytes used when no MSS option is supplied. Windows NT systems use a special method of discovering the connection's path MTU (that is, the largest packet size permitted on an internetwork link between two systems). This method, as defined in RFC 1191, enables the systems to determine the packet sizes permitted on intermediate networks, so that even if the source and destination systems are both connected to Ethernet networks with 1,500-byte MTUs, they can detect an intermediate connection that only supports a 576-byte MTU.

Once the MSS for the connection is established, the systems can begin packaging data for transmission. In the case of an HTTP transaction, the Web browser client transmits the desired URL to the server in a single packet (see Figure 11-24). Notice that the sequence number of this packet (119841004) is the same as that for the previous packet it sent in acknowledgment to the server's SYN message. This is because TCP messages consisting only of an acknowledgment do not increment the sequence counter. The acknowledgment number is also the same as in the previous packet because the client has not yet received the next message from the server. Note also that the PSH bit is set, indicating that the server should send the enclosed data to the application immediately.

After receiving the client's message, the server returns an acknowledgment message, as shown in Figure 11-25, that uses the sequence number expected by the client (116271) and has an acknowledgment number of 119841363. The difference between this acknowledgment number and the sequence number of the client message previously sent is 359; this is correct because the datagram the client sent to the server was 399 bytes long. Subtracting 40 bytes for the IP and TCO headers leaves 359 bytes worth of data. The value in the server's acknowledgment message, therefore, indicates that it has successfully received 359 bytes of data from the client. As each system sends data to the other, they increment their sequence numbers for each byte transmitted.

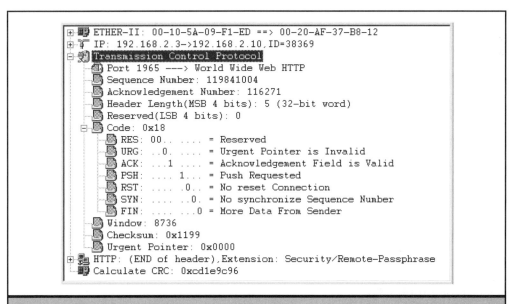

```
⊞▬▶ ETHER-II: 00-10-5A-09-F1-ED ==> 00-20-AF-37-B8-12
⊞▼ IP: 192.168.2.3->192.168.2.10,ID=38369
⊟▒ Transmission Control Protocol
    ▒ Port 1965 ---> World Wide Web HTTP
    ▒ Sequence Number: 119841004
    ▒ Acknowledgement Number: 116271
    ▒ Header Length(MSB 4 bits): 5 (32-bit word)
    ▒ Reserved(LSB 4 bits): 0
  ⊟▒ Code: 0x18
      ▒ RES: 00.. .... = Reserved
      ▒ URG: ..0. .... = Urgent Pointer is Invalid
      ▒ ACK: ...1 .... = Acknowledgement Field is Valid
      ▒ PSH: .... 1... = Push Requested
      ▒ RST: .... .0.. = No reset Connection
      ▒ SYN: .... ..0. = No synchronize Sequence Number
      ▒ FIN: .... ...0 = More Data From Sender
    ▒ Window: 8736
    ▒ Checksum: 0x1199
    ▒ Urgent Pointer: 0x0000
  ⊞▒ HTTP: (END of header),Extension: Security/Remote-Passphrase
    ▬ Calculate CRC: 0xcd1e9c96
```

Figure 11-24.   *The first data packet sent over the connection contains the URL requested by the Web browser*

NETWORK PROTOCOLS

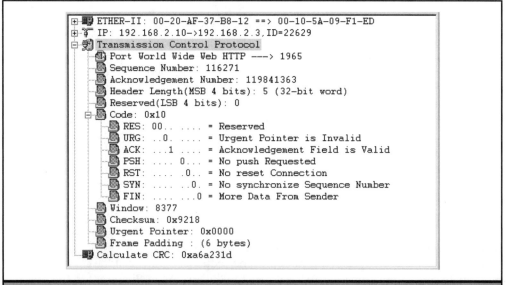

```
ETHER-II: 00-20-AF-37-B8-12 ==> 00-10-5A-09-F1-ED
IP: 192.168.2.10->192.168.2.3,ID=22629
Transmission Control Protocol
    Port World Wide Web HTTP ---> 1965
    Sequence Number: 116271
    Acknowledgement Number: 119841363
    Header Length(MSB 4 bits): 5 (32-bit word)
    Reserved(LSB 4 bits): 0
    Code: 0x10
        RES: 00.. .... = Reserved
        URG: ..0. .... = Urgent Pointer is Invalid
        ACK: ...1 .... = Acknowledgement Field is Valid
        PSH: .... 0... = No push Requested
        RST: .... .0.. = No reset Connection
        SYN: .... ..0. = No synchronize Sequence Number
        FIN: .... ...0 = More Data From Sender
    Window: 8377
    Checksum: 0x9218
    Urgent Pointer: 0x0000
    Frame Padding : (6 bytes)
Calculate CRC: 0xa6a231d
```

Figure 11-25. *The server acknowledges all of the data bytes transmitted by the client*

The next step in the process is for the server to respond to the client's request by sending it the requested HTML file. Using the MSS value, the server creates segments small enough to be transmitted over the network and transmits the first one in the message, as shown in Figure 11-26. The sequence number is again the same as the server's previous message because the previous message contained only an acknowledgment. The acknowledgment number is also the same because the server is sending a second message without any intervening communication from the client.

In addition to the acknowledgment service just described, the TCP header fields provide two additional services:

■ Error correction
■ Flow control

The following sections examine each of these functions.

ERROR CORRECTION　You saw in the previous example how a receiving system uses the acknowledgment number in its ACK message to inform the sender that its data was received correctly. The systems also use this mechanism to indicate when an error has occurred and data is not received correctly.

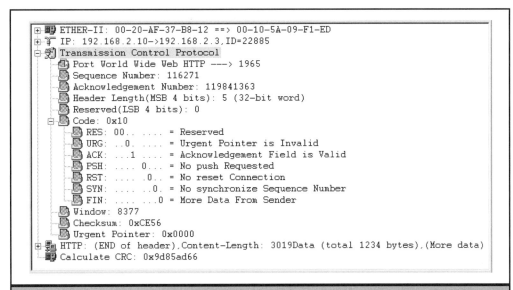

```
⊞ 🖳 ETHER-II: 00-20-AF-37-B8-12 ==> 00-10-5A-09-F1-ED
⊞ 🍿 IP: 192.168.2.10->192.168.2.3,ID=22885
⊟ 🗐 Transmission Control Protocol
     📗 Port World Wide Web HTTP ---> 1965
     📗 Sequence Number: 116271
     📗 Acknowledgement Number: 119841363
     📗 Header Length(MSB 4 bits): 5 (32-bit word)
     📗 Reserved(LSB 4 bits): 0
   ⊟ 📗 Code: 0x10
        📗 RES: 00.. .... = Reserved
        📗 URG: ..0. .... = Urgent Pointer is Invalid
        📗 ACK: ...1 .... = Acknowledgement Field is Valid
        📗 PSH: .... 0... = No push Requested
        📗 RST: .... .0.. = No reset Connection
        📗 SYN: .... ..0. = No synchronize Sequence Number
        📗 FIN: .... ...0 = More Data From Sender
     📗 Window: 8377
     📗 Checksum: 0xCE56
     📗 Urgent Pointer: 0x0000
   ⊞ 🖳 HTTP: (END of header),Content-Length: 3019Data (total 1234 bytes),(More data)
     🖳 Calculate CRC: 0x9d85ad66
```

Figure 11-26.   *In response to the client's request, the server begins to transmit the Web page after splitting it into multiple segments*

TCP/IP systems use a system of *delayed acknowledgments,* meaning that they do not have to send an acknowledgment message for every packet they receive. The method used to determine when acknowledgments are sent is left up to the individual implementation, but each acknowledgment specifies that the data, up to a certain point in the sequence, has been received correctly. These are called *positive acknowledgments* because they indicate that data has been received. *Negative acknowledgments* or *selective acknowledgments,* which specify that data has not been received correctly, are not possible in TCP.

What if, for example, in the course of a single connection, a server transmits five data segments to a client and the third segment must be discarded because of a checksum error? The receiving system must then send an acknowledgment back to the sender indicating that all the messages up through the second segment have been received correctly. Even though the fourth and fifth segments were also received correctly, the third segment was not. Using positive acknowledgments means that the fourth and fifth segments must be retransmitted, in addition to the third.

The mechanism used by TCP is called *positive acknowledgment with retransmission* because the sending system automatically retransmits all of the unacknowledged segments after a certain time interval. The way this works is that the sending system maintains a queue containing all of the segments it has already transmitted. As acknowledgments arrive from the receiver, the sender deletes the segments that have been acknowledged from the queue. After a certain elapsed time, the sending system retransmits all of the unacknowledged segments remaining in the queue. The systems use algorithms documented in RFC 1122 to calculate the timeout values for a connection based on the amount of time it takes for a transmission to travel from one system to the other and back again, called the *round-trip time*.

FLOW CONTROL   *Flow control* is an important element of the TCP protocol because it is designed to transmit large amounts of data. Receiving systems have a buffer in which they store incoming segments waiting to be acknowledged. If a sending system transmits too many segments too quickly, the receiver's buffer fills up and any packets arriving at the system are discarded until space in the buffer is available. TCP uses a mechanism called a *sliding window* for its flow control, which is essentially a means for the receiving system to inform the sender of how much buffer space it has available.

Each acknowledgment message generated by a system receiving TCP data specifies the amount of buffer space it has available in its Window field. As packets arrive at the receiving system, they wait in the buffer until the system generates the message that acknowledges them. The sending system computes the amount of data it can send by taking the Window value from the most recently received acknowledgment and subtracting the number of bytes it has transmitted since it received that acknowledgment. If the result of this computation is zero, the system stops transmitting until it receives acknowledgment of outstanding packets.

Connection Termination

When the exchange of data between the two systems is complete, they terminate the TCP connection. Because two connections are actually involved—one in each direction—both must be individually terminated. The process begins when one machine sends a message in which the FIN control bit is set. This indicates that the system wants to terminate the connection it has been using to send data.

Which system initiates the termination process is dependent on the application generating the traffic. In an HTML transaction, the server can include the FIN bit in the message containing the last segment of data in the sequence, or it can take the form of a separate message. The client receiving the FIN from the server sends an acknowledgment, closing the server's connection, and then sends a FIN message of its own. Note that, unlike the three-way handshake that established the connection, the termination procedure requires four transmissions because client sends its ACK and FIN bits in separate messages. When the server transmits its acknowledgment to the client's FIN, the connection is effectively terminated.

The Complete Reference

Upgrading
&
Troubleshooting
Networks

Chapter 12

NetWare Protocols

Novell NetWare was first designed at a time when proprietary computer networking products were commonplace. As a result, to provide transport services for the NetWare operating system, Novell created its own suite of protocols, usually referred to by the name of the network-layer protocol: IPX, or Internetwork Packet Exchange. As a parallel to TCP/IP, the suite is also sometimes called IPX/SPX, which adds a reference to the Sequenced Packet Exchange (SPX) protocol, which operates at the transport layer. Unlike the combination of TCP and IP, however, which usually accounts for a good deal of the traffic on a TCP/IP network, use of the IPX/SPX combination on a NetWare network is relatively rare.

As the networking industry developed, standardization and interoperability became the most important elements of networking product designs. The rise in popularity of the TCP/IP protocols and the Internet led most of the network operating system developers to adopt TCP/IP as their default protocols, if they were not using them already. Novell, however, held on to its proprietary protocols longer than anyone else, much to the detriment of its market share. It was only with the release of NetWare 5 in 1998 that TCP/IP was fully integrated into NetWare.

The IPX protocols are similar to TCP/IP in several ways. Both protocol suites use a connectionless, unreliable protocol at the network layer (IPX and IP, respectively) to carry datagrams containing the information generated by multiple upper-layer protocols that provide varying degrees of service for different applications. Like IP, IPX is responsible for addressing datagrams and routing them to their destinations on other networks.

Unlike TCP/IP, however, the IPX protocols were designed for use on LANs, and don't have the almost-unlimited scalability of the Internet protocols. IPX does not have a completely self-contained addressing system like IP. Systems on a NetWare network identify other systems using the node address hardcoded into network interface adapters plus a network address assigned by the administrator (or the operating system) during the installation.

IPX also lacks the universality of TCP/IP because of Novell's policy of keeping many of the details regarding the inner workings of the protocols private. In retrospect, this policy can be seen as having worked against Novell. Microsoft seems to have had little difficulty in reverse-engineering IPX for its NWLink protocol; and by not releasing the protocol specifications to other companies, Novell squandered any chance for IPX to become an industry standard.

Data Link–Layer Protocols

IPX datagrams are carried within standard data link–layer protocol frames, just like IP. The IPX protocols have no data link–layer protocols of their own, although you can use them over a PPP connection. On most networks, however, Ethernet or Token Ring frames encapsulate IPX.

The only unusual aspect of configuring NetWare servers to use the Ethernet or Token Ring protocols is that you must specify the frame type (or types) for each network, using names that are less than intuitive. NetWare supports four Ethernet frame types, which differ only in certain aspects of the frame format. While all four are capable of carrying standard IPX traffic, the frame type you select can influence whether or not your network supports the use of other protocol suites (like TCP/IP) concurrently with IPX.

These four Ethernet frame types are as follows:

- **ETHERNET_802.3** Also called "raw Ethernet," this was the default frame type for NetWare versions through 3.11. This frame differs slightly from the exact format defined in the IEEE 802.3 document, which wasn't complete at the time of NetWare's initial release. The frame can be anywhere from 64 to 1,518 bytes long, and the field immediately following the source and destination addresses specifies the length of the packet, not the Ethertype value, as in the DIX Ethernet frame. Because of this, the Ethernet protocol has no means of identifying the network-layer protocol carried in the frame to the receiving system. Therefore, this frame type can only be used on a network running IPX exclusively at the network layer.

- **ETHERNET_802.2** The default frame type for NetWare versions 3.12 and later, the name is confusing because 802.2 refers to the Logical Link Control standard developed by the IEEE for use with all of the 802 protocols. Actually, this frame type uses the standard frame defined in the IEEE 802.3 standard, as well as the 802.2 header in the frame's Data field. Because this frame conforms to the standard, it can be used with other products that support IPX (such as Windows NT). However, the frame still lacks the equivalent of an Ethertype field and can support only IPX traffic.

- **ETHERNET_II** As defined by the DIX Ethernet standard, this frame type differs from the IEEE frame mainly in that it has an Ethertype field that specifies which network-layer protocol generated the data carried in the frame. This, therefore, is the frame type you should use when you are running TCP/IP or other protocols on your network.

- **ETHERNET_SNAP** This frame type is identical to ETHERNET_802.2, except that it includes the SNAP header in the Data field in addition to the LLC header. The SNAP header also has a field that identifies the network-layer protocol, enabling you to use it on networks also running TCP/IP and/or AppleTalk.

NetWare enables you to select as many of these frame types for your Ethernet networks as you need, in order to support the various other systems connected to it. The main concern, apart from using either ETHERNET_II or ETHERNET_SNAP on networks running TCP/IP or other protocols, is that servers and workstations all have at least one frame type in common. On the Windows client systems today, this is not a problem, since the computer detects the frame types in use on the network and configures itself accordingly.

NETWORK PROTOCOLS

| Note | *For more information on Ethernet frames and the standards that define them, see Chapter 8.* |

The Internetwork Packet Exchange (IPX) Protocol

IPX is based on the Internetwork Datagram Packet (IDP) protocol designed for Xerox Network Services (XNS). IPX provides basic connectionless transport between systems on an internetwork, in either broadcast or unicast transmissions. Most of the standard traffic between NetWare servers and between clients and servers is carried within IPX datagrams.

The header on an IPX datagram is 30 bytes long (as compared to IP's 20-byte header). The format for the IPX header is illustrated in Figure 12-1, and the functions of the header fields are as follows:

- **Checksum (2 bytes)**   In the original IDP header, this field contained a CRC value for the datagram. Since the data link–layer protocol performs CRC checking, the function is disabled in IPX datagrams, and always contains the hexadecimal value ffff.

- **Length (2 bytes)**   Specifies the length of the datagram, in bytes, including the IPX header and the data.

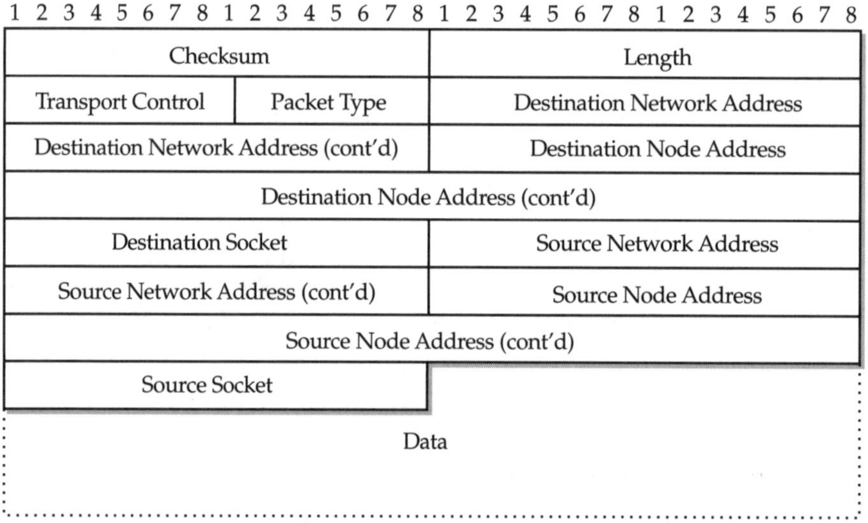

Figure 12-1.   *The IPX datagram format*

■ **Transport Control (1 byte)**   Also known as the *hop count*; specifies the number of routers the datagram has passed through on the way to its destination. Set to 0 by the transmitting system, each router increments the field by one as it processes the packet. If the value reaches 16, the router discards the datagram.

■ **Packet Type (1 byte)**   Identifies the service or upper-layer protocol that generated the data carried in the datagram, using the following values:

   ■ **0**   Unknown Packet Type

   ■ **1**   Routing Information Protocol

   ■ **4**   Service Advertising Protocol

   ■ **5**   Sequenced Packet Exchange

   ■ **17**   NetWare Core Protocol

■ **Destination Network Address (4 bytes)**   Identifies the network on which the destination system is located, using a value assigned by the administrator or the operating system during the NetWare installation.

■ **Destination Node Address (6 bytes)**   Identifies the network interface inside the computer to which the data is to be delivered, using the data link–layer protocol's hardware address. Broadcast messages use the hexadecimal address ffffffffffff.

■ **Destination Socket (2 bytes)**   Identifies the process on the destination system for which the data in the datagram is intended, using the following hexadecimal values:

   ■ **0451**   NetWare Core Protocol

   ■ **0452**   Service Advertising Protocol

   ■ **0453**   Routing Information Protocol

   ■ **0455**   NetBIOS

   ■ **0456**   Diagnostic Packet

   ■ **0457**   Serialization Packet

   ■ **4000–6000**   Custom sockets for server processes

   ■ **9000**   NetWare Link Services Protocol

   ■ **9004**   IPXWAN Protocol

■ **Source Network Address (4 bytes)**   Identifies the network on which the system sending the datagram is located, using a value assigned by the administrator or the operating system during the NetWare installation.

■ **Source Node Address (6 bytes)**   Identifies the network interface inside the computer sending the datagram, using the data link–layer protocol's hardware address.

NETWORK PROTOCOLS

- **Source Socket (2 bytes)**   Identifies the process on the local system from which the data originated, using the same hexadecimal values as the Destination Socket field.
- **Data (variable)**   Contains the data generated by the upper-layer protocol.

To determine a viable route to the destination, NetWare servers use a routing protocol like RIP (Routing Information Protocol) or NLSP (NetWare Link Services Protocol). As with other network-layer protocols, an IPX router strips off the data link–layer protocol frame from each packet and adds a new frame for transmission over another network. The only modification the router makes to the IPX header is to increment the value of the Transport Control field.

 Note   *For more information on routing, see Chapter 6.*

Because IPX is a connectionless protocol, it relies on the upper-layer protocols to affirm that data has been delivered correctly. For example, when a client sends a request to a server using a NetWare Core Protocol (NCP) message in an IPX datagram, it is the response from the server that functions as an acknowledgment of the request.

However, NetWare clients do maintain a response timeout clock that causes them to retransmit an IPX datagram if a response is not received in a given period of time. If there is a condition on the network that intermittently slows down traffic, a client may retransmit a datagram several times before it is received correctly at the destination. You can control the number of times that the system will attempt to retransmit a datagram by changing the client's IPX RETRY COUNT parameter from the default setting of 20. On a Windows NT or 9*x* system with the Novell NetWare client installed, you find this parameter in the Properties dialog box for the IPX protocol module. On a DOS/Windows 3.1 system, you add the following line in the system's Net.cfg file:

```
IPX RETRY COUNT = 30
```

The Sequenced Packet Exchange (SPX) Protocol

Derived from the XNS Sequenced Packet Protocol (SPP), SPX operates at the transport layer and provides a connection-oriented, reliable service with flow control and packet sequencing, much like TCP in the TCP/IP protocol suite. However, NetWare systems use SPX far less often than TCP/IP systems use TCP. Typical file access procedures on a NetWare network use the NetWare Core Protocol, which accounts for the majority of the traffic produced. SPX is only used for tasks that require its services, such as communications between print servers, print queues, and remote printers; RCONSOLE sessions; and network backups.

The SPX header is illustrated in Figure 12-2, and the functions of the fields are as follows:

- **Connection Control (1 byte)** Contains a code that regulates the bidirectional flow of data, using the following hexadecimal values:
  - **10** End of Message
  - **20** Attention
  - **40** Acknowledgment required
  - **80** System packet
- **Datastream Type (1 byte)** Specifies the nature of the data in the message and the upper-layer process for which it is intended, using a value defined by the client or one of the following:
  - **FE** End-of-Connection
  - **FF** End-of-Connection Acknowledgment
- **Source Connection ID (2 bytes)** Contains a unique value used to identify this connection, since a system can have multiple connections open to the same socket simultaneously.
- **Destination Connection ID (2 bytes)** Contains the unique value that the destination system uses to identify this connection. During the initial connection establishment process, the value of this field is ffff, since the other system's connection ID can't be known yet.
- **Sequence Number (2 bytes)** Contains a number, incremented for each message transmitted during the connection, that the receiving system uses to process the messages in the proper order.
- **Acknowledgment Number (2 bytes)** Contains the sequence number of the next message that the system expects to receive from the connected system, thereby acknowledging all of the packets having lower sequence numbers.
- **Allocation Number (2 bytes)** Implements the protocol's flow control mechanism by specifying the number of packet receive buffers available on the system.
- **Data (variable)** Contains the data destined for an upper-layer process or protocol.

As with any connection-oriented protocol, the two systems exchange control messages in order to establish a connection before they transmit any application data. Once the connection is established, the systems send periodic keep-alive messages to maintain the connection when there is no activity. On a network with degraded performance due to heavy traffic or other problems, SPX connections may time out due to transmission delays.

NETWORK PROTOCOLS

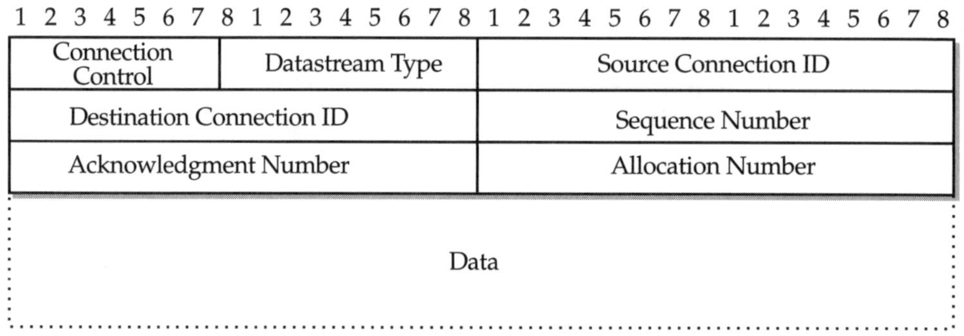

1 2 3 4 5 6 7 8	1 2 3 4 5 6 7 8	1 2 3 4 5 6 7 8 1 2 3 4 5 6 7 8
Connection Control	Datastream Type	Source Connection ID
Destination Connection ID		Sequence Number
Acknowledgment Number		Allocation Number
Data		

Figure 12-2.   *The SPX message format*

Since SPX connections can provide crucial services (such as remote server console sessions), you may want to modify the timeout settings for the protocol if you are experiencing slow network performance. NetWare includes an SPX configuration utility for servers, called Spxconfg.nlm, that enables you to set the following parameters:

■ **SPX Watchdog Abort Timeout**   Specifies the maximum amount of time that an SPX connection can go unused before it's declared invalid. The default value is 540 ticks; the possible values range from 540 to 5,400 ticks (1 tick = 1/18 second).

■ **SPX Watchdog Verify Timeout**   Specifies the amount of time that must pass without a packet received before the system requests a keep-alive message from the connected system. The default value is 108 ticks; possible values range from 0 to 255 ticks.

■ **SPX Ack Wait Timeout**   Specifies the amount of time that a system waits for an acknowledgment before it retransmits an SPX message. The default value is 54 ticks; possible values range from 10 to 3,240 clicks.

■ **SPX Default Retry Count**   Specifies the number of times that a system will retransmit an SPX message without receiving an acknowledgment. The default value is 10; possible values range from 1 to 255.

■ **Maximum Concurrent SPX Sessions**   Specifies the maximum number of SPX sessions that an application can open. The default value is 1,000; possible values range from 100 to 2,000.

■ **Maximum Open IPX Sockets**   Specifies the maximum number of sockets that an application can have open. The default value is 1,200; possible values range from 60 to 65,520.

The NetWare Core Protocol (NCP)

As the name implies, the NetWare Core Protocol is responsible for the majority of the network traffic between NetWare clients and servers. Client systems use NCP to request files on server volumes and send print jobs to print queues. The server uses it to transfer the requested files back to the client. An NCP variant, called the NetWare Core Packet Burst (NCPB) protocol, enables servers to send large amounts of data to a client with the need to acknowledge every packet.

While SPX clearly operates at the transport layer, NCP's place in the OSI reference model is more nebulous. Because clients use NCP messages to log in to a server or NDS tree, the protocol is said to operate at the session layer, but its file transfer and packet acknowledgment capabilities place it in the transport layer. In addition, NCP provides file locking and synchronization services and carries NDS messages, giving it attributes associated with the presentation and application layers. Like SPX, however, NCP messages are carried within standard IPX datagrams.

NCP communications typically follow a request/reply pattern, with the server generating a reply message for every client request. There are different message formats for NCP requests and replies, as outlined in the following sections.

The NCP Request Message

The NCP Request message format is illustrated in Figure 12-3. The functions of the fields are as follows:

- **Request Type (2 bytes)**   Specifies the basic function of the message, using the following values:

  - **1111 – Create a Service Connection**   Initiates a connection with a NetWare server.

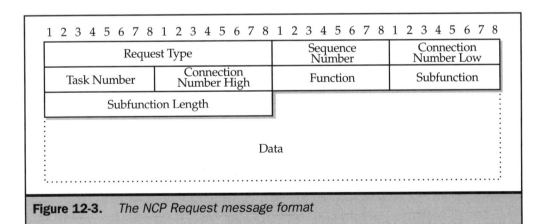

Figure 12-3.   *The NCP Request message format*

- **2222 – File Server Request**   Used to request access to a NetWare server resource.

- **5555 – Connection Destroy**   Terminates a connection with a NetWare server.

- **7777 – Burst Mode Protocol Packet**   Used to request a burst mode transmission from a NetWare server.

- **Sequence Number (1 byte)**   Contains a number that indicates the order in which the NCP messages have been transmitted, so that the receiver can process them in the correct order.

- **Connection Number Low (1 byte)**   Specifies the number of the client's connection to the server, as displayed in the Monitor.nlm utility.

- **Task Number (1 byte)**   Contains a unique value used to associate request messages with replies.

- **Connection Number High (1 byte)**   Unused; contains a value of 00.

- **Function (1 byte)**   Contains a code indicating the specific function of the message.

- **Subfunction (1 byte)**   Contains a code that further defines the function of the message.

- **Subfunction Length (2 bytes)**   Specifies the length of the Data field.

- **Data (variable)**   Contains information pertinent to the processing of the request, such as the location of a file.

NCP is capable of a great many different functions; there are approximately 200 combinations of Function and Subfunction codes, providing services in the following categories:

- **Accounting Services**   Retrieves account status, posts charges, and manages accounts.

- **Bindery Services**   Accesses and modifies NetWare 3.x bindery objects and their properties.

- **Connection Services**   Creates, destroys, and retrieves information about connections to NetWare servers.

- **Directory Services**   Views and manages directories on NetWare volumes and their trustees.

- **File Services**   Accesses, views, and manages files and their attributes on NetWare volumes.

- **File Server Environment**   Retrieves information about NetWare servers and manipulates their properties.

- **Message Services**   Sends and receives broadcast messages.
- **Print Services**   Sends print jobs to spool files in print queues.
- **Queue Services**   Manipulates print queues and the jobs contained in them.
- **Synchronization Services**   Manipulates records, file locks, and semaphores.
- **Transaction Tracking Services**   Manages NetWare Transaction Tracking System (TTS) properties.

The message format for NCP is not absolute. Some of the function codes trigger changes in the format in order to suit their specific purposes. For example, functions that do not take a value for the Subfunction field can eliminate that field from the message completely. Some functions also add their own specialized fields to the end of the message.

The NCP Reply Message

The NCP Reply message format is illustrated in Figure 12-4. The functions of the fields are as follows:

- **Reply/Response Type (2 bytes)**   Specifies the nature of the reply, using one of the following values:
    - **3333 – File Server Reply**   Indicates that the message is a reply to a file server request, with a Request Type value of 2222.
    - **7777 – Burst Mode Protocol**   Indicates that a burst mode transmission process has been successfully initialized.
    - **9999 – Positive Acknowledgment**   Indicates that a request is being processed and that the reply is being sent only to prevent the client from timing out.

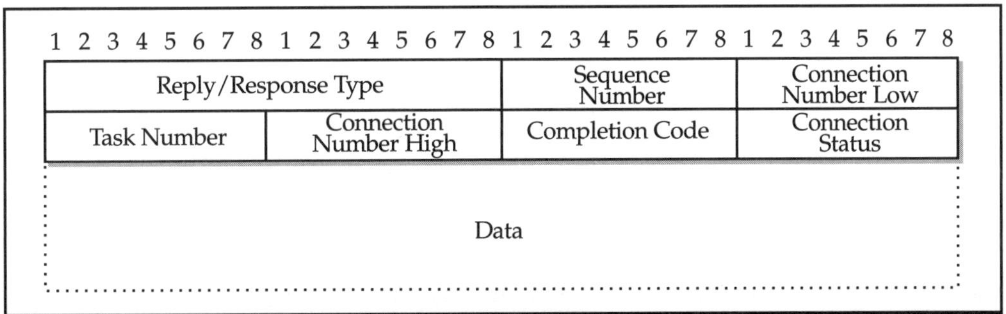

1 2 3 4 5 6 7 8	1 2 3 4 5 6 7 8	1 2 3 4 5 6 7 8	1 2 3 4 5 6 7 8
Reply/Response Type		Sequence Number	Connection Number Low
Task Number	Connection Number High	Completion Code	Connection Status
Data			

Figure 12-4.   *The NCP Reply message format*

NETWORK PROTOCOLS

- **Sequence Number (1 byte)** Contains a number that indicates the order in which the NCP messages have been transmitted, so that the receiver can process them in the correct order.

- **Connection Number Low (1 byte)** Specifies the number of the client's connection to the server, as displayed in the Monitor.nlm utility.

- **Task Number (1 byte)** Contains a unique value used to associate reply messages with requests.

- **Connection Number High (1 byte)** Unused; contains a value of 00.

- **Completion Code (1 byte)** Indicates the success or failure of the associated request. A value of 0 indicates successful completion of the request; nonzero values indicate that the request failed.

- **Connection Status (1 byte)** Indicates whether or not the connection between the client and the server is still active. A value of 0 indicates that the connection is active; a value of 1 indicates that it is not.

- **Data (variable)** Contains data sent by the server in response to the associated request.

The NetWare Core Packet Burst (NCPB) Protocol

The standard NCP protocol requires a response message for every request, which is sensible for some of its many functions, but not for others. For example, when a user logs in to a server, it makes sense for a message requesting the establishment of a connection to be answered immediately with a reply. However, for functions that involve the transfer of data sufficient to require multiple packets, this method is impractical.

When a client uses standard NCP messages to request a file from a server volume, the process is broken down into as many request/reply exchanges as are needed to transfer the file. The client begins by requesting the first part of the file, which it receives in a reply message. The client must then request the second part, receive it, request the third part, and so on. When transferring large files, the number of redundant request messages significantly erodes the efficiency of the protocol.

The NetWare Core Packet Burst Protocol was designed to address this shortcoming by making it possible for servers to send multiple data packets consecutively, without the need for individual replies or acknowledgments. Packet burst transmissions can send up to 64KB of data in a single burst, with only a single acknowledgment.

NCPB was first implemented as an add-on product to NetWare 3.11 that took the form of a server module called Pburst.nlm and a client shell called Bnetx.exe. Beginning with NetWare version 3.12 and the VLM client, NCPB is fully integrated into the protocol suite and is used automatically when a client accesses a file on a server, without any modification to the application generating the access request.

To provide this type of service, the NCPB protocol requires substantial changes to the NCP message format. The NCPB message format is illustrated in Figure 12-5, and the functions of the fields are as follows:

- **Request Type (2 bytes)**   Specifies the basic function of the message, as in the NCP protocol. For packet burst messages, the value is always 7777.
- **Flags (1 byte)**   Contains flags specifying the nature of the message or the data contained in it, using the following values:
  - **Bit 1 – SYS**   Indicates that the packet contains a system message only and does not have any packet burst data associated with it.
  - **Bit 2 – SAK**   Instructs the receiver to transmit its missing fragment list.
  - **Bit 3 – Unused**
  - **Bit 4 – EOB**   Indicates that the message contains the last data fragment in the burst.
  - **Bit 5 – BSY**   Indicates that the server is busy and that the client should continue to wait for a response.
  - **Bit 6 – ABT**   Indicates that the connection has been aborted and is no longer valid.
  - **Bit 7 – Unused**
  - **Bit 8 – Unused**
- **Stream Type (1 byte)**   Specifies whether the server should respond to the request with a packet burst transmission. The only valid (hexadecimal) value is 02, signifying a "big send burst."
- **Source Connection ID (4 bytes)**   Contains a unique value (different from the NCP Connection ID value) derived by the sender from the current time of day, which is used to identify this packet burst connection.
- **Destination Connection ID (4 bytes)**   Contains the connection identifier (equivalent to the Source Connection ID) generated by the destination system.
- **Packet Sequence Number (4 bytes)**   Contains an incremental identifier for this individual packet (not to be confused with the Burst Sequence Number).
- **Send Delay Time (4 bytes)**   Specifies the delay between the sender's packet transmissions (also called the *interpacket gap*), measured in units of 100 microseconds.
- **Burst Sequence Number (2 bytes)**   Contains an incremental identifier for the packet burst (which consists of a sequence of packets containing a contiguous stream of data).
- **Acknowledgment Sequence Number (2 bytes)**   Contains the Burst Sequence Number value that the system expects to see in the next burst, indicating that the previous burst was received successfully.

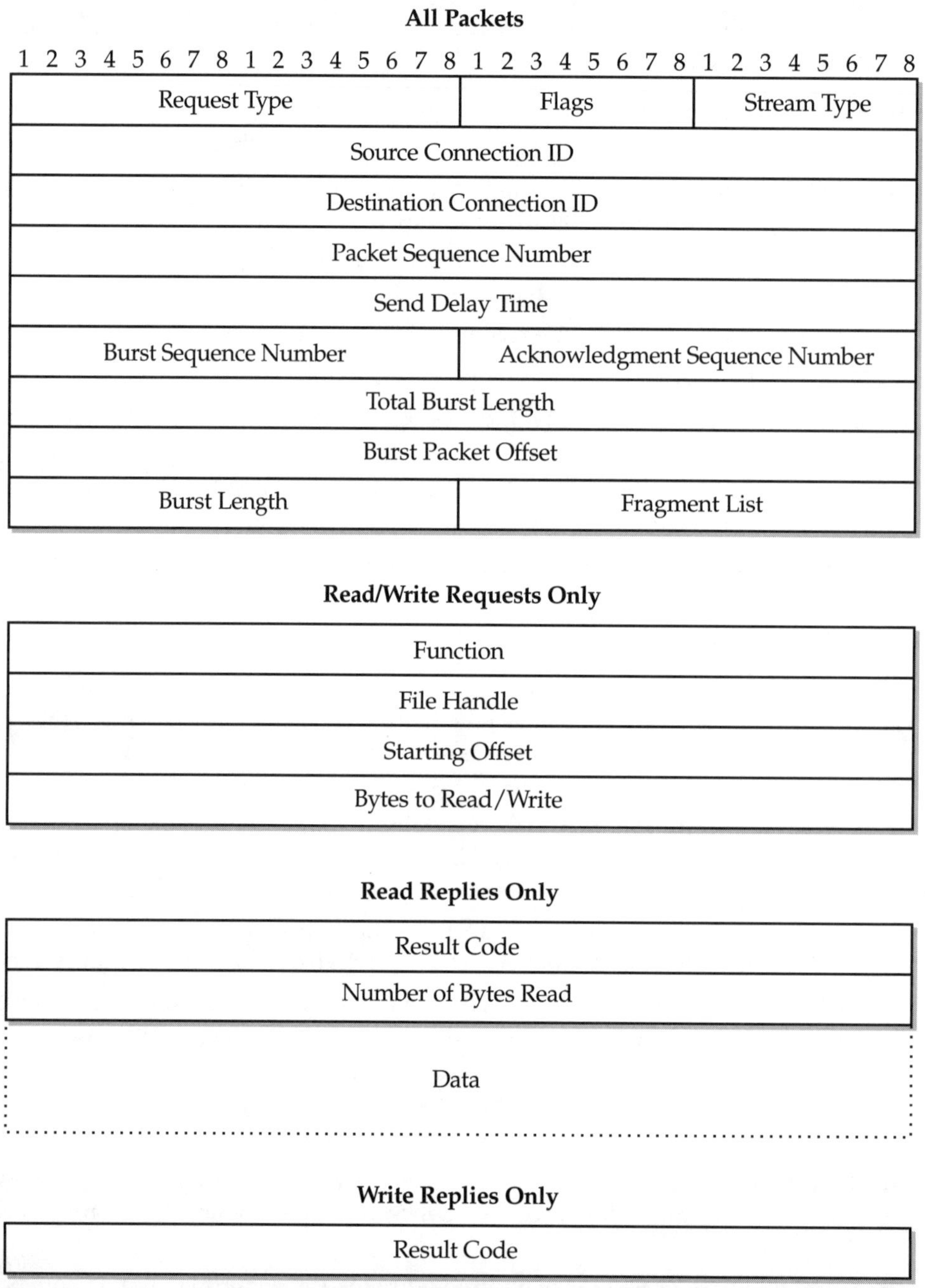

All Packets

1 2 3 4 5 6 7 8	1 2 3 4 5 6 7 8	1 2 3 4 5 6 7 8	1 2 3 4 5 6 7 8
Request Type		Flags	Stream Type
Source Connection ID			
Destination Connection ID			
Packet Sequence Number			
Send Delay Time			
Burst Sequence Number		Acknowledgment Sequence Number	
Total Burst Length			
Burst Packet Offset			
Burst Length		Fragment List	

Read/Write Requests Only

Function
File Handle
Starting Offset
Bytes to Read/Write

Read Replies Only

Result Code
Number of Bytes Read
Data

Write Replies Only

Result Code

Figure 12-5. *The NCPB message format*

- **Total Burst Length (4 bytes)**   Specifies the total length of the data being transmitted in the current burst (in bytes). A system can adjust this value to implement NCPB's sliding window flow control mechanism.
- **Burst Packet Offset (4 bytes)**   Specifies the location of this packet within the current burst.
- **Burst Length (2 bytes)**   Specifies how much of the Total Burst Length is included in this message.
- **Fragment List (2 bytes)**   Contains a list of fragments still to be transmitted to complete the burst. The field initially contains a list of all of the fragments in the burst. As fragments are successfully transmitted, they are removed from the list. Any fragments remaining after the transmission is completed are considered to have been damaged or lost and must be retransmitted.

In addition to the preceding fields, NCPB messages requesting a file read or write operation have the following fields:

- **Function (4 bytes)**   Specifies whether the current transaction is a read or write operation.
- **File Handle (4 bytes)**   Contains a code identifying the file to be read or written.
- **Starting Offset (4 bytes)**   Specifies the portion of the file indicated in the File Handle field that should be included in this packet.
- **Bytes to Read/Write (4 bytes)**   Specifies the number of bytes (beginning at the point specified in the Starting Offset field) that should be included in this packet.

NCPB Reply messages generated in response to a read request have the following fields, in addition to the basic message format:

- **Result Code (4 bytes)**   Specifies whether or not the associated request was successfully fulfilled, using the following values:
  - **0**   No error
  - **1**   Initial error
  - **2**   I/O error
  - **3**   No data read
- **Number of Bytes Read (4 bytes)**   Specifies the number of bytes that were successfully read.
- **Data (variable)**   Contains part of the data being transmitted in reply to the associated request.

NCPB Reply messages generated in response to a write request include the following field, in addition to the basic message format:

■ **Result Code (4 bytes)**   Specifies whether or not the associated request was successfully fulfilled, using the following values:

■ **0**   No error

■ **1**   Write error

Packet Burst Transactions

NCPB is a connection-oriented protocol that is invoked when a client requests a burst mode connection from a server using an NCP request with 101 as its function code and no subfunction code. The request also includes the client's maximum packet size and its maximum send and receive sizes, as shown in the captured packet in Figure 12-6. The server will use this information when packaging the data for transmission to the client.

When the server replies to the request, it transmits an NCP Service Reply message (Reply Type 3333) with a Completion Code value of 0 (see Figure 12-7).

At this time, the client switches to the NCPB message format (Request Type 7777) and sends a Read request for a particular file (see Figure 12-8).

Figure 12-6.   *The NCP Packet Burst Connection Request message*

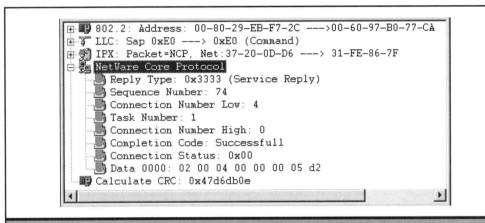

```
⊞ 🖳 802.2: Address: 00–80–29–EB–F7–2C --->00–60–97–B0–77–CA
⊞ 📶 LLC: Sap 0xE0 ---> 0xE0 (Command)
⊞ 📶 IPX: Packet=NCP, Net:37–20–0D–D6 ---> 31–FE–86–7F
⊟ 📑 NetWare Core Protocol
   📄 Reply Type: 0x3333 (Service Reply)
   📄 Sequence Number: 74
   📄 Connection Number Low: 4
   📄 Task Number: 1
   📄 Connection Number High: 0
   📄 Completion Code: Successfull
   📄 Connection Status: 0x00
   📄 Data 0000: 02 00 04 00 00 00 05 d2
   🖳 Calculate CRC: 0x47d6db0e
```

Figure 12-7. *The NCP Service Reply message completes the connection establishment process*

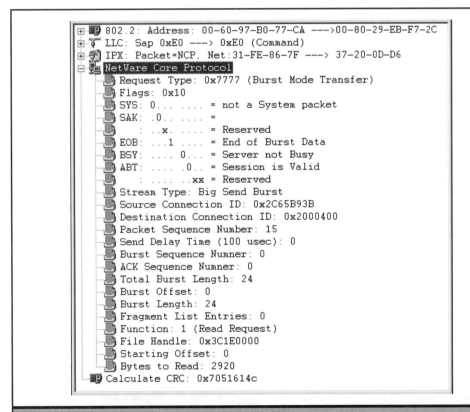

```
⊞ 🖳 802.2: Address: 00–60–97–B0–77–CA --->00–80–29–EB–F7–2C
⊞ 📶 LLC: Sap 0xE0 ---> 0xE0 (Command)
⊞ 📶 IPX: Packet=NCP, Net:31–FE–86–7F ---> 37–20–0D–D6
⊟ 📑 NetWare Core Protocol
   📄 Request Type: 0x7777 (Burst Mode Transfer)
   📄 Flags: 0x10
   📄 SYS: 0... .... = not a System packet
   📄 SAK: .0.. .... =
   📄      : ..x. .... = Reserved
   📄 EOB: ...1 .... = End of Burst Data
   📄 BSY: .... 0... = Server not Busy
   📄 ABT: .... .0.. = Session is Valid
   📄      : .... ..xx = Reserved
   📄 Stream Type: Big Send Burst
   📄 Source Connection ID: 0x2C65B93B
   📄 Destination Connection ID: 0x2000400
   📄 Packet Sequence Number: 15
   📄 Send Delay Time (100 usec): 0
   📄 Burst Sequence Numner: 0
   📄 ACK Sequence Numner: 0
   📄 Total Burst Length: 24
   📄 Burst Offset: 0
   📄 Burst Length: 24
   📄 Fragment List Entries: 0
   📄 Function: 1 (Read Request)
   📄 File Handle: 0x3C1E0000
   📄 Starting Offset: 0
   📄 Bytes to Read: 2920
   🖳 Calculate CRC: 0x7051614c
```

Figure 12-8. *Once the connection is established, the client sends an NCPB Read request message*

NETWORK PROTOCOLS

The server replies with a message containing the first fragment of the requested file (see Figure 12-9). In this case, the size of the requested file is shown in the Total Burst Length field as 2,928 bytes. Notice that the Burst Offset value is 0, indicating that this message contains the beginning of the file, and that the amount of data included in this packet, specified by the Burst Length field, is 1,424.

After transmitting a second message containing the next 1,424 bytes of the file, the server sends the message shown in Figure 12-10. Here, the Burst Offset value is 2,848 and the Burst Length is 80. Since 2,848 and 80 adds up to 2,928, the value of the Total Burst Length field, it is clear that this message contains the last 80 bytes of the requested file, even without noticing that the EOB (End of Burst Data) flag is set.

Once the packet burst transfer is complete, the client reverts back to NCP messages, and requests that the server close the file, as shown in Figure 12-11. Once the server returns a reply indicating that the request was completed successfully, the transaction is completed.

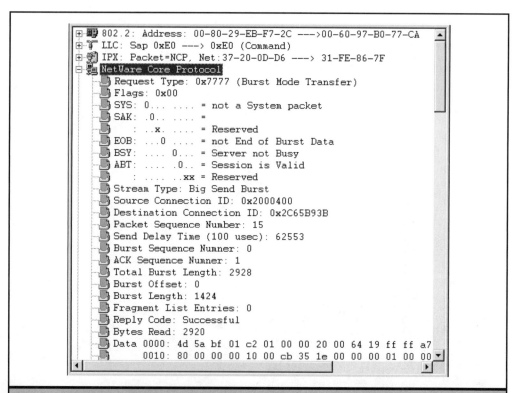

Figure 12-9. *In response to the client's request, the server sends a reply message containing the first data fragment*

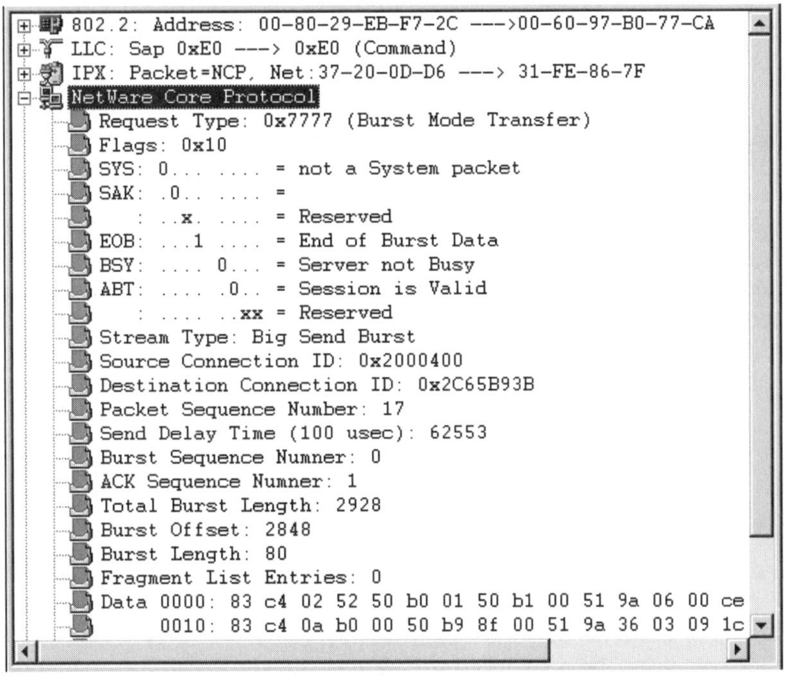

```
⊞ 802.2: Address: 00-80-29-EB-F7-2C --->00-60-97-B0-77-CA
⊞ LLC: Sap 0xE0 ---> 0xE0 (Command)
⊞ IPX: Packet=NCP, Net:37-20-0D-D6 ---> 31-FE-86-7F
⊟ NetWare Core Protocol
     Request Type: 0x7777 (Burst Mode Transfer)
     Flags: 0x10
     SYS: 0... .... = not a System packet
     SAK: .0.. .... =
        : ..x. .... = Reserved
     EOB: ...1 .... = End of Burst Data
     BSY: .... 0... = Server not Busy
     ABT: .... .0.. = Session is Valid
        : .... ..xx = Reserved
     Stream Type: Big Send Burst
     Source Connection ID: 0x2000400
     Destination Connection ID: 0x2C65B93B
     Packet Sequence Number: 17
     Send Delay Time (100 usec): 62553
     Burst Sequence Numner: 0
     ACK Sequence Numner: 1
     Total Burst Length: 2928
     Burst Offset: 2848
     Burst Length: 80
     Fragment List Entries: 0
     Data 0000: 83 c4 02 52 50 b0 01 50 b1 00 51 9a 06 00 ce
          0010: 83 c4 0a b0 00 50 b9 8f 00 51 9a 36 03 09 1c
```

Figure 12-10. *The server transmits the last fragment of the transaction in a message with the EOB flag set*

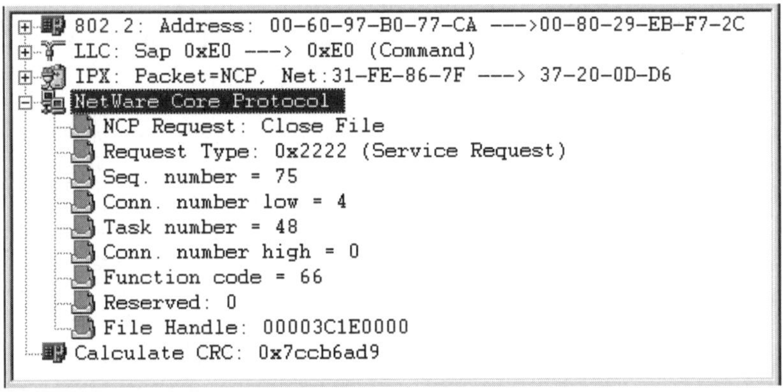

```
⊞ 802.2: Address: 00-60-97-B0-77-CA --->00-80-29-EB-F7-2C
⊞ LLC: Sap 0xE0 ---> 0xE0 (Command)
⊞ IPX: Packet=NCP, Net:31-FE-86-7F ---> 37-20-0D-D6
⊟ NetWare Core Protocol
     NCP Request: Close File
     Request Type: 0x2222 (Service Request)
     Seq. number = 75
     Conn. number low = 4
     Task number = 48
     Conn. number high = 0
     Function code = 66
     Reserved: 0
     File Handle: 00003C1E0000
  ⊞ Calculate CRC: 0x7ccb6ad9
```

Figure 12-11. *Once the file transfer is completed, the client switches back to NCP messages to close the file*

Individual packet burst file transfers are typically integrated throughout a NetWare Core Protocol communications session. The packet burst connection to the server need not be terminated after every completed file transfer, as with TCP.

Packet Retransmission

One advantage of NCPB over TCP and most other connection-oriented protocols is its ability to carry a list of the fragments that need to be transmitted. Most protocols acknowledge packets by specifying a single point in the sequence, thus implying that all of the packets up to that point have been received successfully. When one packet in the sequence is lost, then the whole sequence must be retransmitted from that point forward, even if subsequent packets were transmitted successfully. The NCPB fragment list enables the server to retransmit only the fragments that were lost.

The Service Advertising Protocol

NetWare systems use the *Service Advertising Protocol* (*SAP*) to compile and maintain a list of the file servers, print servers, gateway servers, and multiprotocol routers on the network, and the servers use SAP to inform the other systems of their presence. A NetWare client must learn about the servers on the network from SAP messages before it can send requests to them. Every server broadcasts a SAP message every 60 seconds, by default, containing its name, address, and the services that it provides. The other systems on the network, upon receiving a SAP message, create a temporary entry in its NDS or bindery database for each server listed in the message, in order to store the accompanying information.

In addition to these automatic service information broadcasts, servers can also generate SAP requests in order to solicit information from a particular server. NetWare uses this type of SAP exchange to implement the copy protection feature that prevents two servers with the same license number from running on the same network, and clients use it to locate the server nearest to them. For this type of transaction, there are separate Nearest Server Request and Nearest Server Reply packet types. The regular SAP broadcasts containing server information use the Standard Server Reply packet type. (The Standard Server Request message type is not used.)

SAP requests and replies use different message formats, but all SAP messages are carried in standard IPX datagrams with a Packet Type of 4 and a Destination Socket value of 0452, as shown in Figure 12-12. The message formats are covered in the following sections.

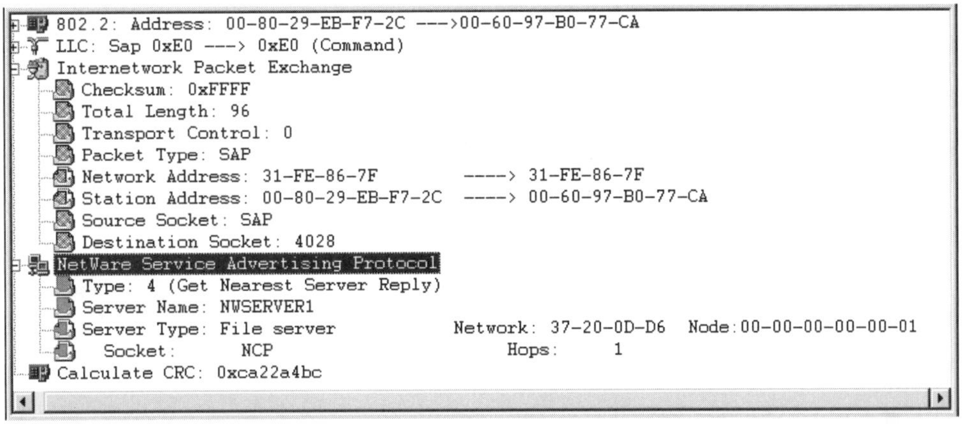

```
⊞-🖳 802.2: Address: 00-80-29-EB-F7-2C --->00-60-97-B0-77-CA
⊞-📶 LLC: Sap 0xE0 ---> 0xE0 (Command)
⊟-📑 Internetwork Packet Exchange
   └-📄 Checksum: 0xFFFF
   └-📄 Total Length: 96
   └-📄 Transport Control: 0
   └-📄 Packet Type: SAP
   └-📑 Network Address: 31-FE-86-7F          ----> 31-FE-86-7F
   └-📑 Station Address: 00-80-29-EB-F7-2C    ----> 00-60-97-B0-77-CA
   └-📄 Source Socket: SAP
   └-📄 Destination Socket: 4028
⊟-📑 NetWare Service Advertising Protocol
   └-📄 Type: 4 (Get Nearest Server Reply)
   └-📄 Server Name: NWSERVER1
   └-📑 Server Type: File server          Network: 37-20-0D-D6   Node:00-00-00-00-00-01
   └-📄    Socket:       NCP              Hops:       1
-🖳 Calculate CRC: 0xca22a4bc
```

Figure 12-12. *The SAP Get Nearest Server Reply message contains identification and routing information about the server*

The SAP Request Frame

The SAP Request message format is used only when a system requests SAP information from a server, such as when client systems locate the nearest server. The messages are transmitted as broadcasts, and all servers receiving the message are expected to reply. The request message contains only two fields, which are as follows:

- **Packet Type (2 bytes)** Specifies the function of the message, using the following hexadecimal values:

  - **1** Standard Server Request (unused)

  - **3** Nearest Server Request

- **Server Type (2 bytes)** Specifies the type of service desired from a server, using the following hexadecimal values:

  - **0000** Unknown

  - **0003** Print Queue

  - **0004** File Server

  - **0005** Job Server

  - **0007** Print Server

- **0009**   Archive Server
- **000a**   Job Queue
- **0021**   NAS SNA Gateway
- **0024**   Remote Bridge Server
- **002d**   Time Synchronization VAP
- **002e**   Dynamic SAP
- **0047**   Advertising Print Server
- **004b**   Btrieve VAP 5.0
- **004c**   SQL VAP
- **007a**   TES-NetWare VMS
- **0098**   NetWare Access Server
- **009a**   Named Pipes Server
- **009e**   Portable NetWare-UNIX
- **0107**   NetWare 386
- **0111**   Test Server
- **0166**   NetWare Management
- **026a**   NetWare Management
- **ffff**   Wildcard

The SAP Reply Frame

The SAP Reply message format is the same for both service information broadcasts and replies to Nearest Server Request messages. The difference between the two is that a Nearest Server Reply contains information about only one server, while the Standard Server Reply can contain information about up to seven servers. For the latter, the entire sequence of fields from Server Type to Intermediate Networks is repeated up to seven times, in sequence.

Since the Standard Server Reply messages are transmitted as broadcasts, they are limited to the local network segment. However, by sharing information about themselves as well as about all of the other servers on the local segment, every server on the network is able to build a complete list of all of the other servers.

The format for SAP Reply messages is illustrated in Figure 12-13, and the functions of the fields are as follows:

- **Packet Type (2 bytes)**   Specifies the function of the message, using the following hexadecimal values:
  - **2**   Standard Server Reply
  - **3**   Nearest Server Reply

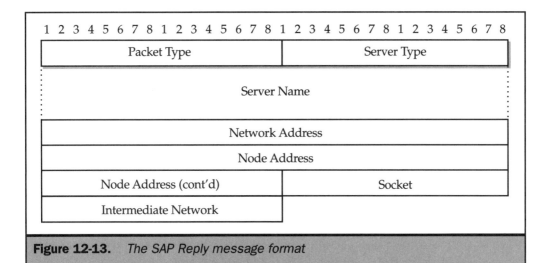

Figure 12-13.   *The SAP Reply message format*

- **Server Type (2 bytes)**   Specifies the type of service provided by the server, using the same values as the message format.
- **Server Name (48 bytes)**   Specifies the name of the server.
- **Network Address (4 bytes)**   Specifies the address of the network on which the server is located.
- **Node Address (6 bytes)**   Specifies the node address of the server.
- **Socket (2 bytes)**   Specifies the socket on which the server will receive service requests.
- **Intermediate Network (2 bytes)**   Specifies the number of hops (that is, routers or network addresses) between the server and the destination.

SAP Problems

One of the frequent criticisms of NetWare throughout its history has been its reliance on SAP and the amount of redundant broadcast traffic it creates on the network. NDS has reduced this traffic by storing the server information in the directory services database. In the course of the normal NDS replication process, the SAP data is replicated throughout the network using unicast messages between servers, rather than broadcasts. Network 5 addresses the problem further by including support for the Service Location Protocol (SLP), a service discovery protocol standardized by the Internet Engineering Task Force (IETF).

Chapter 13

NetBIOS, NetBEUI, and Server Message Blocks

E ven though TCP/IP has become the most popular protocol suite operating at the network and transport layers of the OSI reference model, alternatives still exist. *NetBEUI*, the *NetBIOS Extended User Interface,* is one of the oldest local area networking protocols still in use, yet it continues to be an excellent solution for relatively small networks because it requires less overhead than more comprehensive protocols.

NetBEUI was designed in the mid-1980s to provide network transport services for programs based on *NetBIOS (Network Basic Input/Output System).* NetBEUI is just one method of transporting NetBIOS data across a network. Encapsulating the NetBIOS information using the TCP/IP or the IPX protocols is also possible.

When Microsoft began to introduce networking features into its operating systems, NetBEUI was their protocol of choice. Originally, both Windows for Workgroups and Windows NT used NetBEUI as their default protocols. Only later did Microsoft follow the lead of the rest of the networking industry and began relying on TCP/IP to carry NetBIOS data.

The reasons for the adoption of TCP/IP center around interoperability. The protocols were designed from the ground up to support communications between different computing platforms and operating systems. In addition, as local area networking began to take hold of the business work in a big way, NetBEUI's shortcomings clearly showed it would be unsuitable for anything other than small workgroup networks.

Today, NetBEUI is most commonly used on small Microsoft Windows networks because it provides good performance, requires little or no maintenance (because the protocol is self-configuring and self-tuning), and uses a relatively small amount of memory. Despite the criticisms levied at it in networking circles, if you are running a home or small office network using Windows PCs, NetBEUI is still an excellent protocol solution.

NetBEUI's primary shortcoming is that it is not routable and should generally be used only on networks composed of a single collision domain. This is because the protocol relies on broadcast transmissions for some of its essential functions and has no means of identifying the network on which a system is located. The following sections examine the architecture of the NetBEUI protocol and how it works with NetBIOS and Server Message Blocks to provide basic networking services on Windows networks.

NetBIOS

NetBIOS was designed to provide a standardized programming interface between software applications and the networking hardware to make the applications more easily portable between systems. The interface includes a name space, which Microsoft operating systems still use to identify the computers on the network. The computer name you assign to a Windows system during the installation is, in fact, a NetBIOS name, as are the names of domains and workgroups.

NetBIOS names are 16 bytes long, with the 16th byte used to specify the type of resource the name represents. The first 15 characters can be alphabetical or numeric. The NetBIOS name space performs the same function as the IP addresses used by the TCP/IP protocol suite and the network and node addresses used by the IPX/SPX protocols. They provide a unique identifier for every computer on the network, so systems can send unicast transmissions directly to other systems. For this reason, individual system names are referred to as *unique names*, while NetBIOS names that represent a collection of systems, for purposes of multicasting, are called *group names*.

The main difference between the NetBIOS name space and the TCP/IP and IPX/SPX addresses is that the NetBIOS name space is flat. No naming hierarchy subdivides the network into individual subnetworks. The 32 bits that comprise an IP address are split between host address and network address bits, and the IPX/SPX address is naturally broken into network and node addresses. The NetBIOS name is a single name, however, and contains no identifying information about the network.

Because NetBEUI uses the NetBIOS name space to communicate with other systems and the name space has no inherent mechanism for identifying and addressing networks, NetBEUI cannot address communications to systems on other networks. This is one reason NetBEUI is not routable.

NetBEUI Frame

The point is often made that NetBIOS is an application programming interface (API) and not a protocol, so logically, you can make the same case for NetBEUI by saying an extended user interface for NetBIOS cannot be a protocol either. The Windows operating systems refer to it as such, however, and use the term *NetBEUI Frame* (or sometimes *NetBIOS frame,* or more commonly *NBF*) to describe the actual protocol used to carry NetBEUI information over the network.

> **Note**
> *Unlike TCP/IP and most other protocols, no official standard defines the architecture and functionality of NetBIOS and NetBEUI. Because NetBIOS was originally developed for use on early IBM PC networks, the "IBM LAN Technical Reference IEEE 802.2 and NetBIOS Application Program Interfaces" document is the closest thing there is to a standard. As a result, there have been many NetBIOS implementations over the years that were incompatible and limited to use with specific networking products.*

NBF operates at the session, transport, and network layers of the OSI reference model, although you can argue that NBF has no network layer because it lacks the routing functions that largely define this layer's functionality. On a Windows system, the protocol is used to register the system's NetBIOS names on the network, establish sessions between systems, and carry data generated by several different application layer protocols and APIs. The most important API is *Server Message Blocks (SMB)*, the protocol used to carry shared file and printer data.

In the OSI model, the functionality of the NBF protocol is bounded at the bottom by the NDIS interface, which provides a universal interface to the networking hardware. Data link–layer support is provided by the IEEE 802.2 Logical Link Control (LLC) frame, which surrounds the NBF protocol message. The 802.2 frame for NBF packets uses (hexadecimal) values of F0 for the destination service access point (DSAP) and the source service access point (SSAP).

> **Note** For more information on the LLC frame, see "The Logical Link Control Sublayer" in Chapter 8.

At the top, the protocol either interacts directly with the NetBIOS interface or on Windows NT systems with the *Transport Device Interface (TDI),* an abstraction layer that lies between the NetBIOS interface and the transport layer protocols.

The functions of the NBF protocol are divided into several different services, sometimes referred to as separate protocols in themselves. (The lack of a definitive standard makes the nomenclature difficult.) These services provide name registration and resolution, connectionless datagram delivery, diagnostic and monitoring functions, and session-based delivery, all using the same basic message format, which is shown in Figure 13-1 and consists of the following fields:

- **Length (2 bytes)** Specifies the length of the NBF header field (including the length field)

- **Delimiter (2 bytes)** Indicates the data that follows is intended for the NetBIOS interface

- **Command (1 byte)** Specifies the function of the message, using the following codes. Messages with command codes 00 through 0E are transmitted as unnumbered information (UI) frames, while command codes 0F through 1F are transmitted as information format LLC protocol data units (I-format LPDUs).

  - **00** ADD GROUP NAME QUERY
  - **01** ADD NAME QUERY
  - **02** NAME IN CONFLICT
  - **03** STATUS QUERY
  - **07** TERMINATE TRACE
  - **08** DATAGRAM
  - **09** DATAGRAM BROADCAST
  - **0A** NAME QUERY
  - **0D** ADD NAME RESPONSE

- ■ **0E**   NAME RECOGNIZED
- ■ **0F**   STATUS RESPONSE
- ■ **13**   TERMINATE (local and remote) TRACE
- ■ **14**   DATA ACK
- ■ **15**   DATA FIRST MIDDLE
- ■ **16**   DATA ONLY LAST
- ■ **17**   SESSION CONFIRM
- ■ **18**   SESSION END
- ■ **19**   SESSION INITIALIZE
- ■ **1A**   NO RECEIVE
- ■ **1B**   RECEIVE OUTSTANDING
- ■ **1C**   RECEIVE CONTINUE
- ■ **1F**   SESSION ALIVE

- ■ **Data1 (1 byte)**   Contains optional data specific to the message type
- ■ **Data2 (2 bytes)**   Contains optional data specific to the message type
- ■ **Transmit Correlator (2 bytes)**   Contains a hexadecimal value from 0001 to FFFF used to associate requests and replies
- ■ **Response Correlator (2 bytes)**   Contains a hexadecimal value from 0001 to FFFF that indicates the value expected in the transmit correlator field of the reply to the current message
- ■ **Destination Name (16 bytes)**   Specifies the NetBIOS name of the intended destination system (not included in session service packets)
- ■ **Source Name (16 bytes)**   Specifies the NetBIOS name of the local system (not included in session service packets)
- ■ **Destination Number (1 byte)**   Specifies the session number on the destination system (not included in name, datagram, or diagnostic service packets)
- ■ **Source Number (1 byte)**   Specifies the session number on the destination system (not included in name, datagram, or diagnostic service packets)
- ■ **Optional (variable)**   Contains the actual data carried in session and datagram packets (not included in name or diagnostic service packets)

Four services use NBF messages: the name service, the datagram service, the diagnostic service, and the session service. These are sometimes referred to as separate protocols in themselves. These services are examined in the following sections.

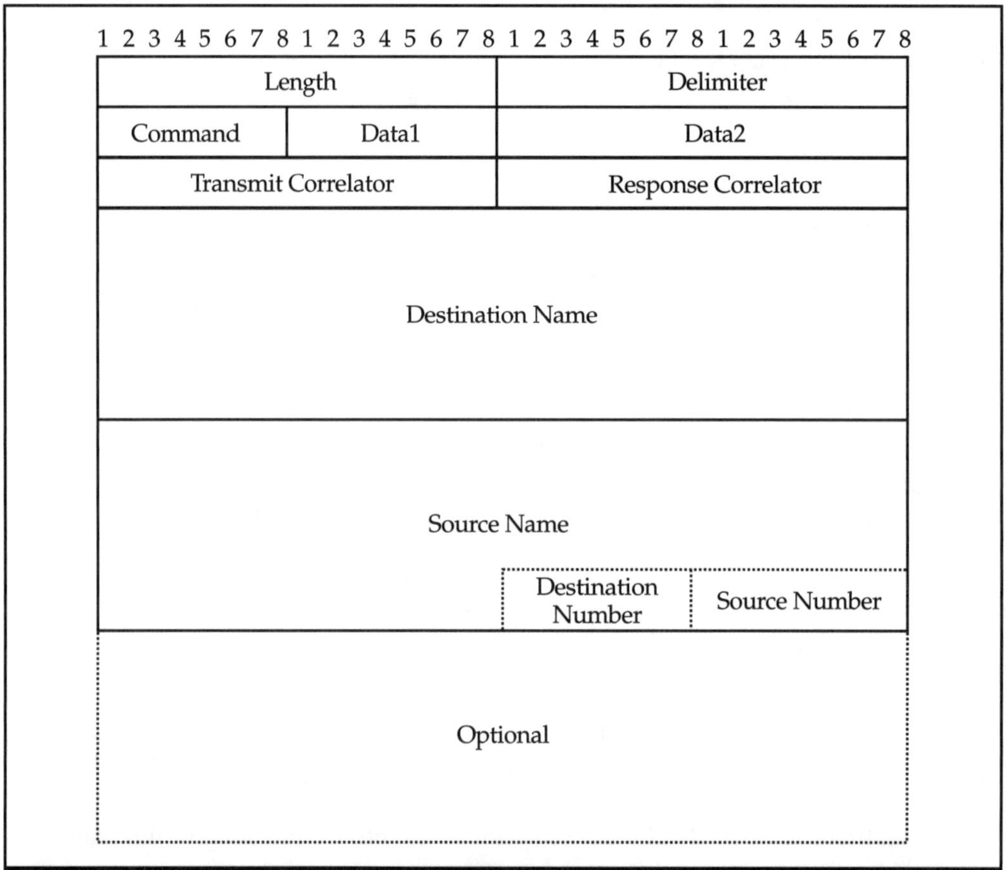

1 2 3 4 5 6 7 8	1 2 3 4 5 6 7 8	1 2 3 4 5 6 7 8	1 2 3 4 5 6 7 8

Length		Delimiter	
Command	Data1	Data2	
Transmit Correlator		Response Correlator	

Destination Name

Source Name
Destination Number	Source Number

Optional

Figure 13-1.   *The NetBEUI Frame message format*

Name Management Protocol

The name service, also called the Name Management Protocol (NMP), provides name registration and resolution services for network systems. When a computer on a Microsoft network boots, the system performs a name registration procedure designed to verify that the computer's NetBIOS name is unique on the network. A name resolution process occurs whenever a system tries to access another computer on the network. Because NetBIOS names have no permanent connection to the hardware addresses used to communicate on the LAN, a system trying to send unicast traffic directly to another system must first discover the hardware address of the intended destination.

Note | *Similar name registration and resolution procedures occur when NetBIOS traffic is encapsulated within the IP protocol, as defined in the standards for NetBIOS over TCP/IP, published as RFCs 1001 and 1002. The primary difference between using TCP/IP as the networking protocol on a Windows network and using NetBEUI is that TCP/IP inserts an intermediate step in the name registration and resolution procedures, in which the NetBIOS name is equated with a specific IP address, instead of the hardware address. A later TCP/IP process converts the IP address into the hardware address using the Address Resolution Protocol (ARP). For more information on name resolution on TCP/IP networks, see Chapter 19.*

Name Registration

The name registration process occurs when a system on a Windows network boots. To determine if another computer is on the network using the same NetBIOS name, the system transmits an ADD NAME QUERY message to the NetBIOS functional address (030000000001). The message contains a command code value of 01 and has the system's NetBIOS name in the source name field (see Figure 13-2).

The other NetBIOS systems on the network are required to respond if they possess the same name as that contained in the message. If the transmitting system receives no responses after repeated retries, the name is considered to be registered. If another machine has the same name, it transmits an ADD NAME RESPONSE message to the sender as a unicast (see Figure 13-3). This denies the name to the original system and forces the user to select a different one.

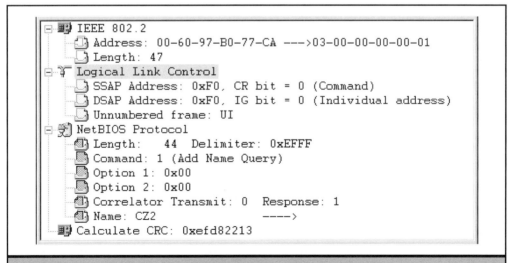

```
├ ░▓ IEEE 802.2
│    ├ ░] Address: 00-60-97-B0-77-CA ---->03-00-00-00-00-01
│    └ ░] Length: 47
├ ¥ Logical Link Control
│    ├ ░] SSAP Address: 0xF0, CR bit = 0 (Command)
│    ├ ░] DSAP Address: 0xF0, IG bit = 0 (Individual address)
│    └ ░] Unnumbered frame: UI
├ ░] NetBIOS Protocol
│    ├ ░] Length:    44  Delimiter: 0xEFFF
│    ├ ░] Command: 1 (Add Name Query)
│    ├ ░] Option 1: 0x00
│    ├ ░] Option 2: 0x00
│    ├ ░] Correlator Transmit: 0  Response: 1
│    └ ░] Name: CZ2                ---->
└ ▓ Calculate CRC: 0xefd82213
```

Figure 13-2. *The NBF ADD NAME QUERY message*

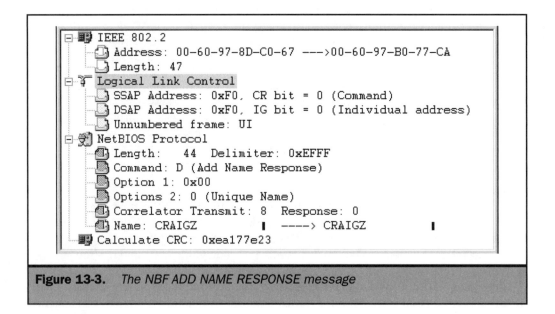

```
IEEE 802.2
   Address: 00-60-97-8D-C0-67 --->00-60-97-B0-77-CA
   Length: 47
Logical Link Control
   SSAP Address: 0xF0, CR bit = 0 (Command)
   DSAP Address: 0xF0, IG bit = 0 (Individual address)
   Unnumbered frame: UI
NetBIOS Protocol
   Length:    44  Delimiter: 0xEFFF
   Command: D (Add Name Response)
   Option 1: 0x00
   Options 2: 0 (Unique Name)
   Correlator Transmit: 8  Response: 0
   Name: CRAIGZ         ----> CRAIGZ
Calculate CRC: 0xea177e23
```

Figure 13-3.   *The NBF ADD NAME RESPONSE message*

The ADD NAME RESPONSE message contains a Command code value of 0D and the name in question in both the Destination Name and Source Name fields. The Data1 field contains a binary flag with one of the following values:

- **0** Signifies that the Add Name procedure is in progress
- **1** Signifies that the Add Name procedure is not in progress

The Data2 field specifies whether the name in question is already in use on the network as a unique name or a group name, using the following values:

- **0** Unique
- **1** Group

The Transmit Correlator field contains the same value as the Response Correlator field in the ADD NAME QUERY message. This is so the system receiving the message can associate it with the correct request.

If the system trying to register the name should receive ADD NAME RESPONSE messages from two or more other systems (or if the same name is registered both as a group name and a unique name), it generates a NAME IN CONFLICT message and transmits it to the NetBIOS functional address. The same message is generated when a system receives multiple ADD NAME RESPONSE replies to an ADD GROUP NAME QUERY message or NAME RECOGNIZED messages from two or more systems in response to a NAME QUERY.

The NAME IN CONFLICT message contains a Command code of 02 and has the name in question in the Destination Name field. The Source Name field contains the special NetBIOS *name number 1* for the transmitting system, which consists of 10 bytes worth of zeros followed by the system's 6-byte hardware address.

If the system is a member of a Windows NT domain, it also transmits an ADD GROUP NAME QUERY containing the name of the domain. This is intended to make sure the group name is not being used by another system as a unique name, in which case the computer using the name generates an ADD NAME RESPONSE message.

Name Resolution

The name resolution process occurs whenever a system attempts to access another NetBIOS system on the network. Before a computer can transmit unicast packets, it must determine the hardware address of the destination system. To do this, the computer generates a NAME QUERY message that it transmits to the NetBIOS functional address. This message contains the Command code 0A and the name of the system to be contacted in the Destination Name field (see Figure 13-4).

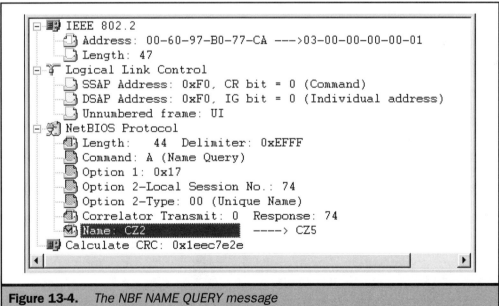

Figure 13-4. *The NBF NAME QUERY message*

The Data1 field is unused, but the Data2 field contains a 2-byte code specifying whether the name being queried is a unique or group name, using the following values:

- **00** Unique name
- **01** Group Name

NetBEUI systems use this NAME QUERY/NAME RECOGNIZED exchange for two purposes: to discover the address of another system or to initiate a session with another system. The second two bytes of the Data2 field contain either 00, indicating that the intent is only to determine the addresses of the system using the name, or a number from 01 to FE that acts as a local identifier for the session the system is trying to establish.

If the system receives no response to the NAME QUERY messages, it assumes the name doesn't exist on the network. Any computer using the name is required to respond with a NAME RECOGNIZED message for each NAME QUERY it receives and transmits as a unicast to the sender. The NAME RECOGNIZED message contains 0E as its Command code (see Figure 13-5). The Destination Name field contains the name of the system that generated the NAME QUERY message and the Source Name field contains the name of the local system.

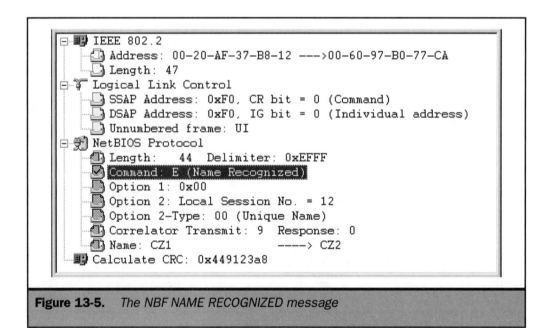

Figure 13-5.   *The NBF NAME RECOGNIZED message*

The Data1 field is again unused, and the Data field begins with the same 2-byte code identifying the name as unique or as that of group, just as in the NAME QUERY message. The second two bytes of the Data2 field specify the state of the name, using the following codes:

- **00**   Indicates that the system is not listening for the SESSION INITIALIZE message from the sender that will initiate a session between the two machines

- **A value from 01 to FE**   Specifies the value the local system will use to identify the session to be established

- **FF**   Indicates that the system is listening for the SESSION INITIALIZE message from the sender, but that it cannot initiate a session between the two machines

User Datagram Protocol

The messages used in the NetBIOS name service exchanges are transmitted as unnumbered information (UI) frames, sometimes called type 1 frames. This is NetBEUI's connectionless, unreliable service, used for brief exchanges in which retransmissions and expected responses eliminate the need for packet acknowledgments and guaranteed delivery. In addition to the name services messages, NBF also supports a datagram service that provides delivery of small amounts of data using the same connectionless, unreliable transmissions. The Server Message Block protocol often uses the datagram service for its request/reply transactions.

This service is sometimes called the User Datagram Protocol (UDP), which is unfortunate because TCP/IP has a transport layer protocol of the same name (that provides basically the same service). In the vast majority of cases, documents that refer to UDP are referring to the TCP/IP protocol, not its NetBEUI equivalent.

The NetBEUI UDP is actually more comparable in function to the IP protocol in the TCP/IP suite, IPX in Novell's IPX/SPX, or AppleTalk's Datagram Delivery Protocol (DDP), except that UDP does not provide services for upper-layer protocols. IP, for example, is used to encapsulate various other protocols, including TCP, (the other) UDP, and ICMP, while NetBEUI's UDP carries only actual application data.

The DATAGRAM messages used to carry UDP data have a Command code of 08 and do not use either of the Data fields or the Correlator fields. The Destination Name field contains the NetBIOS name of the message's intended recipient, and the source name field contains the name of the transmitting system. The Optional field contains the data intended for the destination. There is also a DATAGRAM BROADCAST message used to transmit to the entire network that is identical to the DATAGRAM message except that it has 09 for its Command code and contains no value in the Destination Name field.

NETWORK PROTOCOLS

Diagnostic and Monitoring Protocol

The *Diagnostic and Monitoring Protocol (DMP),* roughly analogous to the Simple Network Management Protocol (SNMP) in TCP/IP, is used to gather functional information about the systems on the network. A typical DMP exchange begins when a system generates a STATUS QUERY message (Command code 03) and transmits it to the NetBIOS functional address. The message contains a code in the Data1 field that indicates the type of request, using the following values:

- **00**   NetBIOS 1.*x* or 2.0 type request
- **01**   Initial NetBIOS 2.1 type request
- **Greater than 01**   NetBIOS 2.1 type request for replies from more systems, where the value indicates the number of replies already received

The value in the Data2 field specifies the length of the system's status buffer. The Destination Name field contains the name of the system for which the status is being requested, and the Source Name field contains the name number 1 for the local system.

In reply to a STATUS QUERY transmission, a computer generates a STATUS RESPONSE message (Command code 0F) that it transmits as a unicast to the querying system. The Data1 field of the message indicates the status of the response, using the following codes:

- **00**   NetBIOS 1.*x* or 2.0 type response
- **01 or greater**   NetBIOS 2.1 type response, where the value indicates the number of replies already received

The Data2 field contains two flags. The first bit is set to 1 if the length of the status data exceeds the frame size; the second bit is set to 1 if the length of the status data exceeds the size of the user's buffer. The remaining 14 bits in the field are used to specify the actual length of the status data. The Destination Name field contains the name of the system receiving the message and the Source Name field contains the NetBIOS name of the sender.

The DMP service also includes two messages used to end a network trace, both with the same name. The TERMINATE TRACE message with Command code 07 terminates the trace activity at a remote system, while the TERMINATE TRACE message with Command code 13 terminates the trace activity at both the local and remote systems. The latter message is never generated by the NetBIOS interface, but it is recognized when generated by another application.

Session Management Protocol

Much of the NetBEUI traffic generated by typical networking tasks on a Windows network is transmitted during a session between two machines. A session occurs when two systems establish a connection before they actually transmit any application data. The connection ensures that each system is prepared to communicate and enables the two machines to regulate the flow of data and acknowledge successful transmissions. The Session Management Protocol (SMP) provides this full-duplex, connection-oriented, reliable service between NetBIOS systems.

Session Establishment

The process of establishing a session between two machines begins with the name resolution procedure described earlier in this chapter. The client computer wishing to establish the session transmits a NAME QUERY message containing a session identifier (that is, a value other than 00) in the Data2 field to all of the NetBIOS systems on the network. The intended destination server responds with a NAME RECOGNIZED message that supplies its hardware address and indicates it is listening for further session messages from the sender.

Note *As is often the case, the roles of client and server are tenuous on a Windows network because the systems can function as both clients and servers. The references here to clients and servers refer to the roles of the computers in this particular transaction. The two machines could just as easily reverse their roles and perform a session establishment originating from the other system.*

Before the next exchange of NBF messages, the two systems perform a session establishment procedure at the LLC level, which consists of the client transmitting a SABME (Set Asynchronous Balance Mode Extended) message, to which the server replies with a UA (Unnumbered Acknowledgment) frame. The client then sends an RR (Receive Ready) message indicating that it is ready to receive data (see Figure 13-6).

Once the session is established at the LLC level, an NBF session establishment transaction is required before the system can begin to transmit actual application data. This procedure begins when the client system transmits a SESSION INITIALIZE message (with a Command code value of 19) as a unicast to the server (see Figure 13-7).

Note *After the initial NAME QUERY message, all the subsequent frames involved in session communications are I-format LPDU unicasts, which use the hardware address discovered during the name resolution process to direct the packets. Any timeouts and retries occurring during the transmissions are handled by the IEEE 802.2 LLC implementation.*

The Data1 field of this message uses the following bit values:

- **Bit 1**   Flag specifying the NetBIOS version, using the following values:
  - **0**   NetBIOS version 2.20 or lower
  - **1**   NetBIOS version higher than 2.20
- **Bits 2–4**   Unused

NETWORK PROTOCOLS

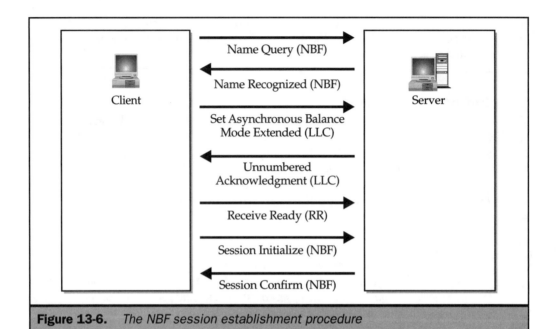

Figure 13-6.   *The NBF session establishment procedure*

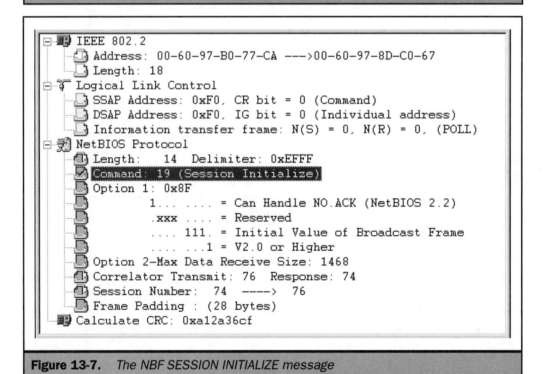

Figure 13-7.   *The NBF SESSION INITIALIZE message*

- **Bits 5–7**   Specify the length of the largest frame value permitted by the MAC protocol
- **Bit 8**   Flag specifying the NetBIOS version, using following values:
  - **0**   NetBIOS version 1.*x*.
  - **1**   NetBIOS version 2.0 or above. This indicates the system is capable of performing a certain type of data transfer that does not require acknowledgments.

The Data2 field specifies the length of the user's receive buffer.

Unlike the messages for the other services, SMP messages do not have Destination Name and Source Name fields. Instead, they have a 1-byte Destination Number and Source Number fields that carry the unique identifiers the systems use to refer to the session. Each computer maintains its own session numbers.

In response to the SESSION INITIALIZE message, the second system generates a SESSION CONFIRM message that completes the initialization of the session (see Figure 13-8). This message has a Command code of 17 and is identical in format to the SESSION INITIALIZE message, except that the bits 5 through 7 of the Data1 field are unused.

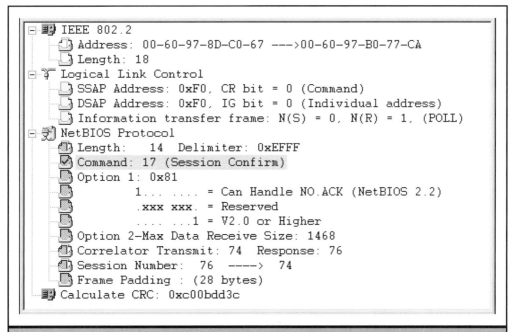

```
⊟ ▦ IEEE 802.2
    ⬜ Address: 00-60-97-8D-C0-67 --->00-60-97-B0-77-CA
    ⬜ Length: 18
⊟ ⋎ Logical Link Control
    ⬜ SSAP Address: 0xF0, CR bit = 0 (Command)
    ⬜ DSAP Address: 0xF0, IG bit = 0 (Individual address)
    ⬜ Information transfer frame: N(S) = 0, N(R) = 1, (POLL)
⊟ ▦ NetBIOS Protocol
    ⬜ Length:   14  Delimiter: 0xEFFF
    ☑ Command: 17 (Session Confirm)
    ⬜ Option 1: 0x81
              1... .... = Can Handle NO.ACK (NetBIOS 2.2)
             .xxx xxx. = Reserved
             .... ...1 = V2.0 or Higher
    ⬜ Option 2-Max Data Receive Size: 1468
    ⬜ Correlator Transmit: 74  Response: 76
    ⬜ Session Number:  76  ----> 74
    ⬜ Frame Padding : (28 bytes)
  ▦ Calculate CRC: 0xc00bdd3c
```

Figure 13-8.   *The NBF SESSION CONFIRM message*

Session Maintenance

During periods of inactivity, the computers involved in a session transmit SESSION ALIVE messages to confirm that the other system is still available and capable of receiving data (see Figure 13-9). The SESSION ALIVE message has a Command code value of 1F; all the subsequent fields are unused.

Data Transfer

Once the session is established, the transfer of data can begin, using NBF messages that may or may not carry data generated by upper-layer protocols (such as SMB). When one computer connects to another to copy files from the server to a local drive, for example, the systems use NBF frames to carry the actual data. When you use a Windows application to open a file on a network drive, the system uses SMB messages (carried with NBF frames) to access the drive and transfer the file.

The NBF frames used to transmit the data depend on the amount of data to be transferred. When copying a file small enough to fit in a single packet, the sending system sends the data in a DATA ONLY LAST message. When the file spans multiple packets because it is too large for either the frame size or the transmit buffer size of the receiving system, all the segments are transmitted in DATA FIRST MIDDLE frames except for the last one, which goes in a DATA ONLY LAST frame.

Note   *The term* message *refers to an entire data sequence, even if it is segmented into multiple packets. All the frames used in the name, datagram, and status services are self-contained messages, but SMP can require many frames to transmit a single message.*

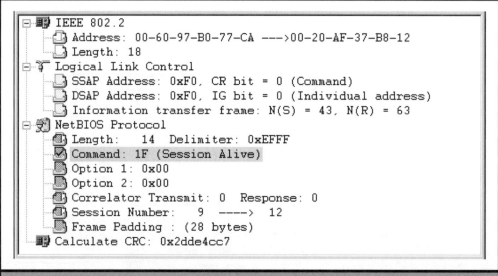

```
⊟ IEEE 802.2
      Address: 00-60-97-B0-77-CA --->00-20-AF-37-B8-12
      Length: 18
⊟ Logical Link Control
      SSAP Address: 0xF0, CR bit = 0 (Command)
      DSAP Address: 0xF0, IG bit = 0 (Individual address)
      Information transfer frame: N(S) = 43, N(R) = 63
⊟ NetBIOS Protocol
      Length:   14  Delimiter: 0xEFFF
      Command: 1F (Session Alive)
      Option 1: 0x00
      Option 2: 0x00
      Correlator Transmit: 0  Response: 0
      Session Number:    9  ----> 12
      Frame Padding : (28 bytes)
   Calculate CRC: 0x2dde4cc7
```

Figure 13-9.   *The NBF SESSION ALIVE message*

The DATA FIRST MIDDLE frame has a Command code of 15 (see Figure 13-10). The Data1 field contains flags that use the following bit values:

- **Bits 1–4**   Unused
- **Bit 5**   Specifies whether an acknowledgment is included with the frame, using the following values:
  - **0**   Acknowledgment not included
  - **1**   Acknowledgment included
- **Bit 6**   Unused
- **Bit 7**   Indicates the version of NetBIOS and whether an acknowledgment is expected from the receiver, using the following values:
  - **0**   NetBIOS version prior to 2.20 (acknowledgment is expected)
  - **1**   NetBIOS version 2.20 or later (acknowledgment is not expected)
- **Bit 8**   Specifies whether or not a RECEIVE CONTINUE message is requested from the receiver, using the following values:
  - **0**   RECEIVE CONTINUE not requested
  - **1**   RECEIVE CONTINUE requested

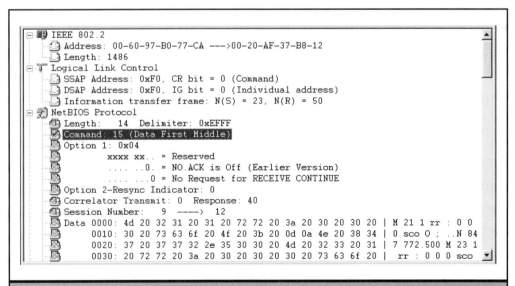

Figure 13-10.   *The NBF DATA FIRST MIDDLE frame*

The sender requests a RECEIVE CONTINUE message from the receiver if the packet contains the first segment sent during the session or if the sender has received any NO RECEIVE responses during the previous message transmission. If the previous message transmission was completed without any NO RECEIVE responses from the receiving system, then the sender does not request a RECEIVE CONTINUE message.

The Data2 field contains a resynchronization indicator with a value of 0001 if this is the first DATA FIRST MIDDLE frame following the receipt of a RECEIPT OUTSTANDING message (which indicates the receiver's ability to accept more data following a NO RECEIVE message). This enables the receiver to resynchronize the transmission sequence with this frame should problems occur during subsequent packet transfers.

The DATA ONLY LAST frame (see Figure 13-11) has a Command code value of 15 and is nearly identical in format to the DATA FIRST MIDDLE frame, except for the flag bits in the Data1 field, which are as follows:

- **Bits 1–4** Unused
- **Bit 5** Specifies whether an acknowledgment is included with the frame, using the following values:
  - **0** Acknowledgment not included
  - **1** Acknowledgment included
- **Bit 6** Specifies whether or not the receiving system can acknowledge the transmission by sending either a DATA ACK message or a data frame in which bit 5 of the data1 field has a value of 1, indicating that an acknowledgment is included with the frame. The acknowledgment with data feature must be supported by the NBF implementations on both systems to be used. The flag takes the following values:
  - **0** Acknowledgment with data not allowed
  - **1** Acknowledgment with data allowed
- **Bit 7** Indicates the version of NetBIOS and whether an acknowledgment is expected from the receiver, using the following values:
  - **0** NetBIOS version prior to 2.20 (acknowledgment is expected)
  - **1** NetBIOS version 2.20 or later (acknowledgment is not expected)
- **Bit 8** Unused

The receiver of a DATA ONLY LAST frame must acknowledge it by responding to the sender with one of the following frames:

- DATA ACK
- NO RECEIVE
- RECEIVE OUTSTANDING
- DATA FIRST MIDDLE or DATA ONLY LAST (with the acknowledgment with data feature enabled)

The DATA ACK message (Command code 14) is a simple frame that does nothing but acknowledge that a DATA ONLY LAST frame was received correctly. Both of the Data fields are unused.

The RECEIVE CONTINUE message is generated by a system that receives a DATA FIRST MIDDLE frame, in which the eighth bit of the Data1 field has a value of 1, indicating that the sender is requesting the response. The RECEIVE CONTINUE message serves as an acknowledgment of the data received thus far and indicates there is more data to transmit. The message itself has a Command code value of 1C and nothing in either of the Data fields.

When a system receives a DATA FIRST MIDDLE or DATA ONLY LAST frame that fill its receive buffer, it generates a NO RECEIVE message with a Command code of 1A. This message contains one flag in the Data1 field, using the following bit values:

- **Bits 1–6**   Unused

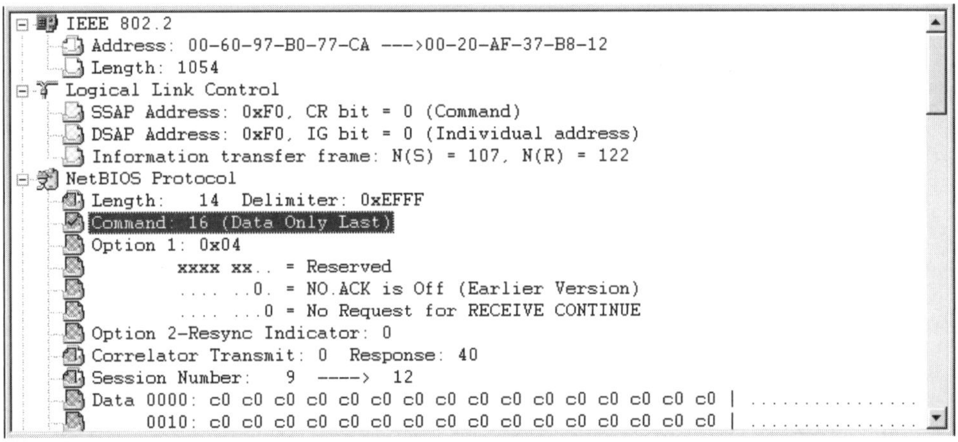

```
☐ ▦ IEEE 802.2
   ┊   🗋 Address: 00-60-97-B0-77-CA --->00-20-AF-37-B8-12
   ┊   🗋 Length: 1054
☐ ⅄ Logical Link Control
   ┊   🗋 SSAP Address: 0xF0, CR bit = 0 (Command)
   ┊   🗋 DSAP Address: 0xF0, IG bit = 0 (Individual address)
   ┊   🗋 Information transfer frame: N(S) = 107, N(R) = 122
☐ 🖳 NetBIOS Protocol
   ┊   🗋 Length:   14   Delimiter: 0xEFFF
   ┊   🗋 Command: 16 (Data Only Last)
   ┊   🗋 Option 1: 0x04
   ┊          xxxx xx.. = Reserved
   ┊          .... ..0. = NO.ACK is Off (Earlier Version)
   ┊          .... ...0 = No Request for RECEIVE CONTINUE
   ┊   🗋 Option 2-Resync Indicator: 0
   ┊   🗋 Correlator Transmit: 0   Response: 40
   ┊   🗋 Session Number:   9 ----> 12
   ┊   🗋 Data 0000: c0 c0 c0 c0 c0 c0 c0 c0 c0 c0 c0 c0 c0 c0 c0 c0 | ................
   ┊   🗋      0010: c0 c0 c0 c0 c0 c0 c0 c0 c0 c0 c0 c0 c0 c0 c0 c0 | ................
```

Figure 13-11.   *The NBF DATA ONLY LAST frame*

- **Bit 7**   Indicates the version of NetBIOS and that the acknowledgment included with the previously transmitted data was either partially received or not received at all, using the following values:
  - **0**   NetBIOS version prior to 2.20
  - **1**   NetBIOS version 2.20 or later (acknowledgment not received)
- **Bit 8**   Unused

The Data2 field specifies how many bytes of data from the last frame were received before the buffer was filled. The sender uses this information when it resumes transmitting to restart the sequence at the point where the receiver left off.

Once the sender receives a NO RECEIVE message, it stops transmitting until it receives a RECEIVE OUTSTANDING message (Command code 1B) from the receiving system. This indicates that room now exists in the receive buffer for more data and that the sender should resume transmitting beginning with the byte immediately after the last byte acknowledged, as specified in the Data2 field.

Session Termination

When the client system wants to terminate the session with the server, it transmits a SESSION END message, with a Command code of 18 (see Figure 13-12). The Data1

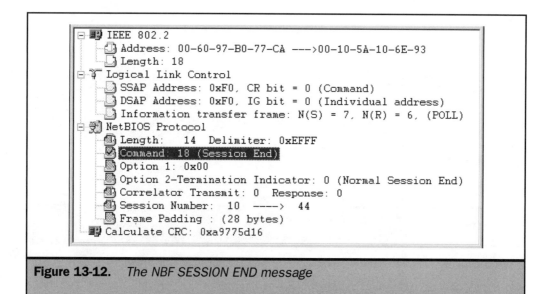

Figure 13-12.   *The NBF SESSION END message*

field of this message is unused, but the Data2 field specifies the reason for the termination of the session, using the following values:

- **00**   Normal session end (due to an application command, for example)
- **01**   Abnormal session end (due to a timeout, for example)

Server Message Blocks

In some cases, the NBF frame is the primary payload of a packet. For example, when a Windows system accesses a file on another system, the file itself is transmitted in NBF data frames. However, NBF messages can also carry upper-layer protocol messages as well. *Server Message Blocks (SMB)* is an application layer protocol that the Windows redirector (the module responsible for sending application requests to the appropriate network resource) uses to perform many different file management and authentication tasks on remote systems. For example, before copying a file from a shared network drive to a local drive, the two systems involved exchange SMB messages that authenticate the user's access to the resource and establish a session with the share.

Note   *The session established at the application layer by the SMB protocol is independent of the other sessions discussed earlier in this chapter: the NBF session and the LLC session. All three session establishment processes must be completed before the two Windows network systems can transfer application data.*

SMB Messages

SMB messages are not restricted to use with NetBEUI, but they are intimately connected with NetBIOS. When a Windows network uses TCP/IP as its network protocol, NetBT (NetBIOS over TCP/IP) frames carry the SMB messages. On a NetBEUI network, SMB messages are carried within the following NBF message types:

- DATAGRAM
- DATAGRAM BROADCAST
- DATA FIRST MIDDLE
- DATA ONLY LAST

Several dozen SMB message types exist, falling into four basic categories:

- **Session control messages**   Used to establish and terminate a connection to a shared resource on a server.
- **File system messages**   Used to access and manipulate the file system on a remote server's shared drive.

■ **Printer messages**   Used to send print jobs generated by local applications to a print queue on a remote server.

■ **Message messages**   Used to carry messages with another system on the network.

Each SMB message includes a 1-byte command field that identifies the function of the message, using the values shown in Table 13-1.

Command	Command Code
CREATE_DIRECTORY	00
DELETE_DIRECTORY	01
OPEN	02
CREATE	03
CLOSE	04
FLUSH	05
DELETE	06
RENAME	07
QUERY_INFORMATION	08
SET_INFORMATION	09
READ	0A
WRITE	0B
LOCK_BYTE_RANGE	0C
UNLOCK_BYTE_RANGE	0D
CREATE_TEMPORARY	0E
CREATE_NEW	0F
CHECK_DIRECTORY	10
PROCESS_EXIT	11
SEEK	12
LOCK_AND_READ	13
WRITE_AND_UNLOCK	14

Table 13-1.   *Server Message Block Protocol Command Codes*

Command	Command Code
READ_RAW	1A
READ_MPX	1B
READ_MPX_SECONDARY	1C
WRITE_RAW	1D
WRITE_MPX	1E
WRITE_COMPLETE	20
SET_INFORMATION2	22
QUERY_INFORMATION2	23
LOCKING_ANDX	24
TRANSACTION	25
TRANSACTION_SECONDARY	26
IOCTL	27
IOCTL_SECONDARY	28
COPY	29
MOVE	2A
ECHO	2B
WRITE_AND_CLOSE	2C
OPEN_ANDX	2D
READ_ANDX	2E
WRITE_ANDX	2F
CLOSE_AND_TREE_DISC	31
TRANSACTION2	32
TRANSACTION2_SECONDARY	33
FIND_CLOSE2	34
FIND_NOTIFY_CLOSE	35
TREE_CONNECT	70
TREE_DISCONNECT	71

Table 13-1.   *Server Message Block Protocol Command Codes* (continued)

NETWORK PROTOCOLS

Command	Command Code
NEGOTIATE	72
SESSION_SETUP_ANDX	73
LOGOFF_ANDX	74
TREE_CONNECT_ANDX	75
QUERY_INFORMATION_DISK	80
SEARCH	81
FIND	82
FIND_UNIQUE	83
NT_TRANSACT	A0
NT_TRANSACT_SECONDARY	A1
NT_CREATE_ANDX	A2
NT_CANCEL	A4
OPEN_PRINT_FILE	C0
WRITE_PRINT_FILE	C1
CLOSE_PRINT_FILE	C2
GET_PRINT_QUEUE	C3
SEND_MESSAGE	D0
SEND_BROADCAST	D1
FORWARD_USER_NAME	D2
CANCEL_FORWARD	D3
GET_MACHINE_NAME	D4
SEND_MULTIBLOCK_MESSAGE	D5
END_MULTIBLOCK_MESSAGE	D6
MULTIBLOCK_MESSAGE_TEXT	D7
READ_BULK	D8
WRITE_BULK	D9
WRITE_BULK_DATA	DA

Table 13-1.   *Server Message Block Protocol Command Codes* (continued)

In addition to the Command code, each SMB message contains a 1-byte Flags field and a 2-byte Flags2 field that specify information about the message and the capabilities of the system generating it, such as whether the system supports long filenames and extended attributes, whether path names should be case sensitive, and whether the message is being sent by a server in response to a client request.

This last flag is included because separate request and reply messages do not exist for each SMB command. A system receiving an SMB message containing a command to perform an action typically responds with a reply that uses the same command code and contains some indication of the success or failure of the procedure. The response flag is set in the reply message to ensure that the receiver associates the reply with its previous request.

The rest of the message fields vary depending on the type and function of the message.

SMB Communications

SMB messages provide networking support services for Windows systems; they do not perform entire transactions by themselves. During a typical client/server process on a NetBEUI network, such as a workstation accessing a file on a shared drive, the communications intersperse LLC, NBF, and SMB messages during the various parts of the procedure. This is illustrated is Figure 13-13, which shows a sequence of packets

No.	Source..	Dest Address	Layer	Summary
1	cz2	NetBIOS	NetBIOS	Cmd: A (Name Query), CZ2 ---->CZ5
2	cz5	cz2	NetBIOS	Cmd: E (Name Recognized), CZ5 ---->CZ2
3	cz2	cz5	LLC	Sap 0xF0 ---> 0xF0 (Command)
4	cz5	cz2	LLC	Sap 0xF0 ---> 0xF0 (Response)
5	cz2	cz5	LLC	Sap 0xF0 ---> 0xF0 (Command)
6	cz5	cz2	LLC	Sap 0xF0 ---> 0xF0 (Response)
7	cz2	cz5	NetBIOS	Cmd: 19 (Session Initialize), 74--->76
8	cz5	cz2	NetBIOS	Cmd: 17 (Session Confirm), 76--->74
9	cz5	cz2	LLC	Sap 0xF0 ---> 0xF0 (Response)
10	cz2	cz5	LLC	Sap 0xF0 ---> 0xF0 (Response)
11	cz2	cz5	SMB	C=Negotiate,Dialect[6]=NT LM 0.12
12	cz5	cz2	LLC	Sap 0xF0 ---> 0xF0 (Response)
13	cz5	cz2	SMB	R=Negotiate,Selected Dialect#=5
14	cz2	cz5	LLC	Sap 0xF0 ---> 0xF0 (Response)
15	cz2	cz5	SMB	C=Session_Setup+X,Account=CRAIGZ, XCmd=Tree_Connect+X,Server=\\CZ5\C
16	cz5	cz2	LLC	Sap 0xF0 ---> 0xF0 (Response)
17	cz5	cz2	NetBIOS	Cmd: 14 (Data Ack), 76--->74
18	cz2	cz5	LLC	Sap 0xF0 ---> 0xF0 (Response)
19	cz5	cz2	SMB	R=Session_Setup+X, XCmd=Tree_Connect+X,Type=A:
20	cz2	cz5	LLC	Sap 0xF0 ---> 0xF0 (Response)
21	cz2	cz5	SMB	C=Open+X,Name=autoexec.bat
22	cz5	cz2	LLC	Sap 0xF0 ---> 0xF0 (Response)
23	cz5	cz2	SMB	R=Open+X,FID=0x41,File Size=0x20
24	cz2	cz5	LLC	Sap 0xF0 ---> 0xF0 (Response)
25	cz2	cz5	SMB	C=Read_Raw,FID=0x41,Read 4096 at 0x0
26	cz5	cz2	LLC	Sap 0xF0 ---> 0xF0 (Response)
27	cz5	cz2	NetBIOS	Cmd: 16 (Data Only Last), 76--->74
28	cz2	cz5	NetBIOS	Cmd: 14 (Data Ack), 74--->76
29	cz5	cz2	LLC	Sap 0xF0 ---> 0xF0 (Response)
30	cz2	cz5	SMB	C=Close_File,FID=0x41
31	cz5	cz2	LLC	Sap 0xF0 ---> 0xF0 (Response)
32	cz5	cz2	SMB	R=Close_File
33	cz2	cz5	LLC	Sap 0xF0 ---> 0xF0 (Response)
34	cz2	cz5	SMB	C=Tree_Disconnect
35	cz5	cz2	SMB	R=Tree_Disconnect
36	cz5	cz2	NetBIOS	Cmd: 14 (Data Ack), 74--->76
37	cz5	cz2	LLC	Sap 0xF0 ---> 0xF0 (Response)

Figure 13-13.   *The LLC, NBF, and SMB protocols working together to provide Windows systems with their networking capability*

captured during a simple transaction in which one Windows system opens the Autoexec.bat file on another system's shared drive using the Wordpad text editor.

The sequence proceeds as follows:

1. **Packets 1–2**   The machine with the NetBIOS name CZ2 sends an NBF NAME QUERY message to the network to locate the machine called CZ5 and resolve its name into a hardware address. CZ5 responds with a NAME RECOGNIZED message containing the address.

2. **Packets 3–6**   CZ2 initiates an LLC session with CZ5 at the data link layer.

3. **Packets 7–10**   CZ2 establishes an NBF session with CZ5, and both systems transmit LLC Receive Ready messages to acknowledge that they are prepared for the next transmission. All subsequent messages with trigger LLC Receive Ready messages in response.

4. **Packets 11–14**   CZ2 sends an SMB NEGOTIATE message (Command code 72) to CZ5, containing the protocol dialects it understands (see Figure 13-14). CZ5 replies with the index number of the dialect it has selected (see Figure 13-15).

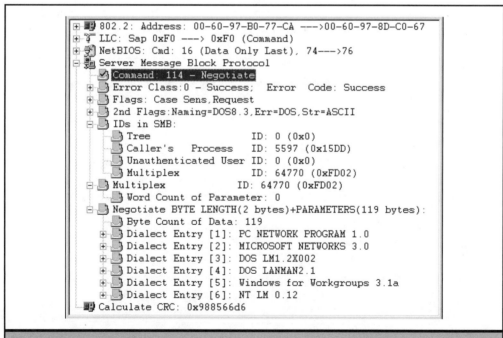

Figure 13-14.   *The SMB NEGOTIATE request message*

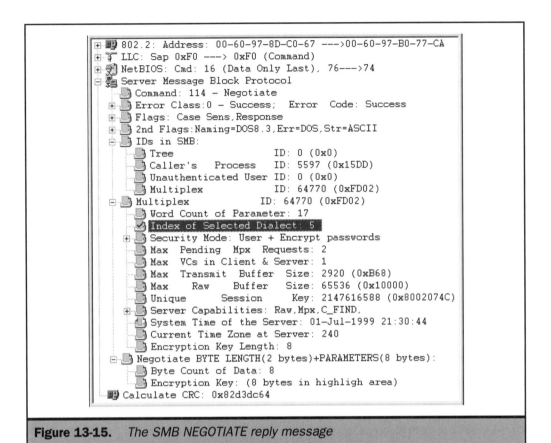

```
⊞ 🖳 802.2: Address: 00-60-97-8D-C0-67 --->00-60-97-B0-77-CA
⊞ 🖫 LLC: Sap 0xF0 ---> 0xF0 (Command)
⊞ 🖫 NetBIOS: Cmd: 16 (Data Only Last), 76--->74
⊟ 🖫 Server Message Block Protocol
    🗋 Command: 114 - Negotiate
  ⊞ 🗋 Error Class:0 - Success;  Error   Code: Success
  ⊞ 🗋 Flags: Case Sens,Response
  ⊞ 🗋 2nd Flags:Naming=DOS8.3,Err=DOS,Str=ASCII
  ⊟ 🗋 IDs in SMB:
      🗋 Tree                    ID:  0 (0x0)
      🗋 Caller's   Process   ID: 5597 (0x15DD)
      🗋 Unauthenticated User ID:  0 (0x0)
      🗋 Multiplex            ID: 64770 (0xFD02)
  ⊟ 🗋 Multiplex              ID: 64770 (0xFD02)
      🗋 Word Count of Parameter: 17
      ☑ Index of Selected Dialect: 5
    ⊞ 🗋 Security Mode: User + Encrypt passwords
      🗋 Max   Pending  Mpx  Requests: 2
      🗋 Max   VCs in Client & Server: 1
      🗋 Max   Transmit  Buffer  Size: 2920 (0xB68)
      🗋 Max    Raw   Buffer  Size: 65536 (0x10000)
      🗋 Unique       Session    Key: 2147616588 (0x8002074C)
    ⊞ 🗋 Server Capabilities: Raw,Mpx,C_FIND,
      🗋 System Time of the Server: 01-Jul-1999 21:30:44
      🗋 Current Time Zone at Server: 240
      🗋 Encryption Key Length: 8
  ⊟ 🗋 Negotiate BYTE LENGTH(2 bytes)+PARAMETERS(8 bytes):
      🗋 Byte Count of Data: 8
      🗋 Encryption Key: (8 bytes in highligh area)
  🖳 Calculate CRC: 0x82d3dc64
```

Figure 13-15.   *The SMB NEGOTIATE reply message*

5. **Packets 15–20**   CZ2 sends an SMB SESSION_SETUP_ANDX message
   (Command code 73) to CZ5, containing a user name, domain name, and
   password for authentication to the server. SMB's ANDX feature enables a
   system to batch multiple commands in the same message. Here, the packet
   contains a secondary TREE_CONNECT_ANDX command (code 75) that
   specifies the share on CZ5 to which CZ2 wants to connect (see Figure 13-16).
   CZ5 sends an NBF DATA ACK message acknowledging the transmission
   and an SMB reply indicating the success of the session establishment and
   tree connection.

6. **Packets 21–24**   CZ2 sends an SMB OPEN_ANDX command (code 2d) to CZ5,
   specifying the name of the file it wants to open: Autoexec.bat (see Figure 13-17).
   CZ5 sends a reply indicating the successful completion of the command;

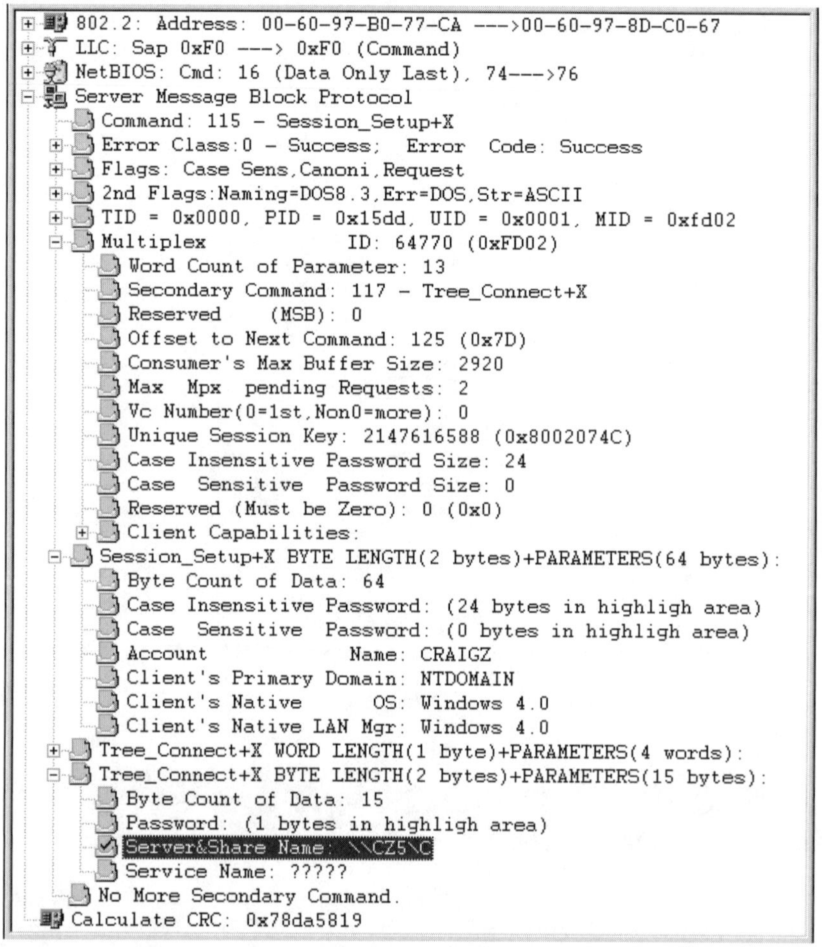

```
⊞ 🌐 802.2: Address: 00-60-97-B0-77-CA --->00-60-97-8D-C0-67
⊞ 🖥 LLC: Sap 0xF0 ---> 0xF0 (Command)
⊞ 🖧 NetBIOS: Cmd: 16 (Data Only Last), 74--->76
⊟ 🖥 Server Message Block Protocol
   ┈🗋 Command: 115 - Session_Setup+X
   ⊞🗋 Error Class:0 - Success; Error Code: Success
   ⊞🗋 Flags: Case Sens,Canoni,Request
   ⊞🗋 2nd Flags:Naming=DOS8.3,Err=DOS,Str=ASCII
   ⊞🗋 TID = 0x0000, PID = 0x15dd, UID = 0x0001, MID = 0xfd02
   ⊟🗋 Multiplex           ID: 64770 (0xFD02)
      🗋 Word Count of Parameter: 13
      🗋 Secondary Command: 117 - Tree_Connect+X
      🗋 Reserved     (MSB): 0
      🗋 Offset to Next Command: 125 (0x7D)
      🗋 Consumer's Max Buffer Size: 2920
      🗋 Max  Mpx  pending Requests: 2
      🗋 Vc Number(0=1st,Non0=more): 0
      🗋 Unique Session Key: 2147616588 (0x8002074C)
      🗋 Case Insensitive Password Size: 24
      🗋 Case  Sensitive  Password Size: 0
      🗋 Reserved (Must be Zero): 0 (0x0)
      ⊞🗋 Client Capabilities:
   ⊟🗋 Session_Setup+X BYTE LENGTH(2 bytes)+PARAMETERS(64 bytes):
      🗋 Byte Count of Data: 64
      🗋 Case Insensitive Password: (24 bytes in highligh area)
      🗋 Case  Sensitive  Password: (0 bytes in highligh area)
      🗋 Account        Name: CRAIGZ
      🗋 Client's Primary Domain: NTDOMAIN
      🗋 Client's Native    OS: Windows 4.0
      🗋 Client's Native LAN Mgr: Windows 4.0
   ⊞🗋 Tree_Connect+X WORD LENGTH(1 byte)+PARAMETERS(4 words):
   ⊟🗋 Tree_Connect+X BYTE LENGTH(2 bytes)+PARAMETERS(15 bytes):
      🗋 Byte Count of Data: 15
      🗋 Password: (1 bytes in highligh area)
      ☑ Server&Share Name: \\CZ5\C
      🗋 Service Name: ?????
   ┈🗋 No More Secondary Command.
   🌐 Calculate CRC: 0x78da5819
```

Figure 13-16.   *The SMB SESSION_SETUP_ANDX message, including a TREE_CONNECT_ANDX command*

assigning a file handle (FID) to Autoexec.bat; and specifying information about the requested file, such as its size and date last modified (see Figure 13-18). CZ2 uses the FID to reference the file in subsequent messages.

7. **Packets 25–26**   CZ2 sends an SMB READ_RAW message (command code 1A) to CZ5 containing the FID of Autoexec.bat, the location in the file where the

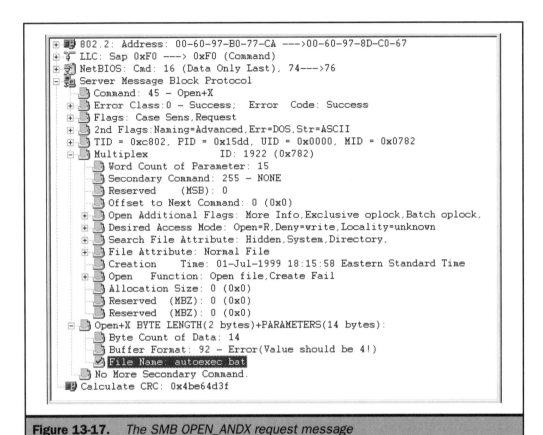

```
⊞ ▓ 802.2: Address: 00-60-97-B0-77-CA --->00-60-97-8D-C0-67
⊞ ⌁ LLC: Sap 0xF0 ---> 0xF0 (Command)
⊞ ▓ NetBIOS: Cmd: 16 (Data Only Last), 74--->76
⊟ ▓ Server Message Block Protocol
   ▓ Command: 45 - Open+X
   ⊞ ▓ Error Class:0 - Success;  Error  Code: Success
   ⊞ ▓ Flags: Case Sens,Request
   ⊞ ▓ 2nd Flags:Naming=Advanced,Err=DOS,Str=ASCII
   ⊞ ▓ TID = 0xc802, PID = 0x15dd, UID = 0x0000, MID = 0x0782
   ⊟ ▓ Multiplex           ID: 1922 (0x782)
      ▓ Word Count of Parameter: 15
      ▓ Secondary Command: 255 - NONE
      ▓ Reserved     (MSB): 0
      ▓ Offset to Next Command: 0 (0x0)
    ⊞ ▓ Open Additional Flags: More Info,Exclusive oplock,Batch oplock,
    ⊞ ▓ Desired Access Mode: Open=R,Deny=write,Locality=unknown
    ⊞ ▓ Search File Attribute: Hidden,System,Directory,
    ⊞ ▓ File Attribute: Normal File
      ▓ Creation    Time: 01-Jul-1999 18:15:58 Eastern Standard Time
    ⊞ ▓ Open  Function: Open file,Create Fail
      ▓ Allocation Size: 0 (0x0)
      ▓ Reserved  (MBZ): 0 (0x0)
      ▓ Reserved  (MBZ): 0 (0x0)
   ⊟ ▓ Open+X BYTE LENGTH(2 bytes)+PARAMETERS(14 bytes):
      ▓ Byte Count of Data: 14
      ▓ Buffer Format: 92 - Error(Value should be 4!)
      ☑ File Name: autoexec.bat
      ▓ No More Secondary Command.
   ▓ Calculate CRC: 0x4be64d3f
```

Figure 13-17.   *The SMB OPEN_ANDX request message*

read should begin (in this case 0, the beginning of the file), and the maximum number of bytes to be returned (see Figure 13-19).

8. **Packets 27–29**   CZ5 reads the file on its local drive as directed and transmits it to CZ2 in a single NBF DATA ONLY LAST frame (see Figure 13-20). If the file was too large to fit in a single frame, the system would use as many DATA FIRST MIDDLE frames as needed, followed by a DATA ONLY LAST frame with the final bits of the file. CZ2 replies with an NBF DATA ACK message.

9. **Packets 30–33**   CZ2 sends an SMB CLOSE message (Command code 04) requesting that CZ5 close the file, using the same FID to reference

```
⊞ 🖳 802.2: Address: 00-60-97-8D-C0-67 --->00-60-97-B0-77-CA
⊞ 🍸 LLC: Sap 0xF0 ---> 0xF0 (Command)
⊞ 🖳 NetBIOS: Cmd: 16 (Data Only Last), 76--->74
⊟ 🖳 Server Message Block Protocol
    📄 Command: 45 - Open+X
  ⊞ 📄 Error Class:0 - Success;  Error  Code: Success
  ⊞ 📄 Flags: Case Sens,Response
  ⊞ 📄 2nd Flags:Naming=Advanced,Err=DOS,Str=ASCII
  ⊞ 📄 TID = 0xc802, PID = 0x15dd, UID = 0x0000, MID = 0x0782
  ⊟ 📄 Multiplex        ID: 1922 (0x782)
      📄 Word Count of Parameter: 15
      📄 Secondary Command: 255 - NONE
      📄 Reserved     (MSB): 0
      📄 Offset to Next Command: 0 (0x0)
      ☑ File Handle: 65 (0x41)
    ⊞ 📄 Open File Attribute: Normal File
      📄 Last Written Time: 31-Jan-1999 13:52:50 Eastern Standard Time
      📄 Current File Size: 32 (0x20)
    ⊞ 📄 Granted Access Mode: Open=R,Deny=write,Locality=unknown
      📄 File Type: 0 - Disk File/Directory
    ⊞ 📄 Device State: Read=byte stream,Type=Byte stream,Consumer end,R/W Block
    ⊞ 📄 Open Function: file existed and was opened,Opened by another user
      📄 Server Unique  File ID: 0 (0x0)
      📄 Reserved      (Must be Zero): 0
  ⊟ 📄 Open+X BYTE LENGTH(2 bytes)+PARAMETERS(0 bytes):
      📄 Byte Count of Data: 0
    📄 No More Secondary Command.
  🖳 Calculate CRC: 0x58aa275c
```

Figure 13-18. *The SMB OPEN_ANDX reply message*

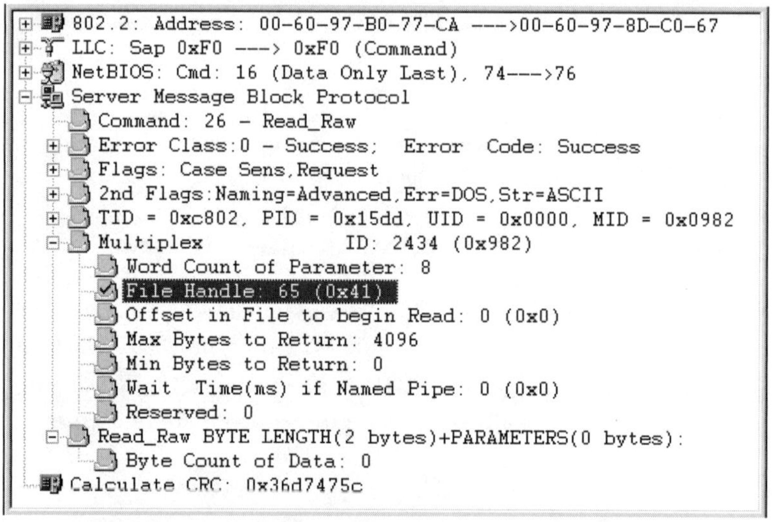

```
⊞ 🖳 802.2: Address: 00-60-97-B0-77-CA --->00-60-97-8D-C0-67
⊞ 🍸 LLC: Sap 0xF0 ---> 0xF0 (Command)
⊞ 🖳 NetBIOS: Cmd: 16 (Data Only Last), 74--->76
⊟ 🖳 Server Message Block Protocol
    📄 Command: 26 - Read_Raw
  ⊞ 📄 Error Class:0 - Success;  Error  Code: Success
  ⊞ 📄 Flags: Case Sens,Request
  ⊞ 📄 2nd Flags:Naming=Advanced,Err=DOS,Str=ASCII
  ⊞ 📄 TID = 0xc802, PID = 0x15dd, UID = 0x0000, MID = 0x0982
  ⊟ 📄 Multiplex        ID: 2434 (0x982)
      📄 Word Count of Parameter: 8
      ☑ File Handle: 65 (0x41)
      📄 Offset in File to begin Read: 0 (0x0)
      📄 Max Bytes to Return: 4096
      📄 Min Bytes to Return: 0
      📄 Wait  Time(ms) if Named Pipe: 0 (0x0)
      📄 Reserved: 0
  ⊟ 📄 Read_Raw BYTE LENGTH(2 bytes)+PARAMETERS(0 bytes):
      📄 Byte Count of Data: 0
  🖳 Calculate CRC: 0x36d7475c
```

Figure 13-19. *The SMB READ_RAW message*

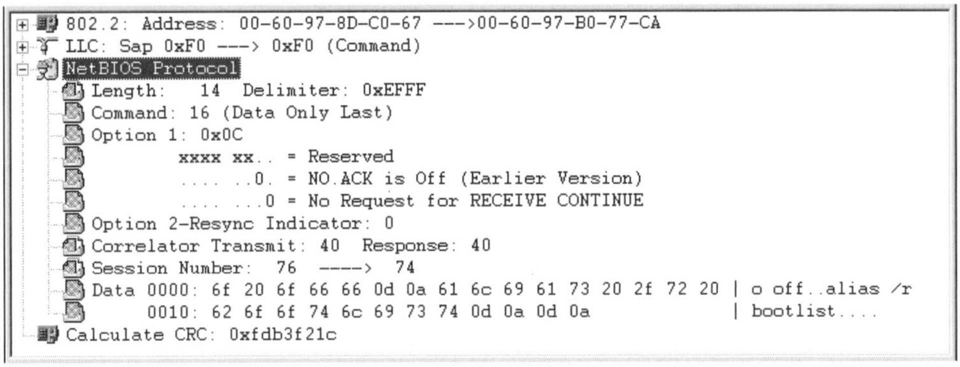

```
⊞ ▇ 802.2: Address: 00-60-97-8D-C0-67 --->00-60-97-B0-77-CA
⊞ ⊤ LLC: Sap 0xF0 ---> 0xF0 (Command)
⊟ ▇ NetBIOS Protocol
   ▇ Length:   14  Delimiter: 0xEFFF
   ▇ Command: 16 (Data Only Last)
   ▇ Option 1: 0x0C
   ▇         xxxx xx.. = Reserved
   ▇         .... ..0. = NO.ACK is Off (Earlier Version)
   ▇         .... ...0 = No Request for RECEIVE CONTINUE
   ▇ Option 2-Resync Indicator: 0
   ▇ Correlator Transmit: 40  Response: 40
   ▇ Session Number:  76  ----> 74
   ▇ Data 0000: 6f 20 6f 66 66 0d 0a 61 6c 69 61 73 20 2f 72 20 | o off..alias /r
   ▇      0010: 62 6f 6f 74 6c 69 73 74 0d 0a 0d 0a             | bootlist....
 ▇ Calculate CRC: 0xfdb3f21c
```

Figure 13-20. *The NBF DATA ONLY LAST message carries the file requested by the SMB sequence*

Autoexec.bat (see Figure 13-21). CZ5 responds, indicating the successful completion of the command.

10. **Packets 34–37** CZ2 sends an SMB TREE_DISCONNECT message (Command code 71) to CZ5, requesting that the connection to the share be terminated (see Figure 13-22). CZ5 responds, indicating a successful disconnection, and transmits a final NBF DATA ACK message.

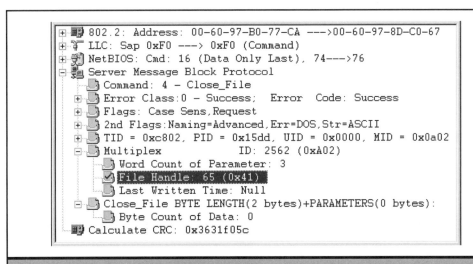

```
⊞ ▇ 802.2: Address: 00-60-97-B0-77-CA --->00-60-97-8D-C0-67
⊞ ⊤ LLC: Sap 0xF0 ---> 0xF0 (Command)
⊞ ▇ NetBIOS: Cmd: 16 (Data Only Last), 74--->76
⊟ ▇ Server Message Block Protocol
   ▇ Command: 4 - Close_File
 ⊞ ▇ Error Class:0 - Success;  Error  Code: Success
 ⊞ ▇ Flags: Case Sens,Request
 ⊞ ▇ 2nd Flags:Naming=Advanced,Err=DOS,Str=ASCII
 ⊞ ▇ TID = 0xc802, PID = 0x15dd, UID = 0x0000, MID = 0x0a02
 ⊟ ▇ Multiplex          ID: 2562 (0xA02)
     ▇ Word Count of Parameter: 3
     ▇ File Handle: 65 (0x41)
     ▇ Last Written Time: Null
 ⊟ ▇ Close_File BYTE LENGTH(2 bytes)+PARAMETERS(0 bytes):
     ▇ Byte Count of Data: 0
 ▇ Calculate CRC: 0x3631f05c
```

Figure 13-21. *The SMB CLOSE message*

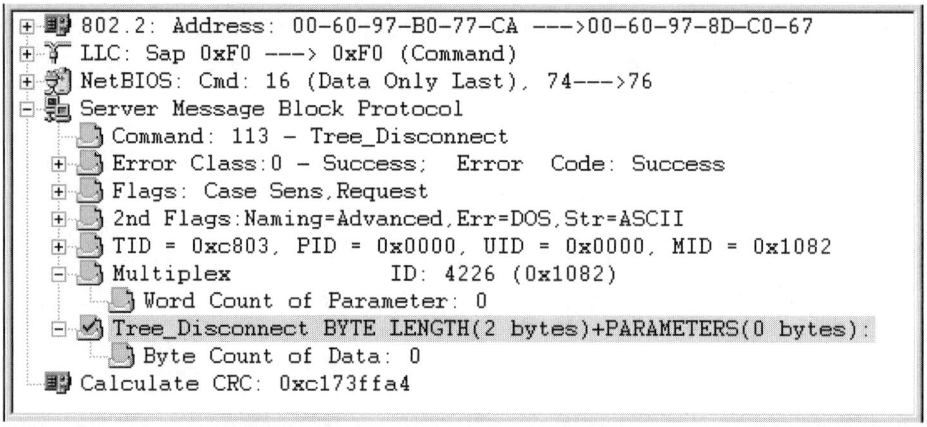

```
⊞ 🖳 802.2: Address: 00-60-97-B0-77-CA --->00-60-97-8D-C0-67
⊞ 🖳 LLC: Sap 0xF0 ---> 0xF0 (Command)
⊞ 🖳 NetBIOS: Cmd: 16 (Data Only Last), 74--->76
⊟ 🖳 Server Message Block Protocol
    🗋 Command: 113 - Tree_Disconnect
  ⊞ 🗋 Error Class:0 - Success;  Error  Code: Success
  ⊞ 🗋 Flags: Case Sens,Request
  ⊞ 🗋 2nd Flags:Naming=Advanced,Err=DOS,Str=ASCII
  ⊞ 🗋 TID = 0xc803, PID = 0x0000, UID = 0x0000, MID = 0x1082
  ⊟ 🗋 Multiplex          ID: 4226 (0x1082)
      🗋 Word Count of Parameter: 0
  ⊟ ☑ Tree_Disconnect BYTE LENGTH(2 bytes)+PARAMETERS(0 bytes):
      🗋 Byte Count of Data: 0
  🖳 Calculate CRC: 0xc173ffa4
```

Figure 13-22.   *The SMB TREE_DISCONNECT message*

The Complete Reference

Upgrading & Troubleshooting Networks

Part IV

Network Operating Systems

Chapter 14

Windows NT and
Windows 2000

Since its initial release in 1993, Microsoft's Windows NT operating system has become the most popular network operating system on the market, taking the place of Novell NetWare. NT's familiar interface and ease of use have enabled relatively unsophisticated users to install and maintain local area networks, making LAN technology an all but ubiquitous part of doing business today. Windows 2000, the latest incarnation of the NT operating system, addresses some of the shortcomings of Windows NT, with the intention of creating one operating system family suitable for use in all PCs, from standalone workstations to the most powerful servers.

The Role of Windows NT/2000 in the Enterprise

The strength of Novell NetWare is traditionally its file and print services, which were the original reason for the development of PC networks. Windows NT still provides these services (though arguably not as well as NetWare), but it also places a much greater emphasis on being an effective application server platform.

Unlike NetWare, which is strictly a client/server platform and uses a proprietary OS at the server, Windows NT operates on a peer-to-peer model, in which each system can function both as a client and as a server. As a result, the familiar Windows interface used in all NT systems simplified its use for both users and software developers. Although applications for Windows NT were some time in coming, they tend to be easier to install and use than NetWare server applications.

At the time of NT's introduction, a NetWare server installation was largely a manual process in which you had to modify the server's configuration files in order to load the appropriate drivers. NT, on the other hand, had an automated installation program much like those of applications. While the process of setting up a NetWare network required considerable expertise, many people discovered that a reasonably savvy PC user could install the NT OS and NT applications with little difficulty. In fact, it was very likely these qualities of NT that led Novell to begin working on a more automated installation process for NetWare.

Although it took several years for the NT operating system to mature, and for large numbers of third-party developers to begin writing applications for it, many administrators began deploying it on their NetWare networks. Its favorable pricing and its ability to coexist with NetWare made NT easy to experiment with and evaluate. In the ensuing years, as Windows replaced DOS on the desktop, NT became the natural choice for high-end workstations and servers; and with the release of Windows 95, software developers were able to design 32-bit applications that ran on either operating system.

Another major factor that contributed to NT's rise in popularity was its adoption of TCP/IP as its default protocols. As the Internet grew in popularity, a market developed for a platform that was easier to use than UNIX that would run Internet and intranet server applications, and NT fit the bill nicely. Eventually, major database engines were running on Windows NT, and the similarity of the client and server platforms streamlined the development process. As it gained a reputation as an application server, NT's popularity grew to the point at which it largely replaced NetWare on business networks.

Today, most of the servers installed on new LANs run Windows NT, and the OS is also making inroads into the desktop workstation market. Until the release of Windows 2000, Microsoft intended Windows 95 and 98 for the average network workstation, and Windows NT Workstation for higher-end applications. These roles will now be filled by the forthcoming Windows Millenium, the final version of the Windows 9*x* OS, and Windows 2000 Professional, the upgrade path for Windows NT Workstation.

Versions

The first version of Windows NT (which was given the version number 3.1, to conform with the then-current version of Windows) was introduced in 1993. The motivation behind it was to create a new 32-bit OS from the ground up that left all vestiges of DOS behind. Although the interface was nearly identical in appearance to that of a Windows 3.1 system, NT was a completely new OS in many fundamental ways. Backward-compatibility with existing applications is a factor that has always hindered advances in operating system design, and once Microsoft decided that running legacy programs was not to be a priority with Windows NT, it was free to implement radical changes.

The various versions of Windows NT can be said to fall into three distinct generations, based on the user interface. The first generation consists of Windows NT 3.1, 3.5, and 3.51, all three of which use the same Windows 3.1–style interface. Version 3.1 used NetBEUI as its default protocol, which immediately limited it to use only on relatively small networks. TCP/IP and IPX support were available, but only through the STREAMS interface. Versions 3.5 and 3.51 shifted the emphasis to TCP/IP, and introduced some of the services that have come to be closely related with Windows NT, such as WINS and DHCP. At this time, there are still some servers running NT 3.51, but any machines still running 3.1 or 3.5 are way out of date, and should be upgraded.

The second generation consists of Windows NT 4.0, which was released in 1996 as an interim upgrade leading toward the major innovation that Microsoft began promising in 1993. NT 4 uses the same interface introduced in Windows 95, and positioned the OS more positively as an Internet platform with the inclusion of the Internet Explorer Web browser and Internet Information Server—a combination World Wide Web, FTP, and Gopher server.

The third generation is Windows 2000, which is the long-awaited release of the operating system that was originally code-named Cairo. The Windows 2000 interface is a refined version of the NT 4/Win95 GUI; but the biggest improvement is the inclusion of Active Directory, an enterprise directory service that represents a quantum leap over the domain-based directory service included in Windows NT.

Windows NT/2000 Products

Every version of Windows NT has been available in separate Workstation and Server editions. However, the core OS is identical in almost every way. The differences between the two are found mostly in the additional services included; the number of users supported; and, of course, the price. Windows NT 4.0 Server, for example, includes the ability to function as a domain controller (DC) for the network, and includes services like DNS, WINS, and DHCP. Windows NT 4.0 Workstation lacks all of these features, but is still able to interact with other workstations on a peer-to-peer basis. Both editions include Internet server capabilities; but while NT 4 Server includes the full IIS package, the Workstation edition includes a scaled-down version intended for intranet use, called Microsoft Peer Web Services.

There are also two special-purpose editions of Windows NT Server 4.0:

- **Windows NT Server Terminal Server Edition**   Used to deliver the Windows NT desktop to Windows-based terminals and thin clients.

- **Windows NT Server Enterprise Edition**   Provides support for large-scale, distributed applications using specialized memory allocation techniques, symmetric multiprocessing (SMP), and server clustering.

Windows 2000 has the same basic product divisions, but with different names. Windows 2000 Server is intended for servers with up to 4 processors, while the Advanced Server and DataCenter Server versions are for systems with up to 8 and up to 32 processors, respectively. The workstation edition is called Windows 2000 Professional, although it, too, has some server capabilities.

Service Packs

Microsoft releases regular updates to the Windows NT products; but unlike Novell, which has traditionally released dozens of small patches for NetWare that addressed specific, individual issues, the NT updates take the form of Service Packs—larger, cumulative updates that are all installed at the same time. The main advantage of this method is that all systems are updated in the same way. Having many separate patches means that a system could be running any number of software combinations, which makes technical support and troubleshooting difficult. Novell has since adopted the same method, calling its updates Support Packs.

Windows NT Service Packs consist of only one release for both the Server and Workstation platforms, and they are cumulative, meaning that each release contains all of the patches included in all of the previous releases for that version of the OS. This leads to the main disadvantage of Service Packs, which is their size. Service Pack 5 for Windows NT 4.0 is over 33MB in size, which makes for an inconvenient download through a dial-up connection. However, you can also order the latest Service Pack on a CD-ROM or receive them automatically as part of a Microsoft TechNet subscription, along with a wealth of other software and information.

Note   *For the network administrator who is heavily committed to the use of Microsoft products, Microsoft TechNet is a subscription-based CD-ROM product that is an invaluable resource for technical information and product updates. The monthly releases typically include six or more CD-ROMs containing Resource Kits, documentation, the entire Knowledge Base for all of the Microsoft products, and a lot of other material as well. TechNet Plus is a new service that, for an additional charge, includes the latest beta releases of the products currently under development.*

Service Packs often consist of more than just bug fixes. They may include upgraded versions of operating system utilities, new features, or entirely new programs. All of the components are installed at the same time by the Service Pack's Setup program. When you download a Service Pack from Microsoft's Web site (at www.microsoft.com/ NTServer/all/downloads.asp) or its FTP site (at ftp://ftp.microsoft.com/bussys/winnt/ winnt-public/fixes/usa), the download takes the form of a single executable archive file (like Sp5i386.exe, for Windows NT 4.0's Service Pack 5) that, when you run it, expands the archive in a temporary directory and launches the installation program. It's also possible to expand the archive without performing the installation, by running the file with the **/X** parameter, as follows:

```
SP5I386 /X
```

The command creates a directory containing the distribution files for the Service Pack, along with a standard Setup.exe installation program.

Generally speaking, it's a good idea to keep the Windows NT systems on your network up to date with the latest Service Pack. However, it's also a good idea to either test out a Service Pack release in a controlled environment or wait a month or two after its release before you install it, to see if any problems arise. Although Microsoft tests the Service Packs before releasing them, problems occasionally do slip by, as was the case with Service Pack 2 for Windows NT 4.0. Once you've decided to install a Service Pack, you should update all of the NT systems on your network, so that they're all operating with the same software.

When you add new components to a Windows NT system that has had a Service Pack installed, such as the Routing and Remote Access service or any other OS update, you must reinstall the Service Pack to ensure that all of the OS files are up to date. Windows 2000, however, includes a feature called *Service Pack Slip-Streaming,* which copies the Service Pack files to an install share and automatically substitutes the latest versions of any modules being installed with a new OS component.

Between Service Pack releases, Microsoft releases *hotfixes,* which are small, interim patch releases intended to address specific issues. You should not install every hotfix that comes along, because they will all be included in the next Service Pack release. The rule of thumb is to install a hotfix only when you have a system that is suffering from the exact problem that the patch addresses. The hotfix releases are available on Microsoft's FTP site, using the same URL previously given for the Service Packs, stored in directories with names that are relative to the last Service Pack release, such as \Hotfixes-PostSP5. Be sure to read all of the documentation included with the hotfix before you install it.

When to Upgrade

At this time, all NT-based computers, both servers and workstations, should be running Windows NT 4.0 with the latest Service Pack or Windows 2000. There are always networks with operating systems that are several versions old, but these are usually stagnant installations with permanent needs that are adequately filled by their current products and thus have no reason to change. However, if you ever install new applications or find new uses for your network, keeping your OS current will make the process of upgrading the other network components easier.

The big question, therefore, is when to upgrade from NT 4.0 to Windows 2000. This question has been weighing heavily on the minds of network administrators everywhere for years, all through the product's excruciatingly long development and testing program. All of the previous Windows NT upgrades are relatively simple affairs. At some point, many networks switched from NetBEUI to TCP/IP as their primary protocol, but this could be a gradual process. Upgrading from NT 4 to Windows 2000, however, is a considerably more complex process, due largely to the introduction of Active Directory, Windows 2000's directory service.

Note	*For more information on the Active Directory design and deployment process, see Chapter 23.*

For small- to medium-sized networks already running Windows NT 4.0, an immediate upgrade to Windows 2000 probably is not necessary, unless you have a specific need for the new features it contains. One important concern is that the new OS has substantially greater system resource requirements than earlier NT versions, meaning that hardware upgrades are likely to be needed in both servers and workstations. There is also a significant learning curve involved for server administrators, since Windows 2000 includes the new Microsoft Management Console (MMC), which performs many of the same tasks as NT 4's individual utilities, but locates the controls in different places. Fortunately, it is possible to deploy Windows 2000 on a gradual basis. The operating system, including Active Directory, can coexist with your current NT network, thus enabling you to install a single server at first and then upgrade the others.

Operating System Overview

Windows NT is a modular OS that is designed to take advantage of the advanced capabilities built into the latest Intel and Alpha processors while leaving behind the memory and storage constraints imposed by DOS-based OSs. Early OSs like DOS were *monolithic*; that is, the entire OS consisted of a single functional unit, which made it difficult to upgrade and modify. By creating an OS composed of many separate components, Microsoft has made it easier to upgrade and modify parts of the operating system without affecting other elements in the overall functionality of the whole.

 Despite a large number of new features, the fundamental architecture of Windows 2000 is quite similar to that of Windows NT, and much of the information in this section is applicable to both.

Kernel Mode Components

The NT operating system is composed of components that run in one of two modes: *kernel mode* and *user mode* (see Figure 14-1). A component running in kernel mode has full access to the system's hardware resources via the *hardware abstraction layer (HAL)*, which is a virtual interface that isolates the kernel from the computer hardware. Abstracting the kernel from the hardware makes it far easier to port the OS to different hardware platforms. While it was at one time available in versions for four processor types, the MIPS and PowerPC versions of Windows NT have been discontinued, leaving only the Alpha and Intel versions—the latter of which is by far the most popular.

The OS kernel itself is responsible for delegating specific tasks to the system processor(s) and other hardware. Tasks consist of *processes*, broken down into *threads*, which are the smallest units that the kernel can schedule for execution by a processor. A thread is a sequence of instructions to which the kernel assigns a priority level that

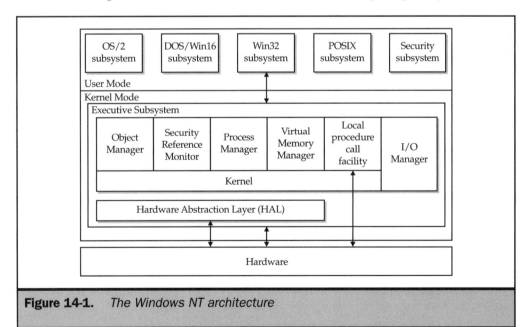

Figure 14-1. *The Windows NT architecture*

determines when it will be executed. When the computer has multiple processors, the kernel runs on all of them simultaneously, sharing access to specific memory areas and allocating threads to specific processors according to their priorities.

In addition to the HAL and the kernel, Windows NT's *executive services* also run in kernel mode. These executive services consist of the following components.

Object Manager

Windows NT creates objects that function as abstract representations of operating system resources, such as hardware devices and file system entities. An *object* consists of information about the resource it represents and a list of *methods*, which are procedures used to access the object. A file object, for example, consists of information like the file's name and methods describing the operations that can be performed on the file, such as open, close, and delete.

The Windows NT *Object Manager* maintains a hierarchical, global name space in which the objects are stored. For example, when the system loads a kernel mode device driver, it registers a device name with the Object Manager, such as \Device\CDRom0 for a CD-ROM drive or \Device\Serial0 for a serial port. The objects themselves are stored in directories similar to those in a file system, but they are not a part of any Windows NT file system. In addition to hardware devices, objects can reference both abstract and concrete entities, including the following:

- Files
- Directories
- Processes
- Threads
- Memory segments
- Semaphores

By using a standard format for all objects, regardless of the type of entities they represent, the Object Manager provides a unified interface for object creation, security, monitoring, and auditing. Access to objects in the name space is provided to system processes using *object handles*, which contain pointers to the objects and to access control information.

Usually, the only places that you see devices referred to by these object names are entries in the registry's HKEY_LOCAL_MACHINE\HARDWARE key and error messages such as those displayed in the infamous "blue screen of death." Applications typically run in the Win32 subsystem, which is a user mode component that cannot use internal Windows NT device names. Instead, the Win32 subsystem references devices using standard MS-DOS device names, like drive letters and port designations such as COM1. These MS-DOS names exist as objects in the Object Manager's name space, in a directory called \??, but they do not have the same properties as the original resources; they are actually only *symbolic links* to the equivalent NT device names.

Security Reference Monitor

Every Windows NT object has an *access control list (ACL)* that contains *access control entries (ACEs)* that specify the *security identifiers (SIDs)* of NT users or groups that are to be permitted access to the object, as well as the specific actions that the user or group can perform. When a user successfully logs on to the computer, Windows NT creates a *security access token (SAT)* that contains the SIDs of the user and all the groups of which the user is a member. Whenever the user attempts to access an object, the *Security Reference Monitor* is responsible for comparing the SAT with the ACL to determine whether the user should be granted that access.

Process Manager

The *Process Manager* is responsible for creating and deleting the process objects that enable software to run on a Windows NT system. A *process object* includes a virtual address space and a collection of resources allocated to the process, as well as threads containing the instructions that will be assigned to the system processor(s).

Virtual Memory Manager

The ability to use virtual memory is one of the major PC computing advancements introduced in the Intel 80386 processor, and Windows NT was designed around this capability. *Virtual memory* is the ability to use the computer's disk space as an extension to the physical memory installed in the machine.

Every process created on a Windows NT system by the Process Manager is assigned a virtual address space that appears to be 4GB in size. The *Virtual Memory Manager (VMM)* is responsible for mapping that virtual address space to actual system memory, as needed, in 4KB units called *pages.* When there is not enough physical memory in the computer to hold all of the pages allocated by the running processes, the VMM swaps the least recently used pages to a file on the system's hard disk drive called Pagefile.sys. This swapping process is known as *memory paging.*

Local Procedure Call Facility

The environmental subsystems that run in Windows NT's user mode (such as the Win32, DOS/Win16, and POSIX subsystems) are utilized by applications (also running in user mode) in a server/client relationship. The messages between the clients and servers are carried by the *local procedure call (LPC)* facility. Local procedure calls are essentially an internalized version of the remote procedure calls used for messaging between systems connected by a network.

When an application (functioning as a client) makes a call for a function that is provided by one of the environmental subsystems, a message containing that call is transmitted to the appropriate subsystem using LPCs. The subsystem (functioning as the server) receives the message and replies using the same type of message. The process is completely transparent to the application, which is not aware that the function is not implemented in its own code.

NETWORK OPERATING SYSTEMS

I/O Manager

The I/O Manager handles all of an NT system's input/output functions by providing a uniform environment for communication between the various drivers loaded on the machine. Using the layered architecture shown in Figure 14-2, the I/O Manager enables each driver to utilize the services of the drivers in the lower layers. For example, when an application needs to access a file on a drive, the I/O Manager passes an *I/O request packet (IRP)* generated by a file system driver down to a disk driver. Since the I/O Manager communicates with all of the drivers in the same way, the request can be satisfied without the file system having any direct knowledge of the disk device where the file is stored.

Window Manager

The Window Manager, along with the *Graphical Device Interface (GDI)*, is responsible for creating the graphical user interface used by Windows NT applications. Applications make calls to Window Manager functions in order to create architectural elements on the screen, such as buttons and windows; and in the same way, the Window Manager informs the application when the user manipulates screen elements by moving the cursor, clicking buttons, or resizing a window.

Prior to NT 4.0, the Window Manager was a user mode process, but it is now implemented as a single, kernel mode driver called Win32k.sys. This change is

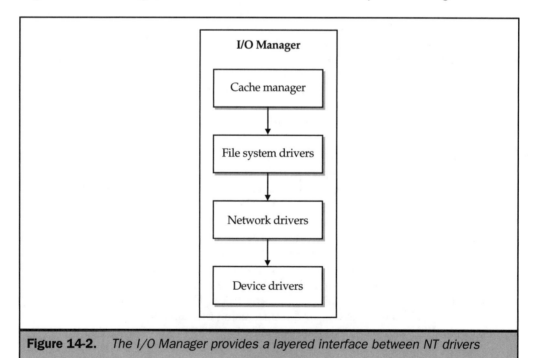

Figure 14-2. *The I/O Manager provides a layered interface between NT drivers*

invisible to application developers, but it improves graphical performance while reducing the amount of memory required.

User Mode Components

In addition to the kernel mode services, Windows NT has two types of protected subsystems that run in user mode: *environment subsystems* and *integral subsystems.* The environment subsystems enable Windows NT to run applications that were designed for various OS environments, such as Win32, OS/2, and POSIX. Integral subsystems, like the security system, perform vital OS functions. User mode subsystems are isolated from each other and from the Windows NT executive services, so that modifications to the subsystem code do not affect the fundamental operability of the OS. If a user mode component like a subsystem or application should crash, the other subsystems and the Windows NT executive services are not affected.

The Win32 Subsystem

Win32 is the primary environment subsystem in Windows NT that provides support for all native NT applications. All of the other environment subsystems included with NT are optional and loaded only when a client application needs them; but Win32 is required and runs at all times because it is responsible for handling the keyboard and mouse inputs and the display output for all of the other subsystems. Since they rely on Win32 API calls, the other environment subsystems can all be said to be clients of Win32.

The DOS/Win16 Subsystem

Unlike Windows 95 and 98, Windows NT does not run a DOS kernel, and as a result, it cannot shell out to a DOS session. Instead, NT emulates DOS using a subsystem that creates *virtual DOS machines (VDMs).* Every DOS application that you run uses a separate VDM that emulates an Intel *x*86 processor in Virtual 86 mode (even on a non-Intel system). All of the application's instructions run natively within the VDM except for I/O functions, which are emulated using *virtual device drivers (VDDs).* VDDs convert the DOS I/O functions into standard Windows NT API calls and feed them to the I/O Manager, which satisfies the calls using the standard NT device drivers.

The use of separate VDMs isolates the DOS applications from the rest of the NT system, and from any other DOS applications that may be running. If a DOS application halts, nothing other than that particular VDM will be affected. Windows NT can run as many VDMs as the installed hardware will support, and once created, VDMs are not destroyed—even when the DOS application terminates. When you execute a DOS application, the system uses an idle VDM if one is available, or creates a new VDM if one is not.

To run 16-bit applications designed for Windows 3.1, NT uses a single VDM with a single additional software layer called *Win16 on Win32,* or *WOW.* The WOW layer emulates the Windows 3.1 environment in standard mode only, not enhanced mode. If you run multiple Win16 apps, they all execute in the same VDM, and NT provides nonpreemptive multitasking between them. (The VDM itself, however, is preemptively multitasked with the other NT components.) This means that Win16 applications running on Windows NT are subject to the same problems as on Windows 3.1. It is possible for one application running on the VDM to use memory allocated for another application, and when one Win16 application crashes, all of the other Win16 apps go down with it (just like on a real Windows 3.1 system).

The OS/2 Subsystem

Windows NT includes an OS/2 subsystem that supports OS/2 1.*x* character-based applications only. It does not support the Presentation Manager or Warp applications. Unlike the other environment subsystems, OS/2 applications are supported on the Intel version of Windows NT only. However, a real mode OS/2 app that can run in a standard DOS session will run in a VDM on a non-Intel NT machine.

The POSIX Subsystem

Windows NT includes support for applications that comply to the POSIX.1 standard as defined by the IEEE Std. 1003.1-1990 document. POSIX stands for *Portable Operating System Interface for Computing Environments,* and is an attempt to create a series of APIs that facilitate the porting of applications between UNIX environments.

Excluding Subsystems

Most of the Windows NT systems installed today have no need for the OS/2 and POSIX subsystems, because they are not used to run those types of applications. At the time of NT's development, OS/2 was a contender in the OS market, but it has now all but disappeared, and the POSIX project has not become a major force either. You can configure the Windows NT installation files to omit these subsystems from your installations, thus conserving system resources.

The Windows NT installation program relies on several scripts for information about what file to copy to specific locations. These scripts are as follows:

- **Dosnet.inf**   Specifies the files and directories that the Winnt.exe (or Winnt32.exe) installation program should copy to the temporary files it creates on the workstation during the DOS mode phase of the installation process.

- **Txtsetup.inf**   Contains a list of the files that the installation program should copy to the NT system directories on the workstation during the text mode phase of the installation process.

- **Layout.inf**   Contains a list of the required files that the installation program should copy to the NT system directories on the workstation during the graphical mode phase of the installation process.

Any modifications that you make to one of these scripts should be made to all three. To exclude the OS/2 and POSIX subsystems from an NT installation, you must edit these files and comment out certain entries. In the Dosnet.inf file, comment out the following entries in the [Files] section by inserting a pound sign (#) at the beginning of each line. For the OS/2 subsystem:

```
d1,doscalls.dll
d1,netapi.os2
d1,os2.exe
d1,os2srv.exe
d1,os2ss.exe
```

For the POSIX subsystem:

```
d1,pax.exe
d1,posix.exe
d1,psxdll.dll
d1,psxss.exe
```

Then, in the Layout.inf file, comment out the following lines by inserting a semicolon (;) at the beginning of each line. For the OS/2 subsystem, comment out these lines in the [SourceDisksFiles.x86] section:

```
doscalls.dll = 1,,12800,,,,,8,0,0
netapi.os2   = 1,,248320,,,,,8,0,0,netapi.dll
os2.exe      = 1,,443904,,,,,2,1,0
os2srv.exe   = 1,,131072,,,,,2,1,0
os2ss.exe    = 1,,9216,,,,,2,1,0
```

For the POSIX subsystem, comment out these lines from the [SourceDisksFiles] section:

```
pax.exe      = 1,,54272,,,,,2,1,0
posix.exe    = 1,,68608,,,,,2,1,0
psxdll.dll   = 1,,36864,,,,,2,1,0
psxss.exe    = 1,,94208,,,,,2,1,0
```

Finally, in the Txtsetup.sif file, comment out the following lines by inserting a semicolon at the beginning of each line. For the OS/2 subsystem, comment out these lines from the [SourceDisksFiles.x86] section:

```
doscalls.dll = 1,,,,,,,8,0,0
netapi.os2   = 1,,,,,,,8,0,0,netapi.dll
```

```
os2.exe      = 1,,,,,,,2,1,0
os2srv.exe   = 1,,,,,,,2,1,0
os2ss.exe    = 1,,,,,,,2,1,0
```

For the POSIX subsystem, comment out these lines from the [SourceDisksFiles] section:

```
pax.exe      = 1,,,,,,,2,1,0
posix.exe    = 1,,,,,,,2,1,0
psxdll.dll   = 1,,,,,,,2,1,0
psxss.exe    = 1,,,,,,,2,1,0
```

To modify the default NT installation, you have to copy the Windows NT distribution files to a hard drive, edit the script files, and install NT from there, since you can't modify the installation scripts on the CD-ROM. You can use this same technique to omit other files from the installation, as well.

Services

A *service* is a program or other component that Windows NT loads with the OS, before a user logs on or sees the desktop interface. Services load automatically and permit no interference from the system user as they're loading. This is in contrast to other mechanisms that load programs automatically, such as the Startup program group. A user with appropriate rights can start, stop, and pause services using the Services Control Panel (see Figure 14-3) or the NET command, and also specify whether a particular service should load when the system starts, not load at all, or require a manual startup.

Users without administrative rights cannot control the services at all, which makes the services a useful tool for network administrators. You can, for example, configure a workstation to load a particular service at startup, and it will run whether a user logs on or not. The Server service, for example, which enables network users to access the system's shares, loads automatically by default. Even if no one logs on to the machine, it is possible to access the shares from the network.

Windows NT includes a large number of services, several of which are required for basic system functions. Some of the fundamental NT services are as follows:

- **Server** Enables the system to share drives and printers with other network systems.
- **Workstation** Enables applications running on the system to access network resources.
- **Browser** Maintains a list of the domains and the Windows computers on the network that the system uses to locate resources.
- **Messenger** Enables administrators or the Alerter service to send and receive messages, either manually or as a result of a system event.

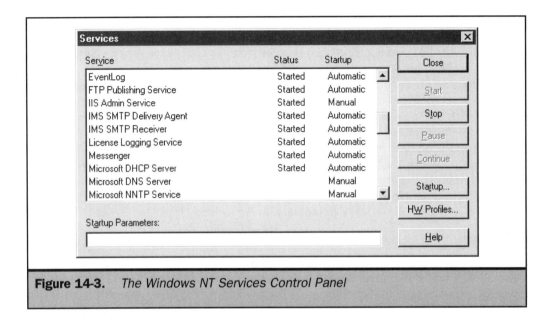

Figure 14-3.   *The Windows NT Services Control Panel*

- **Netlogon**   Enables NT workstations to locate a DC and log on to the domain. Also used by primary domain controllers (PDCs) to replicate the Security Accounts Manager (SAM) database to the backup domain controllers (BDCs). If the system does not participate in a domain, the Netlogon service does not start.

Note   *For more information on Windows NT domains, SAM replication, and the Netlogon service, see Chapter 22.*

In addition to the essential services listed previously, Windows NT includes services that are optional. Windows NT Server includes a great many more than NT Workstation; all of the network servers, such as WINS, DHCP, DNS, and IIS, all run as services. Selecting these components during the NT installation process configures the system to load the services automatically. Many third-party server applications also take the form of services that run continuously in the background.

The Windows NT Server 4.0 Resource Kit includes a utility called Srvany.exe that enables you to run any Windows NT application as a service. When you do this, the application continues to run even while the current user logs off of the system and a new user logs on. In addition, a service can run using the access permissions of a user other than the user who is currently logged on to the system. Srvany.exe itself is actually a service that you install in Windows NT using another Resource Kit utility called Instsrv.exe. Once you've installed Srvany.exe, you specify the path to the application you want to run as a service in a registry entry, which loads that application when the system starts.

File Systems

The 16-bit FAT file system is another holdover from the DOS days that the developers of Windows NT were seeking to transcend. While an adequate solution for a workstation, FAT16 cannot support the large volumes typically used on servers, and it lacks any sort of access control mechanism. As a result, the NT developers again came up with a completely new solution to their problems, without any concern for backward-compatibility. The new NT file system (NTFS) provides the advanced features needed on network servers, at the price of its complete invisibility to DOS. As a result, on Windows NT versions through 4.0, you can select either FAT16 or NTFS as the file system for each drive in the computer. Windows 2000 adds support for FAT32, the next-generation FAT file system first introduced in the OSR2 release of Windows 95, and upgrades NTFS to version 5.

FAT16

The traditional DOS file system divides a hard disk drive into volumes that are composed of uniformly sized clusters and uses a file allocation table (FAT) to keep track of the data stored in each cluster. Each directory on the drive contains a list of the files in that directory and, in addition to the filename and other attributes, specifies the entry in the FAT that represents the cluster containing the beginning of the file. That first FAT entry contains a reference to another entry that references the file's second cluster, the second entry references the third, and so on until enough clusters are allocated to store the entire file. This is known as a *FAT chain*.

Early DOS versions used FAT entries that were 12 bytes long, but DOS version 4.0 increased the size of a FAT entry to 16 bytes, and Windows NT retains this limitation. Because each cluster in a volume must be referenced by a FAT entry, a volume can have no more than 65,536 (2^{16}) clusters. Therefore, as a volume grows larger, the cluster size must increase as well, because the maximum number of clusters remains constant. The largest cluster size supported by DOS is 32KB, meaning that a volume with the maximum of 65,536 clusters at 32,768 bytes each can be no larger than 2,147,482,648 bytes or 2GB. Windows NT, however, supports clusters up to 64KB in size, meaning that a FAT volume can be up to 4GB.

Note   *It was only with the introduction of the FAT32 file system that the traditional FAT file system came to be called FAT16. In most cases, references to a FAT drive without a numerical identifier refer to a FAT16 drive.*

The other limiting factor of the FAT file system is that, as clusters grow larger, more drive space is wasted due to slack. *Slack* is the fraction of a cluster left empty when the last bit of data in a file fails to completely fill the last cluster in the chain. When 3KB of data from a file is left to store, for example, a volume with 4KB clusters will contain 1KB of slack, while a volume with 64KB clusters will waste 61KB. Windows NT is designed to be a server OS, as well as a workstation OS, and servers are naturally expected to have much larger drives. The amount of slack space and the 4GB limit on volume size are not acceptable for a server OS.

The other major shortcoming of the FAT file system is the amount of information about each file that is stored on the disk drive. In addition to the data itself, a FAT drive maintains the following information about each file:

- **Filename**   Limited to an eight-character name plus a three-character extension.
- **Attributes**   Contains four usable file attributes: Read-only, Hidden, System, and Archive.
- **Date/time**   Specifies the date and time that the file was created or last modified.
- **Size**   Specifies the size of the file, in bytes.

Unlike DOS, Windows NT was designed to be a network operating system, and any drive or directory on an NT machine can be shared with network users. To share files effectively, there must be a way to grant specific users access to them, deny access to others, and control the degree of access that is granted. The FAT file system lacks all of these features. A network server is also expected to be able to store the files generated by workstations running other operating systems, files that may use different formats, attributes, and naming conventions. Windows NT improves on the FAT system by enabling files and directories to have names up to 255 characters long, but it cannot provide additional attributes and other elements.

Why Use FAT?

All of this discussion about the deficiencies of the FAT file system raises the question of why Windows NT includes FAT support in the first place, if it is so lacking in the features required for an advanced network OS. One reason is to facilitate access of a computer's drives by other OSs. Windows NT's FAT implementation, despite minor improvements, is wholly compatible with DOS and all DOS-based OSs, including Windows 95 and 98. You can create FAT partitions on NT systems using DOS's standard FDISK and FORMAT tools, as well as with NT's Disk Administrator utility.

ACCESSIBILITY   If you boot a Windows NT system with a DOS boot disk, you can still access the drives, as long as they use the FAT file system. You won't see the long file and directory names, but you can still work with the directories and files using their 8.3 equivalents. You can also use standard FAT disk repair and maintenance tools on Windows NT FAT drives, like Norton Disk Doctor for disk repair and Norton Speed Disk for defragmentation. NTFS drives, on the other hand, are completely invisible to other OSs, such as DOS and Windows 9*x*. When you boot an NT system with NTFS drives using a DOS boot disk, it is as if there are no drives installed in the machine at all. You cannot manipulate the partitions using FDISK or use FAT file system repair tools.

MULTIBOOTING   Quite a few NT systems, especially in lab and classroom environments, are configured with multiple operating systems, and the NT Boot Manager enables a user to select the OS to load as the system starts. When you dual-boot NT with Windows 9x or DOS, at least the boot partition must use the FAT file system to read the non-NT boot files.

To create a multiboot configuration using NT's Boot Manager, you start by installing Windows 9x or DOS on the system in the usual manner. (If you plan to dual-boot with Windows 3.1 or Windows for Workgroups, only the underlying DOS installation is critical at this point, since the 16-bit Windows versions are actually environments that run on top of DOS.) Then, when you launch the Windows NT installation program (Winnt.exe), the Boot Manager will retain the existing OS boot files and add an entry into the boot menu for the Previous Operating System on C:. Once the NT installation is completed, the boot menu enables you to select either Windows NT or the previous OS whenever you boot the machine.

INSTALLING NT USING A FAT DRIVE   Another good reason for using the FAT file system is to facilitate the installation of Windows NT. When installing NT on a new machine, the process goes more quickly if you start with a FAT drive on which you can store the system's boot files. Otherwise, you have to boot the system using the three NT boot disks, which is much more inconvenient. If you have no reason to continue using FAT after the installation is completed, you can convert the drive to NTFS during the installation process, or at any time thereafter.

NTFS

NTFS is the file system intended for use on Windows NT systems. Without it, you cannot implement the file and directory-based permissions needed to secure a drive for network use. Because it uses a completely different structure than FAT drives, you cannot create NTFS drives using the FDISK utility, but the version of FDISK included with Windows 9x is able to identify NTFS drives and delete them (as it can other types of non-DOS partitions).

In the NTFS file system, files take the form of *objects* that consist of a number of *attributes.* Unlike DOS, in which the term "attribute" typically refers only to the Read-only, System, Hidden, and Archive flags, NTFS treats all of the information regarding the file as an attribute, including the flags, the dates, the size, the filename, and even the file data itself. NTFS also differs from FAT in that the attributes are stored with the file, instead of in a separate directory listing.

The equivalent structure to the FAT on an NTFS drive is called the *Master File Table (MFT).* Unlike FAT, however, the MFT contains more than just pointers to other locations on the disk. In the case of relatively small files (up to approximately 1,500 bytes), all of the attributes are included in the MFT, including the file data. When larger amounts of data need to be stored, additional disk clusters called *extents* are allocated, and pointers are included with the file's attributes in the MFT. The attributes stored in the MFT are called *resident attributes*; those stored in extents are *nonresident attributes*.

In addition to the four standard DOS file attributes, an NTFS file includes a Compression flag; two dates/times specifying when the file was created and when it was last modified; and a security descriptor that identifies the owner of the file, lists the users and groups that are permitted to access it, and specifies what access they are to be granted.

Creating NTFS Drives

When you install Windows NT, you can select either an existing volume for the OS or create a new partition out of free space on the drive. The existing volume can use either the FAT or the NTFS file system; and if you choose a FAT drive, you can elect to convert it to NTFS during the installation process. You can also install NT on a FAT volume and convert it to NTFS at any later time. However, NT does not provide the ability to convert an NTFS drive to FAT.

To create a new NTFS drive on a Windows NT system, you can use the Format utility in Windows NT Explorer or the FORMAT command-line utility. In both cases, you can format only hard drives, not floppy disks. As with the DOS FORMAT command, this process is destructive and will erase any data that is currently stored on the drive. To convert a FAT drive to NTFS without destroying the data, you use the Convert.exe utility from the command line, with syntax like the following:

```
CONVERT C: /FS:NTFS
```

When the Convert.exe utility cannot gain exclusive access to the drive to be converted (such as when the \Winnt directory is located on the drive), the file system conversion is performed during the next system reboot.

FAT32

As hard disk drive capacities grew over the years, the limitations of the FAT file system became more of a problem. To address the problem, Microsoft created a file system that uses 32-bit FAT entries instead of 16-bit ones. The larger entries mean that there can be more clusters on a drive. The results are that the maximum size of a FAT32 volume is 2 terabytes (or 2,048GB) instead of 2GB for a FAT16 drive, and the clusters can be much smaller, thus reducing the wastage due to slack space.

The FAT32 file system was introduced in the Windows 95 OSR2 release, and is also included in Windows 98 and Windows 2000. However, Windows NT 4.0 does not support it. You cannot access a FAT32 drive from Windows NT, nor can you boot an NT system from a FAT32 drive. If you want to be able to boot multiple OSs on a single PC, you must format the boot drive using FAT16. The FDISK utility included in Windows 95 OSR2 and Windows 98 prompts you to specify whether or not you want to enable large disk support whenever you load the program. When you answer Yes, FDISK uses FAT32 to create volumes on the system's drives; answering No causes the program to create FAT16 drives, with the standard size limitation.

Note
While Windows NT 4.0 itself cannot access FAT32 drives, there are third-party utilities that make it possible to access existing FAT32 volumes from within Windows NT. FAT32 for Windows NT 4.0, by System Internals, is available in two versions. The freeware version can read FAT32 drives, and the registered version can both read and write to FAT32 drives. In both cases, the program does not make it possible to create new FAT32 volumes, only to read existing ones; and FAT32 still cannot be used on the drive where Windows NT is installed, since support for the new file system is not provided during the system boot process. You can download the freeware version of FAT32 for Windows NT 4.0 or register the full version at www.sysinternals.com/fat32.htm.

FAT32 supports larger volumes and smaller clusters, but it does not provide any appreciable change in performance; and it still does not have the access control capabilities needed for network servers, as NTFS does. For any Windows NT or 2000 system with drives that you plan to share with network users, you should use NTFS to protect the files against unauthorized access or accidental damage.

The Registry

The registry is the database where Windows NT and 2000 store nearly all of their system configuration data. As a system or network administrator, you'll be working with the registry in a variety of ways, since many of the Windows NT/2000 configuration tools function by modifying entries in the registry. The registry is a hierarchical database that is displayed in most registry editor applications as an expandable tree, not unlike a directory tree. At the root of the tree are five containers, called *keys,* with the following names:

- **HKEY_CLASSES_ROOT**   Contains information on file associations; that is, associations between filename extensions and applications.

- **HKEY_CURRENT_USER**   Contains configuration information specific to the user currently logged on to the system. This key is the primary component of a user profile.

- **HKEY_LOCAL_MACHINE**   Contains information on the hardware and software installed in the computer, the system configuration, and the SAM database. The entries in this key apply to all users of the system.

- **HKEY_USERS**   Contains information on the currently loaded user profiles, including the profile for the user that is currently logged on and the default user profile.

- **HKEY_CURRENT_CONFIG**   Contains hardware profile information used during the system boot sequence. This key is not found in Windows NT versions 3.51 and earlier.

In most cases, you work with the entries in the HKEY_LOCAL_MACHINE and HKEY_CURRENT_USER keys (often abbreviated as the HKLM and HKCU, respectively) when you configure an NT system. When the keys are saved as files, as in the case of user profiles, they're often referred to as *hives.* When you expand one of these keys, you see a series of *subkeys,* often in several layers. The keys and subkeys function as organizational containers for the registry *entries,* which contain the actual configuration data for the system. A registry entry consists of three components: the *value name,* the *value type,* and the *value* itself.

The value name identifies the entry for which a value is specified. The value type specifies the nature of the data stored in the entry, such as whether it contains a binary value, an alphanumeric string of a given size, or multiple values. The value types found in the registry are as follows:

- **REG_SZ**   Indicates that the value consists of a string of alphanumeric characters. Many of the user-configurable values in the registry are of this type.

- **REG_DWORD**   Indicates that the value consists of a 4-byte numerical value used to specify information like device parameters, service values, and other numeric configuration parameters.

- **REG_MULTI_SZ**   Same as the REG_SZ value type, except that the entry contains multiple string values.

- **REG_EXPAND_SZ**   Same as the REG_SZ value type, except that the entry contains a variable (such as *%SystemRoot%*) that must be replaced when the value is accessed by an application.

- **REG_BINARY**   Indicates that the value consists of raw binary data, usually used for hardware configuration information. You should not modify these entries manually unless you are familiar with the function of every binary bit in the value.

- **REG_FULL_RESOURCE_DESCRIPTOR**   Indicates that the value holds configuration data for hardware devices in the form of an information record with multiple fields.

The registry hierarchy is large and complex and the names of its keys and entries are often cryptic. Locating the correct entry can be difficult, and the values are often less than intuitive. When you edit the registry manually, you must be careful to supply the correct value for the correct entry or the results can be catastrophic. An incorrect registry modification can halt the system or prevent it from booting, forcing you to reinstall NT.

Because of the registry's sensitivity to improper handling, selecting the proper tool to modify it is crucial. The tradeoff in NT's registry editing tools is between a safe, easy-to-use interface with limited registry access, and comprehensive access using a less intuitive interface. The following sections examine the various registry editing tools included with Windows NT.

NETWORK OPERATING SYSTEMS

The Control Panel

Although it isn't evident from the interface, most of the functions in the Control Panel work by modifying settings in the registry. The Control Panel's graphical interface provides users with simplified access to the registry and prevents them from introducing incorrect values due to typographical errors. You can also use NT's security mechanisms to prevent unauthorized access to certain registry settings through the Control Panel. The main disadvantage of using the Control Panel to modify the registry is that it provides user access to only a small fraction of the registry's settings.

Note *Much of the Control Panel's functionality is duplicated in the Web Administrator for Windows NT Server 4.0 utility, which uses IIS on the server to publish the Control Panel functionality as a Web page that you can access from any Web browser (with the appropriate permissions). Web Administrator is available from Microsoft's Web site at www.microsoft.com/ntserver/nts/downloads/management/NTSWebAdmin.*

The System Policy Editor

System policies are collections of registry settings saved in a *policy file* that you can configure an NT system to load whenever a user logs on to the system or the network. You can create different sets of policies for each of your network users, so that when John Doe logs on to a workstation, his customized registry settings are downloaded to the system and loaded automatically. Windows NT includes a tool called the System Policy Editor that you can use to create policy files; you can also use it to modify the registry directly. Like the Control Panel, the System Policy Editor uses a graphical interface to set registry values (see Figure 14-4), but it is far more configurable than the Control Panel and can provide access to a great many more registry entries.

Note *For more information on using system policies as a network administration tool, see Chapter 27.*

The system policies that the System Policy Editor lists in its hierarchical display are derived from a file called a *policy template.* The template is an ASCII text file with an .adm extension that uses a special format to define how each policy should appear in the System Policy Editor and which registry settings each policy should modify. Windows NT includes several template files that define policies for a wide range of system settings, some of which are also configurable through the Control Panel. Because creating a new system policy is simply a matter of creating a new template, software developers can include with their products template files that define application-specific system policies. You can also create your own templates to modify other registry settings.

The process of setting values for a system policy by using the System Policy Editor consists of navigating through the hierarchical display and selecting a policy. Some

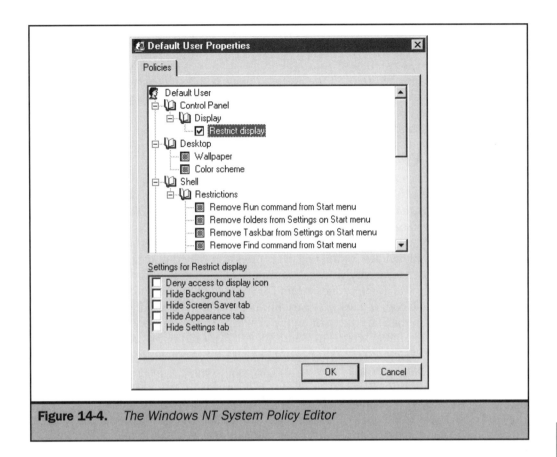

Figure 14-4. *The Windows NT System Policy Editor*

policies consist of a single feature that you can toggle on and off, while others have additional controls in the form of check boxes, pull-down menus, or data entry fields. To create a policy file, you select the policies you want to set, specify values for them, and then save them to a file with a .pol extension.

The System Policy Editor can also directly modify the Windows registry, however. When you select File | Open Registry, the program connects to the registry on the local machine. When you configure a policy, the program applies the necessary changes directly to the registry. In addition, when you choose File | Connect, you can select another Windows NT, 2000, or 9x computer on the network and modify its registry from your remote location.

To access the registry on a Windows 95 or 98 machine from a remote location, the system must be running the Remote Registry service and be configured for user-level access control.

The use of customizable template files makes the System Policy Editor a far more comprehensive registry-editing tool than the Control Panel. You can specify values for a wider range of registry entries, while still retaining the advantages of the graphical interface. Because the changes that the System Policy Editor makes to the registry are controlled by the policy template, the possibility of a misspelled value in a data entry field still exists, but the chances of an incorrect value damaging the system is far less than when editing the registry manually.

The Registry Editors

Windows NT includes two Registry Editors, called Regedt32.exe and Regedit.exe, that provide direct access to the entire registry. There are many Windows NT features that you can configure using the Registry Editors that are not accessible by any other administrative interface. These programs are the most powerful and comprehensive means of modifying registry settings in NT, and also the most dangerous. These editors do not supply friendly names for the registry entries and they do not use pull-down menus or check boxes to specify values. You must locate (or create) the correct entry and supply the correct value in the proper format, or the results can be wildly unpredictable. Windows NT installs both of these Registry Editors with the OS, but it does not create shortcuts for them in the Start menu or on the desktop. You must launch the Registry Editors from the Run dialog box, from Windows NT Explorer, or by creating your own shortcuts. Like the System Policy Editor, both Registry Editors enable you to connect to another Windows system on the network and access its registry.

The Regedit.exe editor (see Figure 14-5) was designed for use with Windows 95, but it was included with Windows NT because it has two important features that Regedt32.exe inexplicably lacks. The program uses an Explorer-like interface that displays an expandable tree of registry keys and subkeys in the left pane. When you select a subkey, the entries it contains are displayed in the right pane. Regedit.exe enables you to make most standard modifications to registry settings as well as create and delete keys and entries, but it lacks certain NT-specific features found in Regedt32.exe, such as the ability to manage registry permissions and support for the REG_MULTI_SZ and REG_EXPAND_SZ value types.

The advantages of using Regedit.exe are that you can search for a string anywhere in the registry, including keys, entries, and their values, while Regedt32.exe can search the keys only. This is an important feature, because it enables you to locate a particular key by searching for its current value. If, for example, you want to know where the system's IP address is stored, you can search for the current address in Regedit.exe to find the correct key. In Regedt32.exe, you have to either find the key by manually browsing through the registry or use a registry reference, such as a book or the Regentry.hlp file included with the Windows NT Server 4.0 Resource Kit.

The other feature found exclusively in Regedit.exe is the ability to import and export registry information using text files with .reg extensions, called *registry scripts*. These scripts contain registry entries along with all of the information associated with

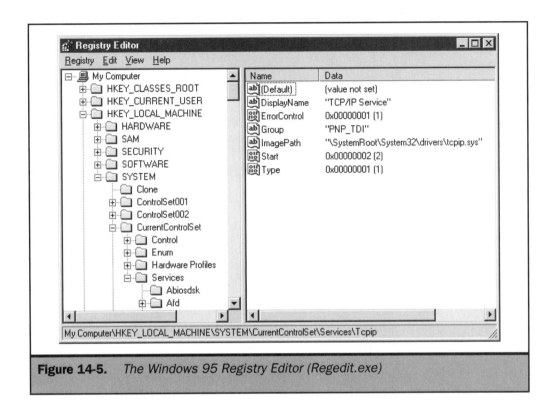

Figure 14-5.   *The Windows 95 Registry Editor (Regedit.exe)*

them, including their locations in the key hierarchy, their value types, and the values themselves. You can select a key at any level in the hierarchy and create a script containing all of the entries and subkeys it contains. You can then apply those registry settings to another machine by running the script with the Regedit.exe program from the NT command prompt. Because you can run scripts from the command line, this capability makes Regedit.exe an excellent tool for network administrators wanting to configure workstations using batch files.

Note   *Regedt32.exe can save the contents of a key to a text file, but the output file is not formatted in such a way that you can apply the settings automatically to another machine, nor can you run Regedt32.exe from the command line.*

Regedt32.exe (see Figure 14-6) is the Registry Editor designed for use with Windows NT 3.*x*. The program opens a separate window for each of the top-level keys in the registry that enables you to navigate through each key independently, to locate the desired entries. Regedt32.exe provides more display options than Regedit.exe; you can view values in binary, decimal, or hexadecimal notation and choose to see the registry

NETWORK OPERATING SYSTEMS

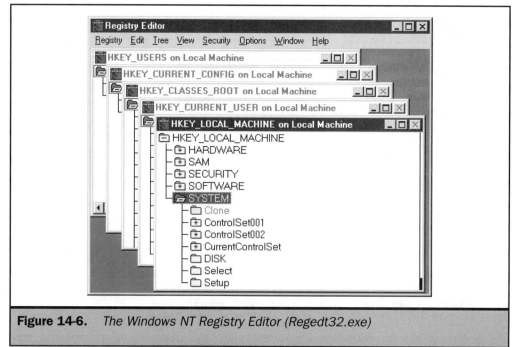

Figure 14-6.   *The Windows NT Registry Editor (Regedt32.exe)*

tree, the data contained in it, or both. When Windows NT is installed on an NTFS drive, Regedt32.exe also enables you to manage permissions for individual registry keys. Just as with file system permissions, you can grant specific users and groups various degrees of access to registry keys and their subkeys.

The Windows NT Networking Architecture

Networking is an integral part of Windows NT, and the OS uses a modular networking architecture that provides a great deal of flexibility for the network administrator. While not perfectly analogous to the OSI reference model, the NT networking architecture is structured in layers that provide interchangeability of modules such as network adapter drivers and protocols. The basic structure of the networking stack is shown in Figure 14-7.

Windows NT relies on two primary interfaces to separate the basic networking functions, called the *NDIS interface* and *Transport Driver Interface (TDI)*. Between these two interfaces are the protocol suites that provide transport services between computers on the network: TCP/IP, NetBEUI, and IPX. Although they have different features, these three sets of protocols are interchangeable when it comes to basic networking services. A Windows NT system can use any of these protocols or all of them simultaneously; the TDI and NDIS interfaces enable the components operating above and below them to address whichever protocol is needed to perform a particular task.

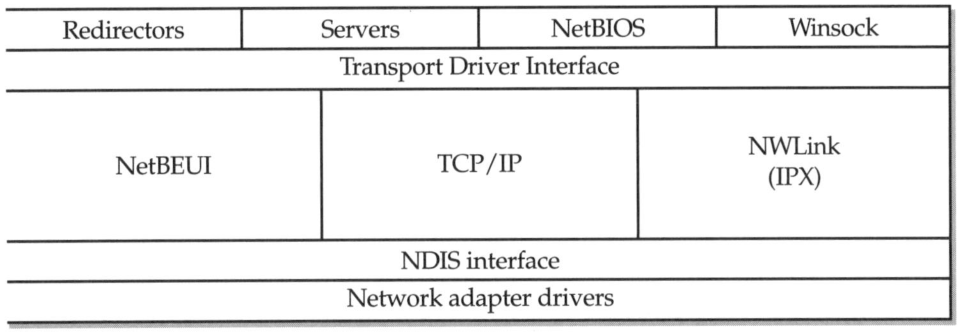

Redirectors	Servers	NetBIOS	Winsock
Transport Driver Interface			
NetBEUI	TCP/IP		NWLink (IPX)
NDIS interface			
Network adapter drivers			

Figure 14-7.   *The Windows NT networking architecture*

For example, on a system with all three protocols loaded, a request for access to an Internet server generated by a Web browser utilizes the TCP/IP protocol, while an application trying to access a Novell NetWare server will use IPX. For applications that can use any of the protocols, the order in which the protocols are bound to the service determines which one the application uses.

 For more information on the protocols used by Windows NT, see Chapters 11, 12, and 13 for coverage of TCP/IP, IPX, and NetBEUI, respectively.

The NDIS Interface

The Network Driver Interface Specification (NDIS) is a standard developed jointly by Microsoft and 3Com that defines an interface between the network-layer protocols and the media access control (MAC) sublayer of the data link–layer protocol. On a Windows NT system, the NDIS interface lies between the network adapter drivers and the protocol drivers. Protocols do not communicate directly with the network adapter; instead, they go through the NDIS interface. This enables an NT system to have any number of network adapters and any number of protocols installed, and any protocol can communicate with any adapter.

NDIS is implemented on a Windows NT system in two parts: the *NDIS wrapper* (Ndis.sys) and the *NDIS MAC driver*. The NDIS wrapper is not device specific; it contains common code that surrounds the MAC drivers and provides the interface between the network adapter drivers and the protocol drivers installed in the computer. This replaces the Protocol Manager (PROTMAN) used by other NDIS versions to regulate access to the network adapter.

NETWORK OPERATING SYSTEMS

The NDIS MAC driver is device specific, and provides the code needed for the system to communicate with the network interface adapter. This includes the mechanism for selecting the hardware resources the device uses, such as the IRQ and I/O port address. All of the network interface adapters in a Windows NT 4.0 system must have an NDIS version 3.0 driver, which is provided by virtually all of the manufacturers producing NICs today.

The Transport Driver Interface

The TDI performs roughly the same function as the NDIS wrapper, but higher up in the networking stack. The TDI functions as the interface between the protocol drivers and the components operating above them, such as the server and the redirector. Traffic moving up and down the stack passes through the interface and can be directed to any of the installed protocols or other components.

Above the TDI, Windows NT has several more components that applications use to access network resources in various ways, using the TDI as the interface to the protocol drivers. Because Windows NT is a peer-to-peer operating system, there are components that handle traffic running in both directions. The most basic of these components are the *Workstation* and *Server* services, which enable the system to access network resources and provide network clients with access to local resources (respectively). Also at this layer are *application programming interfaces (APIs),* such as NetBIOS and Windows Sockets, which provide applications running on the system special access to certain network resources.

The Workstation Service

When you open a file or print a document in an application, the process is the same whether the file or printer is on the local system or on the network, as far as the user and the application are concerned. The Workstation service determines whether the requested file or printer is local or on the network and sends the request to the appropriate driver. By providing access to network resources in this way, the Workstation service is essentially the client half of Windows NT's client/server capability.

The Workstation service consists of two modules: Services.exe, the Service Control Manager, which functions as the user mode interface for all services; and Rdr.sys, the Windows network redirector. When an application requests access to a file, the request goes to the I/O Manager, which passes it to the appropriate file system driver. Depending on what file systems the computer's drives use, there may be NTFS or FAT file system drivers installed on the machine, or both. The *redirector* is also a file system driver; but instead of providing access to a local drive, the redirector transmits the request down through the protocol stack to the appropriate network resource. The I/O Manager treats a redirector no differently from any other file system drivers. Windows NT installs a redirector for the Microsoft Windows network by default, but client software for other network operating systems (like Novell NetWare) can include additional redirectors.

The Multiple UNC Provider

In the case of a system with multiple network clients (and multiple redirectors), Windows NT uses one of two mechanisms for determining which redirector it should use, depending on how an application formats its requests for network resources. The Multiple UNC Provider (MUP) is used for applications that use Uniform Naming Convention (UNC) names to specify the desired resource, and the Multi-Provider Router (MPR) is used for applications that use Win32 network APIs.

The UNC defines the format that Windows NT uses for identifying network resources. UNC names take the following form:

   *server**share*

On a Windows network, the server can be any Windows system, and the share can be any shared drive. On a NetWare network, the *server* and *share* variables correspond to a NetWare server and one of its volumes. When you browse through the shares displayed in the Network Neighborhood and select a file, the system returns a UNC path name whether the file is located on a Windows network share, a Novell NetWare server, or even a local drive. The function of the MUP is to determine which type of resource hosts the file and send the request to the appropriate redirector.

The MUP is implemented as a file called Mup.sys and functions using a trial-and-error method in which it sends the requested UNC name to each of the redirectors on the system in turn and awaits a response from each one. Once the replies are received, the MUP selects the appropriate redirector and transmits the request. If there is only one redirector on the system, obviously this process is simple. If there are two or more redirectors, then it's possible for a resource of the same name to exist on both server types. For example, while you can't have two NT systems with the same NetBIOS name on one network, you can have NT and NetWare servers with the same name. Because of the confusion it can cause, this is a practice that you should generally try to avoid.

If the MUP receives positive responses from two (or more) redirectors, indicating that the requested resource exists on both networks, it sends the request to the redirector with the highest priority. You specify the network priorities in the Network Access Order field in the Network Control Panel's Services page.

The MUP maintains a cache of the UNC names that it has processed within the last 15 minutes, which it consults before sending requested names to any of the redirectors. If it finds the name in the cache, it uses the redirector associated with that name. If the name is not in the cache, the MUP sends the requests to the redirectors *synchronously*, meaning that the MUP sends the request to the redirector with the highest priority and waits for a response before it sends the request to the redirector with the next highest priority.

In some cases, this behavior can result in significant delays while accessing network resources. Prior to the Windows NT 4.0 Service Pack 4 release, the MUP always waited until all of the redirectors had responded to the request before selecting the one that should process it. If the UNC name in question refers to a NetWare server volume, for example, the request has to go through the entire NetBIOS name resolution procedure for the Windows network redirector needlessly. This name resolution procedure, by default, includes repeated broadcast transmissions and WINS server queries, all of which must time out and fail (a process that can take 30 seconds or more) before the request is sent to the NetWare redirector. Service Pack 4 modifies the Mup.sys module so that a request receiving a positive response from the redirector with the highest priority is sent immediately to that redirector for processing.

The Multi-Provider Router

For applications that request access to network resources using the Win32 network APIs (also known as the WNet APIs), the Multi-Provider Router determines which redirector should process the requests. In addition to a redirector, a network client installed on an NT system includes a *provider DLL* that functions as an interface between the MPR and the redirector. The MPR passes the requests that it receives from applications to the appropriate provider DLLs, which pass them to the redirectors.

The Server Service

Just as the Workstation service provides NT's network client capabilities, the Server service enables other clients on the network to access the system's local resources. When the redirector on a client system transmits a request for access to a file on a server, the receiving system passes the request up the protocol stack to the Server service. The Server service is a file system driver (called Srv.sys) that is started by the Service Control Manager, just like the Workstation service, that operates just above the TDI. When the Server service receives a request for access to a file, it generates a read request and sends it to the appropriate local file system driver (such as the NTFS or FAT driver) through the I/O Manager. The local file system driver accesses the requested file in the usual manner and returns it to the Server service, which transmits it across the network to the client. The Server service also provides support for printer sharing, as well as remote procedure calls (RPCs) and named pipes, which are other mechanisms used by applications to communicate over the network.

Bindings

For traffic to pass up and down the protocol stack, the components operating at the various layers must be bound together to form an unbroken path through the stack. In Windows NT, adapter drivers must be bound to protocol drivers, and protocol drivers must be bound to services, for communications to occur. By default, all of the components installed in Windows NT are bound to each other, meaning that all of the installed network adapters are bound to all of the installed protocols, and likewise with the protocols and the services. This makes it possible for a message traveling up or down the stack to take a variety of different paths.

Windows NT also recognizes the order in which the components are bound, and establishes priorities based on that order. If, for example, all of the systems on your network have both the TCP/IP and NetBEUI protocols installed, a request for access to a file on a network share can conceivably use either protocol. The redirector handling the request sends it to all of the available protocol drivers and then selects the protocol with the highest priority that was able to process the request successfully.

On the Bindings page of the Network Control Panel (see Figure 14-8), you can manage the bindings between the installed networking components, creating and deleting bindings and modifying their priorities. The Show Bindings For selector enables you to display the binding information organized by component type: services, protocols, or adapters. By disabling specific bindings, you can eliminate the delays caused by components such as the Server service that have to select from among multiple protocols. If, for example, you use the modem on an NT system exclusively for connecting to the Internet, you can disable the binding between the NetBEUI protocol and the Remote Access WAN Wrapper, which is the adapter driver representing the modem, because only the TCP/IP protocol driver is needed.

Using the Move Up and Move Down buttons, you can control the priority of the bindings. Moving the TCP/IP protocol above the NetBEUI protocol for a particular service, for example, will ensure that the service always uses TCP/IP when both protocols are

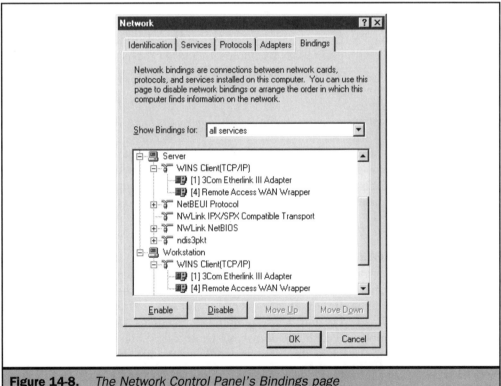

Figure 14-8.   *The Network Control Panel's Bindings page*

available. NetBEUI is used only when the attempt to connect via TCP/IP fails. To set the default protocol for the system, you display the bindings by service and move the desired protocol to the top of the list for both the Server and Workstation services.

APIs

Services are not the only components that interact with the TDI on a Windows NT system. APIs, like NetBIOS and Windows Sockets, also send and receive data through the TDI, enabling certain types of applications to communicate with other network systems without using the Server and Workstation services. NT also supports other APIs that operate higher up in the stack and use the standard services to reach the TDI.

NetBIOS

NetBIOS is an integral component of Microsoft Windows networking, because it provides the name space used to identify the domains, computers, and shares on the network. Because of its dependence on NetBIOS, Windows NT supports it in all of its protocols. NetBEUI is inherently designed for use with NetBIOS communications, and the NetBIOS over TCP/IP (NetBT) standards defined by the Internet Engineering Task Force (IETF) enable its use with the TCP/IP protocols. NWLink, the Windows NT implementation of the IPX protocols, also supports NetBIOS. Windows 2000, while remaining compatible with previous NT versions, relies on DNS names to identify network resources.

Note *For more information on Windows NT's use of NetBIOS and NetBT, see Chapter 19. For more information on NetBEUI and NetBIOS messaging, see Chapter 13.*

In addition to the NetBIOS name space and messaging, Windows NT also supports applications that are designed to use the NetBIOS interface for network communications directly. These applications are relatively rare these days, but NT supports them using a NetBIOS emulator that runs on top of the TDI in kernel mode and the user mode NetBIOS API provided by the Netapi32.dll module.

Windows Sockets

The Windows Sockets specification defines one of the APIs that is most commonly used by applications, because it is the accepted standard for Internet network access. Web browsers, FTP clients, and other Internet client and server applications all use Windows Sockets (Winsock) to gain access to network resources. Unlike NetBIOS, Winsock does not support all of the Windows NT protocols. While it can be used with NWLink (IPX), the overwhelming majority of Winsock applications use TCP/IP exclusively. As with NetBIOS, Winsock is implemented in Windows NT as a kernel mode emulator just above the TDI, and a user mode driver, called Wsock32.dll.

Optional Windows NT Services

In addition to its core services, Windows NT, particularly in its Server version, includes a large collection of optional services that you can choose to install either with the OS or at any time afterward. Some of these services are discussed in the following sections.

Gateway Services for NetWare

In addition to the default Microsoft Windows network client, Windows NT includes a client that enables the system to connect to Novell NetWare servers. NetWare connectivity has been a sore point for Windows NT for several years. Both Microsoft and Novell have provided NetWare clients for NT since soon after its release; but for several years, both clients were limited in their capabilities as well as their performance. Microsoft's own NetWare client provided adequate connectivity, but early versions did not support Novell Directory Services (NDS) connections. The NetWare client in Windows NT 4.0 does support NDS, but it does not provide the full NetWare administration capabilities of Novell's own client for Windows NT.

Note *Novell's client for Windows NT provided NDS support long before Microsoft's client did, and to this day, you must use the Novell client to administer an NDS tree using the NetWare Administrator utility. For more information on the Novell Client for Windows NT, see Chapter 17.*

There are two variants of the NT client for NetWare: NT Workstation includes the Client Services for NetWare (CSNW), and NT Server includes the Gateway Services for NetWare (GSNW). Both of these services provide basic NetWare connectivity in the form of a redirector that enables you to log in to an NDS tree, connect to NetWare servers, and access NetWare volumes and printers in the same manner as Windows network resources. Once connected, you can map drive letters to NetWare volumes or reference them directly using either NetWare notation (*server:volume*) or the standard UNC notation used by Windows NT (*server**volume*).

GSNW is a superset of CSNW that includes the ability to provide Windows network clients with access to NetWare volumes without their having to run a NetWare client themselves. In the GSNW Control Panel (see Figure 14-9), you can use the NetWare client to connect to specific volumes on NetWare servers and publish them as Windows network shares. Other systems on the network see these volumes as shares on the NT server, and can access them as such. These client systems do not have to be running a NetWare client themselves, because the NT server functions as a gateway to the NetWare server.

The use of an NT server as a gateway to NetWare resources is a convenience, but is generally not a solution that is suitable for heavy use. Unless both the NT server and the network connection between the NT server and the NetWare servers are fast enough to support the combined traffic generated by a large number of users, the NT server can end up being a bottleneck that slows down network communications.

NETWORK OPERATING SYSTEMS

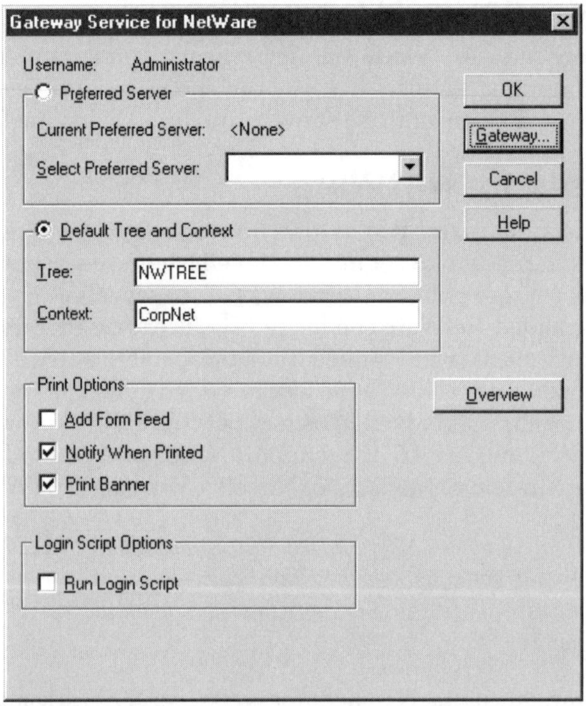

Figure 14-9. *The GSNW Control Panel*

Microsoft DHCP Server

Unlike NetBEUI and IPX, using the TCP/IP protocols on a network requires that each computer be configured with a unique IP address, as well as other important settings. A Dynamic Host Configuration Protocol (DHCP) server is an application designed to automatically supply client systems with TCP/IP configuration settings as needed, thus eliminating a tedious manual network administration chore. For more information about DHCP, see Chapter 18.

Windows Internet Naming Service

Windows Internet Naming Service (WINS) is another service that supports the use of TCP/IP on a Windows network. Windows networks identify systems using NetBIOS names; but in order to transmit a packet to a machine with a given name using TCP/IP, the sender must first discover the IP address associated with that name. WINS is essentially a database server that stores the NetBIOS names of the systems on the network and their associated IP addresses. When a system wants to transmit, it sends a query to a WINS server containing the NetBIOS name of the destination system, and the WINS server replies with its IP address. For more information on NetBIOS naming and NetBEUI, see Chapter 19.

Microsoft DNS Server

The Domain Name System performs a function similar to WINS, in that it facilitates the use of familiar names for computers on a TCP/IP network instead of the IP addresses that they use to communicate. Designed for use on the Internet, DNS servers resolve domain names (Internet domain names, not NT domain names) into IP addresses, either by consulting their own records or by forwarding the request to another DNS server. The DNS server included with Windows NT 4.0 enables an NT server to function on the Internet in this capacity. The role of the DNS is greatly expanded in Windows 2000, however. Windows 2000's Active Directory uses the Microsoft DNS Server instead of WINS to store information about the NT domains on the local network. For more information on the Microsoft DNS Server and its roles on Windows NT and 2000 networks, see Chapter 20.

Routing and Remote Access Server

Windows NT has always included multiprotocol routing capabilities as part of the OS. When two network interfaces are installed in the computer, in the form of either NICs or modem connections, traffic using any of the supported protocols can pass through the system, thus connecting two network segments to form an internetwork. Microsoft later released an additional service for NT 4.0 that enhances NT's routing capabilities, called the *Routing and Remote Access Server (RRAS)*.

RRAS provides NT with the ability to support more complex routing configurations, such as those using WAN and dial-up connections. The service includes dial-on-demand capability, the Open Shortest Path First (OSPF) routing protocol, virtual private networking support using the Point-to-Point Tunneling Protocol (PPTP), and a graphical utility for managing the NT routing table and network connections. For more information on routing and the RRAS service, see Chapter 6.

Distributed File System

The Microsoft Distributed File System (DFS) is a service for Windows NT 4.0 and Windows 2000 that enables you to create a virtual directory tree that is comprised of shared drives or directories located anywhere on the network. Instead of users having to browse to the correct server to find a particular file, they can access all of the share's files from a single DFS tree. There are several advantages to this arrangement, as follows:

- Users are insulated from the actual, physical locations of the files.

- Administrators can relocate files to other volumes or servers without altering the DFS directory structure seen by users.

- The file server traffic load can be distributed among several servers, improving overall network performance.

- A DFS tree can provide fault tolerance by accessing alternate paths to duplicate files on another server in the event of an equipment failure.

When you install DFS, you create a *root volume* on a system running Windows NT Server 4.0 or Windows 2000 Server, and then use the Dfs Administrator graphical utility (see Figure 14-10) or the Dfscmd.exe command-line utility to create the *leaf volumes* that stem from the root. (The Dfs Administrator in Windows 2000 is an MMC snap-in.) The leaf volumes can be located on a computer running any OS that is accessible by Windows NT, including Windows 9x, Windows for Workgroups, and Novell NetWare. Users see the root volume as a share on the NT server, and see the leaf volumes as subdirectories on that share. To a user browsing through the DFS tree, the leaf volumes appear just like subdirectories of the root, even though they are located on other drives or other systems.

Microsoft DFS is included with the three Windows 2000 Server packages, but it is an add-on product for NT Server 4.0 that is available from Microsoft's Web site as a free download, at www.microsoft.com/ntserver/nts/downloads/winfeatures/NTSDistrFile.

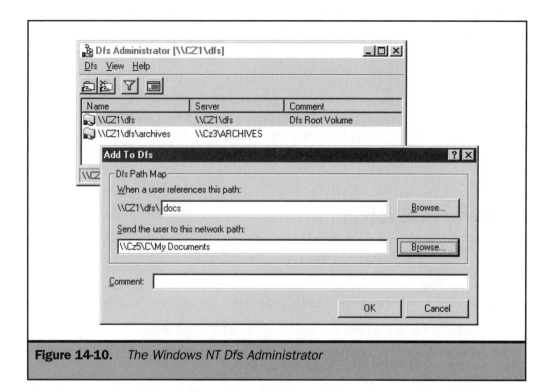

Figure 14-10.   *The Windows NT Dfs Administrator*

DFS provides no additional security of its own. Users who have permission to access a volume, directory, or file in its original location can also access it through the DFS tree. Permission to access the root volume is not needed for a user to access the leaf volumes beneath it.

Internet Information Server

The Internet Information Service (IIS) is Windows NT's Internet server package, which includes Web and FTP servers, as well as other tools for building Web sites and Web-based applications. The original Windows NT 4.0 release included IIS version 2.0, but the current version, 4.0, is part of Windows NT Option Pack 4.0, now included with all Windows NT 4.0 Server products. The Option Pack consists of the following components:

- **Microsoft Internet Information Server 4.0**   Provides HTTP (World Wide Web) and FTP server capabilities.

- **Microsoft Transaction Server 2.0**   Provides component-based transaction processing capabilities for Web-based applications.

- **Microsoft Message Queue Server 1.0**   Enables Web-based applications to send and receive messages over the network.

- **Internet Connection Services for Microsoft RAS**   Provides enhancements to Windows NT's Remote Access Service that enable users to connect to remote networks or ISPs and access the Internet or virtual private networks (VPNs).

- **Microsoft Index Server 2.0**   Provides indexing and search capabilities for Web sites running IIS.

- **Microsoft Certificate Server 1.0**   Creates, revokes, and renews digital certificates used for user authentication to Web-based applications.

- **Microsoft Site Server Express 2.0**   Provides Web site usage analyses and publishing features from the full Site Server product.

- **Personal Web Server for Microsoft Windows 95**   Provides Web server capabilities for Windows 95 and 98 systems.

- **Microsoft Internet Explorer (IE) 4.01**   Provides Web and FTP client capabilities.

Note *The Option Pack is available as a free download from Microsoft's Web site at www.microsoft.com/ntserver/nts/downloads/recommended/NT4OptPk, but the full version is more than 85MB. Users without high-speed Internet connections are better off ordering the Option Pack on a CD-ROM from Microsoft. For more information on IIS, see Chapter 24.*

NETWORK OPERATING SYSTEMS

Load Balancing Service

Windows NT Load Balancing Service (WLBS) is included with NT Server 4.0, Enterprise Edition, and is also available as a free download for the standard NT Server 4.0 product, from Microsoft's Web site at www.microsoft.com/ntserver/nts/downloads/winfeatures/WLBS. WLBS enables up to 32 NT servers to function as a cluster, providing identical services to a large number of TCP/IP clients.

WLBS is designed primarily for use on highly trafficked Web sites in which a single server is not sufficient to support the expected number of users. Since a Web server's DNS name can only be resolved to a single IP address, all client traffic must use that address as its destination. WLBS works by creating a virtual IP address that appears to the clients as though it represents only a single server. In actuality, there are multiple Web servers hosting the same content, all of which communicate through WLBS. The service distributes the incoming traffic evenly among all of the servers in the cluster, enabling them to function as though they were one machine.

The servers in a WLBS cluster continually exchange messages (called *heartbeats*) to inform each other of their continued operation. As the traffic to the Web site increases, administrators can simply add more servers to the cluster. If a server in the cluster malfunctions, the interruption of its heartbeat informs the other systems, and they modify their configurations (using a process called *convergence*) to take up the workload.

Microsoft Cluster Server

Microsoft Cluster Server is another service included with NT Server 4.0, Enterprise Edition and Windows 2000 Advanced Server. In this context, a *cluster* is a pair of NT servers that duplicate all of their functions, not just a single application. To client systems, the cluster appears as a single entity; and if one server malfunctions, the other continues to support the clients. However, the relationship between the servers is not just a fail-over model in which one system sits idle, in case the other one fails. Both servers can run applications independently, and if one server fails, the other launches the applications that the failed server was running and takes over its functions. In addition, applications that are *cluster-aware* can spread their functions across the servers in the cluster to balance the load. Although Cluster Server currently supports only two servers in a cluster, future versions will be able to cluster more machines.

Windows NT Security

Security is an integral part of the Windows NT operating system design, and many of the daily maintenance tasks performed by the network administrator are security related. Simply put, the NT security mechanisms are designed to protect a system's hardware, software, and data from accidental damage and unauthorized access. The goal of the security administration process is to provide users with access to all of the resources they need, while insulating them from those they don't need. This can be a fine line for the administrator to draw, and a difficult one to maintain. Proper use of all of the security administration tools provided by Windows NT is essential to maintaining a secure and productive network.

Windows NT Security Architecture

The security subsystem in Windows NT is integrated throughout the OS and is implemented by a number of different components, as shown in Figure 14-11. Unlike other environmental subsystems running in user mode, such as Win32, the security subsystem is known as an *integral subsystem*, because it is used by the entire OS. All of the security subsystem components interact with Security Reference Monitor, the kernel mode security arbitrator that compares requests for access to a resource to that resource's ACL.

The user mode security subsystem components and their functions are as follows:

- **Logon Process** The mechanism that accepts logon information from the user and initiates the authentication process.

- **Local Security Authority (LSA)** Functions as the central clearinghouse for the security subsystem by initiating the logon process, calling the authentication package, generating access tokens, managing the local security policy, and logging audit messages.

- **Security Accounts Manager (SAM)** Database containing the user and group accounts for the local system and possibly a domain.

- **Security Policy Database** Contains policy information on user rights, auditing, and trust relationships.

- **Audit Log** Contains a record of security-related events and changes made to security policies.

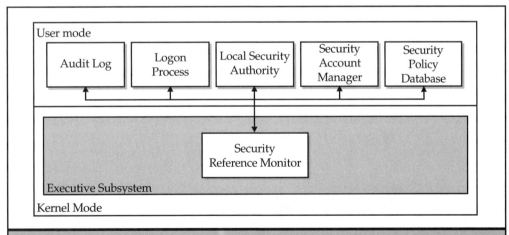

Figure 14-11.   *The Windows NT security architecture*

During a typical user logon, these components interact as follows:

1. The logon process appears in the form of the Logon dialog box produced when the user presses CTRL-ALT-DELETE after the system boots. Other logon processes may be substituted by other network clients (such as the Novell Client for Windows NT). The user then supplies a username and password.

2. The logon process calls the LSA that runs the authentication package.

3. The authentication package checks the username and password against the local SAM database, or if the logon is for a domain, forwards to the authentication package on the DC.

4. When the username and password are verified, the SAM replies to the authentication package with the security IDs of the user and all the groups of which the user is a member.

5. The authentication package creates a logon session and returns it to the LSA with the SIDs.

6. The LSA creates a *security access token* containing the SIDs and the user rights associated with the SIDs, as well as the name of the user and the groups to which the user belongs, and sends it to the logon process, signaling a successful logon. The system will use the SIDs in this token to authenticate the user whenever he or she attempts to access any object on the system.

7. The logon session supplies the access token to the Win32 subsystem, which initiates the process of loading the user's desktop configuration.

Much of the security subsystem's work is transparent to users and administrators. The security component that is most conspicuous in day-to-day activities is the SAM database, which holds all of the NT user, group, and computer accounts. Every NT system has a SAM database for its local accounts, and domains have their own separate SAM database, a copy of which is stored on each DC. Every object on the system that is protected by NT security includes a security descriptor that contains an access control list (ACL). The ACL consists of access control entries (ACEs) that specify which users and groups are to be granted access to the object and what access they are to receive. When you specify the permissions for an object, such as a file, directory, share, or registry key, you are modifying the entries in that object's ACL. The Access Through Share Permissions dialog box for a specific share, for example (see Figure 14-12), displays a list of the users and groups in the SAM database. Selecting users and granting them permission to access the share adds the users to the ACL for that share.

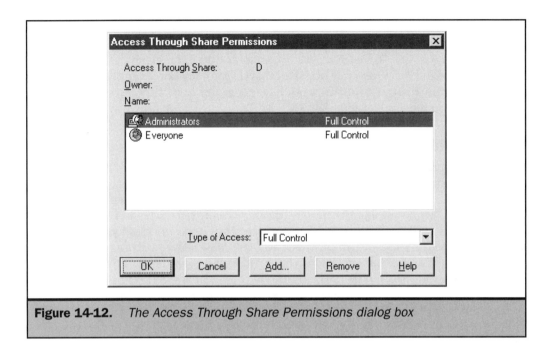

Figure 14-12.   *The Access Through Share Permissions dialog box*

Domains and Security

When you log on to a Windows NT domain, the system accesses a SAM database that is located on one of the network's domain controllers (DCs) for authentication. The user, group, and computer accounts for the domain are stored in the DCs and are accessed whenever you use a utility that modifies the ACLs of system objects. During a domain session, the same Access Through Share Permissions dialog box for a share contains the users and groups in the domain SAM as well as those in the local SAM. You can also select users and groups from other domains on the network, as long as those other domains are trusted by the domain in which the system is currently participating.

 For more information on Windows NT domains, see Chapter 22.

When an NT system is a member of a domain, the local SAM database still exists. The Logon Information dialog box enables you to select a domain for the current session or the local system. Note that the domain and local SAM databases can have user and group accounts with the same name. There is, for example, an Administrator account in the domain and an Administrator account for the local system. These two accounts are not interchangeable. They can have different passwords and different rights and permissions. To install a network adapter driver, for example, you must be logged on as the Administrator of the local system (or an equivalent). By default, a domain Administrator account does not have the rights to modify the hardware configuration on the local system.

User Accounts

Working with user accounts is one of the most basic administrative tasks for Windows NT. One of the most important things to remember about Windows NT account administration is that there can be separate user accounts for a local system and for a domain. An NT workstation, for example, has an Administrator account created in the local SAM by default during the installation process; but if the workstation is a member of a domain, there is another Administrator account in the SAM database on the DC.

These two Administrator accounts can have different passwords, group memberships, and other properties, and should not be confused. A user can log on to either of these Administrator accounts, by selecting either the domain name or the local system name in the Domain field of the Logon Information dialog box. On a DC, there is only one Administrator account, which serves both as the local machine Administrator and the domain Administrator.

Windows NT Workstation and Server systems that are not DCs have the User Manager utility for creating and deleting user and group accounts and managing their properties. Domain controllers have the User Manager for Domains utility (see Figure 14-13), which is functionally similar, but which accesses the SAM databases on the network's PDCs instead of a local SAM.

The User Manager program enables you to create, disable, and delete user accounts, as well as configure the following account properties:

- **Passwords** Specify user passwords, force password changes, and specify whether a user is permitted to change his or her password.
- **Groups** Specify the local and/or global groups of which the user is to be a member.
- **Profile** Specify the location of the user profile and the user's home directory.
- **Hours** Specify the times during which the user is permitted to log on.
- **Logon To** Specify the addresses of the workstations that the user is permitted to use.
- **Account** Specify an expiration date for the account and whether the account is local or global.

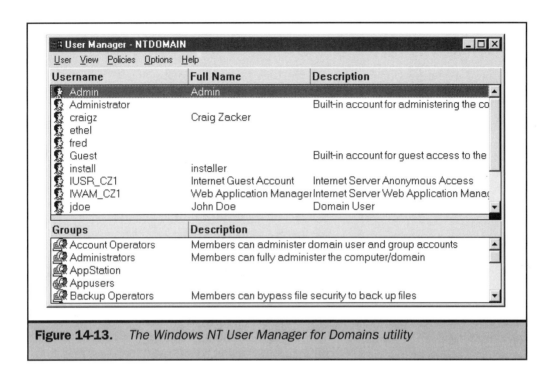

Figure 14-13.   *The Windows NT User Manager for Domains utility*

You don't use the User Manager program to set the permissions for user access to resources, such as shared drives and printers, because this information is not stored in the SAM database. The ACLs for files and directories, for example, are stored as part of the file system; they contain references to the user accounts in the SAM database.

 The User Manager and User Manager for Domains have other important functions besides user account management, as detailed in the following sections.

You do not have to be working at the keyboard of a DC to manage accounts with the User Manager for Domains utility. The \Clients\Srvtools directory on the Windows NT Server 4.0 CD-ROM contains Server Tools collections for Windows NT and Windows 9x that you can install on any network system. Table 14-1 lists the utilities included with each of the Server Tools packages.

There are other utilities that you can use to manage the user accounts on a Windows NT system. User Manager is a convenient and intuitive tool, but as with most graphical utilities, it can be inconvenient to perform tasks that consist of a large

Windows 9*x*	Windows NT
User Manager for Domains	User Manager for Domains
Server Manager	Server Manager
Event Viewer	Event Viewer
	DHCP Administrator
	WINS Administrator
	System Policy Editor
	RAS Administrator
	Remoteboot Manager

Table 14-1.   *Server Tools Applications for Windows 9x and Windows NT*

number of repetitive operations. The NET USER command enables you to create and delete user accounts from the NT command line, using a command like the following:

```
NET USER jdoe /add /fullname:"John Doe"
```

Other parameters enable you to specify values for other account options, as follows:

- **/active:[yes | no]**   Enables or disables the user account.
- **/comment:"*text*"**   Supplies a description for the user account.
- **/expires:[*mm/dd/yy* | never]**   Specifies an expiration date for the user account.
- **/homedir:*pathname***   Specifies the path to the home directory associated with the user account.
- **/homedirreq:[yes | no]**   Specifies whether the user account must have a home directory.
- **/passwordchg:[yes | no]**   Specifies whether the user can change the account password.
- **/passwordreq:[yes | no]**   Specifies whether the user account must have a password.
- **/profilepath:*pathname***   Specifies the location of the user profile associated with the user account.

- **/scriptpath:***pathname*   Specifies the location of the logon script associated with the user account.
- **/times:[***day,time* | **all]**   Specifies the days and times when the user is permitted to log on using the account.
- **/workstations:[***computernames* | ***]**   Specifies the NetBIOS names of up to eight workstations (separated by commas) on which the user can use the account.

For creating large numbers of user accounts, the Windows NT Server 4.0 Resource Kit includes a utility called Addusers.exe that creates accounts from a comma-delimited text file, which you can create easily in a spreadsheet program like Microsoft Excel. By creating a spreadsheet, you can list the values for the various account parameters in columns and later export the data to the comma-delimited text file. You then run Addusers.exe from the NT command line with the text file as a parameter and other options that define the nature of the accounts to be created.

 The Windows NT Server 4.0 Resource Kit Supplement 3 release includes a revised version of Addusers.exe that contains additional command-line options not found in earlier versions, such as parameters that set values for the User Must Change Password At Next Logon, User Cannot Change Password, Password Never Expires, and Account Disabled properties.

Global and Local Groups

Local and domain SAMs both contain groups, but the groups have different properties and functions. The groups in a domain SAM are called *global groups* (or sometimes *domain groups*) because they apply to all of the computers in the domain. *Local groups* are groups that apply only to the system on which they exist. Table 14-2 lists the types of accounts that can be members of each group. The members of a global group must be *domain users*, users in the domain's SAM database. Local system users cannot be a member of a global group, nor can domain users be from another domain. Global groups also cannot have other groups (either local or global) as members. You can grant permissions to a global group, and the domain users who are members of that group will inherit those permissions, no matter what system in the domain they are using.

By contrast, a local group can contain local and domain user accounts as members, as well as global groups from the current domain and trusted domains. By making global groups members of a local group, you can simplify the process of assigning permissions to a system's resources. Suppose, for example, an NT server has five shares and you have five global groups that you want to assign permission to access all of those shares. Rather than add the five global groups to each of the five shares, you can create a single local group on the server that has permission to access all of the shares, and then make the global groups members of that local group. This way, you are creating only 10 new ACEs, instead of 25.

	Global Groups	Local Groups
Local Users	No	Yes
Domain Users	Yes	Yes
Local Groups	No	No
Global Groups	No	Yes
Domain users from Other Trusted Domains	No	Yes
Global Groups from Other Trusted Domains	No	Yes

Table 14-2.   *Global and Local Group Membership Restrictions*

As with user accounts, you create groups and populate them with the User Manager or User Manager for Domains utility. User Manager can work only with local groups, while User Manager for Domains can manage both local and global groups.

From the command line, the NET GROUP command enables you to create or delete a global group and add users to a group. The NET LOCALGROUP command performs the same functions for local groups. The Windows NT Server 4.0 Resource Kit includes other utilities that can help you manage groups, including the following:

- **Global.exe**   Lists the members of a global group in a particular domain or server.
- **Local.exe**   Lists the members of a local group in a particular domain or server.
- **Group Copy (Grpcpy.exe)**   Copies the member list from one existing group to another.
- **Ifmember.exe**   Batch file utility that determines whether a user is a member of a particular group (or groups) and returns its results using an errorlevel value.
- **Showgrps.exe**   Lists the groups of which a particular user is a member.
- **Showmbrs.exe**   Lists the members of a local or global group.
- **Usrtogrp.exe**   Adds users to groups in batches, using a text file for input.

Rights

Windows NT *rights* are rules that identify specific actions a user is allowed to perform on the local system. Many people use the term "rights" incorrectly when they mean permissions, as in "the user has the rights to access the share." By adding a user or group to the ACL for a share, file, or directory, you are modifying permissions, not rights. Rights control access to particular system functions, not to particular system resources. For example, the default NT system configuration assigns the Load and Unload Device Drivers right to the local Administrators group only. Only a member of that group can install the device driver for a new hardware component or delete an existing driver. This is why, on a default NT system, a user logged on with the domain Administrator account cannot load and unload device drivers (as mentioned earlier in this chapter).

Rights apply only to the system on which they are granted, except in the case of DCs. When you grant users or groups a particular right on a DC system, the right applies to all of the DCs in the domain.

In most cases, rights are assigned to groups rather than to individuals. To grant the domain Administrator account the Load and Unload Device Drivers right, for example, you can grant the Administrator user the right directly, grant the Domain Admins global group (of which Administrator is a member) the right, or make the Domain Admins group a member of the local Administrators group, which already has the right.

Users with administrative privileges can modify the rights assignments on an NT system through the User Manager or User Manager for Domains utility. Selecting User Rights from the Policies menu displays the User Rights Policy dialog box, shown in Figure 14-14. When you make a selection in the Right drop-down menu, the Grant To box lists the groups and/or users that currently have that right. You can then add or remove users and groups as needed.

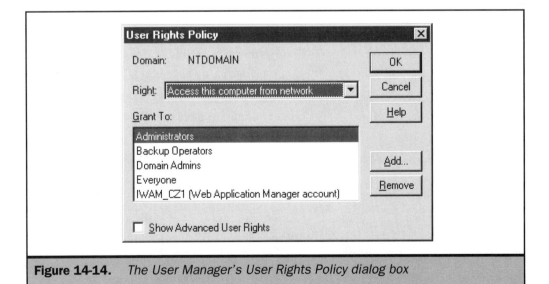

Figure 14-14. *The User Manager's User Rights Policy dialog box*

By default, the Right selector contains only the basic rights for an NT system. When you check the Show Advanced User Rights check box in the User Rights Policy dialog box, additional rights are added to the list. In most cases, there is no need to modify the assignments for these advanced rights. Table 14-3 lists the system names of all the Windows NT rights, both basic and advanced, along with the friendly names displayed in the User Manager utility.

It is also possible to assign rights from the NT command line, using the Ntrights.exe utility included in the Windows NT Server 4.0 Resource Kit. The basic syntax for Ntrights.exe is as follows:

```
ntrights +r|-r right -u groupname [-m computername]
```

where *right* is the system name (as shown in Table 14-3) of the right to be granted or revoked, and *groupname* is the group to receive or lose the right. The *right* variable is case sensitive, and by including the –m parameter and a value for the *computername* variable, you can modify the rights assignments for another computer on the network.

System Name	User Manager Name	Basic/Advanced
SeNetworkLogonRight	Access this computer from the network.	Basic
SeMachineAccountPrivilege	Add workstations to domain.	Basic
SeBackupPrivilege	Back up files and directories.	Basic
SeSystemtimePrivilege	Change the system time.	Basic
SeRemoteShutdownPrivilege	Force shutdown from a remote system.	Basic
SeLoadDriverPrivilege	Load and unload device drivers.	Basic
SeInteractiveLogonRight	Log on locally.	Basic
SeSecurityPrivilege	Manage auditing and security log.	Basic
SeRestorePrivilege	Restore files and directories.	Basic

Table 14-3.   *Windows NT System Rights*

System Name	User Manager Name	Basic/Advanced
SeShutdownPrivilege	Shut down the system.	Basic
SeTakeOwnershipPrivilege	Take ownership of files or other objects.	Basic
SeTcbPrivilege	Act as part of the operating system.	Advanced
SeChangeNotifyPrivilege	Bypass traverse checking.	Advanced
SeCreatePagefilePrivilege	Create a pagefile.	Advanced
SeCreateTokenPrivilege	Create a token object.	Advanced
SeCreatePermanentPrivilege	Create permanent shared objects.	Advanced
SeDebugPrivilege	Debug programs.	Advanced
SeAuditPrivilege	Generate security audits.	Advanced
SeIncreaseQuotaPrivilege	Increase quotas.	Advanced
SeIncreaseBasePriorityPrivilege	Increase scheduling priority.	Advanced
SeLockMemoryPrivilege	Lock pages in memory.	Advanced
SeServiceLogonRight	Log on as a service.	Advanced
SeBatchLogonRight	Log on as a batch job.	Advanced
SeSystemEnvironmentPrivilege	Modify firmware environment values.	Advanced
SeProfileSingleProcessPrivilege	Profile single process.	Advanced
SeSystemProfilePrivilege	Profile system performance.	Advanced
SeUnsolicitedInputPrivilege	Read unsolicited input from a terminal device.	Advanced
SeAssignPrimaryTokenPrivilege	Replace a process-level token.	Advanced

Table 14-3.   *Windows NT System Rights* (continued)

Permissions

Permissions are the most commonly used security element in Windows NT. They protect the NTFS file system and the registry from unauthorized access and accidental damage by users and applications. Granting a user or group permissions to access a resource adds them as an ACE to the resource's ACL. The degree of access that the user or group is granted depends on what permissions they are assigned. NTFS defines six access permissions, as follows:

- **R**   Read
- **W**   Write
- **X**   Execute
- **D**   Delete
- **P**   Change Permissions
- **O**   Take Ownership

These *individual permissions* are the basic building blocks of the NTFS access control system. While you can assign these permissions individually, administrators more commonly use *standard permissions*, which are combinations of individual permissions that fulfill the most common usage scenarios. Tables 14-4 and 14-5 list the standard permissions for NTFS files and directories, respectively.

Standard Permission	Individual Permissions	Definition
Read	RX	User can read and execute files, but cannot modify or delete them.
Change	RWXD	User can read, execute, modify, and delete files.
Full Control	RWXDPO	In addition to reading, executing, modifying, and deleting files, the user can set permissions for them and take ownership of them.
No Access	None	User has no access of any kind.

Table 14-4.   *Standard Permissions for NTFS Files*

Standard Permission	Individual Permissions	Definition
List	RX	User can view the files and subdirectories in the directory.
Read	RX (directory); RX (directory contents)	User can read and execute the files in the directory.
Add	WX	User can add files to the directory but cannot read or modify them.
Add & Read	RWX (directory); RW (directory contents)	User can add files to the directory, as well as read them, but cannot modify them.
Change	RWXD	User can add files to the directory, as well as read, modify, and delete them.
Full Control	RWXDPO	In addition to adding, reading, executing, modifying, and deleting files in the directory, the user can set permissions for the directory and take ownership of it.
No Access	None	User has no access of any kind.

Table 14-5.   *Standard Permissions for NTFS Directories*

NETWORK OPERATING
SYSTEMS

   Permissions are stored as part of the NTFS file system, not in the SAM database. To modify the permissions for a file or directory, you select Permissions from the Security page of the Properties dialog box (see Figure 14-15). Here, you can add users and groups from the local SAM, from the current domain, and from other domains that are trusted. The Type of Access selector lets you choose from among the standard permissions for the file or directory; choosing Special Access enables you to work directly with the individual permissions.

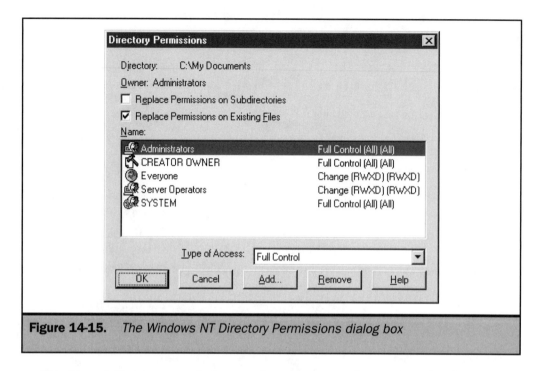

Figure 14-15.   *The Windows NT Directory Permissions dialog box*

The file and directory permissions apply to everyone who accesses the object, either on the local system or through the network. To control network access, however, you can also set permissions on the shares by selecting Permissions from the Sharing tab of a shared directory's Properties dialog box. To access the files on a share, a network user must have permissions for both the share and the files and directories in the share.

Cacls.exe

Windows NT includes a utility called Cacls.exe that enables you to modify NTFS standard permissions from the command line or with a batch file. The syntax for Cacls.exe is as follows:

```
cacls filespec [/t] [/e] [/c] [/g username:permissions] [/r user]
[/p username:permissions] [/d user]
```

- ■ *filespec* Specifies the name of the file(s) or directory for which the permissions are to be set (wildcards are permitted).

- ■ */t* Recurses the subdirectories of a directory specified by the *filespec* variable.

- ■ */e* Edits the ACLs of the files or directories specified by the *filespec* variable instead of replacing them. All existing permissions are retained, except for those overwritten by the command.

- **/c** Continues processing the command despite receiving "access denied" errors.
- **/g** *username:permissions* Creates an entirely new ACL for the files or directories specified by the *filespec* variable, containing only permissions for the user(s) specified by *username* (erasing all previously existing permissions), using the following abbreviations in the *permissions* variable:
  - **R** Read
  - **C** Change
  - **F** Full Control
- **/r** *username* Revokes all permissions held by the specified user for the files or directories specified by the *filespec* variable (requires the /e switch).
- **/p** *username:permissions* Modifies the ACL for the files or directories specified by the *filespec* variable, instead of completely replacing it, as the /g switch does, using the following abbreviations for the *permissions* variable:
  - **N** None
  - **R** Read
  - **C** Change
  - **F** Full Control
- **/d** *username* Denies the specified user all permissions for the files or directories specified by the *filespec* variable.

 Note *When using the /g switch, be sure to include administrative rights for the appropriate users or groups, since the command will erase all existing permissions from the ACL.*

The *username* variable can specify a specific user or a group. If a group name contains spaces, you must enclose it in quotation marks. A single Cacls.exe command can also contain multiple *username:permissions* combinations, as in the following example:

```
cacls C:\Windows /t /g Administrator:F Users:C
```

It is possible to use Cacls.exe commands in a batch file to automate the modification of permissions, but to do this, you have to deal with the confirmation message that the program displays before it actually modifies ACLs. This message requires you to respond with a *y* character before the program will continue processing. To bypass this interruption, you can use the standard DOS pipe redirector to feed the response to the program from the command line, as follows:

```
echo y|cacls C:\Windows /t /g Administrator:F Users:C
```

NETWORK OPERATING SYSTEMS

Xcacls.exe

With Cacls.exe, you can set standard permissions for the NTFS file system, but you cannot work with individual permissions. The Windows NT Server 4.0 Resource Kit includes a utility called Xcacls.exe that uses the same syntax as Cacls.exe, except that you can specify individual as well as standard permissions. The abbreviations used by Xcacls.exe for the standard permissions are the same as those for Cacls.exe (to provide compatibility with existing batch files and scripts); the additional abbreviations for the individual permissions are as follows:

- **P**   Change permissions
- **O**   Take ownership
- **X**   Execute
- **E**   Read
- **W**   Write
- **D**   Delete

The only other difference in the Xcacls.exe syntax is that there is an additional (optional) variable for the /g and /p options called *spec* that enables you to specify permissions for the files in a directory that are different from those that will be assigned to the directory itself, as in the following example:

```
xcacls C:\Documents /t /p jdoe:EW;EWD
```

In this example, the user *jdoe* is granted the Read and Write permissions to the C:\Documents directory, and the Read, Write, Execute, and Delete rights to the files in that directory. This enables the user to delete files in the C:\Documents directory, but he can't delete the directory itself. The *spec* variable can also take one more value, in addition to the individual permissions listed earlier, as follows:

- **T**   Not specified

Windows 2000

Windows 2000 is the latest incarnation of the Windows operating system, and is intended to be the upgrade path for both Windows NT 4.0 and Windows 9x. Windows 2000 retains much of the basic NT system architecture; its advancements are primarily in its additional services. The following sections examine some of the new features included in Windows 2000.

Active Directory

Active Directory, the new enterprise directory service included with the Window 2000 Server products, is the single most comprehensive feature upgrade in Windows 2000. Active Directory is a hierarchical, replicated directory service designed to support networks of virtually unlimited size. For more information on Active Directory, see Chapter 23.

Microsoft Management Console

Microsoft Management Console (MMC) is a new application that provides a centralized administration interface for many of the services included in Windows 2000. Windows NT relies on separate management applications for many of its services, such as the DHCP Manager, WINS Manager, and Disk Administrator. Windows 2000 consolidates all of these applications, and many others, into MMC. Most of the system administration tasks for the OS are now performed through MMC. In many cases, the exact same functions found in the standalone Windows NT utilities are ported to a substantially different MMC interface. The initial Windows 2000 experience for system administrators is typically one of frustration as they search for familiar functions that are now found in very different places.

MMC has no administrative capabilities of its own; it is, essentially, a shell for application modules called *snap-ins* that provide the administrative functions for many of Windows 2000's applications and services. Snap-ins take the form of files with an .msc extension that you load either from the command line or interactively through the MMC menus. Windows 2000 supplies snap-in files for all of its tools, but the interface is designed so that third-party software developers can use the MMC architecture to host administration tools for their own applications.

MMC can load multiple snap-ins simultaneously using the Windows multiple-document interface (MDI). You can use this capability to create a customized management interface containing all of the snap-ins you use on a regular basis. When you run MMC (by launching the Mmc.exe file from the Run dialog box) and select Console | New, you get an empty Console Root window. By selecting Console | Add/Remove Snap-in, you can build a list of the installed snap-ins and load them into the console. The various snap-ins appear in an expandable, Explorer-like display in the left pane of MMC's main screen (see Figure 14-16). By selecting Console | Save As, you can save your console configuration as an MSC file and load it again as needed.

Many of Windows 2000's administrative tools are actually preconfigured MMC consoles. Selecting Computer Management from the Programs/Administrative Tools group in the Start menu displays a console that contains a collection of the basic

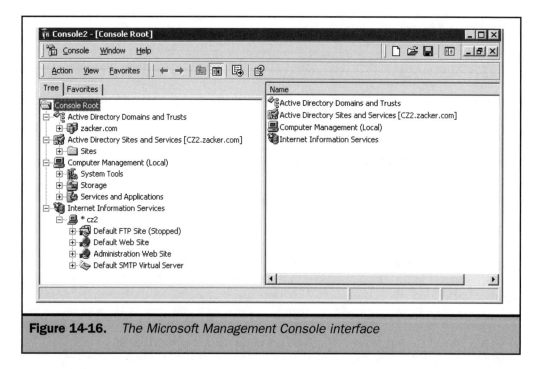

Figure 14-16.   *The Microsoft Management Console interface*

administration tools for a Windows 2000 system, as shown in Figure 14-17. By default, the Computer Management console administers the local system, but you can use all of its tools to manage a remote network system by selecting Action | Connect to Another Computer.

Windows 2000 Security

Windows 2000 includes a number of improvements to its security infrastructure. While much of the basic security architecture is unchanged and the previous technology remains in place for compatibility with Windows NT, some of the mechanisms used to implement the security services are new.

Kerberos

Network authentication in Windows 2000 is provided by a security protocol called Kerberos, as defined in the RFC 1510 document published by the IETF. A Kerberos Key Distribution Center (KDC) service is installed with Active Directory on the network's DCs, and every Windows 2000 system (both Server and Professional) has a client Kerberos authentication provider. There is also a directory services client for Windows 9*x* that provides Kerberos support.

Kerberos authentication is based on the exchange of *tickets* that contain an encrypted password that verifies a user's identity. When a user on a Windows 2000 client system

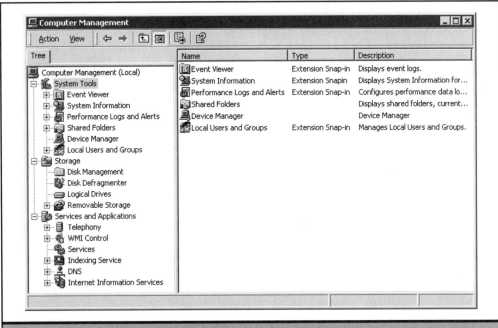

Figure 14-17.   *The Windows 2000 Computer Management Console*

logs on to a domain, the KDC on the domain controller issues a *ticket-granting ticket (TGT)* that includes the user's SID, the network address of the client system, a timestamp that helps to prevent unauthorized access, and the session key that is used to encrypt the data. The TGT is retained by the client system, to be used as a license for future authentication events. Once a client has a TGT, it can use it to identify the user, thus eliminating the need to repeatedly supply a password when accessing various network resources.

When the user attempts to access a resource on a network server, the client sends a request that identifies the user and the resource server, and includes a copy of the TGT, to a *ticket-granting service (TGS)* on the domain controller. The TGS then returns a *service ticket* to the client that grants the user access to that particular resource only. The client then sends an access request to the resource server that contains the user's ID and the service ticket. The resource server decrypts the service ticket, and as long as the user ID matches the ID in the ticket, access is granted to the requested resource. A client system may retain multiple service tickets to provide future access to various network resources. This system protects both the server and the user, because it provides mutual authentication; the client is authenticated to the server and the server to the client.

Public Key Infrastructure

Windows 2000 contains a *public key infrastructure (PKI)* that strengthens its protection against hacking and other forms of unauthorized access. In traditional cryptography, also called *secret key cryptography*, a single key is used to encrypt and decrypt data. For two entities to communicate, they must both possess the key, which implies the need for some previous communication during which the key is exchanged.

The fundamental principle of a PKI is that the encryption and decryption keys for a transmission are different. Each system has a *public key* and a *private key.* By supplying your public key to other systems, you enable them to encrypt data so that you can decrypt it using your private key. However, the public key cannot be used to decrypt the data once it has been encrypted. Thus, while intruders may intercept the public keys as they are transmitted across the network, they are useless to them unless they have the private keys as well, which are never transmitted.

The use of a PKI makes it possible to transmit authentication data across a Windows 2000 network with greater security than with Windows NT. However, a PKI also provides the capability to use digital signatures to positively identify the sender of a message. A *digital signature* is a method for encrypting data with a particular user's private key. Other users receiving the transmission can verify the signature with the user's public key. Changing even one bit of the data invalidates the signature. When the transmission arrives intact, the valid signature proves not only that the transmission has not been changed in any way, but also that it unquestionably originated from the sending user. Thus, the potential exists for a digitally signed transmission to eventually carry as much legal and ethical weight as a signed paper document.

Certificates

A *certificate* is a digitally signed statement, issued by a *certificate authority (CA)*, that binds a user, computer, or service holding a private key with its corresponding public key. Windows 2000 Server includes Certificate Services, which can function as the CA for the network. It's also possible to use an outsourced CA, such as VeriSign. A certificate typically contains the following information:

- **Subject identifier information**   Name, e-mail address, or other data identifying the user or computer to which the certificate is being issued.

- **Subject public key value**   The public key associated with the user or computer to which the certificate is being issued.

- **Validity period**   Specifies how long the certificate will remain valid.

- **Issuer identifier information**   Identifies the system issuing the certificate.

- **Issuer digital signature**   Ensures the validity of the certificate by positively identifying its source.

Windows 2000 can use certificates to authenticate users to Web servers, send secure e-mail, and (optionally) authenticate users to domains. For the most part, the use of certificates is transparent to users, but administrators can manage them manually using the Certificates snap-in for the Microsoft Management Console.

Smart Cards

The security of Windows 2000's PKI relies on the private keys remaining private. Typically, the private key is stored on the workstation, which makes it susceptible to both physical and digital intrusion. To address this problem, Windows 2000 supports the use of *smart cards,* which are external devices that store the private encryption key outside the computer. A system that uses smart cards is equipped with a card reader device. When a user logs on, he or she inserts the card into the reader and supplies the personal identification number (PIN) associated with the card in lieu of a password. The system then accesses the private key from the card as needed, instead of storing it on the system.

Smart cards are a relatively new technology, and obviously they are intended for networks where security is a primary concern. Since they do not store their data in a magnetic strip, like credit cards, smart cards are more difficult to penetrate, but they are by no means impenetrable. There are only a few smart card hardware products on the market as of yet, and it remains to be seen whether the technology is embraced by the industry or remains a niche product.

IP Security Protocol

The IP Security Protocol (IPSec) is a product of the IETF that defines a series of encryption and authentication algorithms that Windows 2000 can use to secure intranet and Internet communications, such as in VPN communications. Because it functions at the network layer, IPSec is an end-to-end security protocol, meaning that the only computers able to read the data are the sender and the ultimate receiver. Intermediate systems, such as routers, only relay the data in its encrypted form.

Security Configuration and Analysis

The Windows 2000 Security Configuration and Analysis tool is an MMC snap-in that enables you to create security policies that consist of settings for the operating system's various security areas, and apply them to different computers, using the interface shown in Figure 14-18. The security policies are stored in templates that are text files with an .inf extension, and that contain registry settings, access control lists, and other security configuration parameters.

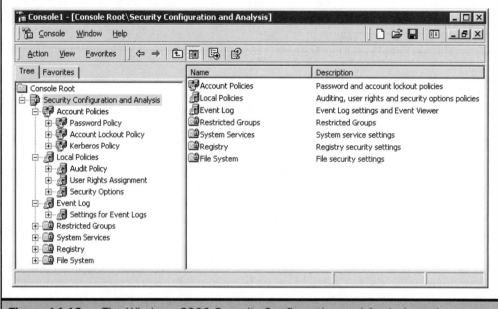

Figure 14-18. *The Windows 2000 Security Configuration and Analysis tool*

IntelliMirror

Microsoft's Zero Administration Initiative for Windows is intended to simplify the administration of network systems and lower their total cost of ownership by limiting user access to the OS and maximizing remote administration capabilities. The Zero Administration Kit defines a methodology for automating the installation of the workstation OS and applications, and for using NTFS permissions and system policies to lock down the Windows NT desktop.

One byproduct of these techniques is the ability to store user profile information on a network drive, thus enabling users to log on to the network from any workstation and retrieve basic configuration settings, such as desktop icons and Start menu program groups. IntelliMirror takes this concept further by enabling more of a user's computing environment to follow him or her around the network, including applications and data files, as well as system and application configuration settings.

IntelliMirror consists of three basic features:

- **User Data Management** Provides users with access to their data files from any workstation on the network, or even when disconnected from the network, using the Windows 2000 Synchronization Manager to replicate folders on the local drive.

- **Software Installation and Maintenance**   Installs applications and other software to any workstation on which they're needed.
- **User Settings Management**   Provides users with access to their desktop environment, application configuration settings, and personal preferences on any network workstation.

In addition to providing users with access to their workstation resources from any computer, IntelliMirror also simplifies the process of building a new workstation. In the event of a hardware failure that puts a user's PC out of commission, an administrator can use IntelliMirror's capabilities to configure a new system quickly, with the user's exact same working configuration.

 For more information on IntelliMirror and the Zero Administration Initiative for Windows, see Chapter 27.

Networking Services

As with Windows NT, networking is integral to Windows 2000, and the OS includes upgraded versions of many of its network services, some of which are discussed in the following sections.

DHCP and DNS

The Domain Name System (DNS) plays a much more important role in Windows 2000 than it did in Windows NT. Active Directory stores information about domain controllers in Service (SRV) resource records on DNS servers, and clients generate DNS queries to locate the DCs. Windows NT, by contrast, uses WINS to track the locations of network resources.

To accommodate the needs of Active Directory, the DNS server included with Windows 2000 supports the new dynamic DNS (DDNS) standard, which enables the DCs to automatically update their resource records. In addition, the DHCP server included with Windows 2000 now works with the DNS server to dynamically update the records for network systems as they are assigned new IP addresses. For more information about DHCP, see Chapter 18. For more information about DNS and its role in Active Directory, see Chapters 20 and 23.

Quality of Service

Quality of Service (QoS) is essentially the result of assigning priorities to various types of network traffic and adapting systems to transmit packets based on the priority they've been assigned, thus guaranteeing the timely delivery of information. Certain applications can benefit from the ability to transmit their data immediately, without delays incurred by traffic volume. Multimedia applications are the typical example used in the design of QoS protocols, because delivering audio and video over a network in real time requires a continuous data stream to avoid interruptions. However, other applications, such as e-mail, can also take advantage of QoS prioritizing. QoS also makes it possible to reserve a certain amount of bandwidth for use by a particular application, whether it is currently using it or not.

There are several different QoS standards and technologies available. Windows 2000 supports the following:

- **Differentiated Quality of Service**   IETF standards (published as RFCs 2474 and 2475) that define a *differentiated services field* (also called the *diff-serve* or *DS* field) for the IPv4 and IPv6 headers, which provide *classes of service* that can be assigned to specific types of applications.

- **Admission Control Service (ACS)**   Enables administrators to reserve bandwidth for specific users, applications, or sites, using the QoS Admission Control MMC plug-in (see Figure 14-19) to create QoS policies stored in Active Directory. Clients that support the IETF's Subnet Bandwidth Management (SBM) standard can request priority bandwidth from the service.

- **IEEE 802.1p**   Defines a frame format extension for Ethernet, Token Ring, FDDI, and other data link–layer protocols that carries the extra bits used to specify the priority of the packet. There are eight service classes, ranging from 0, which has the lowest priority, to 7, which has the highest.

- **Resource Reservation Protocol (RSVP)**   IETF standard (published as RFC 2205) that provides guaranteed, on-time delivery of data over an IP network in cooperation with the diff-serve standard by reserving bandwidth in response to client requests.

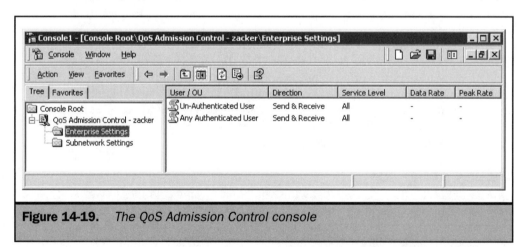

Figure 14-19.   *The QoS Admission Control console*

Network Address Translation

Windows 2000 includes a Network Address Translation (NAT) server that enables a network to use private, unregistered IP addresses for its workstations. When a system on the network connects to the Internet, the unregistered IP address in its packets is translated to a registered address by the NAT server. This enables the NAT server to use a few registered addresses to service many clients, and protects the systems on the network from unauthorized access from the Internet. For more information on NAT, see Chapter 6.

Windows Terminal Support

Windows 2000 Server includes terminal services like those provided by Windows NT Server 4.0, Terminal Server Edition as part of the base OS. With this technology, you can use the server to run the 32-bit Windows interface on legacy desktop systems (such as 16-bit Windows, Macintosh, or UNIX) and on Windows-based terminals.

File System Features

Windows 2000 includes the NTFS 5.0 file system, which improves on the file system included with Windows NT by adding features like support for file encryption and the ability to enlarge volumes without rebooting. Windows 2000 requires NTFS 5.0 volumes to host the Active Directory database; new NTFS volumes created with Windows 2000 use NTFS 5.0, and NTFS volumes that already exist prior to an OS upgrade are converted to the new file system.

One of the most frequent complaints of network administrators about Windows NT's file system concerns its inability to restrict the amount of disk space utilized by a user. NetWare has had this capability for many years, and Microsoft has finally incorporated it into Windows 2000. On the Quota tab of an NTFS drive's Properties dialog box (see Figure 14-20), you can specify the maximum amount of space to be allotted to a new user, as well as the behavior of the system when the user approaches and exceeds the limit. As users access the volume, the system lists them in the Quota Entries window (see Figure 14-21). From here, you can modify the quotas for individual users and monitor the amount of space they have in use.

Windows 2000 also includes a disk defragmentation utility (finally). Like disk quotas, this is a tool that has been lacking ever since the initial Windows NT release. Windows 2000 Server and Professional both can improve disk efficiency by defragmenting volumes that use the NTFS, FAT16, or FAT32 file system.

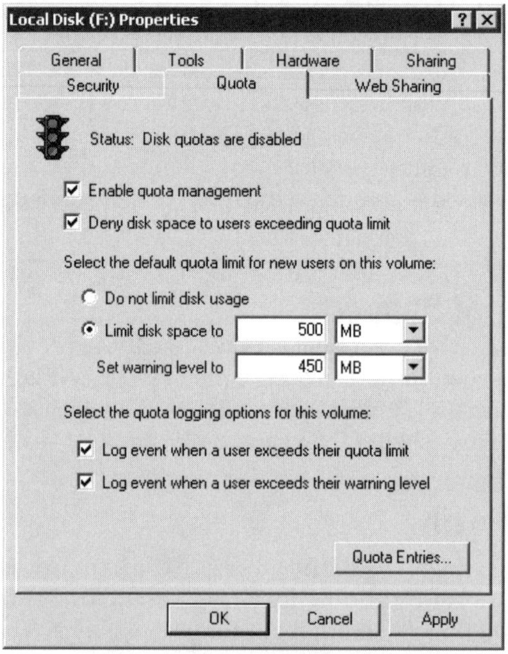

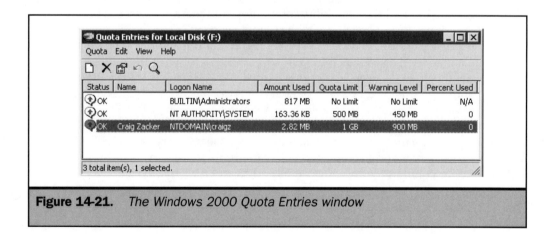

Figure 14-20.   *The Quota tab of a disk's Properties dialog box*

Figure 14-21.   *The Windows 2000 Quota Entries window*

The Complete Reference

Upgrading & Troubleshooting Networks

Chapter 15

Novell NetWare

Novell NetWare was one of the first commercial network operating systems designed for use on PC LANs and is certainly the oldest one still in general use today. In the early 1980s, PC networks were concerned primarily with providing basic functions, such as file and printer sharing, and NetWare has always done this very well. For many years, NetWare was the leader in a market that had little commercial competition that could touch it.

As a platform for third-party application development, however, and particularly as a platform for Internet services, NetWare has failed to keep up with its competition in the 1990s and has lost much of the market share it once enjoyed. NetWare is still used on a great many legacy networks, often in combination with other network operating systems like Windows NT or UNIX; but its deployment on new networks has reduced considerably, despite its obvious strength in certain areas, such as directory services.

Unlike Windows NT and UNIX, NetWare is a dedicated client/server operating system, meaning that NetWare servers contain no client capabilities, and NetWare clients communicate only with servers, not with each other (unless another NOS client is also installed). A NetWare server runs a proprietary OS that launches from a DOS prompt but that runs independently from DOS once loaded. NetWare clients are DOS or Windows systems with a client package installed that provides server connectivity. Microsoft supplies a basic NetWare client with the Windows 9*x*, NT, and 2000 operating systems, but Novell's own client software provides more complete NetWare functionality. Additional software packages provide client connectivity for other operating systems, such as Macintosh and UNIX.

The NetWare server OS provides the ability to run applications developed by Novell and third parties, using executable program files called *NetWare Loadable Modules (NLMs)*. The server console uses a character-based interface, with some utilities driven by ASCII-character menus, as shown in Figure 15-1. The latest version, NetWare 5, includes a Java-based console that for the first time provides a graphical server interface.

NetWare's Role in the Enterprise

NetWare is best known for providing users with the basic file and print services that are the core of any network's functionality. To this day, these services are what NetWare does best, better than operating systems like Windows NT that have taken its place as the market leader. The traditional file system is scaleable and secure, and the printing subsystem is simple to use and administer. Current versions of NetWare include updated versions of these elements, such as Novell Storage Services (NSS) and the Novell Distributed Print System (NDPS), but support for the older versions remains in place, because a great many sites continue to use NetWare as part of an "if it ain't broke, don't fix it" philosophy.

As a platform for application development, NetWare is necessarily more problematic than Windows NT, which has made its name as an application server platform. Network software development for Windows operating systems uses the

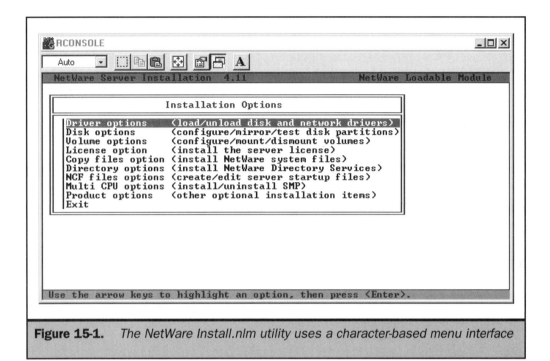

Figure 15-1. *The NetWare Install.nlm utility uses a character-based menu interface*

same types of executables on both servers and clients, whereas NetWare servers require the use of the proprietary NLM executable. In fact, its tendency to rely on proprietary elements is one of the primary causes of NetWare's decline in the network marketplace. The server NLMs and the IPX protocols are both Novell developments that it has retained long after the rest of the industry has moved to other, more publicly documented alternatives.

The single most redeeming factor in the NetWare camp today is Novell Directory Services (NDS), a hierarchical, X.500-based directory service that was originally deployed in 1993 and is now far more mature than anything available for Windows or UNIX. NDS is an extremely flexible repository for all sorts of information about network elements, including hardware and software, as well as users, groups, and other incorporeal entities. In the years since its introduction, NDS has been tested and deployed on more networks than any other directory service, and there are now many third-party products that utilize its capabilities. As good as Microsoft's Active Directory is, it still will require a great deal of testing and development before it can be said to be as reliable as NDS, since Novell has had a seven-year head start.

As an Internet platform, NetWare was the last of the major network operating systems to adopt the TCP/IP protocols. It was only with the release of NetWare version 5 that the operating system was able to use TCP/IP for its core file and print services. Previous versions supported the protocols and included Internet applications, such as Web and FTP servers, but client/server LAN communications relied on the proprietary IPX protocols until very recently.

The NetWare product, as it stands now, contains all the features that are expected in an enterprise NOS, as well as some exciting new ideas, but the continued viability of Novell in the marketplace is definitely in question. An organization that is already committed to NetWare might well benefit from an upgrade to the latest version, but large-scale deployment of the operating system on a new network or migration from Windows NT or UNIX would not, in most cases, be a wise decision at this time.

NetWare Versions

Novell began producing networking products in the early 1980s, and was involved in PC networking almost from the introduction of the first IBM PC. The product has developed steadily over the years, culminating in the current NetWare 5 release. However, many NetWare shops continue to rely on older versions of the product. Table 15-1 lists the versions that are currently available and compares their features and capabilities. The following sections examine in more detail the differences between the major releases of the NetWare product.

Note   *During the course of the year 2000, Novell will be discontinuing support for all NetWare 3.x versions prior to 3.2 and NetWare 4.x versions prior to 4.2.*

	NetWare 3.2	NetWare 4.2	NetWare 5
System Requirements	Intel 80386 or better processor; 6MB RAM; 30MB hard disk space	Intel 80386 or better processor; 16MB RAM; 105MB hard disk space	Intel Pentium or better processor; 64MB RAM; 550MB hard disk space
Directory Service	Bindery	NDS	NDS
File System	NetWare file system	NetWare file system	NetWare file system; Novell Storage Services (NSS)
Maximum Number of Connections Supported per Server	250	Thousands	Thousands

Table 15-1.   *Comparison of NetWare Versions and Features*

	NetWare 3.2	NetWare 4.2	NetWare 5
Maximum Number of Volumes per Server	64	64	Unlimited
Maximum Disk Storage Capacity	32TB	32TB	Unlimited
Maximum File Size	4GB	4GB	8TB
Maximum Volume Size	32GB	32GB	8TB on 32-bit systems; 8 exabytes (EB) on 64-bit systems
Maximum Concurrent Open Files per Server	100,000	100,000	1,000,000
Maximum Directory Entries per Volume	2,097,152	16,000,000	2^{64}
Maximum Number of Server Processors Supported	1	8	32
Core Protocols Supported	IPX; IP (using NetWare/IP encapsulation only)	IPX only; IP (using NetWare/IP encapsulation only)	IPX and/or IP
Internet Services Included	Netscape Communicator	Netscape FastTrack Server; Netscape Communicator; DHCP Server (v2.10); DNS Server (v2); IPX/IP Gateway (free download); FTP Services; CGI Scripting and NetBasic support; Multiprotocol WAN Router	Netscape FastTrack Server; Netscape Communicator; DHCP Server (v3); DNS Server (v3); LDAP 3 Service; FTP Services; Network Address Translation (with Support Pack 1); CGI Scripting and NetBasic support; Multiprotocol WAN Router
Retail Price (100 users)	$6,995	Server plus 5 users: $1,095; 100-user additive license: $6,695	Server plus 5 users: $1,195; 100-user additive license: $6,995

Table 15-1.   *Comparison of NetWare Versions and Features* (continued)

NetWare 2.*x*

The NetWare 2.*x* operating systems culminated in version 2.2, which is no longer sold or supported by Novell. Any network running a 2.*x* version of NetWare must purchase a full version of NetWare 3.12, 4.2, or 5 to upgrade, as there is no longer an upgrade path from this early product.

NetWare 2.*x* was designed to support PCs built around Intel processors up to the 80286 and is subject to limitations that seem absurd by today's standards, but which represented the state of the art back then. A NetWare 2.*x* server could have as much as 12MB of RAM installed and could support up to 2GB of hard disk space, which had to be divided into volumes no larger than 256MB.

Designed primarily to provide file and print services, NetWare 2.*x* included limited support for server applications in the form of *value-added processes (VAPs)*. VAPs enabled servers to run relatively simple applications, such as server backups. NetWare 2.*x* was also the last version of the operating system that enabled the server to be installed in nondedicated mode, meaning that the server computer could be used as a DOS workstation while performing server tasks in the background. This arrangement resulted in unsatisfactory performance of both workstation and server, however, and all subsequent versions of NetWare required a dedicated server.

NetWare 3.*x*

In 1989, Novell released NetWare 386, version 3, which was a major upgrade of the OS designed to take advantage of the (then) new Intel 80386 processor. Several maintenance releases followed, culminating in the NetWare 3.12 release in September 1993. Version 3.12 was planned to be the ultimate version of the NetWare 3.*x* generation, but Novell later decided that a 3.2 version was warranted, primarily to make the operating system Y2K compliant. Even though development of the 3.*x* product has ceased, it is still supported by Novell and used on many small- to medium-sized networks that never saw a reason to upgrade to NetWare 4.*x*. NetWare 3.*x* requires a server with at least a 386 processor, 6MB of RAM, and 30MB of disk space.

Unlike version 2.*x*, NetWare 3.*x* is a 32-bit OS that introduced many of the elements that have come to be associated with NetWare, including multitasking; support for large amounts of RAM (up to 4GB) and disk space (up to 32TB); and NetWare Loadable Modules (NLMs), the application development platform that is still used in the latest NetWare versions. In the course of its release history, NetWare 3.*x* has added support for industry-standard technologies as they arrived, including CD-ROM drives and the TCP/IP protocols. Version 3.2 adds a Windows-based interface for server administration, but the fundamental structure of the operating system has remained intact throughout its ten-year history.

Designed for use on LANs, NetWare 3.*x* is not intended to be an enterprise NOS (as NetWare 4.*x* and 5 are). The OS is organized around a nonhierarchical database called the *bindery*, which consists of *objects* representing users and groups, as well as hardware and software entities found on the network. As in most directory services, the objects are database records that contain attributes called *properties,* which can have one or more *values.* For example, an object representing a user will have a property that consists of a list of the groups of which the user is a member.

Every server on a NetWare network contains its own bindery, and there is no communication between the binderies on different servers. This is one of the reasons why NetWare 3.*x* is not a suitable OS for large networks that must rely on centralized management techniques. A new user who requires access to five different servers must have a separate bindery account on each server.

For its intended purposes, though, NetWare 3.*x* is an excellent solution that has continued to retain a staunch following throughout the years. Many of its devotees have even shunned later releases, like NetWare 4.*x* and 5, in favor of what they have determined to be the right tool for the job.

NetWare 4.*x*

The next generation of NetWare was introduced in April 1993 with version 4. Several maintenance versions ensued during the next three years, and NetWare 4.11 was released in October 1996. This version persisted until early 1999, when version 4.2 was released to provide Y2K revisions and add updated versions of the intraNetWare utilities. Like version 3.*x*, NetWare 4.*x* will run on any server with at least a 386 processor, but requires 16MB or more of RAM and 105MB of disk space.

The primary innovation in NetWare 4 was NetWare Directory Services (NDS), which later was renamed Novell Directory Services to reflect its newly implemented cross-platform compatibility. NDS is a hierarchical, partitioned, replicated directory service that is intended to support enterprise networks of virtually any size. Like the bindery, NDS consists of objects, properties, and values, but the objects here are organized in a tree-like display that can represent a very large organization. An enterprise typically maintains a single NDS database that is split among several servers and replicated to provide fault tolerance and load balancing.

NDS took several years to refine and mature to the point that it could be considered reliable on mission-critical networks, and several years more for third-party developers to take advantage of its services and write applications that store information in the NDS database.

NetWare 4.*x* also included server administration tools for the Windows platform for the first time. The NetWare Administrator (NWADMIN) provides GUI access to the NDS tree and the NetWare file system, although a similar utility for DOS, called NETADMIN, is included as well.

Note *For more information about NetWare Administrator and NDS, see Chapter 21.*

intraNetWare

The intraNetWare release (formerly known as IntranetWare—go figure) is a bundle that combines NetWare 4.11 with a collection of Internet/intranet utilities at the same price as NetWare 4.11 alone. In addition to NetWare 4.11 itself, the package contains the following:

- Novell Web Server 2.51
- Novell FTP Server
- Novell DHCP Server
- Netscape Navigator
- NetWare Internet Access Server
- Novell Multi-Protocol Route 3.1
- NetWare/IP
- Novell IPX/IP Gateway

NetWare 4.2

Instead of continuing the intraNetWare brand, Novell elected to release its next operating system upgrade simply as NetWare 4.2. However, this release includes the latest versions of all the bundled intraNetWare components, making it the functional equivalent of intraNetWare, using the NetWare name. NetWare 4.2 is likely to be the ultimate release of the NetWare 4.x generation, and is intended for use by organizations that are not yet motivated to upgrade to NetWare 5, but that want the latest revisions of the bundled utilities, as well as the assurance that the OS is Y2K compliant.

NetWare 4.2 includes the following components:

- **Netscape Fast-Track Server**   Beginning in NetWare 4.2 and in NetWare 5, Novell began bundling Netscape's entry-level Web server with NetWare, instead of its own Web server. A license for the Netscape Enterprise Web server (available as a free download) is also included with the product.

- **Novell DHCP Server v2.10**   Dynamically allocates TCP/IP configuration settings to network clients.

- **Novell DNS Server v2.0**   Enables client systems to resolve DNS names into the IP addresses required for TCP/IP communications.

- **Novell Multi-Protocol WAN Router**   Enables a NetWare server to function as a WAN router using multiple transport and routing protocols on a number of industry-standard WAN communications technologies.

- **Novell FTP Server**   Enables a NetWare server to function as an FTP server, providing TCP/IP file transfer services to local and remote clients.

- **Netscape Communicator**   Includes a license (equivalent to the NetWare user license) for the Netscape Web browser and e-mail client package.

- **Symmetrical multiprocessing (SMP) support**   Supports up to eight server processors using a separate multiprocessing NLM.
- **Oracle8**   Includes a five-user version of the Oracle database server.

NetWare 5

NetWare 5 is the latest release of the operating system and represents a major step forward in many ways. Most importantly, this is the first version of NetWare that can use TCP/IP as its native protocols. Previous versions supported TCP/IP, but the core file and print services still relied on Novell's own IPX protocols. NetWare 5 can eliminate IPX from the network completely, which is something that users for years have been clamoring for.

NetWare 5 also expands the role of NDS in the enterprise, by including DNS and DHCP servers that store their data in the NDS database. The DNS server also supports the dynamic DNS standard (RFC 2136) that enables DHCP-assigned IP addresses to be automatically reflected in DNS resource records. This new version of NetWare also reflects Novell's commitment to the Java language by including, for the first time, a Java-based GUI installation program and a network administration utility called ConsoleOne.

NetWare Installation

NetWare versions 3.*x* and higher are launched from a single DOS executable file called Server.exe. Installing the OS requires a DOS partition on the server that is large enough to hold this file and a collection of drivers and other support files used during the OS loading process. For troubleshooting purposes, it is also a good idea to leave enough free space on the DOS partition to hold a core dump of the OS, which means having as much free space as there is memory in the computer. A *core dump* is an exact copy of the server's memory content at the time that a fault (called an *abend*, or abnormal ending) occurs. In the event of a serious problem, Novell technicians can determine from the core dump exactly what was happening at the time the error occurred.

Tip   *Many people place the blame for a failure to resolve a problem on the software manufacturer's technical support staff when, in fact, the real cause lies with the user who fails to provide the information needed to determine the cause of the problem. The information in a NetWare core dump is meaningless to all but a small percentage of network administrators, but it is an invaluable diagnostic tool for the Novell engineers.*

The Server.exe file alone loads the NetWare OS, and the rest of the installation process consists of the selection and configuration of the drivers to support the server's storage subsystem, network interface cards (NICs), and protocols. The server console provides a command-line interface through which you can interactively perform these tasks using

NetWare's internal console commands. For example, all NetWare drivers and executables must be loaded into memory using the LOAD command. In addition to the server console command line, various menu-driven utilities enable you to configure the properties of the server, its drivers, and applications. These utilities, such as MONITOR and INETCFG, are not graphical; they use ASCII characters only to create a cursor-driven menu system known as the *C-worthy interface* (see Figure 15-2).

Disk Drivers

Until NetWare version 4.11 was released, support for disk drives and other storage devices in NetWare was provided by separate, monolithic drivers with a .dsk extension. Development of the DSK drivers ceased in January 1997, however. NetWare 4.11 introduced the NetWare Peripheral Architecture (NPA) that consists of modular drivers called HAMs (host adapter modules) and CDMs (custom device modules). During the installation process, you install a HAM for the host adapter installed in the server and install individual CDMs for each of the devices connected to that host adapter.

For example, when the installation program detects a SCSI adapter in the system, it loads a HAM driver such as Scsi154x.ham. Loading this driver *spawns* (that is, autoloads) the main NPA program: Nwpa.nlm. Once the HAM is loaded, the system loads CDMs for each of the storage devices connected to the adapter, such as Scsihd.cdm for hard disk drives and Scsicd.cdm for CD-ROMs. If you are running NetWare 4.11 or higher with the

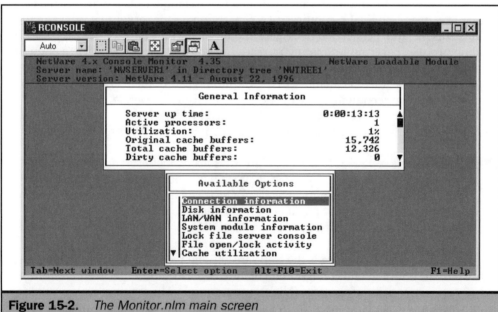

Figure 15-2.   *The Monitor.nlm main screen*

old-style DSK drivers, then it is recommended that you switch to NPA if you plan to upgrade the hardware in your server.

Tip
The NetWare installation program encounters a conflict whenever it attempts to install OS support for the computer's CD-ROM drive. This is because you must load DOS CD-ROM drivers in order to install NetWare from the distribution CD-ROM disk. In most cases, the installation program will generate an error while trying to load the NetWare CD-ROM drivers, because the DOS drivers are already addressing the device. Be sure to remove the commands loading the DOS drivers from the computer's boot device once the installation process is completed, and the NetWare drivers for the CD-ROM should load without a problem the next time you start NetWare.

NIC and Protocol Drivers

In order for a server to be able to communicate on the network, you must install drivers for the network interface card(s) in the computer and for the protocols that the server will use to communicate with other systems. The NIC drivers have a LAN extension, and use parameters on the LOAD command line to specify the hardware resources that the card requires. When you have multiple NICs in a NetWare server, the operating system routes traffic between the different networks by default.

In addition to the NIC drivers that address the network hardware, you must also install drivers for the protocols that you will run on the network. With the exception of NetWare 5, all NetWare versions require Novell's proprietary IPX protocols to communicate with clients. IPX is a connectionless datagram protocol that carries the messages generated by several upper-layer protocols, including SPX and the NetWare Core Protocol. These are the protocols that clients use to access files and printers on servers and perform other standard NetWare functions.

Note
For more information on the IPX protocol suite, see Chapter 12.

NetWare 3.x and 4.x support other protocols, such as TCP/IP, but not for NetWare client/server communications. If, for example, you run a Web server or other Internet service on a NetWare server, you must install the TCP/IP driver in order for Web browsers or other clients to communicate with the server.

You load protocols in the same manner as other drivers, using the LOAD command with appropriate parameters. To use a loaded protocol, you must bind it to one or all of the NIC drivers installed in the system. In the case of a server with multiple NICs, the use of individual bindings enables you to control which protocols are routed between the connected networks. To bind a protocol to a NIC driver, you use the BIND console command to associate a particular protocol driver with a particular NIC driver. In the case of TCP/IP, the BIND command contains the IP address and subnet mask for the NIC (since these will be different for each interface bound to the TCP/IP protocol driver).

Building NCF Files

As on a DOS system, a NetWare server runs batch files when it starts, to configure the OS and load drivers and applications. Instead of using Config.sys and Autoexec.bat, however, NetWare servers use two files called Startup.ncf and Autoexec.ncf. An NCF (NetWare Command File) is simply a text file containing a series of console commands with parameters, just like those that you can issue from the server command prompt. Startup.ncf is stored on the server's DOS partition, because it contains the commands that load the disk drivers. These drivers must load before the server can mount its SYS volume, which contains the other batch file, Autoexec.ncf.

One of the functions of the installation program is to detect the hardware in the computer and build these batch files with commands appropriate to the hardware and to the environment specified by the installer. As NetWare progressed through its various versions, the installation program became increasingly sophisticated. Early 3.*x* versions did virtually no hardware detection and left much of the system configuration up to the installer. By the time version 4.11 was released, the installation process was much easier, because the program was capable of detecting most of the common hardware in modern systems and contained default values for most of the configuration parameters that worked on a majority of systems.

The installation program also enables you to create partitions and volumes on the server's hard disk drives, and then it creates the directory service (either bindery or NDS) on the default SYS volume. Once the installation program has completed all of these tasks, the server restarts and executes all of the commands in the NCF files. At this point, the server is functional and ready to accept connections from clients.

Once the NetWare server is installed, you can modify its startup configuration by editing the Startup.ncf and Autoexec.ncf files directly, using a text editor like the Edit.nlm program included with NetWare, or by using NetWare's Install.nlm utility and the server console. Alternatively, NetWare versions 4.*x* and higher include an Internetworking Configuration utility (Inetcfg.nlm) that enables you to create more complex multinetwork configurations using WAN connections and routing protocols. The first time that you run Inetcfg.nlm on the server console, it removes the commands from Autoexec.ncf that load and bind the NIC and protocol drivers, and imports them into its databases. From this point on, you must use Inetcfg to modify your server's networking configuration. Inetcfg provides a menu-driven interface that makes it easier to reconfigure your server and explore NetWare's WAN and routing capabilities (see Figure 15-3).

NetWare Updates

As with most other operating systems, Novell issues patches between major releases to correct problems and sometimes to provide new features. The original model that Novell used for providing these fixes was to release each patch individually, sometimes resulting in dozens of individual patches that administrators had to download, evaluate, and install. This method is not only inconvenient, it can also result in problems due to

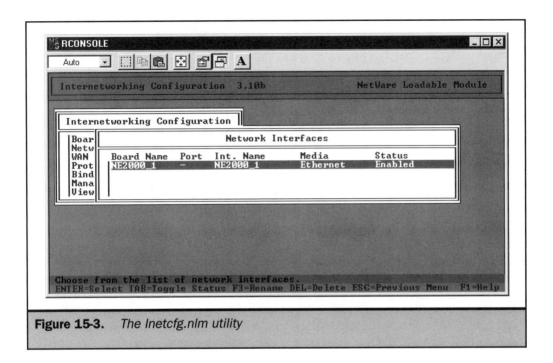

Figure 15-3.   *The Inetcfg.nlm utility*

incompatible modules. The more fixes there are to install, the greater the number of combinations that may be found on a particular server. If a server has only some of the patch releases installed, it may react differently from a server running all of the patches, or a different combination of patches.

To some extent, this is the model that is still used for NetWare 3.12, although some of the fixes have been bundled into packages that simplify the update process. As of this writing, 12 collections of patches are needed to bring NetWare 3.12 up to date. Note, however, that these are the fixes that Novell recommends for every installation. There are other patches addressing highly specific problems that are intended only for sites that are experiencing that problem. There is currently only one patch recommended for NetWare 3.12, since this is a relatively new release.

For NetWare 4.*x* and 5, Novell adopted the method used by Microsoft for its Windows NT (and other product) updates, releasing what it calls Support Packs. Like Microsoft Service Packs, Support Packs are numbered releases containing all of the patches recommended for the OS at that time. The patches are all installed at once, simplifying the process for the administrator, and have all been tested together, simplifying the development process for Novell. Support Pack releases are cumulative, meaning that each release includes all of the material in the previous releases.

The convenience of this practice is dubious, however. It is good for an administrator to be able to download a single file containing all of the fixes for the OS, but once several Support Packs have been released for one OS version, the size of the subsequent downloads can be enormous. The Support Pack 6 release for NetWare 4.11 is 36,707,321 bytes in size. Providing a release containing only the patches added since the last Support Pack would be helpful to a great many administrators.

Support Pack releases are intended for all servers running that NetWare version, but there are other patch releases intended to address only specific problems. In most cases, it is not a good idea to install every patch that comes along; just because it's newer doesn't mean it's better. If you are experiencing the specific problem that a patch addresses, install it, but otherwise your best bet is to leave well enough alone.

The NetWare Storage Subsystem

Unlike peer-to-peer network operating systems such as Windows 9x, NT, and 2000, NetWare only shares the files and directories on designated servers, not on client systems. Because the server is largely dedicated to tasks like this, instead of running a GUI and user applications, the file sharing performance is often better on a NetWare server than on a comparably equipped Windows NT machine.

NetWare uses a proprietary file system that can coexist on a hard disk drive with other types of partition formats, like the DOS FAT and Windows NT NTFS file systems, but it uses no part of these other formats itself. You do not use any of the standard tools (such as FDISK and FORMAT) to create and manage NetWare partitions, nor can you use diagnostic and repair tools like Microsoft's ScanDisk and Norton Disk Doctor on them.

The NetWare file system consists of *partitions,* of which there can be no more than one on a hard disk drive, and *volumes,* into which the partition is divided. A NetWare partition uses a standard partition table entry in the master boot record of a hard disk drive, just as FAT and NTFS partitions do. You create NetWare partitions on drives using the NetWare Install.nlm utility at the server console. When you install NetWare on a server, you must first have a standard FAT partition on the computer's primary drive, to boot the system. The area of the disk that will be used for the NetWare partition should be left as free space.

During the installation process, the NetWare installation program will create a partition on the drive. On that partition, you must create at least one volume, called SYS, which is where the operating system files will be located. You should avoid storing your user data on this volume, so you should be careful not to make it too big; but remember also that this is where NetWare stores the NDS database (even though it doesn't appear as visible files), so be sure to leave enough space for its potential growth.

You can then use any remaining space in the partition to create up to seven additional *segments,* for a total of eight in any one partition. Each segment can be a self-contained volume or part of a volume that spans several segments, either in the same or different partitions. If you have other hard disk drives in the server, you can create partitions and volumes on them in the same way. While it is possible to create a single volume using segments in partitions on separate drives, be aware that if one of the drives fails, you will lose the entire volume. NetWare also includes the ability to create mirrored volumes on separate partitions, which provides fault tolerance at the expense of disk space.

 If you choose to create volumes that are composed of segments on different disk drives or mirrored volumes, be sure to use drives with comparable capabilities. If one segment of a volume or one mirror image is hosted by a drive that is demonstrably slower than the others, the performance of the entire volume will be degraded by the slower device.

Once you have created a volume, you must mount it in before server processes or clients on the network can access it. A server's Autoexec.ncf file typically includes the MOUNT ALL command, which takes care of this task automatically each time the server starts. However, you can manually mount and dismount volumes at any time by using the MOUNT and DISMOUNT commands at the server console prompt.

Disk Allocation Blocks

When you create a volume, you must select the size for the blocks it will use: 4, 8, 16, 32, or 64KB. The volume is divided into *disk allocation blocks* (much like a FAT drive). A disk allocation block was originally the smallest unit of disk space that the server was able to allocate when storing a file. For example, if you specify a 4KB block size, a 9KB file would require three blocks, or 12KB, with the remaining 3KB going to waste. NetWare 4.*x* introduced a feature called *block suballocation,* which mitigated some of this wastage.

Unlike FAT drives, which automatically determine the block size based on the size of the volume, NetWare enables you to specify the block size for each volume you create. Selecting the appropriate block size can be an important element of building a high-performance storage subsystem. To use block sizes most efficiently, you have to consider the type of data that you intend to store on the server, and then organize your volumes accordingly.

If, for example, you intend to store large database files on a server, the best course of action is to dedicate a volume to those large files and use a larger block size for it. This will increase file access efficiency in several ways, such as the following:

- **Fewer blocks read** Using smaller blocks means a larger number of disk read operations are required to access a file. Using larger blocks reduces the mechanical overhead required for the hard disk drive to access the file.

- **Less server memory required** Each block requires an entry in the FAT for that drive. Larger blocks means that fewer entries are required for a given file and that less memory is needed to read them.

- **Faster read-aheads** NetWare's file system attempts to anticipate users' needs when they request a file, by reading the subsequent files on the disk into memory before they are actually requested. Larger blocks enable the server to read more of this data into memory faster than small blocks will.

The drawback to a large block size is that if you store small files on the volume, the amount of wasted space will increase. To use the previous example, storing a 9KB file on a volume with a 64KB block size will waste 55KB of space. Multiply this by a large number of small files, and a great deal of the volume's capacity can end up being wasted.

By default, NetWare 3.x sets a block size of 4KB on all new volumes. NetWare versions 4.x and higher select a block size based on the volume's size, much like the FAT file system. For all volumes larger than 500MB, the default block size is 64KB, because the NetWare 4.x block suballocation feature enables the server to allocate space in increments smaller than the block size. You can select any valid block size for your volumes as you create them, even different sizes for volumes on the same hard disk. However, you cannot change the block size once the volume has been created without destroying the volume (erasing the data) and re-creating it.

DETs and FATs

The *directory entry table (DET)* is where NetWare volumes store all of the information about the files stored on the volume, except for the file data itself. The directory structure you see when you look at a NetWare volume in Windows Explorer or another utility is not actually reflected in the storage of the data on the drive. The directory tree hierarchy is actually a virtual construction that exists physically only as information in the DET.

Each NetWare volume contains two copies of its DET, which is composed of 4KB blocks (no matter what block size you choose for the volume). Every file and directory on the volume has an entry in the DET that contains the following information:

- Whether the element is a file or directory
- The name of the file or directory
- The owner, attributes, and dates (created, last accessed, and last modified) of the file or directory
- The name of the file or directory's parent directory
- If a file, the location of the FAT entry for the first data segment in that file
- The location of name space information associated with the file or directory
- The trustee list for the file or directory

NetWare servers use the DET for all file management functions that do not access the actual file data. For example, when you view the contents of a directory, the server is actually scanning the DET for all entries specifying that directory as its parent.

NetWare volumes use file allocation tables (FATs) to keep track of the blocks used to store a particular file, just like DOS volumes do. Since the blocks containing the data for a single file are usually not stored contiguously on the disk, the FAT maintains the record of which blocks contain the data for that file. There is a numbered entry in the FAT for each block in the volume, and the DET specifies the number of the block containing the first data segment for each file. The first FAT entry for a file contains a reference to the FAT entry for the second data segment, the second entry contains a reference to the entry for the third segment, and so on, until the *FAT chain* reaches the entry representing the file's last data segment.

Name Spaces

NetWare uses the standard DOS 8.3 file and directory naming convention by default, but it also supports other file systems using *name spaces,* which take the form of additional DET entries that contain further information about the file or directory. For example, to support the long file and directory names created by Windows systems, you must install long name space support by loading a module called Long.nam at the server console. Since a standard DET entry cannot hold a file or directory name that is 255 characters long, the server uses additional entries to store the long name and includes references to the additional entries in the file's original DET entry.

When you load a name space module for the first time, you must execute the ADD NAME SPACE command at the server console prompt with the name space to be added and the volume to which it should be added, as in the following example:

```
ADD NAME SPACE LONG TO SYS
```

NetWare includes name space modules (all of which have an .nam extension) that support the following file systems:

- Windows VFAT
- Macintosh
- OS/2 HPFS
- NFS
- FTAM

Long file and directory names are only one feature that can be provided by name space modules. The capabilities that an individual name space adds to NetWare volumes depends on the file system that the name space supports.

While it may be tempting to add all of the available name spaces to your volumes, to provide maximum storage flexibility, you should avoid this practice. Each name space you install on a volume adds an entry to the DET for each file and directory on the volume. One name space, therefore, doubles the size of the DET. Adding many name spaces drastically increases the size of the table, causing it to occupy more disk space, and reducing the number of DET records cached in server memory.

NetWare servers store the most recently used DET entries in a memory cache, for rapid access should they be needed again. Adding a name space cuts the number of cached files and directories in half, since two DET entries are required for each file or directory. Fewer entries in the cache means that the server is more likely to have to access the DET information on the volume, instead of finding it in the cache. If you install too many name spaces on a volume, this can palpably degrade the performance of the volume.

Therefore, it is a good idea to only install the name spaces you actually need on a NetWare volume. In addition, it is a good idea to avoid using multiple name spaces on one volume, by designating specific volumes for storage of certain types of data. For example, allocating one volume for Macintosh file storage is a better solution than adding the MAC name space to all of your volumes, in case someone wants to store Macintosh files there.

It is also possible to adjust the amount of memory that a server uses for caching DET entries. The SET MINIMUM DIRECTORY CACHE BUFFERS command specifies the number of buffers that are automatically allocated for DET caching when the server is started. The default value for this parameter is 20, but you can set it to any value from 10 to 8,000. As the server runs, it allocates additional buffers to the DET cache as needed, up to the maximum specified by the SET MAXIMUM DIRECTORY CACHE BUFFERS command, which defaults to 500. You can set this parameter to any value from 20 to 20,000.

Assuming that you have sufficient memory in the server, you can increase the maximum in cases where you must install name spaces, in order to maintain (or perhaps improve) file system performance. Each 4KB memory buffer that you add to the cache can hold eight DET entries. Thus, to double the size both of the initial cache and the maximum cache, you would issue the following commands from the server console prompt (or add them to the Autoexec.ncf file):

```
SET MINIMUM DIRECTORY CACHE BUFFERS = 40
SET MAXIMUM DIRECTORY CACHE BUFFERS = 1000
```

NetWare 4.x File System Improvements

The basic NetWare file system as described in the preceding sections persists to this day, but the NetWare 4 release introduced several new features. For example, NetWare 4.x volumes can optionally use on-the-fly compression to increase their disk capacity. At a specified time each day or night, the server compresses all of the data on a volume in place. The next time that a user or application requests access to that file, the server automatically decompresses the file before delivering it to the requestor. The file then remains in the decompressed state, ready for further use, until the next compression cycle. This type of compression does have an effect on the performance of the volume, as well as the server's processor utilization; but in some cases, the additional storage space provided is worth the expenditure in other areas.

Another feature of the NetWare 4.x storage system is *block suballocation,* a mechanism that addresses the problem of wasted storage space caused by blocks that are not completely filled. Using small 4KB blocks minimizes the waste, but the ever-increasing capacity of today's hard disk drives makes the use of small blocks increasingly impractical. By dividing blocks into smaller, 512-byte units, it is possible to store files more efficiently, with a minimum of waste.

When a volume's block suballocation feature is activated, the server creates a number of *suballocation reserved blocks (SRBs)*. These are blocks that are divided into 512-byte segments and allocated for the storage of file fragments of various sizes. When writing a file to the volume, the server fills as many full blocks as it can and then uses the size of the leftover fragment to determine which SRB it should use to store the remaining data. As a result of this technique, the amount of space wasted in the worst possible case is no more than 512 bytes per file, which is a significant improvement over a volume that is not suballocated, even when it uses small 4KB blocks.

Block suballocation is an optional feature that is enabled by default and that you can control for each volume individually from the Install.nlm utility. However, there is rarely a good reason to disable it, because it functions completely invisibly and causes no obvious degeneration of system performance. If you do decide not to use block suballocation for a particular volume, you will probably want to modify the default 64KB block size for drives over 500MB. Without suballocation, a block size this large can lead to a great deal of wasted space.

Novell Storage Services

The NetWare 5 release introduced another improvement to the file system, called Novell Storage Services (NSS). NSS is a 64-bit, indexed storage service that uses the free space on multiple storage devices to create a single virtual partition that you can use to create an unlimited number of volumes. Volumes can be up to 8TB in size on today's 32-bit servers and up to 8 exabytes (that's 8×10^{64} bytes) on 64-bit servers. An NSS volume can store billions of files, with individual files up to 8TB in size. NSS also greatly increases the speed at which volumes mount, the slowness of which was a frequent complaint of the standard NetWare file system (which Novell has dubbed NWFS, now that it has something to compare it to).

Other NetWare Information

Novell Directory Services is one of the most important features of the NetWare 4.*x* and 5 operating systems, and is discussed in detail in Chapter 21. The IPX protocols used by NetWare for its client/server communications are covered in Chapter 12. The NetWare printing subsystem is discussed in Chapter 25.

The
Complete
Reference

Upgrading
&
Troubleshooting
Networks

Chapter 16

UNIX

U NIX is a multiuser, multitasking operating system (OS) with roots that date
back to the late 1960s. It was developed throughout the '70s by researchers at
AT&T's Bell Labs, finally culminating in UNIX System V Release 1 in 1983.
During this time, and since then, many other organizations have built their own
variants on the UNIX formula, and now dozens of different operating systems function
using the same basic UNIX components. This was possible because, from the
beginning, UNIX has been more of a collaborative research project than a commercial
product. Unlike companies such as Microsoft and Novell, which jealously guard the
source code to their operating systems, UNIX developers generally tend to make their
code freely available. This enables anyone with the appropriate skills to modify the OS
to their own specifications.

UNIX is not a user-friendly OS, nor is it commonly found on the desktop of the
average personal computer user. To its detractors, UNIX is an outdated OS that relies
primarily on an archaic, character-based interface. To its proponents, however, UNIX is
the most powerful, flexible, and stable OS available. As is usually the case, both
opinions are correct, to some degree.

Although its popularity is growing tremendously, you are not going to see racks of
UNIX-based games and other recreational software at the computer store any time
soon, nor are you likely to see offices full of employees running productivity
applications, such as word processors and spreadsheets, on UNIX systems. However,
when you use a browser to connect to a site on the Web, there's a good chance that the
server hosting the site is running some form of UNIX. In addition, many of the vertical
applications designed for specific industries, such as those used when you book a hotel
room or rent a car, run on UNIX systems.

Despite all this talk of its power and complexity, however, it is not impossible to
provide a user with a UNIX system that has a GUI and runs applications such as word
processors and Web browsers that function very much like their Windows
counterparts. GUIs are not as completely integrated into the UNIX operating systems
as they are in the various versions of Windows. Many of the most powerful UNIX
features require the use of the command prompt, and in many cases, the GUI is just
another program running on the computer rather than an integral part of the OS.

As a server operating system, UNIX has a reputation for being stable enough to
support mission-critical applications, portable enough to run on many different
hardware platforms, and scaleable enough to support a user base of almost any size.
All UNIX systems use TCP/IP as their native protocols, so they are naturally suited for
use on the Internet and for networking with other OSs. In fact, UNIX systems were
instrumental in the development of the Internet from an experiment in decentralized,
packet-switched networking to the worldwide phenomenon it is today.

UNIX Principles

More than other operating systems, UNIX is based on a principle of simplicity that
makes it highly adaptable to many different needs. This is not necessarily to say that

UNIX is simple to use, because generally it isn't. Rather, it means that the OS is based on guiding principles that treat the various elements of the computer in a simple and consistent way. For example, a UNIX system treats physical devices in the computer, such as printers, the keyboard, and the display, in exactly the same way as it treats the files and directories on its drives. You can copy a file to the display or to a printer just as you would copy it to another directory, and use the devices with any other appropriate file-based tools.

Another fundamental principle of UNIX is the use of small, simple tools that perform specific functions and that can easily work together with other tools to provide more complex functions. Instead of large applications with many built-in features, UNIX operating systems are far more likely to utilize a small tool that provides a basic service to other tools. A good example is the **sort** command, which takes the contents of a text file; sorts it according to user-supplied parameters; and sends the results to an output device, such as the display or a printer. In addition to applying the command to an existing text file, you can use it to sort the output of other commands before displaying or printing it.

The element that enables you to join tools together in this way is called a *pipe*, which enables you to use one tool to provide input to or accept output from another tool. DOS can use pipes to redirect standard input and output in various ways, but UNIX includes a much wider variety of tools and commands that can be combined to provide elaborate and powerful tools.

Thus, UNIX is based on relatively simple elements, but its ability to combine those elements makes it quite complex. While a large application attempts to anticipate the needs of the user by combining its functions in various predetermined ways, UNIX supplies users with the tools that provide the basic functions, and lets them combine the tools to suit their own needs. The result is an OS with great flexibility and extensibility, but that requires an operator with more than the average computer user's skills to take full advantage of it.

Because of this guiding principle, UNIX is in many ways a "programmer's operating system," because if a tool to perform a certain task is not included, you usually have the resources available to fashion one yourself. This is not to say that you have to be a programmer to use UNIX, but many of the techniques that programmers use when writing code are instrumental to the use of multiple tools on the UNIX command line.

The various UNIX OSs are built around basic elements that are fundamentally the same, but they include various collections of tools and programs. Depending on which variant you choose and whether it is a commercial product or a free download, you may find either that the OS comes complete with modules such as Web and DNS servers and other programs, or that you have to obtain these yourself. However, one of the other principles of UNIX development that has endured through the years is the custom of making the source code for UNIX software freely available to everyone. The result of this open source movement is a wealth of UNIX tools, applications, and other software that is freely available for download from the Internet.

In some cases, programmers modify existing UNIX modules for their own purposes and then release those modifications to the public domain so that they can be of help to others. Some programmers collaborate on UNIX software projects as something of a hobby and release the results to the public. One of the best examples of this is the Linux OS, which was designed from the beginning to be a free product and which has now become one of the most popular UNIX variants in use today.

UNIX Architecture

Because UNIX is available in so many variants, UNIX operating systems can run on a variety of hardware platforms, from simple Intel 80386-based PCs to dedicated workstations costing hundreds of thousands of dollars. Many of the UNIX variants are proprietary versions created by specific manufacturers to run on their own hardware platforms. Sun Microsystems' Solaris, Hewlett-Packard's HP-UX, IBM's AIX, and Silicon Graphics' IRIX are all examples of OSs that are packaged with a workstation built by the same manufacturer. Most of the software-only UNIX solutions run on Intel-based PCs, and some are available in versions for multiple platforms. Solaris, for example, comes in a version for Sun's proprietary SPARC platform and in an Intel version.

The hardware requirements for the various UNIX platforms vary greatly, depending on the functions required of the machine. You can run Linux on an old 386, for example, as long as you don't expect to use a GUI or run a server supporting a large number of users. At the high end, some of the proprietary workstation platforms, like those from Silicon Graphics, are massively powerful (and massively expensive) machines that the movie industry uses to create state-of-the-art special effects.

No matter what hardware a UNIX system uses, however, the basic software components are the same (see Figure 16-1). The *kernel* is the core module that insulates the programs running on the computer from the hardware. The kernel contains device drivers that interact with the specific hardware devices installed in the computer, to perform basic functions like memory management, input/output, interrupt handling, and access control.

The kernel provides approximately 100 system calls that programs can use to execute certain tasks, such as opening a file, executing a program, and terminating a process. These are the building blocks that programmers use to integrate hardware-related functions into their applications' more complex tasks. The system calls can vary between the different UNIX versions to some extent, particularly in the way that the system internals perform the different functions.

Above the kernel is the shell, which provides the interface that you use to issue commands and execute programs. The shell is a command interpreter, much like Command.com in DOS and Cmd.exe in Windows NT/2000, which provides a character-based command prompt that you use to interact with the system. The shell

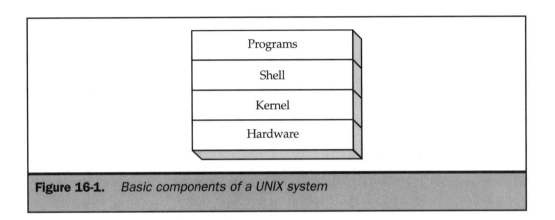

Figure 16-1.   *Basic components of a UNIX system*

also functions as a programming language that you can use to create scripts, which are functionally similar to DOS batch files but much more versatile and powerful.

Unlike DOS and Windows NT, which limit you to a single command interpreter, UNIX traditionally has several shells that you can choose from, with different capabilities. The shells that are included with particular UNIX OSs vary, but others are available as free downloads. Often, the selection of a shell is a matter of personal preference, guided by the user's previous experience. The basic commands used for file management and other standard system tasks are the same in all of the shells. The differences become more evident when you run more complex commands and create scripts.

The original UNIX shell is a program called *sh* that was created by Steve Bourne, and is commonly known as the *Bourne shell*. Some of the other common shells are as follows:

- **csh**   Known as the C shell, and originally created for use with BSD UNIX; utilizes a syntax similar to that of the C language and introduces features such as a command history list, job control, and aliases. Scripts written for the Bourne shell usually need some modification to run in the C shell.

- **ksh**   Known as the *Korn shell*; builds on the Bourne shell and adds elements of the C shell, as well as other improvements. Scripts written for the Bourne shell usually can run in the Korn shell without modification.

- **bash**   The default shell used by Linux; closely related to the Korn shell, with elements of the C shell.

In addition to the character-based shells, it is also possible to use a GUI to interact with a UNIX system. Many different GUIs are available for the various UNIX versions, such as Motif and Open Look. Some UNIX variants, such as Solaris, include their own proprietary GUI implementation, while others, such as Linux, use an X Windows server that enables you to run any one of many window managers, such as the K Desktop Environment (KDE). In response to the popularity of Windows, UNIX GUIs have advanced considerably in quality and capability in recent years, to the point at which they rival the Windows interface in functionality (see Figure 16-2).

Above the shell are the commands that you use to perform tasks on the system. UNIX includes hundreds of small programs, usually called *tools* or *commands*, that you can combine on the command line to perform complex tasks. Hundreds of other tools are available on the Internet that you can combine with those provided with the OS. UNIX command-line tools are programs, but don't confuse them with the complex applications used by other OSs, such as Windows. UNIX has full-blown applications, as well, but its real power lies in these small programs. Adding a new tool on a UNIX system does not require an installation procedure; you simply have to specify the appropriate location of the tool in the file system in order for the shell to run it.

Figure 16-2.   *The K Desktop Environment can be configured to look like Windows*

UNIX Versions

The sheer number of UNIX variants can be bewildering to anyone trying to find the appropriate operating system for a particular application. However, apart from systems intended for special purposes, virtually any UNIX OS can perform well in a variety of roles, and the selection you make may be based more on economic factors, hardware platform, or personal taste than on anything else. If, for example, you decide to purchase proprietary UNIX workstations, you'll be using the version of the OS intended for the machine. If you intend to run UNIX on Intel-based computers, then you might choose the OS based on the GUI that you feel most comfortable with; or, you might be looking for the best bargain you can find, and limit yourself to the versions available as free downloads. The following sections discuss some of the major UNIX versions available.

UNIX System V

UNIX System V is the culmination of the original UNIX work begun by AT&T's Bell Labs in the 1970s. Up until release 3.2, the project was wholly developed by AT&T, even while other UNIX work was ongoing at the University of California, Berkeley, and other places. UNIX System V Release 4 (SVR4), released in the late 1980s, consolidated the benefits of the SVR operating system with those of Berkeley's BSD, Sun's SunOS, and Microsoft's Xenix. This release brought together some of the most important elements that are now indelibly associated with the name UNIX, including networking elements like the TCP/IP Internet Package from BSD, which includes file transfer, remote login, and remote program execution capabilities, and the Network File System (NFS) from SunOS.

AT&T eventually split its UNIX development project off into a subsidiary called UNIX System Laboratories (USL), which released System V Release 4.2. In 1993, AT&T sold USL to Novell, which released its own version of SVR4 under the name UnixWare. In light of pressure from the other companies involved in UNIX development, Novell transferred the UNIX trademark to a consortium called X/Open, thus enabling any manufacturer to describe its product as a UNIX OS. In 1995, Novell sold all of its interest in UNIX SVR4 and UnixWare to the Santa Cruz Operation (SCO), which owns it to this day. In 1997, SCO released UNIX System V Release 5 (SVR5) under the name OpenServer, as well as version 7 of its UnixWare product. These are the descendents of the original AT&T products, and are still on the market.

BSD UNIX

In 1975, one of the original developers of UNIX, Ken Thompson, took a sabbatical at the University of California, Berkeley, and while there, he ported his current UNIX version to a PDP-11/70 system. The seed he planted took root, and Berkeley became a major developer of UNIX in its own right. BSD UNIX introduced several of the major features associated with most UNIX versions, including the C shell and the vi text editor. Several versions of BSD UNIX appeared throughout the 1970s, culminating in 3BSD. In 1979, the U.S. Department of Defense's Advanced Research Projects Agency (DARPA) funded the development of 4BSD, which was coincident with the development and adoption of the TCP/IP networking protocols.

Eventually, BSD UNIX came to be the OS that many other organizations used as the basis for their own UNIX products, including Sun Microsystems' SunOS. The result of this is that many of the programs written for one BSD-based UNIX version are binary-compatible with other versions. Once the SVR4 release consolidated the best features of BSD and several other UNIX versions into one product, the BSD product became less influential, and culminated in the 4.4BSD version in 1992.

Although many of the UNIX variants that are popular today owe a great debt to the BSD development project, the versions of BSD that are still commonly used are public domain OSs, like FreeBSD, NetBSD, and Open BSD. All of these OSs are based on Berkeley's 4.4BSD release and can be downloaded from the Internet free of charge and used for private and commercial applications at no cost.

FreeBSD

FreeBSD, available at http://www.freebsd.org in versions for the Intel and Alpha platforms, is based on the Berkeley 4.4BSD-Lite2 release, and is binary-compatible with Linux, SCO, SVR4, and NetBSD applications. The FreeBSD development project is divided into two branches: the STABLE branch, which includes only well-tested bug fixes and incremental enhancements, and the CURRENT branch, which includes all of the latest code and is intended primarily for developers, testers, and enthusiasts. The current stable version as of December 1999 is 3.4.

NetBSD

NetBSD, available at http://www.netbsd.org, is derived from the same sources as FreeBSD, but places portability as one of its highest priorities. NetBSD is available in formal releases for 15 different hardware platforms, ranging from Intel and Alpha to Macintosh, SPARC, and MIPS processors, including those designed for handheld Windows CE devices. Many other ports are in the developmental and experimental stages. NetBSD's binary compatibility enables it to support applications written for many other UNIX variants, including BSD, FreeBSD, HP/UX, Linux, SVR4, Solaris, SunOS, and others. Networking capabilities supported directly by the kernel include NFS, IPv6, Network Address Translation (NAT), and packet filtering. The latest version of NetBSD, released in August 1999, is 1.4.1.

OpenBSD

OpenBSD is available at http://www.openbsd.org; the current version is 2.6, released in December 1999. Like the other BSD-derived OSs, OpenBSD is binary-compatible with most of its peers, including FreeBSD, SVR4, Solaris, SunOS, and HP/UX, and currently supports 11 hardware platforms, including Intel, Alpha, SPARC, PowerPC, and others. However, the top priority of OpenBSD's developers is security and cryptography. Because OpenBSD is a noncommercial product, its developers feel that they can take a more uncompromising stance on security issues and disclose more information about security than commercial software developers. Also, because it is developed in and distributed from Canada, OpenBSD is not subject to the American laws that prohibit the export of cryptographic software to other countries. The developers are, therefore, more likely than American-based companies to take a cryptographic approach to security solutions.

Linux

Developed as a college project by Linus Torvalds of Sweden, Linux has emerged as one of the most popular UNIX variants in recent years. Like FreeBSD, NetBSD, and OpenBSD, Linux is available as a free download from the Internet in versions for most of the standard hardware platforms, and is continually refined by an ad hoc group of programmers that communicate mainly through Internet mailing lists and newsgroups. Because of its popularity, a lot of people are working on the development of Linux modules and applications. Many new features and capabilities are the result of programmers adapting the existing software for their own uses and then posting their code for others to use. As the product increases in popularity, more people work on it in this way, and the development process accelerates.

This flurry of activity has also led to the fragmentation of the Linux development process. Many different Linux versions are now available, which are similar in their kernel functions but vary in the features they include. As with the various BSD OSs now available, some of these Linux packages are available for download on the Internet, but the growth in the popularity of the OS has led to some semicommercial distribution releases as well.

The most popular version of Linux right now is called Red Hat Linux, distributed by a company whose success is based on the packaging and sales of a free product for a more general audience. The popularity of Linux has reached the point at which it is expanding beyond UNIX's traditional market of computer professionals and technical hobbyists. In part, this is due to a backlash against Microsoft, which some people believe is close to holding a monopoly on OSs. When you pay for a "commercial" Linux release like Red Hat, you get not only the OS and source code on CD-ROM, but also a variety of applications, product documentation, and technical support, which are often lacking in the free download releases. Other distributors, such as Slackware, Debian, and Caldera, provide similar products and services, but this does not necessarily mean that these Linux versions are binary-compatible. In some cases, software written for one distribution will not run on another one.

The free Linux distributions provide much of the same functionality as the commercial ones, but in a less convenient package. The downloads can be very large and time-consuming, and you may find yourself interrupting the installation process frequently to track down some essential piece of information or to download an additional module you didn't know you needed. Generally speaking, the commercial

Linux products offer a slicker package with a smoother installation process and the knowledge that you have on the CD-ROMs all of the software you need to get a system up and running. You also have better documentation and someone to contact for help when you need it, all for a minimal cost (about $50 to $100).

Sun Solaris

Sun Microsystems (http://www.sun.com) has been involved in UNIX development since the early 1980s, when its operating system was known as SunOS. In 1991, Sun created a subsidiary called SunSoft that began work on a new UNIX version based on SVR4, which it called Solaris. Several versions later, Solaris 8 is one of the most popular (if not the most popular) commercial UNIX versions on the market.

Aside from the SunOS kernel, the Solaris OS includes the OpenWindows 3.x GUI, which is X Windows-based. Sun also manufactures its own proprietary computer hardware, based around a processor called SPARC, and Solaris is naturally designed to take full advantage of the platform, although it is available in a version for Intel systems as well. Although Solaris is a commercial product, Sun also supplies the OS to noncommercial users both as a free download or on CD-ROM for the cost of the media and shipping.

UNIX Networking

UNIX is a peer-to-peer network operating system, in that every computer is capable of both accessing resources on other systems and sharing its own resources. These networking capabilities take three basic forms, as follows:

- The ability to open a session on another machine and execute commands on its shell.
- The ability to access the file system on another machine, using a service like NFS.
- The ability to run a service (called a *daemon*) on one system and access it using a client on another system.

The TCP/IP protocols are an integral part of all UNIX OSs, and many of the TCP/IP programs and services that may be familiar to you from working with the Internet are also implemented on UNIX networks. For example, UNIX networks can use DNS servers to resolve host names into IP addresses and use BOOTP or DHCP servers to automatically configure TCP/IP clients. Standard Internet services like FTP and Telnet have long been a vital element of UNIX networking, as are utilities like ping and traceroute.

The following sections examine the types of network access used on UNIX systems and the tools involved in implementing them.

For more information on the TCP/IP protocols, see Chapter 11; for more information on DHCP and DNS, see Chapters 18 and 20.

Using Remote Commands

One form of network access that is far more commonly used on UNIX than on other network operating systems is the remote console session, in which a user connects to another computer on the network and executes commands on that system. Once the connection is established, commands entered by the user at the client system are executed by the remote server and the output is redirected over the network back to the client's display.

Because UNIX relies heavily on the command prompt, character-based remote sessions are more useful than they are in a more graphically oriented environment like that of Windows NT. Although a remote console application is available for Windows NT (as part of the Windows NT 4.0 Server Resource Kit), its command-line capabilities are relatively limited when compared to those of UNIX.

Berkeley Remote Commands

The Berkeley Remote Commands were originally a part of BSD UNIX, and have since been adopted by virtually every other UNIX OS. Sometimes known as the r* commands, these tools are intended primarily for use on LANs, rather than over WAN or Internet links. These commands enable you not only to open a session on a remote system, but also to perform specific tasks on a remote system without logging in and working interactively with a shell prompt.

rlogin

The rlogin command establishes a connection to another system on the network and provides access to its shell. Once connected, any commands you enter are executed by the other computer using its processor, file system, and other components. To connect to another machine on the network, you use a command like the following:

```
rlogin [-l username] hostname
```

where the *hostname* variable specifies the name of the system to which you want to connect.

Authentication is required for the target system to establish the connection, which can happen using either host-level or user-level security. To use host-level security, the client system must be trusted by the server by having its host name listed in the /etc/host.equiv file on the server. When this is the case, the client logs in without a username or password, because it is automatically trusted by the server no matter who's using the system.

NETWORK OPERATING SYSTEMS

User-level security requires the use of a username and sometimes a password, in addition to the host name. By default, rlogin supplies the name of the user currently logged in on the client system to the remote system, as well as information about the type of terminal used to connect, which is taken from the value of the TERM variable. The named user must have an account in the remote system's password database; and if the client system is not trusted by the remote system, the remote system may then prompt the client for the password associated with that username. It's also possible to log in using a different username by specifying it on the rlogin command line with the –l switch.

For the username to be authenticated by the remote system without using a password, it must be defined as an equivalent user by being listed in a .rhosts file located in the user's home directory on that system. The .rhosts file contains a list of host names and usernames that specify whether a user working on a specific machine should be granted immediate access to the command prompt. Depending on the security requirements for the remote system, the .rhosts files can be owned either by the remote users themselves or the root account on the system. Adding users to your .rhosts file is a simple way of giving them access to your account on that machine without giving them the password.

Once you have successfully established a connection to a remote system, you can execute any command in its shell that you would on your local system, except for those that launch graphical applications. You can also use rlogin from the remote shell to connect to a third computer, giving you simultaneous access to all three. To terminate the connection to a remote system, you can use the exit command, press the CTRL-D key combination, or type a tilde followed by a period (~.).

rsh

In some instances, you may want to execute a single command on a remote system and view the resulting output without actually logging in. You can do this with the rsh command, using the following syntax:

```
rsh hostname command
```

where the *hostname* variable specifies the system on which you want to open a remote shell, and the *command* variable is the command to be executed on the remote system. Unlike rlogin, interactive authentication is not possible with rsh; so for the command to work, the user must have either a properly configured .rhosts file on the remote system or an entry in the /etc/host.equiv file. The rsh command provides essentially the same command-line capabilities as rlogin, except that it works for only a single command and does not maintain an open session.

 Note   *The rsh command is called remsh on HP-UX systems. There are many cases in which commands providing identical functions have different names on various UNIX OSs.*

rcp

The rcp command is used to copy files to or from a remote system across a network without performing an interactive login. The rcp functions much like the cp command used to copy files on the local system, using the following syntax:

```
rcp [-r] sourcehost:filename desthost:filename
```

where the *sourcehost:filename* variable specifies the host name of the source system and the name of the file to be copied, and the *desthost:filename* variable specifies the host name of the destination system and the name that the file should be given on that system. You can also copy entire directories by adding the –r parameter to the command and specifying directory names instead of filenames. As with rsh, there is no login procedure; so to use rcp, either the client system must be trusted by the remote system or the user must be listed in the .rhosts file.

Secure Shell Commands

The downside of the Berkeley Remote Commands is that they are inherently insecure. Passwords are transmitted over the network in cleartext, making it possible for intruders to intercept them. Because of this susceptibility to compromise, some administrators prohibit the use of these commands. To address this problem, there is a Secure Shell program that provides the same functions as rlogin, rsh, and rcp, but with greater security. The equivalent programs in the Secure Shell are called slogin, ssh, and scp. The primary differences in using these commands are that the connection is authenticated on both sides and all passwords are transmitted in encrypted form.

 For more information about the Secure Shell, see http://www.ssh.fi.

DARPA Commands

The Berkeley Remote Commands are designed for use on like UNIX systems; but the DARPA commands were designed as part of the TCP/IP protocol suite, and can be used by any two systems that support TCP/IP. Virtually all UNIX OSs include both the client and server programs for telnet, ftp, and tftp, and install them by default, although some administrators may choose to disable them later.

telnet

The telnet program is similar in its functionality to rlogin, except that telnet does not send any information about the user on the client system to the server. You must always supply a username and password to be authenticated. As with all of the DARPA commands, you can use a telnet client to connect to any computer running a telnet server, even if it is running a different version of UNIX or a non-UNIX OS. The commands you can use while connected, however, are wholly dependent on the OS running the telnet server. If, for example, you install a third-party telnet server on a Windows NT system (since NT ships with a telnet client but not a server), you can connect to it from a UNIX client, but once connected, you can only use commands recognized by NT. Since NT is not primarily a character-based OS, its command-line capabilities are relatively limited, unless you install outside programs.

ftp

The ftp command provides more comprehensive file transfer capabilities than rcp, and enables a client to access the file system on any computer running an ftp server. However, instead of accessing files in place on the other system, ftp provides only the ability to transfer files to and from the remote system. For example, you cannot edit a file on a remote system, but you can download it to your own system, edit it there, and then upload the new version back to the original location. As with telnet, users must authenticate themselves to an ftp server before they are granted access to the file system. Many systems running ftp, such as those on the Internet, support anonymous access, but even this requires an authentication process in which the user supplies the name "anonymous" and the server is configured to accept any password.

Note   *For more information on the FTP protocol, see Chapter 26.*

tftp

The tftp command uses the Trivial File Transfer Protocol to copy files to or from a remote system. Whereas ftp relies on the Transmission Control Protocol (TCP) at the transport layer, tftp uses the User Datagram Protocol (UDP) instead. Because UDP is a connectionless protocol, no authentication by the remote system is needed. However, this limits the command to copying only files that are publicly available on the remote system.

Network File System (NFS)

Sharing files is an essential part of computer networking, and UNIX systems use several mechanisms to access files on other systems without first transferring them to a local drive, as with ftp and rcp. The most commonly used of these mechanisms is the Network File System (NFS), which was developed by Sun Microsystems in the 1980s and has now been published by the Internet Engineering Task Force (IETF) as RFC 1094 (NFS Version 2) and RFC 1813 (NFS Version 3). By allowing NFS to be published as an open standard, Sun made it possible for anyone to implement the service, and the result is that NFS support is available for virtually every OS in use today.

Practically every UNIX variant available includes support for NFS, which makes it possible to share files among systems running different UNIX versions. Non-UNIX OSs, such as Windows NT and NetWare, can also support NFS, but a separate product (marketed by either the manufacturer or a third party) is required. Since Windows and NetWare have their own internal file-sharing mechanisms, these other OSs mostly use NFS to integrate UNIX systems into their networks.

NFS is a client/server application in which a server makes all or part of its file system available to clients (using a process called *exporting* or *sharing*), and a client accesses the remote file system by *mounting* it, which makes it appear just like part of the local file system. NFS does not communicate directly with the kernel on the local computer, but rather relies on the remote procedure calls (RPC) service, also developed by Sun, to handle communications with the remote system. RPC has also been released as an open standard by Sun, and published as an IETF document called RFC 1057. The data transmitted by NFS is encoded using a method called *External Data Representation (XDR)*, as defined in RFC 1014. In most cases, the service uses the UDP protocol for network transport and listens on port 2049.

NFS is designed to keep the server side of the application as simple as possible. NFS servers are *stateless*, meaning they do not have to maintain information about the state of a client to function properly. In other words, the server does not maintain information about which clients have files open. In the event that a server crashes, clients simply continue to send their requests until the server responds. If a client crashes, the server continues to operate normally. There is no need for a complicated reconnection sequence. Because repeated iterations of the same activities can be the consequence of this statelessness, NFS is also designed to be as *idempotent* as possible, meaning that the repeated performance of the same task will not have a deleterious effect on the performance of the system. NFS servers also take no part in the adaptation of the exported file system to the client's requirements. The server supplies file system information in a generalized form, and it is up to the client to integrate it into its own file system so that applications can make use of it.

The communication between NFS clients and servers is based on a series of RPC procedures defined in the NFS standard and listed in Table 16-1. These basic functions enable the client to interact with the file system on the server in all of the ways expected by a typical application.

On a system configured to function as an NFS server, you can control which parts of the file system are accessible to clients by using commands such as share on Solaris and SVR4 systems, and exportfs on Linux and HP-UX. Using these commands, you specify which directories clients can access and what degree of access they are provided. You can choose to share a directory on a read-only basis, for example, or grant read/write access, and you can also designate different access permissions for specific users.

Client systems access the directories that have been shared by a server by using the mount command to integrate them into the local file system. The mount command specifies a directory shared by a server, the access that client applications should have to the remote directory (such as read/write or read/only), and the mount point for the remote files. The *mount point* is a directory on the local system in which the shared files and directories will appear. Applications and commands running on the client system can reference the remote files just as if they were located on a local drive.

NETWORK OPERATING SYSTEMS

Procedure Number	Procedure Name	Function
0	NULL	Does not do any work; used for server response testing and timing.
1	GETATTR	Retrieves attributes for a specified file system object.
2	SETATTR	Changes one or more of the attributes of a file system object on the server.
3	LOOKUP	Searches a directory for a specific name and returns the file handle for the corresponding file system object.
4	ACCESS	Determines the access rights that a user has with respect to a file system object.
5	READLINK	Reads the data associated with a symbolic link.
6	READ	Reads data from a file.
7	WRITE	Writes data to a file.
8	CREATE	Creates a regular file.
9	MKDIR	Creates a new subdirectory.
10	SYMLINK	Creates a new symbolic link.
11	MKNOD	Creates a new special file.
12	REMOVE	Deletes a file from a directory.
13	RMDIR	Deletes a subdirectory from a directory.
14	RENAME	Renames a file or directory.
15	LINK	Creates a link to an object.
16	READDIR	Retrieves a variable number of entries from a directory and returns the name and file identifier for each.
17	READDIRPLUS	Retrieves a variable number of entries from a file system directory and returns complete information about each.

Table 16-1.   *RPC Procedures Supplied by an NFS Version 3 Protocol Server*

Procedure Number	Procedure Name	Function
18	FSSTAT	Retrieves volatile file system state information.
19	FSINFO	Retrieves nonvolatile file system state information and general information about the NFS Version 3 protocol server implementation.
20	PATHCONF	Retrieves POSIX information for a file or directory.
21	COMMIT	Forces or flushes data to stable storage that was previously written with a WRITE procedure call with the stable field set to UNSTABLE.

Table 16-1. *RPC Procedures Supplied by an NFS Version 3 Protocol Server* (continued)

Client/Server Networking

Client/server computing is the basis for networking on UNIX systems, as it is on many other computing platforms. UNIX is a popular application server platform largely because its relative simplicity and flexibility enables the computer to devote more of its resources toward its primary function. On a Windows NT server, for example, a significant amount of system resources are devoted to running the GUI and other subsystems that may have little or nothing to do with the server applications that are its primary functions. When you dedicate a computer to functioning as a Web server, for example, and you want it to be able to service as many clients as possible, it makes sense to disable all extraneous functions, which is something that is far easier to do on a UNIX system than on Windows NT.

Server applications on UNIX systems typically run as *daemons*, which are background processes that run continuously, regardless of the system's other activities. There are many commercial server products available for various UNIX versions, and also a great many that are available free of charge. Because the TCP/IP protocols were largely developed on the UNIX platform, UNIX server software is available for every TCP/IP application in existence. For example, a computer running Linux as its OS and Apache as its Web server software is a powerful combination that is easily equal or superior to most of the commercial products on the market—and the software is completely free.

The Complete Reference

Upgrading & Troubleshooting Networks

Chapter 17

Network Clients

W hile network administrators frequently spend a lot of time installing and configuring servers, the primary reason for the servers' existence is the clients. The choice of applications and operating systems for your servers should be based in part on the client platforms and operating systems that have to access them. Generally speaking, it is possible for any client platform to connect to any server, one way or another, but this doesn't mean that you should choose client and server platforms freely and expect them all to work well together in every combination.

For ease of administration, it's a good idea to use the same operating system on your client workstations wherever possible. Most network installations use standard Intel-based PCs running some version of Microsoft Windows; but even if you choose to standardize on Windows, you may have some users with special needs that require a different platform. Graphic artists, for example, are often accustomed to working on Macintosh systems, and other users may need UNIX workstations. When selecting server platforms, you should consider what is needed to enable users on various client platforms to access them. Table 17-1 lists the most common server and workstation platforms and the clients most often used to connect them.

When you run various server platforms along with multiple clients, the process becomes even more complicated, because each workstation might require multiple clients. The impact of multiple network clients on the performance of the computer depends on exactly which clients are involved, but in some instances, the effect can be significant in terms of speed, troubleshooting, and resource utilization. This chapter examines the client platforms commonly used on networks today, and the software used to connect them to various servers.

Windows Network Clients

Although Microsoft Windows began as a standalone operating system, networking soon became a ubiquitous part of Windows, and all versions now include a client that enables them to connect to any other Windows system. Windows networking was first introduced in the Windows NT 3.1 and Windows for Workgroups releases in 1993. The Windows networking architecture is based on network adapter drivers written to the Network Device Interface Specification (NDIS) standard and, originally, on the NetBEUI protocol. Later, TCP/IP became the default networking protocol.

Windows networking is a peer-to-peer system that enables any computer on the network to access resources on any other computer. At the time that Microsoft introduced networking into Windows, the predominant network operating system was Novell NetWare, which uses the client/server model that enables clients to access server resources only. Adding peer-to-peer networking to an already popular, user-friendly operating system like Windows led to its rapid growth in the business LAN industry and its eventual encroachment into NetWare's market share.

	Windows NT/2000 Servers	Novell NetWare Servers	UNIX Servers
DOS Client	Microsoft Client 3.0 for MS-DOS	Novell Client for DOS/Windows	Third-party clients only
Windows for Workgroups Client	Microsoft Windows Network internal client; TCP/IP-32	Novell Client for DOS/Windows	DARPA Commands (using Winsock and Telnet/FTP clients supplied in TCP/IP-32)
Windows 95/98 Clients	Microsoft Client for Microsoft Networks	Microsoft Client for NetWare Networks; Novell Client for Windows 95/98	DARPA Commands (FTP and Telnet)
Windows NT Workstation/ Windows 2000 Professional Clients	Microsoft Windows Network internal client	Microsoft Client Service for NetWare; Novell Client for Windows NT	DARPA Commands (FTP and Telnet); Microsoft Windows NT Services for UNIX
MacOS Clients	Microsoft Services for Macintosh	Novell Client for MacOS; Novell NetWare AppleTalk	DARPA Commands (FTP and Telnet)
UNIX Clients	Microsoft Windows NT Services for UNIX (SAMBA, at www.samba.org)	NFS Services for NetWare	Berkeley Remote Commands; DARPA Commands (FTP and Telnet); NFS

Table 17-1. *Network Client/Server Connectivity Matrix*

Windows Networking Architecture

Windows 3.1 and 3.11 were the only major versions of the operating environment that lacked a networking stack of their own, but it is possible to use Microsoft Client 3.0 for MS-DOS to connect them to a Windows network. All of the other Windows versions, including Windows for Workgroups, Windows 95/98, and Windows NT/2000, have built-in networking capabilities that enable the system to participate on a Windows network.

The basic architecture of the Windows network client is the same in all of the operating systems, although the implementations differ substantially. In its simplest form, the client functionality uses the modules shown in Figure 17-1. At the bottom of the protocol stack is an NDIS network adapter driver that provides the interface to the network interface card (NIC) installed in the computer. Above the network adapter driver are drivers for the individual protocols running on the system. At the top of the stack is the client itself, which takes the form of one or more services on the 32-bit operating systems.

Note *Because Windows uses peer-to-peer networking, all of the operating systems can function as clients as well as servers. This means that all of the information about the Windows network clients pertains equally to the Windows NT and 2000 Server operating systems.*

These three layers form a complete protocol stack running from the application layer of the OSI model down to the physical layer. Applications generate requests for

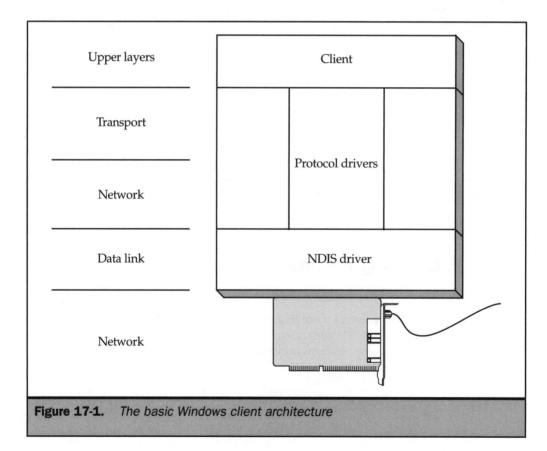

Figure 17-1. *The basic Windows client architecture*

specific resources that pass through a mechanism that determines whether the resource is located on a local device or on the network. Requests for network resources are redirected down through the networking stack to the NIC, where they are transmitted to the appropriate device.

The following sections examine these elements in more detail.

NDIS Drivers

The Network Device Interface Specification was designed by Microsoft and 3Com to provide an interface between the data link and network layers of the OSI model that would enable a single NIC installed in a computer to carry traffic generated by multiple protocols. This interface insulates the protocol drivers and other components at the upper layers of the protocol stack, so that the process of accessing network resources is always the same, no matter what NIC is installed in the machine. As long as there is an NDIS-compatible NIC driver available, the interface can pass the requests from the various protocol drivers to the card, as needed, for transmission over the network.

The various Windows network clients use different versions of NDIS for their adapter drivers, as shown in Table 17-2. NDIS 2 is the only version of the interface that runs in the Intel processor's real mode, using conventional rather than extended memory, and a driver file with a .dos extension. Microsoft Client 3.0 for MS-DOS relies on this version of the specification for network access, but the primary job of NDIS 2 is to function as a real-mode backup for Windows for Workgroups, Windows 95, and Windows 98. All three of these operating systems include later versions of the NDIS specification that run in protected mode, but the real-mode driver is included for situations in which it is impossible to load the protected-mode driver.

For example, when you boot Windows 95 or 98 to the command prompt and load networking support using the NET START command, the system loads the NDIS 2 real-mode driver instead of the default protected-mode driver used by the GUI. The

NDIS Version	Operating Systems
2	Client 3.0 for MS-DOS; Windows 95/98 (real mode)
3	Windows NT 3.1–3.51; Windows for Workgroups 3.11
3.1	Windows 95
4	Windows NT 4.0; Windows 95 OSR2
5	Windows 2000; Windows 98

Table 17-2. *NDIS Versions and the Operating Systems That Use Them*

NETWORK OPERATING SYSTEMS

real-mode driver may not perform as efficiently as the standard driver, but it provides the workstation with basic network access using a minimum of system resources.

The primary advantage of the NDIS 3 drivers included with Windows for Workgroups and the first Windows NT releases is their ability to run in protected mode, which can use both extended and virtual memory. The driver takes the form of an NDIS wrapper, which is generic, and a miniport driver that is device specific. Because most of the interface code is part of the wrapper, the development of miniport drivers by individual NIC manufacturers is relatively simple.

NDIS 3.1, first used in Windows 95, introduced Plug and Play capabilities to the interface, which greatly simplifies the process of installing NICs. NDIS 4 provides additional functionality, such as support for infrared and other new-media and power-management capabilities. NDIS 5 adds connection-oriented service that supports the ATM protocol in its native mode, as well as its Quality of Service functions. In addition, *TCP/IP task offloading* enables enhanced NICs to perform functions normally implemented by the transport-layer protocol, such as checksum computations and data segmenting, which reduces the load on the system processor.

All of the Windows network clients ship with NDIS drivers for an assortment of the most popular NICs that were in use at the time of the product's release. This means, of course, that older clients, like those for DOS and Windows for Workgroups, do not include support for the latest NICs on the market, but the NIC manufacturers all supply NDIS drivers for their products. Even real-mode NDIS 2 drivers are usually included with NICs, because Windows 9*x* can use them in safe mode.

Protocol Drivers

The Windows network clients all support the use of three protocols—NetBEUI, TCP/IP, and IPX—either alone or in combination. When networking was first added to Windows, NetBEUI was the default protocol, because it is closely related to the NetBIOS interface that Windows uses to name the systems on the network. NetBEUI is self-adjusting and requires no configuration or maintenance at all, but its lack of a routing function makes it unsuitable for large networks that consist of multiple segments. This shortcoming, plus the rise in the popularity of the Internet, led to TCP/IP being adopted as the protocol of choice on most networks, despite its need for individual client configuration.

The IPX protocol suite was developed by Novell for its NetWare operating system, which was the most popular networking solution at the time that Windows networking was introduced. As a result, all of the Windows clients include support for the IPX protocol, for compatibility reasons. The Windows IPX implementation is not the actual Novell IPX product, but rather an IPX-compatible protocol that was reverse-engineered to be compatible with NetWare. Therefore, on networks already running NetWare, administrators can implement Windows networking without adding another protocol. Some administrators routinely run two or all three protocols on their networks, but this is usually not necessary on a properly organized network.

Additional protocol modules consume system resources and complicate the process of administering the network.

The protocol drivers take different forms depending on the operating system. The DOS and Windows for Workgroups clients use real- and protected-mode protocol drivers that correspond to the NDIS version, while Windows 95/98 and NT/2000 use 32-bit drivers that conform to their particular architectures.

Client Services

The upper layers of the networking stack in a Windows client take different names and forms, depending on the operating system. On Windows 95 and 98, for example, Client for Microsoft Networks is a service that must be explicitly installed along with at least one protocol and an adapter. A service is a program that runs continuously in the background while the operating system is loaded, the equivalent of a daemon in UNIX. In Windows NT and 2000, however, the client takes the form of a number of separate services that are installed along with the operating system.

In most cases, the Windows networking architecture enables you to install additional client services that can take advantage of the same protocol and adapter modules as the Windows network client. For example, the Client for NetWare Networks and the Client Services for NetWare modules in Windows 9x and Windows NT/2000, respectively, utilize the same protocol and adapter modules as the Windows network client. The exceptions to this are the Microsoft Windows Network client in Windows for Workgroups and Microsoft Client 3.0 for MS-DOS, which are both self-contained clients.

Windows Client Versions

The various Windows operating systems provide most of the same networking capabilities. You can log on to a domain or a workgroup, browse the other computers on the network, map drive letters to specific shares, and redirect print jobs to network printers. However, the clients are slightly different in their implementations. The following sections examine each of the clients and their peculiarities.

Microsoft Client 3.0 for MS-DOS

Windows NT Server 4.0 includes a real-mode client for MS-DOS systems that provides access to Windows networks. Microsoft Client 3.0 for MS-DOS is located in the \Clients\Msclient directory on the Windows NT 4.0 Server CD-ROM, and includes a set of drivers for NICs and support for the three standard protocols (including TCP/IP). In addition to supporting DOS, you can use this client to enable Windows 3.1 systems to access a network. However, Windows for Workgroups uses virtually the same environment as Windows 3.1, except that it includes a protected-mode network client.

If you are committed to a 16-bit Windows environment for your network clients, you should at least consider upgrading Windows 3.1 systems to Windows for

Workgroups. Client for MS-DOS runs in conventional and upper memory only, and therefore occupies a significant amount of the RAM needed to load other programs.

Windows NT Server 4.0 includes a tool called Network Client Administrator that enables you to create installation disks for the MS-DOS client (see Figure 17-2). Using this program, you can create a set of installation disks for the client or create a boot disk that contains a fully configured client. When you boot an MS-DOS system with the disk, the client loads, connects to the network, and runs the client installation program from a shared network drive.

> *Of all the Windows network clients, Client for MS-DOS is the only one that operates exclusively in read-only mode. A workstation running the client can access resources of other Windows systems, but it cannot share its own drives and printers.*

Because it is intended for use on DOS systems, this client does not include any graphical configuration or user tools, but the installation program has a character-based menu interface, as shown in Figure 17-3. From these screens, you choose the adapter and protocol drivers that the program should install, and configure them with the appropriate settings. The client does include a Winsock driver, however, that enables the workstation to run Windows-based Internet applications like Web browsers. The client also includes a standard TCP/IP Ping utility.

The primary tool for controlling the network environment on a DOS client is a command-prompt utility called Net.exe. The Net.exe program is also included with all of the other Windows network clients, even when the operating system provides graphical tools that perform the same functions.

Windows for Workgroups Client

As mentioned earlier, the Microsoft Windows Network client runs in protected mode, which enables it to run mostly in extended memory, freeing up all but 4KB of

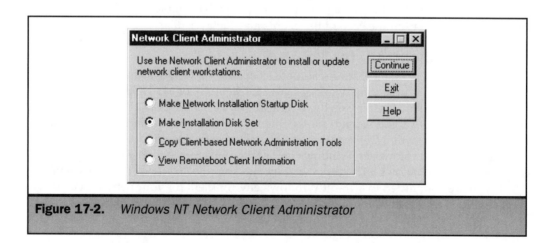

Figure 17-2.   *Windows NT Network Client Administrator*

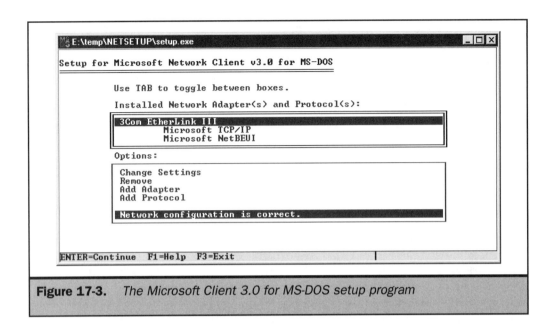

Figure 17-3.   *The Microsoft Client 3.0 for MS-DOS setup program*

conventional memory for use by other programs. Unlike Client for MS-DOS, however, the network client loads with Windows, preventing you from accessing network resources with DOS programs except through a DOS window.

The Microsoft Windows Network client, as it ships with Windows for Workgroups, supports the NetBEUI and IPX protocols only. Support for the TCP/IP protocols is also available, but you must download the TCP/IP-32 protocol package from Microsoft's FTP site and install it after installing Windows for Workgroups.

Note   *The TCP/IP-32 protocol stack for Windows for Workgroups is available as Wfwt32.exe at ftp://ftp.microsoft.com/peropsys/windows/public/tcpip.*

As with Client for MS-DOS, the Windows for Workgroups client enables the workstation to connect to either a workgroup or a domain. The client incorporates networking functions into standard Windows utilities like File Manager and Print Manager, and includes command-line networking tools like Net.exe, Netstat.exe, and Nbtstat.exe. In addition, the TCP/IP-32 package provides a selection of TCP/IP tools, including the Ping, Arp, and Route utilities and a character-based FTP client.

Windows 95/98 Client

Windows 95 and 98 include a 32-bit, protected-mode Windows network client that includes support for all three of the major networking protocols and an extensive set of network adapter drivers. The Windows 95/98 networking architecture is based on

NETWORK OPERATING SYSTEMS

virtual device drivers that enable the NIC and protocol drivers to be shared among multiple clients. For example, after installing the Client for Microsoft Networks service with appropriate protocol and network adapter drivers, you can simply add Client for NetWare Networks to provide access to NetWare servers using the same drivers.

Networking functionality is completely integrated into the Windows 95 and 98 operating systems. The Network Neighborhood program enables you to browse network domains and workgroups and access their resources right alongside those on the local machine. In addition to what are strictly defined as client functions, the Windows operating systems (with the exception of Windows 3.1) include server capabilities that enable you to share the system's drives and printers with other users on the network. These elements are installed along with the client and are also integrated into Windows Explorer and other Windows utilities.

Windows NT/2000 Client

Functionally, Windows NT and 2000 are virtually identical to Windows 95 and 98, as far as networking is concerned. However, the networking architecture of Windows NT and 2000 differ from that of Windows 95 and 98 in that the upper layers of the networking stack are not implemented as a single service. The operating systems have separate Workstation and Server services that both must be running for the system to be able to both access network resources and share its own. Other services, such as the Computer Browser, Messenger, and Netlogon services, provide additional networking functions that contribute to the overall capabilities of the operating system.

NetWare Clients

Novell NetWare dominated the network operating system market at the time that networking was being integrated into the Windows operating systems, so the ability to access legacy NetWare resources while running a Windows network was a priority for Microsoft's development team. The original arrangement was that Novell would supply the NetWare client functionality for Windows NT; but when delays and some unsatisfactory beta releases made this seem unlikely, Microsoft took it upon itself to create its own NetWare client. The original Windows NT release, version 3.1, included the Microsoft version of the IPX protocol suite (called NWLink), but no NetWare client. Microsoft eventually released NetWare Workstation Compatible Service (NWCS) as an add-on to Windows NT 3.1 and incorporated it into version 3.5. Eventually, Novell released its own NetWare client for Windows NT, and ever since, NetWare clients for the Windows operating systems have been available from both Microsoft and Novell.

NetWare and 16-Bit Windows

Neither Windows 3.1 nor Windows for Workgroups includes a NetWare client, but both of them can function with the clients supplied by Novell. In addition, Windows for Workgroups can run a Novell client along with the Microsoft Windows Network client, to provide access to both NetWare and Windows resources. At the time that the 16-bit versions of Windows were released, NetWare clients used either NetWare Shell (NETX) or the NetWare DOS Requestor (VLM) client for the upper-layer functionality, and used either a monolithic or Open Datalink Interface (ODI) driver for the NIC. A monolithic driver is a single executable (called Ipx.com) that includes the driver support for a particular NIC, while ODI is the Novell equivalent of NDIS, a modular interface that permits the use of multiple protocols with a single network card. The combination of an ODI driver and the VLM requestor was the most advanced NetWare client available at that time.

All of these client options loaded from the DOS command line, which meant that they provided network access to DOS applications outside of Windows, but also meant that they utilized large amounts of conventional and upper memory. In fact, without a carefully configured boot sequence or an automated memory management program, it was difficult to keep enough conventional memory free to load applications.

Today, Novell Client for DOS/Windows eliminates this memory management problem and provides full access to all NetWare resources (including Novell Directory Services) while using only 4KB of conventional memory. The main component of the client is NetWare I/O Subsystem (Nios.exe), which works with the DOS extended memory manager (Himem.sys) to provide an area of contiguous protected memory for the rest of the client components. Once Nios.exe is loaded, the ODI network adapter drivers and other client modules are loaded into that memory area. These modules take the form of NetWare Loadable Modules (NLMs), which are traditionally the program files used on NetWare servers. Nios.exe, however, enables client systems to use the same NIC drivers as servers do, and executes them from the command prompt using the LOAD command.

The NLMs needed for the client to function are as follows:

- **Network adapter driver**   The client uses 16- or 32-bit drivers with an .lan extension (the same as those used on NetWare servers) to provide communications with the network adapter.

- **Cmsm.nlm**   The *media support module (MSM)* provides media-specific support in cooperation with *topology support modules (TSMs)* such as Ethertsm.nlm for Ethernet networks and Tokentsm.nlm for Token Ring networks.

- **Lslc32.nlm**   The *link support layer (LSL)* module functions as the interface between the network adapter driver and the protocol drivers operating above it, enabling multiple protocols to use a single adapter.

- **Protocol driver**   The client includes drivers for the IPX protocol suite as well as a full TCP/IP stack, which includes a Winsock driver that enables the workstation to run Web browsers and other Internet applications.

- **Client 32 Requestor**   The Client32.nlm module provides the requestor functions that redirect the resource requests generated by applications to the networking stack. This single module takes the place of the multiple VLM modules used in the earlier NetWare DOS Requestor client.

NetWare and Windows 95/98

With Windows 95 and 98 (as well as Windows NT and 2000), you have a choice between running a NetWare client furnished by Microsoft and one provided by Novell. Generally speaking, the Microsoft client provides better performance, while the Novell client provides more features. The client you choose should be based on what type of access your users need and the resources available in your workstations. For a Windows network that still maintains some NetWare resources, the Microsoft client provides good access and works well together with Client for Microsoft Networks. The Novell client is preferable (or required) in the following client situations:

- Networks that rely exclusively (or heavily) on NetWare for shared network resources
- NetWare administrators that require access to NetWare Administrator and other NDS applications
- Networks that use NetWare 5 servers running TCP/IP as their only protocol

Microsoft Client for NetWare Networks

Windows 95 and 98 both include Client for NetWare Networks, which provides basic connectivity to NetWare resources. To log in to a Novell Directory Services (NDS) tree, you must also install Microsoft Service for NDS, which is also included with the operating system. These services work with the same network adapter and IPX/SPX-compatible protocol modules as Client for Microsoft Networks, and can coexist with the Windows network client as well.

However, although the NDS service enables the user to log in to an NDS tree and access NetWare resources, it does not supply the modules needed to run NDS applications like NetWare Administrator, used to manage the NDS tree. To run these applications, the system must have access to the following files:

- Nwcalls.dll
- Nwlocale.dll
- Nwipxspx.dll
- Nwnet.dll
- Nwgdi.dll
- Nwpsrv.dll

These files are distributed by Novell in its client software and are not included with the Windows 95/98 operating system. You can copy the files to a workstation from a

NetWare distribution disk or client download and use them with the Microsoft client to run NDS applications, as long as you have the appropriate license for the files. Place the files in a directory on the workstation's path, such as C:\Windows.

The Microsoft NetWare client also does not support the use of any protocol other than the IPX/SPX-compatible protocol included with Windows 95/98. You can install TCP/IP on a system running the NetWare client, but you cannot bind the client to the TCP/IP protocol to access NetWare 5 servers. To do this, you must use Novell Client for Windows 95/98.

Windows 95 and 98 also include a real-mode NetWare client that, like the real-mode Windows network client, is intended for use in situations in which the protected-mode client cannot load. This real-mode client lacks some of the more advanced features of the standard client, such as support for long filenames, automatic server reconnection, and the NetWare Core Packet Burst Protocol (NCPB).

Another service included with Windows 95/98, called File and Printer Sharing for NetWare Networks, enables you to configure a Windows machine to share its drives and printers with other NetWare clients on the network. When the service is running, the Windows 95/98 system appears to the network as a NetWare 3.12 server with shared drives appearing as volumes on that server. Users can log in and access the system's resources in the normal manner, unaware that the system they are accessing is actually running Windows.

Novell Client for Windows 95/98

Novell Client for Windows 95/98 includes all the components needed to create a networking stack in the computer, but it also works together with the existing Windows networking architecture. If, for example, you have no networking components in the computer, the Novell client's setup program will install an ODI network adapter driver, Novell's own 32-bit IPX Protocol for the Novell NetWare Client, and the Novell NetWare Client service itself. If you already have Windows' own networking components installed, the Novell client can use the Windows NDIS driver for the NIC, but will still install its own protocols and client service.

 Novell Client for Windows 95/98, as well as the Novell clients for the other Windows operating systems, is available free of charge from Novell's Web site at http://www.novell.com/download.

The protocol drivers that ship with the Novell client are different than Windows' own. Microsoft supplies an IPX/SPX-compatible protocol of its own design, while Novell provides its own version. If you use Microsoft's IPX protocol for your Windows network communications and install the Novell client, there will be two separate IPX implementations running on the system, which is not a problem. NetWare 5 also supports the use of TCP/IP as a native protocol. Previous versions of NetWare could use TCP/IP for Internet services and for standard LAN communications only when IPX data was encapsulated within UDP datagrams. To support NetWare 5, though, the Novell client

NETWORK OPERATING SYSTEMS

now supports TCP/IP communications with NetWare servers (which the Microsoft NetWare client does not), using Windows 95/98's own TCP/IP stack.

With the Novell client installed, you can still log in to an NDS tree or NetWare server and a Windows domain or workgroup using a single username and password, as long as the account exists with the same password in both directories. By default, the Novell client makes itself the primary network client and uses the account name and password you supply for the NetWare login to perform the Windows network logon. If an account with the same name does not exist in the Windows domain, or if the same account exists but uses a different password, the system generates a second authentication dialog box that you can use to log on to the Windows network. If you change the primary network client to Client for Microsoft Networks, the process functions the same way but in reverse; the NetWare client logs in using the Windows network credentials.

The Novell client provides support for all of the latest NetWare features, including Workstation Manager and NetWare Distributed Print Services, as well as other NetWare-related utilities. You can, for example, copy files directly between two NetWare server volumes rather than have them go through the workstation where you are performing the copy; manage NetWare connections through a dedicated interface; log in to two NDS trees simultaneously; and run NetWare utilities like NetWare Administrator and NDS Manager. For network administrators and power NetWare users, these abilities can be useful; but for the average user who simply stores files on NetWare servers and prints to NetWare printers, they are not really necessary.

NetWare and Windows NT/2000

Like Windows 95 and 98, Windows NT and 2000 include Microsoft clients that provide access to NetWare resources, or you can choose to run Novell Client for Windows NT. The development of the NetWare clients for Windows NT was a long and difficult process for both Microsoft and Novell. Early versions of the clients functioned poorly and were lacking in features that users and administrators felt were vital. Today, however, the status of the Windows NT/2000 clients is roughly the same as that of the Windows 95/98 ones. The Microsoft clients provide basic NetWare connectivity, while the Novell client implements the full set of NetWare features.

Microsoft Client Service for NetWare

The Windows NT Workstation and Windows 2000 Professional products include Microsoft Client Service for NetWare (CSNW), which enables the system to log in to an NDS tree or a NetWare server and access its resources. Unlike Windows 95/98, no additional service is required for NDS connectivity. CSNW (and GSNW, the Gateway Service for NetWare client included with Windows NT Server) is *NDS-aware*, but not *NDS compatible*. This means that while the services can log in to an NDS tree, they do not provide full support for NDS applications. As with Windows 95/98, if you want to use NetWare 5 with TCP/IP, NDPS, ZENworks, or other NDS applications, you must install Novell Client for Windows NT.

CSNW is based on NWLink, the Windows NT protocol that provides services compatible with Novell's IPX. NWLink includes modules that emulate the most important protocols in the IPX suite, including IPX itself, SPS, RIP, SAP, and NetBIOS. As with the Windows 98 client, the service uses the same NDIS adapter driver as the Windows network client, and can coexist with the Windows network, providing connectivity to both NetWare and Windows resources simultaneously.

Note *For more information on the IPX protocol suite used by NetWare, see Chapter 12.*

Microsoft Gateway Service for NetWare

The NetWare client included with Windows NT and 2000 Server is called Gateway Service for NetWare (GSNW). GSNW provides the same client services as CSNW, but adds a gateway function that enables Windows client systems to access NetWare resources through the NT or 2000 server. After connecting to the NDS tree or NetWare server using the same elements as CSNW, you can use the gateway to create shares on the NT/2000 server that are associated with particular volumes on NetWare servers (see Figure 17-4). All Windows clients on the network can see the shares and access them in the normal way. The NT or 2000 server accesses the associated NetWare server volumes using its client capabilities and then furnishes the files and directories to the Windows clients. Using GSNW is not a replacement for running NetWare clients on your Windows workstations, but it does provide a quick solution for users who need occasional access to NetWare volumes.

Novell Client for Windows NT

Although the early versions of Novell Client for Windows NT were limited in their functionality, the current release provides full access to all NetWare features, just as the DOS and Windows 95/98 clients do. However, Client for Windows NT does not utilize NetWare I/O Subsystem to run NLMs on the workstation, as the other clients do.

All of the Novell clients have a setup program that simplifies the process of installing all of the individual components. You can also perform the installation in the traditional manner, from the Network Control Panel in Windows. The Novell NT client also includes the capability to integrate the client installation process into the operating system installation, so that an individual client installation procedure is not necessary. Further, the client includes an Automatic Client Upgrade (ACU) feature that checks the version number of a workstation's currently installed client against the version stored on a server. If the server has a newer version, the workstation automatically performs an upgrade. Features like these are designed to simplify the workstation maintenance process for administrators who may be responsible for hundreds or thousands of systems.

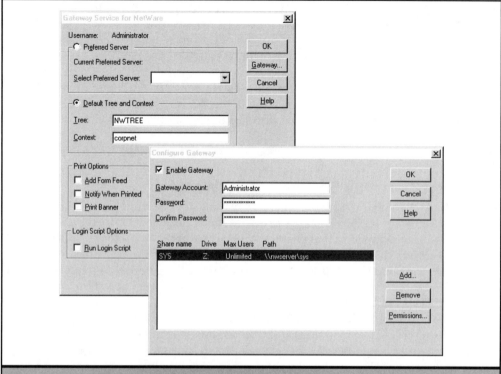

Figure 17-4. *Windows NT Gateway Service for NetWare*

Macintosh Clients

While not nearly as popular as the PC, Macintosh systems have their place in the personal computer world, and you may find yourself needing to connect Mac workstations to your network. All Macintosh systems include an integrated network interface, and this has long been touted as evidence of the platform's simplicity and superiority. However, Macintosh workstations require special treatment to connect them to a network running other platforms, such as Windows NT/2000, NetWare, or UNIX. In most cases, however, you can configure your network to handle Macintosh clients, enabling Mac users to share files with Windows and other clients. If you select applications that are available in compatible versions for the different client platforms you're running, Mac users can even work on the same files as Windows users.

Connecting Macintosh workstations to a network running another platform is usually simply a matter of either configuring your existing servers to use AppleTalk, the native Macintosh networking protocol, or configuring the Macintosh systems to use a protocol supported by the servers, by installing an additional client. The following sections examine the basic procedures for connecting Macs to various types of networks, and the products you may need to implement the connections.

Connecting Macintosh Systems to Windows Networks

Windows NT and 2000 Server include the Microsoft Services for Macintosh product that implements the AppleTalk protocol, enabling Macintosh systems to access file and printer shares on the server. Unlike Windows clients, Mac systems do not participate as peers on the Windows network, however. The relationship between the Mac workstation and the NT or 2000 server is strictly client/server, meaning that the Mac can access the server's files and printers, but it can't share its own drives or access the shares on other network workstations, such as Windows 95/98 machines. It is possible for a Macintosh system to function as a peer with workstations running Windows 95/98 or other operating systems, but a third-party client software product is required.

Using Microsoft Services for Macintosh

Microsoft Services for Macintosh makes it possible for Macintosh systems to access Windows NT/2000 Server shares without modifying the configuration of the workstations. When you install the Services for Macintosh package on a Windows NT or 2000 server from the Network Control Panel, three new modules are added to the machine, as follows:

- **AppleTalk Protocol**   Implements the AppleTalk Phase 2 protocols that enable Macintosh systems to communicate with the server.
- **File Server for Macintosh (MacFile)**   Enables you to create Macintosh-accessible volumes out of directories on the server's NTFS drives.
- **Print Server for Macintosh (MacPrint)**   Enables Macintosh systems to send print jobs to spoolers on the NT server.

Once the installation is complete, you must specify the name of the AppleTalk zone in which the server will participate. The service then creates a directory called *Microsoft UAM Volume* on the server drive. By default, this is the only directory that Macintosh systems can access on the server. The mechanism by which you create and configure Macintosh volumes on the server is wholly separate from the system's standard drive-sharing capability. You can share the \\Microsoft UAM Volume directory in the usual manner, to make it available to standard Windows clients; but to manage its Macintosh-related properties or create new Macintosh volumes on the server, you use the Server Manager program.

Installing Services for Macintosh adds a MacFile menu to Server Manager, as shown in Figure 17-5. Selecting Volumes from this menu displays the Properties of Macintosh-Accessible Volume dialog box, from which you can create new volumes and manage the properties of existing ones. For example, Macintosh users are granted read-only privileges to \\Microsoft UAM Volume, by default. From the Properties dialog box for the volume,

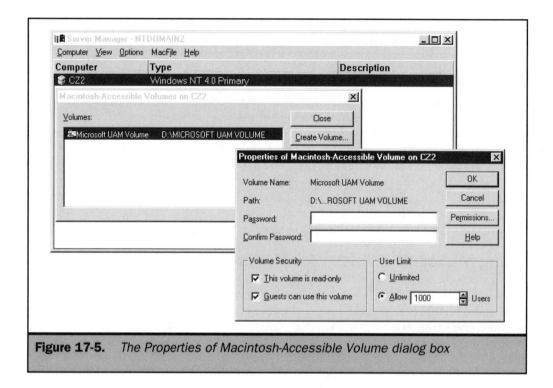

Figure 17-5.   *The Properties of Macintosh-Accessible Volume dialog box*

you can grant users write access, assign a password to the volume, or create access permissions for specific users and groups, with the optional *user authentication module (UAM)*. Installing the UAM on the Macintosh system enables the Mac Chooser to authenticate the system to the NT/2000 server using encrypted Microsoft authentication rather than the cleartext authentication the system uses natively.

Third-Party Macintosh Clients

One of the primary advantages of Windows NT/2000 Services for Macintosh is that the additional networking software needed runs on the network. There is no need to purchase, install, and configure new software on each Macintosh workstation (although you must have a standard Windows NT or 2000 client license for each Mac system that accesses the server). To approach the Mac/Windows networking problem from the other side—that is, by altering the client—you must purchase a third-party product such as Thursby Software Systems, Inc.'s DAVE (www.Thursby.com/products/newin25.htm) or Open Door Networks, Inc.'s ShareWay IP (www2.opendoor.com/shareway/).

DAVE is a peer-to-peer networking solution for Macintosh systems that enables the Mac to access Windows network shares and share its own drives with Windows clients. Unlike NT Services for Macintosh, DAVE enables Macs to access Windows 95/98 and NT Workstation shares as well as those on Windows NT and 2000 Server systems. DAVE also utilizes the TCP/IP protocols instead of AppleTalk and, therefore, requires no changes to the Windows systems on the network. As with any client-based solution, however, you must purchase a copy of DAVE for each Mac client and install it individually. For a relatively small network or a larger network with only a few Macintosh clients, products like DAVE can be an ideal solution.

Connecting Macintosh Systems to NetWare

Novell NetWare provides the same Macintosh connectivity alternatives as Windows. You can configure your NetWare servers to run the AppleTalk protocol, enabling the Macintosh workstations to communicate with the servers in their native mode, or you can install NetWare Client for MacOS on each Macintosh system, which enables the Mac to use the IPX protocols to communicate with NetWare servers. NetWare runs strictly on the client/server model, so both solutions enable workstations to access servers only. The Mac systems do not share their own drives, nor can they access the resources of other clients.

These solutions provide basic client services to Macintosh workstations, such as access to server volumes and printers, but a Mac system is not a suitable platform for NetWare administration. There is no NetWare Administrator utility for the Mac platform, and while a Mac client can log in to an NDS tree and browse through its objects, there is no way for it to create or modify them.

Using NetWare for Macintosh

NetWare for Macintosh is included with the NetWare operating system and installs the AppleTalk protocols on the server, including the AppleTalk Filing Protocol (AFP) and AppleTalk Print Services (ATPS), which provide file and printer sharing services, respectively. You install the product onto an existing server using the Install.nlm utility in the normal manner. Like any other protocol on a NetWare server, AppleTalk must be bound to one or more of the installed NICs, and the Autoexec.ncf file must be modified to load it along with the AFP and ATPS modules automatically with the operating system. You must also add the MAC name space to every NetWare volume on which your clients will store Macintosh files.

Once NetWare for Macintosh is installed and configured on a NetWare server, Mac workstations can connect to it without further modification. However, because no NDS client capability has been added to the Mac system, it can log in to a NetWare 4.x or 5.x server using bindery emulation only. Security for Mac clients is no different than for any other NetWare client. You must create a user object for the person logging in from the Mac system in the server's bindery emulation context and grant the user rights to files and directories in the usual manner.

Using NetWare Client for MacOS

Installing NetWare Client for MacOS enables a Mac workstation to log in to an NDS tree (rather than perform a bindery emulation login) and use NetWare's own IPX protocols rather than AppleTalk. The client also supports NetWare/IP, which is a product that packages IPX traffic within UDP datagrams, a process called *tunneling*. There is not yet a Mac client that supports the use of the TCP/IP protocols in native mode with NetWare 5 servers.

Note *Novell no longer provides NetWare Client for MacOS itself. It has granted an exclusive license for the development and distribution of the client to Prosoft Engineering, Inc. (http://www.prosofteng.com/netware.asp).*

Client for MacOS consists of both server and workstation components. Installing the client on the server adds the Macintosh name space to the volumes you select; enables you to specify the names by which the volumes will appear to the Macintosh systems; and installs Mac OS file system support in the form of a server module called Macfile.nlm, which provides AppleTalk Filing Protocol support.

The workstation components of the client include MacIPX and NW/IP, which provide support for the IPX and NetWare/IP protocols, and an RCONSOLE program that enables Mac systems using IPX to access the server console. The installation process also creates a NetWare Client Utilities folder on the workstation drive that contains the following tools:

- **NetWare Directory Browser**   Enables users to browse (but not modify) the NDS tree.

- **NetWare Print Chooser**   Enables users to select the NetWare printers to which they will send print jobs.

- **NetWare Volume Mounter**   Enables users to mount specific volumes by dragging them from the NetWare Directory Browser window.

Once the client is installed on the workstation, you can log in to NetWare using the Chooser or tree icon on the right side of the menu bar. The tree icon provides NDS login capabilities, and the Chooser lets you select either an NDS or NetWare server login. If you choose to log in to a specific server, the system performs a bindery or bindery emulation login, depending on the NetWare version the server is running.

UNIX Clients

Three primary mechanisms provide client/server access between UNIX systems. Two of these have been ported to many other computing platforms, and you can use them to access UNIX systems from workstations running other operating systems. These three mechanisms are as follows:

- **Berkeley Remote Commands**   Designed for UNIX-to-UNIX networking, these commands provide functions such as remote login (rlogin), remote shell execution (rsh), and remote file copying (rcp).

- **DARPA Commands** Designed to provide basic remote networking tasks, like file transfers (FTP) and terminal emulation (Telnet), the DARPA commands operate independently of the operating system and have been ported to virtually every platform that supports the TCP/IP protocols.

- **Network File System (NFS)** Designed by Sun Microsystems in the 1980s to provide transparent file sharing between network systems, NFS has since been published as RFC 1813, an informational RFC (Request For Comments), by the Internet Engineering Task Force (IETF). NFS is available on a wide range of computing platforms, enabling most client workstations to access the files on UNIX systems.

In most cases, the TCP/IP stacks on client computers include applications providing the DARPA FTP and Telnet commands. Since all UNIX versions run FTP and Telnet server services by default, you can use these client applications to access any UNIX system available on the network. These server applications have been ported to other operating systems as well. For example, Windows NT and 2000 include an FTP server as part of the Internet Information Server package.

All of the Windows TCP/IP clients include FTP and Telnet client applications, with the exception of Microsoft Client 3.0 for MS-DOS. Installing this client provides a TCP/IP stack and the Winsock driver needed to run Internet applications, but the FTP and Telnet programs are not included. You can, however, use third-party FTP and Telnet clients to access UNIX and other server systems, or install Novell Client for DOS/Windows, which also includes FTP and Telnet clients as part of its TCP/IP stack.

While FTP and Telnet provide basic access to a UNIX system, they are not the equivalent of full client capabilities. For example, FTP provides only basic file transfer capabilities. To open a document on a UNIX system using FTP, you must download the file to a local drive and use your application to open it from there. NFS, on the other hand, enables the client system to access a server volume as though it were available locally. NFS downloads only the blocks that the client application needs, instead of the whole file.

Thus, while FTP and Telnet are provided free and are nearly always available, clients that need regular access to UNIX file systems are better off using NFS. There are NFS products for both Windows NT/2000 and Novell NetWare that make file system communications with UNIX systems possible, but both of them are products that must be purchased and installed separately.

Windows NT Services for UNIX is an add-on package that enables Windows NT systems to access UNIX volumes using NFS and to publish their drives as NFS volumes for UNIX clients. The product also includes a Telnet server for Windows NT and a character-based Telnet client that improves on the version included with NT, as well as a password synchronization daemon for UNIX systems. With the services in place, the NT system can map a drive letter to an NFS volume on a UNIX system or reference it using either standard UNC (Universal Naming Convention) names or the UNIX *server:/export* format. UNIX systems can access NT drives just as they would any other NFS volume.

NETWORK OPERATING SYSTEMS

The NFS server feature creates a separate NFS Sharing tab in the Properties dialog box of each drive and directory on the Windows NT system. You create NFS shares and assign permissions to them independently of the standard Windows shares. Windows NT uses its own access control permissions to approximate the security model used on UNIX systems. The password synchronization daemon enables administrators to manage passwords on both UNIX and NT systems from NT.

In addition to the NFS client/server capabilities, Windows NT Services for UNIX includes a toolkit that provides a working environment on the NT system that is similar to that of a UNIX system, including a Korn shell and an assortment of standard UNIX utilities, such as cp, for copying files, mkdir, for creating directories, and vi, the command-line text editor.

Although Windows NT Services for UNIX provides multiple UNIX clients access to NT volumes, it only enables a single NT client to access NFS drives on UNIX systems. Novell's NFS Services for NetWare is a server-based solution that enables UNIX clients to access NetWare volumes and enables NetWare clients to access UNIX NFS volumes using the NetWare server as a gateway. The product also provides UNIX-to-NetWare and NetWare-to-UNIX printing services that enable clients on each platform to access printers on the other.

Both of these products provide basic connectivity between UNIX workstations and PC-based servers running Windows NT/2000 or NetWare. Third-party NFS products also are available that provide similar services. While the interoperability between different platforms is never completely transparent, you should be able to use whatever client operating systems your network users require, and still provide them with access to any resources anywhere on the network.

The
Complete
Reference

Upgrading
&
Troubleshooting
Networks

Part V

Network Connection Services

The Complete Reference

Upgrading & Troubleshooting Networks

Chapter 18

DHCP

Because of their use on the Internet and their compatibility with virtually every network operating system in use today, the TCP/IP family of protocols are nearly ubiquitous on all but the smallest LANs. The chief administrative problem with deploying and maintaining a TCP/IP network is the need to assign each node a unique IP address and to configure the various other TCP/IP parameters with appropriate values. On a large network deployment, performing these tasks manually on individual workstations is not only labor intensive, it also requires careful planning to ensure that no IP addresses are duplicated.

The Dynamic Host Configuration Protocol (DHCP) was developed to address this problem. DHCP takes the form of a service that network administrators configure with ranges of IP addresses and other settings. Workstations configured to run as DHCP clients contact the service at boot time and are assigned a set of appropriate TCP/IP parameters, including a unique IP address. The workstation uses these parameters to configure its TCP/IP client; and network communication commences with no manual configuration necessary at the workstation.

DHCP is a platform-independent service that can configure the TCP/IP parameters on any operating system with DHCP client capabilities. DHCP server software is available for many platforms, including Windows NT, NetWare, and various flavors of UNIX.

Origins

DHCP was developed by Microsoft in the early 1990s as a workstation configuration solution for enterprise networks and, particularly, for its own 35,000-node network rollout. After determining that TCP/IP was the optimum protocol for their needs, Microsoft realized that the task of manually assigning IP addresses to thousands of machines located at various sites in 50 countries was enormous, as was the continued tracking of those addresses as computers were added to and removed from the network.

The concept of server-based IP address assignment was not a new one. DHCP is based on two earlier protocols, called RARP and BOOTP.

RARP

RARP, the Reverse Address Resolution Protocol, does the opposite of ARP, the Address Resolution Protocol used on every TCP/IP system. While ARP converts network layer IP addresses into data link–layer hardware addresses, RARP works by broadcasting a system's hardware address and receiving an IP address in return from a RARP server.

Designed for use with diskless workstations that have no means to store their own TCP/IP configuration information, a RARP server can supply IP addresses to all the systems on a network segment. However, the concept as defined in the Internet

Engineering Task Force's RFC 903 document was not sufficient for Microsoft's needs for several reasons:

- RARP relies on broadcast messages generated by the client because no means exists for the diskless workstation to store the address of the RARP server. There must be a RARP server on every network segment, therefore, to service the workstations on that segment.

- RARP is only capable of supplying client systems with IP addresses. To be useful on today's networks, a protocol must provide values for other configuration parameters as well, such as name servers and default gateways.

- RARP is only a mechanism for the storage and delivery of IP addresses. Administrators must still manually assign addresses to clients by creating a look-up table on the RARP server.

BOOTP

The *Bootstrap Protocol (BOOTP)* is an improvement over RARP and is still in use today, particularly on routers made by Cisco and other manufacturers. DHCP takes much of its functionality from the BOOTP standards (published as RFC 951 with extensions in RFC 1533 and RFC 1542). Also designed for use with diskless workstations, BOOTP is capable of delivering more than just IP addresses; it uses standard UDP/IP datagrams instead of a specialized data link–layer protocol like RARP.

BOOTP servers can use the *Trivial File Transfer Protocol (TFTP)* to deliver an executable boot file to a diskless client system, in addition to an IP address and other TCP/IP configuration parameters. Like RARP, BOOTP clients use broadcast transmissions to contact a server, but the standard calls for the use of BOOTP relay agents to make it possible for one BOOTP server to service clients on multiple network segments.

A *BOOTP relay agent* detects the BOOTP broadcasts on a network segment and transmits them to a server on another segment. Many of the routers on the market support BOOTP relay and, because DHCP uses exactly the same relay system, the DHCP relay feature built into Windows NT and Windows 2000 works with BOOTP traffic as well.

The primary shortcoming of BOOTP is that, like RARP, administrators must manually create a look-up table on the server containing the IP addresses and other configuration parameters to be assigned to the clients. This makes the system subject to many of the same errors and administrative problems as RARP and, for that matter, as manual client configuration.

DHCP Objectives

BOOTP eliminates the need for administrators to travel to every workstation so they can configure the TCP/IP client manually, but the possibility still exists for systems to be assigned duplicate IP addresses because of typographical errors in the look-up table. What was needed was a service that would automatically allocate addresses to systems on demand and keep track of which addresses have been assigned and which are available for use. DHCP improves on the BOOTP concept by enabling administrators to create a pool of IP addresses. As a client system boots, it requests an address from the server, which assigns one from the pool, along with the other static configuration parameters the client needs.

There are problems inherent in this concept, however. One problem is the possibility of a shortage of IP addresses. Once a client system is assigned an address on a particular subnet, what happens to that address if the machine is moved to another department on a different subnet? DHCP will assign the system a different address on the new subnet, but a mechanism must exist to reclaim the old address.

The solution to this problem lies in DHCP's mechanism for leasing IP addresses to client systems. Each time the server assigns an address, it starts a clock that will eventually run out if the system does not renew the lease. Each time the client reboots, the lease is renewed. If the lease runs out, the server releases the assigned IP address and returns it to the pool for reassignment.

The other problem with automatic address assignment is the possibility for a client's IP address to change periodically. If a lease expires for any reason (such as a user going on vacation), the server is likely to assign the system a different address the next time it connects to the network. The reason this can be a problem concerns the name resolution processes on the network.

Client systems are often assigned permanent names in either the DNS or the NetBIOS name service, or in both. In either case, a change of IP address can render the name resolution information invalid. In the NetBIOS name space, the problem arises only if the network relies on LMHOSTS files for name resolution. Networks using broadcasts to resolve names will have no problem with the new IP address because a new resolution is performed each time another system accesses the client. The best solution, however, is WINS, which registers each client system's NetBIOS name and new IP address each time it connects to the network.

Note *For more information on WINS and NetBIOS names, see Chapter 19.*

For DNS names, the problem is more complex because DNS servers traditionally do not dynamically update the resource records containing host names and their equivalent IP addresses. If you have a system on your network that functions as an Internet server (such as a web or an FTP server), its IP address must be permanently assigned. Because of the distributed nature of DNS on the Internet, it takes too long for IP address changes to propagate to all the name servers involved. To address this problem, DHCP makes it possible to create permanent address assignments, as well as dynamic ones.

Note *The DNS server included with the Windows 2000 Server products supports a new feature called Dynamic Update, which provides automatic modification of resource records. Addresses assigned using the Windows 2000 version of Microsoft DHCP Server can be automatically added to DNS records. For more information on DNS, see Chapter 20.*

The overall objectives Microsoft used when designing DHCP are as follows:

- The DHCP server should be able to provide a workstation with all the settings needed to configure the TCP/IP client so that no manual configuration is needed.
- The DHCP server should be able to function as a repository for the TCP/IP configuration parameters for all of a network's clients.
- The DHCP server should assign IP addresses in such a way as to prevent the duplication of addresses on the network.
- The DHCP server should be able to configure clients on other subnets through the use of relay agents.
- DHCP servers should support the assignment of specific IP addresses to specific client systems.
- DHCP clients should be able to retain their TCP/IP configuration parameters despite a reboot of either the client or the server system.

IP Address Assignment

The primary function of DHCP is to assign IP addresses and to accommodate the needs of all types of client systems. The standard defines three types of address assignments, as follows:

- **Manual allocation**   The administrator configures the DHCP server to assign a specific IP address to a given system, which will never change unless it is manually modified. This is the equivalent in functionality to RARP and BOOTP.
- **Automatic allocation**   The DHCP server assigns permanent IP addresses from a pool, which do not change unless they are manually modified by the administrator.
- **Dynamic allocation**   The DHCP server assigns IP addresses from a pool using a limited-time lease, so the address can be reassigned if the client system does periodically renew it.

Tip *Most DHCP server implementations support all three types of address allocation, but they usually do not enable you to select them using these names. For example, with the Microsoft DHCP Server, dynamic allocation is the default. If you want to use automatic allocation, you change the Lease Duration setting for a scope to* unlimited. *For manual allocation, you create what the Microsoft server calls* reservations.

NETWORK CONNECTION SERVICES

Manual allocation is suitable for Internet servers and other machines that require static IP addresses because they rely on DNS name resolution for user access. This form of address allocation is nothing more than a remote configuration solution because the end result is no different than if the administrator manually configured the TCP/IP client. As an organizational aid, however, this method of address assignment is recommended over manual system configuration on a network that uses DHCP for its other machines. Keeping all the address assignments in one database makes it easier to track the assignments and reduces the likelihood of duplication.

Automatic allocation is useful on stable single-segment networks or multisegment networks where machines are not routinely moved to other segments. This method reduces the network traffic by eliminating the address lease renewal procedures. In most cases, the savings are minimal, however. Automatic allocation is also not recommended if your organization is working with a limited supply of registered IP addresses.

Once configured, dynamic allocation provides the greatest amount of flexibility with the least amount of administrative intervention. The DHCP server assigns IP addresses to systems on any subnet and automatically reclaims the addresses no longer in use for reassignment. Also, there is no possibility of duplicate addresses being on the network (as long as DHCP manages all of the systems).

TCP/IP Client Configuration

In addition to IP addresses, DHCP also can provide clients with values for the other parameters needed to configure a TCP/IP client, including a subnet mask, default gateway, and name server addresses. The object is to eliminate the need for any manual TCP/IP configuration on a client system. For example, the Microsoft DHCP server includes over 50 configuration parameters, which it can deliver along with the IP address, even though Windows clients can only use 11 of those parameters. The RFC 2132 document, "DHCP Options and BOOTP Vendor Extensions," defines an extensive list of parameters that compliant servers should support and most of the major DHCP server packages adhere closely to this list. Many of these parameters are designed for use by specific system configurations and are submitted by vendors for inclusion in the standard document.

DHCP Architecture

The architecture of the DHCP system is defined by a public standard published by the IETF as RFC 2131, "Dynamic Host Configuration Protocol," and consists of two basic elements:

- A service that assigns TCP/IP configuration settings to client systems
- A protocol used for communications between DHCP clients and servers

The document defines the message format for the protocol and the sequence of message exchanges that take place between the DHCP client and server.

DHCP Packet Structure

DHCP communications use eight different types of messages, all of which use the same basic packet format. DHCP traffic is carried within standard UDP/IP datagrams, using port 67 at the server and port 68 at the client (the same ports as BOOTP). The packet format is shown in Figure 18-1 and contains the following fields.

- **op (Op Code), 1 byte**   Specifies whether the message is a request or a reply, using the following codes:
  - **1**   BOOTREQUEST
  - **2**   BOOTREPLY
- **htype (Hardware Type), 1 byte**   Specifies the type of hardware address used in the chaddr field, using codes from the ARP section of the IETF "Assigned Numbers" document (RFC 1700), some of which are as follows:
  - **1**   Ethernet (10MB)
  - **4**   Proteon ProNET Token Ring
  - **5**   Chaos
  - **6**   IEEE 802 Networks
  - **7**   ARCNET
  - **11**   LocalTalk
  - **14**   SMDS
  - **15**   Frame Relay
  - **16**   Asynchronous Transmission Mode (ATM)
  - **17**   HDLC
  - **18**   Fibre Channel
  - **19**   Asynchronous Transmission Mode (ATM)
  - **20**   Serial Line
  - **21**   Asynchronous Transmission Mode (ATM)
- **hlen (Hardware Address Length), 1 byte**   Specifies the length (in bytes) of the hardware address found in the chaddr field, according to the value of the htype field (e.g., if htype = 1, indicating an Ethernet hardware address, the value of hlen will be 6 bytes).

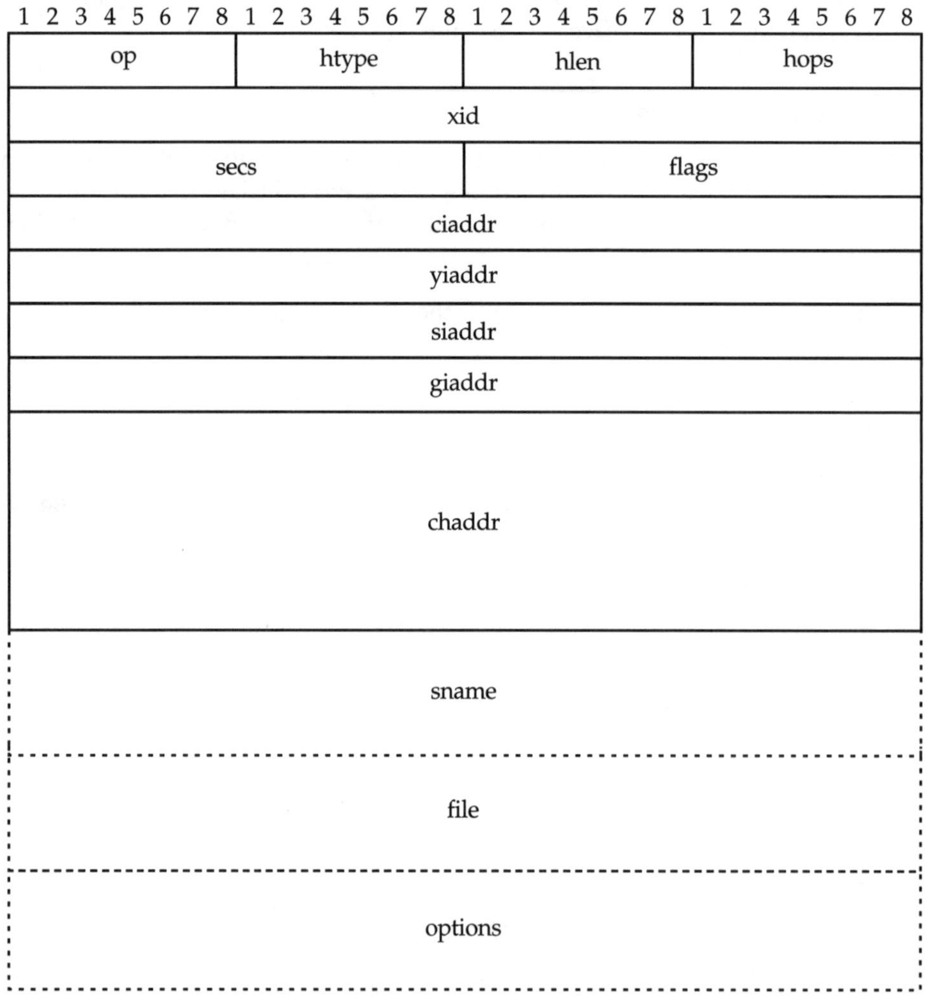

1 2 3 4 5 6 7 8	1 2 3 4 5 6 7 8	1 2 3 4 5 6 7 8	1 2 3 4 5 6 7 8
op	htype	hlen	hops
xid			
secs		flags	
ciaddr			
yiaddr			
siaddr			
giaddr			
chaddr			
sname			
file			
options			

Figure 18-1. *All DHCP messages use the same basic packet format*

- **hops (1 byte)** Specifies the number of network segments between the client and the server. The client sets the value to 0 and each DHCP relay system increments it by 1 during the journey to the server.

- **xid (Transaction ID), 4 bytes** Contains a transaction identifier that systems use to associate the request and response messages of a single DHCP transaction.

- **secs (Seconds), 2 bytes**   Specifies the number of seconds elapsed since the IP address was assigned or the lease last renewed. This enables the systems to distinguish between messages of the same type generated during a single DHCP transaction.

- **flags (2 bytes)**   Contains the broadcast flag as the first bit, which, when set to a value of 1, specifies that DHCP servers and relay agents should use broadcasts to transmit to the client and not unicasts. The remaining bits in the field are unused and must have a value of 0.

- **ciaddr (Client IP Address), 4 bytes**   Specifies the client's IP address in DHCPREQUEST messages transmitted while in the bound, renewal, or rebinding state. At all other times, the value must be 0.

- **yiaddr (Your IP Address), 4 bytes**   Specifies the IP address being offered or assigned by a server in DHCPOFFER or DHCPACK messages. At all other times, the value must be 0.

- **siaddr (Server IP Address), 4 bytes**   Specifies the IP address of the next server in a bootstrap sequence. Servers include this information in DHCPOFFER and DHCPACK messages only when DHCP is configured to supply an executable boot file to clients and the boot files for various client platforms are stored on different servers.

- **giaddr (Gateway IP Address), 4 bytes**   Specifies the IP address of the DHCP relay agent to which a server should send its replies when the client and server are located on different subnets. When the client and server are on the same segment, the value must be 0.

- **chaddr (Client Hardware Address), 16 bytes**   Specifies the hardware address of the client system in DHCPDISCOVER and DHCPREQUEST messages, which the server uses to address its unicast responses to the client. The format of the hardware address is specified by the values of the htype and hlen fields.

- **sname (Server Host Name), 64 bytes**   Specifies the (optional) host name of the DHCP server. The field is more commonly used to hold overflow data from the options field.

- **file (Boot File Name), 128 bytes**   Specifies the name of an executable boot file for diskless client workstations in DHCPDISCOVER messages (in which case a generic filename is supplied) or DHCPOFFER messages (in which the field contains a full path and filename. The field is more commonly used to hold overflow data from the options field.

- **options (variable size, minimum 312 bytes)**   Contains the magic cookie that specifies how the rest of the field should be interpreted and the DHCP Message Type option that defines the function of the message, as well as other options, defined in RFC 2132, that contain configuration data for other TCP/IP client parameters.

DHCP Options

The DHCP message format is almost identical to the BOOTP message defined in RFC 951. The primary difference is the options field, which replaces the 64-byte vend field in the BOOTP message. The options field in a DHCP message is a catchall area designed to carry the various parameters (other than the IP address) used to configure the client system's TCP/IP stack. Because you can configure a DHCP server to deliver many options to clients, defining separate fields for each one would be impractical.

The Magic Cookie

The options field always begins with the so-called *magic cookie*, which informs the server about what is contained in the rest of the field. The magic cookie is a 4-byte subfield containing the dotted decimal value 99.130.83.99.

The Option Format

The individual options in the options field contain various types and amounts of data, but most of them use the same basic structure, which consists of three subfields, as shown in Figure 18-2. The functions of the subfields are as follows:

- **code (1 byte)**   Contains a code specifying the function of the option, as defined in RFC 2132
- **length (1 byte)**   Specifies the length of the data field associated with the option, making it possible for systems that do not support a particular option to skip directly to the next one
- **data (variable)**   Contains information used by the client in various ways depending on the code and the message type

For example, in the Subnet Mask option, the code subfield has a value of 1, the length subfield has a value of 4, and the data field contains the 4-byte mask associated with the IP address assigned to the client.

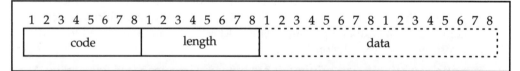

Figure 18-2.   *A DHCP packet's options field contains multiple substructures for individual options, each of which is composed of three fields*

The DHCP Message Type Option

The DHCP Message Type option identifies the overall function of the DHCP message and is required in all DHCP packets. The code subfield for the option is 53 and the length is 1. The data subfield contains one of the following codes:

- **1 – DHCPDISCOVER**   Used by client systems to locate DHCP servers and request an IP address
- **2 – DHCPOFFER**   Used by servers to offer IP addresses to clients
- **3 – DHCPREQUEST**   Used by clients to request specific IP address assignments or to renew leases
- **4 – DHCPDECLINE**   Used by clients to reject an IP address offered by a server
- **5 – DHCPACK**   Used by servers to acknowledge a client's acceptance of an offered IP address
- **6 – DHCPNACK**   Used by servers to reject a client's acceptance of an offered IP address
- **7 – DHCPRELEASE**   Used by clients to terminate a lease
- **8 – DHCPINFORM**   Used by clients that have already been assigned an IP address to request additional configuration parameters

The Pad Option

The *Pad option* is not really an option at all, but is, instead, a filler used to pad out fields so their boundaries fall between 8-byte words. Unlike most other options, the Pad option has no length or data field, and consists only of a 1-byte code field with a value of 0.

The Option Overload Option

Because DHCP messages are carried within UDP datagrams, the packets are limited to a maximum size of 576 bytes and the inclusion of a large number of options can test this limit. Because the DHCP message's sname and file fields are carryovers from the BOOTP protocol that are rarely used today, the DHCP standard allows these fields to be used to contain options that do not fit in the standard options field.

To include options in the sname and/or file fields, the packet's option field must contain the Option Overload option. This option has a value of 52 in the code subfield and a length of 1. The data subfield specifies which of the two auxiliary fields will carry additional options, using the following codes:

- **1**   The file field will carry additional options
- **2**   The sname field will carry additional options
- **3**   Both the file and sname fields will carry additional options

The Vendor-Specific Information Option

An option is defined in the standard as code 43, which is specifically intended for use by vendors to supply information required for the operation of their products. This Vendor-Specific Information option can itself contain multiple options for use by a vendor's products. To identify the vendor of the products for which the information in the Vendor-Specific Information option is intended, a message uses the Vendor Class Identifier option, which has a code value of 60 and a variable length with a minimum of 1 byte.

The Vendor-Specific Information option can contain encapsulated vendor-specific options, which are essentially options within an option. The structure of the encapsulated options is the same as that of the standard DHCP options, with code, length, and data fields. No magic cookie is used, however, and the appearance of the End option (code 255) signals the end of the encapsulated options only—not the end of the entire options field. The codes used in the encapsulated options are not defined by the DHCP standards because they only need to be understandable to systems using the vendor's products.

The End Option

The *End option* signifies the end of the option field. Any bytes in the option field coming after the End option must contain nothing but 0 (Pad option) bytes. Like the Pad option, the End option consists only of a 1-byte code, with no length or data fields. The code has a value of 255.

Other Configuration Options

The DHCP options defined in RFC 2132 fall into several functional categories, which are discussed in the following sections. Each category includes a list containing some of the available options, as well as their code field values.

BOOTP VENDOR INFORMATION EXTENSIONS   These options are included in the DHCP standard exactly as defined in RFC 1497 for use with BOOTP and include many of the basic TCP/IP configuration parameters used by most client systems, such as the following:

- **Pad (code 0)**   See "The Pad Option," earlier in this chapter.
- **End (code 255)**   See "The End Option," earlier in this chapter.
- **Subnet Mask (code 1)**   Specifies which bits of the IP address identify the host system and which bits identify the network where the host system resides.
- **Router (code 3)**   Specifies the IP address of the router (or default gateway) on the local network segment the client should use to transmit to systems on other network segments.
- **Domain Name Server (code 6)**   Specifies the IP addresses of the servers the client will use for DNS name resolution.

- **Host Name (code 12)**   Specifies the DNS host name the client system will use.
- **Domain name (code 15)**   Specifies the name of the DNS domain on which the system will reside.

HOST-SPECIFIC IP LAYER PARAMETERS   These options affect the overall functionality of the IP protocol on the client system.

- **IP Forwarding Enable/Disable (code 19)**   Specifies whether IP forwarding (that is, routing) should be enabled on the client system.
- **Maximum Datagram Reassembly Size (code 22)**   Specifies the largest size datagram the client should reassemble.
- **Default IP Time-to-Live (code 23)**   Specifies the time-to-live value the client should use in its outgoing IP datagrams.

INTERFACE-SPECIFIC IP LAYER PARAMETERS   These options affect the IP protocol functionality of individual network interfaces on the client system. On multihomed systems (that is, systems with two or more network interfaces) these options can have different values for each interface.

- **Interface MTU (code 26)**   Specifies the maximum transfer unit to be used by the Internet Protocol on this network interface only.
- **Broadcast Address (code 28)**   Specifies the address to be used for broadcast messages on this network interface only.
- **Static route (code 33)**   Specifies a list of static routes to be added to the system's routing table.

LINK LAYER PARAMETERS   These options affect the interface-specific functionality of the data link–layer protocol.

- **ARP Cache Timeout (code 35)**   Specifies the amount of time that entries should remain in the system's Address Resolution Protocol cache.
- **Ethernet Encapsulation (code 36)**   Specifies the Ethernet frame type the client will use when transmitting IP traffic.

TCP PARAMETERS   These options affect the interface-specific functionality of the TCP protocol.

- **TCP Default TTL (code 37)**   Specifies the time-to-live value the client should use in its outgoing TCP segments.
- **TCP Keepalive Interval (code 38)**   Specifies the amount of time that should elapse before the client sends a keepalive signal over an idle TCP connection.

APPLICATION AND SERVICE PARAMETERS   These options configure various application layer functions.

- **Network Information Service Domain (code 40)**   Specifies the name of the NIS domain to which the client belongs. The equivalent option for NIS+ uses code 64.

- **Network Information Servers (code 41)**   Specifies the IP addresses of the NIS servers the client will use. The equivalent option for NIS plus uses code 65.

- **Vendor-Specific Information (code 43)**   See "The Vendor-Specific Information Option," earlier in this chapter.

- **NetBIOS over TCP/IP Name Server (code 44)**   Specifies the IP addresses of the servers (usually Windows NT WINS servers) the client will use for NetBIOS name resolution.

- **NetBIOS over TCP/IP Node Type (code 46)**   Specifies the NetBIOS name resolution mechanisms the client will use and the order in which it will use them.

- **Simple Mail Transport Protocol (SMTP) Server (code 69)**   Specifies the IP addresses of the SMTP servers the client will use.

- **Post Office Protocol (POP3) Server (code 70)**   Specifies the IP addresses of the POP servers the client will use.

- **Network News Transport Protocol (NNTP) Server (code 71)**   Specifies the IP addresses of the NNTP servers the client will use.

DHCP EXTENSIONS   These options are used to provide parameters that govern the DHCP lease negotiation and renewal processes, as well as performing basic tasks, such as specifying the function of a message.

- **Requested IP Address (code 50)**   Used by the client to request a particular IP address from the server.

- **IP Address Lease Time (code 51)**   Specifies the duration of a dynamically allocated IP address lease.

- **Option Overload (code 52)**   See "The Option Overload Option," earlier in
- this chapter.

- **DHCP Message Type (code 53)**   See "The DHCP Message Type Option," earlier in this chapter.

- **Server Identifier (code 54)**   Specifies the IP address of the server involved in a DHCP transaction; used by the client to address unicasts to the server.

- **Parameter Request List (code 55)**   Used by the client to send a list of requested configuration options (identified by their code numbers) to the server.

- **Message (code 56)**   Used to carry an error message from the server to the client in a DHCPNAK message.

- **Renewal (T1) time value (code 58)**   Specifies the time period that must elapse before an IP address lease enters the renewing state.
- **Rebinding (T2) time value (code 59)**   Specifies the time period that must elapse before an IP address lease enters the rebinding state.
- **Vendor Class Identifier (code 60)**   Identifies the vendor and configuration of the client. See "The Vendor-Specific Information Option," earlier in this chapter.
- **Client Identifier (code 61)**   Unique identifier for the client delivered to the server for use in its index of client systems.

DHCP Communications

When you configure a workstation to be a DHCP client, the system initiates an exchange of messages with a DHCP server. Whether you are using dynamic, automatic, or manual address allocation, the first exchange of messages, resulting in an IP address assignment for the client, is the same.

IP Address Assignment

The entire IP address negotiation process is illustrated in Figure 18-3. Before the initial client/server exchange can begin, however, the question rises of how the client is to find the server and communicate with it when its TCP/IP stack has not yet been configured. A DHCP client that does not yet have an IP address is said to be in the *init state.* In this state, even though the workstation has no information about the servers on the network and no IP address of its own, it is still capable of sending broadcast transmissions.

The client begins the exchange by broadcasting a series of DHCPDISCOVER messages. In this packet, the DHCP Message Type option has a value of 1 in its data field and the hardware address of the client is included in the chaddr (or client hardware address) field, as shown in Figure 18-4. In most cases, this will be the MAC address hardcoded into the network interface adapter, as identified by the values of the htype and hlen fields. Because the client has no IP address of its own yet, the source address field in the IP header contains the value 0.0.0.0. The message may also contain other options requesting specific information from the server, such as the Requested IP Address option.

 Because the basic DHCP message format is the same as that of BOOTP, some protocol analyzer programs interpret DHCP traffic using BOOTP labels, as in the packet captures shown in Figures 18-4 through 18-7.

Each of the servers receiving the DHCPDISCOVER packet responds to the client with a DHCPOFFER message that contains an IP address in the yiaddr (or your IP address) field. This is the address the server is offering for the client's use. Whether the server transmits its DHCPOFFER and other messages to the client as unicasts or broadcasts is determined by the status of the Broadcast flag in the client's

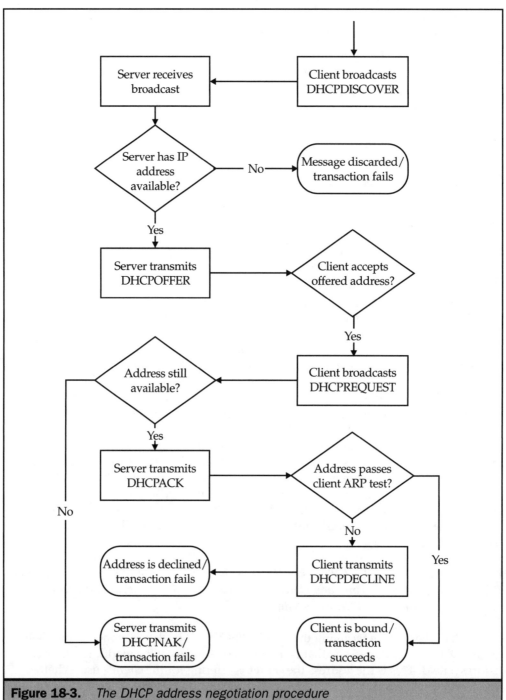

Figure 18-3. *The DHCP address negotiation procedure*

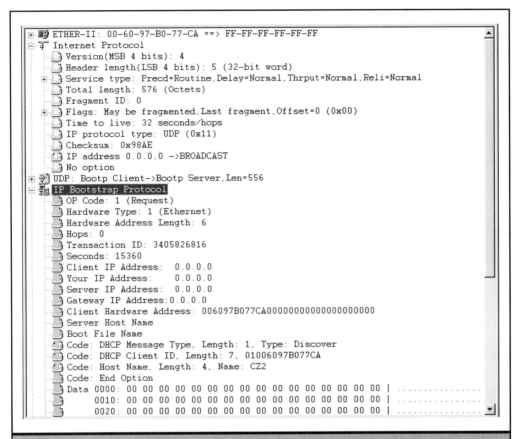

```
⊞ ▨ ETHER-II: 00-60-97-B0-77-CA ==> FF-FF-FF-FF-FF-FF
⊟ ▼ Internet Protocol
   ─ ▢ Version(MSB 4 bits): 4
   ─ ▢ Header length(LSB 4 bits): 5 (32-bit word)
   ⊞ ▢ Service type: Precd=Routine,Delay=Normal,Thrput=Normal,Reli=Normal
   ─ ▢ Total length: 576 (Octets)
   ─ ▢ Fragment ID: 0
   ⊞ ▢ Flags: May be fragmented,Last fragment,Offset=0 (0x00)
   ─ ▢ Time to live: 32 seconds/hops
   ─ ▢ IP protocol type: UDP (0x11)
   ─ ▢ Checksum: 0x98AE
   ─ ▢ IP address 0.0.0.0 ->BROADCAST
   ─ ▢ No option
⊞ ▨ UDP: Bootp Client->Bootp Server,Len=556
⊟ ▨ IP Bootstrap Protocol
   ─ ▢ OP Code: 1 (Request)
   ─ ▢ Hardware Type: 1 (Ethernet)
   ─ ▢ Hardware Address Length: 6
   ─ ▢ Hops: 0
   ─ ▢ Transaction ID: 3405826816
   ─ ▢ Seconds: 15360
   ─ ▢ Client IP Address:  0.0.0.0
   ─ ▢ Your IP Address:    0.0.0.0
   ─ ▢ Server IP Address:  0.0.0.0
   ─ ▢ Gateway IP Address:0.0.0.0
   ─ ▢ Client Hardware Address: 006097B077CA00000000000000000000
   ─ ▢ Server Host Name
   ─ ▢ Boot File Name
   ─ ▢ Code: DHCP Message Type, Length: 1, Type: Discover
   ─ ▢ Code: DHCP Client ID, Length: 7, 01006097B077CA
   ─ ▢ Code: Host Name, Length: 4, Name: CZ2
   ─ ▢ Code: End Option
   ─ ▢ Data 0000: 00 00 00 00 00 00 00 00 00 00 00 00 00 00 00 00 | ................
   ─ ▢      0010: 00 00 00 00 00 00 00 00 00 00 00 00 00 00 00 00 | ................
   ─ ▢      0020: 00 00 00 00 00 00 00 00 00 00 00 00 00 00 00 00 | ................
```

Figure 18-4.   *The DHCPDISCOVER message, as captured in a network analyzer program*

DHCPDISCOVER message (which the observant reader will note is not displayed in the packet captures shown here), as well as the capabilities of the server. The message will also contain options specifying values for the other TCP/IP parameters that the server is configured to deliver, as well as the DHCP extension options, as shown in Figure 18-5. Because each DHCP server on the network operates independently, the client may receive several offers, each with a different IP address.

Note   *If systems are functioning as DHCP (or BOOTP) relay agents on the same network segment as the client, the agent systems will propagate the broadcasts to other segments, resulting in additional DHCPOFFER messages from remote servers being transmitted back to the client through the agent. See "Relay Agents," later in this chapter, for more information.*

```
⊞ ▓ ETHER-II: 00-20-AF-37-B8-12 ==> 00-60-97-B0-77-CA
⊞ ▒ IP: 192.168.2.10->192.168.2.22,ID=40705
⊞ ▒ UDP: Bootp Server->Bootp Client,Len=308
⊟ ▒ IP Bootstrap Protocol
    ▒ OP Code: 2 (Reply)
    ▒ Hardware Type: 1 (Ethernet)
    ▒ Hardware Address Length: 6
    ▒ Hops: 0
    ▒ Transaction ID: 3982093657
    ▒ Seconds: 0
    ▒ Client IP Address:  0.0.0.0
    ▒ Your IP Address:    192.168.2.22
    ▒ Server IP Address:  0.0.0.0
    ▒ Gateway IP Address:0.0.0.0
    ▒ Client Hardware Address: 006097B077CA00000000000000000000
    ▒ Server Host Name
    ▒ Boot File Name
    ▒ Code: DHCP Message Type, Length: 1, Type: Offer
    ▒ Code: Subnet Mask, Length: 4        Address255.255.255.0
    ▒ Code: DHCP Renewal (T1) Time, Length: 4, Value:129600
    ▒ Code: DHCP Rebinding  (T2) Time, Length: 4, Value:226800
    ▒ Code: DHCP IP Address Lease Time, Length: 4, Value:259200
    ▒ Code: DHCP Server ID, Length: 4
    ▒          Address: 192.168.2.10
    ▒ Code: Router, Length: 4
    ▒          Address: 192.168.2.100
    ▒ Code: Domain Name Server, Length: 8
    ▒          Address: 199.224.86.15
    ▒          Address: 199.224.86.16
    ▒ Code: NetBIOS Name Server, Length: 4
    ▒          Address: 192.168.2.10
    ▒ Code: NetBIOS over TCP/IP, Length: 1, Node Type:0x8 H-node
    ▒ Code: End Option
    ▒ Data 0000: 00                          | .
  ▓ Calculate CRC: 0xfab71c9d
```

Figure 18-5.   *The DHCPOFFER message, returned to the client by a server*

After a predetermined interval, the client stops broadcasting DHCPDISCOVER messages and selects one of the offers it has received. If the client receives no DHCPOFFER messages, it retries its broadcasts and eventually times out with an error message. No other TCP/IP communications are possible while the machine is in this state.

When the client accepts an IP address offered by a server, it generates a DHCPREQUEST message that contains the name of the selected server in the Server Identifier option and the offered IP address (taken from the yiaddr field of the DHCPOFFER message) in the Requested IP Address option (see Figure 18-6). The client also uses the DHCP Parameter Request List option to request additional parameters from the server.

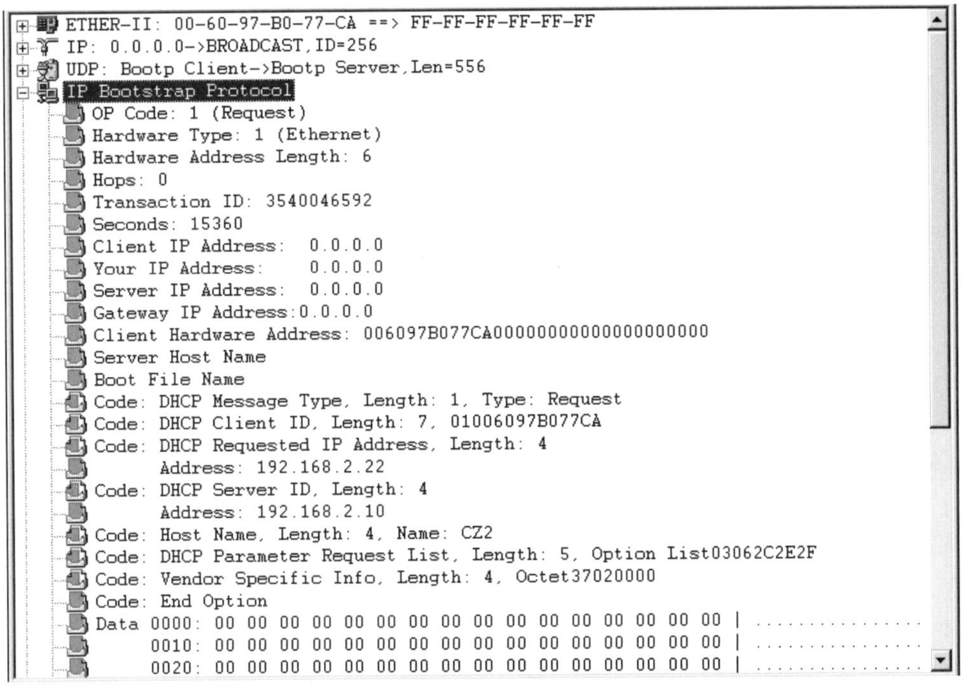

```
ETHER-II: 00-60-97-B0-77-CA ==> FF-FF-FF-FF-FF-FF
IP: 0.0.0.0->BROADCAST,ID=256
UDP: Bootp Client->Bootp Server,Len=556
IP Bootstrap Protocol
  OP Code: 1 (Request)
  Hardware Type: 1 (Ethernet)
  Hardware Address Length: 6
  Hops: 0
  Transaction ID: 3540046592
  Seconds: 15360
  Client IP Address:  0.0.0.0
  Your IP Address:    0.0.0.0
  Server IP Address:  0.0.0.0
  Gateway IP Address:0.0.0.0
  Client Hardware Address: 006097B077CA00000000000000000000
  Server Host Name
  Boot File Name
  Code: DHCP Message Type, Length: 1, Type: Request
  Code: DHCP Client ID, Length: 7, 01006097B077CA
  Code: DHCP Requested IP Address, Length: 4
        Address: 192.168.2.22
  Code: DHCP Server ID, Length: 4
        Address: 192.168.2.10
  Code: Host Name, Length: 4, Name: CZ2
  Code: DHCP Parameter Request List, Length: 5, Option List03062C2E2F
  Code: Vendor Specific Info, Length: 4, Octet37020000
  Code: End Option
  Data 0000: 00 00 00 00 00 00 00 00 00 00 00 00 00 00 00 00 | ...............
       0010: 00 00 00 00 00 00 00 00 00 00 00 00 00 00 00 00 | ...............
       0020: 00 00 00 00 00 00 00 00 00 00 00 00 00 00 00 00 | ...............
```

Figure 18-6. *The DHCPREQUEST message, sent by a client to a server to accept its offered address*

The client transmits the DHCPREQUEST message as a broadcast because the message not only informs the selected server that the client has accepted its offer, it also informs the other servers that their offers have been declined. The message must have the same value in the secs field and use the same broadcast address as the DHCPDISCOVER messages the client previously transmitted. This is so that the broadcast is certain to reach all the servers that responded with offers (including those on other segments that require the assistance of relay agents).

At the time a server generates a DHCPOFFER message, the IP address it offers is not yet exclusively allocated to that client. If addresses are in short supply or if the client takes too long to respond, the server may offer that address to another client in the interim. When the server receives the DHCPREQUEST message saying its offer has been accepted, it generates either a DHCPACK message indicating that the IP address assignment has been completed (see Figure 18-7) or a DHCPNAK message indicating that the offered address is no longer available. The DHCPACK message contains all the

```
⊞ 📠 ETHER-II: 00-20-AF-37-B8-12 ==> 00-60-97-B0-77-CA
⊞ 🖳 IP: 192.168.2.10->192.168.2.22,ID=40961
⊞ 🖳 UDP: Bootp Server->Bootp Client,Len=308
⊟ 🖳 IP Bootstrap Protocol
    ─🗋 OP Code: 2 (Reply)
    ─🗋 Hardware Type: 1 (Ethernet)
    ─🗋 Hardware Address Length: 6
    ─🗋 Hops: 0
    ─🗋 Transaction ID: 3982093657
    ─🗋 Seconds: 0
    ─🗋 Client IP Address:  0.0.0.0
    ─🗋 Your IP Address:    192.168.2.22
    ─🗋 Server IP Address:  0.0.0.0
    ─🗋 Gateway IP Address:0.0.0.0
    ─🗋 Client Hardware Address: 006097B077CA00000000000000000000
    ─🗋 Server Host Name
    ─🗋 Boot File Name
    ─🗋 Code: DHCP Message Type, Length: 1, Type: Ack
    ─🗋 Code: DHCP Renewal (T1) Time, Length: 4, Value:129600
    ─🗋 Code: DHCP Rebinding  (T2) Time, Length: 4, Value:226800
    ─🗋 Code: DHCP IP Address Lease Time, Length: 4, Value:259200
    ─🗋 Code: DHCP Server ID, Length: 4
    ─🗋      Address: 192.168.2.10
    ─🗋 Code: Subnet Mask, Length: 4      Address255.255.255.0
    ─🗋 Code: Router, Length: 4
    ─🗋      Address: 192.168.2.100
    ─🗋 Code: Domain Name Server, Length: 8
    ─🗋      Address: 199.224.86.15
    ─🗋      Address: 199.224.86.16
    ─🗋 Code: NetBIOS Name Server, Length: 4
    ─🗋      Address: 192.168.2.10
    ─🗋 Code: NetBIOS over TCP/IP, Length: 1, Node Type:0x8 H-node
    ─🗋 Code: End Option
    ─🗋 Data 0000: 00                                    |  .
  📠 Calculate CRC: 0xb86b5951
```

Figure 18-7. *The DHCPACK message, confirming that the server has bound the offered address to the client*

options requested by the client in the DHCPREQUEST message and, as with the DHCPOFFER message, can be unicast or broadcast depending on the value of the Broadcast flag in the client's messages.

When the server generates a DHCPACK message, it creates an entry in its database that commits the offered IP address to the client's hardware address. The combination of these two addresses will, from this point until the address is released, function as a unique identifier for that client, called the *lease identification cookie*. If the server sends a DHCPNAK message to the client, the entire transaction is nullified and the client must begin the whole process again by generating new DHCPDISCOVER messages.

As a final test of its newly assigned address, the client can (but is not required to) use the ARP protocol to make sure no other system on the network is using the IP address furnished to it by the server. If the address is in use, the client sends a

DHCPDECLINE message to the server, nullifying the transaction. If the address is not in use, the address assignment process is completed and the client enters what is known as the *bound state.*

DHCPINFORM

The addition of a new message type to the DHCP standard makes it possible for clients to request TCP/IP configuration parameters without being assigned an IP address. When a server receives a DHCPINFORM message from a client, it generates a DHCPACK message containing the appropriate options for the client without including the lease time options or an IP address in the yiaddr field. The assumption is the client has already been manually configured with an IP address and does not require regular renewals or any other maintenance beyond the initial parameter assignment.

The most obvious application for the DHCPINFORM message is to configure DHCP servers themselves, which typically cannot use a DHCP-supplied IP address. The server must have a manually configured IP address, but administrators can use DHCPINFORM messages to request values for the other required TCP/IP configuration parameters. This eliminates the need for administrators to configure any of the client parameters apart from the IP address manually.

Lease Renewal

When a DHCP server is configured to use manual or automatic address allocation, no further contact occurs with the client unless (or until) the client manually releases the address. When using dynamic allocation, however, the DHCPOFFER messages sent to the client contain options that specify the nature of the address lease agreement. These options include the IP Address Lease Time, the Renewal (T1) Time Value, and the Rebinding (T2) Time Value.

These time values are supplied to the client in units of seconds and do not include specific clock times (to account for possible discrepancies between the client and server system clocks). Administrators can specify values for these intervals in the DHCP server configuration. As an example, the Microsoft DHCP Server has a default IP Address Lease Time of three days. The Renewal (T1) Time Value defaults to 50 percent of the lease time and the Rebinding (T2) Time Value to 87.5 percent of the lease time. Because the IP Address Lease Time option uses a 4-byte data subfield to specify the number of seconds, the maximum possible absolute value is approximately 136 years. A hexadecimal value of 0xffffffff (or a binary value of 32 ones) indicates infinity.

Once a client system with a leased address has entered the bound state, it has no further communications with the server until the system restarts or it reaches the T1, or renewal time. The lease renewal transaction that begins at this time is illustrated in Figure 18-8.

When the client's lease reaches the T1 time, it enters the *renewing* state and begins transmitting DHCPREQUEST messages to the server that assigned its IP address. The messages contain the client's lease identification cookie and are transmitted to the

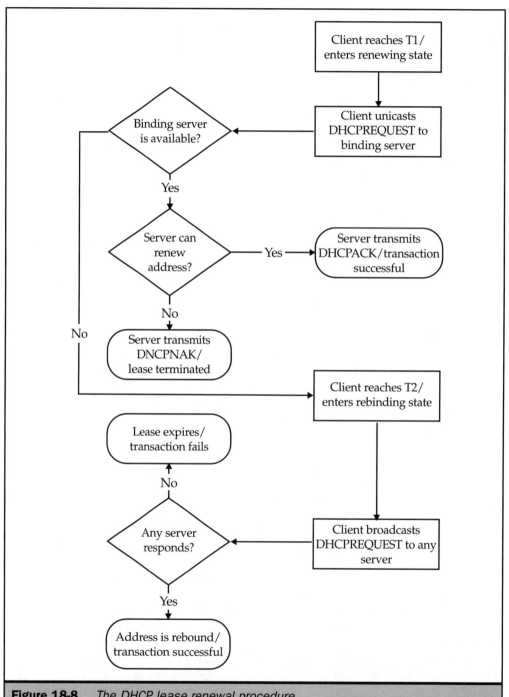

Figure 18-8. *The DHCP lease renewal procedure*

server as unicasts (unlike the DHCPREQUEST messages in the initial lease negotiation, which are broadcasts). If the server receives the message and is capable of renewing the lease, it responds with a DHCPACK message and the client returns to the bound state with a reset lease time. No further communication is necessary until the next renewal.

If the server cannot renew the lease, it responds with a DHCPNAK message, which terminates the transaction and the lease. The client must then restart the entire lease negotiation process with a new sequence of DHCPDISCOVER broadcasts.

Note *This is virtually the same message exchange that occurs each time a DHCP client system reboots, except the client remains in the bound state. Usually, the server will respond to the DHCPREQUEST message with a DHCPNAK only when the client system has been moved to a different subnet and requires an IP address with a different network identifier. If the server fails to respond at all after repeated retransmissions, the client continues to use the address until the lease reaches the T1 time, at which point it enters the renewing state and begins the lease renewal process.*

If the client receives no response to its unicast DHCPREQUEST, it retransmits the message each time half the interval between the current time and the T2 time has expired. Thus, using the default time values for the Microsoft server, the lease duration is 72 hours (three days), the T1 time is 36 hours (50 percent of 72), and the T2 time is 63 hours (87.5 percent of 72). The client will send its first DHCPREQUEST message to the server at 36 hours into the lease (the T1 time) and then retransmit at 49.5 hours (half the time until T2), 55.75 hours (half the remaining time until T2), 59.375 hours, and so on until it reaches the T2 time.

Once the lease time hits the T2 point, the client enters the *rebinding state* and begins transmitting its DHCPREQUEST messages as broadcasts to solicit an IP address assignment from any available server. Once again, the client awaits either a DHCPACK or DHCPNAK reply from a server. If no replies occur, the client continues retransmitting whenever half the remaining time in the lease expires. If the lease time does expire with no response from the server, the client releases the IP address and returns to the init state. It cannot send any further TCP/IP transmissions with the exception of DHCPDISCOVER broadcasts.

Address Release

While in the bound state, a DHCP client can relinquish its possession of an IP address (whether leased or permanent) by transmitting a unicast DHCPRELEASE message to the server, containing the client's lease identification cookie. This returns the client to the unbound state, preventing any further TCP/IP transmissions, except for DHCPDISCOVER broadcasts, and causes the server to place the IP address back into its pool of available addresses. In most cases, an address release like this only occurs when the user of a client workstation explicitly requests it, using a utility such as Ipconfig.exe in Windows NT or Winipcfg.exe in Windows 9x.

Relay Agents

Because of its reliance on broadcast transmissions—at least from the client side—it would seem that DHCP clients and servers must be located on the same network segment in order to communicate. If this were the case, however, DHCP would not be a practical solution for enterprise networks. To resolve this problem, DHCP takes its cue from BOOTP and uses relay agents as intermediaries between clients and servers. In fact, DHCP uses BOOTP relay agents exactly as defined in RFC 1542, "Clarifications and Extensions for the Bootstrap Protocol."

A *DHCP relay agent* (or *BOOTP relay agent*—the names are interchangeable) is a module located in a workstation or router on a particular network segment, which enables the other systems on that segment to be serviced by a DHCP server located on a remote segment. The relay agent works by monitoring UDP port 67 for DHCP messages being broadcast by clients on the local network. Normally, a workstation or router would ignore these messages because they do not contain a valid source address but, like the DHCP server, the relay agent is designed to accept a source address of 0.0.0.0.

When the relay agent receives these messages, it inserts its own IP address into the giaddr field of the DHCP message, increments the value of the hops field, and retransmits the packets to a DHCP server located on another segment. Depending on the location of the relay agent, this retransmission can take two forms. For an agent built into a router, the device may be able to broadcast the message using a different interface than the one over which it received the message. For a relay agent running on a workstation, it is necessary to send the message to the DHCP server on another segment as a unicast.

A message can be passed along by more than one relay agent on the way to the DHCP server. An agent only inserts its IP address into the giaddr field if this field has a value of 0. In addition, the agent must silently discard messages that have a value greater than 16 in the hops field (unless this limit is configurable and has been adjusted by the network administrator). This prevents DHCP messages from cycling endlessly around the network.

When a DHCP server receives messages from a relay agent, it processes them in the normal manner, but transmits them back to the address in the giaddr field, rather than to the client. The relay agent may then use either a broadcast or a unicast (depending on the state of the Broadcast flag) to transmit the reply, unchanged, to the client.

For an entire internetwork to be serviced by DHCP, every segment must have either a DHCP server or a relay agent on it. Most of the routers on the market today have DHCP/BOOTP relay agent functionality built into them but, for those that don't, the server versions of Windows NT 4.0 and Windows 2000 also include a relay agent service.

DHCP Implementations

Most of the operating systems in use today are capable of functioning as DHCP clients and DHCP servers are available on many different platforms. Novell includes a DHCP server in its NetWare 4.2, intraNetWare, and NetWare 5 products; and DHCP server products (many of them are open source) exist for several flavors of UNIX, including Linux. By far, however, the most popular implementation is the Microsoft DHCP Server.

Most of the DHCP products conform to the IETF standards, although you should be aware that some implementations support the older version of the DHCP standard, RFC 1541. The latest standard, RFC 2131, was published in March 1997. The most important modifications to the standard are

- The inclusion of a new message type—DHCPINFORM—that clients already having an IP address can use to request other local configuration parameters from a server.
- The addition of vendor-specific options that make it possible for a DHCP server to supply nonstandardized information to clients based on vendor class identifiers.

When you are evaluating DHCP servers for use on your network, you will find that while the basic functionality in most of the server implementations is the same, the options supported by each one can differ greatly. All DHCP servers will certainly support the basic parameters required by all TCP/IP clients, such as the Subnet Mask, Router, and Domain Name Server options, but the other options they support may be limited. Certain products may also include nonstandardized options intended for specific clients. For example, the Novell DHCP server includes options to support its NetWare/IP clients.

If you are running a variety of different clients on your network, then you should list the options you need to supply to each one and try to find a server to satisfy them all. Mixing DHCP servers from different manufacturers on the same internetwork is also possible but, because the clients use broadcast transmissions for their DHCPDISCOVER messages, no sure way exists to predict which server will configure which client.

Microsoft DHCP Server

Microsoft's DHCP Server is supplied with the Windows NT 4.0 and Windows 2000 server operating systems. While obviously intended for use with the Microsoft client operating systems, the server also supports all the options defined in the DHCP standards, many of which are not used by Microsoft clients. The DHCP server included in Windows NT 4.0 is designed to support the RFC 1533, 1534, 1541, and 1542 standards because the operating system was released in 1996, before RFC 2131 and 2132 were published. The Windows 2000 version supports the newer standards.

Creating Scopes

The Microsoft server enables you to define a range of IP addresses, called a *scope*, for each subnet on the network, and to specify the lease duration for that scope (see Figure 18-9). When a client on another subnet solicits an address from the server through a relay agent, the server uses the information added to the message by the agent to assign an IP address on the proper subnet. You then specify values for the options you want to deliver with each IP address the server assigns. You can assign options for individual scopes, global option that will be applied to all scopes, and default options.

One of the persistent problems with DHCP has always been that no communication exists between servers. Each server operates independently and assigning IP addresses from a single, common pool shared by multiple servers can result in workstations with duplicate addresses. Thus, if you intend to allocate the addresses from 192.168.10.100 to

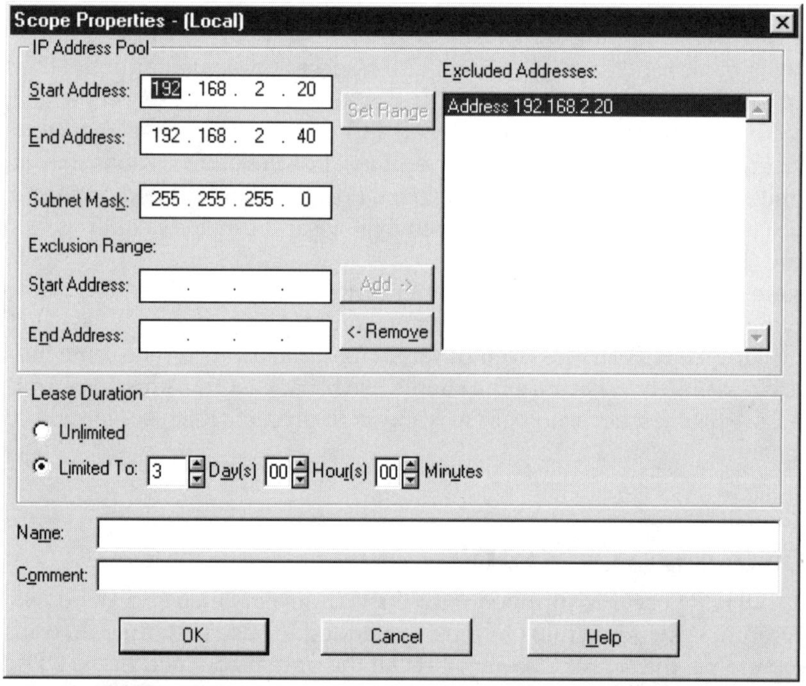

Figure 18-9.   *The Microsoft DHCP Server enables you to define a range of addresses to be excluded from a scope, as well as leases of varying duration*

192.168.10.200 using two DHCP servers, you traditionally must split the addresses between two scopes, one on each server. If one server should fail, the addresses allocated by that server become unavailable for renewal or reallocation unless an administrator modifies the scope on the remaining server.

The Microsoft DHCP server enables you to specify multiple address ranges to exclude from a scope. When using two or more DHCP servers to service a single subnet for fault tolerance purposes, Microsoft recommends you create a single identical scope for each subnet on each server and then exclude different address ranges on each one in an 80/20 split. Thus, to continue the example, you would configure both DHCP servers with a scope of addresses running from 192.168.10.100 to 192.168.10.200, but one server would exclude addresses 192.168.10.181 to 192.168.10.200, while the other would exclude 192.168.10.100 to 192.168.10.180. This technique makes it easy for an administrator to modify the configuration by altering the excluded range, should one of the servers become unavailable.

Since the release of Service Pack 3 for Windows NT 4.0, however, another solution to this problem has existed. The DHCP standards state that a client may use a gratuitous ARP request to determine if the IP address it has just been assigned is already in use on the network. If the address is in use, the client sends a DHCPDECLINE message to the server, which nullifies the entire transaction. If all clients did this, it would be possible to create identical scopes on different DHCP servers without having identically configured clients as a result. Some DHCP clients (most notably those in Windows 95 and 98), however, do not perform this gratuitous ARP test.

The Service Pack 3 (and later) releases for Windows NT 4.0 (as well as Windows 2000) improve on this concept. This update modifies the DHCP server to include a *conflict detection* mechanism that uses ICMP Echo messages (pings) to verify that an address is not in use before it is assigned to a client. This is better than the client-side ARP check because it occurs earlier in the lease negotiation process, saving both time and network traffic. When you enable conflict detection on all your DHCP servers, you can configure them with identical scopes and the only negative result will be some additional "bad address" error messages in the event logs.

To enable conflict detection, you highlight the server icon in the DHCP Manager display and select Properties from the Server menu to display the dialog box shown in Figure 18-10. You can select the number of pings the server uses to test each address before assigning it. On a Windows 2000 server, the Conflict Detection Attempts control is located on the Advanced page of the server's Properties dialog box.

Server to Client Transmissions

By default, the Microsoft DHCP Server included with Windows NT 4.0 ignores the state of the Broadcast flag in the DHCPDISCOVER and other messages transmitted by the client and broadcasts all its responses. This significantly increases the overall amount of network traffic generated by the DHCP address allocation process. In prior

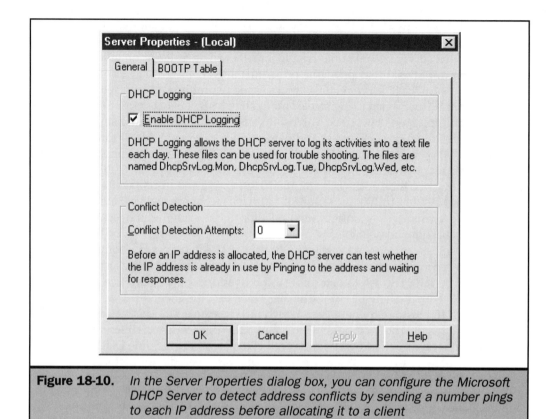

Figure 18-10.   *In the Server Properties dialog box, you can configure the Microsoft DHCP Server to detect address conflicts by sending a number pings to each IP address before allocating it to a client*

versions of Windows NT, this behavior was not controllable, but Windows NT 4.0 supports a registry entry that forces the DHCP server to use the Broadcast flag to determine how it will transmit its responses to DHCP clients. The entry is called IgnoreBroadcastFlag and you create it in the following registry key:

```
HKEY_LOCAL_MACHINE\System\CurrentControlSet\Services\DHCPServer\
Parameters
```

Create IgnoreBroadcastFlag as a REG_DWORD entry and configure it using one of the following values:

- **0**   DHCP transmissions from the server are controlled by the status of the Broadcast flag in the previous client messages
- **1**   All DHCP transmissions from the server are sent as broadcasts

Microsoft Client Utilities

Little client-side control is available for the Microsoft DHCP clients, mainly because little is needed. Simply enabling DHCP instead of manually configuring the TCP/IP stack is all that is needed to use the client. However, the operating systems do include a utility you can use to the view the settings assigned to the client by the DHCP server, as well as manually release and renew the current configuration.

Microsoft Client 3.0 for MS-DOS, Windows for Workgroups (with TCP/IP-32 installed), Windows NT, and Windows 2000 include a utility called Ipconfig.exe, which runs from the command line. The syntax for Ipconfig.exe is as follows:

```
Ipconfig [/all] [/release {adaptername}] [/renew {adaptername}]
```

- **/all**   Displays a complete listing of the TCP/IP parameters for all interfaces installed in the system
- **/release {adaptername}**   Terminates the DHCP lease for a specific adapter installed in the system, or if no adapter name is supplied, for all of the adapters installed in the system
- **/renew {adaptername}**   Initiates a new DHCP lease negotiation procedure for a specific adapter installed in the system, or if no adapter name is supplied, for all of the adapters installed in the system

Running Ipconfig from the command line with no parameters produces a basic TCP/IP client configuration display. Running the program with the /all parameter produces a more detailed display, as follows:

```
Windows NT IP Configuration
        Host Name . . . . . . . . . : cz1
        DNS Servers . . . . . . . . : 199.224.86.15
                                      199.224.86.16
        Node Type . . . . . . . . . : Hybrid
        NetBIOS Scope ID. . . . . . :
        IP Routing Enabled. . . . . : No
        WINS Proxy Enabled. . . . . : No
        NetBIOS Resolution Uses DNS : Yes
Ethernet adapter Elnk31:
        Description . . . . . . . . : ELNK3 Ethernet Adapter.
        Physical Address. . . . . . : 00-20-AF-37-B8-12
        DHCP Enabled. . . . . . . . : Yes
        IP Address. . . . . . . . . : 192.168.2.10
        Subnet Mask . . . . . . . . : 255.255.255.0
        Default Gateway . . . . . . : 192.168.2.100
        Primary WINS Server . . . . : 192.168.2.10
```

```
Lease Obtained. . . . . . : Sunday, June 27, 1999 4:32:59 PM
Lease Expires . . . . . . : Wednesday, June 30, 1999 4:32:59 PM
```

This display provides the network adapter names you can use when you manipulate the DHCP client using the /release and /renew command-line parameters.

Windows 95 and Windows 98 have a GUI version of the same utility called Winipcfg.exe. Executing this program from the Run dialog box produces a display like that shown in Figure 18-11. You can use the buttons to release and renew the DHCP client, just as you would with Ipconfig.exe's command-line parameters.

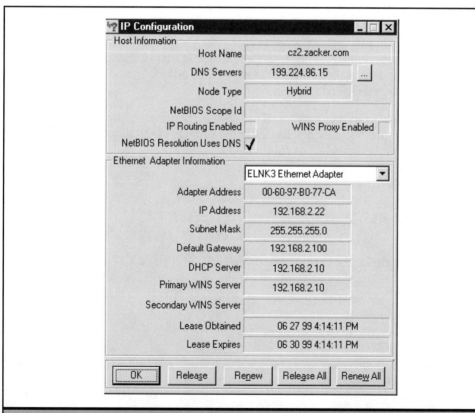

Figure 18-11. *Winipcfg.exe provides the same functions as Ipconfig.exe, using a graphical interface*

Client Option Support

Even though the Microsoft DHCP Server supports all the options defined in the IETF standards, this does not mean the DHCP client in the Microsoft operating systems supports them all as well. In fact, the clients support only a few of the available options, even though they could conceivably make good use of them. In addition to the DHCP extension options required for control of the lease negotiation process, the options supported by the DHCP clients in Microsoft Client 3.0 for MS-DOS, Windows for Workgroups (with TCP/IP-32 installed), Windows 95, Windows 98, and Windows NT are as follows:

- Subnet Mask
- Router
- Domain Name Server
- Domain name
- NetBIOS over TCP/IP Name Server
- NetBIOS over TCP/IP Node Type
- NetBIOS over TCP/IP Scope

The Windows 2000 client also supports these and adds support for vendor-specific information using vendor and client class identifiers.

 For more information on the DHCP support in Windows 2000, see "Windows 2000 and DHCP," later in this chapter.

DHCP Lease Duration

Once configured, DHCP servers require little or no monitoring. Depending on the volatility of the network and the availability of IP addresses, administrators can modify the lease duration to minimize the network traffic generated by DHCP communications. On an unregistered TCP/IP network, no shortage of IP addresses should occur, so you can safely increase the duration of the lease to make renewals less frequent.

By increasing the lease from the default of 3 days to 30 days, for example, a system would have to run continuously for 15 days before attempting to renew its address. If some addresses were to remain allocated for a few weeks after a machine was moved to another subnet, little harm would be done.

On a network that uses registered IP addresses and that has a limited supply of them, however, you can decrease the duration of the lease to prevent addresses from being orphaned for too long a period. Of course, on a stable network—that is, one on which computers are rarely moved around—it may not be necessary to have the leases expire at all.

If the users of a network turn their computers off at the end of the day's work, the lease will be rebound each time the machine is turned on again. Be aware that DHCP activity occurs during the system startup process, not during the network logon. Simply logging off the network at the end of the day, instead of shutting the machine down, will not trigger a renewal at the next logon.

Moving a DHCP Server

If at any time you want to use a different Windows NT machine as your DHCP server, it is possible to migrate the database and configuration settings to another system without interrupting service to the clients. To do this, you must move the DHCP database files themselves as well as the registry entries that govern the DHCP server's operations.

The DHCP database is located in the *\%SystemRoot%\System32\dhcp* directory on the server, which, by default, would be *C:\Winnt\System32\dhcp*. After installing the Microsoft DHCP Server service on the new machine, you must stop the service (from the Services Control Panel) on both machines and copy the entire contents of this directory from the existing DHCP server (including all subdirectories and their contents) to the same location on the new system.

The next step is to launch the Regedit.exe program to export the entire contents of the following registry key to a registry script file:

```
HKEY_LOCAL_MACHINE\SYSTEM\CurrentControlSet\Services\DHCPServer\
Configuration
```

Once you have created a registry script file (with a .reg extension) containing these settings, you import them on the new machine by double-clicking the filename in Windows NT Explorer (or by using the Import Registry Key command on the File menu). At this point, you can restart the service on the new one and the clients will be serviced by the new server from that point forward.

Do not allow the DHCP service to restart on the old system or you may end up with clients on your network that have duplicate IP addresses. Modify the Startup Type of the Microsoft DHCP Server on the old machine in the Services Control Panel to prevent it from starting automatically when the server boots, deactivate the scopes duplicated on the new server, or modify the scopes to assign different IP addresses.

DHCP Maintenance

DHCP address allocation on a large network is a rather disk-intensive process. This is particularly true on networks where a large number of users all turn on their computers at the same time each day. The PCs to be used as DHCP servers should be selected with an eye toward disk efficiency—RAID arrays, high-speed disk drives, and other such disk technologies are a good idea.

Another good idea is to compact the DHCP database on a regular basis, to keep it running at maximum efficiency. Windows NT includes a command-line utility called Jetpack.exe, which enables you to create a batch file that performs the compression. You can execute the batch file manually on a regular basis, or use the AT scheduler to automate the process. The batch file used to compress the DHCP database should appear as follows:

```
cd %SystemRoot%\System32\dhcp
net stop dhcpserver
jetpack Dhcp.mdb Tmp.mdb
net start dhcpserver
```

 This same batch file, run from the\%SystemRoot%\System32\wins directory with the Wins.mdb filename, will compress the WINS database.

The Jetpack.exe program reads the first filename on the command line and compacts it to the second filename. After the process completes, the program deletes the original database file and renames the new, compacted version to the original filename.

 The Jetpack.exe program creates another temporary file called Temp.mdb during the database compression process. Do not use this filename on the command line and be sure no file of this name exists in the database directory before you launch Jetpack.exe.

Windows 2000 and DHCP

The DHCP server included with the Windows 2000 Server operating systems adds several features not found in the Windows NT 4.0 version. The server is now compliant with the newer DHCP standards, published as RFC 2131 and 2132, and is also committed to compliance with emerging standards, such as those defining interaction between DHCP and dynamic DNS and DHCP server-to-server communications.

DHCP and DNS

The Windows NT 4.0 version of the Microsoft DHCP Server can interact with WINS by entering its IP address assignments into the WINS database as they are assigned. In Windows 2000, DNS largely replaces the functionality of WINS, but DNS servers must traditionally be manually updated with new information. The Microsoft DNS Server included with Windows 2000 Server, however, supports dynamic updates of the DNS, as defined in RFC 2136.

As a result of this technology, it is also possible for a DHCP server to update address (A) and pointer (PTR) records on a DNS server with new IP addresses as they are assigned. The draft standard that defines this interaction also calls for a new DHCP option (assigned code number 81), which enables a client to supply its fully qualified domain name to a DHCP server. This capability makes it possible for a Windows 2000 DHCP server to function as a proxy for clients that do not themselves support dynamic DNS updates, like those running Windows 9x and Windows NT 4.0.

Note *The interaction between DHCP and DNS requires all the DNS servers on the network to support the dynamic update feature. This makes the technology suitable for a Windows network that uses only Microsoft DNS servers, but not for the Internet, which uses many different DNS servers. Using DHCP to assign IP addresses to Web servers and other machines accessible from the Internet can result in periodic address changes that may be reflected immediately in the records of the local DNS server, but still take hours or days to propagate throughout the Internet.*

Superscopes

Windows 2000's DHCP server also includes a new feature, called *superscopes*, that resolves one of the problems that occur when you divide the IP addresses to be assigned on a particular subnet between two servers, for fault tolerance purposes. If you divide 100 IP addresses between two separate scopes, a client in the rebinding state (that is, one that has reached the T2 time interval) that broadcasts DHCPREQUEST messages in an attempt to renew its address lease may receive a DHCPNAK message from a server that does not have that address in its scope. This message would terminate the lease and force a renegotiation for a new address. This can occur even when you create identical scopes on both servers and exclude different address ranges on each one, as recommended in "Creating Scopes," earlier in this chapter.

Tip *Deactivating a scope also causes a server to issue DHCPNACK messages when a client attempts to renew an address in that scope. If you want to disable the allocation of certain addresses temporarily, it is better to exclude the address ranges from the active scope than to deactivate the scope entirely.*

You can prevent the generation of these DHCPNAK messages, however, by using Windows 2000 to run your DHCP servers and create superscopes on both that contain all the IP addresses for the subnet (including the excluded ones). Because both servers are aware of all the addresses assigned to the subnet (even those assigned by the other server), they are able to determine which addresses should receive DHCPNAK messages and which should not.

New DHCP Options

The DHCP implementation in Windows 2000 includes support for assignment of vendor-specific options, as well as TCP/IP configurations based on user classes.

Vendor-specific options are defined in RFC 2132 and they are essentially a mechanism for supplying product-specific configuration data to certain clients without the need to put new options through the standardization process. For example, the Windows 2000 DHCP server defines a vendor class for Microsoft clients that includes three new options, as follows:

- **Microsoft Disable NetBIOS option** Disables NetBIOS support on the client.
- **Microsoft Release DHCP Lease on Shutdown option** Causes the client to release its IP address lease each time it shuts down.
- **Microsoft Default Router Metric Base** Specifies the default metric to be used for new entries to the client's routing table.

These options are useful only to Microsoft DHCP clients; so, rather than go through the time and effort of submitting them for inclusion in the DHCP standard, the server delivers them only to clients identifying themselves as Microsoft systems with an appropriate Vendor Class Identifier. The options themselves are delivered as suboptions within the Vendor-Specific Options option.

Another method Windows 2000 uses to supply customized configurations to clients is through user classes. A *user class* is a category of users defined by the administrator and associated with a set of options and their values. In the past, DHCP servers treated all clients equally; every system on a particular subnet received the same combination of options with its IP address. With user classes, it's possible to assign different options or different option values to systems based on any criteria. If, for example, you want to balance the traffic load generated by your clients between two DNS servers, you can create two separate classes, each specifying different values for the Domain Name Server option.

DHCPINFORM

Windows 2000 supports the new DHCPINFORM message type defined in the RFC 2131 standard for supplying configuration parameters to clients without including an IP address. Windows 2000 also uses this message for communications between DHCP servers, however, to verify all the servers operating on the network are authorized.

Windows 2000 includes a DhcpServer object type in Active Directory that you can use to register the DHCP servers operating on the network and to authorize them for use. Whenever the DHCP service starts on a Windows 2000 machine, it broadcasts DHCPINFORM messages, looking for the other DHCP servers on the network. These servers respond with DHCPACK messages containing their DS enterprise root in the Vendor-Specific Options field. The initializing server builds a list of the other DHCP servers on the network, all of which should have the same root. The server also communicates with the directory service by requesting a list of the machines that have been authorized to function as DHCP servers. As long as the server finds its own address on the list, it provides DHCP services to the clients on the network. If its address is not on the list, the DHCP service fails to initialize.

The
Complete
Reference

Upgrading
&
Troubleshooting
Networks

Chapter 19

WINS and NetBIOS
Name Resolution

569

The *Windows Internet Naming Service (WINS)* is a NetBIOS name server (NBNS) as defined in the RFC 1001 and 1002 standards published by the Internet Engineering Task Force (IETF). These standards define the use of NetBIOS over a TCP/IP network, called *NetBT* for short. Windows NT and Windows 2000 servers include WINS as a means of registering the NetBIOS names of the computers on a network and resolving those names into their equivalent IP addresses. Using WINS can significantly reduce the amount of broadcast traffic on your network and simplify the administration of Windows networks that span multiple segments.

NetBIOS Names

Windows networks use computer (NetBIOS) names to uniquely identify each of the systems on the network. When you browse through the Network Neighborhood on a Windows system, the domain, workgroup, and computer names you see in the display are actually NetBIOS names. The NetBIOS name space is flat (not hierarchical), meaning that each name can be used only once on a network. The NetBIOS name space also calls for names up to 16 characters in length, the last character of which Windows systems use for a resource identifier that identifies the function of the system, leaving 15 characters for the actual name supplied during the installation.

For example, when a system is sharing a drive or directory with another computer on the network, its NetBIOS name consists of the computer name assigned during the installation of the operating system, plus a sufficient number of spaces to pad the name out to 15 characters (if necessary), followed by the resource identifier. In this case, the resource identifier has a hexadecimal value of 20, indicating that the system is functioning as a file server. The possible values for the NetBIOS name resource identifier are shown in Table 19-1.

When Windows systems communicate using the NetBEUI protocol at the network and transport layers, they use the NetBIOS names to determine the hardware address to which they send their packets. To communicate using TCP/IP, however, a system requires the IP address of the intended destination. The process of converting a name into an address is known as *name resolution*. Windows systems on a TCP/IP network resolve NetBIOS names by using a look-up table that lists the names of the computers on the network and their equivalent IP addresses.

Note *DNS servers also perform name resolutions, except that they resolve the DNS names of computers into IP addresses, not the NetBIOS names. For more information on DNS, see Chapter 20.*

NetBIOS names must be unique on the network, so that traffic is always sent to the correct machine. To make sure that no two computers on a network have the same NetBIOS name, Windows systems use a name registration mechanism to check for duplicates during the network logon process. The *name registration mechanism* is how the system compiles the look-up table it will use for name resolutions.

Resource Name	Resource Identifier (hex)	Resource Type	Function
computername	00	U	Workstation Service
computername	01	U	Messenger Service
\\--__MSBROWSE__	01	G	Master Browser
computername	03	U	Messenger Service
computername	06	U	RAS Server Service
computername	1F	U	NetDDE Service
computername	20	U	File Server Service
computername	21	U	RAS Client Service
computername	22	U	Microsoft Exchange Interchange(MSMail Connector)
computername	23	U	Microsoft Exchange Store
computername	24	U	Microsoft Exchange Directory
computername	30	U	Modem Sharing Server Service
computername	31	U	Modem Sharing Client Service
computername	43	U	SMS Clients Remote Control
computername	44	U	SMS Administrators Remote Control Tool
computername	45	U	SMS Clients Remote Chat
computername	46	U	SMS Clients Remote Transfer
computername	4C	U	DEC Pathworks TCP/IP service on Windows NT
computername	52	U	DEC Pathworks TCP/IP service on Windows NT
computername	87	U	Microsoft Exchange MTA

Table 19-1.   *Windows NetBIOS Resource Identifiers (16th Character Codes)*

Resource Name	Resource Identifier (hex)	Resource Type	Function
computername	6A	U	Microsoft Exchange IMC
computername	BE	U	Network Monitor Agent
computername	BF	U	Network Monitor Application
username	03	U	Messenger Service
domain	00	G	Domain Name
domain	1B	U	Domain Master Browser
domain	1C	G	Domain Controllers
domain	1D	U	Master Browser
domain	1E	G	Browser Service Elections
INet~Services	1C	G	IIS
IS~*computername*	00	U	IIS
computername	[2B]	U	Lotus Notes Server Service
IRISMULTICAST	[2F]	G	Lotus Notes
IRISNAMESERVER	[33]	G	Lotus Notes
Forte_$ND800ZA	[20]	U	DCA IrmaLan Gateway Server Service

Table 19-1. *Windows NetBIOS Resource Identifiers (16th Character Codes)* (continued)

The NetBT standards define the message exchanges that systems use during their name registration and resolution activities, as well as the formats of the messages themselves.

Windows systems can use three different mechanisms to perform both name registration and name resolutions, which are as follows:

- **LMHOSTS** A manually created text file containing a look-up table of NetBIOS names and IP addresses

- **Broadcasts** A process by which systems broadcast NetBT messages to the entire network segment and rely on the responses from other systems for NetBIOS name information

■ **WINS**   A service running on a Windows NT server that maintains a dynamic database of NetBIOS names and IP addresses

The following sections examine the advantages and drawbacks of these methods and explain how WINS, in most cases, is the best solution for both.

Name Registration Methods

During name registration, a system "claims" a NetBIOS name for its own use and, in some cases, prevents other systems from taking the same name. The name, in some cases, is also added to the look-up table systems will use for name resolution.

LMHOSTS Name Registration

LMHOSTS is a simple text file that contains the NetBIOS names of the systems on the network and their IP addresses, much like the HOSTS file performs the same functions for DNS names on TCP/IP systems. Because the file must be manually created, the name registration process for a system occurs when a user or administrator edits the file and adds the computer's NetBIOS name and IP address.

The only mechanism in an LMHOSTS file that prevents the existence of duplicate NetBIOS names is that systems parse the file from top to bottom and use only the first entry they find for a particular NetBIOS name. All subsequent entries in the file are ignored.

Broadcast Name Registration

When using the broadcast method, a TCP/IP system transmits a series of broadcast messages to the local network that contain the NetBIOS name assigned to the computer during its operating system installation. These NAME REGISTRATION REQUEST messages are carried within a User Datagram Protocol (UDP) packet using a format defined in the NetBT standards. The system repeats the broadcasts three times at 250 millisecond intervals.

All the computers on the local network receiving the broadcasts are required to reply if they are using the same NetBIOS name as the broadcasting system. If this is the case, the computer with the duplicate name transmits a NEGATIVE NAME REGISTRATION RESPONSE message back to the original system as a unicast. When this occurs, the registration of the name fails and the system prompts the user for a different NetBIOS name. This prevents any duplicate NetBIOS names from existing on the same network segment.

If the system receives no replies to its NAME REGISTRATION REQUEST broadcasts, it broadcasts a NAME OVERWRITE DEMAND message that declares its possession of the NetBIOS name in question. No replies are expected to demand-type messages, as they are unequivocal declarations of an operating condition. This entire broadcast name registration process is illustrated in Figure 19-1.

NETWORK CONNECTION SERVICES

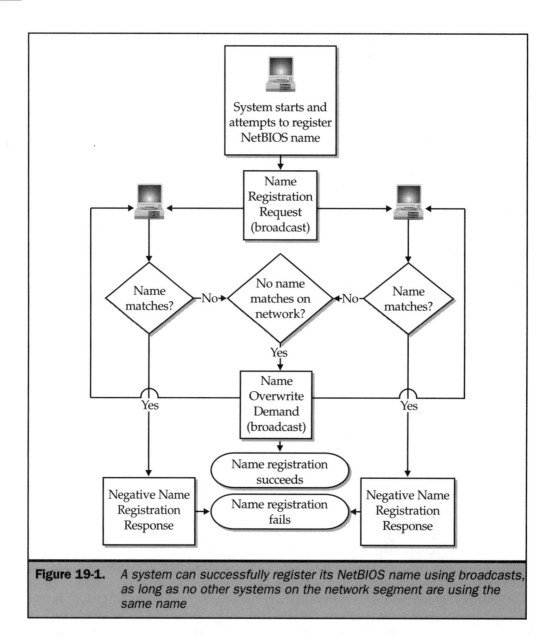

Figure 19-1. *A system can successfully register its NetBIOS name using broadcasts, as long as no other systems on the network segment are using the same name*

Strictly speaking, no permanent look-up table is associated with the broadcast name registration method. Each Windows system on the network does maintain a NetBIOS name cache, however, in which names and their equivalent addresses are stored temporarily, to prevent repetitive name resolution procedures.

Because broadcast transmissions are propagated only within the collision domain in which they originate, this method of name registration does nothing to prevent systems on other network segments from using duplicate NetBIOS names. Also, on a properly configured network (that is, one without duplicate NetBIOS names), these name registration broadcasts generate a lot of network traffic for no good purpose.

WINS Name Registration

When a system configured to use WINS logs on to the network, it also generates a NAME REGISTRATION REQUEST message; but instead of broadcasting it to the entire network, the message is sent as a unicast to the WINS server specified in the system's TCP/IP client configuration using UDP port 137. The only differences in the message itself are the values of a few minor fields (see "NetBT Message Formats," later in this chapter).

The WINS server maintains a database of the NetBIOS names assigned to other systems on the network along with their IP addresses. When it receives a NAME REGISTRATION REQUEST unicast, it checks to see if the NetBIOS name specified in the request has already been registered by another system. If the name is not in use, the WINS server adds it to its database and returns a POSITIVE NAME REGISTRATION RESPONSE back to the sender. This message contains a *time-to-live (TTL)* value that specifies how long the name registration will remain in the database without being renewed by the client. This prevents a NetBIOS name from being perpetually assigned to a system that is no longer running.

WINS Name Challenges

If the WINS server already has the requested NetBIOS name in its database, it initiates a name challenge procedure. This is to ensure that the name in question is actually in use. If, for example, you were to move a computer physically to another location, it might be connected to another subnet, which would give it a different IP address. As far as WINS is concerned, however, the NetBIOS name is still in use by the original IP address. The name challenge determines whether the system to which the name is registered is actually using it. In this example, because the registered system no longer exists at the old IP address, it will not respond to the challenge and the name will be released.

The name challenge process begins when the WINS server transmits a series of unicast NAME QUERY REQUEST messages to the IP address of the system registered as using the NetBIOS name. If the system is still using the name, it replies to the server with a POSITIVE NAME QUERY RESPONSE message. The server then transmits a NEGATIVE NAME REGISTRATION RESPONSE message to the original client, denying the client the registration and forcing the selection of a new NetBIOS name.

If the registered client does not respond to the server's NAME QUERY REQUEST message, the server retransmits up to three times at 500 millisecond intervals. If no responses occur or if the registered client returns a NEGATIVE NAME QUERY

RESPONSE, indicating that it is no longer using the name, then the server purges the record from the WINS server's database and assigns the name to the new client system. The WINS name registration and name challenge process is illustrated in Figure 19-2.

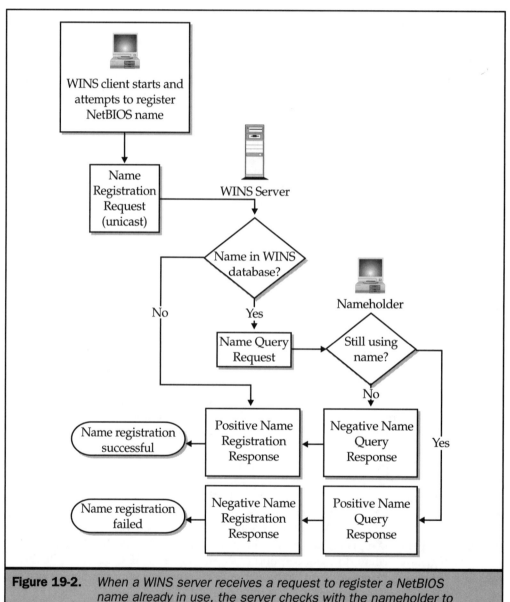

Figure 19-2. *When a WINS server receives a request to register a NetBIOS name already in use, the server checks with the nameholder to verify its status*

WINS name registration is a great improvement over the broadcast method because all its communications are in the form of unicast messages instead of broadcasts. This minimizes the amount of network traffic generated by the name registration process. In addition, because it uses unicast transmissions, WINS can handle name registration and resolution for an entire internetwork, not just for a single segment.

WINS Name Renewal

By default, the TTL interval assigned to each WINS name registration is six days, although network administrators can modify this value. The TTL clock for a given system resets itself to the default interval each time it logs on to the network. When a system remains logged on continuously for half the TTL interval (three days, by default), it begins attempting to renew the name registration.

The name renewal process begins when the client transmits a NAME REFRESH REQUEST message to the WINS server. The server then replies with either a POSITIVE NAME REFRESH RESPONSE message containing a new TTL interval or a NEGATIVE NAME REFRESH RESPONSE that forces the client to register a different name.

If the server fails to respond to the request, the client retransmits at two-minute intervals until half the remaining TTL interval (1.5 days, by default) remains. At this point, the client begins sending NAME REFRESH REQUEST messages to the secondary WINS server specified in the client's TCP/IP configuration. If the client receives no response, it continues transmitting requests to the secondary server until half the remaining TTL interval is left and then switches back to the primary server.

This process continues, with the client switching servers each time it reaches half the remaining time, until it either receives a response from one of the servers or the TTL interval expires. Once the TTL interval expires, the client reverts to the broadcast name registration method.

WINS Name Release

As part of its normal shutdown sequence, a client system transmits a NAME RELEASE REQUEST message to the WINS server. The server replies with either a POSITIVE NAME RELEASE RESPONSE message, in which case the client continues the shutdown process, or a NEGATIVE NAME RELEASE RESPONSE, which only occurs when the IP address in the server's record for that NetBIOS name contains an IP address different from that in the message.

Once the release sequence is complete, the WINS server can reassign the NetBIOS name to any other system that requests it. If a client system's TTL interval expires without the WINS server receiving any renewal messages from the client, the server purges the associated record from its database and releases the NetBIOS name.

Name Resolution Methods

Name resolution is the process by which a client system discovers the IP address of a computer on the network using a particular NetBIOS name. The methods for resolving names correspond to the methods for registering them.

NetBIOS Name Cache Resolution

By far, the fastest method of resolving NetBIOS names uses a look-up table stored in the client system's memory, called the *NetBIOS name cache*. Whenever the client system resolves a name using one of the other methods, the information is stored in the cache for a limited amount of time to prevent the need for repeated resolutions of the same name. Because accessing the cache requires no network communications or even disk drive access, it is much faster than any other method. Windows systems always check the cache before they attempt any other name resolution method.

You can view the current contents of the NetBIOS name cache on a Windows system at any time by running the Nbtstat.exe program at the command line with the –c switch, as shown:

```
c:\>nbtstat -c
Node IpAddress: [192.168.2.5] Scope Id: []
                NetBIOS Remote Cache Name Table
     Name              Type       Host Address      Life [sec]
    ---------------------------------------------------------------
    CZ3           <20>  UNIQUE     192.168.2.3          360
    CZ1           <20>  UNIQUE     192.168.2.10         360
    CZ1           <00>  UNIQUE     192.168.2.10         360
    CZ1           <03>  UNIQUE     192.168.2.10         360
```

The number in angle brackets that follows the NetBIOS name is the value assigned to the NetBIOS name's resource identifier, the 16th character that defines the function of the machine. Because a Windows system can perform multiple functions at the same time (such as client and server), you may see multiple entries in the cache for the same computer, with different resource identifiers.

Entries in the NetBIOS name cache have a limited life, so outdated information does not remain cached indefinitely. Preloading the cache by including entries in the LMHOSTS file that are marked with the #PRE tag is possible, however. When a Windows system boots, it reads the LMHOSTS file and loads the #PRE-tagged entries into the cache without assigning them a time limit. This makes bypassing the other name resolution methods for specific systems and providing virtually instantaneous access to the resolution information possible.

LMHOSTS Name Resolution

The LMHOSTS file is the simplest method of name resolution because it does not require any additional network communications. To resolve a name, a system simply opens the LMHOSTS text file on the local drive, searches for the desired NetBIOS name, and reads its equivalent IP address. The process is fast because there are no network traffic delays, but it also suffers from a major problem.

To function properly, an LMHOSTS file must contain the NetBIOS names and IP addresses of all the computers on the network and no mechanism exists to update the file automatically. A user or administrator must manually update the file on each computer whenever a change occurs in the network configuration. Obviously, once you get beyond a handful of systems on a network, this method becomes far too labor intensive.

In most cases, the LMHOSTS file is only used as a companion to the broadcast name resolution method. Because broadcasts are limited to the local network segment, administrators use an LMHOSTS file to resolve the names of servers and other key systems on other networks. Even for this purpose, however, the maintenance required is usually more than most administrators find convenient.

Broadcast Name Resolution

In the broadcast name resolution method, a system resolves a given NetBIOS name by generating a series of NAME QUERY REQUEST messages and broadcasting them to the local network segment. Each system on the network examines the request, and if it contains that system's NetBIOS name, replies with a POSITIVE NAME QUERY RESPONSE (see Figure 19-3). When the names do not match, the system discards the packet.

The broadcast method works quite well on a small network, but its main problem lies in the excess traffic it generates. Just as with broadcast name registration, every

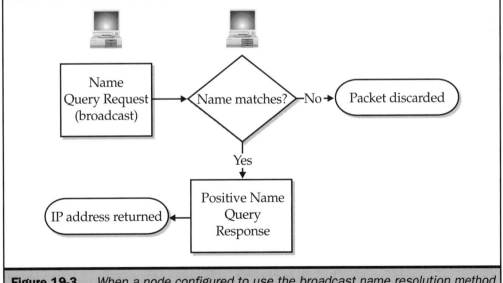

Figure 19-3.   *When a node configured to use the broadcast name resolution method receives a NAME QUERY REQUEST containing its own name, the node must respond with its IP address*

successful name resolution also results in a failed resolution for every other system on the network segment. The impact of these failures is not limited to the excess traffic volume transmitted over the network.

The data link–layer protocol of each system receiving a NAME QUERY REQUEST must pass the message up through the layers of the protocol stack. Not until the message reaches the NetBIOS interface, roughly corresponding to the session layer in the OSI reference model, does the system reads the NetBIOS name in the request and either responds to it or discards it. This requires a certain number of processor cycles on the client computer, which is multiplied by the total number of broadcast messages generated by all the systems on the network.

One factor that does reduce this burden, to some degree, is the NetBIOS name cache on every Windows machine. After successfully resolving a name into an IP address, a system adds the information to the cache it keeps in memory. This prevents the machine from having to perform repeated resolutions of the same name while transmitting a large number of packets to a single destination. This cache is volatile, however, meaning the information is purged whenever the system is restarted. This prevents the computer from using outdated name resolution information when transmitting data.

The other drawback of the broadcast method is its limitation to the local network segment. Data link–layer broadcasts are not propagated to other network segments by routers, switches, and other such devices. While configuring a router to do this would be possible, the amount of traffic generated by having all the broadcasts from all the networks propagated throughout the enterprise would be enormous.

WINS Name Resolution

As with name registration, WINS makes the name resolution process more efficient by using only unicast transmissions. A system trying to resolve a NetBIOS name transmits a NAME QUERY REQUEST message, just as in the broadcast method, except it transmits the message as a unicast to the WINS server specified in its TCP/IP configuration. The server consults its database and replies with either a POSITIVE NAME QUERY RESPONSE containing the equivalent IP address for the requested name or a NEGATIVE NAME QUERY RESPONSE informing the system that the name does not exist in the database.

The server may also send interim WAIT FOR ACKNOWLEDGMENT RESPONSE (WACK) messages back to the client if some delay occurs in satisfying the request to prevent the client from timing out. If the client receives a negative response or no response at all from the server, it sends the same request to the secondary WINS server specified in its TCP/IP configuration (see Figure 19-4). If the secondary server also fails to reply with a positive response, the client switches to a different name resolution method, according to its node type.

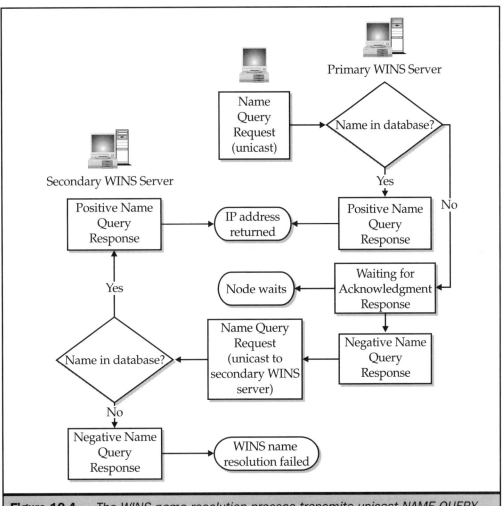

Figure 19-4. *The WINS name resolution process transmits unicast NAME QUERY REQUEST messages to both WINS servers, if necessary*

WINS, therefore, reduces the amount of network traffic devoted to NetBIOS name resolution and eliminates the need for systems to process extraneous broadcast messages. Because unicast messages (unlike broadcasts) can be transmitted to any location in an internetwork, WINS can provide name resolution services for the entire enterprise. In addition, because the WINS name registration process automatically compiles its database of NetBIOS names and IP addresses, there is no need for administrators to edit a look-up table manually.

WINS and Internetwork Browsing

In addition to name registration and resolution services, WINS also makes it possible for client systems to browse the shares on other network segments, without any manual configuration by the administrator. Browsing on a Windows network is the ability to see the domains, workgroups, computers, and shares in the Windows Network Neighborhood display. Browsing the shares on the network is entirely separate from actually accessing the shares. A user may, for example, be unable to see the shares in the Network Neighborhood, but still have the ability to access those shares by mapping a drive letter directly to a UNC name.

Note *Do not confuse the concept of the Windows network browser with World Wide Web browsers like Internet Explorer and Netscape Navigator. These are applications, while the Windows network browser is a service performed by Windows machines.*

On every segment of a Windows network, one system is elected to the role of master browser. The *master browser* is responsible for compiling a definitive list of all the computers and shares on the network and replicating it to other systems that function as *backup browsers*. In the event that the master browser fails or is shut down, a new election delegates a system to take its place.

When WINS servers are present on a network, the master browser gets its information about the systems on the network from WINS, instead of from the systems directly. WINS also simplifies the communications process between browsers on different network segments. Without WINS, the systems functioning as browsers must be listed in the LMHOSTS file of the browsers on other network segments for their names to be resolved during the browser replication process.

Node Types

The NetBIOS name registration and resolution methods a system uses and the order in which it uses them are specified by the computer's node type, as defined in the NetBT standards. Each node type defines a name registration method and a primary name resolution method and, in some cases, a series of fallbacks to use should the primary resolution method fail. The three possible node types defined in the standards are as follows:

- **B-node (broadcast node)** Uses the broadcast method for name registration and resolution exclusively
- **P-node (point-to-point node)** Uses NetBIOS name servers for name registration and resolution exclusively

- **M-node (mixed mode node)**   Uses the broadcast method for name registration exclusively; uses broadcasts for name resolution and NetBIOS name servers if broadcasts fail to resolve a name

Microsoft Node Types

The node types as defined in the standards are not particularly well suited to the capabilities of Windows systems. On a b-node system, a name resolution fails completely if the requested name is located on another network segment. On a P-node system, the name resolutions fail completely if the NetBIOS name servers are not functioning. M-node systems are intended for situations in which a NetBIOS name server is used only for resolving names on other segments. This is impractical on a Windows network because WINS is designed to completely replace broadcasts. As a result of these inadequacies, Microsoft created three additional node types for use with its operating systems, which are as follows:

- **Modified b-node**   Uses the broadcast method for name registration exclusively; uses broadcast for name resolution and the LMHOSTS file if that broadcast fails to resolve a name. This is the default node type for a Windows system that is not configured to use WINS.

- **H-node (hybrid node)**   Uses NetBIOS name servers for name registration exclusively; uses NetBIOS name servers for name resolution and the broadcast method if NetBIOS name servers fail. The system then reverts back to using the name servers as soon as they become available. This is the default node type for a WINS-enabled client.

- **Microsoft-Enhanced h-node**   Windows NT systems include options that can supplement an h-node system with LMHOSTS name resolution, as well as Windows Sockets calls to a DNS server and a HOSTS file, all to be used if both WINS servers and broadcasts fail to resolve a name.

> **Note**   *The DNS option, which appears as an Enable DNS For Windows Resolution check box on the WINS Address page of the Microsoft TCP/IP Properties dialog box on Windows NT systems, enables users to specify a DNS name in a UNC path. The DNS name of a system need not be identical to its NetBIOS name, but because both are associated with the same IP address, the end result is the same.*

With all of its options enabled, a Microsoft-Enhanced h-node uses all the name resolution mechanisms available to it, in the manner shown in Figure 19-5.

> **Tip**   *Systems configured to use WINS do not reply to the NAME REGISTRATION REQUEST broadcasts generated by b-node, modified b-node, and m-node systems. For this reason, it is recommended that you do not mix node types on your network.*

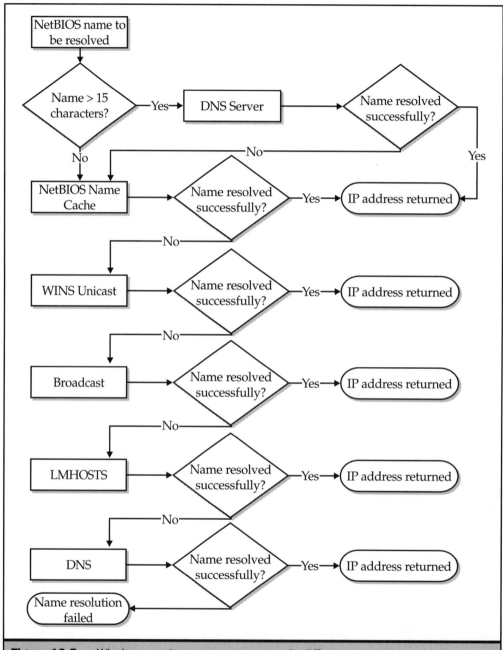

Figure 19-5. *Windows systems can use up to six different mechanisms in an attempt to resolve a NetBIOS name*

Setting Node Types

The node type on a Windows system is determined by the status of the WINS client and whether the WINS client is activated manually or by using DHCP. Generally speaking, systems that use WINS are h-nodes, while systems that do not use WINS are b-nodes.

When you use DHCP to activate a system's WINS client by supplying a value for the WINS/NBNS Servers option (option 044), the node type is set to h-node by default. When you don't activate WINS using DHCP, the system is a b-node. You can set the node type independently of the WINS client, however, by modifying the DHCP WINS/NBT Node Type option (option 046). When you enable the WINS client manually by supplying WINS server addresses in the system's TCP/IP Properties dialog box, the settings override the DHCP options for WINS and the node type, and make the client an h-node.

You can also manually set the node type on a workstation that is not using DHCP by modifying the registry directly. On a Windows NT or Windows 2000 system, you create a registry entry called **NodeType** in the following key:

```
HKEY_LOCAL_MACHINE\System\CurrentControlSet\Services\NetBT\Parameters
```

Assign the new entry one of the following REG_DWORD values:

- 0x00000001 for b-node
- 0x00000002 for p-node
- 0x00000004 for m-node
- 0x00000008 for h-node

On a Windows 95 or 98 system, create the NodeType entry (if it does not already exist) as a string value in the following registry key:

```
HKEY_LOCAL_MACHINE\System\CurrentControlSet\Services\VxD\MSTCP
```

Use the following values for the NodeType entry:

- 1 for b-node
- 2 for p-node
- 4 for m-node
- 8 for h-node

The mechanism for the incorporation of the Microsoft enhancements to these node type settings depends on which operating system the client is running. Windows NT and Windows 2000, for example, have a check box on the WINS Address page of the

Microsoft TCP/IP Properties dialog box that enables LMHOSTS lookups. You can also import an LMHOSTS file from a network drive in this dialog box, which simplifies the process of deploying the same LMHOSTS file on systems throughout a network. Windows 95 and 98 b-node systems, on the other hand, parse the LMHOSTS file automatically during the system startup and do not have the import option (although you can specify an alternate location for the LMHOSTS file by modifying the value of the LMHostFile entry in the registry's \MSTCP key).

Note   *A problem currently exists with the TCP/IP client in Windows 95 and 98 that prevents them from using the LMHOSTS file for NetBIOS name resolution when the DNS client is enabled. However, the system does preload the LMHOSTS entries tagged with the #PRE option into the NetBIOS name cache during the system startup process. You can use this as a workaround until a fix becomes available.*

In most cases, however, WINS clients on a properly configured network should rarely, if ever, have to use any name resolution mechanism other than WINS. A properly configured WINS implementation consists of multiple WINS servers that replicate their database information on a regular basis, so that even if one server fails, clients can access another.

NetBT Message Formats

The name service messages used during the Windows name registration and resolution procedures have the basic form of the message packets for the Domain Name Service (DNS). As with DNS messages, they are typically carried within UDP datagrams, which limits their length to 576 bytes. The packet consists of header fields that contain codes defining the function of the message, plus question and/or resource record sections to carry the query and response data (that is, NetBIOS names and IP addresses), as shown in Figure 19-6. The message format provides the capability to carry multiple resource records in response packets, in separate sections called the answer, authority, and additional sections, but this is not necessary in the NetBIOS name server messages used in Windows networking.

The functions of the name service message fields are explained in the following sections:

The Header Section

Every name service message has a header section that defines the basic type of message carried in the packet and whether it is a request or a response. The header fields are as follows:

- **NAME_TRN_ID (16 bits)**   Contains a transaction ID used to match requests with responses.

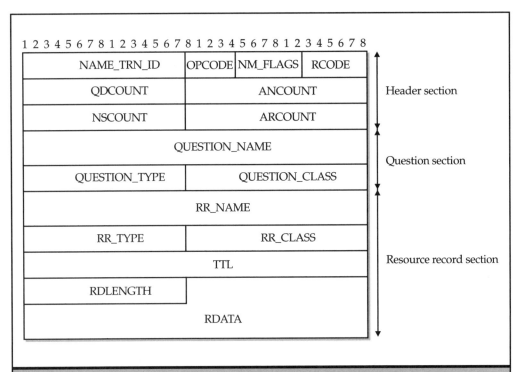

1 2 3 4 5 6 7 8 1 2 3 4 5 6 7 8 1 2 3 4 5 6 7 8 1 2 3 4 5 6 7 8

NAME_TRN_ID	OPCODE	NM_FLAGS	RCODE	Header section
QDCOUNT	ANCOUNT			
NSCOUNT	ARCOUNT			
QUESTION_NAME				Question section
QUESTION_TYPE	QUESTION_CLASS			
RR_NAME				Resource record section
RR_TYPE	RR_CLASS			
TTL				
RDLENGTH				
RDATA				

Figure 19-6.   *Windows systems use the same name service message format for all of their name registration and resolution procedures*

- **OPCODE (5 bits)**   The first bit is the R flag, which specifies whether the message is a request or a response, using the following values:

  - **0**   request
  - **1**   response

  The remaining four bits specify the type of message contained in the packet, using the following values:

  - **0**   query
  - **5**   registration
  - **6**   release
  - **7**   WACK
  - **8**   refresh

- **NM_FLAGS (7 bits)**   Contains five 1-bit flags (and 2 null bits) with the following functions:

- **AA – Authoritative Answer**   Specifies whether the response is being furnished by an authoritative source. In request messages (where the R flag in the OPCODE field is 0), the value of this flag is always 0. WINS servers always set the value of this flag to 1.

- **TC – Truncation**   Specifies whether the message had to be truncated to fit into a UDP datagram; serves as a signal to retransmit using TCP. Because packet length is not a problem in NetBIOS Name Service messaging, the value of this flag is always 0.

- **RD – Recursion Desired**   Used in NBNS request messages to obtain information about the name server's recursive capabilities. Windows clients always set this flag to a value of 1, indicating that recursion is desired.

- **RA – Recursion Available**   Used in NBNS response messages to indicate the name server supports recursive queries, registrations, and releases. For most types of messages (WACK messages are the exception), WINS servers set this value to 1, indicating that recursion is available.

    - **0**   Null bit
    - **0**   Null bit

- **B – Broadcast**   Specifies whether the packet was broadcast or unicast, using the following values:

    - **0**   unicast
    - **1**   broadcast or multicast

- **RCODE (4 bits)**   Used in response packets to specify the results of a particular request, using the following codes:

    - **0**   No Error
    - **1 – FMT_ERR**   Format Error (request was formatted incorrectly)
    - **2 – SRV_ERR**   Server Failure (request could not be processed due to NBNS malfunction)
    - **3 – NAM_ERR**   Name Error (requested name does not exist in the name server)
    - **4 – IMP_ERR**   Unsupported Request Error (used only when an NBNS is challenged by an update type registration request)
    - **5 – RFS_ERR**   Refused Error (policy prevents the server from registering the requested name to this host)
    - **6 – ACT_ERR**   Active Error (requested name is already owned by another node)
    - **7 – CFT_ERR**   Name in Conflict Error (a unique NetBIOS name is already owned by another node)

- **QDCOUNT (16 bits)** Specifies the number of entries in the question section of the message. Windows NetBIOS Name Service messages always contain only one question entry.

- **ANCOUNT (16 bits)** Specifies the number of resource records in the answer section of the message. Windows NetBIOS Name Service messages always contain only one answer section entry.

- **NSCOUNT (16 bits)** Specifies the number of resource records in the authority section of the message. The authority section is not used in Windows NetBIOS Name Service messages.

- **NRCOUNT (16 bits)** Specifies the number of resource records in the additional section of the message. The additional section is not used in Windows NetBIOS Name Service messages.

Note *The name service messages used in name registration and resolution procedures are nearly identical, whether the client system uses the broadcast or the WINS method. The primary difference between the two is the state of the Broadcast bit in the NM_FLAGS field.*

From the values of these header fields, you can determine exactly what kind of message is included in the packet. For example, a message with an R flag value of 0, an OPCODE value of 0, a B flag value of 0, and a QDCOUNT value of 1 would be a NAME QUERY REQUEST packet sent to a WINS server with a NetBIOS name in the question section. If the WINS server replies with a message that changes the R flag to 1, the QDCOUNT field to 0, and the ANCOUNT field to 1, this would be a POSITIVE NAME QUERY RESPONSE with the IP address for the requested NetBIOS name in the resource record section. If the server did not have the name in its database, the resulting NEGATIVE NAME QUERY RESPONSE message would have QDCOUNT and ANCOUNT fields with values of 0 and an RCODE field with a value of 3.

The Question Section

The question section contains the NetBIOS name to be registered or resolved, and appears only in request and demand packets, such as the following:

- NAME REGISTRATION REQUEST
- NAME OVERWRITE DEMAND
- NAME QUERY REQUEST
- NAME REFRESH REQUEST
- NAME RELEASE REQUEST

NETWORK CONNECTION SERVICES

The question section fields are as follows:

- **QUESTION_NAME (variable)**   Contains the NetBIOS name to be registered or resolved.
- **QUESTION_TYPE (16 bits)**   Specifies the type of request, using the following values:
  - **0x0020**   NB (NetBIOS Name Service resource record)
  - **0x0021**   NBSTAT (NetBIOS Node Status resource record)
- **QUESTION_CLASS (16 bits)**   Specifies the class of the request, for which only one possible value exists, as follows:
  - **0x0001**   Internet Class

The Resource Record Section

A resource record section appears in positive response packets, like the following, as well as in WACK packets:

- POSITIVE NAME REGISTRATION RESPONSE
- POSITIVE NAME QUERY RESPONSE
- POSITIVE NAME REFRESH RESPONSE
- POSITIVE NAME RELEASE RESPONSE
- WAIT FOR ACKNOWLEDGMENT RESPONSE

Although resource records can appear in any of three sections—answer, authority, and additional—Windows NetBIOS Name Service messages only carry a single resource record, typically in the answer or additional section. The resource record section fields are as follows:

- **RR_NAME (variable)**   Contains the NetBIOS name from the request message to which this is the response.
- **RR_TYPE (16 bits)**   Specifies the type of resource record, using the following values:
  - **0x0001**   A (IP Address resource record)
  - **0x0002**   NS (name server resource record)
  - **0x000A**   NULL (null resource record)

- ■ **0x0020**   NB (NetBIOS Name Service resource record)
- ■ **0x0021**   NBSTAT (NetBIOS Node Status resource record)
- ■ **RR_CLASS (16 bits)**   Specifies the class of the resource record, for which only one possible value exists, as follows:
  - ■ **0x0001**   Internet Class
- ■ **TTL (32 bits)**   Specifies the time-to-live for the information in the resource record.
- ■ **RDLENGTH (16 bits)**   Specifies the number of bytes in the RDATA field.
- ■ **RDATA (variable)**   Specifies the IP address of the system identified by the value of the RR_NAME field. When the RR_TYPE field contains the NB code (as WINS server responses do), the RDATA field begins with 32 NB_FLAGS bits, broken down as follows:
  - ■ **G (1 bit) – Group Name Flag**   Specifies whether the name supplied in the RR_NAME field is a unique or group NetBIOS name, using the following values:
    - ■ **0**   Unique
    - ■ **1**   Group
  - ■ **ONT (2 bits) – Owner Node Type**   Specifies the node type of the system identified in the RR_NAME field, using the following values:
    - ■ **00**   B-node
    - ■ **01**   P-node
    - ■ **10**   M-node
    - ■ **11**   reserved for future use
- ■ **Reserved for Future Use (13 bits)**

Sample Transactions

The following figures show the contents of packets captured with a protocol analyzer during some of the basic NetBIOS Name Service transactions that occur regularly on a Windows network. Figure 19-7 shows the NAME REGISTRATION REQUEST being sent to a WINS server.

Notice that the desired name (CZ2) is supplied in the question section, but that an additional section also contains the name and the IP address the client is requesting be

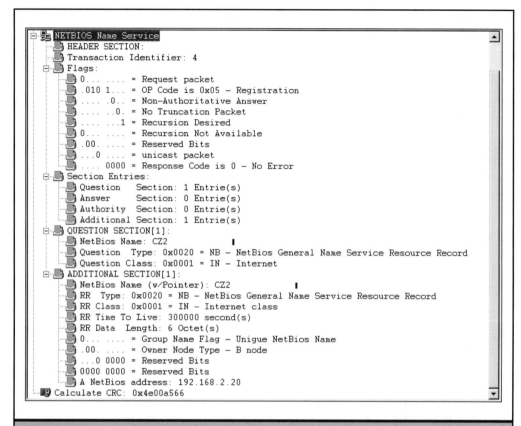

```
NETBIOS Name Service
   HEADER SECTION:
   Transaction Identifier: 4
   Flags:
       0... .... = Request packet
       .010 1... = OP Code is 0x05 - Registration
       .... .0.. = Non-Authoritative Answer
       .... ..0. = No Truncation Packet
       .... ...1 = Recursion Desired
       0... .... = Recursion Not Available
       .00. .... = Reserved Bits
       ...0 .... = unicast packet
       .... 0000 = Response Code is 0 - No Error
   Section Entries:
       Question    Section: 1 Entrie(s)
       Answer      Section: 0 Entrie(s)
       Authority   Section: 0 Entrie(s)
       Additional Section: 1 Entrie(s)
   QUESTION SECTION[1]:
       NetBios Name: CZ2               ▮
       Question  Type: 0x0020 = NB - NetBios General Name Service Resource Record
       Question Class: 0x0001 = IN - Internet
   ADDITIONAL SECTION[1]:
       NetBios Name (w/Pointer): CZ2        ▮
       RR  Type: 0x0020 = NB - NetBios General Name Service Resource Record
       RR Class: 0x0001 = IN - Internet class
       RR Time To Live: 300000 second(s)
       RR Data  Length: 6 Octet(s)
       0... .... = Group Name Flag - Unique NetBios Name
       .00. .... = Owner Node Type - B node
       ...0 0000 = Reserved Bits
       0000 0000 = Reserved Bits
       A NetBios address: 192.168.2.20
   Calculate CRC: 0x4e00a566
```

Figure 19-7.   *A NAME REGISTRATION REQUEST message sent to a WINS server*

added to the WINS name service. Figure 19-8 shows a POSTIVE NAME
REGISTRATION RESPONSE message from the server containing the same
information in the answer section, indicating that it has been successfully added
to the WINS database.

   The next two packet captures show the responses from the WINS server during a
failed name registration attempt. While trying to process the request, the server sends
a WAIT FOR ACKNOWLEDGMENT RESPONSE, or WACK, packet to the client, as

```
⊞ ETHER-II: 00-20-AF-37-B8-12 ==> 00-60-97-B0-77-CA
⊞ IP: 192.168.2.10->192.168.2.20,ID=11950
⊞ UDP: NETBIOS Name Service->NETBIOS Name Service,Len=70
⊟ NETBIOS Name Service
  ⌐ HEADER SECTION:
  ⌐ Transaction Identifier: 4
  ⊟ Flags:
    ⌐ 1... .... = Response packet
    ⌐ .010 1... = OP Code is 0x05 - Registration
    ⌐ .... .1.. = Authoritative Answer
    ⌐ .... ..0. = No Truncation Packet
    ⌐ .... ...1 = Recursion Desired
    ⌐ 1... .... = Recursion Available
    ⌐ .00. .... = Reserved Bits
    ⌐ ...0 .... = unicast packet
    ⌐ .... 0000 = Response Code is 0 - No Error
  ⊟ Section Entries:
    ⌐ Question   Section: 0 Entrie(s)
    ⌐ Answer     Section: 1 Entrie(s)
    ⌐ Authority  Section: 0 Entrie(s)
    ⌐ Additional Section: 0 Entrie(s)
  ⊟ ANSWER SECTION[1]:
    ⌐ NetBios Name: CZ2           I
    ⌐ RR Type: 0x0020 = NB - NetBios General Name Service Resource Record
    ⌐ RR Class: 0x0001 = IN - Internet class
    ⌐ RR Time To Live: 518400 second(s)
    ⌐ RR Data Length: 6 Octet(s)
    ⌐ 0... .... = Group Name Flag - Unique NetBios Name
    ⌐ .00. .... = Owner Node Type - B node
    ⌐ ...0 0000 = Reserved Bits
    ⌐ 0000 0000 = Reserved Bits
    ⌐ A NetBios address: 192.168.2.20
  ⌐ Calculate CRC: 0x757da172
```

Figure 19-8.   *The POSITIVE NAME REGISTRATION RESPONSE message returned to a client by the WINS server*

shown in Figure 19-9. The answer section of this message contains a five-second time-to-live value, so the client does not time out and revert to the broadcast name registration method.

When the server finally generates a reply, as shown in Figure 19-10, the message includes the answer section a POSITIVE NAME REGISTRATION RESPONSE would have; but, in fact, this is a NEGATIVE NAME REGISTRATION RESPONSE, as demonstrated by the value of the response code (RCODE) field. This value indicates that an Active Error has occurred because the requested name is already in use by another system.

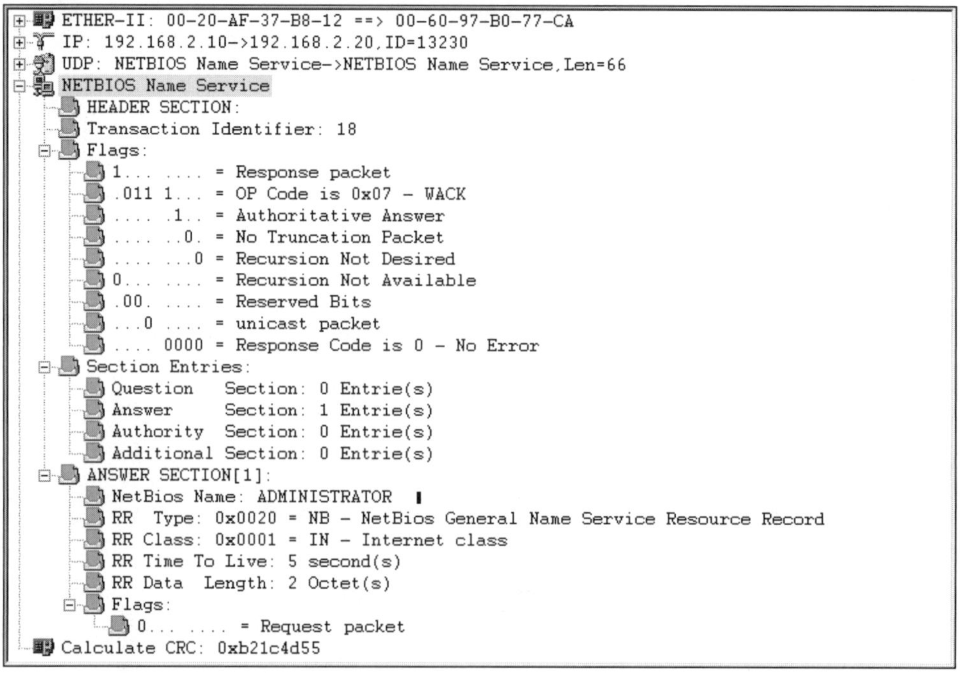

```
ETHER-II: 00-20-AF-37-B8-12 ==> 00-60-97-B0-77-CA
IP: 192.168.2.10->192.168.2.20,ID=13230
UDP: NETBIOS Name Service->NETBIOS Name Service,Len=66
NETBIOS Name Service
    HEADER SECTION:
    Transaction Identifier: 18
    Flags:
        1... .... = Response packet
        .011 1... = OP Code is 0x07 - WACK
        .... .1.. = Authoritative Answer
        .... ..0. = No Truncation Packet
        .... ...0 = Recursion Not Desired
        0... .... = Recursion Not Available
        .00. .... = Reserved Bits
        ...0 .... = unicast packet
        .... 0000 = Response Code is 0 - No Error
    Section Entries:
        Question   Section: 0 Entrie(s)
        Answer     Section: 1 Entrie(s)
        Authority  Section: 0 Entrie(s)
        Additional Section: 0 Entrie(s)
    ANSWER SECTION[1]:
        NetBios Name: ADMINISTRATOR
        RR  Type: 0x0020 = NB - NetBios General Name Service Resource Record
        RR Class: 0x0001 = IN - Internet class
        RR Time To Live: 5 second(s)
        RR Data  Length: 2 Octet(s)
        Flags:
            0... .... = Request packet
Calculate CRC: 0xb21c4d55
```

Figure 19-9. *The WAIT FOR ACKNOWEDGMENT message generated by a WINS server experiencing a delay*

Once it has been registered, a WINS client system can begin using the WINS server to resolve the NetBIOS names of other systems on the network. A NAME QUERY REQUEST sent to a WINS server, as shown in Figure 19-11, contains a question section that specifies the name the client seeks to resolve.

The POSITIVE NAME QUERY RESPONSE message (see Figure 19-12) contains an answer section supplying the requested IP address.

As you can see in Figure 19-13, a broadcast NAME QUERY REQUEST is almost exactly the same as the unicast version sent to a WINS server. The B flag indicates that the message is a broadcast, but the messages are otherwise identical.

```
⊞ ▦ ETHER-II: 00-20-AF-37-B8-12 ==> 00-60-97-B0-77-CA
⊞ ⌇ IP: 192.168.2.10->192.168.2.20,ID=13998
⊞ ▨ UDP: NETBIOS Name Service->NETBIOS Name Service,Len=70
⊟ ▥ NETBIOS Name Service
    ▢ HEADER SECTION:
    ▢ Transaction Identifier: 18
  ⊟ ▢ Flags:
      ▢ 1... .... = Response packet
      ▢ .010 1... = OP Code is 0x05 - Registration
      ▢ .... .1.. = Authoritative Answer
      ▢ .... ..0. = No Truncation Packet
      ▢ .... ...1 = Recursion Desired
      ▢ 1... .... = Recursion Available
      ▢ .00. .... = Reserved Bits
      ▢ ...0 .... = unicast packet
      ▢ .... 0110 = Response Code is 6 - Active Error
  ⊟ ▢ Section Entries:
      ▢ Question   Section: 0 Entrie(s)
      ▢ Answer     Section: 1 Entrie(s)
      ▢ Authority  Section: 0 Entrie(s)
      ▢ Additional Section: 0 Entrie(s)
  ⊟ ▢ ANSWER SECTION[1]:
      ▢ NetBios Name: ADMINISTRATOR  ▮
      ▢ RR  Type: 0x0020 = NB - NetBios General Name Service Resource Record
      ▢ RR Class: 0x0001 = IN - Internet class
      ▢ RR Time To Live: 43114464 second(s)
      ▢ RR Data  Length: 6 Octet(s)
      ▢ 0... .... = Group Name Flag - Unique NetBios Name
      ▢ .00. .... = Owner Node Type - B node
      ▢ ...0 0000 = Reserved Bits
      ▢ 0000 0000 = Reserved Bits
      ▢ A NetBios address: 192.168.2.20
  ▦ Calculate CRC: 0x5bbd8295
```

Figure 19-10. *The NEGATIVE NAME REGISTRATION RESPONSE message generated by a WINS server when a requested NetBIOS name is already in use*

Using LMHOSTS

To use an LMHOSTS file for NetBIOS name resolution, you must first create the file by adding the names you want to resolve and their IP addresses. The basic format of the file is simple; each IP address should appear in a separate line along with its NetBIOS name, separated by at least one space, as shown in the following listing.

```
192.168.2.2        CZ2
192.168.2.3        CZ3
192.168.2.10       CZ1
```

LMHOSTS also supports the use of tags that provide special functions for specific entries. In most cases, you use a tag by adding it to an LMHOSTS entry after the NetBIOS name, separated by at least one space. The tags recognized by Windows systems are as follows:

- **#PRE**   Adding the #PRE tag to an LMHOSTS entry causes the computer to preload the entry into the NetBIOS name cache during system startup. Name resolutions performed using cached information are faster than any other method. Because Windows systems parse the LMHOSTS file from top to bottom, you should place #PRE-tagged entries at the bottom to provide the best possible speed for standard name resolutions.

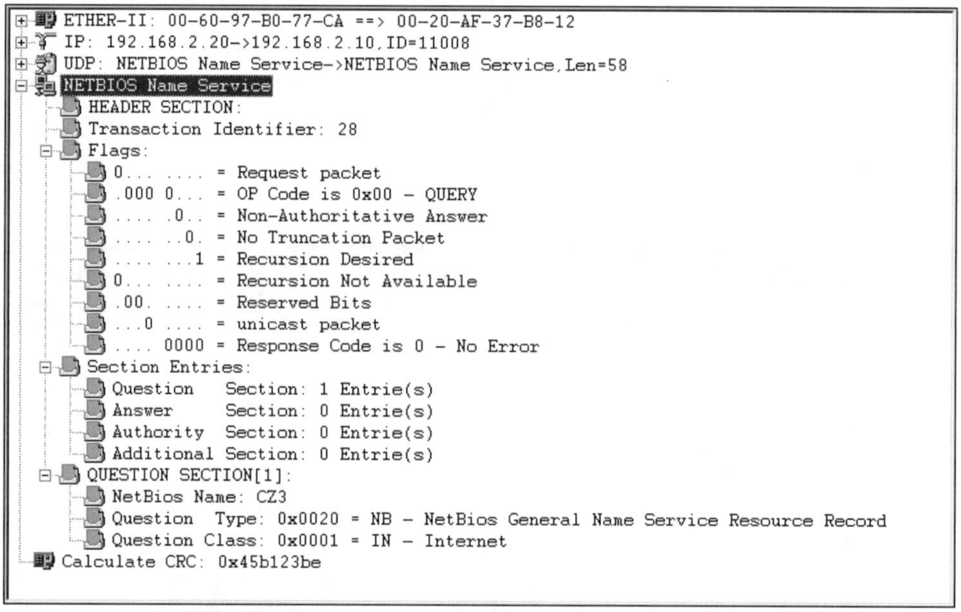

```
⊞ ▦ ETHER-II: 00-60-97-B0-77-CA ==> 00-20-AF-37-B8-12
⊞ ▼ IP: 192.168.2.20->192.168.2.10,ID=11008
⊞ ▦ UDP: NETBIOS Name Service->NETBIOS Name Service,Len=58
⊟ ▦ NETBIOS Name Service
    ─ ▩ HEADER SECTION:
    ─ ▩ Transaction Identifier: 28
  ⊟ ▩ Flags:
      ─ ▩ 0... .... = Request packet
      ─ ▩ .000 0... = OP Code is 0x00 - QUERY
      ─ ▩ .... .0.. = Non-Authoritative Answer
      ─ ▩ .... ..0. = No Truncation Packet
      ─ ▩ .... ...1 = Recursion Desired
      ─ ▩ 0... .... = Recursion Not Available
      ─ ▩ .00. .... = Reserved Bits
      ─ ▩ ...0 .... = unicast packet
      ─ ▩ .... 0000 = Response Code is 0 - No Error
  ⊟ ▩ Section Entries:
      ─ ▩ Question   Section: 1 Entrie(s)
      ─ ▩ Answer     Section: 0 Entrie(s)
      ─ ▩ Authority  Section: 0 Entrie(s)
      ─ ▩ Additional Section: 0 Entrie(s)
  ⊟ ▩ QUESTION SECTION[1]:
      ─ ▩ NetBios Name: CZ3
      ─ ▩ Question Type: 0x0020 = NB - NetBios General Name Service Resource Record
      ─ ▩ Question Class: 0x0001 = IN - Internet
    ─ ▦ Calculate CRC: 0x45b123be
```

Figure 19-11.   *A NAME QUERY REQUEST message sent to a WINS server*

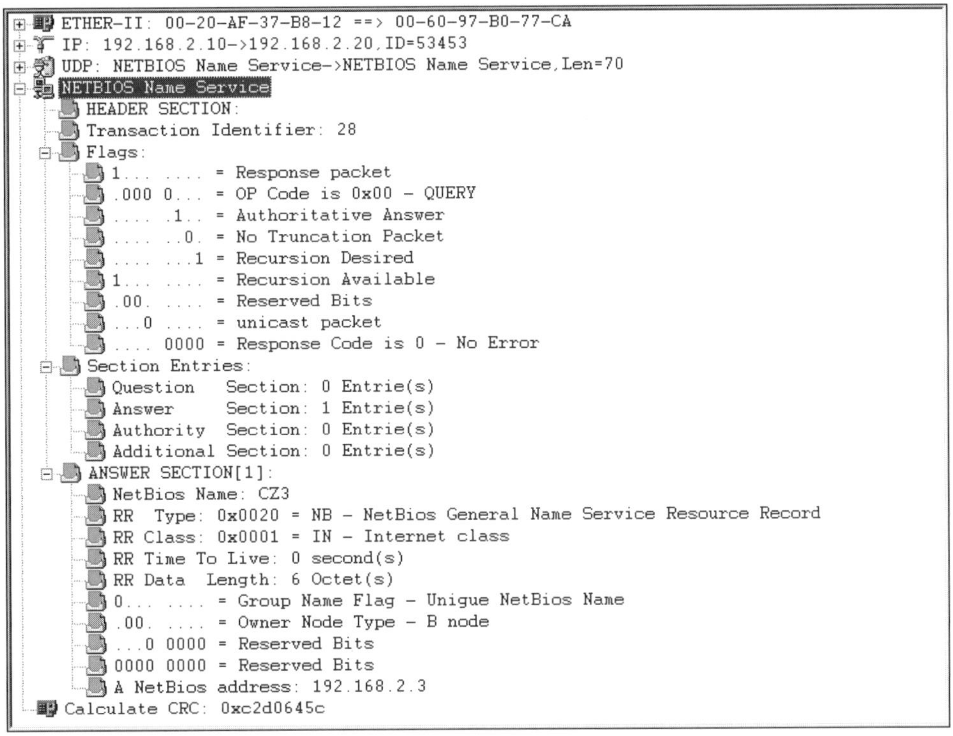

```
ETHER-II: 00-20-AF-37-B8-12 ==> 00-60-97-B0-77-CA
IP: 192.168.2.10->192.168.2.20,ID=53453
UDP: NETBIOS Name Service->NETBIOS Name Service,Len=70
NETBIOS Name Service
   HEADER SECTION:
   Transaction Identifier: 28
   Flags:
      1... .... = Response packet
      .000 0... = OP Code is 0x00 - QUERY
      .... .1.. = Authoritative Answer
      .... ..0. = No Truncation Packet
      .... ...1 = Recursion Desired
      1... .... = Recursion Available
      .00. .... = Reserved Bits
      ...0 .... = unicast packet
      .... 0000 = Response Code is 0 - No Error
   Section Entries:
      Question  Section: 0 Entrie(s)
      Answer    Section: 1 Entrie(s)
      Authority Section: 0 Entrie(s)
      Additional Section: 0 Entrie(s)
   ANSWER SECTION[1]:
      NetBios Name: CZ3
      RR Type: 0x0020 = NB - NetBios General Name Service Resource Record
      RR Class: 0x0001 = IN - Internet class
      RR Time To Live: 0 second(s)
      RR Data Length: 6 Octet(s)
      0... .... = Group Name Flag - Unique NetBios Name
      .00. .... = Owner Node Type - B node
      ...0 0000 = Reserved Bits
      0000 0000 = Reserved Bits
      A NetBios address: 192.168.2.3
Calculate CRC: 0xc2d0645c
```

Figure 19-12. *The POSITIVE NAME QUERY RESPONSE returned by the WINS server when it has successfully resolved a NetBIOS name*

- **#DOM:*domainname*** Use the #DOM tag to identify Windows NT domain controllers located on other network segments, where *domainname* is the name of the domain. This tag adds the entry to the system's domain name cache, making it possible for a non-WINS system to send unicasts directly to domain controllers on other segments. Use #DOM in combination with the #PRE tag to preload the domain controller entries into the cache, as follows:

  ```
  192.168.2.10     CZ1        #PRE#DOM:NTDOMAIN
  ```

- **#MH** Use the #MH tag for multihomed systems (that is, computers with more than one IP address). You can have up to 25 separate #MH entries containing different IP addresses for a single NetBIOS name.

```
⊞ 📠 ETHER-II: 00-80-29-EB-F7-2C ==> FF-FF-FF-FF-FF-FF
⊞ 📠 IP: 192.168.2.22->192.168.2.255,ID=49096
⊞ 📠 UDP: NETBIOS Name Service->NETBIOS Name Service,Len=58
⊟ 📠 NETBIOS Name Service
    ┈ 📄 HEADER SECTION:
    ┈ 📄 Transaction Identifier: 41978
    ⊟ 📄 Flags:
        ┈ 📄 0... .... = Request packet
        ┈ 📄 .000 0... = OP Code is 0x00 - QUERY
        ┈ 📄 .... .0.. = Non-Authoritative Answer
        ┈ 📄 .... ..0. = No Truncation Packet
        ┈ 📄 .... ...1 = Recursion Desired
        ┈ 📄 0... .... = Recursion Not Available
        ┈ 📄 .00. .... = Reserved Bits
        ┈ 📄 ...1 .... = broadcast or multicast packet
        ┈ 📄 .... 0000 = Response Code is 0 - No Error
    ⊟ 📄 Section Entries:
        ┈ 📄 Question   Section: 1 Entrie(s)
        ┈ 📄 Answer     Section: 0 Entrie(s)
        ┈ 📄 Authority  Section: 0 Entrie(s)
        ┈ 📄 Additional Section: 0 Entrie(s)
    ⊟ 📄 QUESTION SECTION[1]:
        ┈ 📄 NetBios Name: NTDOMAIN3    ▌
        ┈ 📄 Question  Type: 0x0020 = NB - NetBios General Name Service Resource Record
        ┈ 📄 Question Class: 0x0001 = IN - Internet
    ┈ 📠 Calculate CRC: 0x4e88c0c8
```

Figure 19-13.   *The header of a broadcast NAME QUERY REQUEST message differs from the unicast version in the value of only one bit*

■ **#SG:*groupname***   Use the #SG tag to create a NetBIOS group with the name specified by the *groupname* variable. Each group can have up to 25 members, each of which must have its own entry in the LMHOSTS file.

■ **\0x##**   Use the \0x## tag to specify the hexadecimal value for a nonprinting character as part of a NetBIOS name. To use the tag, you enclose the entire NetBIOS name in double quotation marks and insert \0x## in place of the desired character, where ## is the hexadecimal value for that character. Note, that when you enclose the NetBIOS name in quotation marks, you must account for all 16 characters of the name. For example, to specify a nonprinting character as the 16th character of the name, you must pad out the preceding 15 characters with spaces or other characters.

■ **#INCLUDE *filename***   Use the #INCLUDE tag to specify the location of an alternate LMHOSTS file on a shared network drive. This enables network administrators to maintain a single LMHOSTS file and to have multiple client systems access it. Place the #INCLUDE tag on its own line of the LMHOSTS file and replace *filename* with the full UNC path to the desired alternate file, as shown. If the UNC name uses a NetBIOS name to identify the system, be sure to preload it into the name cache by creating a separate entry with the #PRE tag.

```
#INCLUDE \\CZ1\C\WINNT\LMHOSTS
```

■ **#BEGIN_ALTERNATE/#END_ALTERNATE**   Use the #BEGIN_ALTERNATE
tag on a separate line to mark the beginning of a subroutine that contains
multiple #INCLUDE commands, followed by the #END_ALTERNATE tag, also
on a separate line. When parsing the LMHOSTS file, the system will attempt to
access each of the alternative LMHOSTS files specified in the #INCLUDE
commands until it successfully locates one. This provides fault tolerance if the
system hosting the LMHOSTS file is unavailable.

```
#BEGIN_ALTERNATE
#INCLUDE \\CZ1\C\WINNT\LMHOSTS
#INCLUDE \\CZ2\D\WINNT\LMHOSTS
#INCLUDE \\CZ3\C\WINDOWS\LMHOSTS
#END_ALTERNATE
```

Using Broadcasts

The broadcast method of NetBIOS name resolution is the default for Windows systems
that are not configured to use WINS. On a relatively small, single-segment network,
broadcasts are an effective solution that should not have an adverse effect on network
performance (unless your bandwidth is already being stretched to the limit). For a
network with more than one segment, you can use broadcasts in combination with
LMHOSTS files (to resolve names on other segments), but this rapidly becomes an
administrative problem best resolved by the addition of one or more WINS servers.

Using WINS

Deploying a single WINS server is a simple matter. Once you install the service itself
on a Windows NT or Windows 2000 server, the default settings are sufficient for most
network environments. It is recommended that a network have at least two WINS
servers to provide fault tolerance in case one fails.

On a single-segment network, having two servers is not strictly necessary because
the client systems will fall back to broadcast name resolution if they can't contact the
WINS server. When multiple segments are involved, however, WINS quickly becomes
an essential element of the network configuration, unless the administrators continue
to maintain the LMHOSTS files that will be needed if the WINS server fails.

WINS Replication

To provide true fault tolerance, WINS servers on the same network must replicate
their data. This makes it possible for a client that has registered its NetBIOS name
with one WINS server to appear in the databases of all WINS servers on the network.
Replication between WINS servers is not automatic. The network administrator must
devise a proper replication strategy that keeps all the servers updated at reasonable
intervals without overloading the network with traffic.

WINS server replication traffic is unidirectional. You can configure a server to push its data to another server or to pull data from another server. To replicate in both directions, you must configure the traffic in each direction separately. This capability makes it possible to deploy a series of WINS servers and create a *replication ring.*

On a WINS replication ring, each server pushes its data to its nearest downstream neighbor and pulls data from its nearest upstream neighbor, as shown in Figure 19-14. The relationship between two WINS servers is known as a *partnership,* with one machine being referenced as the *pull partner* or *push partner* of the other. The ring of partnerships, however, is purely a logical construction that has no correspondence to the physical location of the servers.

WINS Architecture

On a network in which all the segments are connected by LAN links, the number of WINS servers required is governed solely by the number of clients to support. Microsoft states that a single WINS server can support as many as 1,500 name registrations per minute and 4,500 queries per minute. Assuming the existence of

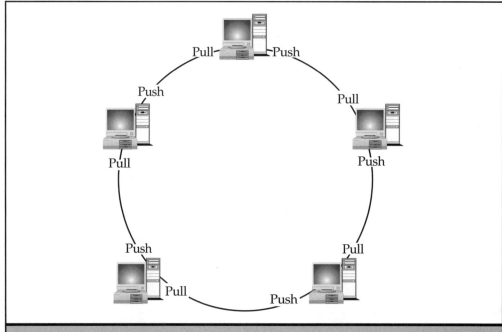

Figure 19-14.   *A WINS replication ring uses push and pull partnerships to see to it that every server has identical information in its database*

traditional peak use times (such as a specific time of day in which many users arrive at the office and turn on their computers, triggering a large number of name registration requests), this works out to approximately 10,000 users who can be supported by a single WINS server.

Thus, two WINS servers (and two are required only for fault-tolerance reasons) can support all but the largest networks in a single location. Because the communications among WINS servers and among clients and servers are all unicasts, the servers can be located on different segments, anywhere on the internetwork.

When an internetwork spans several locations connected by WAN links, the design of the WINS architecture becomes considerably more complex. Because WAN links are usually slower and more expensive than LAN connections (and sometimes much slower and more expensive), having at least two WINS servers at every site makes it possible for every client system on the network to register and resolve NetBIOS names without sending traffic over a WAN link.

In an enterprise that consists of a large number of small offices, however, this may not be practical. It is important to consider how much network traffic actually travels between the sites. In an environment where the majority of the traffic remains within the boundaries of each site, using remote WINS servers and allowing small, individual LANs to fall back to broadcast name registration and resolution if the WAN link fails may be perfectly feasible.

Replication traffic, however, must go over the WAN links and you should configure your servers to replicate themselves in such a way as to provide backup connections if one or more WAN links should go down. A ring arrangement, where each server replicates its data to one other server down the line, doesn't work well in this case because one nonfunctioning WAN link between two sites breaks the chain and prevents the database information from being identical on all servers.

One way to maintain the database replication in a failure is to create a double-ring configuration, as shown in Figure 19-15. With data traveling in both directions, all the servers will continue to be updated, even if a WAN link fails.

When you have more than two WINS servers at a particular site, no need exists to make all the servers part of the ring (or double ring) connecting the WAN sites. For large networks, creating a separate replication ring within each site and then joining the sites with a separate ring is best. Every site should have more than one machine that replicates with the other sites, however. You don't want to have the WINS servers at an entire site cut off from the rest of the enterprise due to the failure of one computer.

Note *For more information on designing a WINS architecture for a large enterprise network, see the Microsoft white paper on "The Windows Internet Naming Service Architecture and Capacity Planning" at http://www.microsoft.com/ntserver/nts/techdetails/techspecs/WINSwp98.asp.*

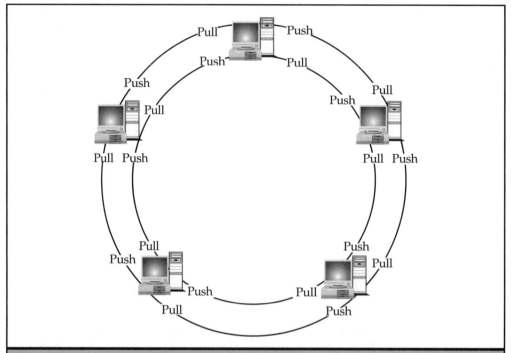

Figure 19-15.   *With a double ring that has traffic flowing in both directions, no single connection failure can prevent the servers from being replicated*

WINS Proxies

Mixing b-node and h-node systems on the same network segment is not a good idea, but sometimes a situation arises when a separate segment of b-nodes is connected to a WINS network. Rather than use LMHOSTS files on the b-node systems to resolve NetBIOS names on other segments, it is possible to configure a Windows NT machine on the b-node segment to function as a WINS proxy.

A *WINS proxy* is a WINS client system configured to listen and respond to broadcast NAME QUERY REQUEST messages on the local network. When a b-node broadcasts a request, the WINS proxy system tries to satisfy the request using the information in its name cache. If this is not possible, the proxy system transmits the request as a unicast to the WINS server (presumably on another segment) specified in its TCP/IP configuration. The WINS server replies to the proxy, which then relays the POSITIVE NAME QUERY RESPONSE message to the original b-node.

WINS proxies, in essence, enable a large number of b-node systems to take advantage of WINS without configuring each individual machine to be a WINS client.

Naturally, the name resolution process takes longer when an intervening proxy is involved; but as a temporary measure, WINS proxies can be quite useful.

To configure a Windows NT system to function as a WINS proxy, you must configure it as a normal WINS client by specifying the IP address of one or more WINS servers in the WINS Address page of the Microsoft TCP/IP Properties dialog box. Then, you must modify the registry by creating a REG_DWORD entry called **EnableProxy** with a value of 1 in the following key:

```
HKEY_LOCAL_MACHINE\SYSTEM\CurrentControlSet\Services\NetBT\Parameters
```

The
Complete
Reference

Upgrading
&
Troubleshooting
Networks

Chapter 20

The Domain Name
System

omputers are designed to work with numbers, while humans are more comfortable working with words. This fundamental dichotomy is the reason why the Domain Name System (DNS) came to be. Back in the dark days of the 1970s, when the Internet was the ARPANET and the entire experimental network consisted of only a few hundred systems, a need was recognized for a mechanism that would permit users to refer to the network's computers by name, rather than by address. The introduction of the TCP/IP protocols in the early '80s led to the use of 32-bit IP addresses, which even in dotted decimal form were difficult to remember.

Host Tables

The first mechanism for assigning human-friendly names to addresses was called a *host table*, which took the form of a file called /etc/hosts on UNIX systems. The host table was a simple ASCII file that contained a list of network system addresses and their equivalent host names. When users wanted to access resources on other network systems, they would specify a host name in the application, and the system would resolve the name into the appropriate address by looking it up in the host table. This host table still exists on all TCP/IP systems today, usually in the form of a file called Hosts somewhere on the local disk drive. If nothing else, the host table contains the following entry, which assigns to the standard IP loopback address the host name localhost:

```
127.0.0.1       localhost
```

Today, the Domain Name System has replaced the host table almost universally, but when TCP/IP systems attempt to resolve a host name into an IP address, it is still possible to configure them to check the Hosts file first before using DNS. If you have a small network of TCP/IP systems that is not connected to the Internet, you can use host tables on your machines to maintain friendly host names for your computers. The name resolution process will be very fast, because no network communications are necessary, and you will not need a DNS server.

Host Table Problems

The use of host tables on TCP/IP systems caused several problems, all of which were exacerbated as the fledgling Internet grew from a small "family" of networked computers into a much larger entity. The most fundamental problem was that each computer had to have its own host table, which listed the names and addresses of all of the other computers on the network. When a new computer was connected to the network, you could not access it until an entry for it was added to your computer's host table.

In order for everyone to keep their host tables updated, it was necessary for administrators to be informed when a system was added to the network or a name or address change occurred. Having every administrator of an ARPANET system e-mail every other administrator each time they made a change was obviously not a practical solution, so it was necessary to designate a registrar that would maintain a master list of the systems on the network, their addresses, and their host names.

The task of maintaining this registry was given to the Network Information Center (NIC) at the Stanford Research Institute (SRI), in Menlo Park, CA. The master list was stored in a file called Hosts.txt on a computer with the host name SRI-NIC. Administrators of ARPANET systems would e-mail their modifications to the NIC, who would update the Hosts.txt file periodically. To keep their systems updated, the administrators would use FTP to download the latest Hosts.txt file from SRI-NIC and compile it into a new Hosts file for their systems.

Initially, this was an adequate solution; but as the network continued to grow, it became increasingly unworkable. As more systems were added to the network, the Hosts.txt file grew larger and more people were accessing SRI-NIC to download it on a regular basis. The amount of network traffic generated by this simple maintenance task became excessive, and changes started occurring so fast that it was difficult for administrators to keep their systems updated.

Another serious problem was that there was no control over the host names used to represent the systems on the network. Once TCP/IP came into general use, the NIC was responsible for assigning network addresses, but administrators chose their own host names for the computers on their networks. The accidental use of duplicate host names resulted in misrouted traffic and disruption of communications. Imagine the chaos that would result today if anyone on the Internet was allowed to set up a Web server and use the name www.microsoft.com for it. Clearly, a better solution was needed, and this led to the development of the Domain Name System.

DNS Objectives

To address the problems resulting from the use of host tables for name registration and resolution, the people responsible for the ARPANET decided to design a completely new mechanism. Their primary objectives at first seemed to be contradictory: to design a mechanism that would enable administrators to assign host names to their own systems without creating duplicate names, and to make that host name information globally available to other administrators without relying on a single access point that could become a traffic bottleneck and a single point of failure. In addition, the mechanism had to be able to support information about systems that use various protocols with different types of addresses, and it had to be adaptable for use by multiple applications.

The solution was the Domain Name System, designed by Peter Mockapetris and published in 1983 as two IETF (Internet Engineering Task Force) documents called RFC 882, "Domain Names: Concepts and Facilities," and RFC 883, "Domain Names: Implementation Specification." These documents were updated in 1987, published as RFC 1034 and RFC 1035, respectively, and ratified as an IETF standard. Since that time, numerous other RFCs have updated the information in the standard to address current networking issues. Some of these additional documents are proposed standards, while others are experimental. These documents include the following:

- **RFC 1101** "DNS Encoding of Network Names and Other Types"
- **RFC 1183** "New DNS RR Definitions"
- **RFC 1348** "DNS NSAP RRs"
- **RFC 1794** "DNS Support for Load Balancing"
- **RFC 1876** "A Means for Expressing Location Information in the Domain Name System"
- **RFC 1982** "Serial Number Arithmetic"
- **RFC 1995** "Incremental Zone Transfer in DNS"
- **RFC 1996** "A Mechanism for Prompt Notification of Zone Changes (DNS NOTIFY)"
- **RFC 2052** "A DNS RR for Specifying the Location of Services (DNS SRV)"
- **RFC 2181** "Clarifications to the DNS Specification"
- **RFC 2136** "Dynamic Updates in the Domain Name System (DNS UPDATE)"
- **RFC 2137** "Secure Domain Name System Dynamic Update"
- **RFC 2308** "Negative Caching of DNS Queries (DNS NCACHE)"
- **RFC 2535** "Domain Name System Security Extensions"

The DNS, as designed by Mockapetris, consists of three basic elements:

- A hierarchical name space that divides the host system database into discrete elements called "domains."
- Domain name servers that contain information about the host and subdomains within a given domain.
- Resolvers that generate requests for information from domain name servers.

These elements are discussed in the following sections.

Domain Naming

The Domain Name System achieves the designated objectives by using a hierarchical system, both in the name space used to name the hosts and in the database that contains the host name information. Before the DNS was developed, administrators assigned simple host names to the computers on their networks. The names sometimes reflected the computer's function or its location, as with SRI-NIC, but there was no policy in place that required this. At that time, there were few enough computers on the network to make this a practical solution.

To support the network as it grew larger, Mockapetris developed a hierarchical name space that made it possible for individual network administrators to name their systems, while identifying the organization that owns the systems and preventing the duplication of names on the Internet. The DNS name space is based on domains, which exist in a hierarchical structure not unlike the directory tree in a file system. A *domain* is the equivalent of a directory, in that it can contain either subdomains (subdirectories) or hosts (files), forming a structure called the DNS tree (see Figure 20-1). By delegating the responsibility for specific domains to network administrators all over the Internet, the result is a *distributed database* scattered on systems all over the network.

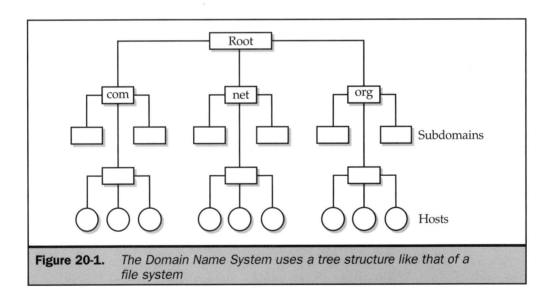

Figure 20-1. *The Domain Name System uses a tree structure like that of a file system*

Note

The term "domain" has more than one meaning in the networking industry. Windows NT, for example, uses the term to refer to an administrative grouping of computers on a private network, identified by a NetBIOS name. This type of domain is completely independent of, and has nothing to do with, a DNS domain. A system on a Windows network can be a member of either a Windows NT domain or a DNS domain, or both, but the domains perform different functions and can have different names. Sun Microsystems' Network Information Service (NIS) also uses the term "domain" to refer to a group of hosts, but this, too, is not synonymous with a DNS domain.

To assign unique IP addresses to computers all over the Internet, a two-tiered system was devised in which administrators receive the network identifiers that form the first part of the IP addresses, and then assign host identifiers to individual computers themselves, to form the second part of the addresses. This distributes the address assignment tasks among thousands of network administrators all over the world. The DNS name space functions in the same way: administrators are assigned domain names, and are then responsible for specifying host names to systems within that domain.

The result is that every computer on the Internet is uniquely identifiable by a *DNS name* that consists of a host name plus the names of all of its parent domains, stretching up to the root of the DNS tree, separated by periods. Each name can be up to 63 characters long, with a total length of 255 characters for a complete DNS name, including the host and all of its parent domains. Domain and host names are not case sensitive, and can take any value except the null value (no characters), which represents the root of the DNS tree.

In Figure 20-2, a computer in the mycorp domain functions as a Web server, and the administrator has therefore given it the host name www. This administrator is responsible for the mycorp domain, and can therefore assign systems in that domain any host name he wants to. Because mycorp is a subdomain of com, the full DNS name for that Web server is www.mycorp.com. Thus, a DNS name is something like a postal address, in which the top-level domain is the equivalent of the state, the second-level domain is the city, and the host name is the street address.

Because a complete DNS name traces the domain path all the way up the tree structure to the root, it should theoretically end with a period, indicating the division between the top-level domain and the root. However, this trailing period is nearly always omitted in common use, except in cases in which it serves to distinguish an absolute domain name from a relative domain name. An *absolute domain name* (also called a *fully qualified domain name,* or *FQDN*) does specify the path all the way to the root, while a *relative domain name* specifies only the subdomain relative to a specific domain context. For example, when working on a complex network called zacker.com that uses several levels of subdomains, I might refer to a system using a relative domain name of mail.paris without a period, because it's understood by my colleagues that I'm actually referring to a system with an absolute name of mail.paris.zacker.com. (with a period).

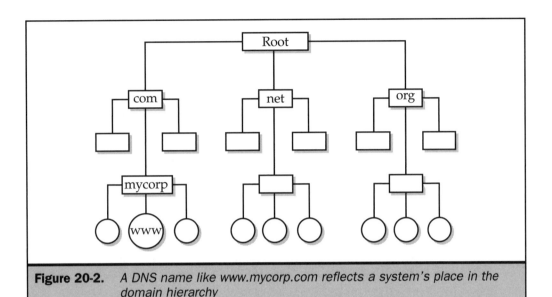

Figure 20-2. *A DNS name like www.mycorp.com reflects a system's place in the domain hierarchy*

It's also important to understand that DNS names have no inherent connection to IP addresses, or any other type of address. Theoretically, the host systems in a particular domain can be located on different networks, thousands of miles apart.

Top-Level Domains

In every DNS name, the first word on the right represents the domain at the highest level in the DNS tree, called a *top-level domain.* These top-level domains essentially function as registrars for the domains at the second level. For example, the administrator of zacker.com went to the com top-level domain and registered the name zacker. In return for a fee, that administrator now has exclusive use of the name zacker.com and can create any host or subdomain names in that domain that he wishes. It doesn't matter that thousands of other network administrators have named their Web servers www, because they all have their own individual domain names. The host name www may be duplicated anywhere, as long as the DNS name www.zacker.com is unique.

The original DNS name space called for seven top-level domains, dedicated to specific purposes, as follows:

- **com** Commercial organizations
- **edu** Four-year, degree-granting educational institutions in North America
- **gov** United States government institutions
- **int** Organizations established by international treaty

- **mil** United States military applications
- **net** Networking organizations
- **org** Noncommercial organizations

The edu, gov, int, and mil domains are reserved for use by certified organizations, but the com, org, and net domains are called *global domains,* because organizations anywhere in the world can register second-level domains within them. Since 1993, these top-level domains have been managed by a company called Network Solutions, Inc. (NSI, formerly known as InterNIC, the Internet Network Information Center) as a result of cooperative agreement with the United States government. You can still go to its Web site at http://www.networksolutions.com and register names in these top-level domains.

In 1998, however, the agreement with the U.S. government was changed to permit other organizations to compete with NSI in providing domain registrations. An organization called the Internet Corporation for Assigned Names and Numbers (ICANN) is responsible for the accreditation of domain name registrars. Under this new policy, the procedures and fees for registering names in the com, net, and org domains may vary, but there will be no difference in the functionality of the domain names, nor will duplicate names be permitted.

Note	*In addition to NSI, some of the organizations currently registering domain names in the com, net, and org domains include the following:*

- **CORE** http://www.corenic.org
- **register.com** http://www.register.com
- **Oleane (France Telecom)** http://www.oleane.com
- **Melbourne IT** http://www.internetnamesww.com

com Domain Conflicts

The com top-level domain is the one most closely associated with commercial Internet interests, and names of certain types in the com domain are becoming scarce. For example, it is difficult at this time to come up with a snappy name for an Internet technology company that includes the word "net" that has not already been registered in the com domain.

There have also been conflicts between organizations that both feel they have a right to a particular domain name. Trademark law permits two companies to have the same name, as long as they are not directly competitive in the marketplace. However, A1 Auto Parts Company and A1 Software, Inc. may both feel that they have a right to the a1.com domain, and lawsuits have arisen in some cases. In other instances, forward-thinking private individuals who registered domains using their own names several years ago have later been confronted by corporations with the same name who want to jump on the Internet bandwagon and feel that they have a right to that name. If a certain individual of Scottish extraction registers his domain, only to find out some years later that a fast-food company (for example) is very anxious to acquire that domain name, the end result can be either a profitable settlement for the individual or a nasty court case.

This phenomenon has also given rise to a particular breed of Internet bottom-feeder known as *domain name speculators.* These are people who register large numbers of domain names that they think some company might want someday, hoping that they can receive a large fee in return for selling them the domain name. Another unscrupulous practice is for a company in a particular business to register domains using the names of their competitors. Thus, when Internet users go to www.pizzaman.com, expecting to find Ray the Pizza Man's Web site, they instead find themselves redirected to the site for Bob's Pizza Palace. Both of these practices have resulted in civil suits, but neither one is illegal.

Generic Top-Level Domains

ICANN is also researching the possibility of creating additional top-level domains, to address this perceived depletion of available names. There have been several proposals for the establishment of *generic top-level domain (gTLD)* names, which are domains that address specific markets. Some of the proposed domain names are arts, shop, store, news, sex, firm, and law. There has been no decision made by ICANN yet regarding whether or not gTLDs will ever become a reality, although there are some companies already taking reservations for names in these domains. Companies that are unable to obtain a name in the com top-level domain that reflects their brand or trademark sometimes settle for the org or net top-level domain, or use one of the country-code domains.

Country-Code Domains

There are 191 *country-code domains* (also called *international domains*), named for specific countries in their own languages, such as *fr* for France and *de* for Deutschland (Germany). Eighty of these 191 countries allow free registration of second-level domains to anyone, without restrictions. For the other 111 countries, an organization must conform to some sort of local presence, tax, or trademark guidelines in order to register a second-level domain. Each of these country-code domains is managed by an organization in that country, which establishes its own domain name registration policies.

Note | *For a list of the country codes, as maintained by the ISO (the International Organization for Standardization), see http://www.din.de/gremien/nas/nabd/iso3166ma/codlstp1/ en_listp1.html.*

Some of the countries that permit free registration of second-level domains have been more aggressive than others in pursuing registrations of company domains, which has resulted in the fairly common appearance of top-level domains from obscure island countries, such as *nu* (Niue), *to* (Tonga), and *cc* (Cocos-Keeling Islands).

There is also a *us* top-level domain that is a viable alternative for organizations unable to obtain a satisfactory name in the com domain. The us domain is administered by the Information Sciences Institute of the University of Southern California, which registers second-level domains to businesses and individuals, as well as to government agencies, educational institutions, and other organizations. The only restriction is that all us domains must conform to a naming hierarchy that uses two-letter state abbreviations at the third level and uses local city or county names at the fourth level. Thus, an example of a valid domain name would be something like zacker.chicago.il.us.

Second-Level Domains

The registrars of the top-level domains are responsible for registering second-level domain names, in return for a subscription fee. As long as an organization continues to pay the fees for its domain name, it has exclusive rights to that name. The domain registrar maintains records that identify the owner of each second-level domain and specify three contacts within the registrant's organization—an administrative contact, a billing contact, and a technical contact. In addition, the registrar must have the IP addresses of two DNS servers that function as the source for further information about the domain. This is the only information maintained by the top-level domain. The administrators of the registrant's network can create as many hosts and subdomains within the second-level domain as they want without informing the registrars at all.

To host a second-level domain, an organization must have two DNS servers. A DNS server is a software program that runs on a computer. DNS server products are available for all of the major network operating systems. The DNS servers do not have to be located on the registrant's network; many companies outsource their Internet server hosting chores and use their service provider's DNS servers. The DNS servers identified in the top-level domain's record are the *authority* for the second-level domain. This means that these servers are the ultimate source for information about that domain. When network administrators want to add a host to the network or create a new subdomain, they do so in their own DNS servers. In addition, whenever a user application somewhere on the Internet has to discover the IP address associated with a particular host name, the request eventually ends up at one of the domain's authoritative servers.

Thus, in its simplest form, the Domain Name System works by referring requests for the address of a particular host name to a top-level domain server, which in turn passes the request to the authoritative server for the second-level domain, which responds with the requested information. This is why the DNS is described as a *distributed database.* The information about the hosts in specific domains is stored on their authoritative servers, which can be located anywhere. There is no single list of all the host names on the entire Internet, which is actually a good thing, because at the time that the DNS was developed, no one would have predicted that the Internet would grow as large as it has.

This distributed nature of the DNS database eliminates the traffic-congestion problem caused by the use of a host table maintained on a single computer. The top-level domain server handles millions of requests a day, but they are requests only for the DNS servers associated with second-level domains. If the top-level domains had to maintain records for every host in every second-level domain they have registered, the resulting traffic would bring the entire system to its knees.

Distributing the database in this way also splits the chores of administering the database among thousands of network administrators around the world. Domain name registrants are each responsible for their own area of the name space, and can maintain it as they wish with complete autonomy.

Subdomains

Many of the domains on the Internet stop at two levels, meaning that the second-level domain contains only host systems. However, it is possible for the administrators of a second-level domain to create subdomains that form additional levels. The us top-level domain, for example, requires a minimum of three levels: the country code, the state code, and the local city or county code. There is no limit on the number of levels you can create within a domain, except for those imposed by practicality and the 255-character maximum DNS name length.

In some cases, large organizations use subdomains to subdivide their networks according to geographical or organizational boundaries. A large corporation might create a third-level domain for each city or country in which it has an office, such as paris.zacker.com and newyork.zacker.com, or for each of several departments, such as sales.zacker.com and mis.zacker.com. The organizational paradigm for each domain is left completely up to its administrators.

The use of subdomains can make it easier to identify hosts on a large network, but many organizations also use them to delegate domain maintenance chores. The DNS servers for a top-level domain contain the addresses for each second-level domain's authoritative servers. In the same way, a second-level domain's servers can refer to authoritative servers for third-level administrators at each site to maintain their own DNS servers.

To make this delegation possible, DNS servers can break up a domain's name space into administrative units called *zones*. A domain with only two levels consists of only a single zone, which is synonymous with the domain. A three-level domain, however, can be divided into multiple zones. A zone can be any contiguous branch of a DNS tree, and can include domains on multiple levels. For example, in the diagram shown in Figure 20-3, the paris.zacker.com domain, including all of its subdomains and hosts, is one zone, represented by its own DNS servers. The rest of the zacker.com domain, including newyork.zacker.com, chicago.zacker.com, and zacker.com itself, is another

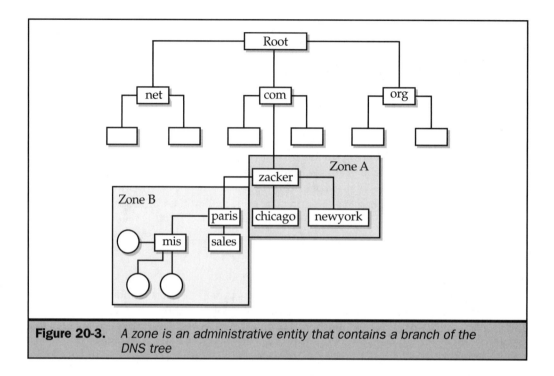

Figure 20-3.   *A zone is an administrative entity that contains a branch of the DNS tree*

zone. Thus, a *zone* can be defined as any part of a domain, including its subdomains, that is not designated as part of another zone.

Each zone must be represented by DNS servers that are the authority for that zone. A single DNS server can be authoritative for multiple zones, so you could conceivably create a separate zone for each of the third-level domains in zacker.com and still only have two sets of DNS servers.

DNS Functions

DNS servers are a ubiquitous part of most TCP/IP networks, even if you aren't aware of it. If you connect to the Internet, you use a DNS server each time you enter a server name or URL to resolve the name of the system you specified into an IP address. When a standalone computer connects to an Internet service provider (ISP), the ISP's server usually supplies the addresses of the DNS servers that the system will use. On a TCP/IP network, administrators or users configure clients with the addresses of the DNS servers they will use. This can be a manual process performed for each workstation, or an automatic process performed using a service such as DHCP (Dynamic Host Configuration Protocol).

TCP/IP communications are based solely on IP addresses. Before one system can communicate with another, it must know its IP address. Often, the user supplies a friendly name (such as a DNS name) for a desired server to a client application. The application must then resolve that server name into an IP address before it can transmit a message to it. If the name resolution mechanism fails to function, no communication with the server is possible.

Virtually all TCP/IP networks use some form of friendly name for host systems and include a mechanism for resolving those names into the IP addresses needed to initiate communications between systems. If the network is connected to the Internet, DNS name resolution is a necessity. Private networks do not necessarily need it, however. Microsoft Windows networks, for example, use NetBIOS names to identify their systems, and have their own mechanisms for resolving those names into IP addresses. These mechanisms include WINS, the Windows Internet Naming System, and also the transmission of broadcast messages to every system on the network. NetBIOS names and name resolution mechanisms do not replace the DNS; they are intended for use on relatively small, private networks and would not be practical on the Internet. A computer can have both a NetBIOS name and a DNS host name, and use both types of name resolution.

For more information on NetBIOS naming and Windows network name resolution, see Chapter 19.

Resource Records

DNS servers are basically database servers that store information about the hosts and subdomain for which they are responsible in *resource records (RRs)*. When you run your own DNS server, you create a resource record for each host name that you want to be accessible by the rest of the network. There are several different types of resource records used by DNS servers, the most important of which are as follows:

- **SOA (Start of Authority)**   Indicates that the server is the best authoritative source for data concerning the zone. Each zone must have an SOA record, and only one SOA record can be in a zone.

- **NS (Name Server)**   Identifies a DNS server functioning as an authority for the zone. Each DNS server in the zone (whether primary master or slave) must be represented by an NS record.

- **A (Address)**   Provides a name-to-address mapping that supplies an IP address for a specific DNS name. This record type performs the primary function of the DNS, converting names to addresses.

- **PTR**   Provides an address-to-name mapping that supplies a DNS name for a specific address in the in-addr.arpa domain. This is the functional opposite of an A record, used for reverse lookups only.

- **CNAME (Canonical Name)**   Creates an alias that points to the *canonical* name (that is, the "real" name) of a host identified by an A record. CNAME records are used to provide alternative names by which systems can be identified. For example, you may have a system with the name server1.zacker.com on your network that you use as a Web server. Changing the host name of the computer would confuse your users, but you want to use the traditional name of www to identify the Web server in your domain. Once you create a CNAME record for the name www.zacker.com that points to server1.zacker.com, the system is addressable using either name.

- **MX (Mail Exchanger)**   Identifies a system that will direct e-mail traffic sent to an address in the domain to the individual recipient, a mail gateway, or another mail server.

In addition to functioning as the authority for a small section of the DNS name space, servers process client name resolution requests by either consulting their own resource records or forwarding the request to another DNS server on the network. The process of forwarding a request is called a *referral*, and this is how all of the DNS servers on the Internet work together to provide a unified information resource for the entire domain name space.

DNS Name Resolution

Although all Internet applications use DNS to resolve host names into IP addresses, this name resolution process is particularly easy to see when you're using the Microsoft Internet Explorer browser to access a Web site. When you type a URL containing a DNS name (like www.microsoft.com, for example) into the browser's Address field and press the ENTER key, if you look quickly at the status bar in the lower-left corner, you'll see a message that says "Finding Site: www.microsoft.com." In a few seconds, you'll then see a message that says "Connecting to," followed by an IP address. It is during this interval that the DNS name resolution process occurs.

From the client's perspective, the procedure that occurs during these few seconds consists of the application sending a query message to its designated DNS server that contains the name to be resolved. The server then replies with a message containing the IP address corresponding to that name. Using the supplied address, the application can then transmit a message to the intended destination. It is only when you examine the DNS server's role in the process that you see how complex the procedure really is.

Resolvers

The component in the client system that generates the DNS query is called a *resolver*. In most cases, the resolver is a simple set of library routines in the operating system that generates the queries to be sent to the DNS server, reads the response information from the server's replies, and feeds the response to the application that originally requested it. In addition, a resolver can resend a query if no reply is forthcoming after a given timeout period, and can process error messages returned by the server, such as when it fails to resolve a given name.

DNS Requests

A TCP/IP client usually is configured with the addresses of two DNS servers to which it can send queries. A client can send a query to any DNS server; it does not have to use the authoritative server for the domain in which it belongs, nor does the server have to be on the local network. Using the DNS server that is closest to the client is best, however, because it minimizes the time needed for messages to travel between the two systems. A client only needs access to one DNS server, but two are usually specified, to provide a backup in case one server is unavailable.

There are two types of DNS queries: recursive and iterative. When a server receives a *recursive query*, it is responsible for trying to resolve the requested name and for transmitting a reply back to the requestor. Even if the server does not possess the required information itself, it must send its own queries to other DNS servers until it obtains the requested information or an error message stating why the information was unavailable, and must then relay the information back to the requestor. The system that generated the query, therefore, receives a reply only from the original server to which it sent the query. The resolvers in client systems nearly always send recursive queries to DNS servers.

When a server receives an *iterative query* (also called a *nonrecursive query*), it can either respond with information from its own database or refer the requestor to another DNS server. The recipient of the query responds with the best answer it currently possesses, but is not responsible for searching for the information, as with a recursive query. DNS servers processing a recursive query from a client typically use iterative queries to request information from other servers. It is possible for a DNS server to send a recursive query to another server, thus in effect "passing the buck" and forcing the other server to search for the requested information, but this is considered to be bad form and is rarely done without permission.

One of the scenarios in which DNS servers do send recursive queries to other servers is when you configure a server to function as a *forwarder*. On a network running several DNS servers, you may not want all of the servers sending queries to other DNS servers on the Internet. If the network has a relatively slow connection to the Internet, for example, several servers transmitting repeated queries may use too much of the available bandwidth.

To prevent this, some DNS implementations enable you to configure one server to function as the forwarder for all Internet queries generated by the other servers on the network. Any time that a server has to resolve the DNS name of an Internet system, and fails to find the needed information in its cache, it transmits a recursive query to the forwarder, which is then responsible for sending its own iterative queries over the Internet connection. Once the forwarder resolves the name, it sends a reply back to the original DNS server, which relays it to the client.

This request-forwarding behavior is a function of the original server only. The forwarder simply receives standard recursive queries from the original server and processes them normally. A server can be configured to use a forwarder in either exclusive or nonexclusive mode. In *exclusive mode,* the server relies completely on the forwarder to resolve the requested name. If the forwarder's resolution attempt fails, then the server relays a failure message back to the client. A server that uses a forwarder in exclusive mode is called a *slave.* In *nonexclusive mode,* if the forwarder fails to resolve the name and transmits an error message to the original server, that server makes its own resolution attempt before responding to the client.

Root Name Servers

In most cases, DNS servers that do not possess the information needed to resolve a name requested by a client send their first iterative query to one of the Internet's root name servers. The *root name servers* possess information about all of the top-level domains in the DNS name space. When you first install a DNS server, the only addresses that it needs to process client requests are those of the root name servers, because these servers can send a request for a name in any domain on its way to the appropriate authority.

The root name servers contain the addresses of the authoritative servers for all of the top-level domains on the Internet. In fact, the root name servers are the authorities for certain top-level domains, but they can also refer queries to the appropriate server for any of the other top-level domains, including the country-code domains, which are scattered all over the world. There are currently 13 root name servers, and they process millions of requests each day. The servers are also scattered widely and connected to different network trunks, so the chances of all of them being unavailable are minimal. If this were to occur, virtually all DNS name resolution would cease and the Internet would be crippled.

Resolving a Domain Name

With the preceding pieces in place, you are now ready to see how the DNS servers work together to resolve the name of a server on the Internet (see Figure 20-4). The process is as follows:

1. A user on a client system specifies the DNS name of an Internet server in an application such as a Web browser or FTP client.

2. The application generates an API call to the resolver on the client system, and the resolver creates a DNS recursive query message containing the server name.

3. The client system transmits the recursive query message to the DNS server identified in its TCP/IP configuration.

4. The client's DNS server, after receiving the query, checks its resource records to see if it is the authoritative source for the zone containing the requested server

name. If it is the authority, it generates a reply message and transmits it back to the client. If the DNS server is not the authority for the domain in which the requested server is located, it generates an iterative query and submits it to one of the root name servers.

5. The root name server examines the name requested by the original DNS server and consults its resource records to identify the authoritative servers for the name's top-level domain. Because the root name server received an iterative request, it does not send its own request to the top-level domain server. Instead, it transmits a reply to the original DNS server that contains a referral to the top-level domain server addresses.

6. The original DNS server then generates a new iterative query and transmits it to the top-level domain server. The top-level domain server examines the second-level domain in the requested name and transmits to the original server a referral containing the addresses of authoritative servers for that second-level domain.

7. The original server generates yet another iterative query and transmits it to the second-level domain server. If the requested name contains additional domain names, the second-level domain server replies with another referral to the third-level domain servers. The second-level domain server may also refer the original server to the authorities for a different zone. This process continues until the original server receives a referral to the domain server that is the authority for the domain or zone containing the requested host.

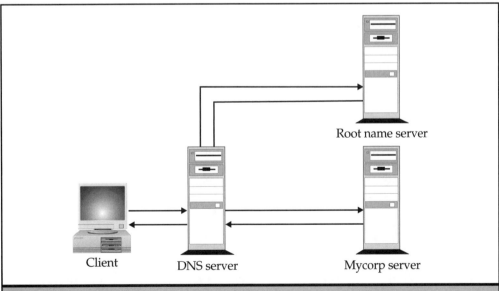

Root name server

Client   DNS server   Mycorp server

Figure 20-4.   *DNS servers communicate among themselves to locate the information requested by a client*

8. Once the authoritative server for the domain or zone containing the host receives a query from the original server, it consults its resource records to determine the IP address of the requested system and transmits it in a reply message back to that original server.

9. The original server receives the reply from the authoritative server and transmits the IP address back to the resolver on the client system. The resolver relays the address to the application, which can then initiate communications with the system specified by the user.

This procedure assumes a successful completion of the name resolution procedure. If any of the authoritative DNS servers queried returns an error message to the original server stating, for example, that one of the domains in the name does not exist, then this error message is relayed back to the client and the name resolution process is said to have failed.

DNS Server Caching

This process may seem extremely long and complex, but in many cases, it isn't necessary for the client's DNS server to send queries to the servers for each domain specified in the requested DNS name, because DNS servers are capable of retaining the information they learn about the DNS name space in the course of their name resolution procedures and storing it in a cache on the local drive.

A DNS server that receives requests from clients, for example, caches the addresses of the requested systems, as well as the addresses for particular domains' authoritative servers. The next time that a client transmits a request for a previously resolved name, the server can respond immediately with the cached information. In addition, if a client requests another name in one of the same domains, the server can send a query directly to an authoritative server for that domain, and not to a root name server. Thus, users should generally find that names in commonly accessed domains resolve more quickly, because one of the servers along the line has information about the domain in its cache, while names in obscure domains take longer, because the entire request/referral process is needed.

NEGATIVE CACHING   In addition to storing information that aids in the name resolution process, most modern DNS server implementations are also capable of negative caching. *Negative caching* occurs when a DNS server retains information about names that do not exist in a domain. If, for example, a client sends a query to its DNS server containing a name in which the second-level domain does not exist, the top-level domain server will return a reply containing an error message to that effect. The client's DNS server will then retain the error message information in its cache. The next time a client requests a name in that domain, the DNS server will be able to respond immediately with its own error message, without consulting the top-level domain.

CACHE DATA PERSISTENCE   Caching is a vital element of the DNS architecture, because it reduces the number of requests sent to the root name and top-level domain servers, which, being at the top of the DNS tree, are the most likely to act as a bottleneck for the whole system. However, caches must be purged eventually, and there is a fine line between effective and ineffective caching. Because DNS servers retain resource records in their caches, it can take hours or even days for changes made in an authoritative server to be propagated around the Internet. During this period, users may receive incorrect information in response to a query. If information remains in server caches too long, then the changes that administrators make to the data in their DNS servers take too long to propagate around the Internet. If caches are purged too quickly, then the number of requests sent to the root name and top-level domain servers increases precipitously.

The amount of time that DNS data remains cached on a server is called its *time to live*. Unlike most data caches, the time to live is not specified by the administrator of the server where the cache is stored. Instead, the administrators of each authoritative DNS server specify how long the data for the resource records in their domains or zones should be retained in the servers where it is cached. This enables administrators to specify a time to live value based on the volatility of their server data. On a network where changes in IP addresses or the addition of new resource records is frequent, a lower time to live value increases the likelihood that clients will receive current data. On a network that rarely changes, you can use a longer time to live value, and minimize the number of requests sent to the parent servers of your domain or zone.

DNS Load Balancing

In most cases, DNS servers maintain one IP address for each host name. However, there are situations in which more than one IP address is required. In the case of a highly trafficked Web site, for example, one server may not be sufficient to support all of the clients. To have multiple, identical servers with their own IP addresses hosting the same site, however, some mechanism is needed to ensure that client requests are balanced among the machines.

One way of doing this is to control how the authoritative servers for the domain on which the site is located resolve the DNS name of the Web server. Some DNS server implementations enable you to create multiple resource records with different IP addresses for the same host name. As the server responds to queries requesting resolution of that name, it uses the resource records in a round-robin fashion to supply the IP address of a different machine to each client.

DNS caching tends to defeat the effectiveness of this round-robin system, because servers use the cached information about the site, rather than issuing a new query and possibly receiving the address for another system. As a result, it is generally recommended that you use a relatively short time to live value for the duplicated resource records.

Reverse Name Resolution

The Domain Name System is designed to facilitate the resolution of DNS names into IP addresses, but there are also instances in which IP addresses have to be resolved into DNS names. These instances are relatively rare. In log files, for example, some systems convert IP addresses to DNS names to make the data more readily accessible to human readers. Certain systems also use reverse name resolution in the course of authentication procedures.

The structure of the DNS name space and the method by which it's distributed among various servers is based on the domain name hierarchy. When the entire database is located on one system, such as in the case of a host table, searching for a particular address to find out its associated name is no different from searching for a name to find an address. However, locating a particular address in the DNS name space would seem to require a search of all of the Internet's DNS servers, which is obviously impractical.

To make reverse name resolution possible without performing a massive search across the entire Internet, the DNS tree includes a special branch that uses the dotted decimal values of IP addresses as domain names. This branch stems from a domain called in-addr.arpa, which is located just beneath the root of the DNS tree, as shown in Figure 20-5. Just beneath the in-addr domain, there are 256 subdomains named

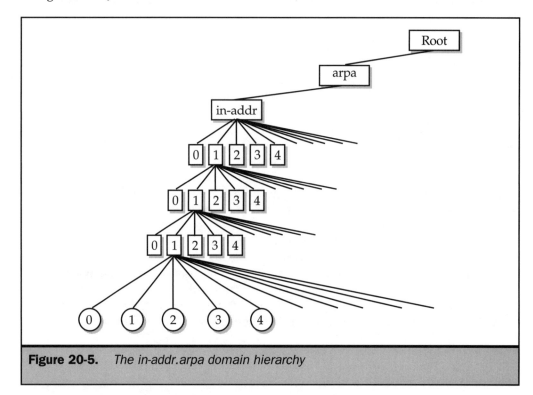

Figure 20-5.   *The in-addr.arpa domain hierarchy*

using the numbers 0 to 255, to represent the possible values of an IP address's first byte. Each of these subdomains contains another 256 subdomains representing the possible values of the second byte. The next level has another 256 domains, each of which can have up to 256 numbered hosts, which represent the third and fourth bytes of the address.

Using the in-addr.arpa domain structure, each of the hosts represented by a standard name on a DNS server also has an equivalent DNS name constructed using its IP address. Therefore, if a system with the IP address 192.168.214.23 is listed in the DNS server for the zacker.com domain with the host name www, then there is also a resource record for that system with the DNS name 23.214.168.192.in-addr.arpa, meaning that there is a host with the name 23 in a domain called 214.168.192.in-addr.arpa, as shown in Figure 20-6. This domain structure makes it possible for a system to search for the IP address of a host in a domain (or zone) without having to consult other servers in the DNS tree. In most cases, you can configure a DNS server to automatically create an equivalent resource record in the in-addr.arpa domain for every host you add to the standard domain name space.

The byte values of IP addresses are reversed in the in-addr.arpa domain, because in a DNS name, the least significant word comes first, whereas in IP addresses, the least significant byte comes last. In other words, a DNS name is structured with the root of the DNS tree on the right side and the host name on the left. In an IP address, the host identifier is on the right and the network identifier is on the left. It would be possible

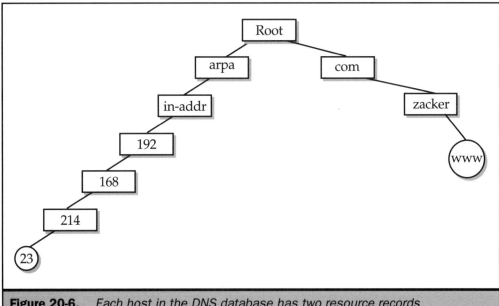

Figure 20-6.   *Each host in the DNS database has two resource records*

to create a domain structure using the IP address bytes in their regular order, but this would complicate the administration process by making it harder to delegate maintenance tasks based on network addresses.

If, for example, a corporate internetwork consists of three branch offices, each with its own Class C IP address (192.168.1, 192.168.2, and 192.168.3), it is possible to have a different person administer the reverse lookup domain for each site, because the domains would have the following names:

```
1.168.192.in-addr.arpa
2.168.192.in-addr.arpa
3.168.192.in-addr.arpa
```

If the in-addr.arpa name space was constructed using the byte values for the IP addresses in their traditional order, the third-level domain would be named using the host identifier (that is, the fourth byte) from the IP address. You might need up to 256 third-level domains to represent these three networks instead of 1. Delegating administration chores would be all but impossible, because the 72.in-addr.arpa domain (for example) could contain a host from all three networks.

DNS Name Registration

As you have already learned, name resolution is the process by which IP address information for a host name is extracted from the DNS database. The process by which host names and their addresses are added to the database is called *name registration.* Name registration refers to the process of creating new resource records on a DNS server, thus making them accessible to all of the other DNS servers on the network.

The name registration process on a traditional DNS server is decidedly low-tech. There is no mechanism by which the server can detect the systems on the network and enter their host names and IP addresses into resource records. In fact, a computer may not even be aware of its host name, because it receives all of its communications using IP addresses and never has to answer to its name.

To register a host in the DNS name space, an administrator has to manually create a resource record on the server. The method for creating resource records varies depending on the DNS server implementation. UNIX-based servers require you to edit a text file, while Microsoft DNS Server uses a graphical interface.

Manual Name Registration

The manual name registration process is basically an adaptation of the host table for use on a DNS server. It is easy to see how, in the early days, administrators were able to implement DNS servers on their network by using their host tables with slight modifications. Today, however, the manual name registration process can be problematic on some networks.

If you have a large number of hosts, manually creating resource records for all of them can be a tedious affair, even with a graphical interface. However, depending on the nature of the network, it may not be necessary to register every system in the DNS. If, for example, your network is composed of Windows workstations and uses unregistered IP addresses, you may not need your own DNS server at all, except possibly to process client name resolution requests. Windows networks have their own NetBIOS naming system and name resolution mechanisms, and you generally don't need to refer to them using DNS names.

The exceptions to this would be systems with registered IP addresses that you use as Web servers or other types of Internet servers. These must be visible to Internet users and, therefore, must have a host name in a DNS domain. In most cases, however, the number of systems like this on a network is small, so manually creating the resource records is not much of a problem. If you have UNIX systems on your network, however, you have to use DNS to identify them using names and you must create resource records for them.

Dynamic Updates

As networks grow larger and more complex, the biggest problem arising from manual name registration stems from the increasing use of DHCP servers to dynamically assign IP addresses to network workstations. The manual configuration of TCP/IP clients is another long-standing network administration chore that is gradually being phased out in favor of an automated solution. However, assigning IP addresses dynamically means that workstations can have different addresses from one day to the next, and the original DNS standard has no way of keeping up with the changes.

On networks where only a few servers have to be visible to the Internet, it isn't too great an inconvenience to configure them manually with static IP addresses and use DHCP for the unregistered systems. However, this situation has changed with the advent of Windows 2000 and Active Directory, its new enterprise directory service. Windows NT networks use WINS to resolve NetBIOS names into IP addresses, but name registration is automatic with WINS. WINS automatically updates its database record for a workstation that is assigned a new IP address by a DHCP server, so that no administrator intervention is required. Active Directory, however, relies heavily on DNS instead of WINS to resolve the names of systems on the network and to keep track of the domain controllers that are available for use by client workstations.

To make the use of DNS practical with technologies like Active Directory that require regular updates to resource records, members of the IETF have developed a new specification, published as RFC 2136, "Dynamic Updates in the Domain Name System," that is currently a proposed standard. This document defines a new DNS message type, called an *Update*, that systems like domain controllers and DHCP servers can generate and transmit to a DNS server. These Update messages can modify or delete existing resource records or create new ones, based on prerequisites specified by the administrator. For Active Directory, the Update message can contain the information for the new SVR resource record type, as defined in RFC 2052, that specifies the locations of servers that perform particular functions.

| Note | *For more information on the role of DNS on an Active Directory network, see Chapter 23.* |

Zone Transfers

Most networks use at least two DNS servers, to provide fault tolerance and to give clients access to a nearby server. Because the resource records (in most cases) have to be created and updated manually by administrators, the DNS standards define a mechanism that replicates the DNS data among the servers, thus enabling administrators to make the changes only once.

The standards define two DNS server roles: the primary master and the secondary master, or slave. The *primary master* server loads its resource records and other information from the database files on the local drive. The *slave* (or *secondary master*) server receives its data from another server in a process called a *zone transfer*, which the slave performs each time it starts and periodically thereafter. The server from which the slave receives its data is called its *master server*, but it need not be the primary master. A slave can receive data from the primary master or another slave.

Zone transfers are performed for individual zones, and because a single server can be the authority for multiple zones, more than one transfer may be needed to update all of a slave server's data. In addition, the primary master and slave roles are also zone specific. A server can be the primary master for one zone and the slave for another, although this practice generally should not be necessary and is likely to generate some confusion.

Although slave servers receive periodic zone transfers from their primaries, they are also able to load database files from their local drives. When a slave server receives a zone transfer, it updates the local database files. Each time the slave server starts up, it loads the most current resource records it has from the database files and then checks this data with the primary master to see whether an update is needed. This prevents zone transfers from being performed needlessly.

DNS Messaging

DNS name resolution transactions use UDP (User Datagram Protocol) datagrams on port 53 for servers and on an ephemeral port number for clients. Communication between two servers uses port 53 on both machines. In cases in which the data to be transmitted does not fit in a single UDP datagram, in the case of zone transfers, the two systems establish a standard TCP connection, also using port 53 on both machines, and transmit the data using as many packets as needed.

The Domain Name System uses a single message format for all of its communications that consists of the following five sections:

- **Header**   Contains information about the nature of the message.
- **Question**   Contains the information requested from the destination server.

- **Answer**   Contains RRs supplying the information requested in the Question section.

- **Authority**   Contains RRs pointing to an authority for the information requested in the Question section.

- **Additional**   Contains RRs containing additional information in response to the Question section.

Every DNS message has a Header section, and the other four sections are included only if they contain data. For example, a query message contains the DNS name to be resolved in the Question section, but the Answer, Authority, and Additional sections aren't needed. When the server receiving the query constructs its reply, it makes some changes to the Header section, leaves the Question section intact, and adds entries to one or more of the remaining three sections. Each section can have multiple entries, so that a server can send more than one resource record in a single message.

The DNS Header Section

The Header section of the DNS message contains codes and flags that specify the function of the message and the type of service requested from or supplied by a server. The format of the Header section is shown in Figure 20-7.

The functions of the Header fields are as follows:

- **ID, 2 bytes**   Contains an identifier value used to associate queries with replies.

- **Flags, 2 bytes**   Contains flag bits used to identify the functions and properties of the message, as follows:

  - **QR, 1 bit**   Specifies whether the message is a query (value 0) or a response (value 1).

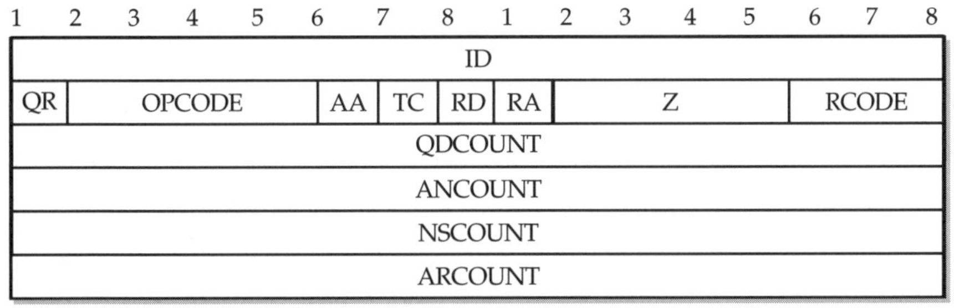

1	2	3	4	5	6	7	8	1	2	3	4	5	6	7	8
ID															
QR	OPCODE				AA	TC	RD	RA	Z				RCODE		
QDCOUNT															
ANCOUNT															
NSCOUNT															
ARCOUNT															

Figure 20-7.   *The DNS Header section format*

- **OPCODE, 4 bits**   Specifies the type of query that generated the message. Response messages retain the same value for this field as the query to which they are responding. Possible values are as follows:
  - **0**   Standard query (QUERY).
  - **1**   Inverse query (IQUERY).
  - **2**   Server status request (STATUS).
  - **3–15**   Unused.
- **AA (Authoritative Answer), 1 bit**   Indicates that a response message has been generated by a server that is the authority for the domain or zone in which the requested name is located.
- **TC (Truncation), 1 bit**   Indicates that the message has been truncated because the amount of data exceeds the maximum size for the current transport mechanism. In most DNS implementations, this bit functions as a signal that the message should be transmitted using a TCP connection rather than a UDP datagram.
- **RD (Recursion Desired), 1 bit**   In a query, indicates that the destination server should treat the message as a recursive query. In a response, indicates that the message is the response to a recursive query. The absence of this flag indicates that the query is iterative.
- **RA (Recursion Available), 1 bit**   Specifies whether a server is configured to process recursive queries.
- **Z, 3 bits**   Unused.
- **RCODE (Response Code), 4 bits**   Specifies the nature of a response message, indicating when an error has occurred and what type of error, using the following values:
  - **0**   No error has occurred.
  - **1 – Format Error**   Indicates that the server was unable to understand the query.
  - **2 – Server Failure**   Indicates that the server was unable to process the query.
  - **3 – Name Error**   Used by authoritative servers only to indicate that a requested name or subdomain does not exist in the domain.
  - **4 – Not Implemented**   Indicates that the server does not support the type of query received.
  - **5 – Refused**   Indicates that server policies (such as security policies) have prevented the processing of the query.
  - **6–15**   Unused.

- **QDCOUNT (2 bytes)** Specifies the number of entries in the Question section.
- **ANCOUNT (2 bytes)** Specifies the number of entries in the Answer section.
- **NSCOUNT (2 bytes)** Specifies the number of name server RRs in the Authority section.
- **ARCOUNT (2 bytes)** Specifies the number of entries in the Additional section.

The DNS Question Section

The Question section of a DNS message contains the number of entries specified in the header's QDCOUNT field. In most cases, there is only one entry. Each entry is formatted as shown in Figure 20-8.

The functions of the fields are as follows:

- **QNAME, variable** Contains the DNS, domain, or zone name about which information is being requested.
- **QTYPE, 2 bytes** Contains a code that specifies the type of RR the query is requesting.
- **QCLASS, 2 bytes** Contains a code that specifies the class of the RR being requested.

DNS Resource Record Sections

The three remaining sections of a DNS message, the Answer, Authority, and Additional sections, each contains resource records that use the format shown in Figure 20-9. The numbers of resource records in each section is specified in the header's ANCOUNT, NSCOUNT, and RCOUNT fields.

The functions of the fields are as follows:

- **NAME, variable** Contains the DNS, domain, or zone name about which information is being supplied.

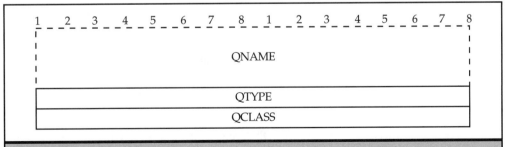

Figure 20-8. *The DNS Question section format*

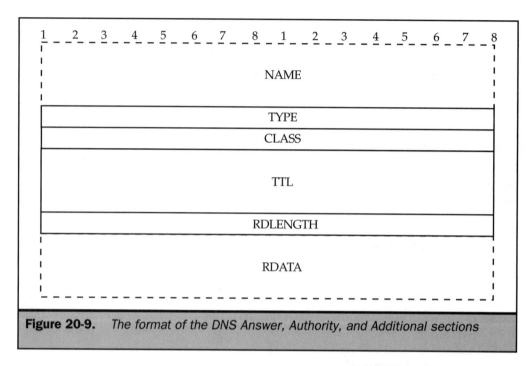

Figure 20-9. *The format of the DNS Answer, Authority, and Additional sections*

- **TYPE, 2 bytes** Contains a code that specifies the type of RR the entry contains.
- **CLASS, 2 bytes** Contains a code that specifies the class of the RR.
- **TTL, 4 bytes** Specifies the amount of time (in seconds) that the RR should be cached in the server to which it is being supplied.
- **RDLENGTH, 2 bytes** Specifies the length (in bytes) of the RDATA field.
- **RDATA, variable** Contains RR data, the nature of which is dependent on its TYPE and CLASS. For an A-type record in the IN class, for example, this field contains the IP address associated with the DNS name supplied in the NAME field.

Different types of resource records have different functions and, therefore, may contain different types of information in the RDATA field. Most resource records, such as the NS, A, PTR, and CNAME types, have only a single name or address in this field, while others have multiple subfields. The SOA resource record is the most complex in the Domain Name System. For this record, the RDATA field is broken up into seven subfields, as shown in Figure 20-10.

The functions of the SOA resource record subfields are as follows:

- **MNAME, variable** Specifies the DNS name of the primary master server that was the source for the information about the zone.
- **RNAME, variable** Specifies the e-mail address of the administrator responsible for the zone data. This field has no actual purpose as far as the server is concerned; it is strictly informational. The value for this field takes

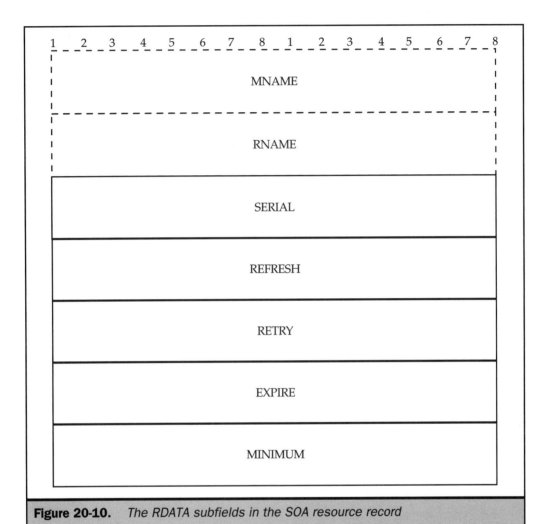

Figure 20-10.   *The RDATA subfields in the SOA resource record*

the form of a DNS name. Standard practice calls for the period after the first word to be converted to the @ symbol, in order to use the value as an e-mail address. For example, a value of administrator.zacker.com is equivalent to the e-mail address administrator@zacker.com.

■ **SERIAL, 4 bytes**   Contains a serial number that is used to track modifications to the zone data on the primary master server. The value of this field is incremented (either manually or automatically) on the primary master server each time the zone data is modified, and the slave compares its value to the one supplied by the primary master, to determine if a zone transfer is necessary.

■ **REFRESH, 4 bytes**   Specifies the time interval (in seconds) at which the slave should transmit an SOA query to the primary master to determine if a zone transfer is needed.

- **RETRY, 4 bytes** Specifies the time interval (in seconds) at which the slave should make repeat attempts to connect to the primary master after its initial attempt fails.

- **EXPIRE, 4 bytes** Specifies the time interval (in seconds) after which the slave server's data should expire, in the event that it cannot contact the primary master server. Once the data has expired, the slave server stops responding to queries.

- **MINIMUM, 4 bytes** Specifies the time to live interval (in seconds) that the server should supply for all of the resource records in its responses to queries.

DNS Message Notation

The latter four sections of the DNS message are largely consistent in how they notate the information in their fields. DNS, domain, and zone names are all expressed in the same way, and the sections all use the same values for the resource record type and class codes. The only exceptions are a few additional codes that are used only in the Question section, called QTYPES and QCLASSES, respectively. The following sections describe how these values are expressed in the DNS message.

DNS Name Notation

Depending on the function of the message, any or all of the four sections can contain the fully qualified name of a host system, the name of a domain, or the name of a zone on a server. These names are expressed as a series of units, called *labels*, each of which represents a single word in the name. The periods between the words are not included; so to delineate the words, each label begins with a single byte that specifies the length of the word (in bytes), after which the specified number of bytes follows. This is repeated for each word in the name. After the final word of a fully qualified name, a byte with the value of 0 is included to represent the null value of the root domain. Thus, to express the DNS name www.zacker.com, the value of the QNAME or NAME field would appear as follows, in decimal form:

```
3 w w w 5 m y c o r p 3 c o m 0
```

Resource Record Types

All of the data distributed by the Domain Name System is stored in resource records. Query messages request certain resource records from servers, and the servers reply with those resource records. The QTYPE field in a Question section entry specifies the type of resource record being requested from the server, and the TYPE fields in the Answer, Authority, and Additional section entries specify the type of resource record supplied by the server in each entry. Table 20-1 contains the resource record types and the codes used to represent them in these fields. All of the values in this table are valid for both the QTYPE and TYPE fields. Table 20-2 contains four additional values that represent sets of resource records that are valid for the QTYPE field in Question section entries only.

Type	Type Code	Function
A	1	Host address
NS	2	Authoritative name server
MD	3	Mail destination (Obsolete)
MF	4	Mail forwarder (Obsolete)
CNAME	5	Canonical name for an alias
SOA	6	Start of a zone of authority
MB	7	Mailbox domain name (Experimental)
MG	8	Mail group member (Experimental)
MR	9	Mail rename domain name (Experimental)
NULL	10	Null RR (Experimental)
WKS	11	Well-known service description
PTR	12	Domain name pointer
HINFO	13	Host information
MINFO	14	Mailbox or mail list information
MX	15	Mail exchange
TXT	16	Text strings
SVR	33	Network server

Table 20-1. *DNS Resource Record Types and Values for Use in the TYPE or QTYPE Field*

QTYPE	QTYPE Code	Function
AXFR	252	Request for transfer of an entire zone
MAILB	253	Request for mailbox-related records (MB, MG, or MR)
MAILA	254	Request for mail agent RRs (Obsolete)
*	255	Request for all records

Table 20-2. *Additional Values Representing Sets of Resource Records for Use in the QTYPE Field Only*

Class Types

The QCLASS field in the Question section and the CLASS field in the Answer, Authority, and Additional sections specify the type of network for which information is being requested or supplied. Although they performed a valid function at one time, these fields are now essentially meaningless, as virtually all DNS messages use the IN class. CSNET and CHAOS class networks are obsolete, and the Hesiod class is used only for a few experimental networks at MIT. For academic purposes only, the values for the CLASS and QCLASS values are shown in Tables 20-3 and 20-4.

Name Resolution Messages

The process of resolving a DNS name into an IP address begins with the generation of a query by the resolver on the client system. Figure 20-11 shows a query message, captured in a network monitor program, generated by a Web browser trying to connect to the URL http://www.zacker.com. The Value of the message's OPCODE flag is 0, indicating that this is a regular query, and the RD flag has a value of 1, indicating that this is a recursive query. As a result, the DNS server receiving the query (which is called CZ1) will be responsible for resolving the DNS name and returning the results to the client. The QDCOUNT field indicates that there is one entry in the Question section, and no entries in the three resource record sections, which is standard for a query message. The Question section specifies the DNS name to be resolved (www.zacker.com) and the type (1 - A) and class (1 - IN) of the resource record being requested.

CZ1 is not the authoritative server for the zacker.com domain, nor does it have the requested information in its cache, so it must generate its own queries. CZ1 first generates a query message (see Figure 20-12) and transmits it to one of the root name servers (198.41.0.4) configured into the server software. The entry in the Question section is identical to that of the client's query message. The only differences in this query are that the server has included a different value in the ID field (4114) and has changed the value of the RD flag to 0, indicating that this is an iterative query.

Class	Class Code	Function
IN	1	Internet
CS	2	CSNET
CH	3	CHAOS
HS	4	Hesiod

Table 20-3.   *Values for the Resource Record CLASS and QCLASS Fields*

QCLASS	QCLASS Code	Function
*	255	Any Class

Table 20-4. *Additional Value for the Resource Record QCLASS Field Only*

The response that CZ1 receives from the root name server bypasses one step of the process, because this root name server is also the authoritative server for the com top-level domain. As a result, the response contains the resource record that identifies the authoritative server for the zacker.com domain. If the requested DNS name had been in a top-level domain for which the root name server was not authoritative, such as one of the country-code domains, the response would contain a resource record identifying the proper authoritative servers.

The response message from the root domain server (see Figure 20-13) has a QR bit that has a value of 1, indicating that this is a response message, and the same ID value as the request, enabling CZ1 to associate the two messages. The QDCOUNT field again has a value of 1, because the response retains the Question section, unmodified, from

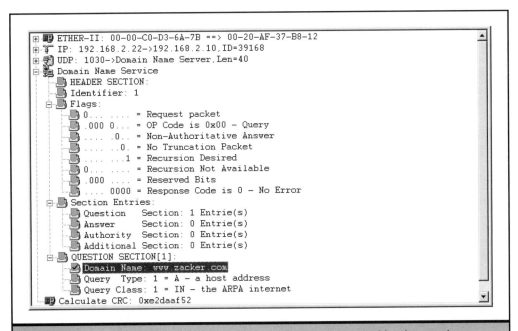

```
⊞ ▦ ETHER-II: 00-00-C0-D3-6A-7B ==> 00-20-AF-37-B8-12
⊞ ⌼ IP: 192.168.2.22->192.168.2.10,ID=39168
⊞ ▦ UDP: 1030->Domain Name Server,Len=40
⊟ ▦ Domain Name Service
    ▬ HEADER SECTION:
    ▬ Identifier: 1
  ⊟ ▬ Flags:
      ▬ 0... .... = Request packet
      ▬ .000 0... = OP Code is 0x00 - Query
      ▬ .... .0.. = Non-Authoritative Answer
      ▬ .... ..0. = No Truncation Packet
      ▬ .... ...1 = Recursion Desired
      ▬ 0... .... = Recursion Not Available
      ▬ .000 .... = Reserved Bits
      ▬ .... 0000 = Response Code is 0 - No Error
  ⊟ ▬ Section Entries:
      ▬ Question   Section: 1 Entrie(s)
      ▬ Answer     Section: 0 Entrie(s)
      ▬ Authority  Section: 0 Entrie(s)
      ▬ Additional Section: 0 Entrie(s)
  ⊟ ▬ QUESTION SECTION[1]:
      ☑ Domain Name: www.zacker.com
      ▬ Query Type: 1 = A - a host address
      ▬ Query Class: 1 = IN - the ARPA internet
    ▦ Calculate CRC: 0xe2daaf52
```

Figure 20-11. *The name resolution query message generated by the resolver*

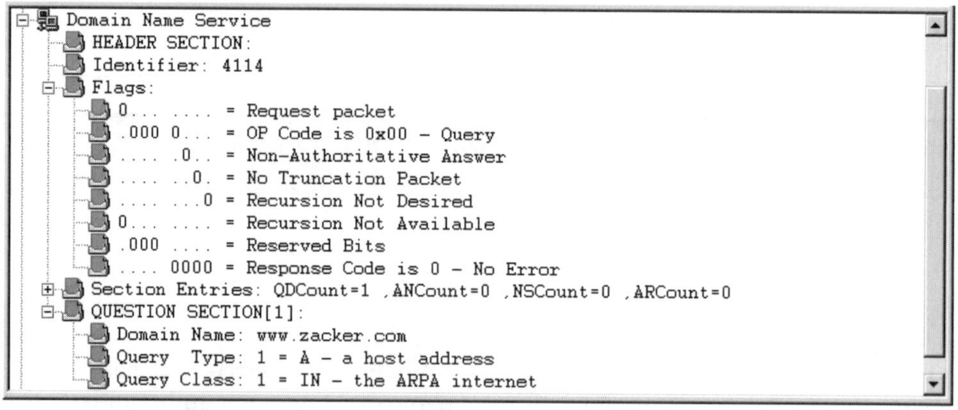

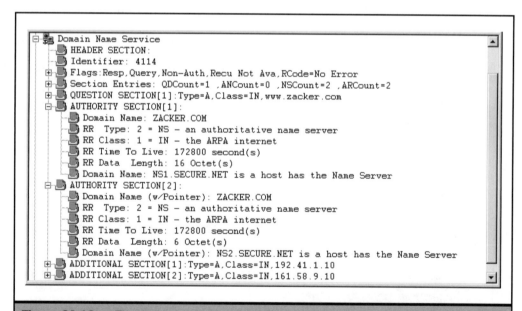

Figure 20-12. The query message sent to the root name server

Figure 20-13. The Authority section from the root name server's response message

the query message. The NSCOUNT and ARCOUNT fields indicate that there are two entries each in the Authority and Additional sections. The first entry in the Authority section contains the NS resource record for one of the authoritative servers for zacker.com known to the root name/top-level domain server, and the second entry contains the NS record for the other. The type and class values are the same as those requested in the query message; the time to live value assigned to both records is 172,800 seconds (48 hours). The RDATA field in the first entry is 16 bytes long and contains the DNS name of the first authoritative server (ns1.secure.net). The RDATA field in the second entry is only 6 bytes long, and contains only the host name (ns2) for the other authoritative server, since it's in the same domain as the first one.

These Authority section entries identify the servers that CZ1 needs to contact to resolve the www.zacker.com domain name, but it does so using DNS names. In order to prevent CZ1 from having to go through this whole process again to resolve ns1.secure.net and ns2.secure.net into IP addresses, there are two entries in the Additional section that contain the A resource records for these two servers, which include their IP addresses, as shown in Figure 20-14.

Using the information contained in the previous response, CZ1 transmits a query to the first authoritative server for the zacker.com domain (ns1.secure.net – 192.41.1.10).

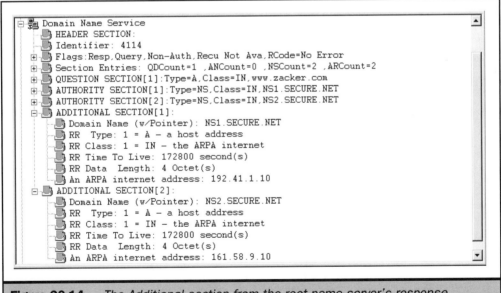

Figure 20-14.   *The Additional section from the root name server's response message*

Except for the destination address, this query is identical to the one that CZ1 sent to the root name server. The response message, shown in Figure 20-15, that CZ1 receives from the ns1.secure.net server (finally) contains the information that the client originally requested. This message contains the original Question section entry and two entries each in the Answer, Authority, and Additional sections.

The first entry in the Answer section contains a resource record with a TYPE value of 5 (CNAME) and a time to live value of 86,400 seconds (24 hours). The inclusion of a CNAME resource record in a response to a query requesting an A record indicates that the host name www exists in the zacker.com domain only as a canonical name (that is, an alias for another name), which is specified in the RDATA field as zacker.com. The second entry in the Answer section contains the A resource record for the name zacker.com, which specifies the IP address 192.41.15.74 in the RDATA field. This is the IP address that the client system must use to reach the www.zacker.com Web server. The entries in the Authority and Additional sections specify the names and addresses of the authoritative server for zacker.com, and are identical to the equivalent entries in the response message from the root name server.

Root Name Server Discovery

Each time the DNS server starts, it loads the information stored in its database files. One of these files is the Cache.dns file, which contains root name server hints. Actually, this file contains the names and addresses of all of the root name servers, but the DNS

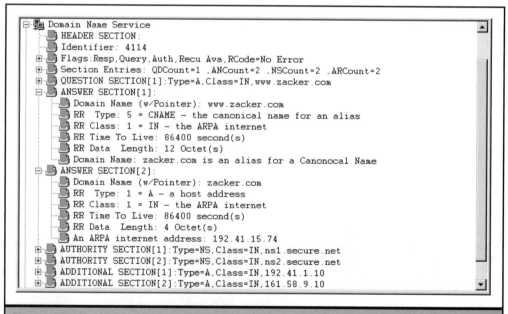

Figure 20-15.   *The response message from the authoritative server for the requested domain*

server, instead of relying on this data, uses it to send a query to the first of the root name servers, requesting that it identify the authoritative servers for the root domain. This is to ensure that the server is using the most current information. The query (see Figure 20-16) is just like that for a name resolution request, except that there is no value in the NAME field.

The reply returned by the root name server contains 13 entries in both the Authority and Additional sections, corresponding to the 13 root name servers currently in operation (see Figure 20-17). Each entry in the Answer section contains the NS resource record for one of the root name servers, which specifies its DNS name, and the corresponding entry in the Additional section contains the A record for that server, which specifies its IP address. All of these servers are located in a domain called root-server.net and have incremental host names from *a* to *m*. Because the information about these servers does not change often, if at all, their resource records can have a long time to live value: 518,400 seconds (144 hours or 6 days) for the NS records and 3,600,000 (1,000 hours or 41.67 days) for the A records.

Zone Transfer Messages

A zone transfer is initiated by a DNS server that functions as a slave for one or more zones whenever the server software is started. The process begins with an iterative query for an SOA resource record that the slave sends to the primary master to ensure that it is the best source for information about the zone (see Figure 20-18). The single Question section entry contains the name of the zone in the QNAME field and a value of 6 for the QTYPE field, indicating that the server is requesting the SOA resource record.

The primary master then replies to the slave with a response that includes the original Question section and a single Answer section containing the SOA resource

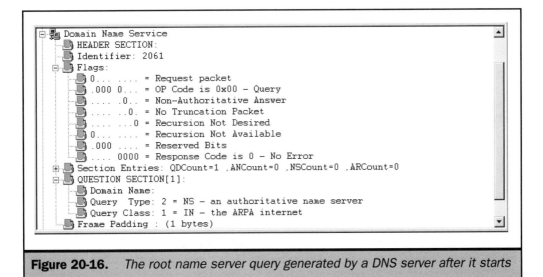

Figure 20-16.   *The root name server query generated by a DNS server after it starts*

```
⊟  🖳 Domain Name Service                                                    ▲
   └ 🗋 HEADER SECTION:
   └ 🗋 Identifier: 2061
   ⊞ 🗋 Flags:Resp,Query,Auth,Recu Not Ava,RCode=No Error
   ⊞ 🗋 Section Entries: QDCount=1 ,ANCount=13 ,NSCount=0 ,ARCount=13
   ⊞ 🗋 QUESTION SECTION[1]:Type=NS,Class=IN,
   ⊟ 🗋 ANSWER SECTION[1]:
      └ 🗋 Domain Name:
      └ 🗋 RR Type: 2 = NS - an authoritative name server
      └ 🗋 RR Class: 1 = IN - the ARPA internet
      └ 🗋 RR Time To Live: 518400 second(s)
      └ 🗋 RR Data  Length: 20 Octet(s)
      └ 🗋 Domain Name: A.ROOT-SERVERS.NET is a host has the Name Server
   ⊞ 🗋 ANSWER SECTION[2]:Type=NS,Class=IN,H.ROOT-SERVERS.NET
   ⊞ 🗋 ANSWER SECTION[3]:Type=NS,Class=IN,C.ROOT-SERVERS.NET
   ⊞ 🗋 ANSWER SECTION[4]:Type=NS,Class=IN,G.ROOT-SERVERS.NET
   ⊞ 🗋 ANSWER SECTION[5]:Type=NS,Class=IN,F.ROOT-SERVERS.NET
   ⊞ 🗋 ANSWER SECTION[6]:Type=NS,Class=IN,B.ROOT-SERVERS.NET
   ⊞ 🗋 ANSWER SECTION[7]:Type=NS,Class=IN,J.ROOT-SERVERS.NET
   ⊞ 🗋 ANSWER SECTION[8]:Type=NS,Class=IN,K.ROOT-SERVERS.NET
   ⊞ 🗋 ANSWER SECTION[9]:Type=NS,Class=IN,L.ROOT-SERVERS.NET
   ⊞ 🗋 ANSWER SECTION[10]:Type=NS,Class=IN,M.ROOT-SERVERS.NET
   ⊞ 🗋 ANSWER SECTION[11]:Type=NS,Class=IN,I.ROOT-SERVERS.NET
   ⊞ 🗋 ANSWER SECTION[12]:Type=NS,Class=IN,E.ROOT-SERVERS.NET
   ⊞ 🗋 ANSWER SECTION[13]:Type=NS,Class=IN,D.ROOT-SERVERS.NET
   ⊟ 🗋 ADDITIONAL SECTION[1]:
      └ 🗋 Domain Name (w/Pointer): A.ROOT-SERVERS.NET
      └ 🗋 RR Type: 1 = A - a host address
      └ 🗋 RR Class: 1 = IN - the ARPA internet
      └ 🗋 RR Time To Live: 3600000 second(s)
      └ 🗋 RR Data  Length: 4 Octet(s)
      └ 🗋 An ARPA internet address: 198.41.0.4
   ⊞ 🗋 ADDITIONAL SECTION[2]:Type=A,Class=IN,128.63.2.53
   ⊞ 🗋 ADDITIONAL SECTION[3]:Type=A,Class=IN,192.33.4.12
   ⊞ 🗋 ADDITIONAL SECTION[4]:Type=A,Class=IN,192.112.36.4
   ⊞ 🗋 ADDITIONAL SECTION[5]:Type=A,Class=IN,192.5.5.241
   ⊞ 🗋 ADDITIONAL SECTION[6]:Type=A,Class=IN,128.9.0.107
   ⊞ 🗋 ADDITIONAL SECTION[7]:Type=A,Class=IN,198.41.0.10
   ⊞ 🗋 ADDITIONAL SECTION[8]:Type=A,Class=IN,193.0.14.129
   ⊞ 🗋 ADDITIONAL SECTION[9]:Type=A,Class=IN,198.32.64.12
   ⊞ 🗋 ADDITIONAL SECTION[10]:Type=A,Class=IN,202.12.27.33
   ⊞ 🗋 ADDITIONAL SECTION[11]:Type=A,Class=IN,192.36.148.17
   ⊞ 🗋 ADDITIONAL SECTION[12]:Type=A,Class=IN,192.203.230.10
   ⊞ 🗋 ADDITIONAL SECTION[13]:Type=A,Class=IN,128.8.10.90      ▼
```

Figure 20-17. *The root name server's response message, containing the RRs for all 13 root name servers*

record for the zone (see Figure 20-19). The slave uses the information in the response to verify the primary master's authority and to determine whether a zone transfer is needed. If the value of the SOA record's SERIAL field, as furnished by the primary master, is greater than the equivalent field on the slave server, then a zone transfer is required.

A zone transfer request is a standard DNS query message with a QTYPE value of 252, which corresponds to the AXFR type. AXFR is the abbreviation for a resource record set that consists of all of the records in the zone. However, in most cases, all of the resource records in the zone will not fit into a single UDP datagram. UDP is a

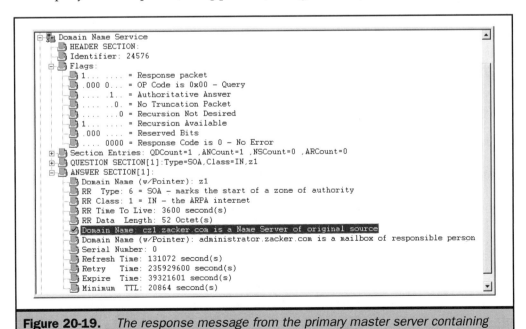

```
┌─────────────────────────────────────────────────────────────────────────┐
│ ⊟ 🖳 Domain Name Service                                                ▲ │
│   ─ 🗋 HEADER SECTION:                                                     │
│   ─ 🗋 Identifier: 24576                                                   │
│   ⊟ 🗋 Flags:                                                              │
│       ─ 🗋 0... .... = Request packet                                      │
│       ─ 🗋 .000 0... = OP Code is 0x00 - Query                             │
│       ─ 🗋 .... .0.. = Non-Authoritative Answer                           │
│       ─ 🗋 .... ..0. = No Truncation Packet                                │
│       ─ 🗋 .... ...0 = Recursion Not Desired                               │
│       ─ 🗋 0... .... = Recursion Not Available                             │
│       ─ 🗋 .000 .... = Reserved Bits                                       │
│       ─ 🗋 .... 0000 = Response Code is 0 - No Error                       │
│   ⊞ 🗋 Section Entries: QDCount=1 ,ANCount=0 ,NSCount=0 ,ARCount=0         │
│   ⊟ 🗋 QUESTION SECTION[1]:                                                │
│       ─ ☑ Domain Name: z1                                                  │
│       ─ 🗋 Query Type: 6 = SOA - marks the start of a zone of authority    │
│       ─ 🗋 Query Class: 1 = IN - the ARPA internet                       ▼ │
└─────────────────────────────────────────────────────────────────────────┘
```

Figure 20-18. *The SOA query message generated by a slave server to determine if a zone transfer is warranted*

connectionless, unreliable protocol in which there can be only one response message for each query, because the response message functions as the acknowledgment of the query. Because the primary master will almost certainly have to use multiple packets in order to send all of the resource records in the zone to the slave, a different protocol is needed. Therefore, before it transmits the zone transfer request message, the slave server initiates a TCP connection with the primary master using the standard three-way handshake. Once the connection is established, the slave transmits the AXFR query in a TCP packet, using port 53 (see Figure 20-20).

```
┌─────────────────────────────────────────────────────────────────────────┐
│ ⊟ 🖳 Domain Name Service                                                ▲ │
│   ─ 🗋 HEADER SECTION:                                                     │
│   ─ 🗋 Identifier: 24576                                                   │
│   ⊟ 🗋 Flags:                                                              │
│       ─ 🗋 1... .... = Response packet                                     │
│       ─ 🗋 .000 0... = OP Code is 0x00 - Query                             │
│       ─ 🗋 .... .1.. = Authoritative Answer                               │
│       ─ 🗋 .... ..0. = No Truncation Packet                                │
│       ─ 🗋 .... ...0 = Recursion Not Desired                               │
│       ─ 🗋 1... .... = Recursion Available                                 │
│       ─ 🗋 .000 .... = Reserved Bits                                       │
│       ─ 🗋 .... 0000 = Response Code is 0 - No Error                       │
│   ⊞ 🗋 Section Entries: QDCount=1 ,ANCount=1 ,NSCount=0 ,ARCount=0         │
│   ⊞ 🗋 QUESTION SECTION[1]:Type=SOA,Class=IN,z1                            │
│   ⊟ 🗋 ANSWER SECTION[1]:                                                  │
│       ─ 🗋 Domain Name (w/Pointer): z1                                     │
│       ─ 🗋 RR Type: 6 = SOA - marks the start of a zone of authority       │
│       ─ 🗋 RR Class: 1 = IN - the ARPA internet                           │
│       ─ 🗋 RR Time To Live: 3600 second(s)                                 │
│       ─ 🗋 RR Data Length: 52 Octet(s)                                     │
│       ─ ☑ Domain Name: cz1.zacker.com is a Name Server of original source │
│       ─ 🗋 Domain Name (w/Pointer): administrator.zacker.com is a mailbox of responsible person │
│       ─ 🗋 Serial Number: 0                                                │
│       ─ 🗋 Refresh Time: 131072 second(s)                                  │
│       ─ 🗋 Retry Time: 235929600 second(s)                                 │
│       ─ 🗋 Expire Time: 39321601 second(s)                                 │
│       ─ 🗋 Minimum TTL: 20864 second(s)                                  ▼ │
└─────────────────────────────────────────────────────────────────────────┘
```

Figure 20-19. *The response message from the primary master server containing the SOA resource record*

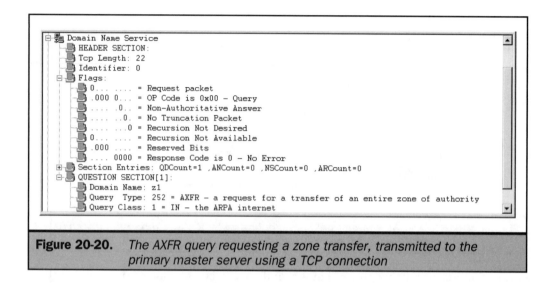

```
☐ 🖳 Domain Name Service
   ⬛ HEADER SECTION:
   ⬛ Tcp Length: 22
   ⬛ Identifier: 0
   ☐ ⬛ Flags:
      ⬛ 0... .... = Request packet
      ⬛ .000 0... = OP Code is 0x00 - Query
      ⬛ .... .0.. = Non-Authoritative Answer
      ⬛ .... ..0. = No Truncation Packet
      ⬛ .... ...0 = Recursion Not Desired
      ⬛ 0... .... = Recursion Not Available
      ⬛ .000 .... = Reserved Bits
      ⬛ .... 0000 = Response Code is 0 - No Error
   ⊞ ⬛ Section Entries: QDCount=1 ,ANCount=0 ,NSCount=0 ,ARCount=0
   ☐ ⬛ QUESTION SECTION[1]:
      ⬛ Domain Name: z1
      ⬛ Query Type: 252 = AXFR - a request for a transfer of an entire zone of authority
      ⬛ Query Class: 1 = IN - the ARPA internet
```

Figure 20-20.   *The AXFR query requesting a zone transfer, transmitted to the primary master server using a TCP connection*

In response to the query, the primary master server transmits all of the resource records in the requested zone as entries in the Answer section, as shown in Figure 20-21. Once all of the data has been transmitted, the two systems terminate the TCP connection in the usual manner, and the zone transfer is completed.

Obtaining DNS Services

On a private network that is connected to the Internet, you still can use your ISP's DNS servers, or you can run your own. If you are not running your own domain, then the network only needs the client capabilities of the DNS servers to resolve names into addresses. An organization that is hosting a domain must have DNS servers to function as the authority for that domain. NIS and other domain registrars require addresses for two DNS servers, for fault-tolerance purposes. Again, even if you are hosting a domain, you can still use your ISP's DNS servers. However, there will usually be an additional fee for domain hosting, whereas client access to the servers is virtually always included in the Internet access fee.

Domain Name Service
  HEADER SECTION:
  Tcp Length: 216
  Identifier: 0
  Flags:Resp,Query,Non-Auth,Recu Ava,RCode=No Error
  Section Entries: QDCount=1 ,ANCount=4 ,NSCount=0 ,ARCount=0
  QUESTION SECTION[1]:Type=AXFR,Class=IN,z1
  ANSWER SECTION[1]:
    Domain Name (w/Pointer):
    RR Type: 6 = SOA - marks the start of a zone of authority
    RR Class: 1 = IN - the ARPA internet
    RR Time To Live: 3600 second(s)
    RR Data Length: 62 Octet(s)
    Domain Name: cz1.zacker.com is a Name Server of original source
    Domain Name: administrator.zacker.com is a mailbox of responsible person
    Serial Number: 0
    Refresh Time: 131072 second(s)
    Retry   Time: 235929600 second(s)
    Expire Time: 39321601 second(s)
    Minimum TTL: 20864 second(s)
  ANSWER SECTION[2]:Type=MINFO,Class=-,
  ANSWER SECTION[3]:
    Domain Name (w/Pointer): cz1
    RR Type: 1 = A - a host address
    RR Class: 1 = IN - the ARPA internet
    RR Time To Live: 3600 second(s)
    RR Data Length: 4 Octet(s)
    An ARPA internet address: 192.168.2.10
  ANSWER SECTION[4]:
    Domain Name (w/Pointer):
    RR Type: 6 = SOA - marks the start of a zone of authority
    RR Class: 1 = IN - the ARPA internet
    RR Time To Live: 3600 second(s)
    RR Data Length: 62 Octet(s)
    Domain Name: cz1.zacker.com is a Name Server of original source
    Domain Name: administrator.zacker.com is a mailbox of responsible person
    Serial Number: 0
    Refresh Time: 131072 second(s)
    Retry   Time: 235929600 second(s)
    Expire Time: 39321601 second(s)
    Minimum TTL: 20864 second(s)

Figure 20-21.   *One packet from a zone transfer transmitted by the primary master server*

Outsourcing DNS Services

The advantages of using the ISP's DNS servers are convenience, accessibility, and fault tolerance. Having the ISP maintain the DNS records for your domain is certainly easier than doing it yourself, and a reliable ISP will have redundant, high-speed Internet connections that ensure your domain's continuous availability to Internet users. A good ISP should also have fault-tolerance mechanisms available to keep its servers running, such as backup power supplies and redundant disk arrays.

The disadvantages of outsourcing your domain hosting chores are the expense and maintenance delays that can result. To make a change in your DNS configuration, you have to call your ISP, who may or may not perform the requested task in a timely manner. In addition, some ISPs charge you for each change that you make to the DNS records, in addition to a monthly hosting fee. This means that every new host or e-mail address you want to add to your domain will cost you money.

Another thing to watch out for are ISPs that offer complete domain hosting packages in which they fill out the forms and send them to the domain registrar, all for one price that includes the registration fee. This can be a nice convenience, but some ISPs supply themselves as all three of the contacts required by the registrar. Only the three people designated as the billing, technical, and administrative contacts are permitted to modify the domain registration information. If you ever decide to change ISPs, the domain records must be changed to reflect different DNS servers, and your old provider is not likely to do this for you after you've dumped it for a competitor. You may, therefore, lose control of the domain name that you've paid for.

To prevent this from happening, you should always register the domain name yourself. NSI provides online forms at its Web site that make the process quite easy, and you can charge the fee to a credit card. Be sure to supply contact names of people who you know will be involved in the organization for some time to come.

Running Your Own DNS Servers

The practicality of running DNS servers on your own network depends on several factors, including which DNS server implementation you will use, how large your network is, and how much maintenance is required. On a UNIX network, for example, all of the workstations usually have to be registered in the DNS server's database, while a Windows or NetWare network might need only a few registered hosts.

Most of the DNS servers on the Internet today run a variation of UNIX, Windows NT, or Windows 2000. Novell also has a DNS server product that runs on a NetWare server. All of these servers are compliant with the core DNS standards and provide basically the same functions in the same way, but with different interfaces. Windows NT and 2000 are by far the easiest to install, configure, and maintain, because they provide a graphical interface to the server's database files. The DNS Manager in Windows NT Server 4.0 and the DNS snap-in for Microsoft Management Console in Windows 2000 Server both enable you to view the information in the DNS database and in the cache (see Figure 20-22). Creating and modifying resource records and configuring server properties is a simple matter of navigating standard Windows dialog boxes and controls.

As is usually the case, the DNS servers included with most UNIX variants are powerful, flexible, and far less user friendly than their Windows counterparts. The

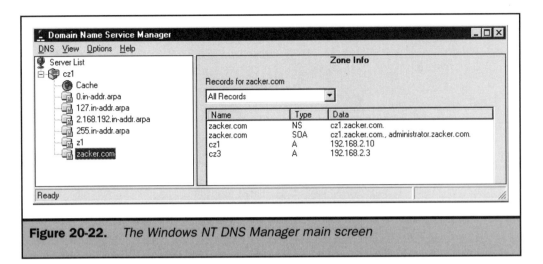

Figure 20-22. *The Windows NT DNS Manager main screen*

most popular of these is BIND (Berkeley Internet Name Domain), which was written
for use with BSD UNIX and has since been ported to many other operating systems,
including Windows NT. As with most UNIX programs, BIND does not have a fancy
interface. To configure the server or add and modify resource records, you must
edit the program's database files directly, the syntax for which can be rather cryptic.
Virtually anyone can create a new resource record in Windows NT's DNS Manager,
but working with BIND is more difficult, and less forgiving of mistakes.

Despite its relative ease of use, however, the NT/2000 DNS servers remain
compatible with the UNIX implementations, because they store most of their data in
the same database files that BIND uses. In fact, the primary function of the Microsoft
DNS Manager utility and the Windows 2000 DNS snap-in is to provide a graphical
editor for these database files.

The usability of NetWare's DNS server falls somewhere between that of Windows
NT and UNIX. You configure the program and create resource records using UNICON,
a character-based, menu-driven utility that runs on the NetWare server.

With one important exception, you can use any of these DNS server implementations
on your network, or even a combination of them. As long as a DNS server is compliant
with the RFC 1034 and RFC 1035 standards, it will be able to interact with another
compliant server. Therefore, you can run a primary master server on Windows NT and
a slave on UNIX if you wish, or any other combination.

The exception is when you are running a Windows 2000 network that uses Active
Directory. Active Directory relies heavily on DNS, and the DNS server included with
the Windows 2000 Server products is compliant with RFC 2052, which implements the
SVR resource record type, and RFC 2136, which provides the Update message. Active
Directory needs these additional features in order to register its domain controllers in
the DNS database and keep the information current. Therefore, you should stick to
Windows 2000 DNS servers if you are using Active Directory.

The Complete Reference

Upgrading & Troubleshooting Networks

Part VI

Network Directory Services

Chapter 21

Novell Directory
Services

As originally conceived, Novell NetWare was an operating system designed to provide multiple users with access to file and print resources on a common server. To control access to the server, NetWare included a flat file database called the *bindery*, which consisted of user accounts, passwords, and other basic properties. Administrators granted access to specific resources on the server by selecting users from the bindery.

As NetWare grew in popularity, it became common for an organization to have multiple servers, each of which had its own bindery. To add a new user, administrators had to create an account in the bindery of each server to which the user needed access. When the network had a handful of servers, this repetitive chore could be irritating, but it was still possible. When large networks grew to the point of having dozens or hundreds of NetWare servers, maintaining individual binderies on each machine became increasingly impractical.

To address this problem, Novell created a directory service that would function as a central repository for information about an entire enterprise network. Administrators create a single account for each user in the directory service, and then can use that account to grant the user access to resources anywhere in the enterprise. Based largely on the X.500 standard developed by the International Organization for Standardization (ISO), NetWare Directory Services (NDS) first appeared as part of the NetWare 4 operating system in 1993. While somewhat unstable at first, NDS has had a long time to mature, and has also undergone a name change from NetWare Directory Services to Novell Directory Services, which reflects the utility of the product for applications and operating systems other than NetWare.

In the commercial networking industry, NDS has become the pattern for the development, deployment, and adaptation of a directory service into a general-purpose networking tool. Microsoft's Active Directory service, first released in Windows 2000, clearly builds on the foundation created by NDS. The use of a single storehouse for information about all of a network's hardware, software, human, and organizational resources greatly simplifies the job of the network administrator, and Novell was the first company to create a commercial enterprise directory service and deploy it on a large scale.

NDS can now run on UNIX and Windows NT servers as well as on NetWare, and is the most widely deployed directory service on the planet. The popularity of NetWare has certainly suffered in the face of competition from Windows NT and Windows 2000, but Novell has had a huge head start in its directory service, and NDS remains far ahead of the competition in its flexibility and stability. Even though Active Directory has a great deal of potential, the fact remains that Novell and its partners have had seven years to exploit the capabilities of NDS, while AD is just leaving the starting gate.

NDS Architecture

NDS is essentially a database that is comprised of objects arranged in a hierarchical tree, just like that of a file system (see Figure 21-1). At the top of the tree is a theoretical object called [Root], from which all the other objects stem. *Objects* are logical entities that can represent users, hardware, software, and organizational components. Each object consists of a collection of *properties* that contain information about the object. For example, an object representing a user called John Doe might be called jdoe, and might contain a property called Telephone Number, and the value of that property would be John Doe's telephone number. The other properties for a user object contain identification information about the user, as well as a list of the groups to which the user belongs, the user's permissions to other objects in the NDS tree, and many other account restrictions.

Administrators can use any one of three tools to create objects and specify values for their properties. NetWare Administrator is a Windows application, available in versions for Windows 3.*x*, 9*x*, NT, and 2000, that provides a graphical view of the NDS tree and its elements (see Figure 21-2). NetWare Administrator is the easiest and most versatile tool to use for these and other NDS maintenance tasks. Each object in the tree has its own Details dialog box that enables you to modify the object's property values.

Netadmin.exe is a menu-driven, character-based utility that you can run from the command prompt in any DOS-based operating system (see Figure 21-3). The interface is not as intuitive as that of NetWare Administrator, and does not perform all of the same functions, but the program has the advantage of being very fast.

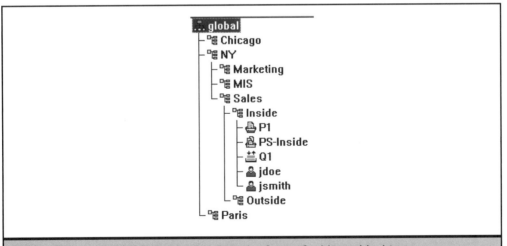

Figure 21-1.   *The NDS database takes the form of a hierarchical tree*

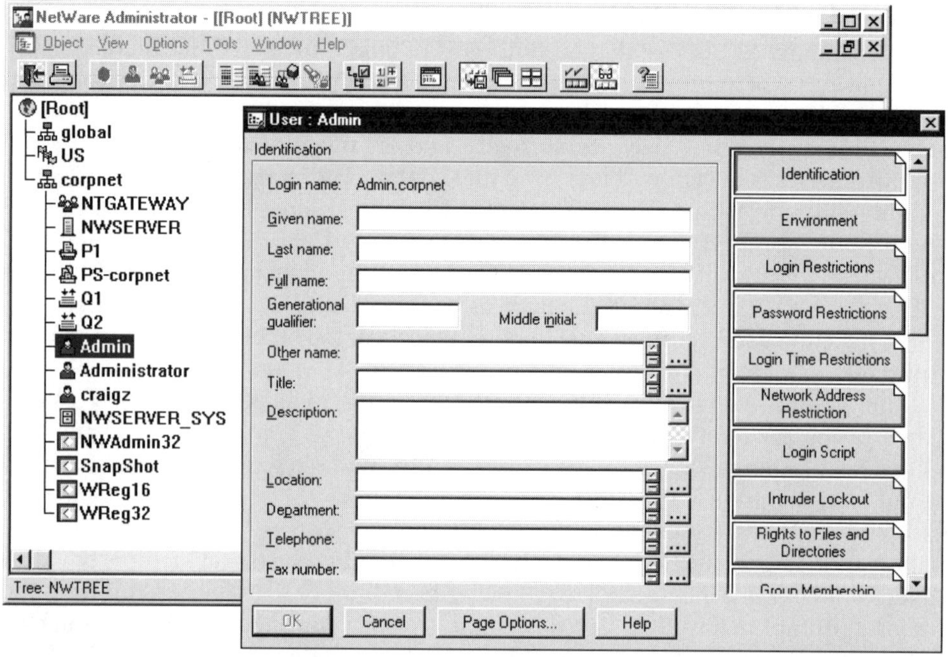

Figure 21-2. *NetWare Administrator tree display and Details dialog box*

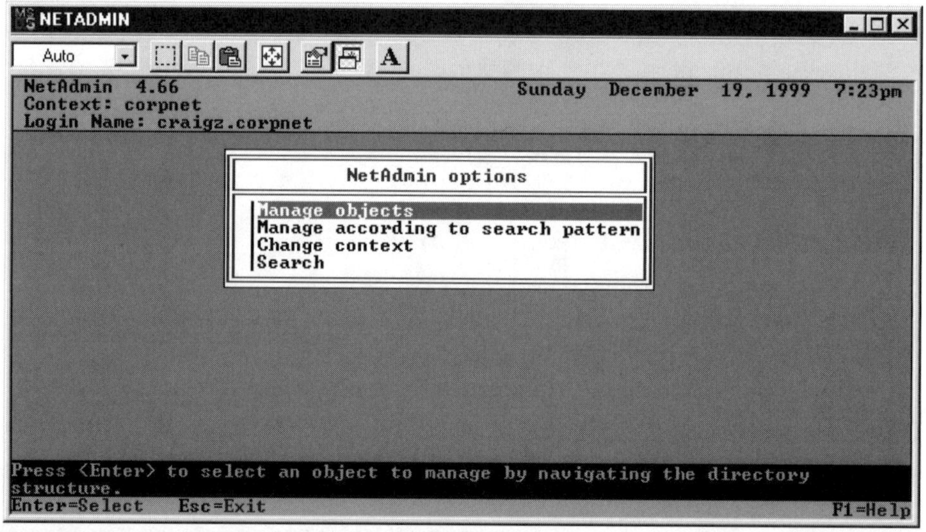

Figure 21-3. *Netadmin.exe main screen*

ConsoleOne is a Java-based administration console (see Figure 21-4) first introduced in NetWare 5 that is designed for use with large enterprise networks. ConsoleOne provides NetWare and NDS administration capabilities on any platform that supports Java, including NetWare servers. A Web browser version of ConsoleOne enables any user with a Java-capable browser to work with the NDS database, even if no other NDS client is installed on the workstation.

Containers and Leaves

There are two types of objects used to build the NDS tree, called *container objects* and *leaf objects*. As the name implies, a container object is one that has other objects subordinate to it, forming a branch of the tree. A leaf object cannot contain other objects, just as the leaves of a tree represent the endpoints of a branch.

Most of the container objects in an NDS tree are purely theoretical constructs that need not have any relationship to the physical objects they contain. For example, country, organization, and organizational unit objects exist only to form the hierarchy of the tree and to contain other objects. You can build the tree using these container objects to represent geographical locations, political divisions in your organization (such as departments), or any other paradigm. These objects simplify the process of assigning the same property values to multiple objects. When you modify a property of a container object, all of the objects in that container inherit the value for that property. For example, you can grant a container object the right to access a specific directory on a server, and every user object in that container will inherit that right.

Apart from user objects, there are other types of leaf objects in an NDS tree, representing NetWare servers, printers, applications, and other elements. Each object type has properties that are specific to the entity that the object represents. In addition to the default objects that you can create in the NDS database, it is possible for software developers to create new object types, or new properties for existing object types. The

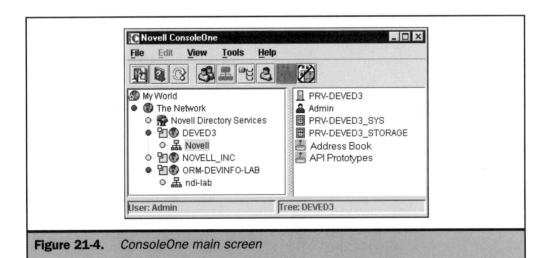

Figure 21-4.   *ConsoleOne main screen*

capabilities of NDS are defined by its schema, which specifies what kind of objects can exist in the database, the properties of those objects, and the relationships between the different object types. Applications can modify the schema by adding new object types that are specifically designed for use by that application. For example, Novell's ZENworks product modifies the schema to enable the creation of objects representing network workstations. Novell has also published software developer's kits (SDKs) that enable third-party developers to create their own schema modifications.

Objects and Properties

The object types included by default with NetWare 4.*x*, their functions, and their icons in NetWare Administrator are listed in Table 21-1. You can create objects of these types using the NDS management utilities immediately upon installing NetWare.

Object Icon	Object Name	Description
	AFP Server	Represents an AppleTalk Filing Protocol server.
	Alias	Functions as a duplicate of another object in the tree; enables the same object to exist in multiple contexts.
	Country	Represents a country in which the network has resources.
	Directory Map	References a particular directory on a NetWare file server; enables NetWare-aware utilities to reference the literal directory using the directory map object name.
	Group	Represents a group of users located anywhere in the NDS tree.
	Locality	Represents a geographical location in the NDS tree.
	NetWare Server	Represents a server running the NetWare operating system.

Table 21-1. *Default NetWare 4.11 Object Types*

Object Icon	Object Name	Description
	Organization	Container object that represents an organization or company.
	Organizational Role	Represents a job responsibility that requires specific access rights to network resources.
	Organizational Unit	Container object that represents a department or division of an organization or company.
	Print Queue	Represents a NetWare print queue.
	Print Server (Non NDPS)	Represents a NetWare print server.
	Printer (Non NDPS)	Represents a NetWare printer.
	Profile	Represents a login script that can be assigned to users.
	Template	A leaf object that enables the rapid creation of multiple leaf objects with similar characteristics.
	User	Represents a network user.
	Volume	Represents a NetWare server volume.

Table 21-1. *Default NetWare 4.11 Object Types* (continued)

As an example of NDS's expandability, the current Novell client software packages ship with the ZENworks Starter Pack, which includes the Novell Application Launcher and Workstation Manager. Both of these applications include schema extensions that add the new object types shown in Table 21-2.

Object Icon	Object Name	Description
	Application	Represents a networked application.
	Application Folder	Container for application objects displayed in Novell Application Launcher.
	Computer	Represents a nonserver computer on the network.
	Policy Package	Contains a collection of policies related to specific object types.
	Workstation	Represents a client workstation on the network.
	Workstation Group	Container holding a collection of workstation objects.

Table 21-2. *Object Types Added by the ZENworks Starter Pack*

The schema also defines the properties for each type of object in the NDS database, which are dependent on the function of the object. Some properties are mandatory, meaning that the object must have a value for them, while others are optional and can be left blank. Object properties carry information that falls into any of four categories, which are as follows:

■ **Names**   Every object must have a name, of course, by which it is referenced in the NDS tree; but other properties can carry more complete naming information, such as a user's full name (for example, John Doe), as well as the object name (for example, jdoe).

■ **Addresses**   Objects that represent hardware components, such as servers and printers, can have network addresses; but mailing addresses, telephone numbers, and other contact information are optional properties, often overlooked by administrators, that can be useful both to other users and to support personnel.

■ **Descriptions**   Informational properties may not have technical functions, but taking the time to provide information about the type of equipment that an object represents, for example, or its exact location, can greatly reduce the support burden for network resources.

■ **Memberships** The relationships of an object to other objects in the tree are among the most important types of property information. Group objects, for example, contain a list of their members, and virtually all objects contain a list of their trustees.

NDS Object Naming

The hierarchical structure of the NDS database functions not only as an organizational paradigm, but also as a means of uniquely identifying each object in the tree. In a flat file database like the bindery in older NetWare versions, every object has a single name that must be unique. This is practical for a single server solution like the bindery, but for an enterprise directory service like NDS, it is far more likely that you will run into a situation in which you want to have two objects with the same name. If, for example, there is a Joanne Smith who works in the Marketing department and a Joe Smith in Sales, your naming convention for user objects might require that both people have the username jsmith.

In an NDS tree, you can have two objects with the same name, as long as they are in different contexts. The *context* of an object is simply its location in the NDS tree, as identified by the names of the containers in which it resides, stretching all the way up to the root, and separated by periods. Each object in the NDS tree is uniquely identified by a combination of the object name and its context. This combination is called the object's *distinguished name (DN)*. Thus, these two users can both exist in the tree with the same object name, using the following DNs:

```
jsmith.NY.Sales.corpnet
jsmith.Chicago.Marketing.corpnet
```

In these names, the context specifies the path from the [Root] object at the right (theoretically, since [Root] never actually appears in a distinguished name) down through the NDS tree to the object. The corpnet container is an organization object at the top layer of the tree, closest to the [Root], and is therefore said to be the *most significant* object in the name. The object that is farthest away from the root is the *least significant* object.

Using the Context

All applications and operating system functions that request information from the NDS database do so using the distinguished name of the object needed. However, when you perform an operation that triggers an NDS call, like entering your username into a login dialog box, you never type the entire distinguished name of your user object, because the application automatically appends your current context to whatever object name you specify.

The user's default context is somehow specified in the client software that provides access to NDS, such as in a Windows registry or Net.cfg file entry, depending on the client operating system used. With the default context in place, the user can reference any other object in the same context using only its object name, which in this case would be called a *relative distinguished name* or *partial name*.

This automatic use of the context by applications and other software is why it is best to design your NDS tree so that users tend to be in the same container as the resources they access most often. To access files on a server in the same context, for example, a user can simply specify the server name. If the server is in a different context, however, the user has to specify either the complete distinguished name of the server or a context qualifier to indicate the name of the context in which the server is located.

It is possible to change your current context after logging in to the NDS tree using the NetWare Administrator, Netadmin.exe, or Cx.exe utility, enabling you to identify resources in the new context by using only their object names. However, most users have no conception of what the NDS tree is and how contexts work, and will not usually do this. The most common method used today to reference objects in other contexts is to browse through the containers in the NDS tree using a graphical dialog box like that shown in Figure 21-5. Selecting an object in another container automatically returns the distinguished name of that object to the application.

Thus, for clients logged in to the NDS tree, the primary function of the context is to simplify the process of referring to other objects in the same container. Contexts

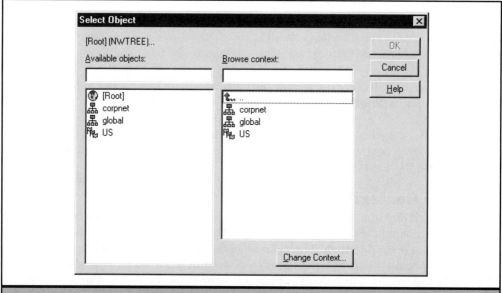

Figure 21-5.   *The Select Object dialog box enables users to browse through the NDS tree to locate a specific object*

also serve a function on NetWare servers, however. When clients who do not support NDS log in to a network, NetWare 4.*x* and 5.*x* servers can emulate the bindery used by NetWare 3.*x* and earlier versions. In order to support *bindery emulation,* you have to create one or more bindery contexts on a NetWare server using SET commands. These commands identify the only contexts that bindery clients can access. To the client, it appears as though the system is logging in to a bindery server, when actually it is logging in to a limited area of the NDS tree.

Typeful and Typeless Names

There are two ways of notating the distinguished name of any object in an NDS tree. The names used as examples so far are called *typeless* names, because they do not specify the object type for each name. A *typeful* name includes an abbreviation for each object name that specifies its type, in the following format:

```
CN=jsmith.OU=NY.OU=Sales.O=corpnet
CN=jsmith.OU=Chicago.OU=Marketing.O=corpnet
```

The abbreviations that can be used in typeful names are as follows:

- **C** Country
- **O** Organization
- **OU** Organizational Unit
- **CN (Common Name)** All leaf objects

The distinguished names supplied by applications and operating systems making NDS calls are always typeful names; however, a user almost never has to supply a typeful name manually because clients use the *default typing rules*, which usually function correctly, to add the abbreviations to distinguished names. The default typing rules are as follows:

- The least significant partial name in a distinguished name should be designated as a leaf object and given the CN abbreviation.
- The most significant partial name in a distinguished name should be designated as an organization object and given the O abbreviation.
- All of the partial names between the least significant name and the most significant name should be designated as organizational unit objects and given the OU abbreviation.

Virtually the only time when these rules do not function properly is when the NDS tree uses Country objects at its top layer. Country objects are a vestige from X.500, which was designed to be a true global directory service. It is because of the default typing rules that the use of Country objects in an NDS tree is generally discouraged, even for multinational organizations.

| Note | *When applying the default typing rules, an NDS client makes no attempt to check whether or not an object of the type it assigns actually exists. If, for example, you use Country objects in your NDS tree, clients will submit names typed using these rules, and the names will all fail, because even though the name of the most significant container object will be correct, the type will be wrong.* |

Using Context Qualifiers

If, for any reason, you want to enter the name of an object in another context into an application, you can usually do so without typing the object's entire distinguished name, but you must be conscious of your current context when you do so. When you specify the name of a leaf object, your NDS client appends your current context to it. Thus, suppose a user is logged in to an NDS tree using the following default context:

```
OU=NY.OU=Sales.O=corpnet
```

When the user attempts to access a server called NW1 and manually types that name into an application dialog box, the NDS client uses the following distinguished name for the server in its call to the NDS database:

```
CN=NW1.OU=NY.OU=Sales.O=corpnet
```

If there is a second server, called NW2, that is located in the Chicago.Sales.corpnet container, the user can avoid typing the server's entire distinguished name by supplying only the name of the server object itself and that of its least significant container, which is the only part that is different from the user's current context. However, if the user supplies the name NW2.Chicago in the application, the client still appends the user's context, resulting in the following nonexistent name:

```
CN=NW2.OU=Chicago.OU=NY.OU=Sales.O=corpnet
```

The user wants to replace the NY container in the name with Chicago, not just add the Chicago container. To do this, you use a *context qualifier*, which essentially is a signal to the client instructing it to suppress a certain part of the context when it appends it to the name supplied by the user.

TRIMMED MASKING   The most commonly used type of context qualifier is called *trimmed masking,* which consists of adding a period to the end of the partial name supplied to the application for each container that you want omitted from the context when it is appended to that name. Thus, if you supply the name NW2.Chicago.

(including the trailing period), the client will omit the NY container from the context and append only OU=Sales.O=corpnet, resulting in the following name, which is correct:

```
CN=NW2.OU=Chicago.OU=Sales.O=corpnet
```

If the user were to supply the name NW2.Chicago.. (including two trailing periods), the client would omit both the NY and Sales containers from the context, resulting in the following incorrect name:

```
CN=NW2.OU=Chicago.O=corpnet
```

PRECEDING PERIODS   Another form of context identifier involves the insertion of a period before the name supplied to an application. When you do this, the client applies the object types of the user's current context to the object names supplied after the period. Thus, if a user with the context OU=NY.OU=Sales.O=corpnet.C=US enters the name .NW2.Paris.Marketing.corpnet.FR into an application, the client will take the object type from each of the four containers in the context and apply them to the names supplied, resulting in the following distinguished name:

```
CN=NW2.OU=Paris.OU=Marketing.O=corpnet.C=FR
```

The only time this technique is necessary is when the NDS tree uses Country objects, and the default typing rules would result in an incorrect name. When you use the preceding period, the name you supply to the application must include the same number of container names as in the context. In other words, you supply a typeless distinguished name, and the preceding period enables the client to type it correctly.

Note   *Context qualifiers are not often needed anymore, because most operating systems enable users to browse the NDS tree in a GUI and select an object, rather than type the object's name. One of the instances in which you might use these techniques is when changing your current context using the NetWare CX utility. Cx.exe is a command-line program that enables you to navigate the NDS tree, much as the DOS CD command enables you to move around in a computer's file system.*

Partitions and Replicas

For NDS to be an effective repository for information about an entire enterprise network, the database can't be located on a single server. Not only would this be inefficient for access by systems that are separated from that server by relatively slow WAN links, but the failure of that one server could bring the entire network to a halt. To protect the database and make it accessible to users and administrators all over the network, NDS can be both partitioned and replicated.

Partitioning refers to splitting the database into segments, each of which is stored on a different server. Each partition is, in effect, a branch of the NDS tree. Creating partitions makes it possible to keep the objects in the NDS tree near to the physical entities they represent. For example, a company with four offices in remote cities connected by WAN links can split its NDS database into four partitions, each containing the users, servers, and other objects for one site and stored on a server at that site. This way, users logging in to the network do not have to access their user objects on a server at another site over a slow WAN link.

Even when WAN links are not involved, however, creating partitions on several servers helps to spread the NDS traffic around the network. When the entire database is stored on one server, every process that requires access to NDS objects must send traffic to that server. This may not be a problem if the server is located on a backbone or other high-speed network that can handle the traffic, but creating partitions on servers connected to different LANs balances the traffic load among several different network segments.

Replica Types

Partitioning the NDS tree creates a measure of fault tolerance, because the failure of one server does not render the entire database unavailable. However, it's possible to make the database even more fault-tolerant by replicating it. A *replica* is an exact duplicate of an NDS partition or the entire database that is stored on another server. You can create as many replicas of a partition as you want, with each one on a different server. The replicas of a specific partition are known collectively as a *replica ring*. If a server containing part of the NDS tree should fail, users and applications can still access the database from one of its replicas.

NDS recognizes four different types of replicas, as follows:

- **Master replica**   The primary copy of a particular partition. There can only be one master replica of a partition. All partition management tasks, such as the creation of new replicas, must be performed on this replica, during which time all other replicas are locked.

- **Read-write replica**   A copy of a partition that users and applications can access to process login and authentication requests, and that administrators can access to make changes to the database.

- **Read-only replica**   A copy of a partition that users and applications can access to process login and authentication requests, but which cannot be modified by an administration utility. This type of replica is updated only by the NDS synchronization process.

- **Subordinate reference replica**   Special-purpose replicas of subordinate partitions created on a server to point to the locations of those subordinate partitions on other servers. When a read-write or read-only replica of a subordinate partition is created on the same server as the parent partition, the subordinate reference replica for that partition is deleted.

Creating Partitions and Replicas

Administrators create partitions using either NDS Manager or Partition Manager. NDS Manager is a Windows utility that provides a graphical view of all of an NDS database's partitions and replicas (see Figure 21-6). Partition Manager is a DOS-based alternative that provides roughly the same functions without the comprehensive overview.

Creating a partition is simply a matter of selecting a container in the tree. That container plus all of the objects in it (both containers and leaves) become part of the new partition. The selected container is then known as the *partition root object*. The partition root object tracks both the replicas of the partition that exist elsewhere on the network and the status of the replica synchronization process. Partitions with root objects that are closer to the [Root] of the NDS tree are said to be *superior* to the partition, and those with root objects farther from the [Root] are said to be *subordinate*.

Once you have created a partition, you can at any time select a container object within that partition and split it off into a partition of its own. You can also create new replicas of a partition at any time. The NDS tree can, therefore, grow to accommodate your network.

The number of partitions and replicas that you create should be based on the number of servers you have available, the capabilities of those servers, the needs of the network's users, and the layout of the network itself. In the case of the network mentioned earlier, consisting of four WAN-connected sites, creating a separate partition for each site is a logical solution. In addition, creating read-write replicas of the other three partitions on each of the four servers is a good idea (assuming that the servers are capable of hosting them), because then the users at each site can access the entire NDS database locally. The only directory service traffic that passes over the WAN links is for the synchronization of the database.

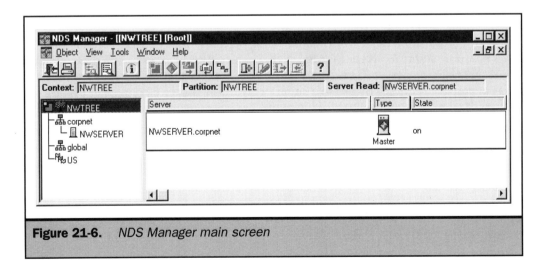

Figure 21-6.   *NDS Manager main screen*

Walking the Tree

No matter how many partitions and replicas an NDS tree has and no matter where they're located, the NDS tree always appears as a single functional entity to the applications that utilize it. Every server that hosts any replica of an NDS partition functions as a *name server* and can locate the resource referenced by any NDS object name. Object name requests always specify the full distinguished name of the requested object. When a name server receives the request, it first checks its own partitions for the object. When the requested object does not exist in the server's own partitions, it must search for it on the network's other name servers. The process by which the server does this is called *walking the tree,* which involves searching the partitions on the other name servers for the requested name in a systematic fashion.

The partition root object of every partition contains a list of the other partitions that are directly superior and directly subordinate to it. If the server recognizes any of the containers in the requested name as being part of a subordinate partition, it can pass the request downward through the tree to the appropriate name server. If the name server makes no such recognition, then it must pass the request farther up the tree toward the [Root] object.

Any object in the tree can be located by searching from the [Root] object, but this is not a practical method, because it would overburden the server containing the [Root] partition and possibly create multiple delays if that server is connected using a slow WAN link. Instead, a name server processing a request passes it to the name server that is immediately superior to it in the tree hierarchy. That server then searches its own partitions and satisfies the request, or passes it down to a subordinate name server of its own, or passes it up to the next-superior server. Eventually, a name server will recognize one of the containers in the request name and be able to route the request down to the server containing the correct partition. This way, the request only gets passed up as far as is needed to find the name.

For example, consider the name server hierarchy shown in Figure 21-7. Suppose that an application sends a request for a user object called jdoe.Chicago.Sales to Server D. The partition on Server D contains the objects in the NY.Sales container, but it has no information about Chicago.Sales. Since the partition subordinate to Server D (Inside.NY.Sales on Server F) must have NY.Sales in its context, Server D knows that it has to pass the request upward to a superior partition. Server B contains the Sales partition and recognizes that part of the requested object name, but it does not contain the Chicago.Sales partition. However, Server B does recognize that Chicago.Sales must be subordinate to Sales, so it passes the request to Server E, which does contain the Chicago.Sales partition. This server can therefore locate the jdoe.Chicago.Sales object and supply the requested information.

In this particular case, the difference between using the tree-walking process and simply sending the request to the [Root] partition is only one layer in the tree; but in a larger network with more layers of partitions, walking the tree can be much faster than querying the [Root] partition. This scenario also assumes that the name servers

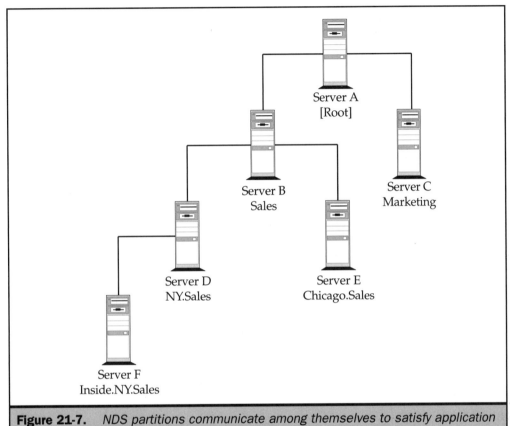

Figure 21-7.   *NDS partitions communicate among themselves to satisfy application requests*

each host only a single partition. Creating replicas of several partitions on a name server reduces the number of other servers involved in the tree-walking process.

NDS Synchronization

The messages exchanged by the name servers during the tree-walking process are only one of the ways in which the various NDS replicas communicate with each other. In the same way that an application can use any name server to access the entire NDS database, an administrator modifying the database can make changes to any replica that permits writes (which means the master replica or any read-write replica). Once the changes have been made, however, they must be propagated to all of the other replicas of that partition, so that applications accessing the NDS database retrieve the same information, no matter which replica they use. This process is called *synchronization,* and it is responsible for most of the traffic between NDS name servers.

A directory service that functions this way is said to use *multiple master replication,* meaning that you can make changes to any one of several replicas. In a *single master replication* system, such as that used by Windows NT domains, all changes to the database must be made to one specific replica (the primary domain controller, in Windows NT), and then that system propagates the changes to the other replicas. The pattern of replication traffic in the two systems is shown in Figure 21-8.

The advantage of multiple master replication is that administrators can perform their database maintenance activities on a local replica, rather than having to access a name server that may be a long distance away or on the other side of a WAN link. The disadvantage is that the synchronization process is much more complicated. In a single master replication system, the synchronization traffic travels in only one direction, and there is no possibility of conflicting information. In a system that uses multiple master replication, it is possible for two administrators to make changes to different replicas of the same partition at nearly the same time. Each of the replicas must then send the modifications to all of the other replicas. If both administrators have modified the same datum, the synchronization processes will conflict, and there must be a mechanism for determining which version takes priority.

For example, suppose that two NDS administrators modify the same user object on two different replicas at roughly the same time. One administrator changes the user's telephone number, and the other administrator modifies the user's account password. The synchronization system must function so that, at the end of the synchronization process, the object in both replicas has the new telephone number and the new password. Thus, in this case, the process is not simply a matter of overwriting the

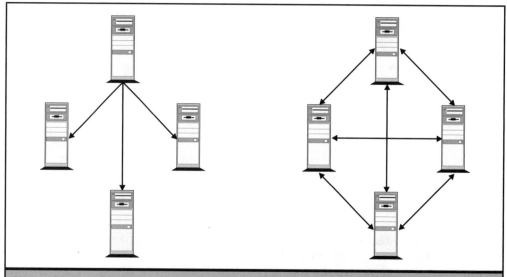

Figure 21-8. *Single master replication traffic moves in one direction, while in multiple master replication, servers communicate bidirectionally*

object on one replica with the object from another. The data in both copies of the object must be combined.

To complicate matters further, it is also possible for the modifications themselves to conflict. Suppose, for example, that a user calls a network administrator to give the administrator the user's new telephone number, realizes soon after that he has given the administrator the wrong number, and then calls again to remedy the error, but talks to a different administrator this time. The first administrator modifies the user's object on one replica by entering the new (incorrect) number, and a few seconds later, before the synchronization process can take place, the second administrator modifies the same object on another replica, entering the correct phone number this time. When the synchronization process begins, the systems must have a way of determining which version of the data should take precedence over the other.

The NDS synchronization process can overcome both of these problems; but while it is quite efficient, it isn't perfect, because it can't update all of the replicas in real time. It is still possible for an application to access outdated information from the database during the brief period before the synchronization process has completed. For this reason, the NDS database is said to be *loosely synchronized*. Replicas that are in the process of synchronizing are said to be *converging*. When the convergence process is completed and the replicas of each partition are identical, the database is said to be *fully synchronized*.

Time Synchronization

The NDS synchronization process is based on *time stamps* that are assigned to each modification made to the database. Name servers use these time stamps to determine which data should take precedence when a conflict occurs. In order for the time stamps to be accurate, it is essential that all of the name servers on an NDS network have their clocks synchronized. Keeping the clocks in synch on a collection of computers is more complicated than it may seem. The first problem is that the servers may be located at different sites, in different time zones, and with different daylight saving time policies. The second problem is that PC clocks are notorious for being wildly inaccurate.

To keep their clocks synchronized, NetWare servers use a program called Timesync.nlm. Each of the servers uses SAP (Service Advertising Protocol) messages to transmit messages containing a UTC (Universal Time Coordinated) signal, which is the same as Greenwich Mean Time. Every NetWare NDS server on the network also includes a series of SET commands in its Autoexec.ncf file that specify how the server should keep time. These commands appear as follows:

```
SET TIME ZONE = EST5EDT
SET DAYLIGHT SAVINGS TIME OFFSET = 1
SET START OF DAYLIGHT SAVINGS TIME = (APRIL SUNDAY FIRST  2:00:00 AM)
SET END OF DAYLIGHT SAVINGS TIME = (OCTOBER SUNDAY LAST  2:00:00 AM)
SET DEFAULT TIME SERVER TYPE = REFERENCE
```

The functions of the first four commands are self-explanatory, and can contain various values depending on the geographical location of the server. The last command specifies how the server should interact with the other servers on the network when processing time signals. The possible values are as follows:

- **Primary**   Exchanges time signal messages with the other primary and reference time servers on the network to compute the average time and adjust its clock.

- **Secondary**   Periodically requests a time signal from a primary or reference server and adjusts its clock accordingly.

- **Single Reference**   Maintains a unilateral time setting without communicating with other servers. Used on a network with only one time server.

- **Reference**   Participates in the computation of average server time, but unlike primary and secondary time servers, does not adjust its clock, because the server is assumed to be calibrated by an external time source—such as a radio clock or modem connection.

Note	*It is not necessarily imperative that all of the name servers participating in an NDS tree keep the correct time, only that they are synchronized to exactly the same time.*

Creating an effective time-synchronization strategy on a medium-to-large network is a tradeoff between the amount of network traffic generated by the process and the fault tolerance of the system. You can designate all of your NDS servers as primary or reference time servers, but then these systems will constantly be exchanging messages in order to compute the average time. At the other extreme, you can create one primary or reference server and designate all of the others as secondaries; but then if the primary time server should fail, you lose calibration for the entire network. A reasonable medium between these two extremes is the best solution.

NDS Tree Design

One of the most important elements of using NDS effectively is designing a tree that is suitable for your enterprise. This is not a task to be taken lightly or improvised as you create the objects in the tree. For all but the smallest networks, the tree design will have an immediate effect on the efficiency of the network. A badly designed tree will slow down user logins and access to network resources and make the task of administering the NDS database more difficult.

It isn't easy to sit down with a blank sheet of paper and design an NDS tree. It takes experience with the administration tools and with the effects of design changes on network performance to become an NDS expert. None of the tree design decisions that you make are irrevocable. In fact, just the opposite is the case. The tools provided with NDS enable you to create a tree that can evolve both with your increasing expertise and with the changes in your network. You can move objects to different containers and even shift whole branches to other locations in the tree. Just as with the file system on a network server, though, making drastic changes like these can confuse the other people who access the tree.

When you install the first NDS name server on your network, the installation program enables you to create a simple tree hierarchy that consists of an organization object and (optionally) a few organizational unit objects. An object representing the new server is then created in one of these containers. For a simple, one-server network, this is all the tree structure you need. Just create your user objects in the same container as the server object, and you are ready to go. In this capacity, the way NDS functions isn't much different from how the old NetWare bindery functioned. However, NDS was designed for use on larger networks, even truly huge ones, and the tree-design process naturally gets more complex when this is the case.

Tree Design Rules

An effective NDS tree must be logical in its construction, to make it easy for users and administrators to locate particular objects. You can, for example, create container objects using the colors of the rainbow as names and randomly distribute your network's user and server objects among them; but this artificial construct would make it very difficult to find anything, and the relationships between the objects would be difficult to manage.

Two fundamental concepts should guide virtually all of your NDS tree design decisions: *rights inheritance* and *ease of access*. In an NDS tree, rights flow downward through the tree, and this policy greatly simplifies the administration process. When an administrator grants access rights to a container, all the objects in that container inherit those rights. Assigning rights to a single container object is far easier than assigning them individually to many different user objects.

Rights inheritance is one of the main reasons why you should try to group together users with similar access requirements. You could conceivably create a tree with containers named for the letters of the alphabet and then create each user object in the container with the same name as the user's initial, but then you could not use the container objects to grant the users access to specific resources. You would have to create individual rights for each user instead, complicating the process enormously.

Ease of access means that users should be located in containers with the network resources they access most often. Most users remain blissfully unaware of the intricacies of the network they're using and are not the least bit interested in learning about NDS tree design. They simply want to access the printer across the room as easily as possible. Placing all of the printer objects in their own separate container for the sake of organizational consistency might look nice on paper, but it won't work well in real life. The users in a workgroup or department who routinely access specific resources, such as servers and printers, should be represented by objects in a container with those resources whenever possible.

Instead of using arbitrary container names and object groupings, NDS trees are typically designed using one or more of the organizational paradigms examined in the following sections. In many cases, the best solution is to use a combination of criteria to design an effective tree. Strict adherence to any one of these paradigms can force you to make impractical design choices in order to conform to a preexisting plan. Practicality is the cornerstone of any tree design, and you should feel free to violate your established design rules if the result is easier access or administration.

Partitions and WAN Links

The communication capabilities of your network are of principle importance when designing an NDS tree. If your network consists of multiple sites connected by WAN links that are slower and/or more expensive than your LANs, then the tree design should reflect those WAN divisions. The general rule when dealing with WAN-connected sites is to create a separate NDS partition at each site containing objects representing the resources at that site. The intention behind this is to keep the majority of NDS communications internal to each site. A user wanting to connect to a server in the next room should not have to exchange messages with a name server a thousand miles away in order to be authenticated.

Thus, when you have multiple sites connected by WAN links, you should create a container object representing each one of those sites as high up as possible in the NDS tree hierarchy. The usual course of action is to create a single organization object and then an organizational unit object named for each site, as shown in Figure 21-9. The organization object enables you to assign property values that are inherited by the entire enterprise, and the organizational units enable you to create a separate partition and specify separate property values for each site.

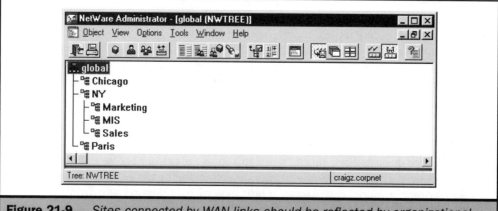

Figure 21-9.   *Sites connected by WAN links should be reflected by organizational unit objects placed as high as possible in the tree*

> **Note** *NetWare 5.x includes a utility called the WAN Traffic Manager, which enables you to exercise precise control over the NDS traffic that passes over WAN links. The utility works by extending the NDS schema to include a new object type called a LAN area object. A snap-in for NetWare Administrator enables you to create LAN area objects and define WAN traffic policies, which exist as properties of either server or LAN area objects. These policies specify the conditions under which NDS traffic should be transmitted over a link connecting LAN areas, and every NDS name server on the network runs a program called Wtm.nlm, which applies the policies.*

Partitioning the NDS database is often a good idea (for load balancing and fault tolerance) even when WAN links aren't involved, and the tree design can center around those partitions as well, even though the network traffic issues are not as critical. Creating a separate partition for each of your network segments, for example, and storing it in a server on that segment, is a good way to maximize the efficiency of your network and reduce the burden on the routers or switches connecting the networks. If you choose to do this, the distribution of the partitions in your tree design should take precedence over any other organizational method you plan to use. If, for example, your tree design is based primarily around geographical locations, such as the rooms in which your users work, you should let the partitions dictate the arrangement of the upper-layer containers, and then apply your geographical method as you work your way down through the tree.

Geographical Divisions

Creating a tree based on the physical locations of the resources the NDS objects represent can be an effective way of grouping users with the objects they need to access. You can create a hierarchy of organizational units that corresponds to the layout of the buildings, floors, wings, or rooms that your network services, as shown in Figure 21-10. Navigating a geographical tree is easy for anyone who is familiar with the layout of the facility, and since users often work near the resources they access regularly, such as servers and printers, administrators can readily place them in the same container.

However, a strict adherence to geographical locations is not necessarily good. If, for example, all of the network's servers are located in a data center, creating a single container for all of the server objects may not be a good idea, because all of your users would have to access servers in another context. It would be better to locate the server for each department or workgroup with the users that actually access it. The same holds true if some users associated with particular resources are not physically near them. For example, even though all of the vice presidents in a corporation might have offices in a separate executive wing, it may be better to place their user objects in the containers associated with their respective departments, rather than in a single container with the other vice presidents.

A geographically designed tree can also be a problem if the organization moves to a new facility or if departments are shifted around within the current facilities. The question then arises of whether you should upset the entire tree design to make it

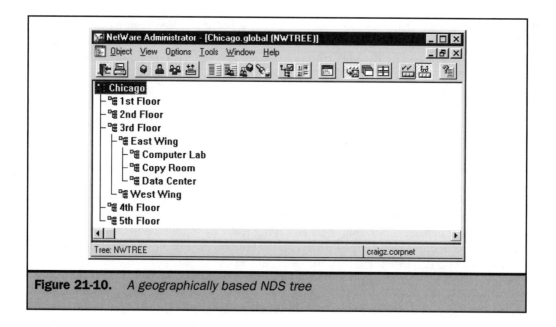

Figure 21-10.   *A geographically based NDS tree*

correspond with the new locations or keep it the way it is despite its increasing discrepancy from the physical layout of the network.

   Most of the problems that arise as a result of using a geographical tree design can be addressed through the judicious use of alias objects, as described in "Using Aliases," later in this chapter.

Departmental Divisions

Another solution that you can use when designing your tree is to take advantage of the divisions that already exist in your organization, such as departments and workgroups. Containers in the higher layers of the tree would represent corporate divisions or departments, such as Sales, with lower-layer containers subdividing each department into smaller units, such as Inside Sales and Outside Sales. This arrangement provides natural groupings of users with the resources they access, regardless of their respective locations, making it easily possible to assign rights using container objects.

A departmental tree could be as easy or even easier to navigate than a geographical one. In a very large organization, users might be more aware of other people's functions than of their exact locations. In addition, the modifications needed to keep the tree up to date would naturally correspond to the practical changes needed. When users move to other departments, they are likely to need access to different network resources, and simply moving their user objects to containers representing their new departments can provide them with that access, if the appropriate rights have been granted to the container. A purely geographical tree would likely require modifications that reflect only the movement of people and equipment from one place to another, and that serves no practical purpose other than to maintain the fidelity of the tree.

Physical Network Divisions

Another method for designing a tree, and one that in some ways functions as a lesson in what not to do, is to follow the physical layout of your network. You can create containers that represent the network segments and place objects in them that represent the equipment connected to those segments. This concept may be intuitive for the network administrator who has designed the network from the ground up, but not for the average network user.

However, while not a suitable model for the whole tree, the network layout can have an effect on the tree design. As mentioned earlier, creating partitions around WAN links must take priority over other more arbitrary design criteria. Therefore, on a network with WAN links, the top layer of the tree may appear to use the geographical method, by having containers named for cities, when it is actually conforming to the layout of the network. Beneath this layer, you can revert to a departmental or geographical design for the rest of the tree.

There is no reason why you can't "mix your metaphors" while designing a tree, as long as the result is intuitive to both users and administrators. You can have your upper-layer containers conform to sites separated by WAN links, and use departmental divisions for the next layer of containers and geographical designations for the layers below that, as shown in Figure 21-11.

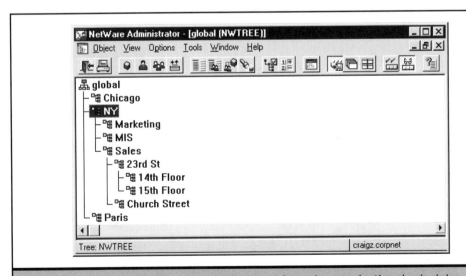

Figure 21-11. *An effective tree design can also mix organizational principles*

Balancing the Tree

In order to make the NDS database function as efficiently as possible, Novell recommends building what it calls a *balanced tree*, using a cone as the optimal shape for the design, as shown in Figure 21-12. When the tree isn't balanced, such as when there are too many containers in the top layer, or just too many layers, its performance can suffer. If your organization has a large number of departments, or branch offices, or other elements that lead you toward the creation of too many top-layer containers, try to find some logical criterion that you can use to group them, to keep the top layer relatively small.

Having too many layers in the tree can also have a negative effect on NDS performance. Aside from making the distinguished names of objects longer than necessary and complicating the tree-navigation process, the need to pass inherited rights down through many layers increases the processing time for each object. It is important not to let the organizational paradigm you've selected for your tree design take precedence over the tree's performance. Just because your workforce is ultimately broken down into five-person teams doesn't mean that you have to create dozens of tiny container objects to represent each one.

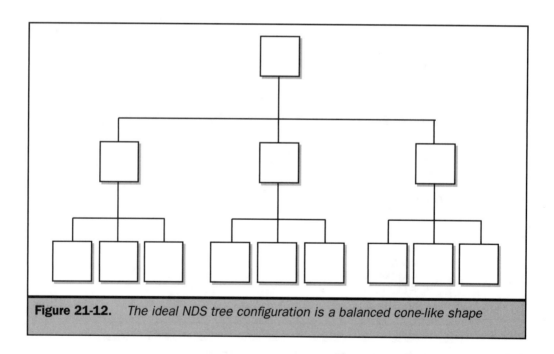

Figure 21-12. *The ideal NDS tree configuration is a balanced cone-like shape*

Building the Tree

After you decide how you will structure your NDS tree, it's time to think about the actual construction process. Creating objects is not difficult in itself, but you must consider the future maintenance of the tree as well. For example, part of the task of designing your tree should involve the ways in which you can assign trustee rights using containers instead of individual objects. It may seem easy to create individual trustee rights as part of the user objects, but later, when it comes time to modify the rights, you'll wish you could change a single container object's rights rather than those of multiple user objects.

The following sections examine some of the elements you should consider, as well as some of the techniques you can use to simplify the object-creation process.

Object Naming Conventions

The names that you select for the objects in your NDS tree can be as important as the structure of the tree itself. Objects that are logically named can more easily be identified by both users and administrators. The primary rule to follow in this respect is *consistency*. User object names, for example, should follow a specific formula, such as the user's first initial and surname. Allowing people to select their own usernames only makes the process of working with the user objects more difficult later on, especially when there are several people maintaining the tree.

In the same way, the names for objects representing hardware resources should be in some way informational. For a small network, calling your servers SERVER1 and SERVER2 can be acceptable; but in a large enterprise, a department name, location, or function, such as SALES1 or DBASE1, is more functional.

Note also that while object names can be up to 64 characters in length, excessively long names are not recommended. Originally, the reason for keeping names short was because people had to type them. This is still a possibility, but most users and administrators today navigate the tree using a graphical interface. Even in a GUI program, however, an object name like NETWARE_SERVER_THIRD_FLOOR_ EAST_WING_BY_THE_WINDOW, while descriptive, will probably not display properly in a dialog box.

Object Relationships

The NDS schema determines the relationships between the various types of objects in the tree; that is, which objects can be superior and subordinate to other objects. For example, you cannot have a container object subordinate to a leaf object, or even a leaf subordinate to a leaf. The top layer of containers in the tree must be either country or organization objects. For the reasons given earlier, you should avoid using country objects, so you must create organizations directly beneath the [Root]. Off of the organization units, you create organizational units for the rest of the layers.

Fortunately, applications like NetWare Administrator enforce these relationships for you. When you highlight the [Root] and attempt to create an object, for example, the program only enables you to create a country, organization, or alias object.

Using Aliases

One method for resolving many tree design problems is through the use of Alias objects. *Aliases* are objects that function as copies of other objects located elsewhere in the tree, enabling them to appear as though they are in another container. For example, if your organization keeps all of the network servers in a data center, you can put all of your server objects into a single container representing the data center and then create an alias object for each server in the same container as the users who regularly access it.

You can create an alias for any object in the NDS tree, and use them for many different purposes. If you have users (such as technical support personnel) who log in to the network from many different workstations, you can create aliases of their user objects and place them in various contexts, so that the users can log in using any workstation's default context. Printer aliases permit users in multiple containers to access the same printer without having to browse the tree. When you use NetWare Administrator to move a container object to another location in the tree, the program offers to leave an alias object behind in the original location, so that any references to the container in its original location will not be orphaned.

When you open the Details dialog box for an alias object in NetWare Administrator, the properties the program displays are those of the original object, not the alias itself (with one exception). The process of displaying the original alias's properties is known as *dereferencing*. The only exception in which NetWare Administrator displays the properties of the alias object itself is for the list of trustees maintained by the alias object separately from the original object's trustees. You can control which trustee list NetWare Administrator displays by selecting either Get Alias Trustees or Get Aliased Object Trustees from the Options menu.

An alias of an object that you've created in a different container has exactly the same property values as the original. This includes values inherited from the container objects in which the original object resides. An alias of a user object, for example, will run the login script of the original object's container, but will not inherit rights to printers from the alias's own container. Therefore, to enable a user to access the local resources when logging in from a different context using an alias, you must explicitly grant the original user object rights to those resources.

Aliases must maintain the same relationships as the objects they reflect; you can only create an alias of an organization object directly beneath the [Root] or a country object, for example. Aliases are also dynamically connected with the objects they reflect. When you change the properties of the original object, the properties of the alias change as well, and when you delete the original object, all of its aliases are deleted.

Using Templates

When building a large NDS tree, setting property values on a large number of user objects can slow down the creation process. There are several methods you can use to simplify the user object-creation process, chief of which is the use of property values inherited from container objects instead of user object property values. However, when you must assign the same property values to multiple user objects, you can do so using a template.

A *template* is an object type that functions as a pattern for the creation of new user objects. You can create a template and configure it with property values like those for a user object. Then, when you use the template to create new user objects, each one is given the same property values as the template.

Note   *The template was first introduced as a separate object type in the NetWare 4.11 release. Prior NetWare 4.x versions enabled you to create a USER_TEMPLATE entity from an existing user object, and then use it to create additional user objects with the same property values.*

You can use template objects to create any number of new user objects, but you cannot apply a template to a user object that already exists. In addition, you must be aware that NDS utilities access the properties of the template object only when creating a new user object. Modifying the template object's property values has no effect on the user objects that have already been created using the template.

Using Groups

The NetWare bindery relied on groups as the sole mechanism for applying trustee rights to multiple users at once. In NDS, the various container objects, such as organization and organizational units, would seem to make groups superfluous, because they perform roughly the same function. However, group objects in NDS differ from the containers in that they enable you to assign rights to a collection of users who are not all located in the same context.

However, because group members can be located anywhere in the tree, including opposite sides of a WAN link, processing the trustee rights assigned to a group object is much more complicated than processing container object rights. For this reason, you should minimize the use of group objects in your tree design wherever possible and assign rights using containers instead. For example, placing the user objects for vice presidents into the containers with the rest of their departments enables them to access the same departmental resources as the other workers. However, you may want to create a group object with the vice presidents of all the departments as members, in order to grant them rights that only executives should have.

Security Equivalences and Organizational Roles

Another method for assigning a user object specific property values is to make it the *security equivalent* of another user object. When you do this, the new object inherits all of the rights granted to its equivalent. The problem with this method, however, is that it's dynamic. Changing property values in the original object causes the same changes to be reflected in its equivalent. If, for example, you assign access rights to a user object called jdoe, and then make all of the other users in the department security equivalents to jdoe, what happens when jdoe is fired or transferred to another department? The communication required between the security equivalents can also slow down NDS performance, particularly when the two objects are separated by a WAN link.

As an alternative to security equivalences, NDS includes an object called an *organizational role,* which defines a particular job, rather than a person performing that job. You can create an organizational role object, assign it access rights, and then specify a list of users that will occupy that role. Changing the property values of the organizational role will dynamically change the properties of the users occupying it.

Bindery Migration

If you are upgrading to NetWare 4.*x* or 5.*x* from a bindery-based NetWare version, you can get a head start on constructing your NDS tree by importing the binderies from your existing NetWare servers. The DS Migrate tool included in NetWare versions 4.11 and above is a separate program that reads the information from your NetWare binderies and stores it in a temporary database. Once there, you can model the bindery information into an NDS tree structure by creating container objects, moving user and group objects to other containers, and modifying object properties. After creating the tree structure you want, you can commit it to the real NDS database. Then, using the NetWare File Migration Utility, you can migrate the files from the volumes on your bindery servers to NetWare 4.*x* or 5.*x* volumes, keeping intact the trustee rights you migrated with the bindery objects.

Merging Trees

Dsmerge.nlm is a server console utility that enables you to combine two separate NDS trees into a single database. You can use this tool when companies or divisions with separate NDS trees merge, or to incorporate an experimental database into your enterprise network tree. DSMERGE simply combines the roots of the two trees you specify. It does not combine objects or reconcile conflicts between similarly named objects. Therefore, you must be sure that there are no duplicate container names in the top layer of each tree before you perform the merge.

NDS Security

Just like a file system, a directory services database contains valuable information that must be secured against intrusion, unauthorized modification, and inadvertent deletion. NDS includes its own system of trustee rights that is independent from the trustee rights you assign to the files and directories on NetWare volumes. You can use these trustee rights to specify which users should be permitted access to the various objects in the tree and their properties. This way, you can delegate NDS maintenance tasks for a portion of the tree to certain administrators without giving them access to the entire tree, and grant users the ability to read information in the NDS database without giving them the ability to modify it. However, because NDS rights and file system rights are separate, it is possible for users to have access to the files and directories on a particular NetWare volume without their having access to the volume object in the NDS tree.

You manage NDS security rights using the same tools that you use to create and configure objects. NetWare Administrator uses a dialog box like that shown in Figure 21-13 to manage all aspects of the object and property rights for a particular object, as well as its inherited rights filters and effective rights. Netadmin.exe provides the same capabilities, using a character-based menu interface.

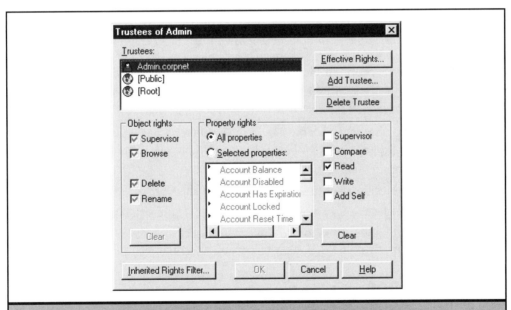

Figure 21-13. *A NetWare Administrator Trustees dialog box*

Object and Property Rights

NDS uses both *object rights* and *property rights,* which enables you to grant users control over an entire object and all of its properties, or just specific properties. Like file system rights, the various object rights grant specific types of access to the trustees that possess them. The types of object rights are as follows:

- **Supervisor**   Grants full control over an object, including the other four rights, all property rights, and the ability to grant rights to other users.

- **Browse**   Enables the user to view the object in the directory tree. To a user who lacks this right, the object and all of its subordinate objects are invisible. By default, all users receive the Browse right to the [Root] object, enabling them to see the entire tree.

- **Create**   Enables the user to create new objects in the tree, subordinate to the current object.

- **Delete**   Enables the user to remove the current object from the tree.

- **Rename**   Enables the user to change the name of the current object.

Object rights enable users to manipulate the objects themselves, but not the properties of those objects. The one exception to this is the Supervisor object right, which grants the trustee full control over all of the object's properties as well. When users do not have the Supervisor object right, they must be granted separate property rights in order to modify the value of specific properties.

Each of an object's properties has its own individual rights. You can grant a user rights to all of an object's properties at once, or to specific properties individually. The rights that you can grant to properties are as follows:

- **Supervisor**   Grants full control over the value for a particular property.

- **Compare**   Enables the user to check a property value for equality with another property value.

- **Read**   Enables the user to see the value of a property.

- **Write**   Enables the user to add, modify, or delete the value for a property.

- **Add Self**   Enables users to add their own user objects to (or remove them from) a property value that accepts a list of object names.

Rights Inheritance

As with file system rights, NDS object and property rights flow downward through the tree. Any rights that you grant to a container object are inherited by the objects in that container. For example, the Admin user object created by default when you install your first NDS server is automatically granted the Supervisor object right to the tree's [Root]. This gives the user full control over all of the objects in the tree and their properties.

In addition, by inheriting the Supervisor object right from the [Root] object, the Admin user also receives full control over the file system on all NetWare server volumes. This is one of the few areas in which the NDS rights and file system rights converge. If you grant any user Supervisor object rights to a server object, the user gets not only the rights to manipulate the object, but rights to the server's volumes as well.

The Admin user is not inherently different from any other user object in the NDS tree, except for the object rights that it has been granted. Unlike the Supervisor in the NetWare bindery, you can delete the Admin user and modify its object rights. However, before you do this, be sure that every object in the tree has at least one user with the Supervisor object right to it. Otherwise, it is possible to orphan parts of the NDS tree by having no one with the rights needed to administer them.

As mentioned earlier, every user object in an NDS tree is granted the Browse right to every other object in the tree. This is not a right that is individually granted to each user on its creation. Instead, this right is granted through the use of a special entity called [Public]. This object doesn't actually appear in the tree, but it is listed in utilities like NetWare Administrator as an object to which you can grant rights. Any rights that you grant to the [Public] object are inherited by all of the objects in the tree, as well as all NDS clients that have not yet logged in to the tree. The Browse object right to the [Root] object that is granted to [Public] is what makes the entire tree visible to all users and enables clients to browse the tree (such as when selecting a context) before they log in.

Inherited Rights Filters

In some cases, you may want to prevent rights from flowing down through the tree, and you can do this by applying an *inherited rights filter (IRF)* to a container object. An IRF functions like a dam, preventing the flow of specific object and property rights. When you create an IRF in a container to filter the Create object right, for example, all the other rights the container possesses will flow down to the objects in the container, but the Create right will not.

IRFs only prevent the inheritance of rights from superior objects; they do not block rights that are explicitly granted to an object below the filter. Thus, if you want to create a secret branch of your tree for experimental purposes or any other reason, you can create an IRF that filters out all inherited rights. The denial of the Browse object right will even make the tree branch invisible to other users. For those users who require access to the hidden branch, you can grant the necessary rights to their user objects or create a group object for that purpose.

Effective Rights

As you have seen, the object and property rights that a particular object possesses can come from several different sources, and all of those rights are combined in the final object. For example, a user can have some property rights to an object granted by inheritance from a container while other rights are explicitly granted by an administrator. The end result is a combination of those rights. Add the [Public] object, group objects, inherited rights filters, and several layers of container objects, and it can sometimes be quite difficult to determine what the user's effective rights actually are.

The *effective rights* of an object are the net result of all of the mechanisms that can grant or revoke object or property rights. The rights explicitly granted to an object or granted through security equivalences or group memberships take precedence over those inherited from containers or the [Public] object. Specifically, effective rights are the combination of all of the following influences:

- Rights explicitly granted to the object.
- Rights received through security equivalences and group memberships.
- Rights received through the [Public] object.
- Rights inherited from container objects.
- Inherited rights blocked by inherited rights filters.

While it is possible to ascertain the effective rights of an object by comparing the effects of all of these influences, it is fortunate that NDS tools like NetWare Administrator and Netadmin.exe can display the effective rights for a particular object, as shown in Figure 21-14.

It is important for everyone who takes part in the maintenance of your NDS tree to understand the concept of effective rights and the various mechanisms you are using to assign object and property rights. Many administrators limit the mechanisms they use to assign rights in order to simplify maintenance tasks, and there must be specific policies in effect so that everyone knows which mechanisms they should use. One new staff member that is fond of using inherited rights filters can create a great deal of confusion if no one else is familiar with them.

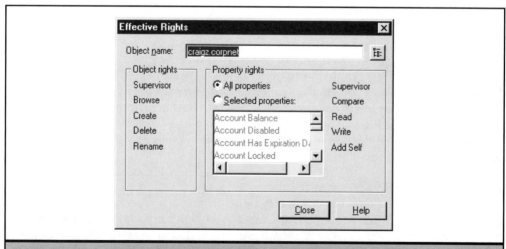

Figure 21-14.   *The NetWare Administrator Effective Rights dialog box*

The Complete Reference

Upgrading
&
Troubleshooting
Networks

Chapter 22

Windows NT Domains

685

Probably the most obvious shortcoming in the Windows NT operating system is its lack of a full-featured directory service. The domains that NT uses to organize and manage the computers on a network are serviceable, but lack the scalability and expandability of products like Novell Directory Services. For a small- to medium-sized network, the NT directory service is sufficient; but as you move into larger enterprises, NT domains become difficult to administer and customize for specific purposes. Windows 2000 addresses these shortcomings with Active Directory, a hierarchical directory service that can support networks of virtually any size; but until Windows 2000 completely replaces NT, there will still be a great many NT domain networks for years to come.

Note   *For more information on Active Directory, see Chapter 23.*

The use of the term *domain* by Windows NT to describe a group of computers managed as a unit is unfortunate. At the time the concept was developed, the Internet was nowhere near as ubiquitous an entity as it is today, and the use of a term previously adopted for the Internet infrastructure was not expected to be a problem. Now, however, even people who have never used a computer are familiar with the phrase "dot com," and there can be some confusion at times between an Internet domain and a Windows NT domain.

The primary difference between the two types of domains is that whereas the Internet's Domain Name Service (DNS) is hierarchical, Windows NT domains are not. An NT domain is simply a group of computers on a network that share a security model and use a common *Security Accounts Manager (SAM)* database of user and group information stored on one or more systems that have been designated as *domain controllers.* A diagram of the computers in a Windows NT domain consists of two layers only: the domains and the computers in those domains (see Figure 22-1). The domains used on the Internet can have any number of layers, with a minimum of three: the top-level domain (such as com), the second-level domain, and the computers in the

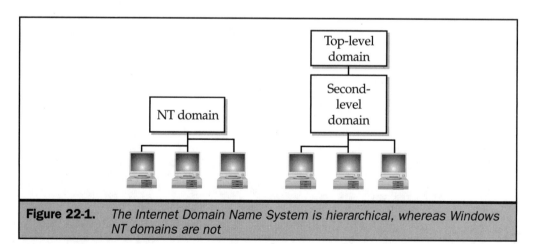

Figure 22-1.   *The Internet Domain Name System is hierarchical, whereas Windows NT domains are not*

second-level domain. The owner of a second-level domain is free to create any number of subdomain layers, while an NT network is limited to a single domain layer.

The alternative to the use of domains in Windows NT is a *workgroup,* an informal grouping of computers in which each system maintains its own SAM database, containing user and group accounts that are valid on that system only. For a very small network (up to approximately 20 workstations) that does not require stringent security, a workgroup is sufficient. You can run a workgroup network with any combination of Windows systems, including Windows 2000 Professional, Windows NT Workstation, Windows 95 and 98, and even Windows for Workgroups. Although you can have Windows NT Server and Windows 2000 Server machines on a workgroup network, they are not needed for administration purposes as they are on a domain network.

From the standpoint of the network administrator, a workgroup network requires that users have individual accounts on each machine whose shares they will access. Either each user must be responsible for maintaining the accounts on his or her machine, or an administrator has to travel to each workstation to maintain it. On a domain network, a single domain user account provides the ability to access the shared resources on any machine in the domain. An administrator can perform account maintenance tasks for the entire domain from any workstation on the network.

Workgroups also function as an organizational resource only, whereas domains can provide security boundaries that restrict user access. In other words, there is nothing to prevent a user logged on to a system in one workgroup from accessing the resources on a system in another workgroup. A member of one domain, however, cannot access resources in another domain, unless an administrator has implemented a trust relationship between the domains.

Domain Controllers

The core of a Windows NT domain is its domain controllers. These are Windows NT Server machines that have been designated as domain controllers during the operating system installation. You cannot make an NT system into a domain controller after the OS installation is complete, nor can you change an existing domain controller back into a regular server. In either case, you must reinstall the operating system to change its domain controller status.

One of the major improvements in Windows 2000's Active Directory is that you can convert a server into a domain controller at any time and then convert it back to a regular server as needed.

Two types of domain controllers can be in a Windows NT domain, called primary and backup. Every domain must have one (and only one) *primary domain controller (PDC).* This is the computer that contains the only read-write copy of the SAM database for the domain, including its users and groups and their password information. Whenever you create a new user or group or modify the properties of an existing one, you are modifying the SAM database on the PDC.

A *backup domain controller (BDC)*, as the name implies, functions as a backup to the PDC, in the event of a system failure or a break in network communications. If the PDC should become unavailable, you can promote a BDC to a PDC to take its place, using the Windows NT Server Manager utility. Promoting any BDC to a PDC causes the existing PDC to be demoted to a BDC; so once the original PDC server is back in operation, you can promote it back to its original role—which causes the temporary PDC to revert back to a BDC. A domain can have any number of backup domain controllers, or none at all, but at least one is recommended for every domain. Without a domain controller, a domain is useless, because no one can log on to the network or access network resources.

Replication

Every BDC on the network contains a replica of the master database stored on the PDC, which is updated at regular intervals by the system's Netlogon service. The replication of the domain database always flows in one direction from the PDC to each of the BDCs. This is called *single master replication,* because there is only one master copy of the database, to which all modifications are made, and which is replicated to all of the other copies. The alternative, as used in NDS and Active Directory, is *multiple master replication,* in which changes can be made to any copy of the database, and these changes are replicated to all of the other copies (see Figure 22-2).

The use of single master replication is one of the limiting factors of Windows NT domains that makes using the directory service on large enterprise networks connected by WAN links inconvenient. As a general rule, a large network that consists of multiple sites connected by WAN links should have at least one domain controller at each site, so that users can log on to the network locally (that is, without having to traverse a WAN connection to reach a domain controller). However, even though a BDC can authenticate users and grant them access to network resources, its copy of the SAM database is read-only. All modifications to the SAM database are made to the PDC, and an administrator at a remote location may have to connect to the PDC using a relatively slow, expensive WAN connection. With multiple master replication, an administrator can make changes to any copy of the SAM database, and the system will eventually propagate those changes to all of the other replicas automatically.

| Note | *Active Directory, the directory service included with Windows 2000, provides multiple master replication, as does Novell Directory Services.* |

Understanding the Replication Process

Because Windows NT uses single master replication, the process of synchronizing the SAM databases on the domain controllers is relatively simple. During the replication process, SAM data travels only in one direction, from the PDC to the BDCs. By default,

NETWORK DIRECTORY
SERVICES

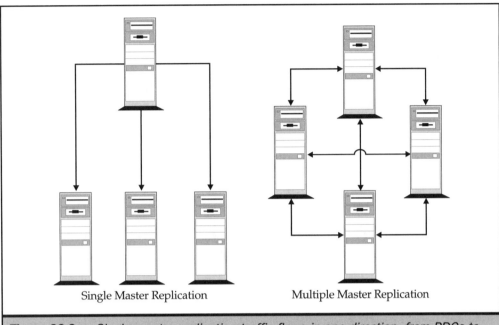

Single Master Replication   Multiple Master Replication

Figure 22-2.   *Single master replication traffic flows in one direction, from PDCs to*
BDCs, while in multiple master replication, all domain controllers
update each other

a domain's PDC sends pulses to the BDCs every five minutes, indicating that the BDCs
should transmit a request for a database update to the PDC. The BDCs' requests are
staggered, so that too many BDCs are not synchronizing at the same time. The PDC
then responds to the requests with the changes that have been made to the database
since each BDC's last update. This is known as a *partial synchronization.*

Note
The PDC sends no pulses when there are no changes made to the SAM database during
the time since the last BDC synchronization.

   Most of the domain replication events that occur on the network are partial
synchronizations. The PDC maintains a change log that lists all of the modifications
to the SAM database, including password changes, the addition of new users and
groups, and the modification of existing ones. The change log has a fixed size (64KB,
by default); the oldest entries are deleted as new ones are added. The update request
sent by a BDC to the PDC specifies the last change that it received, and the PDC's
reply includes all of the modifications made since that time.
   If the BDC's request specifies a last change received that has been purged from the
change log, then the PDC must perform a *full synchronization* and transmit the entire

SAM database to the BDC. This typically occurs when a BDC has been down for an extended period of time, or when a new BDC is added to the network. Depending on the size of the network, a full synchronization can require the transmission of much more data than a partial one, and should be avoided whenever possible.

Modifying Replication Parameters

The frequency of the synchronization events and the size of the change log maintained by the PDC are controlled by registry entries located in the following key:

    HKEY_LOCAL_MACHINE\SYSTEM\CurrentControlSet\Services\Netlogon\Parameters

If the following entries do not already exist in the registry, you can create them to modify the default settings for the Windows NT Server.

ChangeLogSize is a REG_DWORD entry that defines the size of the PDC's change log. The log exists in memory, as well as on the hard drive as a file called Netlogon.chg in the \%SystemRoot% directory (C:\Winnt, by default). Each entry in the log is typically 32 bytes long (with some being longer, but none shorter), which enables the default 64KB log file to hold approximately 2,000 entries. However, you can modify the ChangeLogSize registry entry in order to maintain a log up to 4MB in size (by changing the hexadecimal value of the entry to 4000000). Increasing the size of the log does not degrade the performance of the system in any way, and it greatly reduces the chance that the PDC will have to perform a full synchronization because entries needed by a BDC have aged out of the log.

> **Note** *When modifying the value of the ChangeLogSize registry entry on the PDC, be sure to change the entry on all of the BDCs to the same value. Only the log on the PDC is actually used, but if a BDC ever has to be promoted to a PDC, it should have the same size change log.*

The Pulse REG_DWORD entry specifies the interval at which the PDC should transmit the pulses to the BDCs that trigger their synchronization requests to the PDC. By default, the value is 300 seconds (5 minutes), with possible values ranging from 60 to 172,800 seconds (48 hours). If you increase the size of the change log, you can conceivably increase the Pulse value as well, reducing the amount of network traffic generated by the replication process without forcing the PDC to perform full synchronizations. However, this also means that it will take longer for new user and group accounts to be propagated to all of the domain's BDCs.

Trust Relationships

Because an NT domain is not a hierarchical directory service, there is a point at which an NT domain can grow too large to be practically managed. Therefore, on larger networks, administrators create multiple domains. Theoretically, a single domain can support up to 26,000 users and approximately 250 groups, but you may find that splitting the network into multiple domains is advantageous for several reasons, including the following:

- **Delegating administration tasks**   By creating separate domains, you can grant support personnel administrative access to one domain while preventing them from accessing the other domains.

- **Creating security boundaries**   Domains are inherently secure from access by users outside the domain, unless administrators explicitly create trust relationships between the domains.

- **Improving performance**   On enterprise networks connected using WAN links, separate domains can help to keep network traffic within a site and help to minimize the WAN traffic.

When users log on to the network from a workstation, they must log on using an account in a specific domain, which makes it possible for them to access resources in that domain, but not the resources in other domains. In order for users to access resources outside of their domain, the network administrator must create *trust relationships* between the various domains.

When one domain trusts another domain, the authentication process that grants users access to their home domain also grants them access to the other domain. If Domain A trusts Domain B, then a user logging on to Domain A can access resources in Domain B. However, this does not mean that users logging on to Domain B can automatically access resources in Domain A. Trust relationships operate in one direction; for two domains to mutually trust each other, administrators must create trusts relationships running in both directions.

Trust relationships are also not transitive. If Domain A trusts Domain B, and Domain B trusts Domain C, it does not follow that Domain A trusts Domain C. Again, explicit trust relationships must exist between A and C for them to trust each other.

Even when a trust relationship exists between domains, users' access to shared resources on other domains is still subject to the same access permissions as on their local domain. To access a shared drive on a server in Domain B, a user in Domain A must still be granted permission to access that share, even when Domain B already trusts Domain A. When you set the access permissions for a share, you can select users and groups from any domain visible on the network, as shown in Figure 22-3. The domain to which the computer is currently attached is marked with an asterisk.

Creating Trust Relationships

To create trust relationships between domains, you launch the User Manager for Domains utility and select Trust Relationships from the Policies menu to display the dialog box shown in Figure 22-4. The upper box lists the trusted domains (the domains

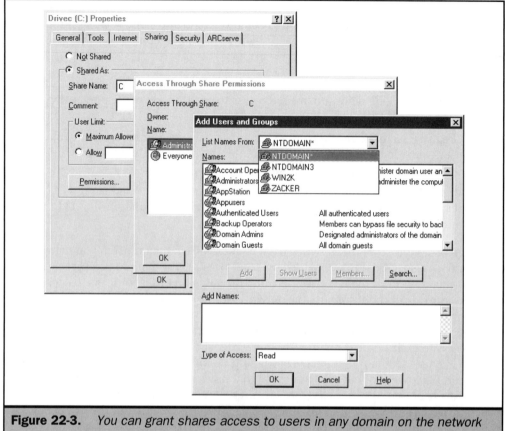

Figure 22-3. *You can grant shares access to users in any domain on the network*

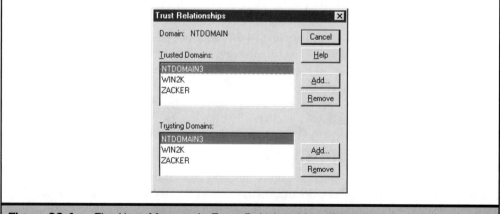

Figure 22-4. *The User Manager's Trust Relationships dialog box*

that the current domain trusts), and the bottom box lists the trusting domains (the domains that will be permitted to trust the current domain).

Note

You can also create trust relationships from the Windows NT command prompt, and perform many other domain-related maintenance tasks, using the Netdom.exe utility included in the Windows NT Server 4.0 Resource Kit. The latest version of Netdom, included in the Supplement 3 release of the Resource Kit, also enables you to create and manage the computer accounts for workstations and BDCs and reset secure channels.

In order for a trust relationship to be established, both of the domains involved must approve. For example, when you, as the administrator of Domain A, add Domain B to the Trusting Domains list, you specify a password to be used for that trust relationship. An administrator of Domain B must then add Domain A to the Trusted Domains list in the same dialog box for their domain, and specify the same password. This establishes a one-way trust relationship in which Domain B trusts Domain A. In other words, users logging on to a machine in Domain A can access resources in Domain B. Domain B users cannot access Domain A resources unless the administrators perform the same process in the other direction.

Note

As a general rule, administrators should configure the Trusting Domain side of the relationship first, and then the Trusted Domain side. This enables the trusted domain to recognize the password and immediately establish the relationship. If the order is reversed, an error message will appear stating that the password could not yet be verified and the relationship will not be established until it is.

During the establishment of the trust relationship, the trusting domain creates a *trusted domain object* on its domain controllers, which contains the name of the trusted domain and its security identifier (SID). Each of the domain controllers in the trusting domain then creates an *LSA (Local Security Authority) secret object* containing the password for the trust relationship.

On the trusted domain, the User Manager program creates an *interdomain trust account* that also stores the password supplied by the administrator. After the trusted domain object, LSA secret object, and interdomain trust account have been created, the Netlogon service on the trusting domain's PDC begins the process of establishing an encrypted communications link called a *secure channel* between the two domains. This secure channel is authenticated by the PDC of the trusted domain, and the trust relationship is established. Once the PDCs on both domains replicate all of these elements to the BDCs, it is possible for any domain controller in the trusting domain to establish a secure channel to any domain controller in the trusted domain.

Each time a domain controller is restarted, it attempts to discover the domain controllers for all of its trusted domains, to reestablish the secure channel. The controller makes three attempts for each trusted domain, at five-second intervals, before the discovery is said to have failed. After a failure, additional discovery attempts occur every 15 minutes, or when a client attempts to access a resource in a trusted domain.

Organizing Trust Relationships

There are a number of different organizational paradigms that you can use when creating multiple domains on a network and establishing trust relationships between them. On a relatively small network, you can establish trust relationships on an ad hoc basis; when users need access to a resource on another domain, you configure it to trust the domain in which those users reside. However, on larger networks, you should consider a more organized methodology that will enable you to use the domains to manage your network more efficiently. Some of the basic types of domain/trust models for an enterprise network are examined in the following sections.

The Single Domain Model

The single domain model requires no trust relationships, since only one domain is involved. This can be a viable alternative, even for a fairly large network, when the entire network is managed by a single group of administrators. Many networks begin as a single domain, and later evolve into one of the other models discussed in the following sections.

The main advantage of this model is that administration is quite simple. There are no trusts to create or maintain, defining groups is easier, and all of the user accounts are located in the one (and only) domain. The disadvantages become increasingly obvious as the network grows in size. Browsing the domain tree slows down as the number of computers and users increases and the lack of groupings provided by separate domains that define departmental or geographical boundaries becomes more of a problem.

The Complete Trust Domain Model

The complete trust domain model consists of multiple domains, each of which has a trust relationship with every other domain, running in both directions (see Figure 22-5). Unlike the master and multiple master domain models, every domain in the complete trust is a peer to all of the other domains, with each one containing its own user accounts. In many cases, this type of network model is the result of the ad hoc trust establishment method described earlier, taken to the nth degree. From a user access standpoint, this arrangement is not much different from having a single, large domain, since every user can be granted access to any resource on the entire network.

As a network grows from a single domain into multiple domains, this model may be viable at first, but it can rapidly become unmanageable. Obviously, this model requires the least amount of planning, and it is best suited to an environment where political or other factors require the use of multiple domains; but users frequently require access to resources all over the network. The main drawbacks of this arrangement are the sheer number of trust relationships that must be established and the fact that user and group accounts are scattered in domains all over the network.

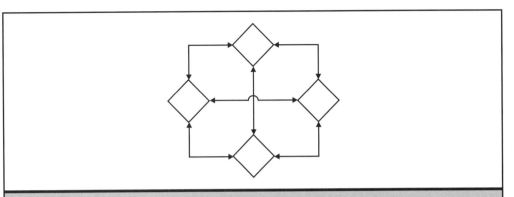

Figure 22-5.   *The complete trust domain model*

Since you create a separate trust relationship in each direction between every pair of domains on the network, the formula for computing the total number of trust relationships needed is $(n–1) \times n$, where n is the number of domains on the network. Thus, a network consisting of 10 domains would require you to create 90 separate trust relationships $[(10–1) \times 9 = 90]$ to form a complete trust domain model, and, as a result of all of this effort, you achieve little more than you would with one large domain.

Managing permissions in this model is difficult, because there is no ready way of knowing which users are members of which domain. If you must grant a specific user rights to a share in the domain for which you are responsible, you either have to know which domain the user account resides in or go searching for it in each of the network's domains.

The Single Master Domain Model

The single master domain model uses standard NT domains in two different roles, called *master domains* and *resource domains.* The arrangement calls for a hierarchy in which there is one master domain that contains the user and group accounts for the entire network (also called the *account domain*), and a series of resource domains that contain the network's workstations, file servers, printers, and other resources, thus breaking up the network into more easily manageable units (see Figure 22-6).

In this model, all of the resource domains have a one-way relationship in which they trust the master domain. Every user logging on to the master domain, therefore, can access resources anywhere on the network (with the appropriate permissions). This eliminates the need to create trust relationships between the resource domains, and all of the user and group accounts are stored in the single master domain for easy centralized administration. Because the trust relationships run in only one direction, from the resource domains to the master domain, any user logging on to an account in one of the resource domains cannot access resources outside of that domain.

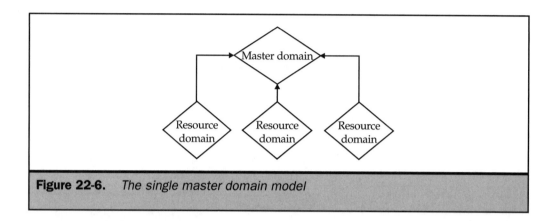

Figure 22-6.   *The single master domain model*

Note, however, that despite the fact that all of the user and group accounts are located in the master domain, the computer accounts should be located in the individual resource domains. When you install a workstation, you specify the NetBIOS name for the computer and join it to the local resource domain, not the master domain. This enables the system to use the domain controllers for the resource domain to provide pass-through authentication during the logon process, and eliminates the need for additional BDCs in the master domain, just to enable workstations not located in the same site as the master domain to log on using a local domain controller.

Note   *See "Logging On to the Network," later in this chapter, for more information on pass-through authentication and the domain logon process.*

In the single master domain model, the master domain is responsible for authenticating all of the users as they log on. However, once the logon process is complete, most of a user's activity will be confined to one or another of the resource domains. This effectively splits the domain processing burden between the master and the resource domains. In addition, the master domain is ultimately responsible for network security, since all of the other domains trust it. Administration of the resource domains can, therefore, be delegated to personnel in the departments hosting the individual domains, without compromising the overall security of the network.

On the down side, however, is the fact that the entire network is reliant on the master domain for authentication services. This single master domain model does not provide the ability to support more users than a single domain, since all of the accounts are still located in the one master domain. Instead, it enables you to use multiple domains for organizational purposes and still maintain all of the user and group accounts in one place. If the network is growing on a regular basis, it is a good idea to have a plan ready for expanding it into a multiple master domain network. Otherwise, it is easy for a well-organized web of trust relationships to degenerate into the confusion of the complete trust domain model.

To further minimize the account administration required at the resource-domain level, you can create local groups in the resource domains and grant them access to the shared resources in those domains. Then, by creating global groups and making them members of the local groups, you can manage access to the resources by adding user accounts to the global groups instead of to the local ones. This makes it possible to perform all of the day-to-day account administration tasks in the master domain, without accessing resource domain accounts at all.

The Multiple Master Domain Model

The multiple master domain model is an extension of the single master domain model that is designed to support larger networks that may have individual administration teams for the organization's divisions or locations. In this model, there are at least two master domains and a number of resource domains. As in the single master model, the master domains contain the user and group accounts for the division, and the resource domains host the shared resources. In this model, however, each of the resource domains trusts all of the master domains, and the master domains all have two-way trust relationships between them (see Figure 22-7). It's also possible for trust relationships to exist between resource domains, but this should not be necessary, unless physical circumstances (such as slow WAN connections) warrant it.

In this arrangement, a user with an account in one of the master domains can access any resource on the network, because all of the resource domains trust all of the master

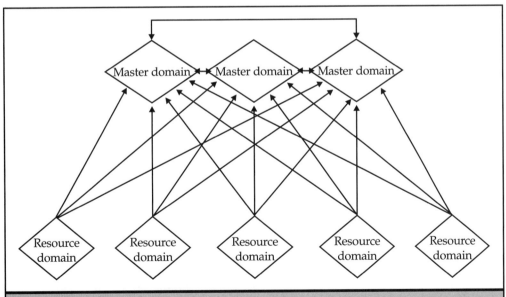

Figure 22-7.   *The multiple master domain model*

domains. The two-way trusts between the master domains enable the users logging directly on to the master domain to access the resources in the other master domains.

The object of this model is to enable each division to maintain its own user and group accounts in its master domain, while still enabling users to access the resources in other divisions. For companies with several branch locations, for example, having a master domain at each site enables the administrators at each location to manage their own accounts.

The main advantage of the multiple master domain model is its potential for almost unlimited growth. By creating additional master domains, you can expand the network in an organized fashion or even join networks together (in the case of a company merger, for example). The number of trust relationships that administrators must create and maintain to support this model can be seen as a disadvantage, but the multiple master domain model requires fewer trusts than the complete trust domain model.

Viewing Trust Relationships

The Windows NT 4.0 Resource Kit includes a graphical utility called Domain Monitor (Dommon.exe) that you can use to examine the secure channels between the domain controllers on your network. When you run the program, you see a list of the domains found on the network, and their trusted domains. Double-clicking an entry in the list produces a display like that shown in Figure 22-8, which displays the status of the domain controllers in the selected domain and the secure channels to the trusted domains.

Domain Monitor is a good way to ensure that all of the secure channels on your network are functioning properly. If the secure channel between a particular resource domain controller and a master domain controller is not functioning, local workstations may be unable to use that resource domain controller for pass-through authentication to the master domain controller. As a result, you may find that your workstations are connecting to another, more distant resource domain controller. If this other resource domain controller is located at another site, the workstation logon process can be delayed considerably, while generating needless traffic over a WAN link.

If you find that there are secure channels on your network that are not functioning properly, you can reset them using the Nltest.exe command-line utility, also included with the Resource Kit. The following command resets the secure channel between the system on which you execute the command and the domain specified by the *domain* variable:

```
NLTEST /SC_RESET:domain
```

If you run the command on a workstation or a server that is not a domain controller, the program resets the secure channel to the domain containing the system's computer account. If you run Nltest on a domain controller, you can reset the secure channel created by the trust relationship with another domain.

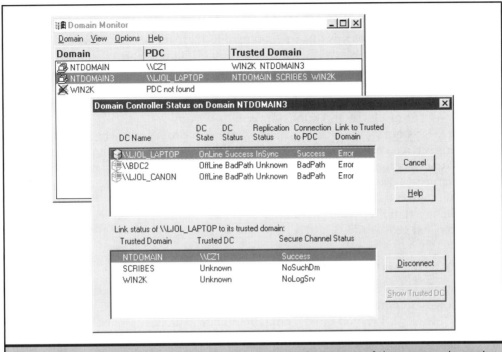

Figure 22-8. *The Domain Monitor utility displays the status of the secure channels between trusted domains*

Note *Nltest.exe is a powerful utility that you can also use to list the domain controllers in a domain, control domain replication, and display the contents of the change log, among other things. For more information, see the documentation included with the Windows NT Server 4.0 Resource Kit.*

Logging On to the Network

When you log on to a domain, the Netlogon service on the workstation performs a series of different processes, depending on how the network's domains are organized. During the boot process of a Windows NT workstation, before you see the screen prompting you to press CTRL-ALT-DEL to log on, the system attempts to locate a domain controller using a process called *discovery*. If the workstation is not configured to log on to a domain, the Netlogon service terminates and no discovery takes place. When it is logging on to a domain, the Netlogon service attempts to locate a domain controller in the domain of which it is a member, and in each of its trusted domains.

Domain Controller Discovery

The Netlogon service does this first by sending queries to its designated WINS server for NetBIOS name entries with 1C as the value of the 16th bit, which identifies them as resource domain controllers. The system then transmits local broadcasts for each of the entries returned by the WINS server. If those broadcasts do not elicit a response, the service begins sending logon requests, one at a time, to each of the entries, in the order that they were furnished by the WINS server.

When the system locates a domain controller for the domain in which the workstation has a computer account, the workstation establishes a secure channel to it. In the same way that the domain controllers involved in trust relationships have secure channels between them, workstations establish secure channels to the domain controller in which their computer account is located. Both the discovery process and the establishment of the secure channel occur before the user is prompted to supply a logon name and password.

Pass-Through Authentication

In the case of a single domain network, all of the domain controllers contain both the workstation's computer account and the user account that will be used to log on to the domain. However, when you build a domain infrastructure using master and resource domains, users logging on to the network can be authenticated by a domain controller in a resource domain, using a process called *pass-through authentication,* even though their user accounts are in the master domain.

On a single or multiple master domain network, the computer accounts for the workstations are located in the resource domains, while the user accounts are located in the master domain. This means that user authentication must ultimately be performed by the domain controller in the master domain, but the workstation will not establish a secure channel directly with the master domain controller.

When you log on to the network from a Windows NT workstation (or from a server that is not functioning as a domain controller), the pull-down menu for the Domain field in the Logon dialog box contains the domain in which the workstation's computer account is located, and all of the domains trusted by that domain. Since your user account is located in the master domain, you select the master domain in this dialog box, even though this is not the domain in which the computer account for the workstation is located.

However, it is the computer account that determines the domain to which the workstation will create a secure channel. Once the secure channel is created between the workstation and the resource domain (where the computer account is located), the resource domain controller passes the authentication information it has received from the workstation (that is, the username and password) to the master domain controller, using the secure channel that it has already created when establishing the trust relationship between the two domains (see Figure 22-9). The master domain controller then attempts to authenticate the user and returns the results to the

Workstation   Resource domain controller   Master domain controller

Figure 22-9. *The workstation creates a secure channel to the resource domain controller, which then uses the existing secure channel to communicate with the master domain controller*

workstation, via the resource domain controller. In this arrangement, it is the master domain controller that supplies the system policy file and logon script to be loaded by the workstation (if any), not the resource domain controller.

The end result of this arrangement is that the workstation can log on using a local resource domain controller, instead of having to establish a secure connection to the master domain controller. In the case of a network that is split into remote sites connected by WAN links, there is no need to have a BDC for the master domain at each location, just so that users can authenticate locally. The resource domain controller performs this function, and uses a secure channel that already exists to communicate with the master domain controller.

Selecting a Windows NT Directory Service

The domain-based directory service is one of the most frequently cited shortcomings of the operating system, particularly in an enterprise network environment. While the NT directory service is quite serviceable for a small- to medium-sized network in which no more than a handful of domains are needed, it becomes increasingly un-wieldy on large networks, especially those with multiple sites connected by a WAN. The multiple master domain model is really a makeshift solution for a directory service that is just not suited for large enterprise networks. For large networks that are expanding on a regular basis, or those that are in need of an overhaul to address out-of-control domain expansion, a hierarchical directory service that is designed to support large networks, such as Active Directory or Novell Directory Services, is recommended.

The Complete Reference

Upgrading & Troubleshooting Networks

Chapter 23

Active Directory

703

T he domain-based directory service used by Windows NT has long come under fire for its inability to scale up to support larger networks. An enterprise network that consists of multiple domains is limited in its communication between those domains to the trust relationships that administrators can establish between them. In addition, because each domain must be maintained individually, the account administration process is complicated enormously. Since the original Windows NT 3.1 release in 1993, Microsoft has promised to deliver a more robust directory service that is better suited for use on large networks; and in Windows 2000's Active Directory, it has finally done that.

Active Directory (AD) is an object-oriented, hierarchical, distributed directory services database system that provides a central storehouse for information about the hardware, software, and human resources of an entire enterprise network. Based on the X.500 standard and similar to Novell Directory Services (NDS) in many ways, network users are represented by objects in the Active Directory tree. Administrators can use those objects to grant users access to resources anywhere on the network, which are also represented by objects in the tree. Unlike Windows NT, which uses a flat, domain-based structure for its directory, Active Directory expands the structure into multiple levels. The fundamental unit of organization in the Active Directory database is still the domain, but a group of domains can now be consolidated into a tree, and a group of trees into a forest. Administrators can manage multiple domains simultaneously by manipulating the tree, and manage multiple trees simultaneously by manipulating a forest.

A directory service is not only a database for the storage of information, however; it also includes the services that make that information available to users, applications, and other services. Active Directory includes a global catalog that makes it possible to search the directory for particular objects using the value of a particular attribute. Applications can use the directory to control access to network resources, and other directory services can interact with AD using a standardized interface and the Lightweight Directory Access Protocol (LDAP).

Caution	*A directory service is a vital and complex part of an enterprise network infrastructure, and should be thoroughly tested before it is deployed on production networks, particularly those that perform critical functions. Windows 2000 and Active Directory are still very new products, and if other directory services are any indication, there may be a period of adjustment before they are deemed to be completely stable.*

Active Directory Architecture

Active Directory is composed of objects, which represent the various resources on a network, such as users, servers, printers, and applications. An *object* is a collection of attributes that define the resource, give it a name, define its capabilities, and specify who should be permitted to use it. Some of an object's attributes are assigned automatically when they're created, such as the globally unique identifier (GUID) assigned to each one, while others are supplied by the network administrator. A user object, for example, has attributes that store information about the user it represents, such as an account name, password, telephone number, and e-mail address, as well as information about the other objects with which the user interacts. There are many different types of objects, each of which has different attributes, depending on its functions.

The primary difference between Active Directory and Windows NT 4.0 domains is that Active Directory provides administrators and users with a global view of the network. Both directory services can use multiple domains, but instead of managing the users of each domain separately, for example, as in Windows NT 4.0, AD administrators create a single object for each user and can use it to grant that user access to resources in any domain.

Each type of object is defined by an object class stored in the directory schema. The schema specifies the attributes that each object must have, the optional attributes it may have, and the object's place in the directory tree. The schema are themselves stored as objects in the Active Directory called *class schema objects* and *attribute schema objects*. A class schema object contains references to the attribute schema objects that together form the object class. This way, an attribute is only defined once, although it can be used in many different object classes.

The schema is extensible, so that applications and services developed by Microsoft or third parties can create new object classes or add new attributes to existing object classes. This enables applications to use Active Directory to store information specific to their functions and provide that information to other applications as needed. For example, rather than maintain its own directory, an e-mail server application can modify the Active Directory schema so that it can use AD to authenticate users and store their e-mail information.

Object Types

There are two basic types of objects in Active Directory, called container objects and leaf objects. A *container object* is simply an object that stores other objects, while a *leaf object* stands alone and cannot store other objects. Container objects essentially function as the branches of the tree, and leaf objects grow off of the branches. Active Directory uses container objects, such as organizational units (OUs) and groups, to store other objects. Containers can store other containers or leaf objects, such as users and computers. The guiding rule of directory tree design is that rights and permissions flow downward through the tree. Assigning a right to a container object means that, by default, all of the objects in the container inherit that right. This enables administrators to control access to network resources by assigning rights and permissions to containers rather than to individual users.

By default, an Active Directory tree is composed of objects that represent the users and computers on the network, the logical entities used to organize them, and the folders and printers they regularly access. These objects, their functions, and the icons used to represent them in tools such as Active Directory Users and Computers are listed in Table 23-1.

Object Naming

Every object in the Active Directory database is uniquely identified by a name that can be expressed in several forms. The naming conventions are based on the LDAP standard defined in RFC 2251, published by the Internet Engineering Task Force (IETF). The distinguished name (DN) of an object consists of the name of the domain in which the object is located, plus the path down the domain tree through the container objects to the object itself. The part of an object's name that is stored in the object itself is called its *relative distinguished name (RDN)*.

By specifying the name of the object and the names of its parent containers up to the root of the domain, the object is uniquely identified within the domain, even if the object has the same name as another object in a different container. Thus, if you have two users, called John Doe and Jane Doe, you can use the RDN jdoe for both of them. As long as they are located in different containers, they will have different DNs.

Canonical Names

Most Active Directory applications refer to objects using their canonical names. A *canonical name* is a DN in which the domain name comes first, followed by the names of the object's parent containers working down from the root of the domain and separated by forward slashes, followed by the object's RDN, as follows:

    zacker.com/sales/inside/jdoe

In this example, jdoe is a user object in the inside container, which is in the sales container, which is in the NY.zacker.com domain.

LDAP Notation

The same DN can also be expressed in LDAP notation, which would appear as follows:

    cn=jdoe,ou=inside,ou=sales,dc=zacker.dc=com

This notation reverses the order of the object names, starting with the RDN on the left and the domain name on the right. The elements are separated by commas and include the LDAP abbreviations that define each type of element. These abbreviations are as follows:

- **cn**   Common name
- **ou**   Organizational unit
- **dc**   Domain component

Icon	Object Type	Function
	Domain	Container object that stores organizational unit objects and their contents.
	Organizational unit	Container object that stores computer, user, and group objects within the tree structure.
	User	Leaf object that represents a network user and stores identification and authentication data about that user.
	Computer	Leaf object that represents a computer on the network, stores information about the computer, and provides the machine account needed for the system to log on to the domain.
	Contact	Leaf object that represents a user outside the domain for specific purposes, such as e-mail delivery; does not enable the user to log on to the domain.
	Group	Container objects that represent logical groupings of users, computers, and/or other groups that are independent of the AD tree structure. Group members can be located in any organizational unit or domain in the tree.
	Shared folder	Represents a shared folder on a Windows 2000 system.
	Shared printer	Represents a shared printer on a Windows 2000 system.

Table 23-1. *Active Directory Object Types*

In most cases, LDAP names do not include the abbreviations, and they can be omitted without altering the uniqueness or the functionality of the name. It is also

possible to express an LDAP name in a URL format, as defined in RFC 1959, which
appears as follows:

```
ldap://cz1.zacker.com/cn=jdoe,ou=inside,ou=sales,dc=zacker.dc=com
```

This format differs in that the name of a server hosting the directory service must
appear immediately following the ldap:// identifier, followed by the same LDAP
name as shown earlier. This notation enables users to access Active Directory
information using a standard Web browser.

Globally Unique Identifiers

In addition to its DN, every object in the tree has a *globally unique identifier (GUID)*,
which is a 128-bit number that is automatically assigned by the Directory System Agent
when the object is created. Unlike the DN, which changes if you move the object to a
different container or rename it, the GUID is permanent and serves as the ultimate
identifier for an object.

User Principal Names

Distinguished names are used by applications and services when they communicate
with Active Directory, but they are not easy for users to understand, type, or
remember. Therefore, each user object has a *user principle name (UPN)* that consists of a
username and a suffix, separated by an @ symbol, just like the standard Internet e-mail
address format defined in RFC 822. This name provides users with a simplified
identity on the network and insulates them from the need to know their place in the
domain tree hierarchy.

In most cases, the username part of the UPN is the user object's RDN, and the suffix
is the DNS name of the domain in which the user object is located. However, if your
network consists of multiple domains, you can opt to use a single domain name as the
suffix for all of your users' UPNs. This way, the UPN can remain unchanged even if
you move the user object to a different domain.

The UPN is an internal name that is used only on the Windows 2000 network, so it
doesn't have to conform to the user's Internet e-mail address. However, using your
network's e-mail domain name as the suffix is a good idea, so that users only have to
remember one address for accessing e-mail and logging on to the network.

  *You can use the Active Directory Domains and Trusts console to specify alternate UPN
suffixes, so that all of your users can log on to the network using the same suffix.*

Domains, Trees, and Forests

Windows NT has always based its networking paradigm on domains, and all but small
networks require multiple domains to support their users. Windows 2000 makes it
easier to manage multiple domains by combining them into larger units called trees

and forests. When you create a new Active Directory database by promoting a server to domain controller, you create the first domain in the first tree of a new forest. If you create additional domains in the same tree, they all share the same schema, configuration, and Global Catalog Server (GCS), and are connected by transitive trust relationships.

Trust relationships are how domains interact with each other to provide a unified network directory. If Domain A trusts Domain B, then the users in Domain B can access the resources in Domain A. In Windows NT domains, trust relationships operate in one direction only and must be explicitly created by network administrators. If you want to create a full network of trusts between three domains, for example, you must create six separate trust relationships, so that each domain trusts every other domain. Active Directory automatically creates trust relationships between domains in the same tree. These trust relationships flow in both directions, are authenticated using the Kerberos security protocol, and are *transitive,* meaning that if Domain A trusts Domain B and Domain B trusts Domain C, then Domain A automatically trusts Domain C. A *tree,* therefore, is a single administrative unit that encompasses a number of domains. The administrative nightmare of manually creating trust relationships between domains is diminished, and users are able to access resources on other domains.

The domains in a tree share a contiguous name space. Unlike a Windows NT domain, which has a single, flat name, an Active Directory domain has a hierarchical name that is based on the DNS name space, such as mycorp.com. Sharing a contiguous name space means that if the first domain in a tree is given the name mycorp.com, the subsequent domains in that tree will have names that build on the parent domain's name, such as sales.mycorp.com and mis.mycorp.com (see Figure 23-1).

The parent/child relationships in the domain hierarchy are limited solely to the sharing of a name space and the trust relationships between them. Unlike the container hierarchy within a domain, rights and permissions do not flow down the tree from domain to domain.

In most cases, a single tree is sufficient for a network of almost any size. However, it is possible to create multiple trees and join them together in a unit known as a *forest.* All of the domains in a forest, including those in separate trees, share the same schema, configuration, and GCS. Every domain in a forest has a transitive trust relationship with the other domains, regardless of the trees they are in. The only difference between the trees in a forest is that they have separate name spaces. Each tree has its own root domain and child domains that build off of its name. The first domain created in a forest is known as the *forest root domain.*

The most common reason for having multiple trees is the merging of two organizations, both of which already have established domain names that cannot be readily assimilated into one tree. Users are able to access resources in other trees, because the trust relationships between domains in different trees are the same as those within a single tree. It is also possible to create multiple forests on your network, but the need for this is rare.

Different forests do not share the same schema, configuration, and GCS, nor are trust relationships automatically created between forests. It is possible to manually

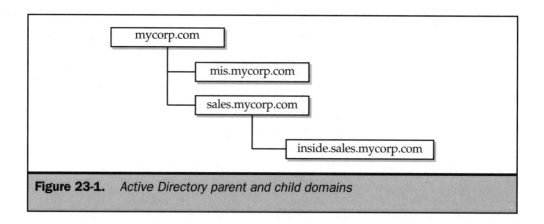

Figure 23-1.   *Active Directory parent and child domains*

create unidirectional trusts between domains in different forests, just as you would on a Windows NT network; but in most cases, the primary reason for creating multiple forests is to completely isolate two areas of the network and prevent interaction between them.

DNS and Active Directory

Windows NT is based on NetBIOS, and uses a NetBIOS name server called *Windows Internet Naming Service (WINS)* to locate computers on the network and resolve their names into IP addresses. The primary limitation of NetBIOS and WINS is that they use a flat name space, whereas Active Directory's name space is hierarchical. The AD name space is based on that of the Domain Name System (DNS), so the directory uses DNS servers instead of WINS to resolve names and locate domain controllers. You must have at least one DNS server running on your network in order for Active Directory to function properly.

The domains in an Active Directory are named using standard DNS domain names, that may or may not be the same as the names your organization uses on the Internet. If, for example, you have already registered the domain name mycorp.com for use with your Internet servers, you can choose to use that same name as the parent domain in your AD tree or create a new name for internal use. The new name doesn't have to be registered, because its use will be limited to your Windows 2000 network only.

DNS is based on resource records (RRs) that contain information about specific machines on the network. Traditionally, administrators must create these records manually; but on a Windows 2000 network, this causes problems. The task of manually creating records for hundreds of computers is long and difficult, and it is compounded by the use of the Dynamic Host Configuration Protocol (DHCP) to automatically assign IP addresses to network systems. Because the IP addresses on DHCP-managed systems can change, there must be a way for the DNS records to be updated to reflect those changes.

Microsoft DNS Server included with Windows 2000 supports the new SRV resource record type that enables client systems to use DNS queries to locate Windows 2000 domain controllers. The Microsoft DNS server also supports dynamic DNS (DDNS), which works together with Microsoft DHCP Server to dynamically update the resource records for specific systems as their IP addresses change. Many of the older DNS server products used today (such as BIND version 4.*xx*) do not support these new features and will not work with Active Directory. However, these new DNS features have been standardized and are being implemented in other manufacturers' products, such as newer versions of BIND. The only one of these new features that is absolutely required by Active Directory is support for the SRV resource record; other features, such as DDNS, secure DDNS, and incremental zone transfers, are recommended but not essential.

Active Directory is still a relatively new product, and is bound to undergo some revisions as it matures, which may affect the relationship between the directory service and DNS. If you are deploying AD on a production network, it is a good idea to stick with Microsoft DNS Server, because it will no doubt be upgraded to conform to any changes made to the directory service itself.

 For more information on the Domain Name System standards and functions, see Chapter 20.

Global Catalog Server

To support large enterprise networks, Active Directory can be both partitioned and replicated, meaning that the directory can be split into sections stored on different servers, and that copies of each section can be maintained on separate servers. Splitting up the directory in this way, however, makes it more difficult for applications to locate specific information. Therefore, Active Directory maintains the *global catalog*, which provides a complete picture of the entire directory structure. While a domain controller contains the Active Directory information for one domain only, the global catalog is a replica of the entire Active Directory, except that it includes only the essential attributes of each object, known as *binding data.*

Because the global catalog consists of a substantially smaller amount of data than the entire directory, it can be stored on a single server and accessed more quickly by users and applications. The global catalog makes it easy for applications to search for specific objects in Active Directory using any of the attributes included in the binding data.

Deploying Active Directory

All of the architectural elements of Active Directory that have been described thus far, such as domains, trees, and forests, are logical components that do not necessarily have any effect on the physical network. In most cases, network administrators create domains, trees, and forests based on the political divisions within an organization, such as workgroups and departments, although geographical elements can come into play as well. Physically, however, an Active Directory installation is manifested as a collection of domain controllers, split into subdivisions called *sites*.

Creating Domain Controllers

A *domain controller (DC)* is a Windows 2000 Server system that hosts all or part of the Active Directory database and provides the services to the rest of the network through which applications access that database. When a user logs on to the network or requests access to a specific network resource, the workstation contacts a domain controller, which authenticates the user and grants access to the network.

Unlike Windows NT 4.0, Active Directory has only one type of domain controller. When installing an NT 4 server, you have to specify whether it should be a primary domain controller (PDC), a backup domain controller (BDC), or a member server. Once a system is installed as a domain controller for a specific domain, there is no way to move it to another domain or change it back to a member server. All Windows 2000 servers start out as member servers; you can then promote them to domain controllers and later demote them back to member servers. Active Directory has no PDCs and BDCs; all domain controllers function as peers.

Anyone who has worked with Windows NT 4.0 domains will understand how the ability to promote servers to domain controllers and demote them at will is a major boon to the network administrator. This capability enables you to add domain controllers when necessary or reassign a domain controller to another domain as needed. This type of flexible deployment enables you to modify Active Directory as the network grows and business conditions change. When a corporation reorganizes its divisions, for example, the network administrators can modify the AD structure by reassigning domain controllers as needed, while Windows NT 4.0 servers would probably have to be completely reinstalled to conform to the new organization.

To promote a Windows 2000 server into a domain controller, you use the Active Directory Installation Wizard utility (see Figure 23-2), which you launch by running the Dcpromo.exe program from the command line. To do this, you must be logged on to the local machine with administrator privileges. The wizard guides you through the process of either creating a new domain or a replica of an existing domain, and of deciding whether the new domain should be the first in a new tree or forest or be the child of an existing domain. If the server is already a domain controller, the wizard enables you to demote it to a member server.

A server that is to function as a domain controller must have at least one NTFS 5.0 drive to hold the Active Directory database, log files, and the system volume, and must have access to a DNS server that supports the SRV resource record and (optionally) dynamic updates. If the computer cannot locate a DNS server that provides these features, it offers to install and configure the Microsoft DNS Server software on the Windows 2000 system.

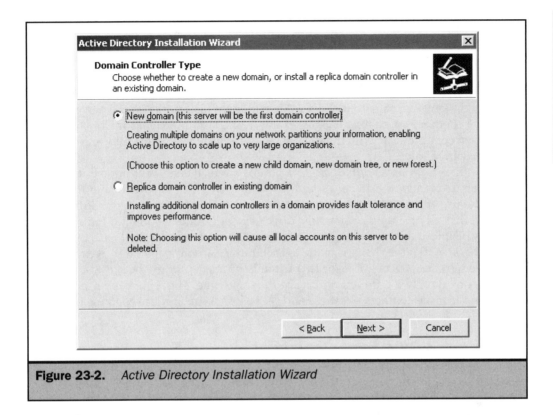

Figure 23-2.   *Active Directory Installation Wizard*

Windows 2000 includes an upgraded version of the NT file system (NTFS 5.0), which you must use to store Active Directory data. You cannot use FAT drives or NTFS drives created by Windows NT, unless you upgrade them during the Windows 2000 installation. The amount of disk space required by Active Directory varies, of course, depending on the size of the network and how you intend to partition the database. A 1GB partition should be the absolute minimum for an Active Directory domain controller.

Directory Replication

Every domain on your network should be represented by at least two domain controllers, for reasons of fault tolerance. Once your network is reliant on Active Directory for authentication and other services, inaccessible domain controllers would be a major problem. Therefore, each domain should be replicated on at least two domain controllers, so that one is always available. Directory service replication is nothing new, but Active Directory replicates its domain data differently from Windows NT.

Windows NT domains are replicated using a technique called *single master replication,* in which a single PDC with read/write capabilities replicates its data to one or more BDCs that are read-only. In this method, replication traffic always travels in one direction, from the PDC to the BDCs. If the PDC fails, one of the BDCs can be promoted to PDC. The drawback of this arrangement is that changes to the directory can only be made to the PDC. When an administrator creates a new user account or modifies an existing one, for example, the User Manager for Domains utility must communicate with the PDC, even if it is located at a distant site connected by a slow WAN link.

Active Directory uses *multiple master replication,* which enables administrators to make changes on any of a domain's replicas. This is why there are no longer PDCs or BDCs. The use of multiple masters makes the replication process far more difficult, however. Instead of simply copying the directory data from one domain controller to another, the information on each domain controller must be compared with that on all of the others, so that the changes made to each replica are propagated to every other replica. In addition, it's possible for two administrators to modify the same attribute of the same object on two different replicas at the same time. The replication process must be able to reconcile conflicts like these and see to it that each replica contains the most up-to-date information.

Multimaster Data Synchronization

Some directory services, such as NDS, base their data synchronization algorithms on timestamps assigned to each database modification. Whichever change has the later timestamp is the one that becomes operative when the replication process is completed. The problem with this method is that the use of timestamps requires the clocks on all of the network's domain controllers to be precisely synchronized, which is difficult to arrange. The Active Directory replication process only relies on timestamps in certain situations. Instead, AD uses *Update Sequence Numbers (USNs),* which are 64-bit values assigned to all modifications written to the directory. Whenever an attribute changes, the domain controller increments the USN and stores it with the attribute, whether the change results from direct action by an administrator or replication traffic received from another domain controller.

In addition to the USN stored with the attributes on the local system, each domain controller maintains a table containing the highest USN value it has received from each of the other domain controllers with which it replicates its data. When the replication process begins, the domain controller requests that its replication partners transmit all modifications with USNs greater than the highest value in the table. Domain controllers also use the USNs to recover from failures or down periods. When the server restarts, it transmits the highest value in its USN table to its replication partners, and the other domain controllers use this information to supply all updates that have occurred since the system went offline.

The only problem with this method is when the same attribute is modified on two different domain controllers. If an administrator changes the value of a specific attribute on Server B before a change made to the same attribute on Server A is fully propagated to all of the replicas, then a *collision* is said to have occurred. To resolve the collision, the domain controllers use property version numbers to determine which value should take precedence. Unlike USNs, which are a single numerical sequence maintained separately by each domain controller, there is only one property version number for each object attribute.

When a domain controller modifies an attribute as a result of direct action by a network administrator, it increments the property version number. However, when a domain controller receives an attribute modification in the replication traffic from another domain controller, it does not modify the property version number. A domain controller detects collisions by comparing the attribute values and property version numbers received during a replication event with those stored in its own database. If an attribute arriving from another domain controller has the same property version number as the local copy of that attribute, but the values don't match, then a collision has occurred. In this case, and only in this case, the system uses the timestamps included with each of the attributes to determine which value is newer and should take precedence over the other.

Sites

A single domain can have any number of domain controllers, all of which contain the same information, thanks to the AD replication system. In addition to providing fault tolerance, you can create additional domain controllers to provide users with local access to the directory. In an organization with offices in multiple locations, connected by WAN links, it would be impractical to have only one or two domain controllers, because workstations would have to communicate with the AD database over a relatively slow, expensive WAN connection. Therefore, administrators typically create a domain controller at each location where there are resources in the domain.

The relatively slow speed and high cost of the average WAN connection also affects the replication process between domain controllers, and for this reason, Active Directory can break a domain up into sites. A site is a collection of domain controllers that are assumed to be well-connected, meaning that all of the systems are connected using the same relatively high-speed LAN technology. The connections between sites are assumed to be WANs that are slower and possibly more expensive.

The actual speed of the intra-site and inter-site connections is not an issue; your LANs can run at 10 to 100 Mbps, and the WAN connections can be anything from dial-ups to T1s. The issue is the relative speed between the domain controllers at the same site and those at different sites. The reason for dividing a domain into logical units that reflect the physical layout of the network is to control the replication traffic that passes over the slower and more expensive WAN links. Active Directory also uses sites to determine which domain controller a workstation should access when authenticating a user. Whenever possible, authentication procedures use a domain controller located on the same site.

Intra-Site Replication

The replication of data between domain controllers located at the same site is completely automatic and self-regulating. A component called the Knowledge Consistency Checker (KCC) dynamically creates connections between the domain controllers as needed to create a replication topology that minimizes latency. *Latency* is the period of time during which the information stored on the domain controllers for a single domain is different; that is, the interval between the modification of an attribute on one domain controller and the propagation of that change to the other domain controllers. The KCC triggers a replication event whenever a change is made to the AD database on any of the site's replicas.

The KCC maintains at least two connections to each domain controller at the site. This way, if a controller goes offline, replication between all of the other domain controllers is still possible. The KCC may create additional connections to maintain timely contact between the remaining domain controllers while the system is unavailable, and then remove them when the system comes back online. In the same way, if you add a new domain controller, the KCC modifies the replication topology to include it in the data synchronization process. As a rule, the KCC creates a replication topology in which each domain controller is no more than three hops away from any other domain controller. Because the domain controllers are all located on the same site, they are assumed to be well-connected, and the KCC is willing to expend network bandwidth in the interest of replication speed. All updates are transmitted in uncompressed form because, even though this requires the transmission of more data, it minimizes the amount of processing needed at each domain controller.

Replication occurs primarily within domains, but when multiple domains are located at the same site, the KCC also creates connections between the global catalog servers for each domain, so that they can exchange information and create a replica of the entire Active Directory containing the subset of attributes that form the binding data.

Inter-Site Replication

By default, a domain consists of a single site, called Default-First-Site-Name, and any additional domains you create are placed within that site. You can, however, use the Active Directory Sites and Services utility to create additional sites and move domains into them. Just as with domains in the same site, Active Directory creates a replication topology between domains in different sites, but with several key differences.

Because the WAN links between sites are assumed to be slower and more expensive, Active Directory attempts to minimize the amount of replication traffic that passes between them. First, there are fewer connections between domain controllers at different sites than with a site; the three-hop rule is not observed for the inter-site replication topology. Second, all replication data transmitted over inter-site connections is compressed, to minimize the amount of bandwidth utilized by the replication process. Finally, replication events between sites are not automatically triggered by modifications to the Active Directory database. Instead, replication can be scheduled to occur at specified times and intervals, to minimize the effect on standard user traffic and to take advantage of lower bandwidth costs during off hours.

Creating and Configuring Sites

Splitting a network into sites has no effect on the hierarchy of domains, trees, and forests that you have created to represent your enterprise. However, sites still appear as objects in Active Directory, along with several other object types that you use to configure your network's replication topology. These objects are only visible in the Active Directory Sites and Services tool, as shown in Figure 23-3. The object called Default-First-Site-Name is created automatically when you promote the first server on your network to a domain controller, along with a server object that appears in the Servers folder beneath it. Server objects are always subordinate to site objects, and represent the domain controllers operating at that site. A site can contain server objects for domain controllers in any number of domains, located in any tree or forest. You can move server objects between sites as needed.

The other two important object types associated with sites and servers are subnet and site link objects. Subnet objects represent the particular IP subnets that you use at your various sites, and are used to define the boundaries of the site. When you create a subnet object, you specify a network address and subnet mask. When you associate a site with a subnet object, server objects for any new domain controllers that you create

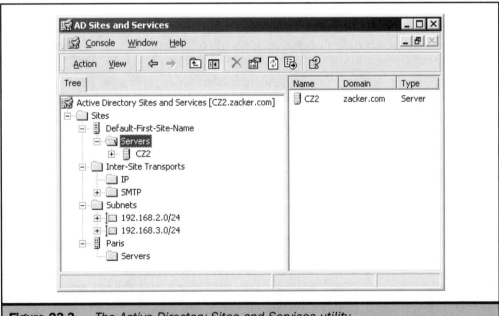

Figure 23-3. *The Active Directory Sites and Services utility*

on that subnet are automatically created in that site. You can associate multiple subnet objects with a particular site, to create a complete picture of your network.

Site link objects represent the WAN links on your network that Active Directory will use to create connections between domain controllers at different sites. Active Directory supports the use of the Internet Protocol (IP) and the Simple Mail Transport Protocol (SMTP) for site links, both of which appear in the Inter-Site Transports folder in Active Directory Sites and Services. IP site links can use any type of WAN connection, such as a dial-up modem connection or a T1. An SMTP site link can take the form of any applications you use to send e-mail using the SMTP protocol. When you create a site link object, you select the sites that are connected by the WAN link the object represents. The attributes of site link objects include various mechanisms for determining when and how often Active Directory should use the link to transmit replication traffic between sites (see Figure 23-4), including the following:

- **Cost**   The cost of a site link can reflect either the monetary cost of the WAN technology involved or the cost in terms of the bandwidth needed for other purposes. For example, the monthly bills for a T1 connection may be astronomical, but if you installed the T1 primarily for the purpose of supporting replication traffic, you don't want to assign it a high cost that results in its not being used. The higher the value of the cost setting, the less frequently AD uses the link for replication traffic.

- **Schedule**   Specifies the hours of the day during each day of the week that the link can be used to carry replication traffic. If you want to minimize the impact of replication on a link used for other types of traffic during work hours, you can create a schedule that enables replication to occur on this link only during non-production times.

- **Replication period**   Specifies the interval between replication procedures that use this link, subject to the schedule described previously.

By default, Active Directory creates an IP site link object, DEFAULTIPSITELINK, that you can use as is or modify to reflect the type of link used to connect your sites. If all of your sites are connected by WAN links of the same type, you don't have to create additional site link objects, because a single set of scheduling attributes should be applicable for all of your inter-site connections. If you use various types of WAN connections, however, you can create a separate site link object for each type and configure its attributes to reflect how you want it to be used.

There is another type of object that you can create in the Inter-Site Transports container, called a *site link bridge object,* that is designed to make it possible to route replication traffic through one remote site to others. By default, the site links that you create are transitive, meaning that they are bridged together, enabling them to route replication traffic. For example, if you have a site link object connecting Site A to Site B, and another one connecting Site B to Site C, then Site A can send replication traffic to Site C. If you want to, you can disable the default bridging by opening the Properties

NETWORK DIRECTORY
SERVICES

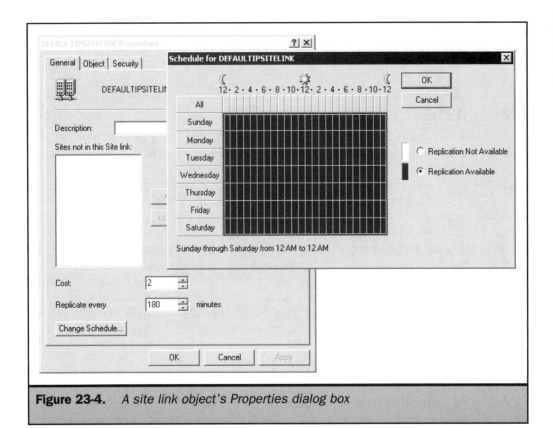

Figure 23-4. *A site link object's Properties dialog box*

dialog box for the IP folder and clearing the Bridge All Site Links check box. If you do this, then you must manually create site link bridge objects in order to route replication traffic in this way. A site link bridge object generally represents a router on the network. While a site link object groups two site objects together, a site link bridge object groups two site link objects together, making it possible for replication traffic to be routed between them.

Once you have created objects representing the sites that form your network and the links that connect them, the KCC can create connections that form the replication topology for the entire internetwork, subject to the limitations imposed by the site link object attributes. The connections created by the KCC, both within and between sites, appear as objects in the NTDS Settings container beneath each server object. A connection object is unidirectional, representing the traffic running from the server under which the object appears to the target server specified as an attribute of the object. In most cases, there should be no need to manually create or configure connection objects, but it is possible to do so. You can customize the replication topology of your network by creating your own connections and scheduling the times during which they may be used. Manually created connection objects cannot be deleted by the KCC to accommodate changing network conditions; they remain in place until you manually remove them.

Designing an Active Directory

As with any enterprise directory service, the process of deploying Active Directory on your network involves much more than simply installing the software. The planning process is, in many cases, more complicated than the construction of the directory itself. Naturally, the larger your network, the more complicated the planning process will be. You should have a clear idea of the form that your AD structure will take and who will maintain each part of it, before you actually begin to deploy domain controllers and create objects.

In many cases, the planning process will require some hands-on testing before you deploy Active Directory on your production network. You may want to set up a test network and try out some forest designs before you commit yourself to any one plan. Although a test network can't fully simulate the effects of hundreds of users working at once, the time that you spend familiarizing yourself with the Active Directory tools and procedures can only help you later when you're building the live directory service.

Planning Domains, Trees, and Forests

To a Windows NT administrator, Windows 2000 and Active Directory may seem like an embarrassment of riches. While NT networks are based solely on domains, Active Directory expands the scope of the directory service by two orders of magnitude by providing trees and forests that you can use to organize multiple domains. In addition, the domains themselves can be subdivided into smaller administrative entities called organizational units. To use these capabilities effectively, you must evaluate your network in light of both its physical layout and the needs of the organization that it serves.

Creating Multiple Trees

In most cases, a single tree with one or more domains is sufficient to support an enterprise network. The main reason for creating multiple trees is if you have two or more existing DNS name spaces that you want to reflect in Active Directory. For example, a corporation that consists of several different companies that operate independently can use multiple trees to create a separate name space for each company. Although there are transitive trust relationships between all of the domains in a tree, separate trees are connected only by trusts between their root domains, as shown in Figure 23-5.

If you have several levels of child domains in each tree, then the process of accessing a resource in a different tree involves the passing of authentication traffic up from the domain containing the requesting system to the root of the tree, across to the root of the other tree, and down to the domain containing the requested resource. If the

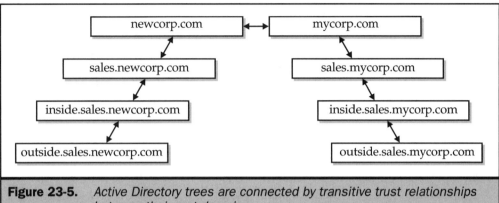

Figure 23-5.   *Active Directory trees are connected by transitive trust relationships between their root domains*

trees operate autonomously, and access requests for resources in other trees are rare, then this may not be much of a problem. If the trust relationships in a directory design like this do cause delays on a regular basis, you can manually create what are known as *shortcut trusts* between child domains lower down in both trees, as shown in Figure 23-6.

Just as you can create multiple trees in a forest, you can create multiple forests in the Active Directory database. Scenarios in which the use of multiple forests is necessary are even rarer than those calling for multiple trees, because forests have no inherent trust relationships between them at all and use a different global catalog, making it more difficult for users even to locate resources. You may want to use a separate forest for a lab-based test network or for a project that you don't want other network users to know even exists.

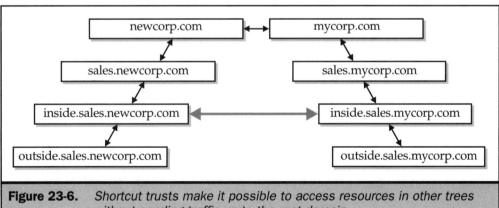

Figure 23-6.   *Shortcut trusts make it possible to access resources in other trees without sending traffic up to the root domain*

Creating Multiple Domains

In Windows NT, the domain is the only administrative available in the directory service. Many administrators have become accustomed to creating separate domains to reflect the department or workgroup divisions in their organizations. Active Directory provides this same capability, but the hierarchical nature of the tree should affect the number of domains that you create. The compound domain names used in Active Directory make it impractical to create a tree that runs to too many layers; the domain names become too long and difficult to use and remember. In many cases, instead of creating a separate domain, it is preferable to create an organizational unit within a domain.

OUs provide administrative boundaries that are similar to those of domains, without extending the domain name space and complicating the network of trust relationships. OUs enable you to assign permissions and create policies for a group of users without modifying their individual user objects. In addition, using OUs instead of domains can yield significant hardware savings, because OUs don't need their own servers to function as domain controllers.

The first element that you should consider when planning your domains is the physical layout of your network, and particularly the WAN links. Splitting a domain among several sites may be desirable in some cases, but you must weigh this against the cost of the bandwidth connecting those sites, the frequency of the changes made to Active Directory, and the location of the people who will maintain the database. If, for example, your AD database is relatively static and your remote sites are relatively small, you can create domain controllers at the different locations, manage them from the central office, and configure the site link objects to perform infrequent database replications. The bandwidth utilized by the replication process will be minimal, and all of the sites will have local access to the resources in the domain.

If you make frequent changes to the AD database, you may be better off creating separate domains at each site, to prevent the need for frequent replication events. Even if you do this, however, there is still some replication traffic that passes across the WAN links, since all of the domains in the forest share a common global catalog, as well as the traffic generated by users accessing resources in domains at other sites.

Another factor that can influence the creation of separate domains is the language used at each site. If your organization has sites in different countries and uses the language indigenous to each country, creating separate domains for each site may be recommended, especially if the sites are located in countries that use non-Roman alphabets, such as Japan or Russia.

Object Naming

One of the most important elements of a directory service plan is the conventions that you will use when naming the objects in the database and the domains that form the network. AD tree designs can be based on several different criteria, including the geographical locations of network resources and the political divisions within an organization; but however you choose to represent the network in the AD design, you should be consistent in the names that you assign objects.

User object names, for example, should consist of a standardized pattern derived from the users' names, such as the first initial plus the surname. In the same way, domains and containers named for geographical locations or departmental divisions should use standardized abbreviations. This type of consistency makes it easier to search for specific objects in the global catalog.

Locating resources on a Windows 2000 network is more complicated than on Windows NT, because the directory service is designed to support networks of almost unlimited size. In Windows NT, each domain is a separate entity and there is no mechanism for performing a global search for a particular resource. Object naming can be a more informal process, because users and administrators are more likely to be intimately familiar with the domain configuration. Active Directory's global catalog, on the other hand, can contain information about thousands of objects located anywhere in the world, and the ability to search successfully for the data needed can be greatly enhanced by the implementation of consistent naming policies for the entire directory.

When it comes to naming domains and trees, the biggest decision you have to make is whether or not you should use the same name space for both your internal network resources and the external resources that are visible to the Internet. Registering one domain name for your organization with a registrar like Network Solutions, Inc. and using it both for your Internet servers and as the root domain name for your AD tree creates a unified name space for your network that has both advantages and disadvantages.

It is important to remember that the average network user is far less acquainted with the infrastructure than the average administrator. Using a single root domain name provides a consistency that makes the network easier for users to understand and also enables them to use their Internet e-mail addresses as their UPNs. The disadvantages of using the same name space are that it can be difficult to distinguish between internal and external resources, and the system is inherently less secure if your domain names are publicly known on the Internet.

Upgrading from Windows NT 4.0

In many cases, Windows 2000 will be installed on an existing Windows NT network, and the domain-based directory service will be upgraded to Active Directory. Windows 2000 and AD are capable of interacting with NT systems, either on a temporary or permanent basis, so there is no need to upgrade the entire network in one weekend. However, as with the installation of a new Windows 2000 network, the upgrade process must be carefully planned in order to proceed smoothly.

Note *This section assumes that the NT systems being upgraded to Windows 2000 are running Windows NT 4.0. There are serious incompatibilities in the authentication methods used by Windows 2000 and Windows NT versions 3.51 and earlier that have led to a recommendation by Microsoft that these two operating systems not be used together.*

Whenever you create an Active Directory domain, the Installation Wizard prompts you for a NetBIOS name for the domain, in addition to the DNS name. By default, the wizard creates the NetBIOS name simply by dropping the .com or other suffix from the DNS name you've supplied for the domain. Downlevel client systems (that is, clients not running Windows 2000) will see the domain using the NetBIOS name rather than the full DNS name.

The basic plan when upgrading an NT network to Windows 2000 is to upgrade the PDCs first, then the BDCs, then the member servers, and finally the clients. You can spread the process out as long as you want, however, and run the NT and 2000 servers together indefinitely. When you upgrade a Windows NT 4.0 PDC to Windows 2000 and promote it to a domain controller, the system functions in mixed mode, meaning that it can use the BDCs for the domain you've upgraded as Active Directory domain controllers. While in mixed mode, the Windows NT 4.0 BDCs operate as fully functional Active Directory domain controllers, capable of multiple master replication and all other AD functions. Once you've upgraded the BDCs to Windows 2000 domain controllers, you can switch the servers to native mode, from the domain's Properties dialog box in the Active Directory Domains and Trusts tool (see Figure 23-7). The drawbacks to running in mixed mode are that you can't nest groups within groups in an Active Directory tree and you can't have groups with members in different domains. Once you've switched to native mode, you can do both of these things.

Note   *Switching from mixed mode to native mode is a one-way process. Once you've switched a server, you cannot switch it back without completely reinstalling it. Be sure that all of your upgraded domain controllers are functioning properly before you make this change.*

If your NT network is relatively simple and based on the single domain model, migrating to Active Directory is simply a matter of upgrading the systems to Windows 2000 in the order previously specified. However, many networks are considerably more complicated, and further planning is required. If your network uses the single master domain model, then you have one account domain containing all of your users and groups and one or more resource domains that contain all of your network's shared resources. This model fits into a single Active Directory tree that may or may not eventually include all of your original domains. For example, you might want to consolidate the tree into a single domain in which the former resource domains are converted to OUs in the original account domain, or even migrate the resource objects directly into the account domain without segregating them in OUs. If you eliminate some domains in this way, you can redeploy some of your servers by creating additional replicas of other domains or demoting them to member servers.

One of the original purposes for using the single master domain model in Windows NT is to limit the number of trust relationships that administrators have to create and maintain. In that model, each of the resource domains has a one-way trust relationship with the account domain. No trusts between resource domains are needed. In Active Directory, the trust relationships between domains are created automatically, so this is

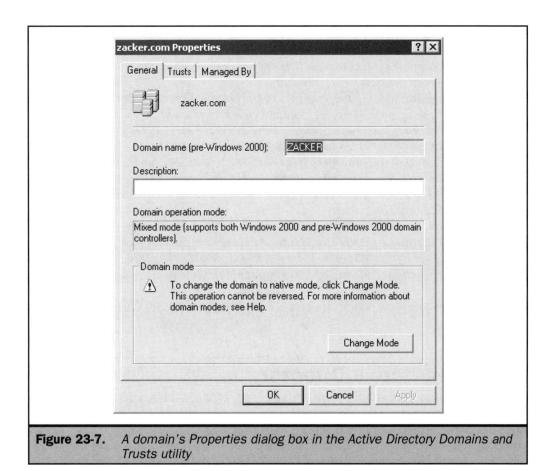

Figure 23-7. *A domain's Properties dialog box in the Active Directory Domains and Trusts utility*

not an issue. You can consolidate the NT domains before you perform the upgrade to AD or after, but you will probably find that the tools for manipulating Active Directory make it easier to consolidate the NT domains after you upgrade the servers.

To start the migration to Active Directory, you must upgrade the PDC in the account domain first, so that it becomes the root domain of the new AD tree. Then, you should upgrade the PDCs of the resource domains, making them children of the root domain and establishing the tree structure. Once the PDC upgrades are completed, you can proceed to upgrade the BDCs for all of the domains, and then modify the tree design to take advantage of Active Directory's capabilities.

If your NT network uses the multiple master domain model, you must examine the reasons for using this model in the first place before you decide on an upgrade strategy. In the multiple master domain model, there are two or more account domains, connected by two-way trust relationships, and a number of resource domains, each of which trusts all of the account domains. In some cases, this model is used simply to support a larger number of users than can comfortably fit in a single account domain. In other cases, multiple masters are needed because the organization uses a decentralized support system in which the network is divided into sites or divisions that each has its own network administrators.

If the deciding factor is the number of users, an Active Directory domain can support many more users than an NT domain, which may lead you to consolidate all of the account domains into one, or create a new directory service design entirely. If you have separate support teams for your domains, you may want to consider creating an Active Directory that uses multiple trees, with each account domain becoming the root of a separate tree. Again, because the trust relationships in AD are created automatically, there is no need to design the directory around the task of manually creating trust relationships.

Once you have made your design decisions, the upgrade process is roughly the same as that for the single master domain model. Upgrade the PDCs of the account domains first, either by selecting one to be the root domain of your tree or by creating a new tree for each account domain, and then upgrade the BDCs.

Note   *For more information on the Windows NT 4.0 domain models, see Chapter 22.*

Managing Active Directory

Once you've designed and built your Active Directory installation, you're ready to populate it with objects. Creating and managing user and group accounts is an everyday task for the typical network administrator, and in Windows 2000, you do this with the Active Directory Users and Computers console, as shown in Figure 23-8. Like most Microsoft Management Console (MMC) snap-ins, the Users and Computers utility consists of a scope pane (on the left) and a result pane (on the right). In this case, the scope pane displays the domains in your tree and the OUs in each domain, and the result pane displays the objects in the highlighted container, such as users and groups.

By default, Active Directory domains contain the following four container objects:

- **Builtin**   Contains various built-in security groups used to delegate system administration tasks.
- **Computers**   Contains computer objects representing the accounts for the machines that are members of the domain.
- **Domain Controllers**   Contains computer objects representing the servers that are functioning as domain controllers for the selected domain.
- **Users**   Contains the default user objects for the domain, such as the Administrator and Guest accounts, and group objects used for delegating domain administrative tasks.

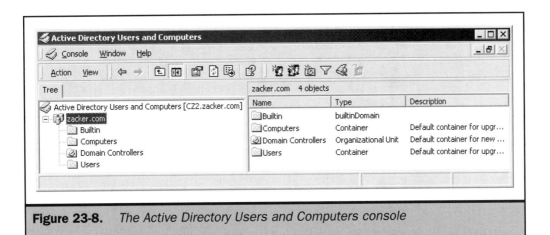

Figure 23-8.   *The Active Directory Users and Computers console*

You can use these existing containers by adding your own user accounts to the Users container and so forth, or you can create your own hierarchy of organizational units and populate it with objects as needed. One of the big differences between creating user objects in Active Directory and in Windows NT is the amount of information that an AD object can store. As you can see in Figure 23-9, the Properties dialog box for each user object has 12 screens that you can use to supply information about the user. For most administrators, the first inclination is to skip all of the informational screens and fields and configure only the attributes that are absolutely needed for the object to function. You should think twice before you do this, however, especially if you are working on a large network. One of the major advantages of Active Directory is the ability to search the entire database for objects, based on the values of specific attributes.

Consider a large corporation with offices in many different cities, for example. There is probably someone in the organization who is responsible for maintaining and publishing a corporate directory that lists all of the employees and vital information about them, such as telephone numbers and e-mail addresses. If you take the time to include just the phone number and e-mail address for each of the user objects that you create, you can eventually eliminate the need to maintain this directory by making it possible for users to search Active Directory for an employee's phone number instead. This is just one example of how Active Directory can become the primary information resource about your network and the people who use it.

Because Active Directory is designed to support networks of almost any size, it is not expected that one administrator will be responsible for the entire directory. There are likely to be situations in which certain administration tasks are delegated to a

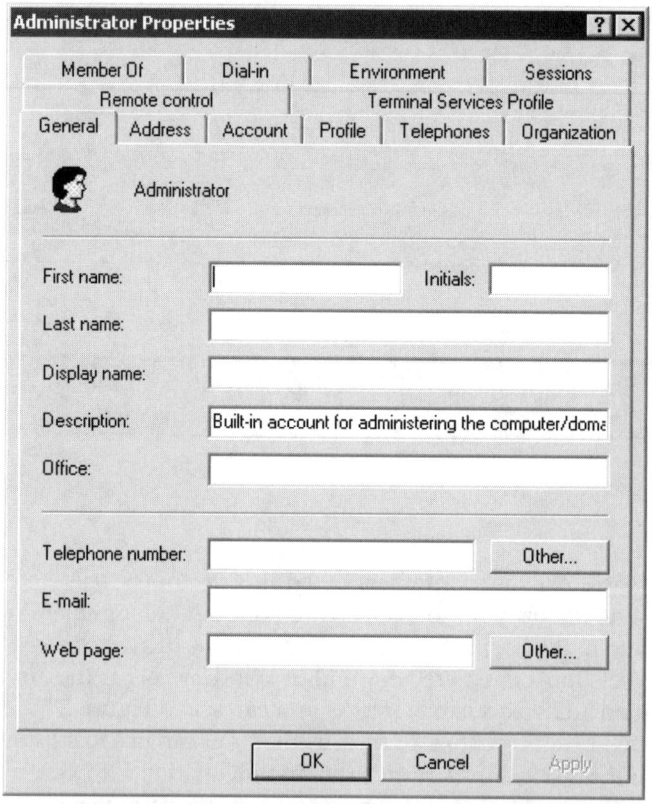

Figure 23-9. A user object's Properties dialog box

variety of individuals, not all of whom should have administrative rights to the entire directory service. To make this possible, Windows 2000 includes a Delegation of Control Wizard that enables you to grant users certain administrative rights to specific users and groups. This way, you can allow managers or supervisors to maintain the accounts of the people who work for them, without endangering the other parts of the directory tree. Once you select the users and groups for whom you want to delegate control and the user who will control them, you specify the tasks that the user can perform, using the dialog box shown in Figure 23-10.

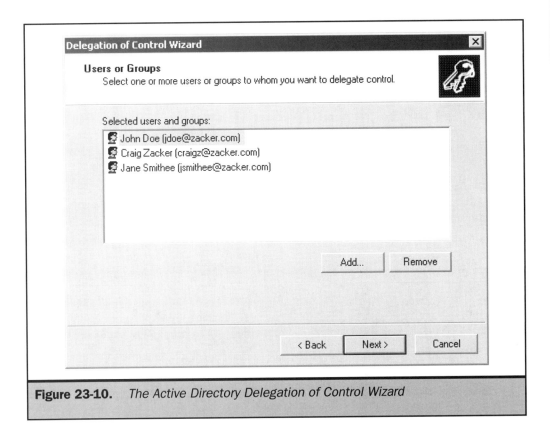

Figure 23-10.   *The Active Directory Delegation of Control Wizard*

The
Complete
Reference

Part VII

Network Services

The Complete Reference

Upgrading & Troubleshooting Networks

Chapter 24

Deploying Internet Servers

A t one time, the term "server" in computer networking was nearly always used in the phrase "file server," referring to a PC running a network operating system (NOS), such as Novell NetWare, that enables users to access shared files and printers. However, the rapid growth of the Internet and the rise of Windows NT as the most popular NOS on the market have changed the common meaning of the term. To average Internet users, servers are the invisible systems that host World Wide Web and FTP sites, or that enable them to send and receive e-mail. For LAN users, servers still fill the traditional file and printer sharing roles, but also provide application-related functions, such as access to databases. Thus, people are gradually learning that a *server* is a software, not a hardware, entity, and that a single computer can actually function in multiple server roles simultaneously.

Internet servers are software products that provide traditional Internet services to clients, whether or not they are actually connected through the Internet. Web, FTP, and e-mail are all services that can be as useful on a LAN as on the Internet, and many sites are deploying them for a variety of reasons. This chapter examines the technology behind these services and the procedures for implementing them on your network.

Web Servers

The Web is rapidly becoming a ubiquitous tool for business, education, and recreation. It seems as though virtually every business these days has a Web site, and the components needed to build and access Web sites are integrated into most operating systems. The basic building blocks of the Web are as follows:

- **Web servers**   Computers running a software program that processes resource requests from clients.

- **Browsers**   Client software that generates resource requests and sends them to Web servers.

- **Hypertext Transfer Protocol (HTTP)**   The TCP/IP application-layer protocol that servers and browsers use to communicate.

- **Hypertext Markup Language (HTML)**   The markup language used to create Web pages.

Why Run Your Own Web Servers?

Most organizations and individuals with Web sites use an Internet service provider (ISP) or other outside service to host their sites. Many ISPs offer subscribers a free site with a subscription to their service, and organizations with more complex sites often do business with a Web hosting company that can provide a wider range of services. However, there are several good reasons why you might want to run one or more Web servers on your own network.

The first of these reasons is for Web site development. If you create your own sites, there is no substitute for testing and debugging on a live Web server. Even though you can open HTML files directly from a local drive, getting the links between pages to function properly requires a server. In addition, if you intend to use scripts, applications, or other advanced technologies on your site, you need a server to test them.

Another reason for running your own Web server is to build an intranet. The term *intranet* is defined as a TCP/IP-based network with access restricted to a specific group of users, but in more common usage, it refers to a Web site running on a private network. An intranet is a tool with which you can publish information for your users in many forms. Standard Web pages can reproduce documents in an easily readable form, but you can also use a Web server to create a library of the files stored on your network.

Shared network drives are an excellent way to provide users with access to files, but it can often be difficult for users to locate the exact information they need. A simple text-based intranet Web site can list the files that are available, along with brief descriptions, and enable users to download them to their workstations using standard hyperlinks. Because an intranet is a read-only medium when used in this way, there is no danger of the files being accidentally modified or deleted. In addition to basic document and file access, an intranet can serve as a development platform for Web-based applications that provide access to databases and other resources using a browser as a client.

This discussion also leads to the question of whether, if you have a Web server on your network, you should host your own site on the Web. You certainly can host your own Web site, but there are several other factors that you must consider before you do so. The Web server is only a small part of running a Web site. In addition to the server itself, you must consider the bandwidth that the Web traffic will consume, the ability of your network infrastructure to tolerate hardware or service faults, and the security of your network. Depending on the nature of your site and your business, the first two of these considerations may be minimized, but security is always a concern.

To run a successful and professional Internet Web site, your network must be capable of coping with the traffic generated by constant access from users, and your server must be continuously available. If, for example, the users on your network access the Internet using the same connection as the Web server, then a period of heavy internal use can reduce the bandwidth available to the server. You should make sure that you have either a separate Internet connection for the Web server or sufficient bandwidth to support both your internal users and the Internet server traffic at the same time.

ISPs typically have large amounts of bandwidth available for their servers, and often provide redundant Internet connections as well. Nothing turns a potential customer off more than an exceedingly slow or unavailable Web site. The impression given is that the company has not made a sufficient commitment to the Internet or that it doesn't care, either of which is worse than having no Web site at all. ISPs often have fault-tolerance mechanisms for their Web servers as well, such as mirrored drives or

RAID arrays, redundant power supplies, and other technologies. There's no reason why you can't have these features as well, but many businesses are not ready to spend an exorbitant sum of money to run a Web server.

Security is another major issue. A computer that is accessible from the Internet also provides a gateway to your network for potential intruders. Most LANs use unregistered IP addresses for their workstations, which makes them invisible to the Internet, but the address of an Internet server must be registered in order for users to connect to it. Most administrators who run their own Web servers place them on the "edge" of the network—that is, on a LAN separate from the unregistered workstations—and use a firewall product to prevent outsiders from accessing the servers using anything other than the prescribed protocol and port.

Selecting a Web Server

A Web server is actually a rather simple device. When you see complex pages full of fancy text and graphics on your monitor, you're actually seeing something that is more the product of the page designer and the browser technology than of the Web server. In its simplest form, a Web server is a software program that processes requests for specific files from browsers and delivers those files back to the browser. The server does not read the contents of the files, nor does it participate in the rendering process that controls how a Web page is displayed in the browser. The differences between Web server products are in the additional features they provide and their ability to handle large numbers of requests.

Web Server Platforms

A Web server does not have to be a big, expensive machine. Depending on your requirements and those of your users, you can run a Web server on any PC, from a basic Windows 98 system to a high-end UNIX workstation. Many of the most popular Web server software products are free, such as Microsoft's Internet Information Server (IIS) and Personal Web Server, as well as the Apache Web server for UNIX and NT, while others can be quite expensive. The computer platform on which you choose to run your server generally does not affect connectivity with clients. Any browser can connect to any server, although certain site-development technologies are platform specific.

Active Server Pages, for example, is a technology created by Microsoft that (not surprisingly) requires the use of a Windows NT or 2000 system to host the site, although any browser can display the resulting pages. Microsoft Front Page is a WYSIWYG Web page editor that requires a Windows system to run, but that can upload pages to a Web server running on virtually any platform, using server extension modules provided with the product.

Web server products are available for all PC platforms, including Windows 9x, Windows NT/2000, NetWare, and many UNIX variants. Windows 9x as a Web server platform is suitable for development purposes and light internal use on a LAN, but generally isn't suitable for use as an Internet server. The Windows 98 operating system includes the Personal Web Server product, which provides basic capabilities that are quite serviceable for personal use. In some organizations, individual users or departments use this combination to create small intranet sites that improve communications between colleagues.

Both Windows NT Workstation 4.0 and NT Server 4.0 include a Web server, as well. NT Server includes IIS, and NT Workstation has Microsoft Peer Web Services (PWS). As with Windows NT Server and Workstation themselves, these Web servers are basically the same product, except that IIS includes additional features and is designed to support an unlimited number of connections, while PWS provides only basic functionality and supports ten connections. Thus, PWS, like Windows 9*x*'s Personal Web Server, is generally limited to light LAN use. There are third-party Web server products, however, that are designed to provide greater functionality on NT Workstation systems, such as O'Reilly's WebSite Professional.

Note   *As Windows NT Workstation 4.0 was being prepared for release in 1996, beta testers protested angrily when Microsoft announced that NT Workstation's ten-user limit on the number of client connections applied not only to Windows network clients on the LAN, but also to TCP clients on the Internet. This meant that using an NT Workstation system as an Internet Web server would be a violation of the license agreement if more than ten users were connected at once. Several of the popular third-party Web server developers at the time recommended the use of NT Workstation as a platform for their products. This made their software economically competitive with IIS, because the cost of the Web server balanced out with the additional cost of purchasing NT Server, which is required to run IIS. Microsoft eventually gave in on this issue, making it legal to run an Internet Web server on an NT Workstation system.*

Internet Information Server is Microsoft's full-featured Web server product, which, like all Microsoft Web servers, is free. The original Windows NT Server 4.0 release includes IIS version 2, but the latest version, IIS 4, is available as part of the Windows NT Server Option Pack (see www.microsoft.com/ntserver/nts/downloads/recommended/NT4OptPk). IIS 4 on NT Server 4.0 is one of the most popular Web server platforms in use today. NT provides the flexibility and the security needed to support a large number of users, and IIS includes a large collection of additional features and services that enable you to create complex, cutting-edge Web sites.

Windows has grown rapidly as a Web server platform, largely due to its ease of installation and administration. All of the Microsoft Web server products include a graphical configuration utility. However, UNIX was the original Web server platform, and it is still used by the majority of sites on the Web. By far the most popular UNIX Web server is Apache, a public-domain product based on the original httpd server created by NCSA (National Computational Science Alliance). The name "Apache" is derived from the fact that the server uses the httpd code plus a collection of patches, thus making it *a patchy server*.

Apache is one of the best examples of open source software. The Apache source code is freely available to anyone (see www.apache.org) and maintained by an informal group of programmers, most of whom have never met, that communicate using e-mail and newsgroups. Many add-on modules are available for the core server, providing more advanced features, such as support for various types of scripts and authentication options. Programmers who create new modules or modify existing ones routinely upload their work to public servers for use by others.

Because Apache is not a commercial product and its source code is freely available, it is far more flexible than any Windows Web server. In the UNIX world, the general rule is that if you don't like how a piece of software runs, then go ahead and change it. Not surprisingly, however, Apache is nowhere near as user friendly as a Windows server, and you'll have a much easier time using Apache if you have the programming skills needed to modify its source code. However, there are also compiled versions of the server available for over 20 UNIX variants, as well as Windows NT and Macintosh, so even a nonprogrammer can get the software up and running. Although not as user friendly as Windows, UNIX is generally thought to be a more stable server platform, and the various UNIX operating systems can run on everything from standard Intel PCs to hugely powerful workstations.

Although UNIX and Windows NT systems account for the vast majority of Web servers, there are products for other platforms, such as NetWare and Macintosh. Novell's intraNetWare was the first version of the operating system to include the Novell Web Server product, but this has since been replaced by Netscape FastTrack Web Server, which is included with NetWare versions 4.2 and 5.x. Macintosh systems do not include a Web server of their own, but there are third-party products available, like StarNine Software's WebStar.

Web Server Functions

A Web server is a program that runs in the background on a computer and listens on a particular TCP port for incoming requests. A program of this type has different names on various operating systems. On Windows NT, it's a *service*; on a UNIX system, it's a *daemon*; on NetWare, it's a *NetWare Loadable Module (NLM)*. The standard TCP port for an HTTP server is 80, although most servers enable you to specify a different port number for a site, and may use a second port number for the server's administrative interface. To access a Web server using a different port, you must specify that port number as part of the URL.

UNIFORM RESOURCE LOCATORS The format of the Uniform Resource Locator (URL) that you type into a browser's Address field to access a particular Web site is defined in the RFC 1738 document published by the Internet Engineering Task Force

(IETF). A URL consists of four elements that identify the resource that you want
to access:

- **Protocol** Specifies the application-layer protocol that the browser will use to
  connect to the server. The values defined in the URL standard are as follows
  (others have been defined by additional standards published since RFC 1738):
  - **http** Hypertext Transfer Protocol
  - **ftp** File Transfer Protocol
  - **gopher** Gopher protocol
  - **mailto** E-mail address
  - **news** USENET news
  - **nntp** USENET news using NNTP access
  - **telnet** Reference to interactive sessions
  - **wais** Wide Area Information Servers
  - **file** Host-specific filenames
  - **prospero** Prospero Directory Service
- **Server name** Specifies the DNS name or IP address of the server.
- **Port number** Specifies the port number that the server is monitoring for
  incoming traffic.
- **Directory and file** Identifies the location of the file that the server should send
  to the browser.

The format of a URL is as follows:

protocol://DNSname:port/directory/file.html

Most of the time, users do not specify the protocol, port, directory, and file in their
URLs, and the browser uses its default values. When you enter just a DNS name, such
as www.zacker.com, the browser assumes the use of the HTTP protocol, port 80, and
the Web server's home directory. Fully expanded, this URL would appear something
like the following:

```
http://www.zacker.com:80/index.html
```

The only element that could vary among different servers is the filename of the default
Web page, here shown as index.html. The default filename is configured on each server,
and specifies the file that the server will send to a client when no filename is specified in

the URL. The traditional default filename for UNIX systems is index.html; for Microsoft Web servers, it is default.htm.

If you configure a Web server to use a port other than 80 to host a site, then users must specify the port number as part of the URL. Most Web users don't even know that port numbers exist, so the use of nonstandard ports is relatively rare. The main exception to this is when the administrator wants to create a site that is hidden from the average user. Some Web server products, for example, are configurable using a Web browser, and the server essentially creates an administrative site containing the configuration controls for the program. During the software installation, the program prompts the administrator for a port number that it should use for the administrative site. Thus, specifying the name of the server on a browser opens the default site on port 80, but specifying the server name with the selected port accesses the administrative site.

The use of a nonstandard port is not really a security measure, because there are programs available that can identify the ports that a Web server is using. The administrative site for a server usually has security in the form of user authentication as well; the port number is just a means of keeping the site hidden from curious users.

CGI   Most of the traffic generated by the Web travels from the Web server to the browser. The upstream traffic from browser to server consists mainly of HTTP requests for specific files. However, there are mechanisms by which browsers can send other types of information to servers. The server can then feed the information to an application for processing. The Common Gateway Interface (CGI) is the most widely supported mechanism of this type. In most cases, the user supplies information in a form built into a Web page using standard HTML tags, and then submits the form to a server. The server, on receiving the data from the browser, executes a CGI script that defines how the information should be used. The server might feed the information as a query to a database server, use it to perform an online financial transaction, or use it for any other purpose.

LOGGING   Virtually all Web servers have the capability to maintain logs that track all client access to the site and any errors that have occurred. The logs typically take the form of a text file, with each server access request or error appearing on a separate line. Each line contains multiple fields, separated by spaces or commas. The information logged by the server identifies who accessed the site and when, as well as the exact documents sent to the client by the server. While it is possible for administrators to examine the logs in their raw format and learn some things about the site's usage, such as which pages receive the most hits, there are a number of third-party statistics programs, such as WebTrends (www.webtrends.com), that take the log files as input and produce detailed reports illustrating trends and traffic patterns.

Most Web servers enable the administrator to choose among several formats for the logs they keep. Some servers use proprietary log formats, which generally are not supported by the statistics programs, while other servers may also be able to log server information to an external database using an interface like ODBC. Most servers, however, support the Common Log File format defined by NCSA. This format consists of nothing but one-line entries with fields separated by spaces. The format for each Common Log File entry and the functions of each field are as follows:

```
remotehost logname username date request status bytes
```

- **remotehost** Specifies the IP address of the remote client system. Some servers also include a DNS reverse lookup feature that resolves the address into a DNS name for logging purposes.

- **logname** Specifies the remote log name of the user at the client system. Most of today's browsers do not supply this information, so the field in the log is filled with a placeholder, such as a dash.

- **username** Specifies the username with which the client was authenticated to the server.

- **date** Specifies the date and time that the request was received by the server. Most servers use the local date and time by default, but may include a Greenwich Mean Time differential, such as –0500 for U.S. Eastern Standard Time.

- **request** Specifies the text of the request received by the server.

- **status** Contains one of the status codes defined in the HTTP standard that specifies whether or not the request was processed successfully, and if not, why.

- **bytes** Specifies the size (in bytes) of the file transmitted to the client by the server in response to the request.

There is also a log file format currently in development by the World Wide Web Consortium (W3C), called the Extended Log File format, that addresses some of the inherent problems of the Common Log File format, such as difficulties in interpreting logged data due to spaces within fields. The Extended Log File provides an extendable format with which administrators can specify the information to be logged or information that shouldn't be logged. The format for the Extended Log File consists of *fields*, as well as *entries*. Fields appear on separate lines, beginning with the # symbol, and specify information about the data contained in the log. The valid field entries are as follows:

- **#Version:** *integer.integer* Specifies the version of the log file format. This field is required in every log file.

- **#Fields:** [*specifiers*] Identifies the type of data carried in each field of a log entry, using abbreviations specified in the Extended Log File format specification. This field is required in every log file.

- **#Software** *string* Identifies the server software that created the log.

- **#Start-Date:** *date time* Specifies the date and time that logging started.

NETWORK SERVICES

■ **#End-Date:** *date time*   Specifies the date and time that logging ceased.

■ **#Date:** *date time*   Specifies the date and time at which a particular entry was added to the log file.

■ **#Remark:** *text*   Contains comment information that should be ignored by all processes.

These fields enable administrators to specify the information to be recorded in the log while making it possible for statistics programs to correctly parse the data in the log entries.

REMOTE ADMINISTRATION   All Web servers need some sort of administrative interface that you can use to configure their operational parameters. Even a no-frills server lets you define a home directory that should function as the root of the site, and other basic features. Some server products include a program that you can run on the computer that provides this interface, but many products have taken the opportunity to include an administrative Web site with the product. With a site like this, you can configure the server from any computer, using a standard Web browser (see Figure 24-1). This is a convenient tool for the network administrator, especially when the Web

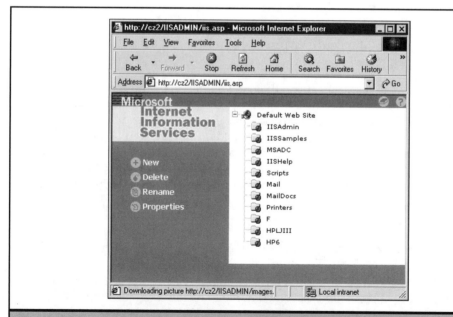

Figure 24-1.   *The IIS Internet Services Manager Web interface*

server system is located in a server closet or other remote location, or when one person is responsible for maintaining several different servers.

The biggest problem with this form of remote administration is security, but there are several different mechanisms that can prevent unauthorized users from modifying the server configuration. The most basic of these mechanisms, as mentioned earlier, is the use of a nonstandard port number for the administrative site. All of Netscape's server products use this method. Servers that use nonstandard ports typically require that you specify the port number during the server installation.

A second method is to include a means by which you can specify the IP addresses of the only systems that are to be permitted access to the administrative interface. IIS includes this method, and, by default, the only system that can access the Web-based interface is the one on which the server is installed (see Figure 24-2). However, you can open up the server to remote administration by specifying the addresses of other workstations to be granted access or by opening up the server to free access and specifying the addresses of systems that are to be denied.

The third method is the use of a directory service to specify which users are permitted to configure the system. IIS uses the accounts in standard Windows NT domains or in Active Directory for this purpose. Netscape provides its own directory

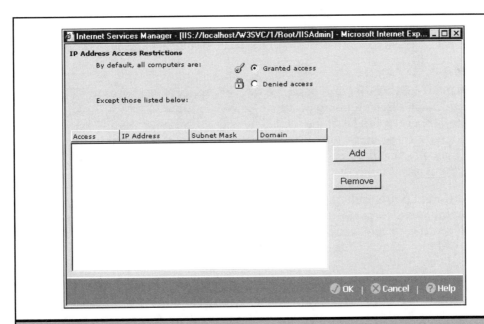

Figure 24-2.   *IIS's Internet Services Manager enables you to grant or deny Web site access to specific computers*

server for access control, and UNIX systems can use any one of several authentication protocols.

VIRTUAL DIRECTORIES   A Web server utilizes a directory on the computer's local drive as the home directory for the Web site it hosts. The server transmits the default filename in that directory to clients when they access the site using a URL that consists only of a DNS name or IP address. Subdirectories beneath that directory also appear as subdirectories on the Web site. IIS, for example, uses the C:\InetPub\wwwroot directory as the default home directory for its Web site. If that Web server is registered in the DNS with the name www.zacker.com, then the default page displayed by a browser accessing that site will be the default.htm file in the wwwroot directory. A file in the C:\InetPub\wwwroot\docs directory on the server will, therefore, appear on the site in http://www.zacker.com/docs.

   Using this system, all the files and directories that are to appear on the Web site must be located beneath the home directory. However, this is not a convenient arrangement for every site. On an intranet, for example, administrators may want to publish documents in existing directories using a Web server without moving them to the home directory. To make this possible, some server products enable you to create virtual directories on the site. A *virtual directory* is a directory at another location—elsewhere on the drive, on another drive, or even on another computer's shared drive—that is published on a Web site using an alias. The administrator specifies the location of the directory and the alias under which it will appear on the site. The alias functions as a subdirectory on the site that users can access in the normal manner, and contains the files and subdirectories from the other drive.

MULTIPLE SITE SUPPORT   A basic Web server product like Microsoft's Personal Web Server enables a computer to host a single Web site, but more advanced products like IIS can host multiple sites at the same time without running multiple copies of the server program. There are several different methods that a single computer can use to host multiple sites, and high-end servers usually give you a choice between them. These methods are as follows:

- **Different port numbers**   When hosting sites using the same IP address but different ports, users must specify a port number in the URL, except for the default site using port 80. This is rarely done, except in cases where an administrator wants to keep a site hidden, because most Internet users are unaware of the use of port numbers; and even if users are aware, there is no easy way of knowing which one to use.

- **Different IP addresses**   It is possible to assign multiple IP addresses to a single network interface, and once you do this, some Web servers enable you to select a different address for each Web site. You can then register each address in the DNS with a different host name, making the sites appear to be completely independent to users, even though they are running on the same computer.

This is a common method for hosting multiple sites, the only drawback being the need for a separate registered IP address for each site.

- **Different DNS names**   Some servers can host multiple sites with different DNS names but only one IP address, using a technique called *virtual hosting*. In this method, each site has its own DNS name, but all of the names are registered in the DNS with the same IP address. When the Web server receives HTTP requests at that address, it uses the contents of the Host field in the message header to determine which site should receive the request. Even though the DNS name specified by the client in the URL is resolved into an IP address before the request is transmitted, the DNS name is retained in the Host field. The advantage of this method is that only one registered IP address is required for the server, but it is also impossible to reach a site by specifying only the IP address in the browser.

SECURITY   Many Web sites have no need for security measures at all beyond those that protect the computer running the server software from outside intrusion. However, two forms of security are needed in some cases: the need to restrict site access to selected users, and the need to protect the data being transmitted between clients and servers.

The first form of security usually takes the form of an authentication protocol that restricts access to specific users with valid passwords. Just as you can protect your server's administration interface by restricting access to selected users, you can protect your Web sites as well. This capability is used more on intranets than on Internet sites, because access to certain documents (such as financial data) may have to be restricted to certain employees. However, some organizations are implementing *extranets,* intranet Web sites that are accessible to selected outside entities via the Internet. Companies use extranets to grant their clients access to information about products and services and to enable them to perform tasks like checking inventory and placing orders.

Some Web servers, such as Apache, maintain their own directories of user accounts, while others use the directory service provided by the operating system, or one running as a separate service. Netscape's Directory Server product, for example, provides authentication services for all of Netscape's other server products, including its Web servers. IIS, on the other hand, uses the internal directory services on Windows NT and 2000 networks.

The other form of security implemented by Web servers enables clients to send and receive data over the Internet using a secure channel that can't easily be intercepted or penetrated by outsiders. The most common application for this type of security is *e-commerce,* the purchasing of products and services over the Web. Securing communications between a client browser and Web server is a matter of authenticating the systems so that the client can be sure of communicating with the correct server, and encrypting the data transmitted between the systems so that anyone intercepting the transmissions will not be able to read them.

The standard protocol for Web server authentication and encryption is Secure Sockets Layer (SSL), a public key encryption protocol developed by Netscape and later submitted to the IETF for standardization. To initiate an SSL connection, the Web site developer creates a hyperlink that uses https as the protocol identifier instead of http, as follows:

```
https://www.zacker.com
```

The use of https initiates the use of the SSL Handshake Protocol between the server and the client using port 443 instead of the standard HTTP port 80. The two systems first perform a certificate negotiation to discover the strongest encryption method that they have in common, and the server sends a *digital certificate* to the client to verify its identity. Digital certificates are encrypted data files provided by trusted third-party companies, called *certificate authorities (CAs),* that uniquely identify a particular company or organization. A client receiving such a certificate from a server can be reasonably sure that the server is actually affiliated with that company or organization. It's also possible for a client to accept an "untrusted" certificate and initiate an SSL session without a certificate signed by a CA.

To read the certificate, the client must possess the public key for the certificate authority that generated the server's digital certificate. The two most common CAs, VeriSign, Inc. and Thawte, Inc., are supported by most browsers. Using the CA's public key, the browser decrypts the certificate and extracts the public key for the server. The server, meanwhile, encrypts the file requested by the server using the SSL Record Protocol and transmits it to the client. The client can then transmit information (such as an order form containing a credit card number, for example) to the server, using the same key. Only a system possessing that key can decrypt the data.

Support for the SSL protocol is provided in the Internet Explorer and Netscape Navigator Web browsers and in most servers, including IIS 4 (available as part of the Windows NT 4.0 Option Pack). Apache servers can use OpenSSL, an open source SSL toolkit available at www.openssl.org.

HTML

HTML, the Hypertext Markup Language, is the *lingua franca* of the Web, but it actually has very little to do with the functions of a Web server. Web servers are programs that deliver requested files to clients. That most of these files contain HTML code is immaterial, because the server does not read them. The only way in which they affect the server's functions is when the client parses the HTML code and requests additional files from the server that are needed to display the Web page in the browser, such as image files. Even in this case, however, the image file requests are just additional requests to the server. It doesn't know that the files contain graphic images or that they are associated with the HTML file it delivered previously.

HTTP

Communication between Web servers and their browser clients is provided by an application-layer protocol called the Hypertext Transfer Protocol. The most current version of the HTTP specification, version 1.1, was published by the IETF as RFC 2616 in June 1999. HTTP is a relatively simple protocol that takes advantage of the services provided by the TCP protocol at the transport layer to transfer files from servers to clients. When a client connects to a Web server by typing a URL in a browser or clicking a hyperlink, the system generates an HTTP request message and transmits it to the server. This is an application-layer process, but before it can happen, communication at the lower layers must be established.

Unless the user or the hyperlink specifies the IP address of the Web server, the first step in establishing the connection between the two systems is to discover the address by sending a name resolution request to a DNS server. This address makes it possible for the IP protocol to address traffic to the server. Once the client system knows the address, it establishes a TCP connection with the server's port 80, using the standard three-way–handshake process defined by that protocol.

Note *For more information on DNS name resolution, see Chapter 20. For more information on the TCP three-way handshake, see Chapter 11.*

Once the TCP connection is established, the browser and the server can exchange HTTP messages. HTTP consists of only two message types, requests and responses. Unlike the messages of most other protocols, HTTP messages take the form of ASCII text strings, not the typical headers with discrete coded fields. In fact, you can connect to a Web server with a Telnet client and request a file by feeding an HTTP command directly to the server. The server will reply with the file you requested in its raw ASCII form.

Each HTTP message consists of the following elements:

- **Start line** Contains a request command or a reply status indicator, plus a series of variables.
- **Headers [optional]** Contains a series of zero or more fields containing information about the message or the system sending it.
- **Empty line** Contains a blank line that identifies the end of the header section.
- **Message body [optional]** Contains the payload being transmitted to the other system.

HTTP Requests

The start line for all HTTP requests is structured as follows:

```
RequestType RequestURI HTTPVersion
```

Version 1.1 of the HTTP standard defines seven types of request messages, which use the following values for the *RequestType* variable:

- **GET** Contains a request for information specified by the *RequestURI* variable. This type of request accounts for the vast majority of request messages.
- **HEAD** Functionally identical to the GET request, except that the reply should contain only a start line and headers; no message body should be included.
- **POST** Requests that the information included in the message body be accepted by the destination system as a new subordinate to the resource specified by the *RequestURI* variable.
- **OPTIONS** Contains a request for information about the communication options available on the request/response chain specified by the *RequestURI* variable.
- **PUT** Requests that the information included in the message body be stored at the destination system in the location specified by the *RequestURI* variable.
- **DELETE** Requests that the destination system delete the resource identified by the *RequestURI* variable.
- **TRACE** Requests that the destination system perform an application-layer loopback of the incoming message and return it to the sender.
- **CONNECT** Reserved for use with proxy servers that provide SSL tunneling.

Note   *The HTTP 1.0 specification (RFC 1945) defines only the GET, HEAD, and POST request types. In addition to the five new request types, version 1.1 also enables a client to establish a persistent connection to a server, so that multiple files can be transmitted during one TCP session. Version 1 requires a separate TCP connection for each file. The new specification also provides better cache management at the browser, which improves the overall client response time. Both the client and the server must support the 1.1 standard in order to use these new features.*

The *RequestURI* variable contains a *Uniform Resource Identifier (URI),* a text string that uniquely identifies a particular resource on the destination system. In most cases, this variable contains the name of a file on a Web server that the client wants the server to send to it, or the name of a directory from which the server should send the default file. The *HTTPVersion* variable identifies the version of the HTTP protocol that is supported by the system generating the request. Currently, the three possible values for this variable are as follows:

- HTTP/0.9
- HTTP/1.0
- HTTP/1.1

Thus, when a user types the name of a Web site into a browser, the request message generated contains a start line that appears as follows:

```
GET / HTTP/1.1
```

The GET command requests that the server send a file. The use of the forward slash as the value for the *RequestURI* variable represents the root of the Web site, so the server will respond by sending the default file located in the server's home directory.

HTTP Headers

Following the start line, any HTTP message can include a series of headers, which are text strings formatted in the following manner:

```
FieldName: FieldValue
```

where the *FieldName* variable identifies the type of information carried in the header, and the *FieldValue* variable contains the information itself. The various headers mostly provide information about the system sending the message and the nature of the request, which the server may or may not use when formatting the reply. The number, choice, and order of the headers included in a message are left to the client implementation, but the HTTP specification recommends that they be ordered using four basic categories. The possible values for the *FieldName* variable defined in the HTTP 1.1 specification are as listed in the following sections, by category.

GENERAL HEADER FIELDS   General headers apply to both request and response messages, but do not apply to the entity (that is, the file or other information in the body of the message). The general header *FieldName* values are as follows:

- **Cache-Control**   Contains directives to be obeyed by caching mechanisms at the destination system.
- **Connection**   Specifies options desired for the current connection, such that it be kept alive for use with multiple requests.
- **Date**   Specifies the date and time that the message was generated.
- **Pragma**   Specifies directives that are specific to the client or server implementation.
- **Trailer**   Indicates that specific header fields are present in the trailer of a message encoded with chunked transfer-coding.
- **Transfer-Encoding**   Specifies what type of transformation (if any) has been applied to the message body in order to safely transmit it to the destination.
- **Upgrade**   Specifies additional communication protocols supported by the client.

- **Via**   Identifies the gateway and proxy servers between the client and the server and the protocols they use.

- **Warning**   Contains additional information about the status or transformation of a message.

REQUEST HEADER FIELDS   Request headers apply only to request messages, and supply information about the request and the system making the request. The request header *FieldName* values are as follows:

- **Accept**   Specifies the media types that are acceptable in the response message.

- **Accept-Charset**   Specifies the character sets that are acceptable in the response message.

- **Accept-Encoding**   Specifies the content codings that are acceptable in the response message.

- **Accept-Language**   Specifies the languages that are acceptable in the response message.

- **Authorization**   Contains credentials with which the client will be authenticated to the server.

- **Expect**   Specifies the behavior that the client expects from the server.

- **From**   Contains an e-mail address for the user generating the request.

- **Host**   Specifies the Internet host name of the resource being requested (usually a URL), plus a port number if different from the default port (80).

- **If-Match**   Used to make a particular request conditional by matching particular entity tags.

- **If-Modified-Since**   Used to make a particular request conditional by specifying the modification date of the client cache entry containing the resource, which the server compares to the actual resource and replies with either the resource or a cache referral.

- **If-None-Match**   Used to make a particular request conditional by not matching particular entity tags.

- **If-Range**   Requests that the server transmit the parts of an entity that the client is missing.

- **If-Unmodified-Since**   Used to make a particular request conditional by specifying a date that the server should use to determine whether or not to supply the requested resource.

- **Max-Forwards**   Limits the number of proxies or gateways that can forward the request to another server.

- **Proxy-Authorization**   Contains credentials with which the client will authenticate itself to a proxy server.

- **Range** Contains one or more byte ranges representing parts of the resource specified by the *ResourceURI* variable that the client is requesting be sent by the server.
- **Referer** Specifies the resource from which the *ResourceURI* value was obtained.
- **TE** Specifies which extension transfer-codings the client can accept in the response and whether or not the client will accept trailer fields in a chunked transfer-coding.
- **User-Agent** Contains information about the browser generating the request.

RESPONSE HEADER FIELDS The response headers apply only to response messages and provide additional information about the message and the server generating the message. The response header *FieldName* values are as follows:

- **Accept-Ranges** Enables a server to indicate its acceptance of range requests for a resource (used in responses only).
- **Age** Specifies the elapsed time since a cached response was generated at a server.
- **Etag** Specifies the current value of the entity tag for the requested variant.
- **Location** Directs the destination system to a location for the requested resource other than that specified by the *RequestURI* variable.
- **Proxy-Authenticate** Specifies the authentication scheme used by a proxy server.
- **Retry-After** Specifies how long a requested resource will be unavailable to the client.
- **Server** Identifies the Web server software used to process the request.
- **Vary** Specifies the header fields used to determine whether a client can use a cached response to a request without revalidation by the server.
- **WWW-Authenticate** Specifies the type of authentication required in order for the client to access the requested resource.

ENTITY HEADER FIELDS The term *entity* is used to describe the data included in the message body of a response message, and the entity headers provide additional information about that data. The entity header *FieldName* values are as follows:

- **Allow** Specifies the request types supported by a resource identified by a particular *RequestURI* value.
- **Content-Encoding** Specifies additional content-coding mechanisms (such as gzip) that have been applied to the data in the body of the message.
- **Content-Language** Specifies the language of the message body.
- **Content-Length** Specifies the length of the message body, in bytes.

- **Content-Location**   Specifies the location from which the information in the message body was derived, when it is separate from the location specified by the *ResourceURI* variable.

- **Content-MD5**   Contains an MD5 digest of the message body (as defined in RFC 1864) that will be used to verify its integrity at the destination.

- **Content-Range**   Identifies the location of the data in the message body within the whole of the requested resource when the message contains only a part of the resource.

- **Content-Type**   Specifies the media type of the data in the message body.

- **Expires**   Specifies the date and time after which the cached response is to be considered stale.

- **Last-Modified**   Specifies the date and time at which the server believes the requested resource was last modified.

- **Extension-Header**   Enables the use of additional entity header fields that must be recognized by both the client and the server.

HTTP Responses

The HTTP responses generated by Web servers use many of the same basic elements as the requests. The start line also consists of three elements, as follows:

```
HTTPVersion StatusCode StatusPhrase
```

The *HTTPVersion* variable specifies the standard supported by the server, using the same values listed earlier. The *StatusCode* and *StatusPhrase* variables indicate whether or not the request has been processed successfully by the server, and if it hasn't, why not. The code is a three-digit number and the phrase is a text string. The code values are defined in the HTTP specification and are used consistently by all Web server implementations. The first digit of the code specifies the general nature of the response, and the second two digits give more specific information. The status phrases are defined by the standard as well, but some Web server products enable you to modify the text strings in order to supply more information to the client. The codes and phrases defined by the standard are listed in the following sections.

INFORMATIONAL CODES   Informational codes are used only in responses with no message bodies, and have the numeral 1 as their first digit. No informational codes were defined in HTTP version 1 and earlier. The only code of this type in the current standard is as follows:

- **100 – Continue**   Indicates that the request message has been received by the server and that the client should either send another message completing the request or continue to wait for a response. A response using this code must be followed by another response containing a code indicating completion of the request.

SUCCESSFUL CODES   Successful codes have a 2 as their first digit and indicate that the client's request message has been successfully received, understood, and accepted. The valid codes are as follows:

- **200 – Ok**   Indicates that the request has been processed successfully and that the response contains the data appropriate for the type of request.

- **201 – Created**   Indicates that the request has been processed successfully and that a new resource has been created.

- **202 – Accepted**   Indicates that the request has been accepted for processing, but that the processing has not yet been completed.

- **203 – Nonauthoritative Information**   Indicates that the information in the headers is not the definitive information supplied by the server, but is gathered from a local or a third-party copy.

- **204 – No Content**   Indicates that the request has been processed successfully, but that the response contains no message body. It may contain header information, however.

- **205 – Reset Content**   Indicates that the request has been processed successfully and that the client browser user should reset the document view. This message typically means that the data from a form has been received and that the browser should reset the display by clearing the form fields.

- **206 – Partial Content**   Indicates that the request has been processed successfully and that the server has fulfilled a request that uses the Range header to specify part of a resource.

REDIRECTION CODES   Redirection codes have a 3 as their first digit and indicate that further action from the client (either the browser or the user) is required to successfully process the request. The valid codes are as follows:

- **300 – Multiple Choices**   Indicates that the response contains a list of resources that can be used to satisfy the request, from which the user should select one.

- **301 – Moved Permanently**   Indicates that the requested resource has been assigned a new permanent URI and that all future references to this resource should use one of the new URIs supplied in the response.

- **302 – Found**   Indicates that the requested resource resides temporarily under a different URI, but that the client should continue to use the same *RequestURI* value for future requests, since the location may change again.

- **303 – See Other**   Indicates that the response to the request can be found under a different URI and that the client should generate another request pointing to the new URI.

- **304 – Not Modified**   Indicates that the version of the requested resource in the client cache is identical to that on the server and that retransmission of the resource is not necessary.

- **305 – Use Proxy**   Indicates that the requested resource must be accessed through the proxy specified in the Location header.

- **306 – Unused**

- **307 – Temporary Redirect**   Indicates that the requested resource resides temporarily under a different URI, but that the client should continue to use the same *RequestURI* value for future requests, since the location may change again.

CLIENT ERROR CODES   Client error codes have a 4 as their first digit and indicate that the request could not be processed due to an error by the client. The valid codes are as follows:

- **400 – Bad Request**   Indicates that the server could not understand the request due to malformed syntax.

- **401 – Unauthorized**   Indicates that the server could not process the request because user authentication is required.

- **402 – Payment Required**   Reserved for future use.

- **403 – Forbidden**   Indicates that the server is refusing to process the request and that it should not be repeated.

- **404 – Not Found**   Indicates that the server could not locate the resource specified by the *RequestURI* variable.

- **405 – Method Not Allowed**   Indicates that the request type cannot be used for the specified *RequestURI*.

- **406 – Not Acceptable**   Indicates that the resource specified by the *RequestURI* variable does not conform to any of the data types specified in the request message's Accept header.

- **407 – Proxy Authentication Required**   Indicates that the client must authenticate itself to a proxy server before it can access the requested resource.

- **408 – Request Timeout**   Indicates that the client did not produce a request within the server's timeout period.

- **409 – Conflict**   Indicates that the request could not be processed because of a conflict with the current state of the requested resource, such as when a PUT command attempts to write data to a resource that is already in use.

- **410 – Gone**   Indicates that the requested resource is no longer available at the server, and that the server is not aware of an alternate location.

- **411 – Length Required**   Indicates that the server has refused to process a request that does not have a Content-Length header.

- **412 – Precondition Failed**   Indicates that the server has failed to satisfy one of the preconditions specified in the request headers.

- **413 – Request Entity Too Large**   Indicates that the server is refusing to process the request because the message is too large.

- **414 – RequestURI Too Long**   Indicates that the server is refusing to process the request because the *RequestURI* value is longer than the server is willing to interpret.

- **415 – Unsupported Media Type**   Indicates that the server is refusing to process the request because the request is in a format not supported by the requested resource for the requested method.

- **416 – Requested Range Not Satisfiable**   Indicates that the server cannot process the request because the data specified by the Range header in the request message does not exist in the requested resource.

- **417 – Expectation Failed**   Indicates that the server could not satisfy the requirements specified in the request message's Expect header.

SERVER ERROR CODES   Server error codes have a 5 as their first digit and indicate that the request could not be processed due to an error by the server. The valid codes are as follows:

- **500 – Internal Server Error**   Indicates that the server encountered an unexpected condition that prevented it from fulfilling the request.

- **501 – Not Implemented**   Indicates that the server does not support the functionality required to satisfy the request.

- **502 – Bad Gateway**   Indicates that a gateway or proxy server has received an invalid response from the upstream server it accessed while attempting to process the request.

- **503 – Service Unavailable**   Indicates that the server cannot process the request due to it being temporarily overloaded or under maintenance.

- **504 – Gateway Timeout**   Indicates that a gateway or proxy server did not receive a timely response from the upstream server specified by the URI or some other auxiliary server needed to complete the request.

- **505 – HTTP Version Not Supported**   Indicates that the server does not support, or refuses to support, the HTTP protocol version used in the request message.

NETWORK SERVICES

After the start line, a response message can contain a series of headers, just like those in a request, that provide information about the server and the response message. The header section concludes with a blank line, after which comes the body of the message, typically containing the contents of the file requested by the client. If the file is larger than can fit in a single packet, then the server generates additional response messages containing message bodies, but no start lines or headers.

HTTP Message Exchanges

In the most basic form of HTTP message exchange, the client browser establishes a TCP connection to a server and then transmits an HTTP request message, like that shown in Figure 24-3.

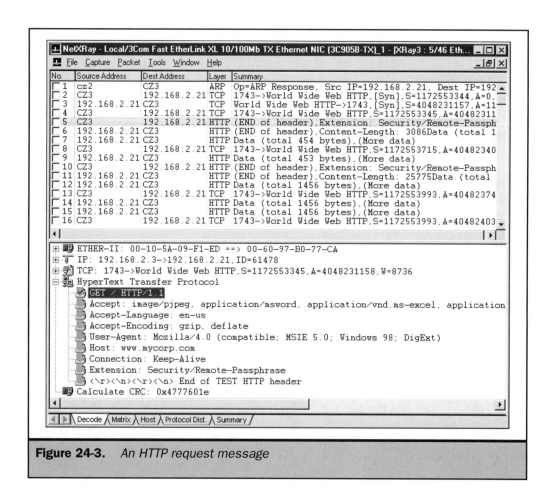

Figure 24-3.   *An HTTP request message*

The start line for the message indicates that it's a GET command, that the *RequestURI* value identifies the default file in the Web site's root directory, and that the client is using HTTP version 1.1. The Accept header lists the media types acceptable in the response, including the */* value, which enables the client to accept any media type. The Accept-Language and Accept-Encoding headers indicate, respectively, that the response should be in U.S. English and that the gzip and deflate compression formats are acceptable. The User-Agent header identifies the browser used by the client (Internet Explorer 5, in this case), and the Host header provides the URL supplied by the user in the browser's Address field. The Connection header contains the Keep-Alive value, indicating that the same TCP connection will be used to transmit multiple files, and the Extension header contains proprietary information about the authentication used by the client to access the server.

Before issuing a response, the server transmits a standard TCP acknowledgment message back to the client, indicating that the request has been received intact. This message is not strictly necessary, since the response also serves as an indication that the request was received, but all HTTP messages are transmitted within a TCP connection and must be acknowledged.

The server's response to the request (shown in Figure 24-4) specifies that the server is also using HTTP version 1.1, and the StatusCode value 200 indicates that the request was processed successfully. The Server header identifies the server as running IIS 5, and other headers specify the date and time that the request was processed and the media type of the requested file. The Content-Location header specifies the name of the file included in the response, which also specifies the default filename that the server is configured to use (that is, the request had only a forward slash for the *RequestURI* value). The Last-Modified header indicates that the requested file has not been modified since October 2, 1999, and the Content-Length header provides the total length of the file. The Etag header provides an entity tag for the file, which has no function here but can conceivably be used with other headers like If-Match and If-None-Match for cache checking.

Because of its size, two additional response messages are required before the entire file is transmitted to the client. Once it has received the file, the client parses its HTML code. Encountering an image tag, the browser generates another request message for a file called 5.gif and transmits it to the server (see Figure 24-5). Because both the browser and the server support persistent connections, the request and response messages for the 5.gif file are both transmitted as part of the same TCP connection. If this was not the case, the server would have begun the connection termination process immediately after sending the last part of the index.html file, and the browser would have had to establish a new connection in order to send the 5.gif request.

Once the client has requested and the server has transmitted all of the files needed to display the home page for the Web site, the server begins the process of terminating the TCP connection with the client. Once this process is completed, there is no further communication between client and server until the user initiates another request by clicking a hyperlink or typing a URL.

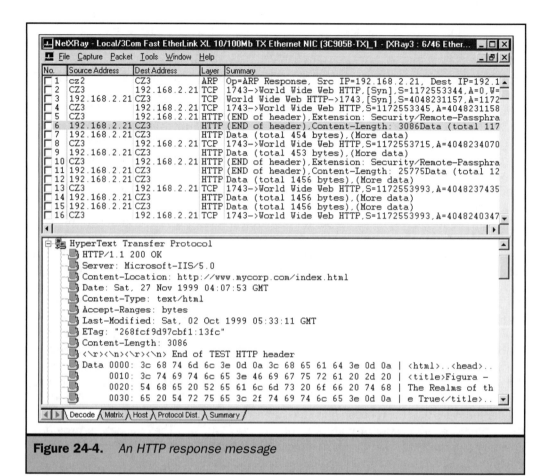

Figure 24-4.   *An HTTP response message*

FTP Servers

FTP, the File Transfer Protocol, is an application-layer TCP/IP protocol that enables an authenticated client to connect to a server and transfer files to and from the other machine. FTP is not the same as sharing a drive with another system on the network. Access is limited to a few basic file management commands, and the primary function of the protocol is to copy files to your local system, not to access them in place on the server.

Defined by the IETF in RFC 959, FTP has been a common fixture on UNIX systems for many years. All UNIX workstations typically run an FTP server daemon and have an FTP server client, and many users rely on the protocol for basic LAN file transfers. FTP is also a staple utility on the Internet, with thousands of public servers available from which users can download files. Although not as ubiquitous as on UNIX, every

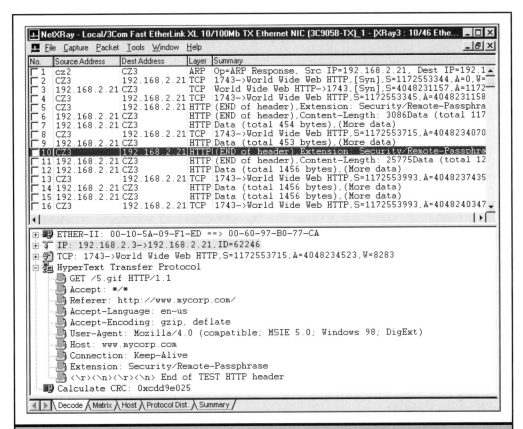

Figure 24-5. *An HTML file can trigger requests for additional files, such as graphic images*

Windows operating system with a TCP/IP stack has a character-based FTP client, and Web browsers can access FTP servers as well. FTP server capabilities are provided as a part of Web server packages such as IIS.

Like HTTP, FTP uses the TCP protocol for its transport services and relies on ASCII text commands for its user interface. All of the original FTP implementations on UNIX are character based, as is the FTP client included with Windows NT and 9*x*. However, there are now many graphical FTP clients available that automate the generation and transmission of the appropriate text commands to a server.

The big difference between FTP and HTTP (as well as most other protocols) is that FTP uses two port numbers in the course of its operations. When an FTP client connects to a server, it uses port 21 to establish a control connection. This connection remains open during the life of the session; the client and server use it to exchange commands and replies. When the client requests a file transfer, the server establishes a second connection on port 20, which it uses to transfer the file and then terminates immediately afterward.

While UNIX systems include FTP client and server capabilities as part of the default operating system installation, running an FTP server on Windows NT, 2000, or 98 requires a separate installation process. Microsoft bundles its FTP server software for Windows NT/2000 with its Web server as part of the IIS product. FTP runs as a service that administrators can configure through the same Internet Service Manager application as the Web server. There are also several popular and robust FTP server products available as freeware/shareware.

The IIS FTP server uses Windows NT domains or Active Directory to authenticate client connections, while UNIX systems typically use a list of approved usernames on the local system for access control. Most FTP access on the Internet is anonymous, but on LANs, more security is often required. While you can protect FTP servers from unauthorized access with passwords, the FTP messages themselves are utterly unprotected. As with HTTP, the communications exchanged by clients and servers over the FTP control connection take the form of ASCII strings, which are transmitted over the control connection in cleartext. If someone is using a network monitor program to capture packets as they travel over the network, the account names and passwords used to authenticate FTP client connections are easily visible.

For this reason, administrators should not use accounts with access to sensitive materials when connecting to an FTP server. For example, when running the IIS FTP server on Windows NT, you can conceivably use the Administrator account for your domain, but this would compromise the security of your entire network. Instead, create a new account that has only the permissions you need when using FTP, one that you can easily change or delete if the password is intercepted.

FTP Commands

An FTP client consists of a user interface, which may be text based or graphical, and a *user protocol interpreter.* The user protocol interpreter communicates with the *server protocol interpreter* using text commands that are passed over the control connection (see Figure 24-6). When the commands call for a data transfer, one of the protocol interpreters triggers a *data transfer process,* which communicates with a like process on the other machine using the data connection. The commands issued by the user protocol interpreter do not necessarily correspond to the traditional text-based user interface commands. For example, to retrieve a file from a server, the traditional user interface command is GET plus the filename; but after the user protocol interpreter receives this command, it sends a RETR command to the server with the same filename. Thus, the user interface can be modified for purposes of language localization or other reasons, but the commands used by the protocol interpreters remain consistent.

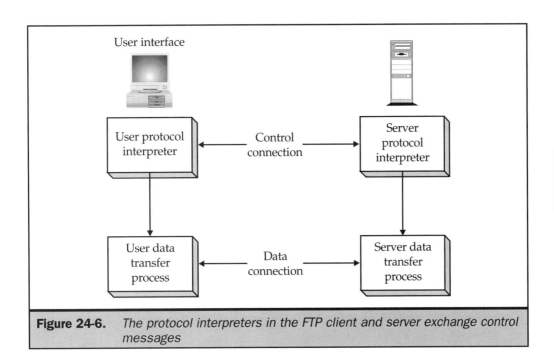

Figure 24-6. *The protocol interpreters in the FTP client and server exchange control messages*

The following sections list the commands used by the FTP protocol interpreters.

Access Control Commands

FTP clients use the access control commands to log in to a server, authenticate the user, and terminate the control connection at the end of the session. These commands are as follows:

- **USER** *username*   Specifies the account name used to authenticate the client to the server.

- **PASS** *password*   Specifies the password associated with the previously furnished username.

- **ACCT** *account*   Specifies an account used for access to specific features of the server file system. The ACCT command can be issued at any time during the session, and not just during the login sequence, as with USER.

- **CWD** *pathname*   Changes the working directory in the server file system to that specified by the *pathname* variable.

- **CDUP**   Shifts the working directory in the server file system one level up to the parent directory.

■ **SMNT** *pathname*   Mounts a different file system data structure on the server, without altering the user account authentication.

■ **REIN**   Terminates the current session, leaving the control connection open and completing any data connection transfer in progress. A new USER command is expected to follow immediately.

■ **QUIT**   Terminates the current session and closes the control connection after completing any data connection transfer in progress.

Transfer Parameter Commands

The transfer parameter commands prepare the systems to initiate a data connection and identify the type of file that is to be transferred. These commands are as follows:

■ **PORT** *host/port*   Notifies the server of the IP address and ephemeral port number that it expects a data connection to use. The *host/port* variable consists of six integers, separated by commas, representing the four bytes of the IP address and two bytes for the port number.

■ **PASV**   Instructs the server to specify a port number that the client will use to establish a data connection. The reply from the server contains a *host/port* variable, like PORT.

■ **TYPE** *typecode*   Specifies the type of file to be transferred over a data connection. Currently used options are as follows:

  ■ **A**   ASCII plain text file
  ■ **I**   Binary file

■ **STRU** *structurecode*   Specifies the structure of a file. The default setting, F (for File), indicates that the file is a contiguous byte stream. Two other options, R (for Record) and P (for Page), are no longer used.

■ **MODE** *modecode*   Specifies the transfer mode for a data connection. The default setting, S (for Stream), indicates that the file will be transferred as a byte stream. Two other options, B (for Block) and C (for Compressed), are no longer used.

FTP Service Commands

The FTP service commands enable the client to manage the file system on the server and initiate file transfers. These commands are as follows:

■ **RETR** *filename*   Instructs the server to transfer the specified file to the client.

■ **STOR** *filename*   Instructs the server to receive the specified file from the client, overwriting an identically named file in the server directory if necessary.

■ **STOU**   Instructs the server to receive the file from the client and give it a unique name in the server directory. The reply from the server must contain the unique name.

- **APPE** *pathname*   Instructs the server to receive the specified file from the client and append it to the identically named file in the server directory. If no file of that name exists, the server creates a new file.

- **ALLO** *bytes*   Allocates a specified number of bytes on the server before the client actually transmits the data.

- **REST** *marker*   Specifies the point in a file at which the file transfer should be restarted.

- **RNFR** *filename*   Specifies the name of a file to be renamed; must be followed by an RNTO command.

- **RNTO** *filename*   Specifies the new name for the file previously referenced in an RNFR command.

- **ABOR**   Aborts the command currently being processed by the server, closing any open data connections.

- **DELE** *filename*   Deletes the specified file on the server.

- **RMD** *pathname*   Deletes the specified directory on the server.

- **MKD** *pathname*   Creates the specified directory on the server.

- **PWD**   Returns the name of the server's current working directory.

- **LIST** *pathname*   Instructs the server to transmit an ASCII file containing a list of the specified directory's contents, including attributes.

- **NLST** *pathname*   Instructs the server to transmit an ASCII file containing a list of the specified directory's contents, with no attributes.

- **SITE** *string*   Carries nonstandard, implementation-specific commands to the server.

- **SYST**   Returns the name of the operating system running on the server.

- **STAT** *filename*   When used during a file transfer, the server returns a status indicator for the current operation. When used with a *filename* argument, the server returns the LIST information for the specified file.

- **HELP** *string*   Returns help information specific to the server implementation.

- **NOOP**   Instructs the server to return an "OK" response. Used as a session keep-alive mechanism; the command performs no other actions.

FTP Reply Codes

An FTP server responds to each command sent by a client with a three-digit reply code and a text string. As with HTTP, these reply codes must be implemented as defined in the FTP standard on all servers, so that the client can determine its next action; but some products enable you to modify the text that is delivered with the code and displayed to the user.

The first digit of the reply code indicates whether the command was completed successfully, unsuccessfully, or not at all. The possible values for this digit are as follows:

■ **1## – Positive preliminary reply**   Indicates that the server is initiating the requested action and that the client should wait for another reply before sending any further commands.

■ **2## – Positive completion reply**   Indicates that the server has successfully completed the requested action.

■ **3## – Positive intermediate reply**   Indicates that the server has accepted the command, but that more information is needed before it can execute it, and that the client should send another command containing the required information.

■ **4## – Transient negative completion reply**   Indicates that the server has not accepted the command or executed the requested action due to a temporary condition, and that the client should send the command again.

■ **5## – Permanent negative completion reply**   Indicates that the server has not accepted the command or executed the requested action, and that the client is discouraged (but not forbidden) from resending the command.

The second digit of the reply code provides more specific information about the nature of the message. The possible values for this digit are as follows:

■ **#0# - Syntax**   Indicates that the command contains a syntax error that has prevented it from being executed.

■ **#1# - Information**   Indicates that the reply contains information that the command requested, such as status or help.

■ **#2# – Connections**   Indicates that the reply refers to the control or data connection.

■ **#3# – Authentication and accounting**   Indicates that the reply refers to the login process or the accounting procedure.

■ **#4# – Unused**

■ **#5# – File system**   Indicates the status of the server file system as a result of the command.

The actual error codes defined by the FTP standard are as follows:

■ 110 Restart marker reply

■ 120 Service ready in *nnn* minutes

■ 125 Data connection already open; transfer starting

■ 150 File status okay; about to open data connection

■ 200 Command okay

■ 202 Command not implemented, superfluous at this site

- 211 System status, or system help reply
- 212 Directory status
- 213 File status
- 214 Help message
- 215 NAME system type
- 220 Service ready for new user
- 221 Service closing control connection
- 225 Data connection open; no transfer in progress
- 226 Closing data connection
- 227 Entering Passive Mode (h1,h2,h3,h4,p1,p2)
- 230 User logged in, proceed
- 250 Requested file action okay, completed
- 257 "PATHNAME" created
- 331 Username okay, need password
- 332 Need account for login
- 350 Requested file action pending further information
- 421 Service not available, closing control connection
- 425 Can't open data connection
- 426 Connection closed; transfer aborted
- 450 Requested file action not taken
- 451 Requested action aborted; local error in processing
- 452 Requested action not taken; insufficient storage space in system
- 500 Syntax error, command unrecognized
- 501 Syntax error in parameters or arguments
- 502 Command not implemented
- 503 Bad sequence of commands
- 504 Command not implemented for that parameter
- 530 Not logged in
- 532 Need account for storing files
- 550 Requested action not taken; file unavailable (e.g., file not found, no access)
- 551 Requested action aborted; page type unknown
- 552 Requested file action aborted; exceeded storage allocation (for current directory or dataset)
- 553 Requested action not taken; filename not allowed

NETWORK SERVICES

FTP Messaging

An FTP session begins with a client establishing a connection with a server by using either a GUI or the command line to specify the server's DNS name or IP address. The first order of business is to establish a TCP connection using the standard three-way handshake. The FTP server is listening on port 21 for incoming messages, and this new TCP connection becomes the FTP control connection that will remain open for the life of the session. The first FTP message is transmitted by the server, announcing and identifying itself, as follows:

```
220 CZ2 Microsoft FTP Service (Version 5.0)
```

As with all messages transmitted over a TCP connection, acknowledgment is required. During the course of the session, the message exchanges will be punctuated by TCP ACK packets from both systems, as needed. After it sends the initial acknowledgment, the client prompts the user for an account name and password and performs the user login sequence, as follows:

```
USER anonymous
331 Anonymous access allowed, send identity (e-mail name) as password.
PASS jdoe@zacker.com
230 Anonymous user logged in.
```

The client then informs the server of its IP address and the port that it will use for data connections on the client system, as follows:

```
PORT 192,168,2,3,7,233
200 PORT command successful.
```

The values 192, 168, 2, and 3 are the four decimal byte values of the IP address, and the 7 and 233 are the 2 bytes of the port number value, which translates as 2025. By converting these 2 port bytes to binary form (00000111 11101001) and then converting the whole 2-byte value to a decimal, you get 2025.

At this point, the client can send commands to the server requesting file transfers or file system procedures, such as the creation and deletion of directories. One typical client command is to request a listing of the files in the server's default directory, as follows:

```
NLST -l
```

In response to this command, the server informs the client that it is going to open a data connection, because the list is transmitted as an ASCII file:

```
150 Opening ASCII mode data connection for /bin/ls.
```

The server then commences the establishment of the second TCP connection, using its own port 20 and the client port 2025 specified earlier in the PORT command. Once the connection is established, the server transmits the file it has created containing the listing for the directory. Depending on the number of files in the directory, the transfer may require the transmission of multiple packets and acknowledgments, after which the server immediately sends the first message in the sequence that terminates the data connection. Once the data connection is closed, the server reverts to the control connection and finishes the file transfer with the following positive completion reply message:

```
226 Transfer complete.
```

At this point, the client is ready to issue another command, such as a request for another file transfer, which repeats the entire process beginning with the PORT command, or some other function that uses only the control connection. When the client is ready to terminate the session by closing the control connection, it sends a QUIT command, and the server responds with an acknowledgment like the following:

```
221
```

The Complete Reference

Upgrading & Troubleshooting Networks

Chapter 25

Network Printing

S haring printers was one of the original motivations for networking computers, and now, decades later, it is still one of the primary reasons to install a LAN. In most cases, users have to print documents on a regular basis, but not continuously, so it is not worth the expense of devoting a separate printer to each user that needs one. In addition to the expense, individual printers occupy valuable desk space and represent an additional support burden for the system administrators.

Network Printing Issues

Sharing printers among multiple users presents several technical and administrative issues that administrators must resolve in the planning phase, preferably before they purchase or install the printers. The most obvious issue is that sharing the printer makes it possible for two or more users to print jobs at the same time. A network printing solution, therefore, must include some means to store pending jobs in a *queue* until the printer is ready to process them. The process of temporarily storing print jobs on a disk drive is called *spooling*.

Print Job Spooling

Depending on the print architecture used, print jobs may be spooled on the machine where they were generated or on a network server directory dedicated to that purpose. The location of the spool file determines how long the user's workstation is involved in the printing process. When print jobs are queued on the local machine, the system processor must continue to expend clock cycles and utilize network bandwidth in order to send the job to the printer when it's ready. Using a network print queue provides better performance for the user, because the job is transmitted immediately to the network server, and the workstation is no longer involved in the printing process.

The location of the queued files can also determine how much control network administrators can exercise over the printing process. When the queue is stored on a network server, administrators can usually manage the jobs by reordering, pausing, and canceling them. When the queued files are stored on individual workstations, it's more difficult for administrators to exercise control over the entire printing process from a centralized location.

Printer Connections

Another important issue is the location of the printers themselves. Finding locations that are convenient to the network users is certainly important, but there are also limitations imposed by the type of connection used to attach the printer to the network. There are three basic types of network printer connections, which are as follows:

- **Server connections**   On a client/server network, such as one using Novell NetWare, connecting the printer to a server can minimize the amount of network traffic generated by the printing process, because the print queue is typically located on the same server. The drawbacks of this method are that the use of parallel or serial connections limits both the maximum distance between the printers and the server and the number of printers you can conveniently connect to the server. If the server is located in a wiring closet or data center, access to the printers by users may be limited.

- **Workstation connections**   Connecting a printer to a workstation is possible on either a client/server or peer-to-peer network. Although workstations use the same parallel or serial connections as servers, with the same limitations on the distance between the printer and the computer, workstations are nearer to the users and are more numerous than servers, which provides greater flexibility in finding convenient printer locations. However, workstations can generate more network traffic if the queue is located on a different machine. In addition, the printing process imposes an additional burden on the workstation's processor. The same is true for server connections, but servers are usually faster machines that can better sustain the additional load.

- **Direct network connections**   One of the most popular network printing solutions is to connect the printers directly to the network cable using a standalone print server that takes the form of either a network interface card that you install into the printer or a dedicated device that connects to the printer with a parallel cable. This method enables you to locate the printer anywhere a network connection is available. Print jobs must always be queued on a computer somewhere on the network, but this can be a server or a workstation, and the administrator can select a system that is powerful enough to service the printer.

The type of connections you use influences the locations that you select for your printers, but you should also consider their proximity to the users. It's inconvenient to have to walk down the hall every time you print a document, but it can be equally inconvenient to have a big laser printer right next to your desk with a constant stream of people using it. In addition, printers make noise that can be intrusive and expel gases that some people think may be harmful. The ideal location for a printer is one that is convenient to users but away from work areas.

Selecting Printers

Virtually any printer can be connected to a network, because it is the operating system that is responsible for tasks like spooling print jobs, not the printer itself. Laser, inkjet, and dot matrix printers all have their uses. Lasers are the most popular type of printer, especially in business environments, because they provide the best print quality. They tend to be the most expensive, but in the past five years, their prices have dropped to the point at which a wide selection is affordable, ranging from small personal printers to large business machines.

Inkjets are less expensive than lasers, but generally print at lower resolutions and with less quality. However, inkjet printers can print in color much more easily and economically. The output quality is far from professional, but good enough for proofs and home use. Inkjet technology is also used in home office devices that combine faxing, printing, and scanning functions in one unit.

Dot matrix printers are the cheapest of the three main printer types, both to purchase and to run; but their poor-quality output, low speed, and noisy operation have relegated them to specialized uses such as forms and receipts.

There are printers that are specifically intended for use on networks, because they have special features that make them more suitable for the network environment. These features can include the following:

- **Higher print speed**   A printer intended for use on a network typically runs faster than a personal printer, to keep up with jobs generated by multiple users. Manufacturers usually produce printers at several speeds (and price points) that are marketed as personal printers, workgroup printers, high-volume printers, and so forth.

- **Higher usage rating**   Printers have a usage rating that specifies the recommended maximum number of pages that should be printed per month. It's a good idea to use this rating when evaluating network printers. Even a high-quality printer is likely to have a shorter operational life if you consistently push it beyond its capabilities.

- **Integrated print server**   Some printers have a built-in print server with a network interface that enables you to plug the network cable directly into the printer. In most cases, the print server takes the form of a card that is installed in an expansion slot inside the printer, so that the device can be removed to accommodate cards for different networks. This is not an essential feature, because you can always purchase a print server separately, but it is a convenience.

- **Multiple paper trays**   A printer with multiple paper trays and/or high-capacity trays can support a variety of print jobs for longer periods without refilling. When users print jobs that call for different-sized pages, a printer with multiple trays and a driver that recognizes them can service the jobs with no manual intervention. If a printer has only one tray, then a job requiring a different page size will cause all print job processing to halt until someone inserts the right size paper.

- **Remote printer administration**   Most printers today have bidirectional communication capabilities that enable administrators to install, configure, monitor, and manage the functions of multiple network printers from a central interface. Using a dedicated program or a Web interface, it is possible to check the printer's operational status and manipulate its controls over the network, just as you would from the control panel on the printer. Note that this is a capability of the printer and its accompanying software, whereas managing a print queue is a function of the operating system.

- **Internal hard disk drive** Some printers can use internal hard drives to store frequently accessed data, such as font files and fax cover sheets, which speeds up the printing process and reduces the traffic sent over the network.

- **Combination devices** Combination devices are a rapidly growing part of the printer market. A copier, for example, is essentially a scanner and a laser printing engine, so it is only logical for manufacturers to add a printer's data processing components and a network interface, creating a hybrid device called a *mopier*. A mopier provides all of the standard copier functions, but enables users to generate documents directly from their computers. Unlike most standard laser printers, a mopier can produce multiple copies of a document without having to process the data for each page multiple times. Some combination devices also enable you to use the scanner for faxing and digitizing documents, in addition to making copies.

None of these features are essential. You can buy any small personal printer with only the most basic features and it will function perfectly well on a network. Your printer selection should be based more on the specific needs of your users than on a set of "network-ready" features that you may or may not need.

Selecting an Operating System

You can use either Windows, NetWare, or UNIX systems as servers to host your network printers. Many networks run more than one or even all of these operating systems, and the question will arise of which one(s) you should use. As with all network planning questions, the answer should be based primarily on the needs of your clients and the capabilities of their workstations.

Windows NT/2000 and NetWare provide comparable printer hosting capabilities. Both operating systems enable you to implement complex printing strategies that support heavy use and a wide variety of printer types. If your network uses mostly Windows workstations, then you can configure them to access either Windows or NetWare network printers, or both. However, you must install a NetWare client on every Windows system that is to use NetWare printers. Generally speaking, running a NetWare client on a Windows workstation just to provide printer access is not recommended, because the client tends to slow down the system in several ways. Therefore, if your workstations don't need NetWare access for other reasons, Windows-based printers are the better choice.

As discussed earlier, Windows NT and 2000 provide better printer hosting capabilities than Windows 9x. If the choice is between using NetWare servers or Windows 9x workstations to host your printers, then NetWare is probably the better solution, particularly if you want to use advanced capabilities like printer pooling.

UNIX workstations complicate the network printing problem further. Windows NT includes an LPD (Line Printer Daemon) implementation called the TCP/IP Print Server service that enables RFC 1179-compliant UNIX clients to send print jobs to Windows NT printers. The NetWare Print Services for UNIX, which is included with NetWare 4.2, intraNetWare, and NetWare 5, provides a bidirectional solution that enables UNIX clients to access NetWare printers, and NetWare clients to access UNIX printers.

Selecting Print Servers

Virtually any computer on your network can host a network printer, but it is important to consider the effect that the role of print server can have on a working system. As mentioned earlier, print jobs can be huge files, and it is important that the system functioning as print server have sufficient disk space and processing power to handle the burden. This is particularly true when the drive where the spooled files are stored also contains the operating system.

On a Windows NT system, for example, the spooling directory is C:\Winnt\System32\Spool by default. If the printer is offline for a long period of time, such as when it runs out of paper, a large number of print jobs can build up in the queue and fill up the disk. If the system drive (that is, the drive on which the operating system is installed) runs out of free space, Windows NT may be unable to write to the registry or the memory paging file, causing serious problems. If the machine happens to be the primary domain controller, the situation can be even more serious.

The same can be true for NetWare if print queues are located on the SYS volume and the server contains part of the NDS (Novell Directory Services) database. Administrators may be unable to make additions or changes to the NDS tree, and the automated database replication events might fail. On NetWare, you can select the volume on which a print queue is to be located when you create it. It is recommended that you not use the SYS volume for this purpose. On Windows NT, you can change the default spooling directory by opening the Printer Control Panel and selecting Server Properties from the File menu. On the Advanced page, you can change the Spool Folder value by specifying a path to a directory on a different drive.

There are also Windows NT registry settings that you can use to specify the location of an alternative spooling directory that the system uses when no disk space is available on the drive on which the main spooling directory is located. To create an alternative spooling directory for all of the printers hosted by the system, create a REG_DZ registry entry called DefaultSpoolDirectory that contains the directory path in the following key:

```
HKEY_LOCAL_MACHINE\SYSTEM\CurrentControlSet\Control\Print\Printers
```

To create an alternative spooling directory for an individual printer, create an entry of the same type called SpoolDirectory in this key:

```
HKEY_LOCAL_MACHINE\SYSTEM\CurrentControlSet\Control\Print\Printers\PrinterName
```

Replace the *PrinterName* variable with the name of the printer that should use the specified directory.

The PCs that you use for your Windows NT/2000 or NetWare servers should have the hardware needed to support the processing and I/O burden of a print server's functionality. However, if you plan to share printers that are connected to workstations, this may not be the case. Print server functions can seriously debilitate the performance of an average workstation, particularly if the print jobs are spooled on the workstation, as in the case of a Windows network printer share. A continual influx of print jobs to the workstation can affect application responses and frustrate the user working on that machine.

The effects of printer processing on a NetWare client with a shared local printer are less debilitating, because the print queue and print server functions are located on other computers, but there can still be a significant I/O burden. If you must use workstations to host your network printers, you should select PCs that have sufficient resources to support the additional functions.

Printer Administration

Printer administration is often more of an organizational issue than a technical one. Often, when a single printer is shared by multiple users, no one wants to take responsibility for it. This can result in a large backlog of queued print jobs because no one bothered to fill the paper tray. There should be someone who is responsible for performing everyday services to the printer, such as filling the paper trays, clearing jams, and replacing the toner or ink cartridge. Depending on the location of the printer and the size of the organization, this could be either an end user or a network support person.

Even if the network users are responsible for basic printer maintenance tasks, there is still a need for a knowledgeable administrator to handle more complex problems. For example, it is important for someone to be available to manage the jobs in the print queue. It is not uncommon for a print job to be garbled on its way to the printer, and if the initial characters of the print job do not follow the correct format, the printer may end up producing hundreds of pages of gibberish. Someone with the knowledge and the permission to manage the jobs in the queue can delete the offending job before too much time and paper is wasted. Depending on the print architecture in use, it may also be possible for an administrator to modify the order in which jobs are printed, or put certain jobs on hold because they would take too long or require a paper change. Apart from operational problems, there are also the inevitable hardware breakdowns and malfunctions, which require an experienced person to troubleshoot.

Windows Network Printing

Printing on a Windows network is a matter of installing a printer on the system that is to function as the print server and then creating a printer share out of it. Users can access the printer by configuring their workstations to send print jobs to the share, rather than to a locally attached printer. Windows printing is based on the concept of a logical printer, which is realized by the installation of a printer driver on both client and server systems. A *logical printer* is the software entity created when you install a printer driver on a Windows machine using the Printers Control Panel. Applications send print jobs to a logical printer, which in turn relays them to the appropriate physical printing device, either on the local machine or a print server on the network.

Logical printers make it possible to create multiple print configurations that are serviced by a single physical printer. If you have a printer that uses both the PCL and PostScript page description languages (PDLs), you can create a separate logical printer for each PDL. You can also create logical printers with different printer configuration settings. For example, one logical printer can use separator pages while another doesn't, and another printer can be configured to print large, complex jobs only during the night hours.

The Windows Printing Process

In the Windows network printing architecture, both the client and server systems must have a logical printer installed. The logical printer on the server points to the physical printer using either a parallel or serial port or a custom port created by an external print server device. A user working at the server can then print jobs locally using that logical printer. After creating a share out of the server's logical printer, clients can create their own logical printers that use a printer driver to create jobs and send them to the share.

Note *External network print servers, like the Hewlett-Packard JetDirect devices, are not print servers in the same sense as a Windows system. They do not store the print jobs internally and do not themselves appear as shares on the network. There must be a computer on the network with a logical printer that is configured to send its jobs to the port created by the print server device.*

The networking printing process as performed by Windows NT systems is illustrated in Figure 25-1. On other Windows operating systems, the file and directory names may be different, but the basic concepts are the same. The printing procedure is as follows:

1. The client loads the printer driver, from either the local drive or the print server. The printer driver consists of three components: a *print graphics driver DLL,* a *printer interface driver DLL,* and either a *minidriver* or a *PostScript Printer Description (PPD)* file. The print graphics driver module provides image rendering and management services and the API calls used by the Windows GDI (Graphical Device Interface) when an application prints a document. The printer interface driver module provides the configuration interface (the printer's Properties dialog box). The minidriver or PPD provides the device-specific configuration parameters for the printer.

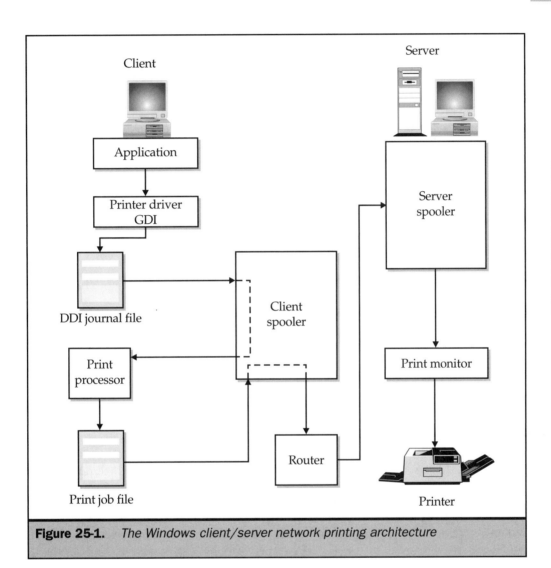

Figure 25-1.   *The Windows client/server network printing architecture*

2. Through the GDI, the application running on the client system creates an output file containing API calls to the printer driver using the *Device Driver Interface (DDI)*. This output file is called a *DDI journal file*.

3. The spooler on the client system receives the DDI journal file and stores it in the C:\Winnt\System32\Spool directory until the print processor can service it. The spooler can also perform a limited amount of rendering on the file, which is completed by the print processor.

4. The print processor (Winprint.dll) receives the DDI journal file from the spooler and processes it to create a print job file using the format specified in the logical

printer's Properties dialog box. The RAW format means that the print job is rendered by the client system and the output is sent to the server. The *EMF (enhanced metafile)* format sends the journal file data to the server for rendering there. After processing, the print job file is returned to the spooler.

5. The print router (Winspool.drv) retrieves the job from the client spooler, locates the printer for which it is intended, and transmits it over the network to the spooler on the print server. The server's spooler assigns a priority to the job and tracks its progress. The print router is also responsible for copying the printer driver from the print server. After the initial driver installation, the print router compares the version of the driver installed on the client system with the version on the print server at regular intervals and updates the client if necessary. This way, network administrators can install new drivers on the server and automatically update all of the clients.

6. The print monitor (Localmon.dll) on the server retrieves the print job file from the spooler and sends it to the parallel, serial, or other port associated with the printer share.

7. Once the print job file is processed by the printer, the print monitor sends a notification message to the client system, informing it of the job's completion. The spooler then deletes the job from the queue. The print monitor is also responsible for handling errors generated by the printer and resubmitting spooled jobs that have to be reprinted due to an error.

Windows Printer Configuration

Virtually all administrative access to the printing architecture in Windows 95, 98, NT, and 2000 is through the Printers Control Panel. The Add Printer wizard walks you through the steps of creating a logical printer, either on a machine that will function as a print server or on a client system. On a Windows NT or 2000 system, you are given the option to create a share whenever you install a local printer; on the other operating systems, you have to share the printer manually after the installation is completed. When installing a client, you select a printer share from an expandable network tree; and if the share is hosted by an NT/2000 server with the appropriate drivers installed, the client automatically downloads the drivers and installs them. Otherwise, you must select the appropriate driver for the printer.

Once you've created a logical printer, you can modify its configuration from its Properties dialog box, accessible from the File menu in the Printers Control Panel. The controls available in this dialog box vary depending on the operating system running on the machine. A Windows 98 system, for example, always displays the Windows 98 dialog box, even if the logical printer is pointing to a Windows NT print server.

Any Windows system can function as a print server, but Windows NT and 2000 systems provide more advanced features that provide the greatest amount of flexibility. Note, however, that you can only control these options from a Windows NT or 2000 system; the Properties dialog box on a Windows 9*x* system does not have the required controls. Some of the advanced printing functions that Windows NT and 2000 provide are examined in the following sections.

Using Printer Pools

While any Windows system can have multiple logical printers that are serviced by one physical printer, a Windows NT/2000 system can have one logical printer that is serviced by multiple physical printers. This is called a *printer pool*, and it enables you to cope with an increasing number of print jobs by adding physical printers to the logical printer, instead of reconfiguring some of the workstations to use a different logical printer.

The printers in a pool can be connected to the local machine, or to remote systems, which makes it possible to create a pool of almost any size. The only limitation is that all of the printers in the pool must be the same model, because the same driver is used to process all of the print jobs. For the convenience of your users, the printers should also be located in the same general area, because there is no way to know which of the printers in the pool will actually print a particular document.

To create a printer pool, you select the Enable Printer Pooling check box on the Ports page of the printer's Properties dialog box (see Figure 25-2). Also on this page, each of the computer's LPT and COM ports is listed with a check box, and you can select all of the ports to which a printer is connected. When you use an external print server to connect a printer to the network, its software creates additional ports that you can add to the pool as well.

Installing Additional Printer Drivers

As part of the process of creating a logical printer on a Windows NT or 2000 system that represents a locally attached device, you install the printer driver for the operating system. However, it is also possible to install additional drivers for other Windows operating systems, including Windows 9*x*; previous versions of Windows NT; and the Windows NT/2000 versions for other platforms, such as Alpha, MIPS, and PowerPC.

Although the system does not run these additional drivers itself, it does make them available to clients. When a user on a client system creates a logical printer that points to a share on the NT/2000 system, the Add Printer wizard contacts the server and specifies what operating system version it is running. If the driver for that operating system is installed on the server, the client automatically copies it to its local drive and installs it. If the proper driver is not available on the server, then the user must select a driver from the standard Windows list of manufacturers and printer models.

To install additional drivers for an existing logical printer on a Windows NT machine, you select the Sharing tab in the printer's Properties dialog box, to display the page shown in Figure 25-3. On a Windows 2000 system, you click the Additional Drivers button on the Sharing page. After you select the operating systems for which you want to install drivers, the system prompts you for the location of the various distribution files needed and copies them to the local drive.

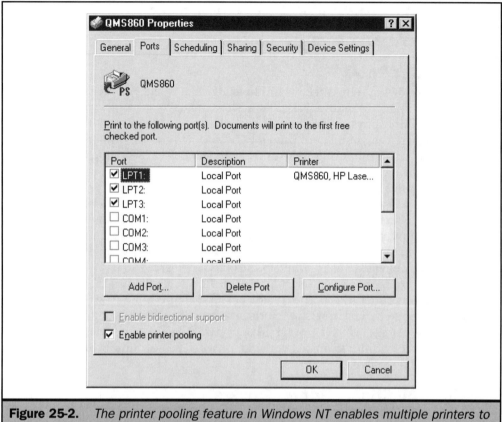

Figure 25-2. *The printer pooling feature in Windows NT enables multiple printers to service a single print queue*

Scheduling and Prioritizing Printers

Some print jobs can monopolize a printer for a long period of time, because they consist of many pages or contain elaborate graphics that take a long time to render. In cases like this, you can configure a logical printer to process jobs only during specific hours of the day. On the Scheduling page of the Properties dialog box (see Figure 25-4), you can specify a range of hours during which the printer is available.

If you can count on your users to understand the difference between them, you can create two shared logical printers on the print server pointing to the same physical printer and configure one of them with access only during nonbusiness hours. This assumes that the users will be conscious of the size of their print jobs and conscientious enough to defer them by using the alternate printer share when necessary.

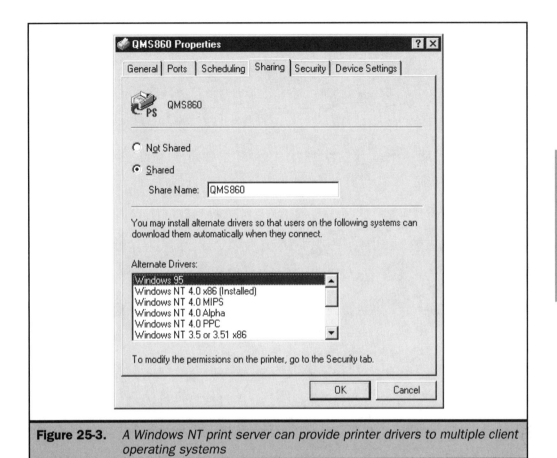

Figure 25-3.   *A Windows NT print server can provide printer drivers to multiple client operating systems*

You can also use this feature to grant users limited access to a special printer. For example, you may not want certain users to send jobs to a color printer during business hours. You can create one logical printer for selected users that permits access to the printer at any time, secure it using share permissions, and then create a second logical printer for all other users that grants access only after business hours.

Another way to control access to a physical printer is to create multiple logical printers with different priority ratings and share permissions. The Priority control on the Scheduling page enables you to assign a priority value between 1 and 99 to the logical printer. The default value for this setting is 1, which is the lowest priority. You can create several logical printers, assign them escalating priority values, and then use permissions to specify which users should have priority access to the printer. When the

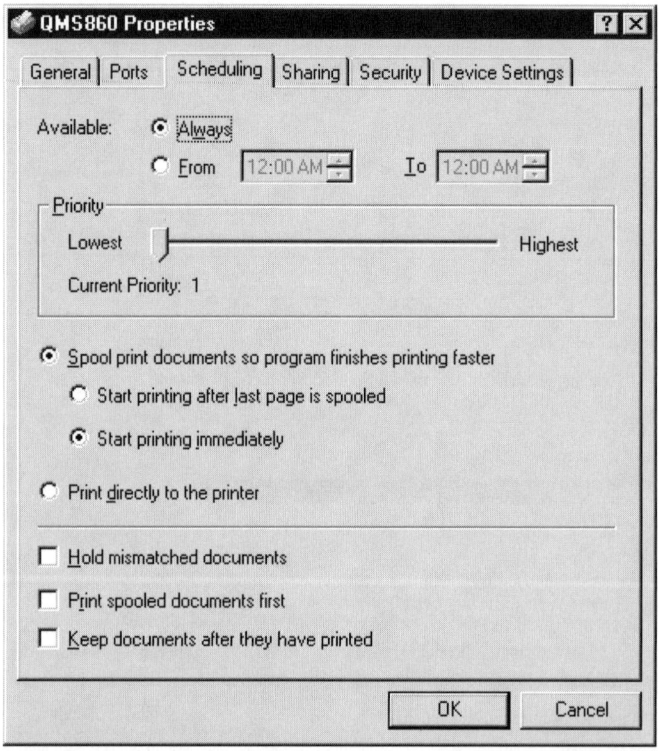

Figure 25-4.   *Windows NT can schedule printer use hours and assign printing priority ratings to various clients*

print queue on the server contains multiple jobs, the jobs with the highest priority are always processed first. However, once a job begins printing, it is not interrupted if a job with a higher priority arrives in the queue.

Securing Printers

All Windows operating systems enable you to restrict access to printer shares with whatever form of access control the system is configured to use. Windows 95 and 98 systems, for example, can use share-level access control to authenticate users with a single share password before granting them access, or use user-level access control to grant specific users and groups access to the printer. In both cases, however, access is granted using an "all or nothing" model. Either the user has full access to the printer or no access at all.

Windows NT and 2000 systems provide a more flexible form of access control that enables you to specify what activities users are permitted to perform. This capability makes it easier to delegate printer administration chores to specific users without giving them complete control over a printer. To do this on a Windows NT system, click the Permissions button on the Security page of the Properties dialog box, to display the window shown in Figure 25-5. Here you can select a user or group and grant them any one of the following four access levels:

- **No Access**   Denies the user or group any and all access to the share. Whereas all of the other permissions are cumulative, No Access overrides all of the other permissions. This means that users who are granted the Print permission through a group membership and the Manage Documents permission through their individual user accounts retain both permissions; but if the user accounts are assigned the No Access permission instead, the Print permission is overridden and no access is granted.

- **Print**   Enables users and groups to print documents but denies them any other access to the printer.

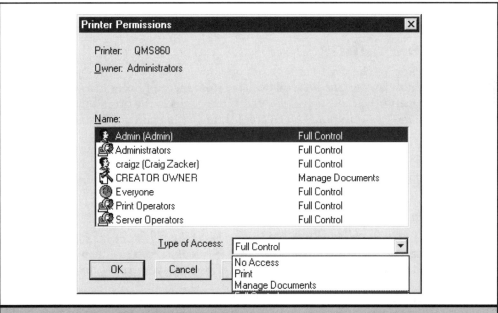

Figure 25-5.   *A standard Windows NT Permissions dialog box controls access to a printer*

- **Manage Documents**   Enables users to pause, resume, restart, and delete jobs from the print queue, as well as control the properties of individual documents.
- **Full Control**   Includes all of the capabilities of the Print and Manage Documents permissions, as well as the ability to pause, resume, and purge the printer; reorder jobs in the print queue; modify the printer properties and permissions; and delete the printer.

Windows 2000 expands this flexibility further by enabling you to allow or deny users and groups the following six permissions for the current printer, for documents only, or for both the printer and the documents:

- Print
- Manage Printers
- Manage Documents
- Read Permissions
- Change Permissions
- Take Ownership

NetWare Printing

Because NetWare is a client/server network operating system, its printing architecture relies more heavily on servers. It is still possible to connect a printer to a server, a workstation, or directly to the network cable, but the jobs in the print queue must be stored on a server. The traditional NetWare printing architecture consists of the following three elements:

- **Printer**   Represents the physical printer itself and contains information about how the printer is connected to the network and which print queues it will service.
- **Print queue**   Represents a directory on a NetWare server volume where print jobs are stored while waiting to be serviced by a printer.
- **Print server**   A hardware or software module that accesses the print jobs stored in a queue and submits them to the appropriate printer.

These elements are represented by NDS objects on a NetWare 4 or 5 network, which makes them configurable using the NetWare Administrator or Pconsole.exe utility. In its simplest form, the NetWare print architecture consists of a printer connected to a server using a standard parallel or serial port, a print queue directory on that same server, and the Pserver.nlm print server, also running on that server, as shown in Figure 25-6. In this case, the printing process would proceed as follows:

1. A NetWare client produces a print job file using its native processes. On a Windows system, this involves the use of the standard drivers for the printer type and the GDI. NetWare print servers do not provide any rendering capabilities; the print job file produced by the client must be ready to be submitted to the printer.

2. The print job file is routed to the print queue on the NetWare server in one of two ways. Either the application is configured to submit jobs directly to the queue, or the print output is captured from a printer port (such as LPT1) and redirected to the queue. Once the job is submitted to the queue, the client's role in the printing process is completed. Once queued, print jobs can be paused, reordered, or scheduled by an administrator.

3. The print server reads the print job from the queue and sends it to the printer using the appropriate port. Once the printing is complete, the job is purged from the queue.

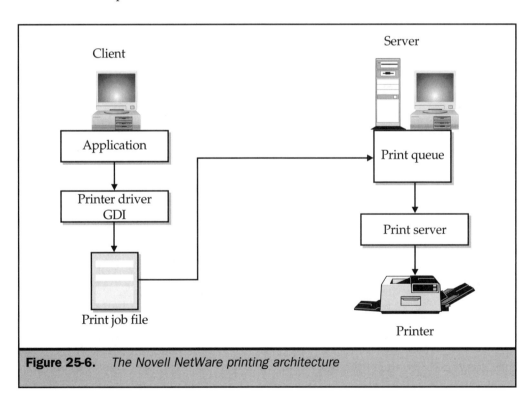

Figure 25-6.   *The Novell NetWare printing architecture*

The relationships between the print objects are configurable through the NetWare Administrator or Pconsole utility. Print server objects are associated with specific printers, and printers, in turn, are associated with specific print queues. In this scenario, all of the print objects are located on the same server, but they can just as easily be separated. You can connect a printer to another server or a workstation using a standard parallel or serial port, but you must then run on that system a program called a *port driver* that enables it to receive jobs from the print server and send them out the appropriate port to the printer. The port driver program for servers is called Nprinter.nlm; for Windows 9*x* systems, you use Nptwin95.exe; and for DOS and Windows 3.*x* systems, Nprinter.exe is used.

In much the same way, the print queue can be located on any volume of any server on the network. As with Windows printing, you can have multiple print queues serviced by one printer, or have multiple printers service one queue. The print server must take the form of either an NLM running on a NetWare server or a standalone device like a HP JetDirect print server. The JetDirect print server enables you to connect the printer directly to the network cable, and services only that one printer. The Pserver.nlm program running on any NetWare server version can manage up to 256 printers connected to servers and workstations all over the network.

While separating the print elements by placing them on different machines can be convenient, you should also consider the impact that it has on your network traffic situation. Print job files can be enormous, because they can contain graphics, fonts, and other data in a raw, uncompressed form. The print output file for a modest word processor document can be several megabytes long, and files with intensive graphics and other elements can be 100MB or more. When all of the print elements are on one server, these files only have to be transmitted over the network once, from the client to the server. However, if you have the printer, print queue, and print server on separate systems, the file must be transmitted three times.

Novell Distributed Print Services

NetWare 5 supports the traditional queue-based NetWare printing system, but the preferred network printing architecture for this new NetWare version is called *Novell Distributed Print Services (NDPS)*. The original NetWare printing architecture was developed long before NDS, and when the directory service was introduced, objects representing the three print elements were included in the directory. NDPS replaces the older print architecture with a single entity called a *Printer Agent (PA)* that performs all the tasks of the printer, print server, and print queue objects.

You can connect NDPS printers to servers, workstations, or the network cable, just as before, and the PA takes the form of either a software program running on a server or a hardware device embedded in the printer. The PA manages the processing of print jobs, controls bidirectional communications between the printer and network clients, and notifies users of job status and printer errors. To create a PA on a server, you must first create an NDPS Manager object on the NDS tree.

An NDPS printer can be configured as either a public access printer or a controlled access printer. A *public access printer* is available to all users on the network, with limited administration and notification capabilities. A *controlled access printer* is represented in the NDS database by a Printer object that not only enables you to use NDS permissions to limit access to the printer, but also provides more comprehensive administration and notification options. For example, an administrator can configure a Printer object to send a notification by pop-up message or e-mail whenever the printer goes offline or experiences a specific error like a paper jam. The administration architecture is also extensible so that third-party developers can create interfaces that provide beeper notification and other features.

NDPS is a protocol-independent print architecture, unlike queue-based printing, which requires the use of IPX. NDPS is also more completely integrated into NDS than the old system. NetWare Administrator functions as the interface to a wide range of printer configuration parameters and status indicators. The functionality is limited only by the bidirectional communication capabilities of the printer itself. You can gather printers together into groups in order to regulate access to them and, by assigning properties to the printer objects, search for printers with certain capabilities.

Novell Print Manager is an NDPS utility for users that enables them to locate printers on the network and install them, as well as modify printer configuration parameters (such as page size) and check the current status of a printer, including the number of jobs currently waiting to be processed. NDPS also provides an automatic driver-download capability, much like that of Windows NT/2000. When a user installs an NDPS printer, the workstation downloads the driver from a database and installs it without the user having to determine the exact printer model.

NetWare Printer Configuration

When the NetWare print architecture was first adapted to NDS, you had to create the Printer, Print Queue, and Print Server objects separately, and then manually configure the associations between them so that the print server could manage the printer and the printer could service the print queue. The NetWare Administrator and Pconsole utilities now have a Print Services Quick Setup feature that creates all three objects at once and automatically configures the relationships between them (see Figure 25-7). Once the utility has created the three basic objects, you can specify values for their properties or add objects to modify your printing strategy.

The Printer object's details dialog box (see Figure 25-8) enables you to both specify which print queues the printer should service and assign a priority value (from 1 to 10) for each queue. As with the Windows NT print server, you can use this feature to grant certain users priority access to the printer. In the Print Queue object's details dialog box, you can view the Printer and Print Server objects that are associated with the queue, but you can't modify them. However, this dialog box is where you view the list of jobs currently in the queue and select both the users that are to be allowed to submit jobs to the queue and the users that are to be designated as queue operators. Queue

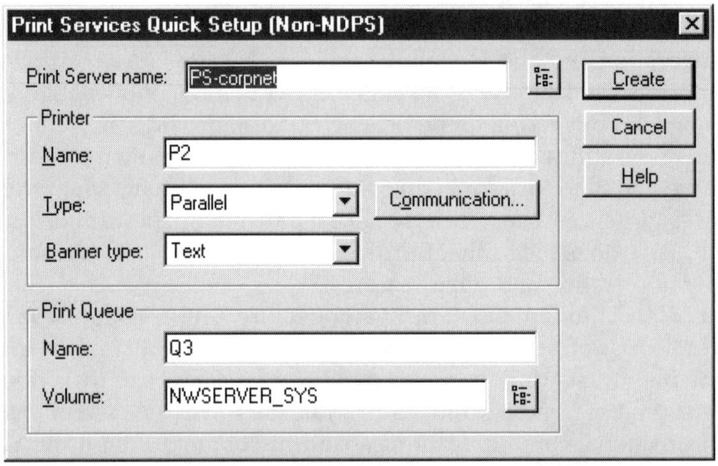

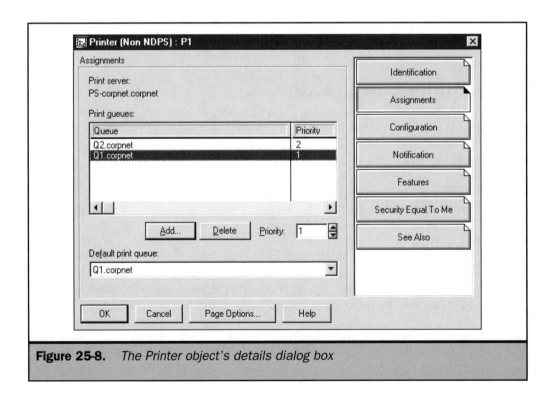

Figure 25-7.   *NetWare Administrator's Print Services Quick Setup tool*

Figure 25-8.   *The Printer object's details dialog box*

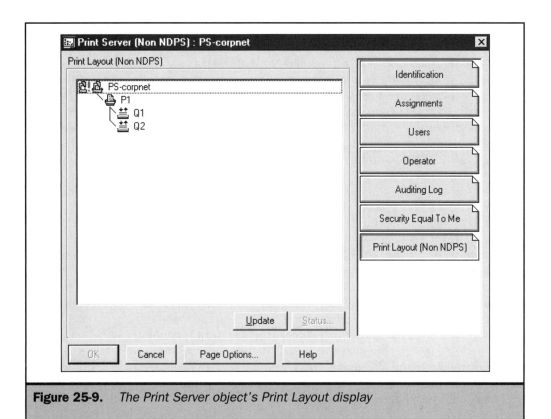

Figure 25-9. *The Print Server object's Print Layout display*

users are permitted to manipulate their own queued jobs, by deleting them or putting them on hold. A queue operator can manage any jobs in the queue by reordering, pausing, or deleting them.

The Print Server object's dialog box enables you to select the printers that the server will manage, grant print server user and print server operator privileges, and display a print layout that diagrams all of the objects associated with that server, as shown in Figure 25-9. On networks with a complex printing infrastructure, this feature provides an excellent high-level view of print operations.

UNIX Printing

The dozens of different UNIX variations use a wide variety of printing solutions, but one of the most common is the *line printer daemon (LPD)* running on a workstation. A *daemon* on a UNIX system is a program that runs continuously in the background, much like a service in Windows NT. LPD is a daemon that causes the system on which it's running to function as a print server. Client systems can send their print jobs to the

LPD system, where they're spooled until the printer can service them. Thus, the basic architecture of UNIX network printing consists of clients, servers, and jobs spooled into a print queue, much like on Windows and NetWare networks.

Once a printer is set up for local use, configuring the system to function as a print server generally consists of creating a spool directory, where the print jobs will be stored while they await processing, and a printer capability database, called a *printcap* file, that specifies the names of the printers the server manages and their capabilities. The daemon accesses the printcap file every time a file is submitted to the spooler for printing. Administrators control access to the printer by listing the names of authorized users in a hosts.lpd file.

The protocol for the communications between the line printer daemon and client systems is defined in the RFC 1179 document, "Line Printer Daemon Protocol," published by the Internet Engineering Task Force (IETF) in August 1990. RFC 1179 is an informational document, not a TCP/IP standard, that specifies the print server functions created for the BSD UNIX operating system in the 1980s. The LPD protocol calls for the print server running the daemon to listen on port 515 for incoming TCP connections from clients. The clients must use a port number ranging from 721 to 731 (inclusive) and, once connected, can send print jobs to the server as well as commands that enable them to check the status of and manage queued jobs.

Most UNIX applications provide direct access to print functions, just like on any other operating system; but client systems can also use a variety of commands to submit print jobs to the LPD and manage existing jobs, the names of which can vary depending on the UNIX implementation. The primary command for submitting jobs is lp (or lpr), the syntax of which is as follows:

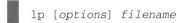

```
lp [options] filename
```

The command has a wide array of options that enable users to specify which printer should receive the job, specify how the job should print, and control the use of banner pages, among other things. The lp command is intended for sending ASCII print jobs to a printer, possibly with a few basic formatting commands. It is also possible to send PostScript files to a printer using the lp command. Other print-related commands are as follows:

- **lprm (or cancel)**   Removes jobs from the print queue
- **lpq (or lpstat)**   Displays the contents of the print queue

An LPD print job consists of two files, one of which contains the actual data to be printed, and a control file that contains information about the data file, such as the name of the document being printed and its attributes. You can send either file to the print server first, but there are some LPD implementations (such as routers that support printers connecting to asynchronous ports) that ignore the contents of the control file because they have no facility for storing large data files, and instead feed them directly to the printer, even if the control file hasn't yet arrived.

The Complete Reference

Upgrading & Troubleshooting Networks

Chapter 26

Adding Internet Access

nternet access has become an all but ubiquitous part of computer networking. Even if employers don't want the staff surfing the Web on company time, they probably do provide Internet e-mail, and may rely on the Internet for other vital business services as well. This chapter examines the process of connecting a network to the Internet, providing users with the services they need, and protecting the network from outside intrusion.

Providing network users with Internet access is a matter of establishing an Internet connection and sharing it with the rest of the network. The basic steps of the procedure are as follows:

1. Contract with an Internet service provider (ISP) for a connection.

2. Install the hardware needed for the connection.

3. Install and configure a router that will connect your LAN to the ISP's network.

4. Configure your client systems to access the Internet using the router.

5. Arrange for the clients to have access to the Internet services they need.

6. Protect your network from unauthorized access by Internet intruders.

Selecting an ISP

The Internet is essentially a pyramid of service providers, stemming from large backbone networks at the top that are connected to regional networks that sell bandwidth to local ISPs, which in turn split the bandwidth into smaller units and resell it to other providers or end users, as shown in Figure 26-1. The providers higher up in the pyramid use high-bandwidth connections to the backbone (sometimes called *fat data pipes*) to handle all the traffic generated by their client ISPs, which use smaller pipes. The place that your organization occupies in the food chain depends on how much bandwidth you need, what type of connection you'll use to get it, and which ISP provides it for you. The bandwidth you obtain from your provider might have been resold several times before it gets to you, but this is not necessarily a bad thing, as long as you obtain your service from a reputable and well-equipped ISP.

In a business environment, Internet access can be crucial. When your users can't exchange e-mail with business partners, and customers can't access your Web site, business suffers. Therefore, it is important that you select an ISP that can be relied on to supply you with a consistent stream of bandwidth. The more bandwidth you require, the better the ISP's facilities have to be to support your connection reliably.

For example, a small, local ISP that services dial-up users might have a T1 connection (running at 1.544 Mbps) to its own provider, which it subdivides into a number of 56 Kbps connections. A single T1 can support 25–30 user connections at this speed, and the ISP might sell 50 or more subscriptions, because it knows that not every user is connected all the time. This also means that it is possible for some users to be unable to connect, because all of the lines are in use. The reliability of the ISP's service

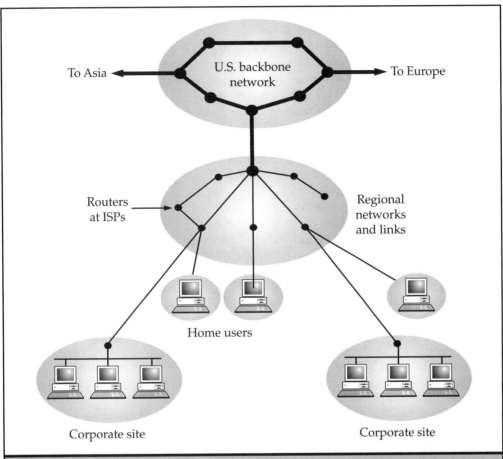

Figure 26-1.   *Most ISPs resell bandwidth that they obtain from their own ISPs*

is based on its ratio of subscribers to available connections. A failure to connect may not be a major problem for a home user, who can simply try again later, but a business has more stringent requirements.

In most cases, businesses do not use dial-up Internet connections, but it is possible to provide a small number of users with basic e-mail access using a shared dial-up that connects on demand or at regular intervals. However, for this arrangement to work, the ISP must have a client/connection ratio that enables the user to connect reliably. There is often no way to determine the reliability of this type of ISP other than to use its service for a while. The size of the provider's company is not necessarily relevant to the quality of its service. One of the largest national ISPs recently came under harsh criticism for signing up far more subscribers than its infrastructure could handle.

However, since this type of connection doesn't require specialized equipment or large installation fees, changing providers is easy.

Connecting a large number of users to the Internet requires more than a dial-up connection. For large organizations, a leased telephone line is a more common solution. A T1 line can provide Internet connectivity for about 100 average users, and fractional T1 services are available in 64 Kbps increments. A leased-line connection to the Internet is an expensive undertaking. There are monthly fees for both the telephone company providing the connection and the ISP providing the service, which can easily run to $2,000 or more. There are also significant installation and equipment fees, and because a leased line is a permanent connection between two sites, changing providers is a major production. Therefore, you must be sure to select an ISP that can adequately and reliably support your needs.

Many of the ISPs that cater primarily to dial-up users also offer T1 connections and other business services, but they may or may not be properly equipped to support them. A provider that offers T1 service should have at least a T3 line of its own (running at 44.736 Mbps) that connects it to the Internet. Remember, any ISP that you deal with has its own ISP, from whom it purchases the bandwidth that it resells to you. If its service goes down, then yours does too. That's why the best providers offering business services have redundant T3s with multiple providers high up in the Internet hierarchy, to ensure that your service is not interrupted. About 90 percent of all Internet traffic is carried by the networks owned by Sprint, Cable & Wireless, and UUnet Worldcom. A provider connected directly to a backbone on one or more of these networks is more likely to provide better service than one that is connected farther down in the pyramid.

ISPs are also just as liable as any other type of business to experience failures of other kinds, such as those caused by power failures and natural disasters. The best providers also have facilities that can keep their services running in spite of these problems, such as backup power supplies in the form of battery arrays and/or generators. ISPs that have advanced capabilities like these are usually quite proud of them and should be more than willing to tell you all about them, or even give you a tour of their facilities. This type of investigation is well worth the effort when you are planning to commit your organization to a contract that will cost you many thousands of dollars a year.

In between the dial-up service and the leased line are other types of Internet connections, such as ISDN, DSL, and cable modems, that are popular in the home market, but that also have potential for widespread business use. All of these technologies are constrained by the limitations of the technology. ISDN and DSL connections require that the telephone company providing the line have a switching office relatively close to your site, and cable modem connections are usually provided by the cable television company that services your area. Of the three connection types, only ISDN offers the possibility of changing service providers without an additional installation fee, as it is a dialed, circuit-switching service. Switching to a new DSL or cable provider requires an entirely new installation, if a competing service is even available.

Connection Types

The following sections examine the technologies that you can use to connect a network to the Internet, and the advantages and drawbacks of each. These various types of Internet connections are essentially wide area network (WAN) links, all of which are discussed in more technical detail in Chapter 7.

Dial-Up Connections

Most users with standalone systems connect to the Internet with a standard asynchronous modem and a dial-up connection using a POTS (Plain Old Telephone Service) line. Although intended for use by a single computer, you can share a connection of this type with a network. The primary drawback is, of course, the relatively low bandwidth. Most ISPs today have the equipment to support 56 Kbps modem connections, but in the real world, the connections are not nearly this fast. The Federal Communications Commission limits the data transfer speed over POTS lines to 53 Kbps, but even this speed is rarely achieved. Connections of 40 to 50 Kbps are more common, due primarily to the condition of the lines connecting the user site to the telephone company's switching office. In addition, this higher speed is for downstream traffic only; that is, traffic from the ISP to the modem. The maximum upstream speed is 33.6 Kbps, which is also the maximum speed for ISPs that do not have the digital links and other equipment needed for the faster connections.

Dial-up connections are the most economical way to connect to the Internet. Although the client is responsible for buying the modem, the market is quite competitive and modems are heavily discounted. A standard telephone line is needed, but there are thousands of ISPs available that provide dial-up service. It should be no problem finding one within your local calling area, thus keeping the telephone charges to a minimum. A typical unlimited dial-up account with an ISP costs about $20 per month, possibly with a small setup fee; but if you plan to share a dial-up connection with a network, you should be aware that ISPs can have different definitions of the term "unlimited." In almost every case, an unlimited account does not enable you to remain connected to the Internet 24 hours a day. Most ISPs impose a limit on their "unlimited" accounts, either in the form of a timeout that disconnects you after a certain number of hours or a maximum number of connected hours you are permitted per month. Therefore, a dial-up connection to the Internet cannot provide network users with continuous access.

There are several methods you can use to overcome these limitations. Some ISPs offer a dedicated dial-up service. This is a dial-up connection with a port and telephone line at the ISP's site that are dedicated solely to your use. You can remain connected continuously for a single monthly fee. The cost of this type of connection is significantly more than that of a standard dial-up account, typically from $100 to $150 per month; but as long as you have local unlimited service for the phone line, there are no additional charges.

Another method is *dial-on-demand*, which is a feature of most of the router products that enable you to share a dial-up connection. Dial-on-demand causes the modem to connect to the ISP whenever a client generates a request to an Internet service. After a specified period of inactivity, the connection is then terminated. This enables the modem to reconnect as needed without manual intervention, while also conforming to the ISP's policies. This method saves money by using the ISP's standard dial-up account, although the savings over a dedicated dial-up are slightly mitigated by the additional telephone calls needed to reestablish the connection.

In addition to these solutions to the problem, there is also the low-tech option, in which you use a standard dial-up account and a user is responsible for periodically disconnecting and reconnecting to the ISP. This may seem like a viable alternative, unless you are the person with that responsibility.

The downside of sharing a dial-up connection is obviously the limited bandwidth. A dial-up connection, though intended for a single user, can conceivably serve two or three users on a network, as long as they don't require superior performance. Shared dial-ups are more common in residential settings than in business settings for this reason. However, it is possible to combine the bandwidth of two or more dial-up connections into a single data pipe. The technique by which this is done is called *inverse multiplexing*; Windows 98, NT, and 2000 call this feature *multilink*.

A multilink installation requires a separate COM port, modem, telephone line, and ISP port for each of the connections to be combined. In addition, the ISP must support the multilink feature, and this is one of the factors that has prevented this technology from achieving widespread use. Another limiting factor is that there are now other, faster connection types available, such as cable modems and DSL, that provide far better service for approximately the same cost.

ISDN

Integrated Services Digital Network is a dial-up service that operates over standard POTS lines but that uses digital connections at higher speeds than standard analog modems. There are two ISDN services: *Basic Rate Interface (BRI)*, which provides 128 Kbps of bandwidth, and *Primary Rate Interface (PRI)*, which runs at up to 1.544 Mbps. BRI service is directed primarily at the home market, whereas PRI is directed at businesses. Both have a far greater installed user base in Europe than in North America.

ISDN was designed as a general-purpose replacement for the current analog phone system and has been around since the mid-1980s, but it received very little commercial attention in the U.S. until the Internet boom sent people searching for faster connections. There are many ISPs that offer ISDN Internet connections, mostly using the BRI service, but the technology has a reputation for being difficult to install and cranky in its operation.

The primary advantages of ISDN are that it provides dedicated digital service at the specified bandwidth and that it is a dial-up service, just like the analog phone system. Once you have the ISDN service installed, if you ever want to change ISPs, all you have to do is change the numbers dialed; no hardware or service modifications are necessary. The PRI service provides the same bandwidth as a T1, but it actually consists of 24 channels of 64 Kbps each that can be combined into a single data pipe or used independently for voice or data traffic.

The ISDN service itself must be installed by a telephone company. No special wiring is required for the BRI service, but the line plugs into a hardware device called an *NT1* at the client site, which in turn is connected to a *terminal adapter,* which provides the interface for the computer or router. In most cases, you must purchase the NT1 and the terminal adapter yourself, although several manufacturers integrate the two into a single device. In addition to the hardware, there is an installation fee from the phone company, a monthly charge, and usually a connection charge of about one cent per minute. Because it is a dial-up service, however, you can disconnect from your ISP during off hours to minimize the connection charges.

These fees are all in addition to the ISP charges for Internet access. Some providers offer a turnkey solution in which they arrange for the ISDN installation by the phone company, while with other providers, you must arrange for the installation yourself. The end result is that ISDN can be an expensive proposition, and compared to newer technologies like DSL and cable modems, the increase in bandwidth for the average home user (from 40 or 50 Kbps to 128 Kbps) is not worth the difficulty and the expense. You can usually share a BRI ISDN connection with a network by using the same hardware or software routers as you would use for a standard dial-up, but the additional bandwidth supports only a few more users.

DSL

Digital Subscriber Line connections provide high-speed Internet access over standard POTS lines, much like ISDN, except that the connection is a permanent link between the client site and the ISP and usually runs at much higher speeds. The most popular DSL service for Internet access is Asymmetrical Digital Subscriber Line (ADSL). An *asymmetrical* connection is one with a downstream speed that differs from the upstream speed. ADSL providers typically offer the service at a variety of speeds and prices, which can range from 640 Kbps downstream and 160 Kbps upstream to 1.544 Mbps downstream and 320 Kbps upstream. The difference in upstream and downstream speeds makes the connection a good choice for Internet client access, which consists mainly of downstream traffic, but not for hosting Internet servers, which require more upstream bandwidth.

In many cases, Symmetrical Digital Subscriber Line (SDSL) service is more suitable for business Internet access, because it provides various bandwidths running at the same speed downstream and upstream. Compared to leased lines and other types of connections providing similar transmission speeds, DSL is an economical alternative that requires a relatively small initial investment.

DSL is the latest Internet access technology to hit the market, and it is being marketed primarily to home users, but there is no reason why DSL connections could not eventually become a popular business solution as well. The only hardware required is a DSL "modem" and a standard Ethernet card for the computer hosting the connection. Most ISPs supply the hardware, on either a leased or purchase basis, as part of a subscription package that includes a monthly fee and an installation charge. No additional wiring is needed, since DSL enables you to continue to use the phone line for voice traffic while you're connected to the Internet.

Note   *For more information on DSL technology and the bandwidths of the various services available, see Chapter 7.*

Cable Modems

Many cable television providers are taking advantage of the broadband fiber-optic networks they have installed in neighborhoods all over North America to supply Internet access in addition to the TV signals. Since most potential subscribers already have the cable wired into their homes, and the cable company already has a fleet of service technicians, the installation process consists of a cable technician putting a splitter on the provider's coaxial cable and connecting it to a modem-like device. This unit functions as the interface to the cable network and also connects to a standard Ethernet card installed in a computer. Since the same company is providing the hardware, the cable, and the Internet access, there is only one bill to think about, which is generally approximately $40 per month (not including the cable TV service). The hardware may be leased, with the cost included in the monthly fee, or you may have the option to buy it from the cable company in return for a lower monthly charge. Be aware, however, that this is relatively new technology that has not yet been standardized in the same way as analog modems. You will very likely not be able to use the same hardware if you move or switch to another cable system.

Cable modems deliver excellent bandwidth, as much as 512 Kbps, but they are asymmetrical, like DSL, so this speed is restricted to downstream traffic. This asymmetry is due to the fact that cable television networks are designed primarily to send signals from the provider to the subscriber. Relatively little upstream bandwidth is available, so the upstream speed is typically capped at 128 Kbps or less. Even this speed, however, is as fast as a BRI ISDN connection and far faster than any dial-up connection. Therefore, while a cable modem connection is an excellent solution for Web surfing and other Internet client applications, even when shared among many network users, you probably would not want to use one to run a heavily trafficked Web server.

The potential downside to cable access is that, unlike all of the other connection types discussed here, the cable network uses a shared network medium. The fiber-optic network owned by the cable system is essentially a *metropolitan area network (MAN)* that joins you to your neighbors on a large Ethernet network. The greater the number of other users accessing the Internet, the less bandwidth that is available to you. As a result, you may notice a slowdown in the service during peak usage hours. In addition, you must be careful to secure your network against intrusion from other users on the same MAN.

Cable companies are used to dealing primarily with residential users, and many of them intend their service for use only on standalone computers, not networks. However, there is no technological reason why you can't share a cable modem connection with a network, as long as the cable company permits it. Some cable systems are new to the Internet-access side of the business, and they might not yet have a policy in place regarding the sharing of the connection. Others might specify a maximum number of users that you can connect to the system for the standard subscription fee, or might charge a much higher rate for a network connection. However, for the amount of bandwidth provided, cable modem access to the Internet is currently the best bargain in the industry.

Leased Lines

Most of the connection types discussed thus far are primarily marketed at home Internet users, but also can be shared with a network in a business environment. Leased lines are the Internet access standard for the business world, however, because they provide a large amount of consistent, continuous bandwidth. The most common type of leased line is the T1, running at 1.544 Mbps, which can function as a single data pipe or be split into 64 Kbps voice channels. Individual 64 Kbps channels are also available from some providers; this is called *fractional T1* service. A leased line is a permanent connection between two sites, installed by a telephone carrier, that runs continuously at a specific bandwidth. The cost of the line itself is based on the distance between the two sites. Since there are many ISPs that offer T1 service, it should not be difficult to find one nearby. However, even a short-distance T1 line can cost $1,500 per month or more, plus a hefty installation fee and the cost of the required hardware, called a *channel service unit/data service unit (CSU/DSU)*, which can be over $1,000. This is in addition to the ISP charges, which will also run at least $1,000 per month. A leased line, therefore, is an expensive proposition, but it can service a large number of Internet users, and enables you to host your own Internet servers.

Because a leased line is a permanent connection, you cannot easily switch ISPs. You must have the old line removed and a new one installed, which can take a great deal of time and money. Therefore, you should be careful to choose a provider that is going to be around for a while and that can provide all of the services you are liable to need in the future.

Frame Relay

Frame relay is an alternative to a leased line that enables you to pay only for the bandwidth you use. When you install a T1 line for Internet access, you pay for the full amount of bandwidth at all times, even when you're not using it. Frame relay is a type of WAN link that uses a leased line to connect to a local provider, which routes your traffic through its network to another provider, which in turn is connected to your destination site using another leased line. The concept is a little different for an ISP connection. You still must install a leased line between your site and the ISP, and pay all of the telephone company charges for that line, but the ISP's fees are substantially lower because you are not paying for bandwidth that goes unused when your company is closed. When you contract with an ISP for frame relay service, you agree to a *committed information rate (CIR)* that specifies the amount of bandwidth that will always be available to you. At times of increased traffic (called *bursts*), you can exceed the CIR, for an additional charge. If your needs increase over time, you can negotiate a new CIR.

Thus, in a typical installation, you would install a T1 line between your site and the ISP, and contract for a CIR of 768 Kbps, for example. You are guaranteed to have 768 Kbps available to you at all times, but you are not paying for bandwidth during times when your offices are closed or not in use. During high-traffic periods, your transmission rate may burst up to the full capacity of the leased line, as long as the ISP has the additional bandwidth available. Frame relay does not affect the cost of the leased line or the hardware needed to connect it to your network, but it can reduce ISP fees from 20 to 40 percent in cases where you do not utilize all of the bandwidth of the T1 (or other leased-line connection).

Bandwidth Requirements

Although the fundamental principles of connecting a LAN to the Internet are always the same, the amount of bandwidth you need for your Internet connection will influence much of the process, from purchasing equipment to selecting an ISP. Table 26-1 lists the most common Internet connection types used today, the bandwidth they supply, and the approximate number of clients they can support for particular applications.

The estimates provided in the table refer to the approximate number of clients of each type that can use the given connection at any one time. They do not indicate that the connection will support the number of all three clients given simultaneously. For example, a 33.6 Kbps dial-up connection will support up to six e-mail users, two Web browsers, or two FTP clients, but not all three at the same time. TCP/IP traffic tends to be "bursty," meaning that the amount of data traveling over the cable is more likely to come in spurts rather than a continuous stream.

The table also refers to users who are actually working in the client programs specified. You may budget a T1 connection as supporting 100 Web users, for example, but you can use that connection to provide Web access to several hundred users, as long as you don't expect too many more than 100 users to be surfing the Web at any one time. In most cases, network users have access to all three of the specified clients, and possibly others as well.

When you are evaluating Internet connection types and the needs of your users, be sure to account for the fact that a single user might be running more than one client at the same time, such as surfing the Web while downloading a file with FTP. You should also try to account for the growth both of your network and of the reliance of your business on the Internet.

Connection Type	Approximate Actual Speed	Applications
Basic dial-up	28.8–33.6 Kbps	E-mail for up to 6 users Web browsing for 1 or 2 simultaneous users Large FTP downloads for 1 or 2 simultaneous users
High-speed dial-up	Up to 53 Kbps	E-mail for up to 10 users Web browsing for 2 to 3 simultaneous users Large FTP downloads for 1 or 2 simultaneous users
ISDN	128 Kbps	E-mail for up to 20 users Web browsing for 6 to 8 simultaneous users Large FTP downloads for 3 or 4 simultaneous users
Cable modem	Up to 512 Kbps downstream; up to 128 Kbps upstream	E-mail for 50 or more users Web browsing for 25 to 30 simultaneous users Large FTP downloads for 12 to 15 simultaneous users
DSL	Up to 640 Kbps downstream; up to 160 Kbps upstream	E-mail for 60 or more users Web browsing for 30 to 35 simultaneous users Large FTP downloads for 15 to 18 simultaneous users
T1	1.544 Mbps	E-mail for 120 or more users Web browsing for 75 to 100 simultaneous users Large FTP downloads for 40 to 50 simultaneous users

Table 26-1. *Internet Connection Types and Estimated Bandwidth Utilization*

NETWORK SERVICES

The following sections examine the most common Internet applications and the issues that affect their bandwidth utilization.

E-mail

E-mail is one of the most basic Internet applications, and the one that in most cases utilizes the least amount of bandwidth. E-mail messages themselves consist of ASCII text, which takes up relatively little bandwidth. Therefore, you can support more e-mail users with a given amount of bandwidth than you can support any other type of Internet client.

The factor that complicates the equation is the ability to attach files of almost any size to e-mail messages. If you use a relatively low-bandwidth connection to provide network users with e-mail access, it is possible for a single large attachment to monopolize the connection for a long period of time. Therefore, you may want to impose a limit at the mail server on the size of the attachments that you permit e-mail users to send and receive. This is particularly true when you are using an asymmetrical connection, such as DSL or a cable modem. In these cases, you should calculate your attachment size limit in relationship to the upstream transmit rate rather than the downstream one, unless you are confident that an internal policy against sending e-mails with large attachments will be observed by your users.

Web Surfing

Web pages are primarily made up of HTML files, which are all ASCII text, and relatively small image files, in most cases. Therefore, the amount of data that makes up a page is fairly modest. However, there are several factors that make Web surfing a more bandwidth-intensive application than e-mail.

E-mail is an application in which a delay between the transmission of a message and the receipt of a reply is expected, and delays caused by a busy Internet connection are generally acceptable, within reason. However, users accessing the World Wide Web expect a more immediate response. Delays in the receipt of the files that make up a Web page are more frustrating to users, especially in a business environment. A large download or other form of congestion on a low-bandwidth connection can bring Web performance to a virtual halt. Another factor is the ability of Web pages to link to other file types that require more bandwidth, such as binary program files, large images, and sound files.

Because of these factors, you should count on an Internet connection supporting fewer Web users than e-mail users. In a home environment where people use the Internet primarily for recreation, two or three users can conceivably share a connection intended for one, because they can more easily wait until later if the delays become too great. However, in a business environment where users are (presumably) using the connection for business purposes, delays can result in reduced productivity and other negative effects.

It's also important to consider the amount of time that you expect your network clients to spend using the Internet connection. The Web is the application most prone to abuse, so you should calculate the amount of time that you would expect the average user to spend surfing for business purposes and double it to account for their other interests, unless you plan on implementing a mechanism that monitors or restricts their access.

Web traffic utilizes much more downstream bandwidth than upstream. The messages generated by Web browsers are mostly small requests for specific URLs transmitted to Web servers. The servers respond by supplying the requested files, which, while usually not enormous in size, are far bigger than the requests. Therefore, asymmetrical Internet connections like those provided by cable modems and DSL are eminently suited for Web browsing.

FTP

Once the mainstay of Internet communications, the File Transfer Protocol has been eclipsed by the Web in popularity, but it is still widely used. Many of the hyperlinks on Web pages that trigger file downloads use the FTP protocol instead of the Hypertext Transfer Protocol (HTTP), the standard for Web communications. The files downloaded using FTP are usually binaries, such as program and image files, and are often larger than the files that make up a home page.

When triggered from Web links, however, FTP communications tend to be intermittent. For example, a typical user might perform one or two FTP downloads in the midst of an hour of Web surfing. Dedicated FTP clients, however, spend the majority of their time performing file transfers, and can consume a great deal more bandwidth than Web browsers. Serious FTP users also tend to transfer larger files, some of which can be enormous. Advanced users involved in software beta testing, for example, might have to download dozens or even hundreds of megabytes worth of program files in the course of the testing process.

Because their bandwidth needs are greater and more continuous, you should count on FTP clients utilizing more bandwidth than virtually any other Internet application. Another difference between Web-triggered FTP and a dedicated FTP client is that Web links produce downstream file transfers only, while an FTP client can transfer files in either direction. Asymmetrical connections are suitable for Web-based FTP transfers, but not for dedicated FTP clients if upstream transfers will be frequent.

Usenet News

Usenet is the Internet news service, but it is not "news" in the traditional sense of the word. Usenet is actually a collection of 30,000 to 40,000 messaging forums, called *newsgroups*, on every topic under the sun, from computer-related subjects to entertainment, that are maintained on news servers located all over the Internet. Users access these forums with a client program called a *newsreader* that downloads the latest messages for particular forums and posts their replies back to the server.

Much of the traffic generated by Usenet is plain ASCII text, much like e-mail, so the burden on an Internet connection is similar to that of an e-mail client. Some of the newsgroups are dedicated to the posting of binaries, such as images or program files, encoded into ASCII text. These binaries are the functional equivalent of files attached to e-mails, as far as bandwidth utilization is concerned.

As long as users are accessing a news server on the Internet or one supplied by your ISP, you can consider a Usenet client as the equivalent of an e-mail client. However, if you plan to run your own news server, the bandwidth requirements are greater than for virtually any other Internet application. A full news feed consists of several gigabytes of data every day, which can tax even the fastest connection.

Web Site and FTP Hosting

The bandwidth needed for client access to the Internet is relatively quantifiable, but when you run your own Web and FTP servers, the traffic is determined by the number of outside users that access them. In most cases, businesses make a concerted effort to draw as much traffic to their Web sites as possible, so you must be sure that you have sufficient bandwidth to support the maximum number of users you can realistically expect.

When running a business Web site, the consequences of having insufficient bandwidth can be far worse than when supporting only internal Internet clients. Temporarily inconveniencing your employees is nothing compared to alienating potential customers and portraying your business in an unprofessional light. If you plan on using promotional activities to draw Internet users to your site, you must be prepared to handle them.

Unlike the traffic generated by Internet client programs, which mostly run downstream, Web and FTP servers generate mostly upstream traffic, so asymmetrical technologies like ADSL and cable modems are unsuitable for this purpose.

Internet Services

At the most basic level, an ISP supplies access to the Internet and nothing more. However, additional services are required to use Internet applications, and you may have to obtain those services from your ISP if you don't plan on running them internally. For example, your clients will need access to DNS servers; you can use your ISP's servers or run your own servers on your local network. ISPs usually can also provide access to mail and news servers, and can host your Web site for you, for additional charges. All of these are services that you can provide yourself, however. For a large network with hundreds of users, running these services in-house is a practical solution; while for small networks, it's generally better to obtain them from the ISP. The following sections examine these services and what's involved in running them.

IP Addresses

One of the few things that you can only get from an ISP, apart from the Internet connection itself, is the registered IP address(es) that Internet systems will use. Every client system connected to the Internet must have an IP address, but only systems with registered IP addresses are visible from the Internet. ISPs obtain registered addresses either from the Internet Assigned Numbers Authority (IANA) or from their own service providers, and sublet them to their clients.

 For more information about registered and unregistered IP addresses, see Chapter 11.

Depending on both the type of connection you use to access the Internet and the configuration of the ISP's own network, registered IP addresses may or may not be available. For example, cable systems typically run their own private, unregistered networks and assign unregistered addresses to the computers connected to it. When this is the case, your clients must all use unregistered addresses, meaning that they can access the Internet, but that Internet users cannot access their machines. This is perfectly acceptable for Internet client applications, but you cannot run a Web or FTP server using this arrangement.

If you have a T1, ISDN, frame relay, or even a dial-up connection, however, your ISP should be able to provide you with as many registered IP addresses as you need, although there may be an additional charge for them. Generally speaking, you should only use registered IP addresses on Web servers and other computers that must be accessible from the Internet. Every system with this type of address is vulnerable to unauthorized access from the Internet and must be protected against intruders.

Note *For more information about protecting your systems from unauthorized access and using unregistered IP addresses to access the Internet, see "Firewalls," later in this chapter.*

DNS

The Domain Name System is the service that converts the friendly names by which Internet servers are known into the IP addresses needed to communicate with them. Internet clients need access to a DNS server in order to process the URLs, server names, and e-mail addresses they supply in their applications. All ISPs have DNS servers, and in many cases a client system is automatically configured to use them when connecting to the provider. For example, a system using a dial-up Internet connection receives an IP address and DNS server addresses from the ISP's server during the network logon sequence. Whenever the user of the client system types a URL or clicks a hyperlink, the computer sends a name resolution request to the ISP's DNS server, which returns the IP address of the specified destination.

A system that is directly connected to the ISP through a modem; or other connection can be automatically configured with the addresses of DNS servers, but when you share the connection with other network users, you must configure the client systems with the DNS server addresses either manually or by using some other means, such as a DHCP (Dynamic Host Configuration Protocol) server.

Internet client systems use the Domain Name System only to resolve the names of the servers on the Internet that they want to access; but if you run Web or FTP servers of your own, you must have a DNS server that is configured with resource records containing your servers' names and their equivalent IP addresses. This is necessary in order for other users on the Internet to be able to access your servers by specifying a name, such as www.zacker.com. When your ISP or a hosting service runs your Web and FTP servers for you, adding the appropriate resource records to the provider's DNS servers is usually part of the package.

To register a domain name, you must contact one of the registrars that are charged with maintaining the records for specific top-level domains, such as com, org, and net. At one time, a company called Network Solutions, Inc. (www.networksolutions.com) was the sole registrar for these domains, but there are now several organizations that function as domain name registrars.

Note *For more information on the Domain Name System, running DNS servers, and registering your own domain name, see Chapter 20.*

You can, however, run your own DNS servers, both for use by your clients and for hosting your own Web and FTP sites. Most server operating systems, such as Windows NT, 2000, UNIX, and NetWare, include DNS server software. The computer functioning as a DNS server must have a registered IP address, so that it is visible from the Internet. If you are hosting your own Internet servers, you must register the addresses of the DNS servers with the authority that provides you with your domain name.

Mail Servers

In order for your users to send and receive Internet e-mail, they must have their own e-mail addresses and access to mail servers. Internet e-mail is based on the Simple Mail Transfer Protocol (SMTP), which carries e-mail traffic between servers and defines the well-known addressing format *username@domain*.com. Most ISPs provide e-mail service to their clients by using two types of mail servers: an SMTP server for sending outgoing mail, and a Post Office Protocol (POP3) or Internet Message Access Protocol (IMAP) server for receiving incoming mail. Both of these servers (which may or may not run on the same computer) have registered IP addresses, so that they are visible from the Internet.

Most of the Internet access accounts provided by ISPs, especially those intended for home users, include at least one e-mail address and access to the provider's mail servers. Some ISPs provide multiple e-mail addresses with the account, either for free or for a nominal additional fee. Unlike DNS servers, you must manually configure each e-mail client to access the appropriate servers, whether the computer is connected directly to the ISP or accesses it through the network.

When you share an Internet connection with a network and use the ISP's mail servers, your provider must either supply an e-mail address and POP3 or IMAP server account for each of your users, or give you a shell account that enables you to connect to the server and create the accounts yourself.

If you choose to run your own mail servers, you can perform all of the account maintenance tasks yourself and create as many accounts as you wish, but there are other factors you must consider. As with DNS servers, the computers running the e-mail server software must have registered IP addresses, and the SMTP server must be connected to the Internet at all times, in order for e-mail messages from outside users to find it. If the server is down or disconnected, mail messages directed to any of the accounts bounce back to the sender. E-mail server software is not included with server operating systems, and prices for e-mail server products can vary greatly. Full-featured e-mail products for Windows NT, like Microsoft Exchange, can be quite expensive, while sendmail, the most popular mail server on the Internet, is free. You must also have your own registered domain name and the appropriate resource records in the DNS, so that e-mail messages sent by users elsewhere on the Internet can find their way to your server.

Hosting your own e-mail servers is a major commitment in both time and resources, and thus is recommended only for network administrators with a large number of users and a full-time, high-speed connection to the Internet, such as a T1.

News Servers

Most ISPs provide access to a Usenet news server; and in most cases, there is no persuasive reason to run your own, because of the enormous amount of data required for a full news feed. However, some companies run news servers in order to host their own newsgroups for technical support purposes or product announcements. A private news server does not have to receive the Usenet news feed, so its bandwidth requirements are no more than that of a Web server.

Web Hosting

Many ISPs offer Web site hosting services, and include a small site with an Internet access account. This level of service is usually only suitable for a personal Web site, however, and if you want a professional site, you will have to pay an additional monthly fee for the disk space and other services. As with e-mail and DNS servers, you can have your ISP or an outside service host your Web site, or you can run it yourself.

As with e-mail servers, Web servers must have registered IP addresses and be visible from the Internet. You also need a permanent connection with sufficient bandwidth for the traffic that your site will generate, so that it is continuously available. Web server software is included with most server operating systems, but there are many reasons why it is better to use a service to host your Web sites instead. Many Web hosting services have redundant Internet connections that provide all the bandwidth you need and fault-tolerant systems that can compensate for potential disasters like power outages and disk failures. Some services can also provide access to advanced features like database servers and e-commerce tools that enable you to build a state-of-the-art Web site. These are all features that you can conceivably provide yourself, and for a large enough company, it may be economical to do so; but for most Web sites, a hosting service can provide a more reliable and consistent presence on the Web.

Internet Routers

To share an Internet connection with a network, you must have a router that provides the interface between your internal LAN and your ISP's network. The ISP network, in turn, is connected to another ISP or to an Internet backbone. Most people envision a router as an expensive standalone device used only on large networks; but an Internet router can also take the form of a software program running on a PC, or a small hardware device designed to provide Internet access to a small network.

The router, in its basic form, receives the packets generated by the workstations on the network that are intended for the Internet, repackages them for transmission over the connection to the ISP, and sends them on to the ISP's server. The ISP then forwards them to the appropriate Internet destination. The format of the packets generated by the router depends on the type of Internet connection you're using. Since the router is a network-layer device and the Internet uses TCP/IP communications exclusively, the packets all contain IP datagrams that may be repackaged several times by different data link–layer protocols on the way to their destination.

At one time, the high-end standalone routers intended for use on large networks performed only the standard functions associated with routers; but today, the routers designed for connecting networks to the Internet often include other features as well, such as firewall capabilities, Network Address Translation (NAT), and DHCP servers. These features are designed to make the process of connecting your network to the Internet easier and safer.

Software Routers

A software router is a program that enables a computer to share its connection to the Internet with other systems on the LAN. Some operating systems, such as Windows NT, can route the IP traffic to the Internet themselves; but others, such as Windows 98, cannot. A software router program provides this IP routing capability, as well as other functions that simplify the process of sharing an Internet connection. Windows 98 Second Edition includes a software routing service called Internet Connection Sharing (ICS), and third-party products, such as ACT Software's NAT32, and ITWIN Technology's WinRoute, provide roughly the same features. These products are designed to work on a small scale, providing Internet access to users on a small LAN; you would not use them to provide access to dozens or hundreds of Internet clients.

Note   *For information on NAT32 and to download a trial version of the program, see www.nat32.com. For information on WinRoute, see www.itwin.com.my/winroute.htm.*

Like any router, the computer providing the Internet access is connected to two networks: the LAN, using a standard network interface card; and the ISP's network, using a modem, ISDN, DSL, or cable modem connection. The Internet connection itself is not modified in any way by the router software. To the ISP and to Internet systems, all of the traffic appears to be coming from the router. While performing its router functions, it is still possible to use the connected system as a normal workstation.

Each of the other workstations on the LAN accesses the Internet by using the router system's IP address as its default gateway. Most Internet client programs can access the Internet through the router with no modification.

Network Address Translation

Software routers are typically used to share connections that are normally intended for single users, such as dial-up, BRI ISDN, and cable modem connections. The providers of these types of connections typically do not furnish registered IP addresses for multiple systems as part of the account, so the router software uses a technique called *Network Address Translation (NAT)* to enable the network clients to use unregistered IP addresses.

Windows NT is capable of routing IP traffic, but to use an Internet-connected NT system as a router, you must use registered IP addresses for all of the client workstations on the network. Not only can this be an expensive proposition, since some ISPs charge $10 to $20 per month for each additional registered address, but it is also a dangerous one, because it can also open up your network to outside intruders. Registered IP addresses make your workstations visible to any user on the Internet that cares to access them, and installations using connection sharing on a small scale are rarely willing to invest in elaborate firewalls to protect the network from intrusion.

With NAT, you assign unregistered IP addresses to your workstations. The IANA has designated three ranges of IP addresses for use on unregistered networks, one for each address class. These addresses are not assigned to any specific network. By using them on your private network, you can be sure that there is no conflict between the addresses of your systems and those of public machines on the Internet. These addresses are listed in Table 26-2.

Class	Private Network Addresses
Class A	10.0.0.0 through 10.255.255.255
Class B	172.16.0.0 through 172.31.255.255
Class C	192.168.0.0 through 192.168.255.255

Table 26-2.   *Unregistered IP Addresses for Use on Private Networks*

When a client system on your network sends a packet to a server on the Internet, the packet's IP header contains the IP address of the sender, which is unregistered. If this packet was to reach the destination server unaltered, the server would transmit its reply to the unregistered IP address. This attempt would fail, because Internet routers do not forward packets with unregistered destination addresses. Therefore, the router on your LAN translates the IP address of the sending system in each packet from the unregistered address of the client to the registered address of the router itself. The destination server can then send its response to the router, which forwards it to the appropriate client.

Thus, NAT enables any number of workstations to access the Internet using a single registered IP address. At the rate that the Internet is currently growing, the 32-bit IP address space is rapidly becoming depleted, and the use of NAT helps to conserve the registered IP addresses by enabling networks to use them only for the systems that must be directly accessible from the Internet. At the same time, the router protects the workstations from direct access by intruders on the Internet. Only the router itself has an address that is visible from outside, making it impossible to address IP traffic directly to a workstation on the LAN.

DHCP

Software router programs are directed at users who have little technical knowledge about networking, so they try to make the process of configuring the workstations to access the router as simple as possible. The program typically includes a DHCP service that automatically configures the TCP/IP client on the LAN workstations with an unregistered IP address and the address of the router as the default gateway. As a result, no manual configuration is required for the client workstations other than to specify that they use DHCP to obtain their TCP/IP settings.

Hardware Routers

There are also hardware-based Internet routers designed for use on networks of various sizes. This type of unit is essentially a special-purpose computer with its own processor, software, and IP addresses that performs all the functions of a software router and typically has other capabilities, such as packet filtering and support for multiple protocols. The primary difference is that, in this case, the router is a completely separate device, not reliant on any single workstation on the network and not as vulnerable as a workstation to interference. When you use a software router, all the clients on the LAN rely on that machine for their Internet access. If the computer goes down or the user must reboot, all Internet communications cease. A hardware router is wholly dedicated to providing Internet access and, unlike a regular workstation, is not subject to failure because of user error or an errant application.

Hardware routers connect both to the local network and to an ISP. Some devices have an Ethernet hub integrated into the unit, enabling you to plug the LAN workstations into it, while others just have an Ethernet interface, which you plug into a port on a standard hub. This latter type provides more versatility, because you can use any size hub, rather than being limited to the number of ports integrated into the former unit. The router also supports a connection to an ISP, with different products supporting various types of connections. Devices intended for use on home or small business networks might have a serial port or PC card slot for a standard modem connection, or they might support BRI ISDN or DSL. Higher-end units might support PRI ISDN, frame relay, or leased lines. Like software routers, these devices typically use NAT to provide client access to the Internet, and might include a DHCP server. Most units also have an integrated Web server that enables you to configure the unit by using a standard browser.

Hardware routers are significantly more expensive than software ones, ranging from a few hundred dollars for small business units to thousands for more advanced models, but they generally provide a more reliable connection-sharing solution.

Client Requirements

Part of the process of providing your network users with Internet access is the configuration of the client systems themselves. The Internet is a TCP/IP-based network, so if you have not already done so, you must configure all of the client workstations that need Internet access to use the TCP/IP protocols. Most LANs today use TCP/IP as their primary networking protocol; unless you have Novell NetWare servers that require IPX, no other protocols are necessary.

Every workstation that will access the Internet must be configured with the following TCP/IP parameters:

- IP address
- Default gateway address
- DNS server addresses

The primary consideration when you are assigning IP addresses is whether they are registered or unregistered. Some network administrators, when designing a private network that will not be connected to the Internet, choose IP addresses arbitrarily because no conflict with the Internet can exist. Then, if they decide to connect the network to the Internet later, they must change all of the addresses.

The type of addresses you use is determined by the type of connection you will have to the Internet and the type of firewall you will use to protect your network from intrusion. If you're going to use NAT, for example, you must use unregistered addresses on your workstations. Other types of firewalls, such as those that filter packets, permit the use of registered IP addresses.

The default gateway address for each workstation is the internal IP address of the router that provides access to the Internet. If the workstation is on the same LAN as the router that is actually connected to the Internet, then that router is the default gateway.

On a multisegment network, the default gateway for some of your workstations will be a router that provides access to the segment on which the Internet router is located. On this type of network, you must configure your internetwork routers so that they know the address of the Internet router, using either a static route or a routing protocol.

Each workstation must also be configured with the IP address of at least one DNS server, either on the local network or the ISP's network. Although it is still possible for a TCP/IP workstation to communicate with another system without a DNS server, the inability to resolve names means that the user must specify the IP address of the target system, instead of a friendly name, which is usually not practical. The addresses of two DNS servers are preferable, but the second one is only used if the first is unavailable.

Firewalls

A *firewall* is a hardware or software entity that protects a network from intrusion by outside users by regulating the traffic that can pass through a router connecting it to another network. The term is most often used in relation to protection from intruders on the Internet, but a firewall can also protect a LAN from users on other LANs, either local or WAN connected. Without some sort of a firewall in place, outside users can access the files on your network, plant viruses, use your servers for their own purposes, or even delete your drives entirely.

Completely isolating a network from communication with other networks is not difficult, but this is not the function of a firewall. A firewall is designed to permit certain types of traffic to pass over the router between the networks, while denying access to all other traffic. For example, you want your client workstations to be able to send HTTP requests from their Web browsers to servers on the Internet, and for the servers to be able to reply, but you don't want outside users on the Internet to be able to access those clients. Firewalls use several different methods to provide varying degrees of protection to network systems. A client workstation has different protection requirements than a Web server, for example.

Depending on the size of your network, the functions of your systems, and the degree of risk, firewalls can take many forms. In fact, the term has come to be used to refer to any sort of protection from outside influences. In fact, a true firewall is really a set of security policies that may be implemented by several different network components that work together to regulate not only the traffic that is permitted into the network, but possibly also the traffic that is permitted out. For example, in addition to preventing Internet users from accessing the systems on your network, you can also use a firewall to prevent certain internal users from surfing the Web, while allowing them the use of Internet e-mail.

An inexpensive software router program uses NAT to enable client workstations on a small network to use unregistered addresses, and in a loose sense of the term, this is a form of firewall. A large corporation with multiple T1 connections to the Internet, however, is more likely to have a system between the internal network and the Internet routers that is running software dedicated to firewall functions. Some firewall capabilities are integrated into a router, while other firewall products are separate software products that you must install on a computer.

Firewall protection can stem from either one of the following two basic policies, the choice of which is generally dependent on the security risks inherent in the network and the needs of the network users:

- Everything not specifically permitted is denied.
- Everything not specifically denied is permitted.

These two policies are essentially a reflection of the phenomenon by which a glass is seen as being either half full or half empty. You can start with a network that is completely secured in every way and open up portals permitting the passage of specific types of traffic, or you can start with a completely open network and block the types of traffic considered to be intrusive. The former method is much more secure, and is generally recommended in all environments. However, it tends to emphasize security over ease of use. The latter method is less secure but makes the network easier to use. This method also forces the administrator to try to anticipate the techniques by which the firewall can be penetrated. If there is one thing that is known for certain about Internet hackers, it is that they are endlessly inventive, and keeping up with their diabolical activities can be difficult.

Network administrators can use a variety of techniques to implement these policies and protect the different types of systems on the network. The following sections examine some of these techniques and the applications for which they're used.

Packet Filters

Packet filtering is a feature implemented on routers and firewalls that uses rules specified by the administrator to determine whether or not a packet should be permitted to pass through the firewall. The rules are based on the information provided in the protocol headers of each packet, including the following:

- IP source and destination addresses
- Encapsulated protocol
- Source and destination port
- ICMP message type
- Incoming and outgoing interface

By using combinations of values for these criteria, you can specify precise conditions under which packets should be admitted through the firewall. For example, you can specify the IP addresses of certain computers on the Internet that should be permitted to use the Telnet protocol to communicate with a specific machine on the local network. As a result, all packets directed to the system with the specified destination IP address and using port 23 (the well-known port for the Telnet protocol) are discarded, except for those with the source IP addresses specified in the rule. Using this rule, the network administrators can permit certain remote users (such as other administrators) to Telnet into network systems, while all others are denied access. This is known as *service-dependent filtering,* because it is designed to control the traffic for a particular service, such as Telnet.

Service-independent filtering is used to prevent specific types of intrusion that are not based on a particular service. For example, a hacker may attempt to access a computer on a private network by generating packets that appear as though they originated from an internal system. This is called *spoofing.* Although the packets might have the IP address of an internal system, they arrive at the router through the interface that is connected to the Internet. A properly configured filter can associate the IP addresses of internal systems with the interface to the internal network, so that packets arriving from the Internet with those source IP addresses can be detected and discarded.

Packet filtering is a feature integrated into many routers, so no extra monetary cost is involved in implementing protection in this way, and no modification to client software or procedures is required. However, creating a collection of filters that provides adequate protection for a network against most types of attack requires a detailed knowledge of the way in which the various protocols and services work, and even then the filters may not be sufficient to prevent some types of intrusion. Packet filtering also creates an additional processing burden on the router, which increases as the filters become more numerous and complex.

Proxy Servers

Proxy servers, also known as *application-level gateways* or *bastion hosts,* provide a much stricter form of security than packet filters, but they are designed to regulate access only for a particular application. In essence, a proxy server functions as the middleman between the client and the server for a particular service. Packet filtering is used to deny all direct communication between the clients and servers for that service; all traffic goes to the proxy server instead (see Figure 26-2).

Because the proxy server has a much more detailed knowledge of the specific application and its functions, it can more precisely regulate the communications generated by that application. A firewall might run individual proxy servers for each of the applications needed by client systems, as shown in Figure 26-3.

The most common form of proxy server used today is for the Web. The client browsers on the network are configured to send all of their requests to the proxy server, instead of to the actual Internet server they want to reach. The proxy server (which does have access to the Internet) then transmits a request for the same document to the appropriate server on the Internet, using its own IP address as the source of the request, receives the reply from the server, and passes the response on to the client that originally generated the request.

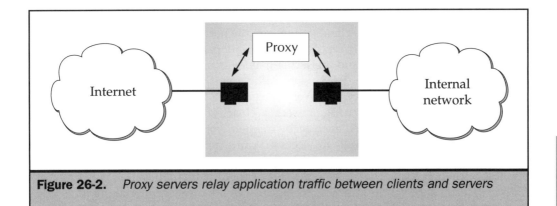

Figure 26-2. *Proxy servers relay application traffic between clients and servers*

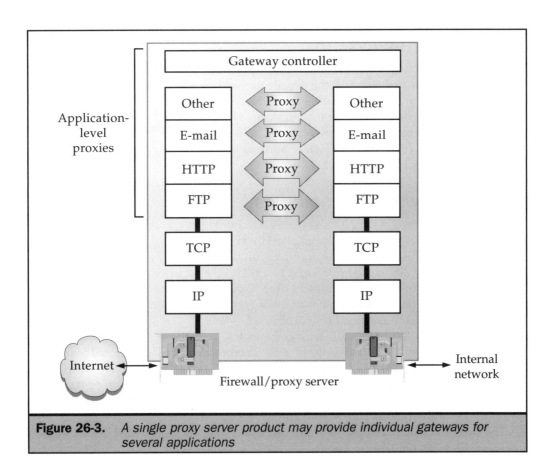

Figure 26-3. *A single proxy server product may provide individual gateways for several applications*

Because only the proxy server's address is visible to the Internet, there is no way for Internet intruders to access the client systems on the network. In addition, the server analyzes each packet arriving from the Internet. Only packets that are responses to a specific request are admitted, and the server may even examine the data itself for dangerous code or content. The proxy server is in a unique position to regulate user traffic with great precision. A typical Web proxy server, for example, enables the network administrator to keep a log of users' Web activities, restrict access to certain sites or certain times of day, and even cache frequently accessed sites on the proxy server itself, enabling other clients to access the same information much more quickly.

The drawbacks of proxy servers are that you need an individual server for every application, and that modifications to the client program are required. A Web browser, for example, must be configured with the address of the proxy server before it can use it. Traditionally, manual configuration of each client browser was needed to do this, but there are now protocols that can enable the browser to automatically detect a proxy server and configure itself accordingly.

Circuit-Level Gateways

A *circuit-level gateway*, a function that is usually provided by application-level gateway products, enables trusted users on the private network to access Internet services with all the security of a proxy server, but without the packet processing and filtering. The gateway creates a conduit between the interface to the private network and the Internet interface, which enables the client system to send traffic through the firewall. The gateway server still substitutes its own IP address for that of the client system, so that the client is still invisible to Internet users.

Combining Firewall Technologies

There are various ways in which these firewall technologies can be combined to protect a network. For a relatively simple installation in which only client access to the Internet is required, packet filtering alone or in combination with a proxy server can provide a sufficient firewall. Adding the proxy server increases the security of the network beyond what packet filtering provides, because a potential intruder has to penetrate two levels of protection. However, if you run servers that must be visible to the Internet, the problem becomes more complicated.

One of the most secure firewall arrangements you can use for this type of environment is called a *screened subnet firewall*. This consists of a *demilitarized zone (DMZ)* network between the private network and the Internet. Using two routers with packet-filtering capabilities, you create a DMZ network that contains your proxy server, as well as your Web, e-mail, and FTP servers, and any other machines that must be visible to the Internet, as shown in Figure 26-4.

The two routers are configured to provide systems on the private network and the Internet with a certain degree of access to certain systems on the DMZ network, but no traffic passes directly through the DMZ. A user from the Internet must then pass

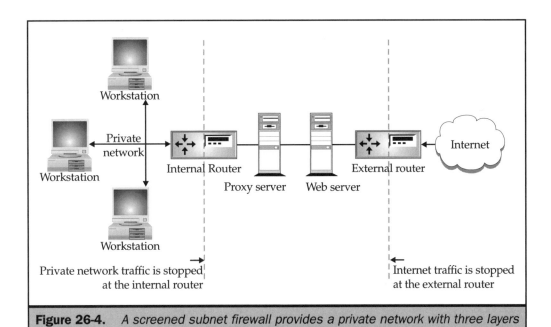

Figure 26-4.   *A screened subnet firewall provides a private network with three layers of protection*

through three separate layers of security (router, proxy, and router) before he or she can access a system on the private network.

Firewalls of this type are complex mechanisms that must be configured specifically for a particular installation, and can require a great deal of time, money, and expertise to implement. The prices of comprehensive firewall software products for enterprise networks can run well into five figures, and deploying them is not simply a matter of running an installation program. However, compared to the potential cost in lost data and productivity of a hacker intrusion, the effort taken to protect your network is not wasted.

Providing users with Internet access is a task that almost every network administrator will have to face at some point or another, and an understanding of all the concepts involved can only make the job easier. Protecting your network against unauthorized access is a crucial element of the task that you should take into consideration throughout the planning and installation process.

The
Complete
Reference

Upgrading
&
Troubleshooting
Networks

Part VIII

Network Administration

The Complete Reference

Upgrading & Troubleshooting Networks

Chapter 27

Windows Network Administration

Although business networks often run a variety of operating systems, particularly on their servers, the majority of user workstations run some form of Windows. Whether or not you agree that the Windows interface is user friendly and intuitive, there is no question that administering a fleet of hundreds or thousands of Windows workstations is an extremely formidable task. Windows 95, Windows 98, Windows NT Workstation, and Windows 2000 Professional all include tools that network administrators can use to simplify the process of installing, managing, and maintaining the operating system on a large number of workstations. This chapter examines some of these tools and how you can use them to configure workstations en masse, rather than working on them one at a time.

One of the primary goals of any network administrator should be to create workstation configurations that are standardized and consistent, so that when problems occur, the support staff is fully acquainted with the user's working environment. Failure to do this can greatly increase the time and effort needed to troubleshoot problems, thus increasing the overall cost of operating the machine. Unfortunately, users have a tendency to experiment with their workstations, such as by modifying the configuration settings or installing unauthorized software. This can make the system unstable and can interfere with the maintenance and troubleshooting processes. Therefore, it is advisable that administrators impose some form of restraints on network workstations, to prevent this unauthorized experimentation.

Features such as user profiles and system policies are basic tools you can use to do this on Windows systems, to whatever degree you judge is necessary for your users. Using these tools, you can limit the programs that a system is able to run, deny access to certain elements of the operating system, and control access to network resources. These tools, and several others, are all part of what Microsoft calls its Zero Administration Initiative (ZAI). The ZAI is misunderstood by many people who think that its goal is a workstation that needs no maintenance or administration of any kind. In actuality, the ZAI is designed to prevent users from performing system administration tasks for which they are not qualified. By installing a workstation environment that has been carefully planned and tested, and then preventing users from changing it, the cost of maintaining workstations can be greatly reduced.

Imposing restrictive policies and limiting users' access to their workstations can be sensitive undertakings, and network administrators should carefully consider the capabilities of their users before making decisions like these. Unsophisticated computer users can benefit and may even appreciate a restricted environment that insulates them from the more confusing elements of the operating system. However, users with more experience might take offense at being limited to a small subset of the computer's features, and their productivity may even be impaired by it.

Locating Applications and Data

One of the basic tasks of the network administrator is to decide where data should be stored on the network. Network workstations require access to operating system files, applications, and data, and the locations where these elements are stored is an important part of creating a safe and stable network environment. Some administrators actually exercise no control over where users store files. Fortunately, most Windows applications install themselves to a default directory located in the C:\Program Files directory on the local system, which provides a measure of consistency if nothing else. Some applications even create default data directories on the local drive, but leaving users to their own devices when it comes to storing their data files is an inherently dangerous practice. Many users have little or no knowledge of their computer's directory structure and no training in file management. This can result in files for different applications all being dumped into a single common directory and left unprotected from accidental damage or erasure.

Server-Based Operating Systems

In the early days of Windows, running the operating system from a server drive was a practical alternative to having individual installations on every workstation. Storing the operating system files on a server enabled the network administrator not only to prevent them from being tampered with or accidentally deleted, but also to upgrade all the workstations at once. The technique also saved disk space on the workstation's local drive. However, as the years passed, the capacity of a typical hard drive on a network workstation grew enormously, as did the size of the Windows operating system itself.

Today, the practice of simply installing a standard operating system onto a mapped server drive is not practical. A workstation running Windows 95/98 or NT/2000 must load many megabytes of files just to boot the system; and when you multiply this by hundreds of computers, the amount of network traffic created could clog even the fastest network. In addition, disk space shortages are not a big problem anymore when workstations routinely ship with drives that hold anywhere from 2 to 8GB of data or more. Installing the operating system onto the local drive is, in most cases, the obvious solution.

However, there are newer technologies available today that are once again making it practical to run a Windows operating system from a server. This time, however, the workstations do not download the entire operating system from the server drive. Instead, the workstations function as client terminals that connect to a terminal server. The workstation operating system and applications actually run on the server, while the terminal functions solely as an input/output device. As a result, the workstations require only minimal resources, because the server takes most of the burden.

The terminals in this arrangement are either relatively modest computers, such as 486s, running a terminal emulation program, or dedicated Windows terminals that are designed solely to run the client software. In either case, the cost of a workstation is far less than that of a new PC with the hardware needed to run an individual copy of Windows NT or 2000. Windows NT 4.0 is available in a special version that supports this technology, called Windows NT Server Terminal Server Edition, while Windows 2000 Server includes the terminal server capability in the basic package. There are also

NETWORK ADMINISTRATION

third-party products that provide the same capabilities, the pioneer of which is WinFrame, by Citrix Systems (http://www.citrix.com).

Running a terminal-based Windows network is a complete departure from a standard LAN, and is not a practical alternative for a network already running full Windows versions on its workstations. However, if you're building a new network or performing a major expansion, then using Windows terminals is an option that you may want to consider.

Server-Based Applications

Running applications from a server drive rather than individual workstation installations is another way to provide a consistent environment for your users and minimize the network's administrative burden. At its simplest, you do this by installing an application in the usual manner and specifying a directory on a network drive instead of a local directory as the location for the program files. However, Windows applications are rarely simple, and the process is usually more complicated.

Running applications from server drives has both advantages and disadvantages. On the plus side, as with server-based operating systems, are the disk space savings on the local drives, the ability to protect the application files against damage or deletion, and the ability to upgrade and maintain a single copy of the application files rather than individual copies on each workstation. The disadvantages are that server-based applications nearly always run more slowly than local ones, generate a substantial amount of network traffic, and do not function when the server is malfunctioning or otherwise unavailable.

In the days of DOS, applications were self-contained and usually consisted of no more than a single program directory that contained all of the application's files. You could install the application to a server drive and then let other systems use it simply by running the executable file. Today's Windows applications are much more complex, however, and the installation program is more than just a means of copying files. In addition to the program files, a Windows application typically consists of registry settings and Windows DLLs that must be installed on the local machine, as well as a procedure for creating the Start menu entries and icons needed to launch the application.

When you want to share a server-based application with multiple workstations, you usually still have to perform a complete installation on each machine. This is to ensure that each workstation has all of the Windows files, registry settings, and icons needed to run the application. One way to implement a server-based application is to perform a complete installation of the program on each workstation, specifying the same server directory as the destination for the program files in each case. This way, each workstation receives all of the necessary files and modifications, and only one copy of the application files are stored on the server.

However, another important issue is the ability to maintain individual configuration settings for each of the workstations accessing the application. For example, when one user modifies the interface of a shared application, you don't want those modifications to affect every other user. As a result, each of the application's users must maintain their own copies of the application configuration settings. Whether or not this is an easy task, or even a possible one, depends on how each individual application stores its configuration settings. If, for example, the settings are stored in the registry or a Windows INI file, the installation process will create a separate configuration on each workstation. However, if the settings are stored with the program files on the server by default, then you must take steps to prevent each user's changes from overwriting those of the other users.

In some cases, it is possible to configure an application to store its configuration settings in an alternate location, enabling you to redirect them to each workstation's local drive or to each user's home directory on a server. If this is not possible, then the application may not be suitable for use in a shared environment.

In many cases, the most practical way to run applications from a server is to select applications that have their own networking capabilities. Microsoft Office, for example, enables you to create an administrative installation point on a server that you can use to install the application on your workstations. When you perform each installation, you can select whether the application files should be copied to the local drive, run from the server drive, or split between the two.

Storing Data Files

On most of today's Windows networks, both the operating system and the applications are installed on local workstation drives, but it is still up to the network administrator to decide where the data files generated and accessed by users should be stored. The two primary concerns that you must evaluate when making this decision are accessibility and security. Users must certainly have access to their own data files, but there are also files that have to be shared by many users. Important data files also have to be protected from modification and deletion by unauthorized personnel, and backed up to an alternative medium to guard against a disaster, such as a fire or disk failure.

Data files come in various types and formats that can affect the way in which you store them. Individual user documents, for example, such as those created in word processor or spreadsheet applications, are designed for use by one person at a time, while databases can support simultaneous access by multiple users. In most cases, database files are stored on the computers running the database server application, so that administrators can regulate access to them with file system permissions and protect them with regular backups. Other types of files may require additional planning, however.

Since Windows 95/98 and NT/2000 are all peer-to-peer network operating systems, you can allow users to store their document files on either their local drive or a server and still share them with other users on the network. However, there are several compelling reasons why it is better for all data files to be stored on servers. The first and most important reason is to protect the files from loss due to a workstation or disk failure. Servers are more likely to have protective measures in place, such as RAID arrays or mirrored drives, and are more easily backed up. Servers also make the data available at all times, while a workstation might be turned off when the user is absent.

The second reason is access control. Although Windows workstations and servers both have the same capabilities when it comes to granting access permissions to specific users, users rarely have the skills or the inclination to protect their own files effectively, and it is far easier for network administrators to manage the permissions on a single server than on many individual workstations. Another important reason is that sharing the drives on every workstation can make it much more difficult to locate information on the network. To look at a Windows NT or 2000 domain and see dozens or hundreds of computers, each with its own shares, makes the task of locating a specific file much more complicated. Limiting the shares to relatively few servers simplifies the process.

As a result, the best strategy for most Windows networks is to install the operating system and applications on local drives and implement a strategy for storing all data files on network servers. The most common practice is to create a home directory for each user on a server, to which they have full access permissions. You should then configure all applications to store their files in that directory, by default, so that no valuable data is stored on local drives. Depending on the needs of your users, you can make the home directories private, so that only the user that owns the directory can access it, or grant all users read-only access to all of the home directories. This makes it possible for users to share files at will simply by giving another user the filename or location.

When you create a user account in a Windows NT domain or a user object in the Windows 2000 Active Directory, you have the option of creating a home directory for the user at the same time in a dialog box like that shown in Figure 27-1. By default,

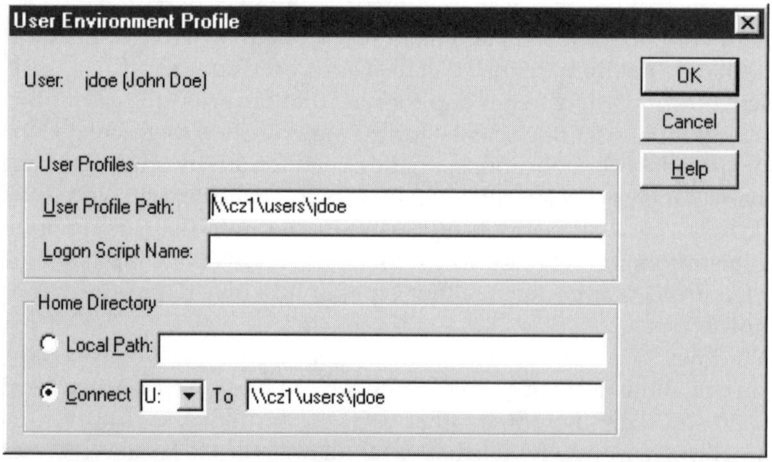

Figure 27-1.   The User Environment Profile dialog box in Windows NT's User Manager for Domains

users are given full control over their home directories, and no one else is given any access at all. You may want to modify these permissions to grant access to the directory to the other users on the network or, at the very least, to administrators.

Controlling the Workstation Environment

In an organization comprised of expert computer users, you can leave everyone to their own devices when it comes to managing their Windows desktops. Experienced users can create their own desktop icons, manage their own Start menu shortcuts, and map their own drive letters. However, not many networks have only power users, and it is better left up to the network administrator to create a viable and consistent workstation environment.

Drive Mappings

Many less sophisticated computer users don't fully understand the concept of a network and how a server drive can be mapped to a drive letter on a local machine. A user may have the drive letter F mapped to a particular server drive and assume that other users' systems are configured the same way. If workstation drive mappings are inconsistent, then confusion results when one user tells another that a file is located on the F drive, and F refers to a different share. To avoid problems like these, administrators should create a consistent drive mapping strategy for users who will be sharing the same resources.

As an example, in most cases users will have a departmental or workgroup server that is their "home" server, and it's a good idea for every workstation to have the same drive letter mapped to that home server. If there are application servers that provide resources to everyone on the network, such as a company database server, then every system should use the same drive letter to reference that server. Implementing minor policies like these can significantly reduce the number of nuisance calls to the help desk generated by puzzled users.

To implement a set of consistent drive mappings for your users, you can create logon script files containing NET USE commands that map drives to the appropriate servers each time the user logs on to the network. By structuring the commands properly, you should be able to create a single logon script for multiple users. For example, to map a drive letter to each user's own home directory, you use a command like the following:

```
NET USE X: /home
```

To designate a command file as a user's logon script, you add it to the User Environment Profile dialog box in Windows NT 4.0's User Manager for Domains

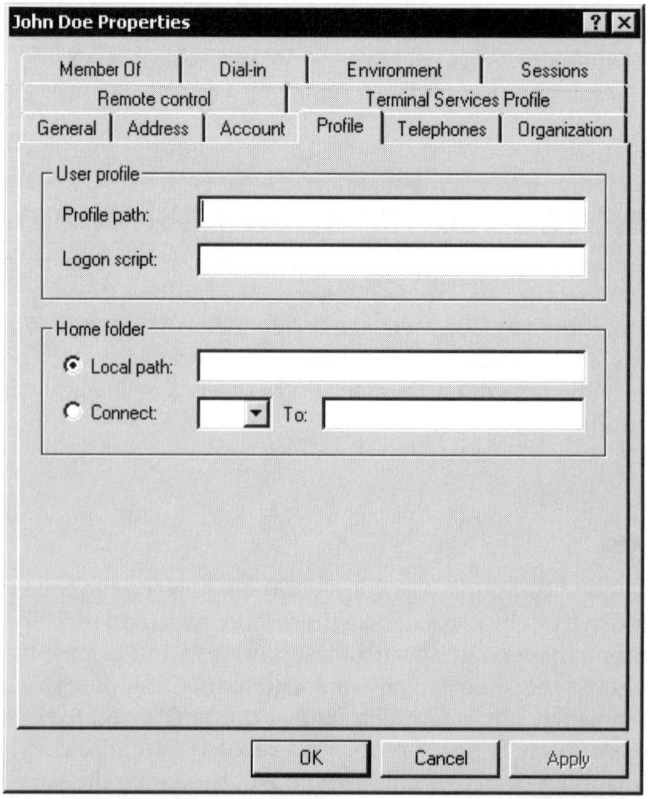

John Doe Properties   ? ✕

| Member Of | Dial-in | Environment | Sessions |

| Remote control | | Terminal Services Profile |

| General | Address | Account | Profile | Telephones | Organization |

┌─ User profile ──────────────────────────────────────┐
│ Profile path: [   ] │
│   │
│ Logon script: [   ] │
└───┘

┌─ Home folder ───────────────────────────────────────┐
│ ⦿ Local path: [   ] │
│   │
│ ○ Connect: [▾] To: [   ] │
└───┘

[OK   ]   [Cancel]   [Apply]

Figure 27-2.   *The Profile page in the Properties dialog box of an Active Directory user object*

utility or to the Profile page in the user object's Properties dialog box in the Windows 2000 Active Directory Users and Computers console (see Figure 27-2).

 For more information on the many uses of the Windows NET command, see Chapter 28.

User Profiles

Creating user profiles is a method of storing the shortcuts and desktop configuration settings for individual users in a directory in which they can be accessed during the system startup sequence. By creating separate profiles for different users, each person can retrieve their own settings when they log on. When you store multiple profiles on a local machine, you make it possible for users to share the same workstation without overwriting each other's settings. When you store the profiles on a network server, users can access their settings from any network workstation; this is called a *roaming profile*. In addition, you can force users to load a specific profile each time they log on to a system, and prevent them from changing it; this is called a *mandatory profile.*

The registry on a Windows 95 or 98 system consists of two files on the local drive, called System.dat and User.dat. User.dat corresponds to the HKEY_CURRENT_USER key in the registry, which contains all of the environmental settings that apply to the user that's currently logged on. On a Windows NT or 2000 system, the corresponding file is called Ntuser.dat. This file, called a *registry hive,* forms the basis of a user profile. By loading a User.dat or Ntuser.dat during the logon sequence, the settings contained in the file are written to the registry and become active on the system.

The user hive contains the following types of system configuration settings:

■ All user-definable settings for Windows Explorer

■ Persistent network drive connections

■ Network printer connections

■ All user-definable settings in the Control Panel, such as the Display settings

■ All taskbar settings

■ All user-definable settings for Windows accessories, such as Calculator, Notepad, Clock, Paint, and HyperTerminal

■ All bookmarks created in the Windows Help system

In addition to the hive, a user profile can include subdirectories that contain shortcuts and other elements that form parts of the workstation environment. These subdirectories are as follows:

■ **Application Data**   Contains application-specific data, such as custom dictionary files.

■ **Cookies**   Contains cookies used by Internet Explorer to store information about the system's interaction with specific Internet sites.

■ **Desktop**   Contains shortcuts to programs and files that appear on the Windows desktop.

■ **Favorites (Windows NT/2000 only)**   Contains shortcuts to programs, files, and URLs that appear in Internet Explorer's Favorites list.

■ **History (Windows 95/98 and NT only)**   Contains shortcuts to the URLs previously visited by the user in Internet Explorer.

■ **My Documents (Windows 2000 only)**   Contains shortcuts to personal documents and other files.

■ **NetHood**   Contains shortcuts that appear in the Network Neighborhood window.

■ **Personal (Windows NT only)**   Contains shortcuts to personal documents and other files.

NETWORK ADMINISTRATION

- **PrintHood (Windows NT/2000 only)**   Contains shortcuts that appear in the Printers window.

- **Recent**   Contains shortcuts to files that appear in the Documents folder in the Start menu.

- **SendTo (Windows NT/2000 only)**   Contains shortcuts to programs and file system locations that appear in the context menu's Send To folder.

- **Start menu**   Contains folders and shortcuts to programs and files that appear in the Start menu.

- **Templates (Windows NT/2000 only)**   Contains shortcuts to document templates.

 The NetHood, PrintHood, and Templates directories are hidden by default. To view them, you must configure Windows Explorer to display hidden files.

Between the hive and the subdirectories, the user profile configures most of a user's workstation environment—including cosmetic elements, such as screen colors and wallpaper, and operational elements, such as desktop icons and Start menu shortcuts. The more concrete elements of the system configuration, such as hardware device drivers and settings, are not included in the user profile. If, for example, you install a new piece of hardware on a system, all users will have access to it, regardless of which profile is in use.

By default, Windows NT creates a user profile for each different user that logs on to the machine, and stores them in the \Winnt\Profiles directory on the system drive. The system also creates a default user profile during the operating system installation process that functions as a template for the creation of new profiles. If there are elements that you want included in all of a system's profiles, you can make changes to the profile in the \Default User directory before any of the users log on. The system will then copy the default profile to a new subdirectory each time a new user logs on.

In Windows 95 and 98, the use of user profiles is optional and controlled by the User Profiles page in the Passwords Control Panel (see Figure 27-3). In this dialog box, you can specify whether or not the system should create a new profile for each user that logs on and whether the profile should include desktop icons, Network Neighborhood settings, the Start menu, and program groups. The profiles are created in the \Windows\Profiles directory on the system drive. Unlike Windows NT, however, there is no default user profile on a Windows 95/98 system.

Creating Roaming Profiles

Both Windows NT/2000 and 95/98 store user profiles on the local machine by default. You can modify this behavior by specifying a location on a network server for a particular user's profile in the same NT User Environment Profile dialog box or Windows 2000 Profile page in which you specified the location of the user's home directory. Windows NT and 2000 systems use the path specified in the Profile field, while Windows 95 and 98 systems use the home directory. The profile server can be

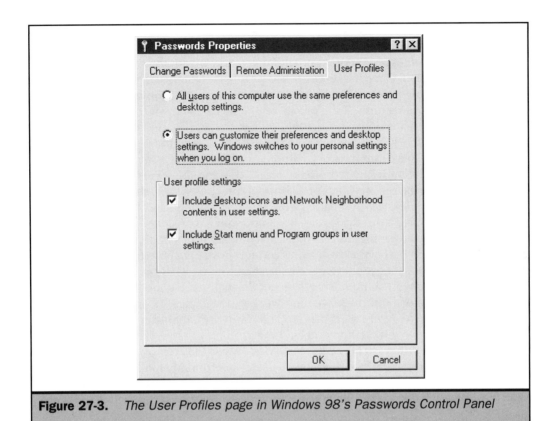

Figure 27-3. *The User Profiles page in Windows 98's Passwords Control Panel*

any system that is accessible by the workstation, running any version of Windows 95/98 or NT/2000, or even Novell NetWare. Once you specify the location for the profile, the operating system on the workstation copies the active profile to the server drive the next time the user logs off the network.

The best way to organize user profiles on the network is to designate a single machine as a profile server and create subdirectories named for your users, in which the profiles will be stored. Then, when you specify the location of the profile directory for each user, you can use the *%UserName%* variable as part of the path, as follows:

```
\\Ntserver\Profiles\%UserName%
```

The system then replaces the *%UserName%* variable with the user's logon name, as long as the variable appears only once in the path, and the variable is the last subdirectory in the path. In other words, the path \\Ntserver\Users\ *%UserName%*\Profile would not be acceptable. However, the system does recognize an extension added to the variable, making \\Ntserver\Profiles\ %UserName%.man an acceptable path.

Storing user profiles on a server does not delete them from the workstation from which they originated. Once the server-based profile is created, each logon by the user triggers the following process: The workstation compares the profile on the server with the profile on the workstation. If the profile on the server is newer than that on the workstation, the system copies the server profile to the workstation drive and loads it from there into memory. If the two profiles are identical, then the workstation loads the profile on the local drive into memory without copying from the server. When the user logs off, the workstation writes to both the local drive and the server any changes that have been made to the registry keys and shortcut directories that make up the profile.

Because the profile is always loaded from the workstation's local drive, even when a new version is copied from the server, it is important to consider the ramifications of making changes to the profile from another machine. If, for example, an administrator modifies a profile on the server by deleting certain shortcuts, these changes will likely have no effect, because those shortcuts still exist on the workstation, and copying the server profile to the workstation drive does not delete them. To modify a profile, you must make changes on both the server and workstation copies.

Once you create a server-based profile for a given user, that user can log on to the network from any workstation and load the profile, with one exception: the user profiles created by Windows NT/2000 and Windows 95/98 are not interchangeable, because the registries of the two operating systems are fundamentally different. A user with a Windows NT/2000 profile on the server cannot log on to a Windows 95 or 98 system and load that same profile or use that same server directory to store a 95/98 profile as well.

One of the potential drawbacks of storing user profiles on a network server is the amount of data that must be transferred on a regular basis. The registry hive and the various shortcut subdirectories are usually not a problem; but if, for example, a Windows 2000 Professional user stores many megabytes worth of files in the \My Documents directory, the time needed to copy that directory to the server and read it back again can produce a noticeable delay during the logoff and logon processes. The reason for including directories such as \My Documents and \Personal in the user profile is to enable users to access their personal documents if they log on to the network using another machine. If you store your users' document files on server drives already, as recommended earlier, this is not necessary and you should instruct your users not to store large amounts of data in these directories.

Creating Mandatory Profiles

When users modify elements of their Windows environment, the workstation writes those changes to their user profiles so that the next time they log on, the changes take effect. However, it's possible for a network administrator to create mandatory profiles that the users are not permitted to change, so that the same workstation environment loads each time they log on, regardless of the changes they made during the last session. To prevent users from modifying their profiles when logging off the system, you simply change the name of the registry hive in the server profile directory from Ntuser.dat to Ntuser.man, or from User.dat to User.man. When the workstation detects the MAN file in the profile directory, it loads that instead of the DAT file and does not write anything back to the profile directory during the logoff procedure.

When creating a mandatory profile, be sure that the user is not logged on to the workstation when you change the registry hive file extension from .dat to .man. Otherwise, the hive will be written back to the profile with a .dat extension during the logoff.

Another modification you can make to enforce the use of the profile is to add a .man extension to the directory in which the profile is stored. This prevents the user from logging on to the network without loading the profile. If the server on which the profile is stored is unavailable, then the user can't log on. If you choose to do this, be sure to add the .man extension both to the directory name itself and to the path specifying the name of the profile directory in the User Environment Profile dialog box (for Windows NT 4.0) or the user object's Properties dialog box (for Windows 2000).

It's important to note that making profiles mandatory does not prevent the users from modifying their workstation environments; it just prevents them from saving those modifications back to the profile. Also, making a profile mandatory does not in itself prevent the user from manually modifying the profile by adding or deleting shortcuts or accessing the registry hive. If you want to exercise greater control over the workstation to prevent users from making any changes to the interface at all, then you must use another mechanism, such as system policies, and be sure to protect the profile directories on the server using file system permissions.

Replicating Profiles

If you intend to rely on server-based user profiles to create workstation environments for your users, you should take pains to ensure that those profiles are always available to your users when they log on. This is particularly true if you intend to use mandatory profiles with .man extensions on the directory names, because if the server on which the profiles are stores is malfunctioning or unavailable, the users cannot log on. One way of doing this is to create your profile directories on a domain controller and then use the Directory Replicator service in Windows NT or 2000 to copy the profile directories to the other domain controllers on the network on a regular basis.

Once you have arranged for the profile directories to be replicated to all of your domain controllers, you can use the *%LogonServer%* variable in each user's profile path to make sure that they can always access the profile when logging on, as in the following example:

```
\\%LogonServer%\users\%UserName%
```

During the logon process, the workstation replaces the *%LogonServer%* variable with the name of the domain controller that authenticated the user. Since the profile directories have been copied to all of the domain controllers, the workstation always has access to the profile as long as it has access to a domain controller. If none of your domain controllers are available, then you have much bigger problems to worry about than user profiles.

Creating a Network Default User Profile

Windows NT and 2000 systems have a default user profile they use as a template for the creation of new profiles. As mentioned earlier, you can modify this default profile so that all of the new profiles created on that machine have certain characteristics. It is also possible to create a default user profile on your network, to provide the same service for all new profiles created on the network. To do this, you create a directory called \Default User in the root of the Netlogon share on your Windows NT or 2000 domain controllers. By default, the Netlogon share is located in the \Winnt\System32\ Repl\Import\Scripts directory on the server's system drive. Then, you copy the entire profile you want to use, including the registry hive and the subdirectories, to the \Default User directory. Whenever new users log on to a Windows NT or 2000 system, their profiles are created by copying the default profile from the domain controller.

   The network default user profile works with Windows NT and Windows 2000 client systems only. Windows 95 and 98 systems do not create new profiles from the network drive.

Controlling the Workstation Registry

The registry is the central repository for configuration data in Windows 95, 98, NT, and 2000 systems, and exercising control over the registry is a major part of a system administrator's job. The ability to access a workstation's registry in either a remote or automated fashion enables you to control virtually any aspect of the system's functionality and also protect the registry from damage due to unauthorized modifications.

Using System Policies

All of the 32-bit Windows operating systems include *system policies,* which enable you to exercise a great deal of control over a workstation's environment. By defining a set of policies and enforcing them, you can control what elements of the operating system your users are able to access, what applications they can run, and the appearance of the desktop. System policies are really nothing more than collections of registry settings that are packaged into a system policy file and stored on a server drive. When a user logs on to the network, the workstation downloads the system policy file from the server and applies the appropriate settings to the workstation's registry. Because workstations load the policy file automatically during the logon process, users can't evade them. This makes system policies an excellent tool for limiting users' access to the Windows interface.

Using system policies is an alternative to modifying registry keys directly, and reduces the possibility of system malfunctions due to typographical or other errors. Instead of browsing through the registry tree, searching for cryptic keys and value names, and entering coded values, you create system policy files using a graphical utility called System Policy Editor (SPE). SPE displays registry settings in the form of *policies*, plain-English phrases with standard Windows dialog box elements arranged in a tree-like hierarchy (see Figure 27-4).

System Policy Templates

System Policy Editor is simply a tool for creating policy files; it has no control over the policies it creates. The policies themselves come from system policy templates, which

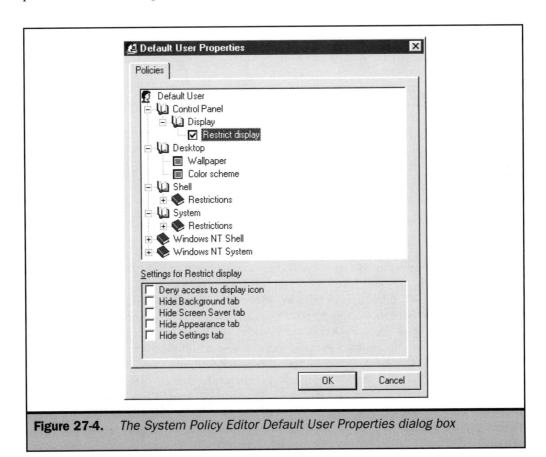

Figure 27-4.   *The System Policy Editor Default User Properties dialog box*

are ASCII files that contain the registry keys, possible values, and explanatory text that make up the policies displayed in SPE. For example, the following excerpt from the Common.adm policy template creates the Remote Update policy shown in Figure 27-5:

```
CATEGORY !!Network
    CATEGORY !!Update
        POLICY !!RemoteUpdate
        KEYNAME System\CurrentControlSet\Control\Update
        ACTIONLISTOFF
            VALUENAME "UpdateMode"          VALUE NUMERIC 0
        END ACTIONLISTOFF
            PART !!UpdateMode               DROPDOWNLIST REQUIRED
            VALUENAME "UpdateMode"
            ITEMLIST
                NAME !!UM_Automatic         VALUE NUMERIC 1
                NAME !!UM_Manual            VALUE NUMERIC 2
            END ITEMLIST
            END PART
            PART !!UM_Manual_Path           EDITTEXT
            VALUENAME "NetworkPath"
            END PART
            PART !!DisplayErrors            CHECKBOX
            VALUENAME "Verbose"
            END PART
            PART !!LoadBalance              CHECKBOX
            VALUENAME "LoadBalance"
            END PART
        END POLICY
    END CATEGORY       ; Update
END CATEGORY       ; Network
```

All of the Windows operating systems include a variety of template files in addition to SPE itself. The three main templates are Winnt.adm, which contains Windows NT policies; Windows.adm, which contains Windows 95/98 policies; and Common.adm, which contains policies that apply to both Windows 95/98 and NT/2000. Other applications, such as Microsoft Office and Internet Explorer, include their own template files containing policies specific to those applications, and you can even create your own custom templates, to modify other registry settings.

By selecting Options | Policy Template, you can load the templates that SPE will use to create policy files. You can load multiple templates into SPE, and the policies in them will be combined in the program's interface. Whenever you launch SPE, it loads the templates that it was using when it was last shut down, as long as the files are still

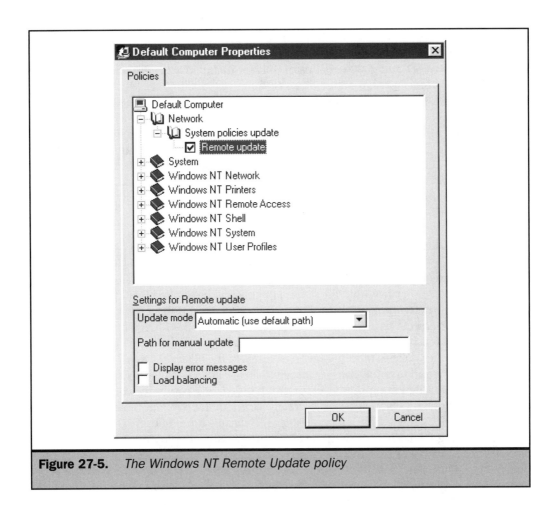

Figure 27-5.   *The Windows NT Remote Update policy*

in the same locations. When you use multiple policy templates in SPE, it is possible for policies defined in two different templates to configure the same registry setting. If this type of duplication occurs, the policy closest to the bottom of the hierarchy in the object's Properties dialog box takes precedence.

System Policy Files

Using SPE, you can create policies that apply only to specific users, groups, and computers, as well as create Default User and Default Computer policies. Policies for multiple network users and computers are stored in a single file that every computer downloads from a server as it logs on to the network. The policy file for Windows NT systems is called Ntconfig.pol, and the file for Windows 95/98 systems is called Config.pol. Windows 95, 98, NT, and 2000 all ship with their own versions of System Policy Editor, and the versions all use the same interface; but Windows 95/98 policy files are different from NT/2000 policy files, so they must be created separately.

The Windows NT and 2000 versions of SPE are installed with the operating system by default, and you can run them on any Windows NT, 2000, 95, or 98 system simply by copying the files to a drive on another computer. However, the type of policy files that SPE creates depends on the operating system on which it's running. You can create NT/2000 policy files by running SPE on an NT or 2000 system, and create 95/98 policy files by running SPE on a Windows 95 or 98 system; but you can't create a 95/98 policy file on an NT or 2000 system, and vice versa. The versions of SPE included with Windows 95 and 98 are not installed by default, must be manually installed (and not just copied) from the distribution CD-ROM, and can create Windows 95/98 policy files only.

CREATING POLICY FILES   Creating a new policy file is a matter of opening SPE and selecting File | New Policy. By default, the program creates Default Computer and Default User objects. Opening an object displays the policies that you can configure for it. Policies that you configure within the default objects will be applied to all workstations logging on to the network. You can also create additional computer and user objects, as well as group objects, that correspond, respectively, to the NetBIOS names of the computers, and to the user and group account names in your Windows NT or 2000 domain. Computer policies modify registry settings in the HKEY_LOCAL_MACHINE key, while group and user policies affect settings in the HKEY_CURRENT_USER key. When you create a new computer, user, or group object, SPE copies the contents of the corresponding default object and creates a new icon, as shown in Figure 27-6. With these tools, you can implement different policies for the various types of users on your network.

After saving the policy file with the appropriate name, deploying it on the network typically is as simple as copying it to the Netlogon share on your domain controllers, which by default is the \Winnt\System32\Repl\Import\Scripts directory on the system drive. Workstations automatically check this share for a policy file during the logon process and, if one is present, download and process it. System policy files are always processed after user profiles are loaded, so the registry settings in the policy file always take precedence over those in the registry hive of a user profile.

POLICY PRIORITIES   It is up to you to create a policy strategy that is easy to maintain and that exercises sufficient control over your workstations. As with most network administration tasks, it is easier to implement policies on a group level than it is to create individual user policies. When creating group policies in SPE, you can specify a priority for each group (by selecting Options | Group Priority) that controls the order in which the policies are applied to a system. When a workstation processes a policy file and the user is a member of more than one group, the system applies the group policies in order, from the lowest priority to the highest, so that the policies with higher priorities can overwrite the registry settings of the lower-priority policies.

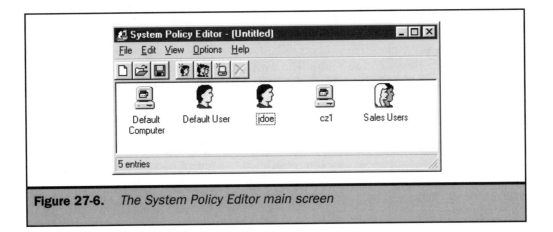

Figure 27-6.   *The System Policy Editor main screen*

When you create individual computer objects in SPE, they take priority over the Default Computer object. When a user logs on to the network from a workstation that is represented by a computer object, the system processes the policies for the individual computer and ignores the Default Computer policies. In the same way, when a user is represented by an individual user object in the policy file, the system loads the policies for that user object and ignores all of the groups to which the user belongs, as well as the Default User policies. User and group policies also take precedence over computer policies in the case of the few registry keys that can exist in either the HKEY_LOCAL_ MACHINE or HKEY_CURRENT_USER key. When a setting exists in both keys, the value in HKEY_CURRENT_USER takes precedence.

 System policies apply to all users, including those with administrative access. If you plan to impose severe restrictions on your users' workstations, be sure to create user or group objects that provide exceptional access for administrators.

Setting Policy Values

Once you have loaded the policy templates into SPE and created a new policy file, you can begin to create new objects and configure their policies. Each computer, user, and group object in a policy file contains a hierarchy of categories that contains the various policies. Each policy appears with a check box that has three possible states, which are as follows:

- **Enabled**   Applies the policy to the registry using the given value
- **Disabled**   Does not apply the policy to the registry and removes it from the registry if it already exists
- **Undefined**   Ignores the policy, making no changes to the registry, whether it exists or not

In addition to the check box, a policy can have a number of other controls associated with it, which appear in the settings area at the bottom of the dialog box when the policy is enabled. These controls can take several forms, including additional check boxes, data fields, and selectors. The way that the controls affect the registry depends on the requirements of the individual setting and the structure of the policy template. Some policies simply create a value name in the registry, while others assign a binary, alphanumeric, or hexadecimal value to a particular setting.

Restricting Workstation Access with System Policies

One of the primary functions of system policies is to prevent users from accessing certain elements of the operating system. There are several reasons for doing this, such as these:

■ Prohibiting users from running unauthorized software

■ Preventing users from adjusting cosmetic elements

■ Insulating users from features they cannot use safely

By doing these things, you can prevent users from wasting time on nonproductive activities and causing workstation malfunctions, through misguided experimentation, that require technical support to fix. The following sections describe how you can use specific system policies to control the workstation environment.

RESTRICTING APPLICATIONS One of the primary causes of instability on Windows workstations is the installation of incompatible applications. Most Windows software packages include dynamic link library modules (DLLs) that get installed to the Windows system directories, and many times these modules overwrite existing files with new versions designed to support that application. The problem with this type of software design is that installing a new version of a particular DLL may affect other applications already installed in the system.

The way to avoid problems stemming from this type of version conflict is to assemble a group of applications that supplies the users' needs, and then test the applications thoroughly together. Once you have determined that the applications are compatible, you install them on your workstations and prevent users from installing other software that can introduce incompatible elements. Restricting the workstation software also prevents users from installing nonproductive applications, like games, that can occupy large amounts of time, disk space, and even network bandwidth.

There are several techniques that you can employ to prevent users from installing unauthorized software on their workstations. One is the brute-force method, in which you simply deny them access to the media with which they would install new software. By purchasing computers without CD-ROM drives, you cut off the primary source of unauthorized software. It is also possible to prevent access to the system's floppy drive, either by installing a physical lock or by running a program such as the FloppyLocker service included with the Microsoft Zero Administration Kit.

The third potential source of unauthorized software is the Internet. If you are going to provide your users with access to services such as the Web, you may want to take steps to prevent them from installing downloaded software. One way of doing this, and of preventing all unauthorized software installations, is to use system policies that prevent users from running the setup program needed to install the software. Some of the policies that can help you do this are as follows:

- **Remove Run Command from Start menu**   Prevents the user from launching application installation programs by preventing access to the Run dialog box.

- **Run Only Allowed Windows Applications**   Enables the administrator to specify a list of executable files that are the only programs the user is permitted to execute. When using this policy, be sure to include executables that are needed for normal Windows operation, such as Systray.exe and Explorer.exe.

- **Disable MS-DOS Prompt**   Prevents Windows 95/98 users from launching programs from the DOS prompt.

LOCKING DOWN THE INTERFACE   There are many elements of the Windows interface that unsophisticated users do not need to access, and suppressing these elements can prevent the more curious among your users from exploring things they don't understand and possibly damaging the system. Some of the policies you can use to do this are as follows:

- **Remove Folders from Settings on Start menu**   Suppresses the appearance of the Control Panel and Printers folders in the Start menu's Settings folder. This policy does not prevent users from accessing the Control Panel in other ways, but it makes the user far less likely to explore it out of idle curiosity. You can also suppress specific Control Panel icons on Windows 95/98 systems using policies such as the following:

  - Restrict Network Control Panel
  - Restrict Printer Settings
  - Restrict Passwords Control Panel
  - Restrict System Control Panel

- **Remove Taskbar from Settings on Start menu**   Prevents users from modifying the Start menu and taskbar configuration settings.

- **Remove Run Command from Start menu**   Prevents users from launching programs or executing commands using the Run dialog box. This policy also provides users with additional insulation from elements such as the Control Panel and the command prompt, both of which can be accessed with Run commands.

- **Hide All Items on Desktop**   Suppresses the display of all icons on the Windows desktop. If you want your users to rely on the Start menu to launch programs, you can use this policy to remove the distraction of the desktop icons.

■ **Disable Registry Editing Tools**   Direct access to the Windows registry should be limited to people who know what they're doing. This policy prevents users from running the registry editing tools included with the operating system.

■ **Disable Context Menus for the Taskbar**   Prevents the system from displaying a context menu when you click the secondary mouse button on a taskbar icon.

You can also use system policies to secure the cosmetic elements of the interface, preventing users from wasting time adjusting the screen colors and desktop wallpaper. In addition, you can configure these items yourself, to create a standardized desktop for all of your network's workstations. These policies are as follows:

■ **Deny Access to Display Icon**   Removes the Display icon from the Control Panel window, preventing users from accessing all display configuration parameters.

■ **Hide Background Tab**   Suppresses the Background tab in the Display Properties dialog box.

■ **Hide Screen Saver Tab**   Suppresses the Screen Saver tab in the Display Properties dialog box.

■ **Hide Appearance Tab**   Suppresses the Appearance tab in the Display Properties dialog box.

■ **Hide Settings Tab**   Suppresses the Settings tab in the Display Properties dialog box.

■ **Wallpaper Name**   Enables you to specify the path and filename of a bitmap image that the system will use as desktop wallpaper.

■ **Color Scheme**   Enables you to specify the colors that the system should use for the various elements of the desktop.

As an alternative to user profiles, system policies enable you to configure with greater precision the shortcuts found on the Windows desktop and in the Start menu. Instead of accessing an entire user profile as a whole, you can specify the locations of individual shortcut directories for various elements of the interface, using policies such as the following:

■ **Custom Programs Folder/Custom Shared Programs Folder**   Specifies the location of a directory containing shortcuts that will appear in the Start menu's Programs folder.

■ **Custom Desktop Icons/Custom Shared Desktop Icons**   Specifies the location of a directory containing shortcuts that will appear on the Windows desktop.

■ **Custom Startup Folder/Custom Shared Startup Folder**   Specifies the location of a directory containing shortcuts that will appear in the Start menu's Startup folder.

- **Custom Start menu/Custom Shared Start menu**   Specifies the location of a directory containing shortcuts that will appear in the Start menu.
- **Hide Start menu Subfolders**   Suppresses the display of the Start menu subfolders included in a user profile, to prevent duplication with the folders specified in the previous policies.

These system policies have different names, depending on whether they apply to Windows 95/98 or Windows NT/2000. The first policy listed in each of these bullets is for Windows 95/98 and the second is for Windows NT/2000.

PROTECTING THE FILE SYSTEM   Limiting access to the file system is another way of protecting your workstations against user tampering. If you preconfigure the operating system and applications on your network workstations and force your users to store all of the data files on server drives, then there is no compelling reason why users should have direct access to the local file system. By blocking this access with system policies, you can prevent users from moving, modifying, or deleting files that are crucial to the operation of the workstation. You can limit users' access to the network also, using policies such as the following:

- **Hide Drives in My Computer**   Suppresses the display of all drive letters in the My Computer window, including both local and network drives.
- **Hide Network Neighborhood**   Suppresses the display of the Network Neighborhood icon on the Windows desktop and disables UNC connectivity. For example, when this policy is enabled, users can't open access network drives by opening a window with a UNC name in the Run dialog box.
- **No Entire Network in Network Neighborhood**   Suppresses the Entire Network icon in the Network Neighborhood window, preventing users from browsing network resources outside the domain or workgroup.
- **No Workgroup Contents in Network Neighborhood**   Suppresses the icons representing the systems in the current domain or workgroup in the Network Neighborhood window.
- **Remove Find Command from Start menu**   Suppresses the Find command, preventing users from accessing drives that may be restricted in other ways. If, for example, you use the Hidden attribute to protect the local file system, the Find command can still search the local drive and display the hidden files.

Locking down the file system is a drastic step, one that you should consider and plan for carefully. Only certain types of users will benefit from this restricted access, and others may severely resent it. In addition to system policies, you should be prepared to use file system permissions and attributes to prevent specific types of user access.

NETWORK ADMINISTRATION

Above all, you must make sure that the system policies you use to restrict access to your workstations do not inhibit the functionality your users need to perform their jobs, and that the features you plan to restrict are not accessible by other methods. For example, you might prevent access to the Control Panel by removing the folder from the Settings group in the Start menu, but users will still be able to access it from the My Computer window or the Run dialog box, unless you restrict access to those as well.

Deploying System Policies

The use of system policies by a Windows system is itself controlled by a policy called Remote Update, which is applicable to all of the Windows operating systems. This policy has three possible settings:

- **Off**   The system does not use system policies at all.
- **Automatic**   The system checks the root directory of the Netlogon share on the authenticating domain controller for a policy file called Ntconfig.pol (for Windows NT/2000 systems) or Config.pol (for Windows 95/98 systems).
- **Manual**   The system checks for a policy file in a directory specified as the value of another policy called Path for Manual Update.

Using the Remote Update policy, you can configure your systems to access policy files from the default location, or from any location you name. In order for workstations to have access to the policy files at all times, it is a good idea to replicate them to all of your domain controllers, either manually or automatically, just as you can do with user profiles.

Remote Registry Editing

In addition to preconfigured methods, such as user profiles and system policies, it is also possible to manage the registry on Windows workstations interactively, even from a remote location, using any one of several different tools. Windows NT and 2000 systems are capable of remote registry access by default, but on Windows 95 and 98 systems, you must install the Remote Registry Service from the distribution CD-ROM and configure the system for user-based access control.

Both the Windows 95/98 registry editor (Regedit.exe) and the Windows NT registry editor (Regedt32.exe) are able to connect to another system on the network and access its registry. In addition, you can use SPE to interactively modify the registry of the local or a remote system. However, the registry access available through SPE is limited to the registry settings that have been defined in the system policy templates that are currently loaded.

Windows 2000 Group Policies

While Windows 2000 systems support the use of Windows NT 4.0 system policies, the operating system also introduces an expanded feature called *group policies* that works in conjunction with Active Directory to create more comprehensive desktop environments. In addition to the registry-based capabilities of NT system policies, group policies can include the following types of policies:

- **Security policies**   Policies containing local computer, domain, and network security settings.

- **Software installation and maintenance policies**   Policies that enable administrators to remotely install, update, repair, and remove workstation software.

- **Script policies**   Policies that can implement specific user logon and logoff scripts using the variety of different scripting languages supported by the Windows Scripting Host.

- **Folder redirection policies**   Policies that redirect users' special folders to network drives, where they can be accessed by any system.

You implement group policies by creating a group policy object in one of the Active Directory consoles included with Windows 2000, such as Active Directory Users and Computers (see Figure 27-7). Once created, you can associate the group policy object with any other object in Active Directory to apply the policies to it.

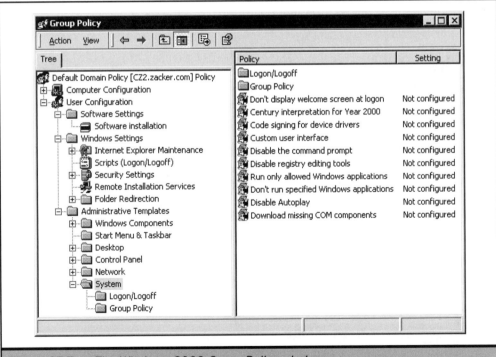

Figure 27-7.   *The Windows 2000 Group Policy window*

Microsoft Zero Administration Initiative for Windows

Microsoft's Zero Administration Initiative (ZAI) is a program that uses tools such as user profiles, system policies, and other elements to build workstation environments that are easy to install and maintain, and that are designed to provide users with all the features they need to do their jobs—and little or no other features. Not a product, per se, the ZAI is more of a theory of workstation deployment that incorporates some elements that have been available in Windows operating systems for years, and other elements that are just being introduced.

The ZAI works from a philosophy of "least privileges." By default, Windows workstations are left wide open when they're installed, meaning that the user has full access to all elements of the operating and file systems. The ZAI works by starting with a completely closed operating system and then granting users access only to the elements they need. This means, in many cases, suppressing all access to system configuration tools, such as the Control Panel and the registry editors, and limiting users to a few carefully selected applications.

The goal of the ZAI is to automate as much of the workstation deployment process as possible and reduce the total cost of ownership by limiting the users' interaction with the operating system, thus preventing them from corrupting the workstation environment by installing unauthorized software and altering the system configuration.

ZAK Environments

Microsoft's Zero Administration Kit (ZAK) has been available for some time, in versions for Windows NT 4.0, Windows 95/98, and Windows NT Terminal Server Edition. The ZAK includes two preconfigured workstation environments and a collection of tools that you can use with the operating systems' own capabilities to deploy those environments. The aim of the ZAK is not to provide a completion zero administration solution for your network, but rather to provide a template for the creation of your own workstation environments, suitable for your users' needs.

Note	*The Zero Administration Kit for Windows is available free of charge from Microsoft's Web site at http://www.microsoft.com/windows/zak.*

The two environments included in the ZAK are called the TaskStation and the AppStation. The *AppStation* is intended for users with a minimum of computing experience who have to perform a limited number of tasks, such as call center workers who are dedicated to basic order entry or customer service tasks. The *TaskStation* system is limited to running a single application (in this case, the Internet Explorer browser) that completely replaces the operating system's Explorer shell. Typically, the application functions as the front end to a database system that provides the users with the functions and information they need to do their jobs.

Because the shell is replaced by the application, the computer has no desktop icons, taskbar, or Start menu, and Internet Explorer loads automatically when the system starts. In addition, the users are completely insulated from the local file system, and have access to network drives only through the single application. Because TaskStation users have no interface with the operating system other than the application, there is no way for them to modify the system configuration, and the protected file system prevents them from disturbing the operating system or application files on the local drive.

The AppStation environment is less restricted than the TaskStation and provides greater flexibility to users. An AppStation system runs a carefully selected group of applications from a server drive and retains the Explorer shell, along with some of the standard Windows navigational controls—such as the taskbar and the Start menu. However, the Start menu is limited to the shortcuts needed to launch the applications, and the users still have file system access that is limited to specific network drives that are accessible only through the applications. Users can't access the Control Panel or any other system configuration controls, nor do they have access to the command line through the Run dialog box or MS-DOS sessions.

The workstation restrictions that are part of the TaskStation and AppStation environments are imposed primarily through the use of system profiles and file system permissions. In addition, the ZAK includes tools that enable you to lock down the floppy drive on your workstations and install the entire workstation, including the operating system and applications, using a scripted procedure that requires no user or administrator interaction.

IntelliMirror

Windows 2000 adds more functionality to the ZAI, particularly in its IntelliMirror feature. IntelliMirror is a service that stores a more complete composite of a workstation's configuration on network servers, so that it can be retrieved by any system at any time. This principle is similar to that of a roaming user profile, except that in addition to the standard profile information, IntelliMirror maintains copies of each user's data and information about the applications stored on each workstation. The final result is that users can log on to any workstation on the network and have their applications, data files, and environment settings downloaded to the system for immediate use. In the same way, if a workstation suffers an equipment failure, support personnel can easily configure a new computer for the user without a loss of data or environmental settings.

The
Complete
Reference

Upgrading
&
Troubleshooting
Networks

Chapter 28

Network Management
and Troubleshooting Tools

849

No matter how well designed and well constructed your network is, there are going to be times when it does not function properly. Part of the job of a network administrator is to monitor the day-to-day performance of the network and cope with any problems that arise. To do this, you must have the appropriate tools. In Chapter 2, you learned about the seven layers of the networking stack as defined in the OSI reference model. Breakdowns can occur at virtually any layer, and the tools used to diagnose problems at the various layers are quite different. Knowing what resources are available to you is a large part of the troubleshooting battle; knowing how to use them properly is another large part.

Operating System Utilities

Many administrators are unaware of the network troubleshooting capabilities that are built into their standard operating systems, and as a result, they sometimes spend money needlessly on third-party products and outside consultants. The following sections examine some of the network troubleshooting tools that are provided with the operating systems commonly used on today's networks.

Windows Utilities

The Windows operating systems include a variety of tools that you can use to manage and troubleshoot network connections. Most of these tools are included in both the 95/98 and NT/2000 packages, although they may take slightly different forms.

NET

The NET command is the primary command-line control for the Windows network client. You can use NET to perform many of the same networking functions that you can perform with graphical utilities, such as Windows Explorer, and because NET is a command-line utility, you can include the commands in logon scripts and batch files. For example, you can use NET to log on and off of the network, map drive letters to specific network shares, start and stop services, and locate shared resources on the network.

The NET command is implemented as a file called Net.exe, which is installed to the system directory (C:\Windows or C:\Winnt) during the operating system installation. To use the program, you execute the file from the command line with a subcommand, which may take additional parameters. Although Windows 95/98 and Windows NT share some of these subcommands, other subcommands are unique to each operating system. These subcommands and their functions are listed in Table 28-1, and some of the key functions are examined in the following sections.

NET Subcommand	Operating Systems Supported	Function
NET ACCOUNTS	Windows NT/2000	Configures settings and policies for all of the accounts on a particular computer or domain
NET COMPUTER	Windows NT/2000	Adds or removes computers from the current domain
NET CONFIG	Windows 95/98	Displays network client information
NET CONFIG SERVER	Windows NT/2000	Configures Server service parameters
NET CONFIG WORKSTATION	Windows NT/2000	Configures Workstation service parameters
NET CONTINUE	Windows NT/2000	Resumes a service that has been paused
NET DIAG	Windows 95/98	Exchanges diagnostic messages with another system to test the network connection
NET FILE	Windows NT/2000	Displays and closes files shared with network users and removes file locks
NET GROUP	Windows NT/2000	Creates or deletes global groups and adds users to or deletes them from those groups
NET HELP	Windows 95/98; Windows NT/2000	Displays help information for specific NET subcommands
NET HELPMSG	Windows NT/2000	Displays additional information about a specific four-digit error code

Table 28-1.   *Windows NET Commands*

NET Subcommand	Operating Systems Supported	Function
NET INIT	Windows 95/98	Loads network adapter and protocol drivers without binding them to the Protocol Manager
NET LOCALGROUP	Windows NT/2000	Creates or deletes local groups and adds users to or deletes them from those groups
NET LOGOFF	Windows 95/98	Logs the user off of the network and severs connections with all shared network resources
NET LOGON	Windows 95/98	Logs a user onto a workgroup or domain
NET NAME	Windows NT/2000	Administers the list of names used by the Messenger service to send messages
NET PASSWORD	Windows 95/98	Changes the current user's logon password
NET PAUSE	Windows NT/2000	Pauses a specific service without unloading it until resumed by the NET CONTINUE command
NET PRINT	Windows 95/98; Windows NT/2000	Administers print queues and the print jobs in them
NET SEND	Windows NT/2000	Transmits a text message to another user or computer using the Messenger service
NET SESSION	Windows NT/2000	Displays information about, and disconnects currently active sessions with, other network users
NET SHARE	Windows NT/2000	Displays, creates, and deletes shares on the current system
NET START	Windows 95/98; Windows NT/2000	Starts a specific network service

Table 28-1.   *Windows NET Commands* (continued)

NET Subcommand	Operating Systems Supported	Function
NET STATISTICS	Windows NT/2000	Displays statistics for the Server or Workstation service
NET STOP	Windows 95/98; Windows NT/2000	Stops a specific network service
NET TIME	Windows 95/98; Windows NT/2000	Displays the time on the current system or synchronizes the time with another system
NET USE	Windows 95/98; Windows NT/2000	Displays information about and administers connections to shared network resources
NET USER	Windows NT/2000	Creates, modifies, and deletes user accounts
NET VER	Windows 95/98	Displays the type and version number of the workgroup redirector currently in use
NET VIEW	Windows 95/98; Windows NT/2000	Displays available resources on the network

Table 28-1.   *Windows NET Commands* (continued)

NETWORK ADMINISTRATION

NET CONFIG   The NET CONFIG command displays network client information about the current system, such as the following:

```
Computer name                 \\CZ5
User name                     CRAIGZ
Workgroup                     NTDOMAIN
Workstation root directory    C:\WINDOWS
Software version              4.00.950
Redirector version            4.00
The command was completed successfully.
```

NET DIAG   The NET DIAG command initiates a low-level diagnostics test between two computers on the network. For this purpose, NET can function as either a diagnostic client or server. When you run the NET DIAG command, the system first attempts to detect a diagnostic server on the network. If it fails to detect a server, it starts functioning as one itself. If the system has both the IPX protocol and a NetBIOS protocol (TCP/IP or NetBEUI) installed, the program prompts you for the protocol it should use for the diagnostic test.

When the system successfully locates a server, it transmits a series of NetBIOS session messages or IPX Service Advertising Protocol (SAP) messages and examines the replies that it receives. During a NetBIOS test, the client establishes a TCP connection or a NetBEUI session with the server and then begins sending session messages containing test data. In an IPX test, the client transmits a SAP broadcast and receives a reply from the server. After that, the client can transmit unicast SAP packets containing test messages to the server.

The NET DIAG command tests the networking functionality of the entire protocol stack, and when used in combination with other diagnostic utilities, you can try to isolate a problem to a particular service or protocol. If, for example, two systems can successfully exchange Ping messages, but the NET DIAG test between the two machines fails, you can deduce that a problem exists somewhere above the network layer of the OSI model.

NET START AND NET STOP The NET START and NET STOP commands are used to start and stop network services on the current system. On a Windows 95 or 98 system, you can use these commands to select which redirector you want to load on the system, using the following syntax, the individual elements of which are described next:

```
NET START [BASIC | NWREDIR | WORKSTATION | NETBIND | NETBEUI |
NWLINK] [/LIST] [/YES] [/VERBOSE]
```

- **BASIC**   Starts the basic redirector
- **NWREDIR**   Starts the Microsoft Client for NetWare Networks redirector
- **WORKSTATION**   Starts the default redirector
- **NETBIND**   Binds protocols and network-adapter drivers
- **NETBEUI**   Starts the NetBIOS interface
- **NWLINK**   Starts the IPX/SPX-compatible interface
- **/LIST**   Displays a list of the services that are running
- **/YES**   Executes the command without user input
- **/VERBOSE**   Displays information about device drivers and services as they are loaded

By default, Windows 95 and 98 load the full workstation redirector, which provides complete access to domains and workgroups on the network. The operating system also includes a basic redirector, however, that you can use for basic network connectivity, using a minimum of system resources. The basic redirector enables you to connect to a workgroup system and access shared resources, but you cannot use it to log on to a Windows NT or 2000 domain.

In situations where elements of the system are not functioning properly, such as when you can't load the GUI, you can load the real-mode network client included with Windows 95/98, using either the NET START BASIC or NET START WORKSTATION command. These commands load the NDIS 2.0 driver for your NIC and the drivers for your installed protocols, and then bind the drivers to the protocol manager.

Once the redirector is fully loaded, the system logs you on to the default workgroup or domain and prompts you for your password. You can then map drive letters to shared network drives using the NET USE command, and access those drives, or execute other commands that perform network functions, such as NET VIEW to display the resources available on the network, or NET DIAG to test network communications. After they're started, you can stop specific services by using the NET STOP command with the same parameters that started the services, such as NET STOP WORKSTATION, but only outside of the Windows GUI. You cannot execute the NET STOP command from a DOS session within Windows.

On Windows NT systems, you can use the NET START and NET STOP commands to start and stop any service running on the machine, or use NET PAUSE and NET CONTINUE to temporarily suspend a service. Typing NET START at the command prompt on an NT/2000 system displays a list of the services currently running, such as the following:

```
These Windows NT services are started:
    Alerter
    Computer Browser
    Content Index
    DHCP Client
    EventLog
    IIS Admin Service
    License Logging Service
    Messenger
    MSDTC
    Net Logon
    NT LM Security Support Provider
    Plug and Play
    Print Server for Macintosh
    Protected Storage
    Remote Procedure Call (RPC) Locator
    Remote Procedure Call (RPC) Service
    Server
```

```
    Spooler
    Task Scheduler
    TCP/IP NetBIOS Helper
    Workstation
    World Wide Web Publishing Service
The command completed successfully.
```

The behavior of the NET START command, without any further parameters, is different on Windows 95/98 and NT/2000 systems. Whereas this command is purely informational on an NT/2000 system, on Windows 95/98 it starts the default redirector.

NET SESSION It is possible, in both Windows NT and 2000, to disable a particular user account in the User Manager or in the user object's Properties dialog box, thus preventing the user from logging on to the network. However, this action doesn't take effect until the next time the user tries to log on. If you want to disconnect a user from a system immediately, you can use the Windows NT Server Manager or the Computer Management Console in Windows 2000, or you can use NET SESSION from the command line.

Running NET SESSION with no parameters displays a list of the current active sessions on the system, like the following:

```
Computer     User name        Client Type      Opens Idle time
---------------------------------------------------------------
\\CZ2        Administrator    Windows NT 1381  5     00:14:51
\\CZ3        JDOE             Windows 4.0      0     00:00:08
\\CZ5        CRAIGZ           Windows 4.0      0     06:02:51
The command completed successfully.
```

To disconnect a session immediately, you use NET SESSION with the following syntax:

```
NET SESSION [\\computername] /delete
```

When you specify the NetBIOS name of a computer on the command line, NET SESSION immediately disconnects all of the sessions from that computer to the current system and closes all open files. If you omit a computer name, NET SESSION terminates all sessions from all computers.

Net Watcher

Net Watcher is a utility included in Windows 95/98 and in Windows NT Server 4.0 Resource Kit that enables you to monitor the network users connected to your computer, the shares that are currently being accessed, and the files that the remote users have open. You can also disconnect a user from a share, forcibly close a file that a user has open, and create or remove shares. Net Watcher is a useful tool for determining who is accessing the files or shares on your system at any given time. However, from a network administration standpoint, the best feature of this application is that you can connect to other computers on the network and perform these actions remotely for those systems.

CONNECTING TO A REMOTE SYSTEM Net Watcher takes the form of an executable file called Netwatch.exe that Windows 95 and 98 install with the operating system by default. When you launch Net Watcher, the program displays the connections to your own machine that are currently open. To monitor the activity of another Windows 95 or 98 workstation on the network, you choose Select Server from the Administer menu and either browse to the computer you want to monitor or specify its NetBIOS name or IP address.

To connect to another Windows 95 or 98 system with Net Watcher, the other computer must have Remote Administration enabled. To do this, a user at the other machine must open the Passwords Control Panel to the Remote Administration page, select the Enable Remote Administration of This Server check box, and specify a password that you will use when connecting to the workstation.

Tip *It is advisable that you use a strong Remote Administration password for systems that contain sensitive data, since a user with remote administration privileges can access all of the system's hard drives and create new shares without limitation.*

When you enable Remote Administration, Windows 98 creates two administrative shares, as follows:

- **ADMIN$** Provides administrators with access to the file system, even when drives are not shared
- **IPC$** Provides an interprocess communication (IPC) channel between the user's computer and the administrator's computer

These shares enable you to interact with the remote system and observe its networking activities.

Note *The Windows 98 Remote Administration feature is not the same as the Remote Registry service that enables you to modify registry settings on other network systems. You can enable Remote Administration on any Windows 98 system, whereas the Remote Registry service requires user-level access control and a Windows NT system on the network.*

USING THE CONNECTIONS WINDOW When you first connect to another system with the Windows 95/98 version of Net Watcher, the program displays the Connections window, which contains a list of the users and computers currently accessing the system's shares, as shown in Figure 28-1. The left pane displays the number of shares and files that each user has open, while the right pane lists the open files in each share. You can disconnect a user from the computer (as well as any shares and files they are accessing) by highlighting a name and selecting Disconnect User from the Administer menu.

As a security tool, Net Watcher enables you to both monitor the network for unauthorized access to specific systems and shares, and take steps to prevent continued intrusion. When you discover someone accessing a share without authorization, you can immediately disconnect that user from the machine, and then switch to the Shared Folders window to change the share's permissions or password.

Disconnecting a user from a system is a drastic step when the user has files open. The connection is severed with no warning to the user, and the interruption can result in data loss.

USING THE SHARED FOLDERS WINDOW   The other two Net Watcher windows display the same information in a different format. The Shared Folders window lists the drive shares on the system, the computers connected to them, and the files opened by each computer (see Figure 28-2). From this window, you can create and delete shares on the remote system and modify the properties of existing shares.

To create a new share, you select Add Shared Folder from the Administer menu and select the desired drive or directory from the Browse for Folder dialog box, shown in Figure 28-3. This dialog box displays the existing shares on the computer, as well as the administrative shares, represented by a drive letter followed by a dollar sign (such

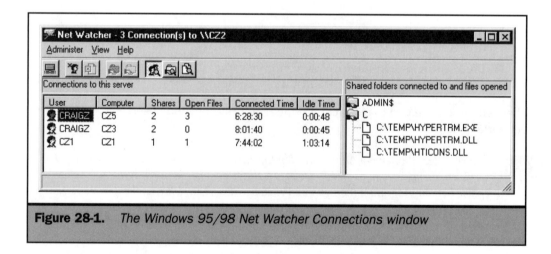

Figure 28-1.   *The Windows 95/98 Net Watcher Connections window*

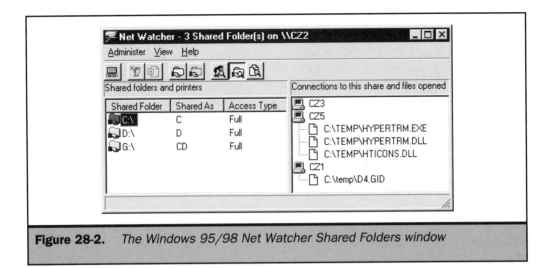

Figure 28-2.   *The Windows 95/98 Net Watcher Shared Folders window*

Figure 28-3.   *The administrative shares for a Windows 95/98 system appear as drive letters followed by a dollar sign*

as C$). You must select one of these administrative shares or a subdirectory of one of these shares as the root directory for your new share. After you make your selection, you see the standard Sharing dialog box (in which you specify a name for the share), the type of access you want to grant to users, and a password.

You can also modify the password for a share, or the share name itself, by selecting a share from the list and choosing Shared Folder Properties from the Administer menu. In the event of a security breech, you can even delete the share entirely to prevent all users from accessing it.

USING THE OPEN FILES WINDOW The Open Files window lists the files that are in use, and identifies who is using them (see Figure 28-4). From this window, you can close an individual file (instead of disconnecting a user completely from the system) by selecting Administer | Close File. For example, if a file is inaccessible because another user has left it open and walked away from their computer, you can close it without disturbing the user's other work.

MONITORING NETWORK ACTIVITY ON WINDOWS NT AND WINDOWS 2000 Windows NT and Windows 2000 both include utilities that provide the same functions as Net Watcher. The Windows NT Server 4.0 Resource Kit includes Net Watch, its own version of the Net Watcher program, which uses a different interface (see Figure 28-5), but can perform all of the same tasks as Net Watcher. The NT version of the Net Watcher program can monitor other NT and 2000 systems, and the Windows 95/98 version can monitor other 95/98 systems, but the two cannot interact.

Instead of the three different windows that Net Watcher displays, Net Watch displays shares, connections, and open files in one hierarchical tree, and you can disconnect users and close files from their context menus. The same functions are

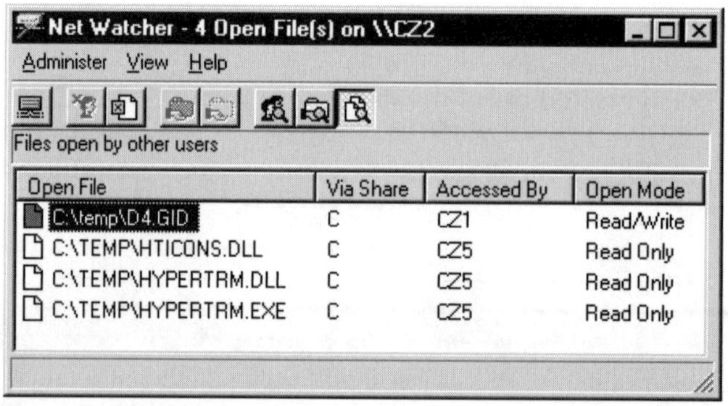

Net Watcher - 4 Open File(s) on \\CZ2
Administer View Help
Files open by other users
Open File
Via Share
Accessed By
Open Mode
C:\temp\D4.GID
C
CZ1
Read/Write
C:\TEMP\HTICONS.DLL
C
CZ5
Read Only
C:\TEMP\HYPERTRM.DLL
C
CZ5
Read Only
C:\TEMP\HYPERTRM.EXE
C
CZ5
Read Only

Figure 28-4. *The Windows 95/98 Net Watcher Open Files window*

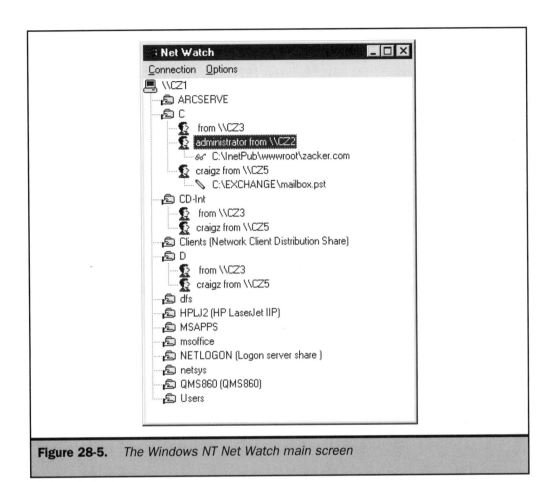

Figure 28-5.   *The Windows NT Net Watch main screen*

provided by the Server Manager utility included with Windows NT, using screens like that shown in Figure 28-6.

In Windows 2000, you find the equivalent functionality in the Computer Management console (see Figure 28-7). The Shares, Sessions, and Open Files panels enable you to monitor the network connections of any system on the network, just as you can with Server Manager and Net Watcher.

Web Administrator

Web Administrator is an add-on product for Microsoft's Internet Information Server (IIS) that enables you to manage many elements of a Windows NT 4.0 Server system using any Java-capable Web browser. Available free of charge from Microsoft's Web site at http://www.microsoft.com/ntserver/nts/downloads/management/NTSWebAdmin, installing the product creates a new subdirectory called \NTADMIN

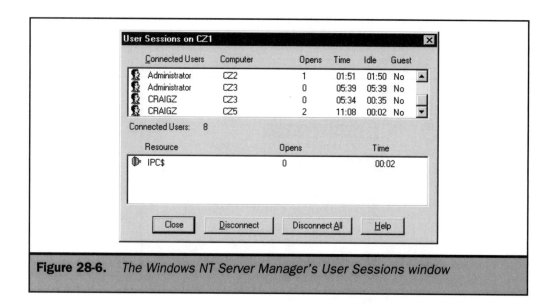

Figure 28-6. *The Windows NT Server Manager's User Sessions window*

on the Web site hosted by your NT Server. When you point a browser to that directory, the main Web Administrator page appears (see Figure 28-8).

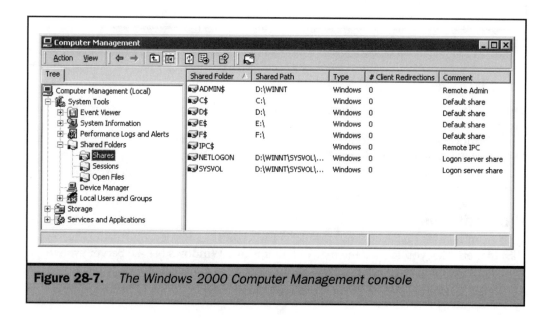

Figure 28-7. *The Windows 2000 Computer Management console*

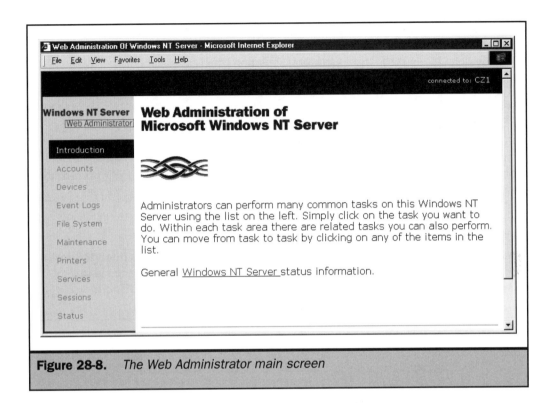

Figure 28-8. *The Web Administrator main screen*

From this screen, you can perform many of the same tasks as you can with the native NT administration programs—such as Control Panel, Server Manager, User Manager, Performance Monitor, and other utilities—including the following:

- Manage local and domain user, group, and computer accounts
- Manage the device drivers installed on the system
- View the NT event logs
- Manage shares and file system permissions
- Send messages to users logged on to the server
- Open a remote console session to the server
- Reboot the server from a remote location
- Manage print queues and their contents
- Start, stop, and pause services running on the server
- Monitor sessions and disconnect users
- View server status and performance statistics

Web Administrator uses Java to simulate the controls found in standard Windows applications, as shown in Figure 28-9. Most of the functionality of the original programs is intact. By default, the Web Administrator installation program sets the IIS permissions so that only a Web browser running on the server itself can access the site. You can modify the permissions so that only specific users or machines with specific IP addresses can access Web Administrator.

The Web Administrator utility is an excellent tool for networks running several different operating systems, because it provides administrative access to an NT server from any computer with a supported browser. Although many of the Windows NT tools can perform their functions for any NT system on the network, Web Administrator enables network support personnel working on other operating systems, such as Windows 95/98, Macintosh, or UNIX, to access native NT functions.

NetMeeting

Microsoft NetMeeting is a conferencing and collaboration tool that is intended for use over the Internet, but it can also be a valuable asset to the network administrator. NetMeeting is a part of the full installation of Internet Explorer 4 and 5, but

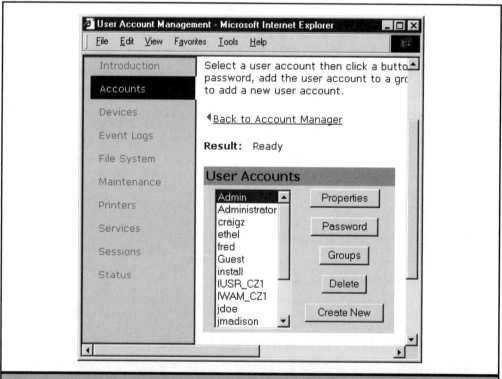

Figure 28-9. *The Web Administrator User Account Management screen*

it is also available separately in versions for Windows 95/98 and NT/2000 (see www.microsoft.com/windows/netmeeting). Unless you have high-speed connections, NetMeeting's performance over the Internet is usually disappointing. However, the program runs much better on a LAN.

Although Internet users are primarily concerned with NetMeeting's audio- and videoconferencing capabilities, network administrators will find that its collaboration features are an excellent means of providing technical support without traveling to the user's location. In addition to audio- and videoconferencing, NetMeeting includes text-based chat and a whiteboard, as well as the ability to collaborate on a specific application.

For example, if a user is having trouble with a particular application, she can call the help desk and arrange to activate a NetMeeting connection with an administrator. When the user shares the application within NetMeeting, the administrator can take control over it to demonstrate a particular procedure. Only one user can have control of the application at a time, but the user is able to see the administrator's keystrokes and mouse clicks, and can learn to use the software interactively. In the same way, the administrator can watch the user try to perform a task, to see what she's doing wrong.

Another NetMeeting feature, called Remote Desktop Sharing, enables a remote user to take full control over a computer. Administrators can use this feature to remotely configure a system, install software, and even launch applications, all without any direct contact with the machine.

TCP/IP Utilities

TCP/IP has become the most commonly used protocol suite in the networking industry, and many network administration and troubleshooting tasks involve working with various elements of these protocols. Because virtually every computing platform supports TCP/IP, a number of basic tools have been ported to many different operating systems, some of which have also been adapted to specific needs. The following sections examine some of these tools, but do so more from the perspective of their basic functionality and usefulness to the network administrator than from the operational elements of specific implementations.

Ping

Ping is unquestionably the most common TCP/IP diagnostic tool, and is included in virtually every implementation of the TCP/IP protocols. In most cases, it is a command-line utility, although some graphical or menu-driven versions are available that use a different interface to perform the same tasks. The basic function of Ping is to send a message to another TCP/IP system on the network to determine if the protocol stack up to the network layer is functioning properly. Because the TCP/IP protocols function in the same way on all systems, you can use Ping to test the connection between any two computers, regardless of processor platform or operating system.

All Windows systems install a command-line Ping program called Ping.exe to the system directory (such as C:\Windows or C:\Winnt) as part of their TCP/IP stacks. In the same way, all of the shells in the various UNIX variants support the ping command. Novell NetWare includes a menu-driven Ping.nlm utility that runs on a server, as well as a server command-line implementation called Tping.nlm.

Ping works by transmitting a series of Echo Request messages to a specific IP address using the Internet Control Message Protocol (ICMP). When the system using that IP address receives the messages, it generates an Echo Reply in response to each Echo Request and transmits it back to the sender. ICMP is a TCP/IP protocol with several dozen types of messages that perform various diagnostic and error-reporting functions. ICMP messages are carried directly within IP datagrams. No transport-layer protocol is involved, so a successful Ping test indicates that the protocol stack is functioning properly from the network layer down. If the sending system receives no replies to its Echo Requests, then something is wrong with either the sending or the receiving system, or the network connection between them.

 For more information on the ICMP protocol and its various functions, refer to Chapter 11.

When Ping is implemented as a command-line utility, you use the following syntax to perform a Ping test:

```
PING destination
```

where the *destination* variable is replaced by the name or address of another system on the network. The destination system can be identified by its IP address, or by a name, assuming that an appropriate mechanism is in place for resolving the name into an IP address. This means that you can use a host name for the destination, as long as you have a DNS server or HOSTS file to resolve the name. On Windows networks, you can also use NetBIOS names, along with any of the standard mechanisms for resolving them, such as WINS servers, broadcast transmissions, or an LMHOSTS file.

The screen output produced by a PING command appears as follows:

```
Pinging cz3 [192.168.2.3] with 32 bytes of data:

Reply from 192.168.2.3: bytes=32 time=1ms TTL=128
Reply from 192.168.2.3: bytes=32 time<10ms TTL=128
Reply from 192.168.2.3: bytes=32 time=1ms TTL=128
Reply from 192.168.2.3: bytes=32 time<10ms TTL=128

Ping statistics for 192.168.2.3:
    Packets: Sent = 4, Received = 4, Lost = 0 (0% loss),
Approximate round trip times in milli-seconds:
    Minimum = 0ms, Maximum =  1ms, Average =  0ms
```

Because most Ping implementations display the IP address resolved from the system name specified on the command line, the program is also a quick and easy tool for determining a given system's IP address.

The program displays a result line for each of the four Echo Request messages it sends by default, specifying the IP address of the recipient, the number of bytes of data transmitted in each message, the amount of time elapsed between the transmission of the request and the receipt of the reply, and the target system's Time to Live, or TTL. The TTL is the number of routers that a packet can pass through before it is discarded.

Ping has other diagnostic uses apart from simply determining whether a system is up and running. If you can successfully ping a system using its IP address, but pings sent to the system's name fail, you know that a malfunction is occurring in the name resolution process. When you're trying to contact an Internet site, this indicates that there is a problem with either your workstation's DNS server configuration or the DNS server itself. If you can ping systems on the local network successfully, but not systems on the Internet, then you know that there is a problem with either your workstation's Default Gateway setting or the connection to the Internet.

Note *Sending a Ping command to a system's loopback address (127.0.0.1) tests the operability of the TCP/IP protocol stack, but it is not an adequate test of the network interface because traffic sent to the loopback address travels down the protocol stack only as far as the network transport layer and is redirected back up without ever leaving the computer through the network interface.*

In most Ping implementations, you can use additional command-line parameters to modify the size and number of the Echo Request messages transmitted by a single Ping command, as well as other operational characteristics. In the Windows Ping.exe program, for example, the parameters are as follows:

```
ping [-t] [-a] [-n count] [-l size] [-f] [-i TTL] [-v TOS] [-r count]
[-s count] [[-j host-list] | [-k host-list]] [-w timeout] destination
```

- ■ **-t** Pings the specified destination until stopped by the user (with CTRL-C)
- ■ **-a** Resolves destination IP addresses to host names
- ■ **-n** *count* Specifies the number of Echo Requests to send
- ■ **-l** *size* Specifies the size of the Echo Request messages to send
- ■ **-f** Sets the IP Don't Fragment flag in each Echo Request packet
- ■ **-i** *TTL* Specifies the IP TTL value for the Echo Request packets
- ■ **-v** *TOS* Specifies the IP Type of Service (TOS) value for the Echo Request packets

- **-r** *count*   Records the IP addresses of the routers for the specified number of hops

- **-s** *count*   Records the timestamp from the routers for the specified number of hops

- **-j** *host-list*   Specifies a partial list of routers that the packets should use

- **-k** *host-list*   Specifies a complete list of routers that the packets should use

- **-w** *timeout*   Specifies the time (in milliseconds) that the system should wait for each reply

There are many different applications for these parameters that can help you manage your network and troubleshoot problems. For example, by creating larger than normal Echo Requests and sending large numbers of them (or sending them continuously), you can simulate user traffic on your network to test its ability to stand up under heavy use. You can also compare the performance of various routes through your network (or through the Internet) by specifying the IP addresses of the routers that the Echo Request packets must use to reach their destinations. The –j parameter provides *loose source routing,* in the which the packets must use the routers whose IP addresses you specify, but can use other routers also. The –k parameter provides *strict source routing,* in which you must specify the address of every router that packets will use to reach their destination.

Traceroute

Traceroute is another utility that is usually implemented as a command-line program and included in most TCP/IP protocol stacks, although it sometimes goes by a different name. On UNIX systems, the command is called traceroute, but Windows implements the same functions in a program called Tracert.exe. The function of this tool is to display the route that IP packets are taking to reach a particular destination system. When you run the program with the name or IP address of a destination system as the command-line parameter, the result is a display like the following:

```
Tracing route to zacker.com [192.41.15.74] over a maximum of 30 hops:
  1    254 ms    194 ms    162 ms   qrvl-67.epix.net [199.224.67.3]
  2    151 ms    135 ms    154 ms   qrvl.epix.net [199.224.67.1]
  3    163 ms    150 ms    173 ms   svcr03-7b.epix.net [199.224.103.125]
  4    136 ms    160 ms    164 ms   router05.epix.net [216.37.155.162]
  5    161 ms    145 ms    170 ms   cpbg01-7.epix.net [199.224.88.62]
  6    165 ms    149 ms    164 ms   Serial1.PH.ALTER.NET [157.130.7.213]
  7    182 ms    242 ms    169 ms   161.ATM2.ALTER.NET [146.188.162.118]
  8    178 ms    149 ms   1839 ms   294.ATM7.ALTER.NET [146.188.160.126]
  9    168 ms    147 ms    155 ms   192.ATM10.ALTER.NET [146.188.160.93]
 10    260 ms    150 ms    176 ms   uu.iad1.verio.net [137.39.23.22]
```

```
11    163 ms    175 ms    166 ms    iad3.dca0.verio.net [129.250.2.62]
12    235 ms    243 ms    244 ms    dca0.pao5.verio.net [129.250.2.245]
13    224 ms    249 ms    255 ms    p4-01.us.bb.verio.net [129.250.2.74]
14    406 ms    272 ms    265 ms    pao6.pvu0.verio.net [129.250.3.26]
15    267 ms    250 ms    271 ms    pvu0.vwh.verio.net [129.250.16.14]
16    257 ms    270 ms    278 ms    zacker.com [192.41.15.74]
Trace complete.
```

Each of the entries in the trace represents a router that processed the packets generated by the traceroute program on the way to their destination. In this case, the packets required 16 hops to get to the zacker.com server. The three numerical figures in each entry specify the round-trip time to that router, in milliseconds, followed by the DNS name and IP address of the router. In a trace like this one, to a destination on the Internet, the round-trip times are relatively high and can provide you with information about the backbone networks your ISP uses (in this case, alter.net) and the geographical path that your traffic takes. For example, when you run a trace to a destination system on another continent, you can sometimes tell when the path crosses an ocean by a sudden increase in the round-trip times. On a private network, you can use traceroute to determine the path through your routers that local traffic typically takes, enabling you to get an idea of how traffic is distributed around your network.

Most traceroute implementations work by transmitting the same type of ICMP Echo Request messages used by Ping, while others use UDP packets by default. The only difference in the messages themselves is that the traceroute program modifies the TTL field for each sequence of three packets. The TTL field is a protective mechanism that prevents IP packets from circulating endlessly around a network. Each router that processes a packet decrements the TTL value by one. If the TTL value of a packet reaches 0, the router discards it and returns an ICMP Time to Live Exceeded in Transit error message to the system that originally transmitted it.

In the first traceroute sequence, the packets have a TTL value of 1, so that the first router receiving the packets discards them and returns error messages back to the source. By calculating the interval between a message's transmission and the arrival of the associated error, traceroute generates the round-trip time and then uses the source IP address in the error message to identify the router. In the second sequence of messages, the TTL value is 2, so the packets reach the second router in their journey before being discarded. The third sequence of packets has a TTL value of 3, and so on, until the messages reach the destination system.

It is important to understand that although traceroute can be a useful tool, a certain amount of imprecision is inherent in the information it provides. Just because a packet transmitted right now takes a certain path to a destination does not mean that a packet transmitted a minute from now to that same destination will take that same path. Networks (and especially those on the Internet) are mutable, and routers are designed to compensate automatically for the changes that occur. The route taken by traceroute packets to their destination can change, even in the midst of a trace, so it is entirely possible for the sequence of routers displayed by the program to be a composite of two or more different paths to the destination, because of changes that occurred in midstream. On a private network, this is less likely to be the case, but it is still possible.

Route

The routing table is a vital part of the networking stack on any TCP/IP system, even those that do not function as routers. The system uses the routing table to determine where it should transmit each packet. The Route.exe program in Windows and the route command included with most UNIX versions enable you to view the routing table and add or delete entries to it.

Note   *For more information on routing tables and the principles of IP routing, refer to Chapter 6.*

Netstat

Netstat is a command-line utility that displays network traffic statistics for the various TCP/IP protocols and, depending on the platform, may display other information, as well. Most UNIX variants support the netstat command, and Windows operating systems include a program called Netstat.exe that is installed by default with the TCP/IP stack. The command-line parameters for Netstat can vary in different implementations, but one of the most basic ones is the –s parameter, which displays the statistics for each of the major TCP/IP protocols, as follows:

```
IP Statistics
  Packets Received                      = 130898
  Received Header Errors                = 0
  Received Address Errors               = 19
  Datagrams Forwarded                   = 0
  Unknown Protocols Received            = 0
  Received Packets Discarded            = 0
  Received Packets Delivered            = 130898
  Output Requests                       = 152294
  Routing Discards                      = 0
  Discarded Output Packets              = 0
  Output Packet No Route                = 0
  Reassembly Required                   = 0
  Reassembly Successful                 = 0
  Reassembly Failures                   = 0
  Datagrams Successfully Fragmented     = 0
  Datagrams Failing Fragmentation       = 0
  Fragments Created                     = 0
```

```
ICMP Statistics
                            Received    Sent
    Messages                499         683
    Errors                  44          0
    Destination Unreachable 0           154
    Time Exceeded           414         0
    Parameter Problems      0           0
    Source Quenchs          0           0
    Redirects               0           0
    Echos                   1           522
    Echo Replies            27          1
    Timestamps              0           0
    Timestamp Replies       0           0
    Address Masks           0           0
    Address Mask Replies    0           0

TCP Statistics
    Active Opens                     = 1893
    Passive Opens                    = 12
    Failed Connection Attempts       = 37
    Reset Connections                = 657
    Current Connections              = 0
    Segments Received                = 117508
    Segments Sent                    = 142099
    Segments Retransmitted           = 378

UDP Statistics
    Datagrams Received   = 12399
    No Ports             = 943
    Receive Errors       = 0
    Datagrams Sent       = 9129
```

Apart from the total number of packets transmitted and received by each protocol, Netstat provides valuable information about error conditions and other processes that can help you troubleshoot network communication problems at various layers of the OSI model. The Windows version of Netstat also can display Ethernet statistics (using the –e parameter), which can help to isolate network hardware problems, such as the following:

```
Interface Statistics
                       Received           Sent
    Bytes              44483612           20434045
```

```
Unicast packets            94653           92824
Non-unicast packets         4543             743
Discards                       0               0
Errors                         0               0
Unknown protocols          15452
```

When executed with the –a parameter, Netstat.exe displays information about the TCP connections currently active on the computer and the UDP services that are listening for input, as follows:

```
Active Connections
  Proto  Local Address        Foreign Address       State
  TCP    cz5:1044             CZ5:0                 LISTENING
  TCP    cz5:1025             CZ5:0                 LISTENING
  TCP    cz5:1025             CZ1:nbsession         ESTABLISHED
  TCP    cz5:137              CZ5:0                 LISTENING
  TCP    cz5:138              CZ5:0                 LISTENING
  TCP    cz5:nbsession        CZ5:0                 LISTENING
  TCP    cz5:nbsession        CZ3:1531              ESTABLISHED
  TCP    cz5:2521             netsurge.com:pop3     TIME_WAIT
  UDP    cz5:1044             *:*
  UDP    cz5:nbname           *:*
  UDP    cz5:nbdatagram       *:*
```

Note *It is also possible to display network traffic statistics for upper-layer protocols, such as Server Message Blocks (SMBs), using the NET STATISTICS command.*

Nslookup

Nslookup is a utility that enables you to send queries directly to a particular DNS server in order to resolve names into IP addresses or request other information. Unlike other name resolution methods, such as using Ping, Nslookup enables you to specify which server you want to receive your commands, so that you can determine if a DNS server is functioning properly and if it contains the correct information. Originally designed for UNIX systems, an Nslookup.exe program is also included with the Windows NT and 2000 TCP/IP clients, but not with Windows 95 and 98. However, third-party Nslookup implementations are available, such as the graphical one included with Luc Neijens' CyberKit (available at www.cyberkit.net).

Nslookup.exe can run in either interactive or noninteractive mode. To transmit a single query, you can use noninteractive mode, using the following syntax from the command prompt:

```
Nslookup hostname nameserver
```

Replace the *hostname* variable with the DNS name or IP address that you want to
resolve, and replace the *nameserver* variable with the name or address of the DNS
server that you want to receive the query. If you omit the *nameserver* value, the
program uses the system's default DNS server. The output of the program in
noninteractive mode on a Windows 2000 system is as follows:

```
Server:  ns1.secure.net
Address:  192.41.1.10

Name:     zacker.com
Address:  192.41.15.74
Aliases:  www.zacker.com
```

To run Nslookup in interactive mode, you execute the program from the command
prompt with no parameters (to use the default DNS server) or with a hyphen in place
of the *hostname* variable, followed by the DNS server name, as follows:

```
Nslookup - nameserver
```

The program produces a prompt in the form of an angle bracket (>), at which you can
type the names or addresses you want to resolve, as well as a large number of commands
that alter the parameters that Nslookup uses to query the name server. You can display
the list of commands by typing **help** at the prompt. To exit the program, press CTRL-C.

Ipconfig

The Ipconfig program is a simple utility for displaying a system's TCP/IP configuration
parameters. This is particularly useful when you are using Dynamic Host Configuration
Protocol (DHCP) servers to automatically configure TCP/IP clients on your network,
because there is no other simple way for users to see what settings have been assigned to
their workstations. All UNIX implementations include the ifconfig command (derived
from *interface configuration*), and Windows 98, NT, and 2000 systems have a command-line
program called Ipconfig.exe. Windows 95 and 98 also include a graphical utility that
performs the same functions, called Winipcfg.exe (see Figure 28-10).

Running Ipconfig.exe on a Windows 2000 system with the /all parameter produces
the following output:

```
Windows 2000 IP Configuration
        Host Name . . . . . . . . . . . . : cz2
        Primary DNS Suffix  . . . . . . . : zacker.com
        Node Type . . . . . . . . . . . . : Hybrid
        IP Routing Enabled. . . . . . . . : No
        WINS Proxy Enabled. . . . . . . . : No
        DNS Suffix Search List. . . . . . : zacker.com
```

```
Ethernet adapter Local Area Connection:
        Connection-specific DNS Suffix  . :
        Description . . . . . . : 3Com EtherLink III (3C509/3C509b)
        Physical Address. . . . : 00-60-97-B0-77-CA
        DHCP Enabled. . . . . . : Yes
        Autoconfiguration Enabled: Yes
        IP Address. . . . . . . : 192.168.2.21
        Subnet Mask . . . . . . : 255.255.255.0
        Default Gateway . . . . : 192.168.2.100
        DHCP Server . . . . . . : 192.168.2.10
        DNS Servers . . . . . . : 199.224.86.15
                                  199.224.86.16
        Primary WINS Server . . : 192.168.2.10
        Lease Obtained. . . . . : Sunday, Feb 06, 2000 10:08:23 PM
        Lease Expires . . . . . : Wednesday, Feb 09, 2000 10:08:23 PM
```

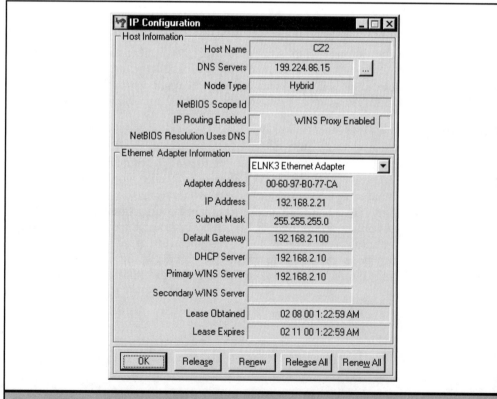

Figure 28-10.   *The Winipcfg.exe IP Configuration dialog box*

You can also use Ipconfig to terminate or renew a workstation's lease with its DHCP server, using the /release and /renew parameters, respectively.

Network Analyzers

A *network analyzer*, sometimes called a *protocol analyzer*, is a device that captures the traffic transmitted over a network and analyzes its properties in a number of different ways. The primary function of the analyzer is to decode and display the contents of the packets captured from your network. For each packet, the software displays the information found in each field of each protocol header, as well as the original application data carried in the payload of the packet (see Figure 28-11). Analyzers often can provide statistics about the traffic carried by the network, as well, such as the number of packets that use a particular protocol and the amount of traffic generated by each system on the network. A network analyzer is also an excellent learning tool. There is no better way to acquaint yourself with networking protocols and their functions than by seeing them in action.

There is a wide variety of network analyzer products, ranging from self-contained hardware devices costing thousands of dollars, to software-only products that are relatively inexpensive or free. Windows NT Server 4.0 and Windows 2000 Server, for example, include an application called Network Monitor (shown in Figure 28-11) that enables you to analyze the traffic on your network.

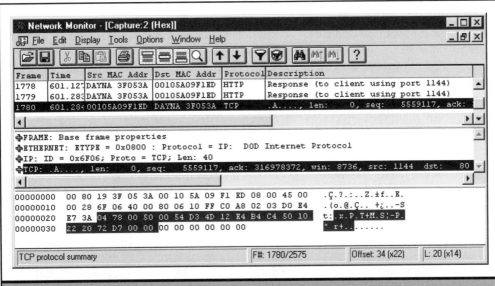

Figure 28-11.   *Network analyzers display packet contents in both raw and decoded form*

A network analyzer is essentially a software application running on a computer with a network interface. This is why products can either include hardware or take the form of software only. A traveling network consultant might have a portable computer with comprehensive network analyzer software and a variety of NICs to support the different networks at various sites, while an administrator supporting a private network might be better served by a less-expensive software-based analyzer that supports only the type of network running at that site.

A network analyzer typically works by switching the NIC in the computer on which it runs into *promiscuous mode.* Normally, a NIC examines the destination address in the data link–layer protocol header of each packet arriving at the computer, and if the packet is not addressed to that computer, the NIC discards it. This prevents the CPU in the system from having to process thousands of extraneous packets. When the NIC is switched into promiscuous mode, however, it accepts all of the packets arriving over the network, regardless of their addresses, and passes them to the network analyzer software for processing. This enables the system to analyze not only the traffic generated by and destined for the system on which the software is running, but also the traffic exchanged by other systems on the network.

Once the application captures the traffic from the network, it stores the entire packets in a buffer from which it can access them later during the analysis. Depending on the size of your network and the amount of traffic it carries, this can be an enormous amount of data, so you can usually specify the size of the buffer, to control the amount of data captured. You can also apply filters to limit the types of data the analyzer captures.

Filtering Data

Because of the sheer amount of data transmitted over many networks, controlling the amount of data captured and processed by a network analyzer is an important element of the product. You exercise this control by applying *filters* either during the capture process or afterward. When you capture raw network data, the results can be bewildering, because all the packets generated by the various applications on many network systems are mixed together in a chronological display. To help make more sense out of the vast amount of data available, you can apply filters that cause the program to display only the data you need to see.

Two types of filters are provided by most network analyzers:

- **Capture filters**   Impose limits on the packets that the analyzer reads into its buffers
- **Display filters**   Limit the captured packets that appear in the display

Usually, both types of filters function in the same way; the only difference is in when they are applied. You can choose to filter the packets as they are being read into the analyzer's buffers, or capture all of the data on the network and use filters to limit the display of that data (or both).

You can filter the data in a network analyzer in several different ways, depending on what you're trying to learn about your network. If you're concerned with the performance of a specific computer, for example, you can create a filter that captures only the packets generated by that machine, destined for that machine, or both. You can also create filters based on the protocols used in the packets, making it possible to capture only the DNS traffic on your network, for example, or on pattern matches, enabling you to capture only packets containing a specific ASCII or hexadecimal string. By combining these capabilities, using Boolean operators such as AND and OR, you can create highly specific filters that display only the exact information you need. Figure 28-12 shows the Capture Filter dialog box from the Microsoft Network Monitor application. In this example, the application is configured to capture all IP packets traveling to or from the machine called LJOL_LAPTOP. Other network analyzers may use a different interface and offer additional features, such as the ability to filter packets based on their size or on specific error conditions, but the basic functionality is the same.

Agents

Hardware-based network analyzers are portable and designed to connect to a network at any point. Software-based products are not as portable, and often include a

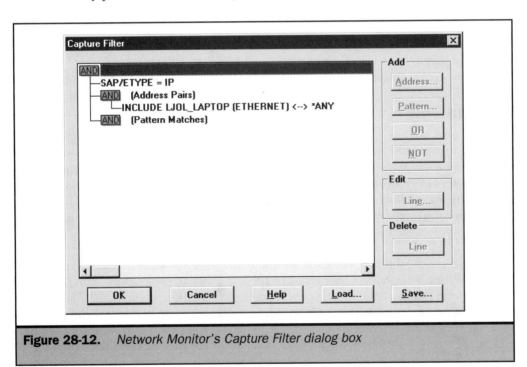

Figure 28-12.   *Network Monitor's Capture Filter dialog box*

mechanism (sometimes called an agent) that enables you to capture network traffic using the NIC in a different computer. Using agents, you can install the analyzer product on one machine and use it to support your entire network. The agent is usually a driver or service that runs on a workstation elsewhere on the network. For example, all versions of Windows 95/98, NT, and 2000 include the Network Monitor Agent that provides remote capture capabilities for the Network Monitor application running on a Windows NT or 2000 server.

Note *The version of Network Monitor that is included with Windows NT 4.0 Server and Windows 2000 Server is limited to capturing only the network traffic sent to or from the computer on which it is running. In other words, it does not switch the NIC into promiscuous mode. To capture all the traffic on your network, you must use the full version of Network Monitor, which is included as part of the Microsoft Systems Management Server (SMS) product.*

When you run a network analyzer on a system with a single network interface, the application captures the data arriving over that interface by default. If the system has more than one interface, either in the form of a second NIC or a modem connection, you can select the interface from which you want to capture data. When the analyzer is capable of using agents, you can use the same dialog box to specify the name or address of another computer on which the agent is running. The application then connects to that computer, uses its NIC to capture network traffic, and transmits it to the buffers in the system running the analyzer. When you use an agent on another network segment, however, it's important to be aware that the transmissions themselves from the agent to the analyzer generate a significant amount of traffic.

Traffic Analysis

Some network analyzers can display statistics about the traffic on the network while it is being captured, such as the number of packets per second, broken down by workstation or protocol. Depending on the product, you may also be able to display these statistics in graphical form. You can use this information to determine how much traffic each network system or each protocol is generating. Network Associates' Sniffer Basic (formerly called NetXRay) can display a matrix that graphically illustrates which computers on the network are communicating with each other, as shown in Figure 28-13.

Using these capabilities, you can determine how much of your network bandwidth is being utilized by specific applications or specific users. If, for example, you notice that user John Doe's workstation is generating a disproportionate amount of HTTP traffic, you might conclude that he is spending too much company time surfing the Web when he should be doing other things. With careful application of capture filters, you can also configure a network analyzer to alert you of specific conditions on your network. Some products can generate alarms when traffic of a particular type reaches certain levels, such as when an Ethernet network experiences too many collisions.

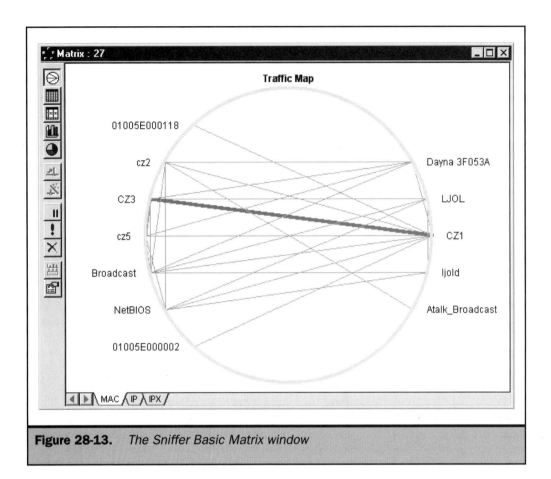

Figure 28-13. *The Sniffer Basic Matrix window*

In addition to capturing packets from the network, some analyzers can also generate them. You can use the analyzer to simulate traffic conditions at precise levels, to verify the operational status of the network or to stress-test equipment.

Protocol Analysis

Once the analyzer has a network traffic sample in its buffers, you can examine the packets in great detail. In most cases, the packets captured during a sample period are displayed chronologically in a table that lists the most important characteristics of each one, such as the addresses of the source and destination systems, and the primary protocol used to create the packet. When you select a packet from the list, you see additional panes that display the contents of the protocol headers and the packet data, usually in both raw and decoded form.

The first application for a tool of this type is that you can see what kinds of traffic are present on your network. If, for example, you have a network that uses WAN links that are slower and more expensive than the LANs, you can use an analyzer to capture the traffic passing over the links, to make sure that their bandwidth is not being squandered on unnecessary communications.

One of the features that differentiates high-end network analyzer products from the cheaper ones is the protocols that the program supports. To correctly decode a packet, the analyzer must support all the protocols used to create that packet at all layers of the OSI reference model. For example, a basic analyzer will support Ethernet and possibly Token Ring at the data link layer, but if you have a network that uses FDDI or ATM, you may have to buy a more elaborate and expensive product. The same is true at the upper layers. Virtually all analyzers support the TCP/IP protocols, and many also support IPX and NetBEUI, but be sure before you make a purchase that the product you select supports all the protocols you use. You should also consider the need for upgrades to support future protocol modifications, such as IPv6.

By decoding a packet, the analyzer is able to interpret the function of each bit and display the various protocol headers in a user-friendly, hierarchical format. In Figure 28-14, for example, you can see that the selected packet contains HTTP data generated by a Web server and transmitted to a Web browser on the network. The analyzer has decoded the protocol headers, and the display indicates that the HTTP data is carried in a TCP segment, which in turn is carried in an IP datagram, which in turn is carried in an Ethernet frame. You can expand each protocol to view the contents of the fields in its header.

A network analyzer is a powerful tool that can just as easily be used for illicit purposes as for network troubleshooting and support. When the program decodes a packet, it displays all of its contents, including what may be sensitive information. The FTP protocol, for example, transmits user passwords in cleartext that is easily visible in a network analyzer when the packets are captured. An unauthorized user running an analyzer can intercept administrative passwords and gain access to protected servers. This is one reason why the version of Network Monitor included with Windows NT and 2000 is limited to capturing the traffic sent to and from the local system.

Cable Testers

Network analyzers can help you diagnose many types of network problems, but they assume that the physical network itself is functioning properly. When there is a problem with the cable installation that forms the network, a different type of tool, called a *cable tester,* is required. Cable testers are usually handheld devices that you connect to a network in order to perform a variety of diagnostic tests on the signal-conducting capabilities of the network cable. As usual, there is a wide range of devices to choose from that vary greatly in their prices and capabilities. Simple units are available for a few hundred dollars, while top-of-the-line models can cost several thousand dollars. Some combination testers can connect to various types of network cables, such as unshielded twisted pair (UTP), shielded twisted pair (STP), and coaxial, while others can test only a single cable type. For completely different signaling technologies, such as fiber-optic cable, you need a separate device.

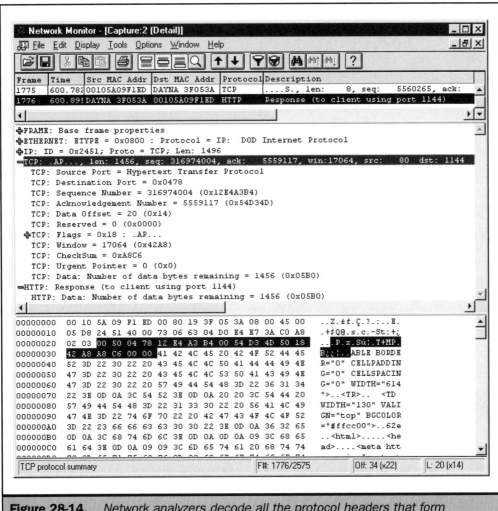

Figure 28-14.   *Network analyzers decode all the protocol headers that form each packet*

Cable testers are rated for specific cable standards, such as Category 5, so that they can determine if a cable's performance is compliant with that standard. This is called *continuity testing*. During a cable installation, a competent technician tests each link to see if it is functioning properly, taking into account problems that can be caused by the quality of the cable itself or by the nature of the installation. For example, a good cable tester tests for electrical noise caused by proximity to fluorescent lights or other electrical equipment; crosstalk caused by signals traveling over an adjacent wire; attenuation caused by excessively long cable segments or improperly rated cable; and kinked or stretched cables, as indicated by specific levels of capacitance.

In addition to testing the viability of an installation, cable testers are good for troubleshooting cabling problems. For example, a tester that functions as a time-delay reflectometer can detect breaks or shorts in a cable by transmitting a high-frequency signal and measuring the amount of time it takes for the signal to reflect back to the source. Using this technique, you can determine that a cable has a break or other fault a certain distance away from the tester. Knowing that the problem is 20 feet away, for example, can prevent you from having to poke your head up into the ceiling every few feet to check the cables running through there. Some testers can also help you locate the route that a cable takes through walls or ceilings, using a tone generator that sends a strong signal over the cable that can be detected by the tester unit when it is nearby.

Network Management

Many of the tools examined thus far in this chapter are for use when a problem occurs, but many network administrators prefer to use a more proactive approach, by continuously monitoring and gathering information about the network by using a network management console, such as Hewlett-Packard's OpenView or Microsoft's Systems Management Server. These products are designed to gather information about various devices located all over the network and display it at a central console. Some products are able to compile a graphical view of the network that enables administrators to select a device and check its status and statistics. When problems occur, causing a device to generate a special event called a *trap*, the console can be configured to notify administrators in a variety of ways, such as by e-mail and pages. Other network management functions include traffic monitoring, network diagnostics, software inventory and metering, and report generation.

There are two network management standards that are currently popular, called the Simple Network Management Protocol (SNMP) and Remote Monitoring (RMON). These standards are similar in their basic architecture, but handle information in different ways. The basic components of a network management system are as follows:

- **Network management console** Receives the information gathered by the agents and collates it for presentation to the administrator in the form of statistical readouts, graphical displays, and/or printed reports.

- **Agents** Programs running on network devices that gather information for eventual transmission to the network management console. Most network hardware devices, such as routers, switches, and hubs, have built-in agents that support SNMP, RMON, or both. On computers, the agent takes the form of a program or service that may be included with the operating system or furnished separately.

- **Management information bases (MIBs)** Store the *managed objects*, the individual pieces of information compiled by an agent.

- **SNMP**   Includes the query language used between the agents and the console, and the UDP-based transport mechanism that carries the information collected by the agents.

While SNMP and RMON use the same basic components, RMON is the newer standard, developed to address the shortcomings of SNMP. In an SNMP installation, the agents are simple components that gather information and transmit it on request. The network management console is responsible for continually polling the agents and retrieving the information they've gathered. This places most of the burden for supporting the network management system on the console, which must constantly gather and process new data, and also generates a considerable amount of network traffic.

RMON also uses a central console and individual agents (which it calls *probes*); but instead of the agents functioning as the clients of the console, as in SNMP, the probes are the servers and the console is the client. RMON probes are more complex than SNMP agents, and are capable of gathering and maintaining information about the devices they serve by themselves. The console only has to retrieve the data from a probe when it is needed for display or processing. This reduces both the burden on the console and the network traffic generated by the process.

Deploying a network management application requires a considerable investment in time, money, and equipment; but on a larger network, it enables administrators to monitor and maintain hundreds or thousands of individual components without traveling to the far reaches of the network installation.

NETWORK
ADMINISTRATION

Index

B

priorities
creating for system policies,
838–839
IEEE 802.1p standard for
implementing, 50
private WAN networks, 154–155
Process Manager, 415
process object, 415
processes in Windows kernel mode,
299
Profile page (Active Directory
Properties dialog box), 828
profiles. *See* user profiles
promiscuous mode, 101, 876
properties
architecture of NDS, 658–659
rights of NDS, 682
Properties dialog box (Active
Directory)
for site link object, 719
upgrading to Active Directory
domains, 724, 725
for user object, 727, 728
protocol analyzers
interpreting DHCP traffic using
BOOTP labels, 547, 549–552
in network analyzers, 879–880
protocol data unit. *See* PDU
protocol drivers
NLMs for Novell Client for
DOS/Windows, 519
for Novell Client for Windows
95/98, 511, 521–522
for Windows network clients,
514–515
protocol stack
availability of TCP/IP-32 stack
for Windows for
Workgroups, 517
data encapsulation within, 18
data link layer and, 26
defined, 16
TCP/IP and OSI, 17, 293–294
vertical communications
within, 19–21
Windows implementation of
OSI model, 512
*See also specific layers listed
individually*
protocols
architecture for Gigabit
Ethernet, 274
ARP, 316–320
ATM, 281–289
architecture of, 282–287
drawbacks of, 287–289
combining data link-,
network layer, and
transport-layer, 33–34

command codes for SMB,
394–396
connection-oriented and
connectionless, 32, 33–34
as factor in selecting NICs,
51–52
FDDI, 257–273
development of as
backbone protocol, 254
layers of, 262–272
standards for, 257–258
symbol values and 5-bit
binary sequences for,
264–265
topology for, 258–261
LAN emulation for ATM
network backbones, 288–289
loading in NetWare, 481
NetBEUI Frame, 375–393
for Novell NetWare
data link-layer protocols
and Ethernet frames,
350–351
IPX, 350, 352–354
NCP, 357–368
SAP, 368–371
SPX, 354–356
origins of NetBEUI, 374
OSI stack intended as prototype
for, 16
protocol functions for OSI
transport layer, 34–36
protocol service combinations
for OSI transport layer, 33–34
routing, 130–137
for SAR sublayer of AAL, 287
on session layer, 36
as standard for network
communication, 11
supporting fiber-optic cabling,
84
used in OSI application layer,
41–42
See also specific protocols by name
proxy servers
firewalls and, 814–816
WINS, 603
public access printer, 787
public key infrastructure (Windows
2000), 464
pull string, 88
pulling cables, 87–88
punchdown block, 87
punchdown tools, 89
push and pull partnerships for
WINS replication ring, 600
PVCs (permanent virtual circuits),
167, 286

PWS (Microsoft Peer Web Services),
737

Q

QAM (quadrature amplitude
modulation), 163
QCLASS field, 636, 637
QoS (quality of service), 50
ATM features enabling
reservation of bandwidth,
281
for Windows 2000, 50, 467–468
QoS Admission Control console,
468
QTYPE field, 634–635
quads, 295
quartet signaling, 247, 251
query messages
AXFR, 643
DNS
name resolution query
generated by resolver,
636, 637
root name server query for
name resolution, 641
sent to root name server,
636, 638
ICMP, 334–336
Echo Request and Echo
Reply messages, 334–335
router solicitations and
advertisements, 334–336
SOA, 641, 643
question section of NetBT message
formats, 589–590
queue, 770
Quota Entries window (Windows
2000, 469, 470
Quota tab (Windows 2000
Properties dialog box), 469, 470

R

RADSL (Rate-Adaptive Digital
Subscriber Line), 162
RARP (Reverse Address Resolution
Protocol), 534–535
Reply messages, 318
Request messages, 318
raw Ethernet, 351
rcp command, 503
RD (route designator), 109, 111
RDATA field of SOA resource
record, 632–634
RDN (relative distinguished name),
660, 706
receive congestion error, 246

pin assignments for 10BaseT
  networks, 188
pin assignments for 100BaseT4
  networks, 211–212
pinouts for twisted-pair
  cabling, 80–82
USOC standard for, 80, 81
rlogin command, 501–502
RMAC (repeater media access
  control) sublayer, 248–250
RMON (Remote Monitoring),
  882–883
roaming user profiles, 828–829,
  830–832
root bridge, 106
root hubs, 248
root name server
  about, 620
  discovery of, 640–641
  query for name resolution, 641
  query messages sent to, 636,
    638
  response message, 641, 642
round trip signal delay time
  calculating for Ethernet, 195,
    196–198
  calculating for Fast Ethernet,
    215–216
  defined, 194
route designators (RDs), 109, 111
Route utility, 125, 870
routed daemon (UNIX), 130
routers, 116–137
  applications for, 117–120
  defined, 10, 116
  fragmenting datagrams, 326
  functions of, 120–128
    for collapsed backbone,
      254–257
    discarding packets, 127
    packet fragmentation,
      127–128
    routing tables, 121–125
    selecting most efficient
      route, 126–127
    static and dynamic routing,
      125–126
  gateway as synonymous with,
    122
  hardware, 810–811
  ICMP solicitations and
    advertisements, 335–336
  improvements offered by
    switches, 137
  Internet, 808–811
    hardware, 810–811
    overview, 808
    software, 808–810
  multi-provider, 436

packet filtering on, 813–814
recognizing zeroes as subnet
  identifier, 301
redirect messages, 333–334
replacing bridging with, 102
as term used with high-speed
  backbone networks, 254
WAN connections using,
  146–147
See also switches
routing
  ICMP and, 128–129
  of IP packets, 327–329
  on OSI network layer, 30–31
  OSPF protocol for, 135–137
  routing control section of RIF,
    110–111
  static and dynamic, 329
  switching vs., 141–143
    layer-3 switches, 143
    virtual LANs, 142–134
  See also RIF; RIP
Routing and Remote Access
  program (Server Manager), 125,
  126
Routing and Remote Access Server
  (RRAS), 441
routing information field. *See* RIF
routing information indicator (RII),
  109, 110
Routing Information Protocol. *See*
  RIP
routing protocols, 130–137
  OSPF, 135–137
  RIP, 130–135
routing tables
  overview, 121
  parsing, 124–125
  UNIX, 123–124
  Windows, 121–123
RR. *See* resource records
RRAS (Routing and Remote Access
  Server), 441
rsh command, 502
runts, 223

S/T interface, 159
SAM (Security Accounts Manager)
  database, 686
SAP (Service Advertising Protocol),
  368–371
  Get Nearest Server Reply
    message, 369
  overview, 368
  problems with, 371

SAP Reply message format,
  370–371
SAP Request message format,
  369–370
SAR (segmentation and reassembly
  sublayer) of ATM adaptation
  layer, 286
SAS (single-attachment stations),
  259
SAT (security access token), 415, 446
SC and ST connectors, 85, 86
scopes
  creating, 558–559
  deactivating, 564, 566
screened subnet firewall, 816, 817
SDSL (Symmetrical Digital
  Subscriber Line), 161, 797
second-level domains, 614–615
secret key cryptography, 464
secure channels and trust
  relationships, 693
Secure Shell commands, 503
Secure Sockets Layer (SSL), 745–746
security
  combining firewall
    technologies for, 816–817
  for FTP servers, 760
  NDS, 681–684
    object and property rights,
      682
    overview, 681
    rights inheritance, 682–684
    security equivalences and
      organizational roles, 680
  remote administration of Web
    servers and, 743
  restricting access
    to applications on
      Windows workstations,
      840–841
    to Windows file system on
      workstations, 843–844
    to Windows interface on
      workstations, 841–843
  for Web servers and sites, 736,
    745-746
  Windows NT, 444-460
    architecture, 445-447
    domains and security,
      447-448
    global and local groups,
      451-452
    overview, 444-445
    permissions, 456-460
    rights, 452-455
    user accounts, 448-451
  Windows 2000, 462-466
    certificates, 464-465
    IP Security Protocol, 465